African Philosophy

BLACKWELL PHILOSOPHY ANTHOLOGIES

Each volume in this outstanding new series provides a comprehensive and authoritative collection of the essential primary readings from philosophy's main fields of study. Designed to complement the *Blackwell Companions to Philosophy* series, each volume represents an unparalleled resource in its own right, and will provide the ideal platform for course use.

1 Cottingham: *Western Philosophy: An Anthology*
2 Cahoone: *From Modernism to Postmodernism: An Anthology*
3 LaFollette: *Ethics in Practice: An Anthology*
4 Goodin & Pettit: *Contemporary Political Philosophy: An Anthology*
5 Eze: *African Philosophy: An Anthology*

Forthcoming

6 McNeill & Feldman: *Modern European Philosophy: An Anthology*
7 Sosa & Kim: *Epistemology: An Anthology*
8 Kim & Sosa: *Metaphysics: An Anthology*

African Philosophy

An Anthology

Edited by *Emmanuel Chukwudi Eze*
Bucknell University

 BLACKWELL
Publishers

Copyright © Blackwell Publishers Ltd, 1998
Preface, selection and arrangement copyright © Emmanuel Chukwudi Eze, 1998

First published 1998
2 4 6 8 10 9 7 5 3 1

Blackwell Publishers Inc.
350 Main Street
Malden, Massachusetts 02148
USA

Blackwell Publishers Ltd
108 Cowley Road
Oxford OX4 1JF
UK

Library of Congress Cataloging-in-Publication Data

African philosophy : an anthology / edited by Emmanuel Chukwudi Eze.
      p.   cm. — (Blackwell philosophy anthologies ; 5)
   Includes index.
   ISBN 0-631-20337-0 (alk. paper). — ISBN 0-631-20338-9 (pbk. : alk. paper)
   1. Philosophy, African. 2. Philosophy, Black. I. Eze, Emmanuel Chukwudi. II. Series.
B5305. A36 1997
199′.6—dc21   96-40926
                                                  CIP

British Library Cataloguing in Publication Data

A CIP catalogue record for this book is available from the British Library.

Typeset in 9 on 11 pt Ehrhardt by Ace Filmsetting Ltd, Frome
Printed and bound in Great Britain by MPG Books Ltd, Bodmin, Cornwall

This book is printed on acid-free paper.

Contents

Contents

Contents

Preface

This major anthology is designed to accomplish two main goals: (a) to serve, for many years to come, as the standard *textbook* on the subject of Africana philosophy, and (b) to fulfill the need for a wide-ranging general *reference* volume for scholars and researchers working in the area of Africana philosophical and cultural studies.

Underneath the two goals stated above are several animating concerns. Within the last ten years, several philosophers and critics have recognized as crucial the need to abandon the sterile and tendentious question of whether or not there exists an "African" philosophy, and instead to focus on actually cultivating and shaping (and re-shaping), for the future, the nature of philosophy as it is practiced both within and outside Africa and among black as well as non-black philosophers. This anthology adopts the novel future-oriented posture: it brings together the canonical texts in Africana philosophy not because it wants to "prove" that Africans also do philosophy but rather because it wants to put into the hands of teachers and students and researchers the best and the most productive textual resources in the modern and ancient African philosophy traditions, in order to encourage the academic and professional consolidation and expansion of the fields of philosophy in question.

The fields of philosophy constructed in this volume, then, are called "African" because they include philosophical materials from: (1) the con-tinent of Africa (the traditional and the modern, of diverse inspirations: secular, Islamic, and Christian); (2) African-America, (3) Afro-Caribbea, and (4) philosophical writings by African-descended European, Black Atlantic, thinkers. The texts gathered here provide a window heretofore unparalleled into the historical and contemporary vitality of philosophical activities in Africa and the African Diaspora.

Although the nature, the boundaries, as well as the institutional manifestations of "Africana" philosophical activities are varied and dynamic and therefore constantly changing, the writings selected in this volume capture as well as problematize in outstanding ways both the idea and the substance of "Africana" in philosophy.

In addition to the goals of consolidating and advancing Africana traditions of philosophy, this anthology is also conceived with multi-cultural and international philosophic dialogues in mind. It is meant to be a strong invitation to dialogue issued by African and African-diasporic or "black" philosophers to their counterparts who teach other philosophic traditions – the European, the Asian, the Latin-American, the feminist, etc. – to include the Africana perspective in their teachings and research. Days are gone when one people, epoch, or tradition could arrogantly claim to have either singularly invented philosophy, or to have a monopoly over the specific yet diverse processes of search for knowledge typical to the discipline of philosophy. It is hoped that all philosophers interested in a diversified or diversifying approach to their research and teaching would find this volume invaluable.

For the purpose of enhancing this desired universal access to the volume, effort has been made to arrange the texts along the lines of traditional thematic divisions of philosophy – "untidy" and overlapping as this arrangement may be. Hence: "What is [African] Philosophy?" (Part 1); "Human Nature: Mind, Body, and Self-Identity" (Part 2); "Philosophy, Politics, and Society" (Part 3); "Ethics" (Part 4); "On Knowledge and Science" (Part 5); "Philosophy and Colonial Encounter" (Part 6); "Philosophy and Race" (Part 7); "Philosophy and Gender" (Part 8); "Philosophy and Transatlantic

African Slavery" (Part 9); "Ontology and the Nature of Art" (Part 10), and "Philosophy of Religion" (Part 11). It should be obvious that a major innovative feature of this volume is that it is the only philosophy textbook that contains thematic-disciplinary units devoted entirely to the questions of race, slavery, and colonialism. As far as I know, it is also the only anthology in Africana philosophy that has this sort of focus and organization. The themes and the chapters on "philosophy and race," "philosophy and slavery," and "philosophy and colonial encounter," as well as "philosophy and gender," make the book useful not only to philosophers but also those who teach or work in the areas of gender and race theory, black, postcolonial, and cultural studies.

Acknowledgments

Constructing an anthology of "African" philosophy that would respond to the needs of students and teachers in Africa, America, and Europe demands of necessity a recognition of some shared historical concerns – intellectual, cultural, and political – that constitute the Diasporic relationships. I have taught Africana philosophy in Africa, in Europe, and North America for the past nine years. After many frustrating and time-consuming experiences of photocopying materials from disparate and elusive sources, I decided in 1994 to travel to Ethiopia, Kenya, Zaire, Nigeria, England, and France, giving lectures and speaking with colleagues there about the difficult issue of assembling suitable classroom as well as reference texts in the area. This book grew out of the classroom experiences in, and the travels to, many colleges and universities on several continents. I would therefore like to thank friends and colleagues in so many places who answered my queries by letters, or invited me to speak in their classrooms and departments. In Africa, may the following accept my thanks: Claude Sumner of Addis Ababa University, Ethiopia; Odera Oruka, F. Ochiang-Odhiambo, Patrick Dikkir, and Jack Odhiambo, all of the Department of Philosophy, University of Nairobi; D. U. Opata, J. A. Eneh, and Chukwudum Okolo of the Department of Philosophy, University of Nigeria, Nsukka; and Sophie Oluwole of the Department of Philosophy, University of Lagos.

In the United States, I am grateful to friends and colleagues in the New York Society for the Study of Black Philosophy (NYSSBP), Society for African Philosophy in North America (SAPINA), and several members of the American Philosophical Association (APA) Committee on Black Experience, whose interests, advice, and encouragement supported this work. I am particularly grateful to members of the NYSSBP from whom I inherited the mandate "to develop and exemplify, through teaching . . . the idea that philosophy can contribute to the clarification and resolution of issues critical in the lives of African-diasporic peoples," and the sense of an urgent need "to fill the gap in philosophy curricula" in regard to "the development and study of African and African-diasporic philosophical texts." I hope my modest effort here finds echo in yours. My thanks to Frank Kirkland, John Pittman, Lucius Outlaw, Lewis Gordon, Tom Slaughter, Tommy Lott, Tsenay Serequeberhan, Jean-Marie Makang, and a long list of others who encouraged this work in so many ways.

I am also particularly grateful to my students over the years and in many places, on whom I "tested" the value of most of the materials contained here. It was their persistent interest and demands that convinced me of the need for this volume, and sustained my own sense of its relevance. In this connection, too, let me mention the institutional and financial support provided by Bucknell University for this project. For the Research Travel Grant provided by the Dean's

Office I am grateful to the Dean and her Associates, Genie Gerdes and Debbie Abowitz. I also thank the directors of the Bucknell Knight Fellowship, especially Professors Doug Cantland and Jim Rice, who provided the stipend that enabled me to retain the assistance of my student, Mike Ashton, over the summer of 1995. Kendra Harmon, a member of another generation of my students at Bucknell, also graciously did for me some administrative work in May 1996. Finally, to my colleagues in the Department of Philosophy: Richard, Jeff, Frank, and Nancy, I say: *Daalu*.

E. C. E.

Pathfinder Press for Malcolm X, "Universal Dimensions of Black Struggle: The Revolution Known as 'The Black Revolution' " in *Malcolm X Speaks* (1965). Copyright © 1965, 1989 by Betty Shabazz and Pathfinder Press; and Malcolm X, "Universal Dimensions of Black Struggle II: Human Rights Versus Civil Rights" in *Two Speeches by Malcolm X*. Copyright © 1965, 1990 by Betty Shabazz and Pathfinder Press;

Présence Africaine for Aimé Césaire, "Discourse on Colonialism" in *Discourse on Colonialism* (*Discours sur le Colonialisme*) (1989); Birago Diop, "Breath" (Souffle) in *Leurres et Lueurs* (1961); and Placide Tempels, "Bantu Ontology" in *Bantu Philosophy* (1959);

Routledge, New York and London, for Tsenay Serequeberhan, "Philosophy and Post-Colonial Africa" and "Colonialism and the Colonized" in *The Hermeneutics of African Philosophy: Horizon and Discourse* (1994);

Rowman & Littlefield Publishers, Inc. for Sandra Harding, "The Curious Coincidence Between Feminine and African Moralities" in *Women and Moral Theory*, eds Eva Kittay and Diana T. Myeres (1987);

Elizabeth Spelman for "The Erasure of Black Women" in *Twenty Questions: An Introduction to Philosophy*, eds G. Lee Bowie, M. W. Michaels and R. Solomin, Harcourt Brace (1995). Copyright © Elizabeth Spelman;

South End Press for bell hooks, "Racism and Feminism" in *Ain't I a Woman?* (1988); bell hooks, "Black Women Shaping Feminist Theory" in *Black Women Shaping Feminist Theory*; and bell hooks and Cornel West, "Black Women and Men: Partnership in the 1990's";

Franz Steiner Verlag Wiesbaden GmbH for Zera Yacob, "God, Faith and the Nature of Knowledge" in *The Source of African Philosophy: The Ethiopian Philosophy of Man* by Claude Sumner (1986);

Temple University Press for material from Kwame Gyekye, "Relations of Ōkra (soul) and Honam (body): An Akan Conception" in *An Essay on African Philosophical Thought* (1995). Copyright © 1995 by Kwame Gyekye;

The University of North Carolina Press for Winthrop D. Jordan, "The Concept of Slavery" in *White Over Black: American Attitudes Toward the Negro, 1550–1812* (1968) published for the Institute of Early American History and Culture. Copyright © 1968 by the University of North Carolina Press;

University Press of America, Inc. for Henry Olela, "The African Foundations of Greek Philosophy" in *African Philosophy: An Introduction*, ed. Richard Wright (1984);

Zed Books Ltd and Monthly Review Press for Kwame Nkrumah, "Consciencism" in *Conscienscism: Philosophy and Idealogy for De-Colonization* (1964). Copyright © 1970 by Monthly Review Press;

Philosophical Forum Inc. for Lucius Outlaw, "African, African American, Africana Philosophy," Bernard Boxill, "Two Traditions in African American Political Philosophy," and Tommy Lott, "Du Bois on the Invention of Race."

Every effort has been made to trace the copyright holders, but if any have been inadvertently overlooked the publishers will be pleased to make the necessary arrangements at the first opportunity.

PART I

What is African Philosophy?

1

African Philosophy: Yesterday and Today

Joseph I. Omoregbe

Philosophy is essentially a reflective activity. To philosophize is to reflect on human experience in search of answers to some fundamental questions. As man takes a reflective look at himself or the world around him, he is filled with "wonder," and some fundamental questions arise in his mind. When he reflects on these fundamental questions in search of answers, he is philosophizing. Both Plato and Aristotle tell us that this "wonder" is the beginning of philosophy. "It is through wonder that men now begin and orginally began to philosophize."[1] Plato echoes this same view in *Republic* when he says that there is no other beginning of philosophy than this "wonder." Thus the first step in the philosophical activity is this "wonder" that accompanies man's experimental contact with himself or the world around him. This wonder gives rise to some fundamental questions, and this is the second step. The third step is taken when man begins to reflect on these fundamental questions in search of answers. At this stage, the man in question is philosophizing, and if he puts down his reflections in writing he has written a philosophical book.

Human experience is the source of the reflective activity known as philosophy. This experience could either be man's own experience of himself (subjectivity) or his experience of the world around him (objectivity). Hence philosophy could start from subjectivity or from objectivity. The early

Greek philosophers began from objectivity. As they observed the world around them they were filled with the philosophic "wonder." They were amazed at two things that struck them with particular interest. First, they were struck by the diversity and the unity in the universe. They observed that things around them were amazingly diverse: but at the same time they also observed that there was a basic unity in the midst of this diversity. Second, they were struck by the fact of change in the universe. They noticed that things were constantly changing: but at the same time they also observed that there was a basic continuity in the midst of these changes. Thus they observed that the universe combined unity with diversity and continuity with changes. These phenomena set the early Greek philosophers thinking, in search of explanations. Thus the marvels of the physical universe led the early Greek philosophers into philosophizing. Indeed such phenomena as the immensity of space, the immensity of the universe, the amazing variety of things, the idea of time, the ceaseless changes going on in the world around us, the continuity in the midst of these changes, the basic unity in the midst of diversity, the seasons of the year; the heavenly bodies and their orderly circular movement, the starry sky, the sun, the moon, etc., have led to deep reflections and philosophizing all over the world. In his *Critique of Practical Reason*, Kant tells us that two things fill him with wonder, namely, the starry sky above and the moral law within.

But, as it has been already mentioned, philosophizing can also start from the human person. Indeed man has within himself a richer source of

From *Philosophy in Africa: Trends and Perspectives*, ed. P. O. Bodunrin, University of Ife Press (1985); reproduced by kind permission of P. O. Bodunrin.

philosophy than the physical universe. For the marvels and the complexities of the human person far exceed those of the physical universe. The brevity of human life, the vicissitudes of life, man's superiority over the rest of nature which he controls and dominates, his power and weaknesses, his joys, sorrows, successes and failures, his finitude, his experience of suffering, misery, disease, death and decay, man's greatness and misery, etc., have led to deep reflection and philosophizing all over the world. Buddha's philosophy, for example, arose from his reflection on human suffering. Reflection on these phenomena of human existence gives rise to some basic questions about the nature of the human being: what kind of being is man, so powerful and yet so weak, so great and yet so miserable? Today he is strong and powerful, tomorrow he is gone, and that is the end of him. Man has a natural yearning for continued existence, his strongest instinct is the instinct of self-preservation – his wish to continue living. Yet his lifespan is brief and is often terminated contrary to his deepest desire, and all his efforts to resist this imposed termination are futile. Man has a strong natural desire to know, he is by nature curious. Yet his knowledge is so limited that he does not know even himself. He does not know why he exists and he has no answers to his own basic questions about himself. He did not choose to come into this world, he simply found himself in it without knowing why: and sooner or later he will be forced out of it. Like everything else in the universe, man simply appears in it and eventually disappears from it. "What a chimera is man!" exclaimed Pascal, a chaos, a subject of contradiction. Thus, man is to himself a problem, a mystery. What is his origin? What is his ultimate destiny? Why is he here? What happens when he is forced out of this life? Is he completely part of nature or does he transcend nature? Is the difference between him and the lower animals a difference in degree or a difference in nature? What is he living for? Has his life any ultimate meaning?[2] Is there a force over and above man that controls all these? If there is such a force can it be known?

These and similar questions are fundamental questions about the human person. They have led to deep reflections all over the world. To reflect on such questions in search of explanations or answers is to philosophize. There is no part of the world where men never reflect on such basic questions about the human person or about the physical universe. In other words, there is no part of the world where men do not philosophize. The ten-

dency to reflect on such fundamental philosophic questions is part of human nature; it is rooted in man's natural instinct of curiosity – the instinct to know.

Human nature and human experience are basically the same all over the world, and the tendency to philosophize is part of human nature. Hence the German philosopher Karl Jaspers says that "man cannot avoid philosophizing."[3] In a certain sense, that is, in a loose sense, every man is a philosopher in as much as every man at one time or another in the course of his life reflects on some of the fundamental philosophic questions about human life or about the physical universe. At funerals, for example, or at the sight of a dead body, or in the face of suffering, sickness, pain, misery etc., men are apt to reflect on the meaning and value of human life. However, in the strict sense of the word, a philosopher is one who devotes a good deal of his time reflecting on these questions and who frequently and habitually does this. There are such people all over the world; they are to be found among all peoples, in all civilizations and in every part of the globe. It is not only in the Western world that men reflect on the fundamental questions about human life or about the universe. Those who, in any civilization, were particularly struck with "wonder" at the marvels and complexities of the human being or the physical universe, and frequently devoted a lot of time reflecting on the fundamental questions arising from these marvels or complexities, constitute the philosophers of these civilizations. It is not necessary to employ Aristotelian or the Russellian logic in this reflective activity before one can be deemed to be philosophizing. It is not necessary to carry out this reflective activity in the same way that the Western thinkers did. Ability to reason logically and coherently is an integral part of man's rationality. The power of logical thinking is identical with the power of rationality. It is therefore false to say that people cannot think logically or reason coherently unless they employ Aristotle's or Russell's form of logic or even the Western-type argumentation. Some people, trained in Western philosophy and its method, assert that there is no philosophy and no philosophizing outside the Western type of philosophy or the Western method of philosophizing (which they call "scientific" or "technical"). In his book *An Introduction to Western Philosophy*, Professor Antony Flew says that philosophy consists of argument "first, last and always," and since there is no argument in Eastern thought (or so he thinks) there is consequently no philosophy in Eastern thought. Similarly, referring to African traditional philosophy, Professor Wiredu has this to say: "without argument and clarification, there is, strictly, no philosophy."[4] African traditional philosophy, according to him, is termed philosophy only on a generous understanding of the term. Professor Wiredu is well-versed in Western philosophy, especially the Anglo-Saxon analytic tradition which sees philosophy essentially in terms of logic, analysis and clarification of terms. This is the impression one gets from his writings. He is certainly one of the leading African philosophers of today and he has contributed a great deal to African philosophy. However, when he says that without argumentation and clarification there is strictly no philosophy, he means Western-type argumentation. In other words, he means that if the reflective activity is not carried out through the Western-type argument and clarification (which the British analytic tradition insists on) then it is not philosophy. In the first place, the essence of philosophy is not argument but reflection, and this does not have to take the form of the Western-type argument. Wherever there is reflection on the fundamental questions about man or about the universe (whatever form this reflection may take) there is philosophy.

We must distinguish between philosophy and its mode of transmission and preservation. Philosophical reflections can be preserved and transmitted in a number of ways. By far the best way to transmit and preserve them is by writing, in the form of books. The advantages in this mode of preservation and transmission are enormous; not only are these reflections preserved and transmitted intact, the philosophers whose reflections are so preserved and transmitted are also identified and known individually. In this way it is possible to know who the original authors of certain ideas or views are, either through their own writings or through the writings of those who wrote about them (as is the case with men like Buddha, Socrates, Jesus Christ who in themselves left no writing behind). The Western world then has been fortunate in this regard since the art of writing has been in existence for a very long time in the West and consequently, this has made it possible to preserve substantially the reflections of its philosophers. We therefore can now talk of Socrates, Plato, Aristotle, Kant, Hegel, etc. But who can say that other civilizations do not have their own philosophers?[5] Who can say that men of other civilizations do not think, do not reflect on the basic philosophic questions about human life or about the universe? Men of the Western world were not the only people blessed with rationality, with intelligence, with thought, with the instinct of curiosity. These are all characteristics of human nature and are to be found among all peoples all over the globe. All civilizations, all people, have their own philosophers – their own Socrates, their own Plato, their own Descartes, their own Hegel, etc. In this Africa cannot be an exception. Unfortunately, due to the absence of records in writing in Africa until recent times, the philosophical reflections of African thinkers were not preserved effectively.

The fact that the philosophical reflections of African thinkers in the past were not preserved or transmitted by writing accounts for the fact that these philosophers remain unknown to us. But this does not mean that they did not exist, for we have fragments of their philosophical reflections and their views preserved and transmitted to us through channels other than writing such as mythologies, formulas of wise-sayings, traditional proverbs, stories, and especially religion. This is to say that writing, though the most effective, is not the only means of transmitting knowledge across generations. Apart from mythologies, wise sayings, worldviews, knowledge can be preserved in the socio-political set-up of the people. These are the channels through which the reflections and views of African philosophers have been preserved and transmitted to us in Africa. These philosophical reflections and views have therefore become, in the process of transmission over ages, part of the African way of life, part of the African culture and heritage. But the individual original authors of these views remain unknown to us. Yet we know that these views must have been the fruits of deep and sustained philosophical reflections by some individual African thinkers in the past. For where there is smoke there must be some fire even when, for some reason, the fire is not seen. The fragments of philosophical reflections, ideas and world-views transmitted to us through the formulas of wise-sayings, through proverbs, stories, socio-political organizations, mythology, through religious doctrines and practices did not originate from a vacuum. They are evidences of deep philosophical reflections by *some gifted individual thinkers* who were the *African philosophers* of the past, the African counterparts of Socrates, Plato, Aristotle, Descartes, Kant, Hegel, etc. Professor Wiredu calls African traditional philosophy "community thought" and says that it "is not the creation of any specifiable set of philosophers."[6] He says it is the common property of all and sundry. Does Professor Wiredu mean that these ideas, these insights, these world-views etc., did not originate from individual thinkers? How then did they originate in the first place? We know that there is no such thing as collective consciousness or community consciousness in the strict sense of the word. For consciousness is always an individual consciousness and thinking is always done by individuals. The term "community thought" can mean nothing other than the thought of individuals in a community, for thinking is always done by individuals. African traditional philosophy must have originated from some particular individual thinkers, individual philosophers who have reflected on the fundamental questions arising from human experience. Professor Wiredu says that they are the common property of all and sundry, but this does not mean that they originated from all and sundry. Thoughts and ideas put forward by individual thinkers do eventually become common property of all and sundry in a given community, but this does not mean that they had no original individual authors. Let us take the example of the Akan concept of the human person described by both W. E. Abraham[7] and Wiredu.[8] According to the Akan, the human person is made up of five elements: (1) *nipadu* – a body, (2) *okra* – a soul, the guiding spirit, (3) *sunsum* – that part of a man which accounts for his character, (4) *ntoro* – that part of man which is passed on from the father and which is the basis of inherited characteristics, (5) *mogya* – that aspect of man which becomes a ghost after death. It is something passed on from the mother and it is what determines one's clan identity. Now, this is a highly complex concept of man and it is obviously the fruit of deep and sustained reflection on the human person. Such a reflection culminating in this complex notion of the human person must have been carried out by some gifted individual thinkers among the Akan people. Although this Akan concept of the human person has become the common property of all and sundry among the Akan, yet it did not originate from all and sundry or from a vacuum. The authors were the Akan philosophers at some time in the past whose ideas have become part of the Akan heritage, part of their culture. These Akan philosophers must evidently have been reflecting on the nature of the human person, and this theory of man is the fruit of their reflection. The fact that we do not know who these philosophers were does not mean that there were no

such people, no such thinkers and that these ideas had no original individual authors. This concept of man is richer and more complex than anything we find in Western philosophy and it evidently has original individual authors. These were the Socrates, the Plato, the Descartes etc. of the Akan people.

Professor Wiredu also says that folk thought consists of bald assertions without supportive arguments.[9] Yet we know that they are not gratuitous assertions, for the original authors of these ideas and views obviously had their reasons for holding and advancing them. They are not bald assertions but the fruit of reflection, the conclusions of a reasoning process. These African thinkers did not just advance these ideas and views without reasons or without thinking and reflecting on the issues in question. They did not put their reasoning in the form of Aristotle's syllogism or Russell's logical form, but they evidently had their reasons. When for example they held the view of reincarnation they evidently reasoned before coming to this conclusion. They must have made some observations about people they knew who had died and those born later. They noticed that certain traits in the former reappeared in the latter. They must have reflected on these phenomena before coming to the conclusion that certain aspects of man are reborn after death. Similar observation and reflection must have led the Akan philosophers to hold the view that the human person is composed of five elements as enumerated above. African philosophers therefore must have gone through a process of observation, reasoning and reflection before arriving at the ideas, views or world-views which they have transmitted to us through the channels of proverbs, wise-sayings, stories, mythology, socio-political organizations, religious doctrines, etc.

Now, how do we find out the reasoning process which led them to hold these views? How do we get at their reason for the ideas, views and doctrines transmitted to us? In a culture whose philosophy is preserved in books, this is an easy task. If for example we want to know why Plato held the view that the soul is immortal all we need do is read the *Phaedo*. But in a culture whose philosophy was preserved by memory through wise-sayings, proverbs, stories, mythology, religion, etc., handed down from generation to generation, elderly people (since they are the nearest we can get to the original thinkers) can be of some help. Since the philosophy was preserved by memory rather than by books, the memory of the elderly people should therefore, as it were, be consulted in order to find out the reasoning process that led to these which have been handed down to us. The memory of the elderly people therefore takes the place of books. In the Western culture research of this nature is normally done in the library. Because of this peculiar situation of African traditional philosophy, there is need for field-work in our researches. This field-work aims at finding out the reasoning process that led to the views handed down to us, by interviewing the old, elderly and the aged. In other parts of the world, if you want to know the philosophy of the given people, says Professor Wiredu, "you do not go to aged peasant or fetish priests or court personalities, but to the individual thinkers in person or in print."[10] In the case of African traditional philosophy, the memory of aged peasants or court personalities can be of immense help.

African traditional philosophy is not the only philosophy of Africa. Contemporary Africans also philosophize. We therefore agree with Professor Wiredu that the term "African Philosophy" should not be understood only in terms of African traditional philosophy since there is also *contemporary* African philosophy.[11] There are contemporary African philosophers and there is contemporary African philosophy. This means that a course on African philosophy should not be confined to traditional philosophy but should include contemporary African philosophers such as Kwame Nkrumah, Leopold S. Senghor, Nyerere and Kwasi Wiredu. The first three are political thinkers and politicians who have contributed immensely to contemporary African political philosophy. The last named, Kwasi Wiredu, is a professional philosopher, a professor of philosophy. There are of course several other professional philosophers in departments of philosophy all over Africa.

Professor Wiredu observes that contemporary African philosophers devote a lot of time on the question of African philosophy, which is distinct from doing African philosophy. He believes it is necessary at this stage to go beyond talking *about* African philosophy and get down to actually doing it.[12] Professor Wiredu accordingly gets down to work and advances two philosophical theses: first, that truth is nothing but opinion, and second, that to be is to be known. The first thesis, i.e., that truth is nothing but opinion, has been criticized by another African philosopher, Dr Oruka. Professor Wiredu has defended himself against both this and other criticisms.[13]

Wiredu denies any distinction between truth and opinion, and holds that "there is nothing called truth as distinct from opinion."[14] Common sense experience, he says, seems to indicate that truth is distinct from opinion. We sometimes hold some opinions as true but only to discover later that we were wrong. From this fact, common experience leads one to make a distinction between truth and opinion. Truth is then seen as an independent, objective reality, categorically distinct from opinion.[15] Wiredu calls this an objectivist view of truth according to which truth is a timeless, eternal and unchanging reality whereas opinions do change. He rejects this objectivist view of truth on the ground that "if truth is categorically different from opinion, then truth is, as a matter of logical principle, unknowable."[16] "Any given claim to truth is merely an opinion advanced from some specific point of view, and categorically different from truth. Hence knowledge of truth as distinct from opinion is a self-contradictory notion."[17] Thus, the objectivist theory implies, according to Wiredu, that truth is unknowable. But this is at variance with common experience, for we sometimes know some propositions to be truth. "Therefore the objectivist theory must be incorrect."[18] Wiredu contends that the element of "point of view" is intrinsic to the concept of truth, that truth is always truth from some point of view. Wiredu simply identifies "point of view" with "opinion" and contends that since truth is always truth from some point of view it follows that truth is always and nothing but opinion. "Truth then is necessarily joined to point of view or better, truth is a view from some point, and there are as many truths as there are points of view."[19]

I cannot subscribe to this subjectivist theory of truth which makes no distinction between truth and opinion. "To be true is to be opined," says Wiredu.[20] Truth is not identical with opinion. Truth is objective whereas opinion is always subjective. Opinion is always the opinion of somebody, a subjective view of something, but truth cannot be said to be the truth of somebody. Wiredu tries to dismiss the distinction between subjectivity and objectivity or to reduce objectivity to subjectivity so that objectivity will disappear. But if objectivity itself were to disappear or if it were reduced to subjectivity, we could no longer talk of subjectivity itself since it would thereby lose its distinctive characteristic which it has, only if and when it is contrasted with objectivity. This applies to truth (objectivity) and opinion (subjectivity). If, as Wiredu contends, truth is nothing but opinion, then opinion itself would lose its meaning which it can have only if and when it is contrasted with truth. Wiredu's assertion that there are as many truths as there are points of view amounts to saying that every point of view is true or that every point of view represents the truth, and this is plainly false. Wiredu implicitly identifies "point of view" with "opinion." But in reality they are not identical. Opinion is always subjective but point of view can be objective. It makes no sense to talk of "an objective opinion" since opinion is always subjective, but one can talk of an "objective point of view," or "from the point of view of objectivity." Consequently, even if it is true that the element of point of view is intrinsic to the concept of truth it still would not follow that it is nothing but an opinion.

Wiredu's other thesis is that "to be is to be known." Just as the cognitive element of point of view is intrinsic to the concept of truth, so is the concept of knowledge intrinsic to the concept of being or existence. To say that an object exists, Wiredu argues, is to assert that the term in question refers to an object. "To be (to exist) then means for a given term 'x' to be asserted to refer to some object."[21] Thus to say that "x" exists is to say that "x" has a reference. It is plain without argument, says Wiredu, that one cannot claim that a term "x" refers to some entity while disclaiming all knowledge about the entity in question. From this it follows that to claim or say that an object exists implies that one has some knowledge of that object.

Hence to exist is to be known.

Again, I cannot subscribe to this thesis. The similarity between this thesis and that of Berkeley (that to be is to be perceived) is obvious. Indeed Wiredu declares that the thesis of Berkeley is irrefutable,[22] and his own thesis is simply another form of that of Berkeley. To say that to be is to be known, as Wiredu does, implies that the existence of an object is dependent on the object being known. But this cannot be the case because knowledge always presupposes an object which is prior to and independent of the knowledge itself. The act of knowing is an activity directed to an object, and this presupposes that the object of knowledge exists prior to, and is independent of, the activity of knowing which is directed to it. It is not the knowing activity that constitutes the object in being. Nothing can be known except it exists prior to and independently of the act of knowing. Objects therefore exist first of all before the activity of knowing is directed to them, thus becoming objects of knowledge. To be can therefore not be to be known. It is true that we cannot assert that an object exists without knowing the object in question, but that does not make the object dependent on our knowledge of it. To know an object is to make the object in question the object to which our knowing activity is directed, and this certainly implies that the object exists prior to and independently of our knowledge of it.

Notes

1 Aristotle, *Metaphysics*, 982b.10.
2 Cf. Karl Britton, *Philosophy and the Meaning of Life*, Cambridge University Press, 1969.
3 K. Jaspers, *Introduction à la philosophie*, Librairie Plon, 1974, p. 1.
4 K. Wiredu, *Philosophy and an African Culture*, Cambridge University Press 1980, p. 47.
5 Hegel, who saw philosophy as the self-consciousness of the Spirit, was led by racism to say that in Africa the Spirit had not yet attained self-consciousness, meaning that there is no philosophy in Africa, no rationality, no thinking.
6 Wiredu, pp. 46–7.
7 W. E. Abraham, *The Mind of Africa*, University of Chicago Press, 1962, pp. 59–61.

8 Wiredu, p. 47.
9 Ibid.
10 Ibid., pp. 47–8.
11 Ibid., p. xi.
12 Ibid.
13 Ibid., p. 174, and the last chapter of the book.
14 Ibid., p. 114.
15 Ibid., p. 114.
16 Ibid., p. 115.
17 Ibid.
18 Ibid.
19 Ibid.
20 Ibid., p. 114.
21 Ibid., p. 127.
22 Ibid., p. 114.

2

Philosophy and Post-Colonial Africa

Tsenay Serequeberhan

For one thing, nothing could be done without friends and loyal companions, and such men were not easy to find ready at hand, since our city was no longer administered according to the standards and practices of our fathers.

– Plato, Letter VII, 325d

For us, contemporary Africans, the condition that has resulted from the colonial obliteration of the "standards and practices of our fathers," to use Plato's words, and the consequent neocolonial inertness of our contemporary situation is the necessary point of departure for any worthwhile or meaningful philosophic engagement. Thus, the closing years of the twentieth century are bound to be for Africa and Africans a time of prolonged, deep reflection and self-examination. Having achieved political "independence," for the most part, we now need to take stock of the victories, defeats, and compromises that constitute and inform our enigmatic present.

The concern with this felt and lived situation seems to be the central focus of post-colonial African literature and intellectual work as a whole. In fact, contemporary developments in African philosophy are themselves interior to this intellectual productivity and occupy a place of fundamental importance in it.[1] However, what has been said thus far notwithstanding, Marcien Towa has correctly observed that

Africa will not really attain its cultural [historic, political, and economic] maturity as long as it does not elevate itself resolutely to a profound thinking of its essential problems, that is to say, to philosophical reflection.[2]

In endorsing Towa's observation, we impose on ourselves the responsibility of properly articulating what these "essential problems" might be and of spelling out the role of "philosophical reflection" in the situation of the present. It was in the guise of introducing the "maturity" of the modern age that European colonialism imposed on Africa its present subordinate status. Thus, to be able to transcend this deplorable situation we contemporary Africans need to confront the question of our "maturity" at its most fundamental level – on the plane of philosophic reflection.

In this initial chapter, I will articulate the situated historicity of contemporary African philosophy as the critical self-reflection of a concrete totality: post-colonial Africa. In doing so, I will establish the parameters within which, in my view, Africa can "elevate itself resolutely to a profound thinking of its essential problems." It is only thus that it can self-consciously confront the question of its historic, cultural, political, and economic subordinate status or "maturity" imposed on it by colonialism, which to this day defines, in all spheres of life, the situation of the present.

From Tsenay Serequeberhan, *The Hermeneutics of African Philosophy* (1994), by kind permission of Routledge, New York and London.

I

As far back as 1958, Frantz Fanon had correctly pointed out, without the benefit of hindsight and from within the lived actuality of the African liberation struggle, that

> The twentieth century, when the future looks back on it, will not only be remembered as the era of atomic discoveries and interplanetary explorations. The second upheaval of this period, unquestionably, is the conquest by the peoples of the lands that belong to them.[3]

But the future will also note – as we do today in the last decade of the twentieth century – that the "conquest by the peoples of the lands that belong to them" was a much more complicated and protracted struggle than it first appeared to be.[4] When "the future looks back on it" – that is, on Fanon's present and our (1990s) immediate post-colonial past – it will register a rather harsh disillusionment and disappointment regarding the promise and the actuality of the immediate post-colonial African situation.[5] For as Enrique Dussel points out:

> The heroes of neocolonial emancipation worked in an ambiguous political sphere. Mahatma Gandhi in India, Abdel Nasser in Egypt, and Patrice Lumumba in the Congo dream of emancipation but are not aware that their nations will [soon] pass from the hands of England, France, or Belgium into the hands of the United States.[6]

Today, in the last decade of the twentieth century, the United States is the dominant superpower and the harbinger of a "new world order" dominated by the West (i.e., NATO).[7] In fact, paraphrasing Lenin and Nkrumah, one could describe this "new world order" as the latest, if not the highest, stage of neocolonialism in which the United States, under the guise of the United Nations, rules the world, and smart bombs enforce "international law." In this context,

> the prolongation of existing socio-economic structures and world relationships, deriving as these do from the colonial period and the world capitalist structure, must inevitably, without a change, produce in Africa a vast international slum.[8]

In fact, the 1970s and the 1980s have already been for Africa a period of "endemic famine"[9] orchestrated by the criminal incompetence and political subservience of African governments – to European, North American, and Soviet interests. Thus, irony of ironies, the official inheritors of the legacy of the African liberation struggle today preside over – or, more appropriately, dictate – the neocolonial demise of the continent. This is the paradox and "dark" enigma of contemporary Africa.

It is appropriate then for the closing decade of the twentieth century to be a period of introspection and self-examination. For the naive mid-century euphoria of "liberation" and "freedom" has come to naught. It has been callously dashed on the historically languid violence of neocolonialism. These very terms, "liberation" and "freedom" – the proud, clear, and popular slogans of yesterday's anti-colonial struggle – are today's opaque, obscure, and ambiguous enigma. In the midst of famine, political terror, Western or Eastern ("democratic" or "socialist," as the case may be) military interventions, "liberation" and "freedom" have become the words with which Occidental power imperiously proclaims its military might and political preeminence.

In contrast to the recent past (i.e., the period of armed anti-colonial liberation struggles), today it is in these very terms that post-colonial "independent" Africa misunderstands itself. What seemed to be clear and unambiguous has become obscure and opaque. Thus the lethargic inertness of neocolonialism passes for the actuality of "freedom" and "liberation." To explore and decipher the source of this vexing "misunderstanding" is the proper task of contemporary African philosophy. For it is only by challenging and contesting this situation at its source that Africa can put behind it the subordinate status imposed on it by European colonialism and perpetuated by neocolonialism.

As Hans-Georg Gadamer, the father of contemporary philosophical hermeneutics puts it, it is precisely this negative situation of "misunderstanding" and the estrangement of meaning within the lived context of a tradition (i.e., a specific historicalness) which is the originative moment of hermeneutics as a particular philosophic orientation. For Gadamer, "understanding becomes a special task only when . . . misunderstandings have arisen."[10] What Gadamer is here enunciating is the grounding insight of the tradition of philosophical hermeneutics within which he operates.[11] This insight is an old, even if at times neglected, truth of philosophy that is abundantly epitomized in the originative moments of Plato's dialogues (which occupy a central paradigmatic place in Gadamer's work) and is categorically affirmed by Hegel when he writes that: "Diremption is the source of *the need for philosophy*."[12]

In our case, the veracity of the above is confirmed by the indisputable historical and violent diremption effected by colonialism and the continued "misunderstanding" of our situation perpetuated by neocolonialism which calls forth and provokes thought in post-colonial Africa.[13] It is in this regard, then, that the proper task of philosophy in Africa is that of systematically elaborating a radical hermeneutics of the contemporary African situation. Having asserted the central and defining claim of this study, we now have to confront Gadamer's strong reservations on this point and the rather contentious remarks of the African historian and philosopher Ernest Wamba-Dia-Wamba.

II

Gadamer forcefully affirms that "hermeneutics has [now] become fashionable and every interpretation [today, 1977] wants to call itself 'hermeneutical.'"[14] On the other hand, Wamba rhetorically asks, almost a decade later, in 1983: Why is hermeneutics "understood by our African philosophers" as the correct response "to the philosophical question in Africa?"[15] From these remarks, especially from Wamba's observations, we can surmise that a hermeneutical orientation, for better or for worse, has already taken root within the indigenous soil of the discourse of contemporary African philosophy.[16]

The net rhetorical effect of these strong remarks, however (expressed, as they are, from within differing philosophical paradigms: philosophical hermeneutics and an "Africanized" Marxism-Leninism), is to question the validity of the "linkage" of hermeneutics to African philosophy. Gadamer charges that hermeneutics is now in vogue and points to a faddish fashionableness without substance. Wamba, on the other hand, following his rhetorical question and without in any way philosophically accounting for the ideological bent of his own ties to European thought, strongly suggests that a hermeneutical position in African philosophy lacks "authenticity" and does not escape neo-colonialism: European tutelage in the realm of theory.

The validity – both philosophical and political – of

the "link" between hermeneutics and African philosophy is thus in doubt. Given the nature of my concerns – named by the title [of the book from which this chapter is extracted]: *The Hermeneutics of African Philosophy: Horizon and Discourse* – it is necessary and beneficial in this initial chapter, to begin by presenting a sustained defense against this double, if disparate, attack. In so doing I will formulate the question of hermeneutics (my response to Gadamer) and of the hermeneuticity of contemporary African philosophy (my response to Wamba) by concretely exploring the way in which philosophic discourse itself originates from and is organically linked to the concrete conditions-of-existence and the life-practices of the horizon within and out of which it is formulated. I will also show, in the process of articulating the above and in line with my subtitle, that this hermeneutical undertaking cannot but be a politically committed and historically specific critical self-reflection that stems from the negativity of our post-colonial present.

III

The hermeneuticity of contemporary African philosophy – as is the case with the hermeneuticity of philosophical discourse as such – consists of the interplay of horizon and discourse. This interplay is grounded on the concrete and lived historicalness of a specific horizon. The terms "horizon" and "discourse," are here used in a rather specialized sense. Horizon designates the historico-hermeneutical and politico-cultural milieu within and out of which specific discourses (philosophic, artistic, scientific, etc.) are articulated. It is the overall existential space within and out of which they occur. Discourse, on the other hand, refers to these articulated concerns interior to the concrete conditions-of-existence made possible by and internal to a specific horizon.[17]

The discourse of modern European philosophy, beginning with Descartes, for example, originates in the concerns arising from the horizon of modern science. Out of these concerns, associated with the names of Galileo and Newton, the discourse of modern philosophy is articulated.[18] It is these concerns that provoked and made possible Kant's Copernican Revolution in philosophy and enshrined the subjectivity of the subject as the originative moment of reflection for modern European thought.

In like manner, but within a radically different horizon, the philosophic discourses of the sixteenth-century Abyssinian philosopher Zar'a Ya'aqob and his disciple Walda Heywat are grounded in the lived concerns of their day. Unlike their European counterparts, the Abyssinian thinkers are concerned with questions of piety and the nature of faith in the context of the acute crisis of Abyssinian Christianity, in confrontation with the subversive work of Jesuit missionaries and aggressive Catholicism. Religiosity, in its differing and thus bewildering claims, manifestations, and contradictory instantiations, is the singular and defining concern of Zar'a Ya'aqob's and Walda Heywat's thinking.[19]

In our case, on the other hand, it is neither the theoretical exigencies of modern science, nor the crisis of faith in confrontation with a foreign and aggressive piety that provokes thought. Rather, it is the politico-existential crisis interior to the horizon of post-colonial Africa which brings forth the concerns and originates the theoretic space for the discourse of contemporary African philosophy. In each case, then, it is out of the concerns and needs of a specific horizon that a particular philosophic discourse is articulated. For as Elungu Pene Elungu puts it:

It is often during periods of perturbation that the human being is called on to affirm and at the same time verify the unfathomable depth from whence springs his action on the world, on himself and on others.[20]

In a similar way Theophilus Okere points out that the various discourses of philosophy are "dictated by the non-philosophy [i.e., horizon]" which is "their own cultural [and historical] background."[21] Elungu and Okere articulate, in slightly differing formulations, the same insight: philosophic discourse is a reflexive and reflective response to the felt crisis of a lived and concrete horizon.

In view of the above, then, to interpretatively engage the present situation in terms of what Africa "*has been*"[22] – both in its ambiguous pre-colonial "greatness"[23] as well as in its colonial and neocolonial demise – is the proper hermeneutical task of African philosophical thought. This interpretative exploration, furthermore, has to be undertaken in view of the future of freedom toward which Africa aspires – as exemplified by its undaunted struggle, and in spite of all its failings, against colonialism and neocolonialism. This historically saturated, ex-

plorative self-reflection is the basic character of philosophy, whether consciously recognized as such or not, and constitutes the explicit self-awareness of hermeneutics as a philosophic orientation.[24]

This then is the radical hermeneutic task of contemporary African philosophy in view of the contradictory and yet fecund legacy of the African liberation struggle. Radical, because such a task is concerned with exploring and exposing the root-sources of the contradictions of our paradoxical present. Hermeneutical, because such a grounding exploration cannot but be a constant and ongoing interpretative and reinterpretative task undertaken in view of the failures and successes of our history as Africans in the contemporary world. As Okonda Okolo puts it:

The cultural [historic] memory is ceaselessly renewed retroactively by new discoveries. Our past, by continually modifying itself through our discoveries, invites us to new appropriations; these appropriations lead us toward a better grasp of our identity.[25]

In this respect, then, the hermeneutical task of contemporary African philosophy is itself interior to the lived and continuous process of self-understanding indigenous to a particular historicalness, to a specific identity.

It is this perpetual process of lived self-understanding, peculiar and internal to human existence as such, that philosophical hermeneutics consciously articulates and cultivates. Moreover, this is the concrete actuality of the contemporary discourse of African philosophy insofar as it is concerned with overcoming the diremptions and misunderstandings of present-day Africa – what Wiredu and Hountondji respectively refer to as the "anachronism" of our situation and the "folklorism"[26] of our theoretic efforts.

The fundamental orientation of this inherently interpretative undertaking is aimed at disclosing a future in congruence with the humanity of the human in African existence. But one might and indeed should ask at this point: What exactly does humanity mean in this context? In this regard I take my cue not from Leopold Sedar Senghor's essentialist humanism of "negroness" (*Négritude*), but from Martin Heidegger's ontological and phenomenological formulation (itself the product of a systematic hermeneutic of modern European existence), that *"the substance of man [the human being] is existence,"*[27] or, put differently, "The "essence" [*Wesen*] of this entity lies in its "to be" [*Zu-sein*]."[28] Heidegger's personal political languidity and Eurocentric anti-semitic racist views notwith-standing,[29] his formulation of the Being (*Sein*) of the human being is grounded in the particular ontologi-cal specificity of the temporalizing ecstatic phenomenality of human existence.[30] To the extent that we recognize both Europe and Africa as sites of human historical becoming, the ontological explorations of the "to be" of human existence, which Heidegger undertakes from within the ontic confines of European modernity, can also be posed from within the ontic confines of other cultures and histories.[31]

In his destructuring reading of the tradition of European metaphysics, starting from the lived ecstatic phenomenality of human life, Heidegger asserts – against the ossified and ossifying ontotheological conceptions of human existence – that human reality (*Dasein*) is not a present-at-hand substance or entity, but the lived fluidity/actuality of its own existence. In this radical destructive hermeneutic critique of the metaphysical tradition, Heidegger explores – in *Being and Time* and in his later works – the "to be" [*Zu-sein*] of European modernity. Seen from the perspective of Heidegger's Being-question, and the grounding ontic-ontologi-cal destructive analysis that derives from it, the modern world is caught in the snare of the *Ge-stell* (en-framing) of modern technology. Thus, the evocations of Heidegger's Being-question are aimed at salvaging the "to be" (i.e., the essential nonsubstantial substance) of European modernity from the beguiling snare of technological catastro-phe. To the very end, Heidegger's efforts were dominated by and directed against this obstinate *Ge-stell*, and oriented toward the striving "to prepare the possibility of a transformed abode of man in the world."[32]

We too – the ex-colonial subjects of this ensnared and ensnaring Europe – suffer from this *Ge-stell*. But for us this situation of enframing is mediated, instituted, and imposed through the persistence of neocolonialism as the continued intrusion of Euro-pean hegemony in present-day Africa. This he-gemony – beyond the overt violence of colonialism and in a much more effective manner – institutes and establishes itself from within and reproduces and perpetuates our subordinate status in the contemporary world. Thus, for us to appropriate the "to be" of our historicalness means to confront

European neocolonial subjugation: the politics of economic, cultural, and scientific subordination.

The insidious nature of neocolonialism is that it internally replicates – in an indigenous guise – what previously was imposed from the outside by the exclusive and explicit use of violence. In view of the above then, and unlike Heidegger, for us, the question of our existence, of our "to be," is an inherently political question. To neglect the politics of this question, in our case, is to disregard the question itself. For, when we ask or reflect on our own humanity, when we examine the actuality, the "substance of our existence" as human beings, there we find and are confronted by an internalized imperious Europe dominant over the contradictory remains of our own indigent and subjected indig-enousness.

It is in this manner that the *Ge-stell* of modern technology shows itself, and is rendered in the form of political domination. As Wamba puts it:

> This is why the expatriate personnel, from imperialist countries, are more at ease in these national [African] state structures, functioning as if they were made by, and for, that personnel, than are the majority of the natives who have to bear [and support] these structures' repressive hierarchical weight. In these conditions, to be intelligent, reason-able, rational, civilized, etc., is to be recep-tive to, and to function according to, the logic and rationality governing these [neocolonial] structures.[33]

This tragicomic obscene duplication of Europe – in Africa and as Africa – is the actual and concrete duplicity which negatively constitutes and posi-tively structures the nonhistoricity of neocolonialism – its historico-existential inertness.

In this manner the technocratic *Ge-stell* of European modernity – compounded by and in the form of political, economic, cultural, and historical dominance – is imposed on us, the ex-colonial subjects of imperial Europe. In the name and in the guise of technological and scientific "assistance" Europe imposes on us its hegemonic political and cultural control. We are thus afflicted by proxy. Precisely for this reason, a concrete hermeneutics of the existentiality of our existence, in order to be adequate, has to confront the actuality of our present. For the "veracity" of this present is the historical duplicity of neocolonialism, which is lived and concretely actualized in and through our existence.[14] In this context the culture of the former colonial power is the ground and the accepted source of hegemonic cultural, technical-economic, and historico-political dominance.

This is the historical and cultural estrangement, internal to our situation, that Fanon systematically inspected as early as 1952 in *Black Skin, White Masks*. It is the estranged and estranging tragic legacy of the European "civilizing mission" to the world. As Basil Davidson points out, the African anti-colonial struggle did not only expel the physical presence of colonialism, but it also put in

> question the smoothly borrowed assumptions of the social hybrids [i.e., Europeanized Africans] about the opposition of "European civilization" to "African barbarism."[35]

Indeed, beyond the physical combat to expel colonialism, contemporary Africa finds itself confronted and hindered, at every turn, by that which this combat has put in question without fundamentally and decisively eradicating.

Thus, present-day African realities are constituted partly by the hybrid remnants of the colonial and pre-colonial past – as embodied at every level in the ossified neocolonial institutional forms of contemporary Africa and in the pathologically negative self-awareness of Europeanized Africans – and partly by the varied forms of struggle aimed at actualizing the possibility of an autonomous and free Africa in the context of the contemporary world. These struggles, furthermore, are not homogenous in their ideological or theoretic orientation. Along with the Africanist essentialism of Senghor, we have Nkrumah's Marxism-Leninism, as well as the historically and hermeneutically astute theoretic perspectives articulated by Fanon and Cabral. All this and more is the mélange that constitutes the lived actuality of post-colonial Africa!

Broadly speaking then, this is the enigmatic and paradoxical inheritance of African "independence": the situation of the present. It is the "ambiguous adventure" of Africa that Cheikh Hamidou Kane articulates so well in his seminal novel of the same title. The inseminative tilling of Africa's "ambiguous adventure" with the Occident is thus the central concern of contemporary African philosophy. It is only by hermeneutically plowing (i.e., turning over) and radically subverting the theoretic space of the post-colonial African situation, with the concrete historicity of our own most distinctive

existential actuality that African philosophic reflection can be part of the practical and theoretic effort aimed at concretely reclaiming the freedom and actuality of the continent.

In the words of Antonio Gramsci:

> The beginning of a critical elaboration is the awareness of that which really is, that is to say a "knowing of one's self" as a product of the process of history that has unfolded thus far and which has left in you an infinity of traces collected without the benefit of an inventory. It is necessary initially to undertake such an inventory.

> Note II. One cannot separate philosophy from the history of philosophy and culture from the history of culture. In a more direct and fitting or proper sense, it is not possible to be philosophers, that is, to have a critically coherent conception of the world, without a consciousness of its historicity, of the phase of development represented by it and of the fact that it is in contradiction with other conceptions or with elements of other conceptions.[36]

In this regard, African philosophy can be true to its own historicity – the historicalness of contemporary Africa out of which it is being secreted and spun – by concretely exploring and confronting the "infinity of traces" left by colonialism and the enduring remains of the pre-colonial past. It is, in this manner, a "knowing of one's self" and an explorative "inventory" aimed at appropriating that which is possible in the context of a specific history.

As Gramsci puts it, "philosophy is the critique and the surpassing [*superamento*, i.e., the Hegelian notion of sublation] of religion and of common sense and in this way it coincides with 'good sense' [*buon senso*] which is counterposed to common sense."[37] This is so, inasmuch as the "religion" of the mass and a historically specific "common sense" are the culturally distinctive self-awareness of a people that structures its historic and politico-economic existence internal to its traditions. Philosophy is thus this critical and explorative engagement of one's own cultural specificity and lived historicalness. It is a critically aware explorative appropriation of our cultural, political, and historical existence.

In view of the above, contemporary African

philosophy has to be conceived as a radically originative hermeneutics of the paradoxical and yet fecund post-colonial present. It is the ardent effort to reclaim the African experience of Being – the historicity of the various modes of African existence – from within the world-historical context of the present, i.e., the implosion of European modernity. In other words, it is an attempt to explore and concretely reappropriate what this modernity closed off at the dawn of its own originative moment of history: the violent self-inception of its own histori-cal actualization.[38]

In this regard, the hermeneutics of contemporary African philosophy or African philosophical hermeneutics is a thinking of new beginnings born out of our enigmatic political "emancipation" and the historical and political crisis of European modernity – the long-awaited weakening, if not the demise, of our subjugators. As Okolo sagaciously points out:

> In Africa, the interest in hermeneutics also arises out of the reality of crisis: a generalized identity crisis due to the presence of a culture – a foreign and dominating tradition – and the necessity for a self-affirmation in the construction of an authentic culture and tradition.[39]

In the paragraph that precedes the sentence just quoted, Okolo points out that in Europe, the "birth and current revival of the hermeneutic movement" is linked to crises: "the crisis of self-identity in German romanticism," and the "crisis of Europe confronted with a technicized [technicises] world and language," which Heidegger, among others, "felt . . . as the forgetting of Being."[40] In each case then, and in terms of differing traditions, the hermeneuticity of philosophy is grounded on the theoretic effort to reconstruct and appropriate meaning within the parameters of a lived inherit-ance and tradition that has become estranged and crisis prone. In other words, philosophic discourse does not just happen; rather, it is the articulation of reflective concerns interior to a negativity arising out of the horizon of a specific cultural and historical totality within which it is located and framed.[41]

For philosophic reflection, the lived life concerns of a culture, a history, a tradition, serve as the source and bedrock on which its own hermeneuticity is grounded. Thus, philosophic discourse is the rhetorically effective enunciation – the bringing to utterance – of the historicity of existence out of and within a specific historicalness. For as Okolo emphatically affirms, ultimately, "hermeneutics [philosophy] exists only in particular traditions."[42]

In view of the fact that one dwells and is immured within the bounds and lived confines of one's tradition or concrete historicalness, how precisely does the hermeneutically oriented phil-osopher engage the particular tradition or histori-calness within which and out of which philosophizing occurs? In this regard, in *An Introduction to Meta-physics*, Heidegger writes:

> But here we may, indeed, we must ask: Which interpretation is the true one, the one which simply takes over a perspective into which it has fallen, because this perspective, this line of sight, presents itself as familiar and self-evident; or the interpretation which questions the customary perspective from top to bottom, because conceivably – and indeed actually – this line of sight does not lead to what is in need of being seen.[43]

In other words, the philosopher/interpreter who works out of the context of the present, as it relates to and arises out of a specific tradition, should not passively adhere to what is given by that tradition. Rather, the relation to tradition is an open-ended encounter in which what is explicitly preserved and implicitly betrayed by tradition is revealed. But how or from what vantage point is the "customary perspective" to be questioned from "top to bot-tom"?

> This is not done shiftily and arbitrarily, nor is it done by clinging to a system set up as a norm, but in and out of historical necessity (*Notwendigkeit*), out of the need (*Not*) of historical being-there.[44]

It is imperative for us to note that by "historical being-there," Heidegger means the concrete and factual (ontic) situation in which human beings find themselves (i.e., the actual lived situation of an individual or a group) within the confines and possibilities of a specific tradition.

In other words, "historical being-there" (i.e., a specific person or a historical community of per-sons) always becomes what it is by projecting itself out of its effective past, its lived inheritance. Its "destiny" is thus always what comes out of itself, its "has been," out of the prospects of its history and the possibilities of its generation. As Okolo explains, "destiny" is here understood as the

> implacable given [actuality] of a people and of an individual, but it is also a task of the future for a people and for an individual. It is the thread of tradition and of interpretations.[45]

It is in a constant process of self-interpretation and ongoing re-interpretations that a history, a people (and an individual within the confines of a people and a generation), constitutes itself and projects its future/destiny – the yet-to-be of its lived presence.

Taking Heidegger's *Being and Time* as his benchmark, Gadamer refers to the actuality of "historical being-there," in its encounter with tradition, as the "effective-historical consciousness."[46] For Gadamer the "effective-historical consciousness" or the hermeneutical encounter with tradition is open to the tradition's claim to truth. In this encounter, tradition/history (i.e., the written or oral past) is not muffled but allowed to challenge the certainties of the present. The interpreter or philosopher in this situation – the embodiment of the "effective-historical consciousness" – is in a questioning and yet released disposition to that which the past holds in its independence and the autonomy of its possibilities.

This openness and willingness to *risk* the standpoint of the present is the critical moment and the moment of critique in the hermeneutical encounter with tradition. The undecided and risky character of the hermeneutical situation, furthermore, arises out of the concrete "need [*Not*]" of the actuality of estrangement, out of which tradition, as the historicalness of the present, is explored and engaged.[47] As I have already pointed out, for us contemporary Africans, that which impels us to thought is precisely the estranged actuality of our present deriving from the colonial experience, the specific particularity of our history. Thus, it is in view of the inert presence of neocolonialism – the diremptions and misunderstandings consequent on colonialism – that a radical hermeneutics becomes the proper task of contemporary African philosophy.

It is necessary at this point to confront squarely the fundamental problem of this whole explication: How can one guard against the political dangers latent in an open-ended and radically interpretative relation with a particular and specific tradition exclusively guided by the "need [*Not*]" of the contemporary moment of history? Or as Drew

Hyland puts it, how is "the 'ontic' [concrete, political, and historical] question of good and evil" to be settled?[48]

One can only say that it is the "effective-history,"[49] to use Gadamer's term, the history that makes itself felt and saturates the lived presence and actuality of the present (in our case, the emancipatory promise and failure of the African liberation struggle) that acts as the normative standard which projects a future/destiny as the actuality of its yet-to-be. This effective past, this felt presence of history, itself is derived from and simultaneously constitutes our hermeneutical appropriation of the heritage that we project as our future.

In other words, if "historical being-there" (i.e., the concretely situated person in community) projects itself out of its past (i.e., out of that which marks the present by its presence while being appropriated by it as its concretely felt "effective-history"), it follows that the emancipatory aspirations of this effective past have a defining and normatively determining relation to our future, our destiny. As Okolo unequivocally points out, our

> hermeneutical situation is that of the formerly colonized, the oppressed, that of the underdeveloped, struggling for more justice and equality. From this point of view, the validity of an interpretation is tied to the validity of a struggle – of its justice and of its justness. Here, we affirm the methodological preeminence of praxis on hermeneutics, praxis understood in the sense of an action tending toward the qualitative transformation of life.[50]

In this context, as Okolo affirms, "Hermeneutical theory is an integral part of hermeneutical practice. Here, theory is not added to practice as a luxurious supplement; it illuminates practice, which, in turn provokes it in a dialectical manner."[51] In this theoretic scenario, emancipatory *praxis* opens and offers the timely issues and concerns in which a hermeneutical perspective incarnates its interrogative and interpretative explorations. Conversely, and as a rejoinder to the dialectical tensions interior to this relation, hermeneutical reflection opens to *praxis* the proper theoretic space to explore and suggest the normative alignment of its emancipatory projects and practical undertakings.

It is imperative to remember, as Amilcar Cabral unequivocally pointed out in 1962, that the *praxis* of the African anti-colonial struggle as affirmed by the "UN resolution on decolonialisation" is now part of the internationally recognized emancipatory legacy of post-colonial humanity.[52] In honoring this legacy we are basically upholding the "justice" and "justness" of our age-old African struggle against colonialism and the continuing efforts against neocolonialism. In view of this:

> When in our country [or Continent] a comrade dies under police torture, is assassinated in prison, is burned alive or falls under the bullets of Portuguese guns, for which cause is he giving his life? He is giving it for the liberation of our people from the colonial yoke, and hence for the UN. In fighting and dying for the liberation of our countries we are giving our lives, in the present context of international legality, for the ideal which the UN itself has defined in its Charter, in its resolutions, and in particular in its resolution on decolonialisation.[53]

The struggle against neocolonialism is, furthermore, a continuation and a hermeneutically critical refining of this emancipatory *praxis* aimed at autonomy and freedom in full recognition of the differing cultural-historical totalities that constitute our world. This then is the moment of critique in the hermeneutical encounter with tradition and the specifics of appropriation within a particular historicalness.

In contradistinction to Heidegger then, and with Cabral and Fanon, on an *ontic* level it is our struggle, grounded in the specificity of our history, which acts as the normative sieve that strains, sifts, and negotiates our orientation to the future. This does not mean that we cling "to a system set up as a norm,"[54] nor that we are beguiled by history, wheresoever it might take us! Rather, in releasing ourselves to the fluidity of our existence and of our future, in and out of this fluidity we firmly resolve that the lived "necessity [*Notwendigkeit*]"[55] out of which this future is being historicized will always be remembered. In so doing we persevere and sustain into the future the "justice" and the "justness" of our concrete engagements. This is how we respond to Hyland's germane question regarding "good and evil."[56]

Thus, African philosophy as the hermeneutics of the post-colonial situation is the critical remembrance, itself interior to the lived emancipatory *praxis* of contemporary Africa, that cultivates, mediates, and revitalizes the origin or the source of this emancipatory *praxis* as the historicity of its effective inheritance. It is the discourse which concretely evokes and evocatively recalls to this emancipatory tradition the "truth" of its originative disclosure. Occasioned by the felt and lived needs of the present, it explores the future embedded and preserved in the possibilities of the heritage of its own enduring horizon. In so doing it explodes the duplicity and sterility of the neocolonial duplication of European modernity (i.e., the en-framing of modern technology) and inaugurates "invention into [contemporary African] existence."[57]

[T]his is how the African liberation struggle – as critically epitomized in the thinking of Fanon and Cabral – actualizes the historicity of the colonized in the process of the anti-colonial struggle. In the apt words of Cheikh Hamidou Kane: "*We* have not had the same past, *you* and ourselves, but we shall have, strictly, the same future. The era of separate destinies has run its course ... no one can any longer live by the simple carrying out of what he himself is." In the sameness of this global future, however, we the formerly colonized, "all of us, Hindus, Chinese, South Americans, Negroes, Arabs, all of us, awkward and pitiful, we the underdeveloped, who feel ourselves to be clumsy in a world of perfect mechanical adjustments," have to reclaim and concretely reinstitute the historicity of our own existence.[58]

This is the "justice" and "justness" that originates out of the disappointed possibilities of our past, from whence we project a future. A future in which the unequivocal recognition of the multiverse that constitutes our – thus far denied – historical and cultural specificity (i.e., our humanity) will become the basis for global earthly solidarity. Thus, heeding Fanon's insightful words, we leave behind Old Europe, with all its transcendental and empty odes to "Man,"[59] and with Nietzsche we "*remain faithful to the earth.*"[60]

IV

The hermeneutical orientation in contemporary African philosophy or African philosophical hermeneutics is thus thematically and historically linked to the demise of direct European colonial dominance and is aimed at the destructuring of the persistence of neocolonial hegemony in contemporary African existence. It is focused on the theoretic consummation of this demise. For the concrete resurrection of Africa beyond the tutelage of Europe requires in all spheres of life a rethinking of the present asphyxiating inertness in terms which are conducive and congenial to Africa and its diverse peoples. This is the indispensable hermeneutic supplement to the historic and concrete process of "re-Africanisation"[61] without which, as Cabral tells us, nothing can be achieved.

As part of the cultural and intellectual production of a diverse continent, the hermeneutic evocations of the African philosopher are interior to the efforts of differing African peoples in "the sphere of thought" to constitute and "keep [themselves] . . . in existence."[62] For the African philosopher the accent is on hermeneutically exploring these differences in view of the common and binding African experience in confronting European modernity – the shared experience of colonialism and neocolonialism.

In the commonality of these differences we need to ascend to and forge a joint future. For beyond the inert present the future still remains "to be discovered."[63] As Okolo fittingly observes:

> We have to acknowledge that our efforts at theorizing interpretation and tradition are inscribed interior to the ways and means that tradition itself secretes and utilizes for its own preservation, renewal, and perpetuation.[64]

The basic task of philosophy in Africa is explicitly giving voice to this needful concern. In contributing to this hermeneutical effort, on its own level of abstraction and in full recognition of its lived historicity, philosophy constitutes itself and fulfills its calling – to think that which evokes thought – in the situatedness of the present. To affirm the above is to recognize that "interpretation [philosophy] presupposes a tradition, and . . . tradition as such is always interpreted."[65] This is the historicity of philosophic thought and reflection in the context of post-colonial Africa. For the historicity of philosophy is always measured against its own conscious awareness – or lack thereof – of its lived presuppositions and its rootedness in a specific tradition and history.

In view of all that has been said thus far, then, the discourse of African philosophy has to be grasped explicitly as a radical hermeneutics of the contemporary African situation. This historically specific situation is that out of which African philosophical hermeneutics spins the thread of its reflexive reflections. Taking its point of departure from the as of yet unfulfilled promise of African "independence," this hermeneutical perspective constitutes the substance of its discourse and critically appropriates as its own the emancipatory horizon of the theoretical and political legacy of the African liberation struggle.[66] As Heidegger aptly puts it:

> Philosophy will never seek to deny its "presuppositions," but neither may it simply admit them. It conceives them, and it unfolds with more and more penetration both the presuppositions themselves and that for which they are presuppositions.[67]

Notes

All emphasis in the original unless otherwise indicated.

1 Theophilus Okere, *African Philosophy: A Historico-Hermeneutical Investigation of the Conditions of Its Possibility* (Lanham, Md.: University Press of America, 1983), p. vii. See also, Elungu Pene Elungu, "La philosophie, condition du développement en Afrique aujourd'hui," *Présence Africaine*, no. 103, (1977), p. 3.
2 Marcien Towa, "Conditions for the Affirmation of a Modern African Philosophical Thought," in *African Philosophy: The Essential Readings*, ed. Tsenay Serequeberhan (New York: Paragon House, 1991), p. 187.
3 Frantz Fanon, *Towards the African Revolution* (New York: Grove Press, 1988), p. 120.
4 Unlike most others, as early as 1961 in his seminal work *The Wretched of the Earth* (New York: Grove Press, 1968), Fanon had pointed out the class and historico-political difficulties that lay ahead for the African anti-colonial struggle. In this regard see particularly the section titled, "The Pitfalls of National Consciousness." On this point Kofi Buenor Hadjor, a one time press aide in the publicity secretariat of the Nkrumah government, pays tribute to Fanon's keen insight at the time of his exile with Nkrumah in Guinea Conakry. "It was in Conakry that I first read Fanon, especially his *Wretched of the Earth* which my exile companion, John K. Tettegah, now Ghana's ambassador to the Soviet Union, gave me as a present. It did not take me long to realize that Fanon's analysis had much more to offer than Machiavelli and many of the other classics. Tettegah and I literally devoured the chapter on 'The Pitfalls of National Consciousness' as we felt its analysis was too true to the Ghanaian situation." *On Transforming*

Africa Discourses with Africa's Leaders (Trenton, N.J.: Africa World Press, 1987), p. 3.

5 Notice that this last sentence projects an African future that will "recognize" in our immediate postcolonial past the disappointments of the hopes and aspirations of the African liberation movement. In so doing it projects into the future the validity of its own assumptions given the situatedness of its own hermeneutical actuality. Now this "recognition" is not the "recognition" of some "objective state of affairs in the future," much less a prediction of what is to come. Rather it is a "recognition" that will be possible or will be possiblized only if the disappointed objectives of the African liberation struggle – yet to be explored in this text – are fulfilled (at least in part and in some way) in the future the sentence projects and on which it stakes its emancipatory hopes. In other words, if the neocolonial present endures into the immediate and remote future of Africa, all of the above will be no more than unfulfilled and lost possibilities of African historical existence.

6 Enrique Dussel, *Philosophy of Liberation* (New York: Orbis Books, 1985), p. 13.

7 This is the basic theme of George Bush's first presidency, the beginning of the "second American century" as he put it in his inaugural address. With the collapse of the Soviet Union (the other superpower) and its Eastern European allies, Bush, in keeping with the rhetoric of his predecessor, has claimed all of these developments as victories for what has come to be known as the Reagan–Bush conservative revolution in contemporary American politics. The 2 August 1990 Iraqi invasion of Kuwait, and the "100 hour" Gulf War unleashed by the United States of America on Iraq (in conjunction with and in the guise of the United Nations) starting 16 January 1991 – all these developments are, by accident or design, framing the character of this "new world order" as extremely bellicose for the non-European world as a whole. American/Occidental military might, as in the days of old, seems to be, in a much more intense manner, the standard of "justice" in this "new world order." In this regard see, Noam Chomsky " 'What We Say Goes': The Middle East in the New World Order," *Z Magazine* (May 1991); Edward W. Said, "Ignorant Armies Clash by Night," *The Nation*, 11 February 1991; Anton Shammas, "A Lost Voice," *The New York Times Magazine*, 28 April 1991; and Eqbal Ahmad, "The Hundred-Hour War," *Dawn*, 17 March 1991.

8 Basil Davidson and Antonio Bronda, *Cross Roads in Africa* (Nottingham, Eng.: Spokesman Press, 1980), p. 36.

9 Ibid.

10 Hans-Georg Gadamer, *Truth and Method* (New York: Crossroad Publishers, 1982), pp. 158–9.

11 Ibid., second part, section I: "Schleiermacher's Project of a Universal Hermeneutics," *passim*.

12 *Hegel: The Difference between the Fichtean and Schellingian Systems of Philosophy*, trans. Dr Jere Paul Surber (Atascadero, Calif.: Ridgeview Publishing Co., 1978), p. 10.

13 In this regard see Abiola Irele, *In Praise of Alienation*, an inaugural lecture delivered on 22 November 1982, at the University of Ibadan (Published by Abiola Irele, 1987), *passim*. It is interesting to note, however, that Irele fails to capitalize on the negative value of alienation when he is concerned with the contemporary developments of African philosophy. In this regard see his substantial introduction to Paulin J. Hountondji's book, *African Philosophy: Myth and Reality* (Bloomington: Indiana University Press, 1983), *passim*.

14 Hans-Georg Gadamer, *Philosophical Apprenticeships* (Cambridge, Mass.: MIT Press, 1985), p. 177. Gadamer is here defending himself against those who have reduced hermeneutics to a fad and use this fad either to hide methodological sterility or as a justification for the absence of method. Even if such a defense is justified, it is ironic that Gadamer – who claims that philosophy is hermeneutical in its very nature – should take offense and react so strongly to the "popular" acclaim of his basic and productive insight. As I hope the reader will see, my use of Gadamer is not "faddish" but concretely grounded in the nature of the questions with which I am concerned.

15 Ernest Wamba-Dia-Wamba, "Philosophy in Africa: Challenges of the African Philosopher," in *African Philosophy: The Essential Readings*, ed. Tsenay Serequeberhan (New York: Paragon House, 1991), p. 230. As Wamba puts it: "Why, indeed, are hermeneutics, phenomenology, Althusserianism, logical positivism, Hegelianism, structuralism, pragmatism, dialectical materialism, Thomism, etc., all products of specific material and symbolic conditions (specific ideological struggles), understood by our African philosophers as so many correct responses to the philosophical question in Africa?" (ibid.). All I would like to say at this point is that Wamba's question has a boomerang effect on his own "Africanized" Marxist-Leninist position, which he does not address. To be sure, the question is to the point and, as I shall show in this chapter, can be adequately engaged – in all its cultural and historico-political richness – only from an Africanist hermeneutic perspective radically and critically informed by and absorbed in its own lived historicalness.

16 V. Y. Mudimbe, "African Gnosis: Philosophy and the Order of Knowledge," *African Studies Review*, vol. 28, nos. 2/3 (June/Sept. 1985), pp. 210–11.

17 I derive this distinction from an exploration of Martin Heidegger, *Discourse on Thinking* (New York: Harper & Row, 1966); Hans-Georg Gadamer, *Truth and Method* (New York: Crossroad Publishers, 1982), second part; and Thomas S. Kuhn, *The Structure of Scientific Revolutions*, 2d edn (Chicago: University of Chicago Press, 1970), *passim*.

18 In this regard see Martin Heidegger's "Modern

Science, Metaphysics, and Mathematics," in *Basic Writings*, ed. David Farrell Krell (New York: Harper & Row, 1977).

19 For the work of these two thinkers, please see *Ethiopian Philosophy*, vol. 2, The Treatise of Zar'a Ya'aqob and Walda Heywat, text and authorship (Addis Abeba: Printed for the Addis Abeba University by Commercial Printing Press, 1976), prepared by Dr Claude Sumner.

20 Elungu, "La philosophie, condition du développement en Afrique aujourd'hui," p. 8, my own translation.

21 Okere, *African Philosophy: A Historico-Hermeneutical Investigation*, p. xiv.

22 Martin Heidegger, *Being and Time* (New York: Harper & Row, 1962), division two, section 69, *passim* and specifically p. 416. See also, section 68 and section 73, *passim* and specifically p. 430. For Heidegger, who is the most important figure in contemporary hermeneutics, the term "has been," which appears sporadically in differing forms in the texts indicated and throughout *Being and Time*, designates the past that is felt and makes itself felt in the presence of the present. It is a living past that structures the lived actuality of historical *Dasein* – the concrete historicity of human existence. As we shall soon see in our further elaboration of this point in this chapter, this is what Gadamer refers to and appropriates as "effective history."

23 I have placed the term "greatness" in quotation marks to indicate that my concern, in using it, is not to praise and extol the "greatness" of ancient Africa but merely to point to the fact that the African past did have moments of greatness embodied in a variety of ancient civilizations, such as Axum, Mali, Soghai, Ghana, and Egypt, with all their contradictions and internal problems. My project is thus not defined by a "Diopian" (to borrow a word from Asante) longing for the "greatness" of ancient Africa, but by a critical and historical engagement with the historicity of the African situation.

24 This is what Gadamer refers to as the "effective-historical consciousness." For a discussion of this term and for a thematic exploration of its origins in Heidegger's Being-question, see my paper, "Heidegger and Gadamer: Thinking as 'Meditative' and as 'Effective-Historical Consciousness,'" *Man and World*, vol. 20, no.1 (1987).

25 Okonda Okolo, "Tradition and Destiny: Horizons of an African Philosophical Hermeneutics," in *African Philosophy: The Essential Readings*, ed. Tsenay Serequeberhan (New York: Paragon House, 1991), p. 207.

26 Kwasi Wiredu, *Philosophy and An African Culture* (New York: Cambridge University Press, 1980), p. 1; Paulin J. Hountondji, *African Philosophy, Myth and Reality*, p. 67.

27 Heidegger, *Being and Time*, p. 255. In this regard see also, "Letter on Humanism," in *Basic Writings*, ed. David Farrell Krell (New York: Harper & Row, 1977), p. 209.

28 Ibid., p. 67

29 For an overview of the discussions provoked by Heidegger's Nazism brought about by Victor Farias's book, *Heidegger and Nazism* (Philadelphia: Temple University Press, 1989), see Kathleen Wright, "The Heidegger Controversy – Updated and Appraised," *Praxis International*, vol. 13, no. 1 (April 1993). For a concise and revealing discussion of this scandalous affair, see, Thomas Sheehan, "Heidegger and the Nazis," in *The New York Review of Books*, vol. 35, no. 10 (16 June 1988). For a variety of views on this question by Gadamer, Habermas, Derrida, Blanchot, Lacoue-Labarthe, and Levinas, all contemporary European philosophers whose work has been critically influenced by Heidegger's Being-question, see *Critical Inquiry*, vol. 15, no. 2 (Winter 1989), "Symposium on Heidegger and Nazism," ed. Arnold I. Davidson. In this regard it is imperative to remember the words of Aimé Césaire, the Martiniquian poet and philosopher of *Négritude* (a *Négritude* fundamentally at odds with Senghor's essentialism of "Negro-ness"). On this point Césaire writes: "Yes, it would be worthwhile to study clinically, in detail, the steps taken by Hitler and Hitlerism and to reveal to the very distinguished, very humanistic, very Christian bourgeois of the twentieth century that without his being aware of it, he has a Hitler inside him, that Hitler *inhabits* him, that Hitler is his *demon*, that if he rails against him, he is being inconsistent and that, at bottom, what he cannot forgive Hitler for is not *crime* in itself, *the crime against man*, it is not *the humiliation of man as such*, it is the crime against the white man, the humiliation of the white man, and the fact that he applied to Europe colonialist procedures which until then had been reserved exclusively for the Arabs of Algeria, the coolies of India, and the blacks of Africa [and, we might add, the exterminated aboriginal populations of Australia, North and South America, and more recently the Palestinian Arabs, at the hands of the victimizing victims of the Holocaust]." *Discourse on Colonialism*, originally published in French in 1955 (New York: Monthly Review Press, 1972), p. 14. Needless to say, not one of the above thinkers – who appropriately lament and condemn Heidegger's Nazi connection – least of all Jürgen Habermas, the "philosopher of modernity" (the age of "imperialist colonialism," to borrow Lenin's phrase), has made racism, colonialism, or the expansionist aggressive nature of European modernity a problem for his thought or the focus of his reflections. This silence, this un-said, might just be the "demon" that needs to be exorcised. But under what "banner" is this exorcism to be performed? Who is to be the exorciser?

30 Martin Heidegger, *Being and Time*, p. 377. As the translators, J. Macquarrie and E. Robinson explain: "The root-meaning of the word 'ecstasis' (Greek εκστασισ; German, *Ekstase*) is 'standing outside'. Used generally in Greek for the 'removal' or 'displacement' of something, it came to be applied to states-of-

mind which we would now call 'ecstatic'. Heidegger usually keeps the basic root-meaning in mind, but he also is keenly aware of its close connection with the root-meaning of the word 'existence' " (p. 377, note 2). This affinity of the terms "ecstatic" and "existence" is central not only for *Being and Time* but for Heidegger"s work as a whole. In "Letter on Humanism" and throughout his later works the term "existence" is rendered as "ek-sistence" in order to accentuate this affinity and to suggest that human existence is the process of its own ecstatic going beyond – hence "standing outside" – itself. The human being is the *Da* – the "there" or openness – of Being which is interior to Being itself. In other words, Heidegger is not merely rejecting humanism out of hand; rather, he is thinking a nonmetaphysical humanism grounded on the *Da*'s interiority to Being. Throughout this chapter and the study as a whole, the reader is advised to keep in mind the above key interpretation of the term "existence" as "ek-sistence." Finally, on p. 205 of the "Letter on Humanism," Heidegger writes that the statement: "The 'essence' of *Dasein* lies in its existence," does not "contain a universal statement about *Dasein*, since the word came into fashion in the eighteenth century as a name for 'object', intending to express the metaphysical concept of the actuality of the actual." As the careful reader can easily ascertain, this refers to the term *Dasein* and its origins and not to the existentiality of human existence which it indicates.

31 Heidegger himself suggests this point in his discussions with a Japanese philosopher in, *On the Way to Language* (New York: Harper & Row, 1982). See the first section titled, "A Dialogue on Language," *passim*. In his already cited book, Theophilus Okere also notes this point. However, in his explication he unduly restricts this fecund suggestion. In this regard see *African Philosophy: A Historico-Hermeneutical Investigation*, pp. 118–19.

32 In this regard, see Heidegger's last statement of his views, "Modern Natural Science and Technology," in *Radical Phenomenology*, ed. J. Sallis (Atlantic Highlands, N.J.: Humanities Press, 1978), p. 4. For Heidegger's overall perspective on technology and the situation of the modern world, see *The Question concerning Technology and Other Essays*, trans. William Lovitt (New York: Harper & Row, 1977). For the sense of the term *Ge-stell* and its English rendering as "enframing," see Lovitt's introduction to the text, p. xxix, and in the text, see p. 19.

33 Wamba, "Philosophy in Africa: Challenges of the African Philosopher," *African Philosophy: The Essential Readings*, p. 239.

34 Heidegger, *Being and Time*, p. 346.

35 Basil Davidson, *Africa in Modern History* (New York: Penguin Books, 1985), p. 44.

36 Antonio Gramsci, *Quaderni Del Carcere*, vol. 2, edizione critica dell'Instituto Gramsci, a cura di Valentino Gerratana (Torino: Giulio Einaudi, 1975), pp. 1376–

7, my own translation.

37 Ibid., p. 1378, my own translation.

38 For a classic description of this momentous moment in the self-institution of modernity and the destruction of the non-European world which justifies and welcomes it as the objective self-unfolding of *Weltgeist*, see Karl Marx and Frederick Engels, *The Communist Manifesto* (New York: International Publishers, 1983), pp. 10–13.

39 Okolo, "Tradition and Destiny: Horizons of an African Philosophical Hermeneutics," in *African Philosophy: The Essential Readings*, p. 201.

40 Ibid.

41 In this regard, see Martin Heidegger, *Discourse on Thinking* (New York: Harper & Row, 1966), the second part, "Conversation on a Country Path about Thinking," *passim*.

42 Okolo, "Tradition and Destiny," p. 204.

43 Martin Heidegger, *An Introduction to Metaphysics* (New Haven, Conn.: Yale University Press, 1977), p. 176.

44 Ibid.

45 Okolo, "Tradition and Destiny," p. 203.

46 Gadamer, *Truth and Method*, p. 325, and pp. 273–4.

47 Hans-Georg Gadamer, *Reason in the Age of Science* (Cambridge, Mass.: MIT Press, 1981), pp. 109–10. In this regard see also my already cited paper, "Heidegger and Gadamer: Thinking as 'Meditative' and as 'Effective-Historical Consciousness,' " p. 56 and pp. 59–60. For an interesting discussion of this point centered on the Habermas–Gadamer debate and on Vico's notion of "sensus communis," see John D. Schaefer, *Sensus Communis* (Durham, N.C.: Duke University Press, 1990), pp. 117–22. I would like to thank Nuhad Jamal for this last reference.

48 Drew Hyland, *The Origins of Philosophy* (New York: Capricorn Books, 1973), p. 289; and by the same author, *The Virtue of Philosophy* (Athens: Ohio University Press, 1981), pp. 12–13. This is a central problem of Heidegger's thought located in the ontic-ontological ambiguity of his ontological analysis and its ontic specificity, or lack thereof, in relation to particular political and historical questions. I cannot here consider, at great length, this important concern except to say that the specific way in which African hermeneutics is here being articulated and the distinctive history out of which it emerges precludes the dangers inherent in Heidegger's position. This is so precisely because the hermeneutical orientation of African philosophy is firmly wedded to an emancipatory political *praxis* and an ontic historical orientation aimed at the recognition and celebration of cultural-historical variety and difference.

49 Gadamer, *Truth and Method*, pp. 267–8. For the source of Gadamer's conception of "effective-history," see Heidegger, *Being and Time*, division two, part five, section 73, p. 430.

50 Okolo, "Tradition and Destiny," p. 208. See also S. K. Dabo, "Negro-African Nationalism as a Quest for Justice," *Présence Africaine*, no. 107, 3d quarterly

(1978), *passim*.

51 Okolo, ibid., p. 205.

52 Amilcar Cabral, "Anonymous Soldiers for the United Nations," in *Revolution in Guinea: Selected Texts* (New York: Monthly Review Press, 1969), pp. 50–2. In view of what has been said in note 7, it should be noted that the United Nations, just as any other complex body that encompasses within itself conflicting and contending forces around formal principles and norms of behavior, is a site of struggle and hegemonic contention. In this regard, what Cabral is affirming is an achievement that is sanctioned by the formal principles of the United Nations and yet has been secured against the interests of the dominant forces within it, i.e., the United States and its NATO allies. For an interesting discussion of the "functioning" of the United Nations in terms of "its" most recent international crisis, the colonial legacy of the non-European world, and in the context of superpower reconciliation, see Erskine B. Childers, "The Use and Abuse of the UN in the Gulf Crisis," *Middle East Report*, no. 169, vol. 21, no. 2 (March/April 1991). For a detailed exposition of the United Nations' partiality in its selective application of international norms and standards, see Norman Finkelstein, "Israel and Iraq: A Double Standard," *Journal of Palestine Studies*, vol. 20, no. 2 (Winter 1991).

53 Cabral, ibid., pp. 51–2.

54 See note 44.

55 See note 44. From within the concrete situation of the Eritrean anti-colonial struggle Issayas Afewerki expresses this view in the following manner: "the attainment of the objectives of our national cause – independence and liberation from Ethiopian colonial rule – take precedence over other issues, and because of various other regional considerations, we have chosen to avoid involvement in any regional conflicts or inter-Arab disputes. We have chosen to concentrate our efforts on our main objective, which is victory over Ethiopian colonial rule." *Foreign Broadcast Information Service*, Daily Report, Sub-Saharan Africa, Thursday 12 July 1990, p. 8.

56 For the relevant quotation in full and reference please see, in this chapter, note 48.

57 Fanon, *Black Skins, White Masks*, p. 229.

58 Cheikh Hamidou Kane, *Ambiguous Adventure* (Portsmouth, N.H.: Heinemann Educational Books, 1989), pp. 79–80, emphasis added. On this point, see also Lucius Outlaw, "African 'Philosophy': Deconstructive and Reconstructive Challenges," in *Contemporary Philosophy: A New Survey*, vol. 5, African Philosophy, ed. Guttorm Floistad (Dordrecht, Netherlands: Martinus Nijhoff, 1987), pp. 35–6.

59 Fanon, *The Wretched of the Earth*, p. 311.

60 *The Portable Nietzsche*, trans. Walter Kaufmann (New York: Viking Press, 1974), p. 125. I would like to thank Robert Gooding-Williams for helping me locate this reference.

61 Cabral, *Revolution in Guinea: Selected Texts*, p. 76.

62 Fanon, *The Wretched of the Earth*, p. 233. It is important to note, as is clear from the context, that Fanon's remarks – which I have slightly modified in quoting – refer in the singular to all the differing historico-cultural totalities that in sum constitute the cultural and historical actuality of the continent in all its diversity and difference.

63 Aimé Césaire, "Letter to Maurice Thorez," English translation, *Présence Africaine* (Paris: Présence Africaine, 1957), pp. 6–7.

64 Okolo, "Tradition and Destiny," p. 209.

65 Ibid., p. 202.

66 For an extremely condensed synopsis of this perspective see my paper, "The African Liberation Struggle: A Hermeneutic Exploration of an African Historical-Political Horizon," *Ultimate Reality and Meaning*, Interdisciplinary Studies in the Philosophy of Understanding (Canadian Journal), vol. 14, no. 1 (March 1991).

67 Heidegger, *Being and Time*, p. 358. Regarding presuppositions and the educational and lived background or context in which and out of which one philosophizes, Kwasi Wiredu writes: "Suppose now that a critic should attribute what I have written to my particular educational background; I am bound to concede as much. In a certain obvious sense we are all children of our circumstances. But were the existence of such a 'bias' proof of falsity, universal silence would be obligatory on all mankind" (*Philosophy and an African Culture*, p. 36). On the same crucial point Ernest Wamba-Dia-Wamba observes that: "The paradox in philosophy is that the selection of a conception or the definition of philosophy one makes is necessarily an expression of one's philosophical position, stand, and outlook." "Philosophy in Africa: Challenges of the African Philosopher," in *African Philosophy: The Essential Readings*, p. 236. In both of these remarks (remarks by contemporary African philosophers) there is a failure to recognize the hermeneutical truth that the lived situatedness of philosophy is not a blemish but the source of philosophical reflection as such. In fact one needs to begin from the recognition that philosophy is "its own time apprehended in thoughts," as Hegel puts it in the preface to the *Philosophy of Right*, trans. T. M. Knox (Oxford University Press, 1973), p. 11. Once this point is grasped the "fear" of "bias" and "paradox" is dissipated and the hermeneutically circular character of philosophy and its practice, grounded on "*Dasein*'s circular Being" (Heidegger, *Being and Time*, p. 363), can properly be seen as the fecund origin of philosophy itself. In this regard, see Theophilus Okere's already cited book, *African Philosophy: A Historico-Hermeneutical Investigation*, ch. 5. See also, Lucius Outlaw, "African and African-American Philosophy: Deconstruction and the Critical Management of Traditions," in *The Journal*, vol. 1, no. 1 (Winter–Spring 1984).

3

African, African American, Africana Philosophy

Lucius Outlaw

Introduction

Nearly fifty years ago, arguments that certain modes of thought of African peoples should be regarded as "philosophy" were advanced – in important instances by persons of European descent – and became a matter of serious debate.[1] Both the context and the debates were structured by the domination and exploitation of Africans by peoples from Europe, and rationalized with strategies drawing on rank-ordering distinctions and infected with racism. That Africans could philosophize was for many a bold declaration or proposal, at the very least, in light of the rationalizing, redefining, and attempted remaking of African peoples as subordinates to "civilized" peoples of Europe.

Today, of course, there are a significant number of formally trained African philosophers throughout the world. And, to a great extent the *explicit* development of discursive formations within the discipline of philosophy that invoke "Africa" has been unfolding through efforts to identify, reconstruct, and create traditions and repositories of thought by African and African-descended persons and peoples, in both oral and written literatures, as forms of philosophy. In the context of such endeavors, persons past and present, who were and are without formal training or degrees in philosophy, are being worked into developing canons as providing instances of reflections, on

Reproduced by kind permission of *Philosophical Forum*, Inc.

various matters, that are appropriately characterized as philosophical.[2]

Similar (and related) circumstances and developments condition efforts to give shape and meaning to African American philosophy as a disciplinary enterprise. When we look through the tables of contents of collections of writings organized under the heading of "American Philosophy," we find, in virtually every case, *no* writings by persons of African descent. Histories of American philosophy tend to be equally silent about thinkings and writings of Africans-becoming-"Americans" as instances of philosophy. There are, of course, long, rich traditions of critical, more or less systematic thought by women and men of African descent articulated in speeches and writings of various kinds that are now being appropriated as instances and traditions of philosophizing.[3] And during the last two decades in particular, with the significant increase in the number of persons of African descent with formal training in philosophy (nonetheless, still a very small number – fewer than one percent of professional philosophers in the United States), many of whom underwent this training during the highly charged historical periods of the civil rights, black power, and African independence movements, efforts to construct a disciplinary formation and to identify and refine traditions of intellectual praxis as distinctively African American philosophy were a major concern of a few engaged and determined persons.[4]

"Africana philosophy" is the phrase I use as a "gathering" notion under which to situate the articulations (writings, speeches, etc.), and traditions of Africans and peoples of African descent collectively, as well as the subdiscipline- or field-forming, tradition-defining or tradition-organizing reconstructive efforts, which are (to be) regarded as philosophy. However, "Africana philosophy" is to include, as well, the work of those persons who are neither African nor of African descent but who recognize the legitimacy and importance of the issues and endeavors that constitute the disciplinary activities of African or African American philosophy and contribute to the efforts – persons whose work justifies their being called "Africanists." Use of the qualifier "Africana" is consistent with the practice of naming intellectual traditions and practices in terms of the national, geographic, cultural, racial, and/or ethnic descriptor or identity of the persons who initiated and were/are the primary practitioners – and/or are the subjects and objects – of the practices and traditions in question (e.g., "American," "British," "French," "German," or "continental" philosophy).

Yet, what is it that is characteristic of the philosophical practices of African and African-descended thinkers that distinguishes – or should distinguish? – the efforts *by virtue of their being those of persons African and/or African-descended*? Is there, or can there be, a properly determined field of philosophy that is constituted by the efforts of persons of a particular racial or ethnic group? Given the global dispersal of African peoples and the subsequent development of regional (e.g., Caribbean), more or less complex local-national (e.g., African American), and nation-state groupings ('Nigerian," "Kenyan"), can we speak of "Africana philosophy" in a cogent way?

These are some of the questions I wish to explore in what follows. In the process, I hope to clarify, for myself especially, the extent to which it makes sense to continue speaking of "Africana philosophy" as an "umbrella" notion under which can be gathered a potentially large collection of traditions of practices, agendas, and resulting literatures of African and African-descended peoples. I propose to review, briefly, developments in what is now referred to as African philosophy and particular instances of African American thought. However, I wish to also explore whether it makes sense to speak of "Africana philosophy" in even stronger terms: as a venture which should be bound by *particular* norms appropriate to discursive practices by and/or in the interests of African peoples (that is to say, which have their origins, justification, and legitimacy in the life-worlds of African peoples) in contrast to norms of the life-worlds of other peoples. In this regard, I intend to test the adequacy of what, in some quarters, is at present the most prominent – and contested – effort to define an agenda and strategies for inquiry about and in the interests of African peoples, namely, Molefi Kete Asante's notion and project of "Afrocentricity."

African Philosophy[5]

On the continent of Africa, the publication in 1945 of Placide Tempels' *La Philosophie Bantoue*, one of the earliest and most influential explicit acknowledgments of African intellectual efforts and achievements as philosophy, marks the initiation of contemporary discussions of African philosophy.[6] Emerging during the apex of European colonization in Africa, the discussion, both in form and content, was shaped by this context, and no less so by subsequent anticolonial struggles. The focus of the discussion was whether African peoples could *have* or *do* philosophy. But this was only the surface issue. The deeper and more pressing question was whether Africans were fully human as defined by the reigning Greek-cum-European philosophical-anthropological paradigm centered around the notion of "rationality."

There were strong reactions to Tempels since the major thesis of the book – that Bantu Africans had a "philosophy" – challenged the rationalizations of the colonization, enslavement, and exploitation of Africans and the resources of Africa. In addition, a significant number of African intellectuals felt that the humanity of Africans as beings of "reason" was defended and vindicated, all the more so by a European. Even further, certain Europeans who were in some ways more knowledgeable of, sympathetic to, and respectful of Africans than was Tempels were likewise happy to see their views confirmed in Tempels' report of African achievements in philosophy.[7]

Tempels challenged the claim that Africans were inherently or developmentally incapable of the level of thought required for "true" philosophy, the standards for which were those operative in the traditions and practices of mainstream European philosophy. Franz Crahay, in his criticism of *Bantu Philosophy*, argued against what he regarded as the mistaken acceptance of the book as an instance of Bantu *philosophy*, rather than as what he termed an "impetus" for philosophy.[8] A "frank appraisal," he argued, required the conclusion that philosophy did *not* exist at present (circa 1965) among the Bantu "within the admissible sense" of "philosophy": that is, as "explicit, abstract analytical reflection, sharply critical and autocritical, which is systematic, at least in principle, and yet open, dealing with experience, its human condition, and the meanings and values that it reveals."[9] Crahay went on to specify what he took to be the necessary "dissociations" constitutive of the appropriate conceptual conditions under which a Bantu philosophy might be founded, conditions, in his judgment, not then fulfilled by Bantu thinkers:

- dissociation of subject and object through reflection; dissociation of I and others;
- dissociation of the natural from the supernatural, of technical action and acts of faith; dissociation of the concrete and the abstract leading to dissociation of the named object and the term;
- dissociation of time and space;
- development from a limited concept of corporeal freedom to a *mature* concept of freedom involving a synthesis of corporeal freedom, the faculty of decision, and the "assumption of responsibility for one's actions and their rationally recognized consequences"; and
- a desirable attitude, i.e., the avoidance of temptations of "shortcuts" or the "cult of difference."[10]

This was the context within which debates regarding the humanity of Africans were forced by Tempels' *Bantu Philosophy* and its reception. Other scholars during the same period (1930s–40s and subsequently) who were investigating the thought-systems of various African peoples made substantial contributions to the debate. It was in this same historical context that the voices of Africans concerned with the liberation of African peoples from colonial domination and with the reclamation of the indigenous cultures of African peoples were raised (for example, during the Négritude movement) to challenge the caricatures of black peoples perpetrated by peoples of European descent. Efforts to identify and elaborate "African philosophy" have to a large extent been endeavors of this kind. And it is this historical, contextual framing that, in part, gives identity to the efforts as comprising a distinct field of discourse, one that is conditioned by European legacies (e.g., in being called "philosophy") while, in many instances, challenging the claims to truth, exclusivity, and predominance that

for centuries were driving forces, theoretically and practically, in the imperialist encounters of European peoples with native peoples in Africa and elsewhere.[11]

That debate has now given way to a broader range of concerns. On the African continent this has resulted in the emergence of different trends or "schools" of thought, the growth of diverse bodies of philosophical literature, the formation of national and international professional philosophical associations, and the development of programs offering advanced degrees in philosophy in African institutions with strong emphasis, in a number of instances, on African philosophy. Critical self-consciousness regarding developments in African philosophy has led to the articulation of various taxonomic overviews or "mappings" of the field. There is H. Odera Oruka's discussion of the four "trends" of African philosophy (i.e., "ethnophilosophy," "philosophic sagacity," "nationalist-ideological" philosophy, and "professional" philosophy).[12] Alphonse J. Smet[13] and O. Nkombe[14] offer a more insightful and nuanced mapping of trends.[15] *Ideological* is their name for a trend that, for them, includes such developments as "African personality,"[16] Pan-Africanism,[17] Négritude,[18] African humanism,[19] African socialism,[20] scientific socialism,[21] Consciencism,[22] and "authenticity."[23] The rule for inclusion in this trend is that all of the works and discussions are geared primarily to redressing the political and cultural situation of African peoples under the conditions of European imperialism, enslavement, and colonization. Their second trend includes works which recognize the existence of philosophy in traditional Africa, examine its philosophical elements as found in its various manifestations, and systematically explore complexes of traditional thought as repositories of wisdom and esoteric knowledge.[24] The principal criterion for placement in this trend is the shared motivation on the part of the thinkers surveyed to contest the pernicious myth that Africans are peoples of a decidedly "primitive mentality."

Smet and Nkombe's third trend, the *critical* school, is shaped by reactions to the first two trends. It is from the critical trend that we get the label "ethnophilosophy" applied to the thinkers in the traditional and ideological groupings as a way of questioning the relevance and validity of their work as instances of philosophy proper.[25] On the other hand, there are those in the critical group who also criticize western conceptions of science and philosophy, particularly in the context of the deployment of those enterprises as part of the European expansion into Africa. Finally, the Nkombe/Smet taxonomy includes a fourth grouping, one they term the *synthetic* trend. Here are to be found the works and practices of persons who use philosophical hermeneutics to explore issues and new problems which emerge in the African context.[26]

The Nkombe/Smet survey of African philosophy has been given even greater detail by Mudimbe who identifies a first group (the principle of placement which Mudimbe uses being the idea that the participants make use of a "wide sense" of the term "philosophy"[27]) that is made up of two subgroups: the *ethnophilosophical*,[28] which includes "works arising from the need to express and to render faithfully the unity and the coherence of traditional philosophies" and the *ideologico-philosophical*, which includes works "qualified by an explicit intention to separate and to analyze present constraints of African society, marking the present and future situation, while remaining true to African ideals . . ."[29]

Mudimbe's second group is made up of persons whose works are structured by the notion of philosophy "in the strict sense" (i.e., in something like the sense articulated by Crahay). Sub-groupings include persons who are involved in reflections on the conditions of possibility of African philosophy (e.g., Fabien Eboussi-Boulaga, Marcien Towa, and Paulin Hountondji) and persons who reflect on the significance of western sciences, the anthropological/ethnological social sciences in particular, both in terms of their developments and their applications as forms of knowledge in African contexts (Stanislas Adotevi, Ngoma-Binda, Mudimbe himself). Writings in a third group (those of Atanganga, Njoh-Mouelle, and other writings of Eboussi-Boulaga), which involve reflections on philosophy "as a critical auxiliary to the process of development," Mudimbe regards as high points in the field. Finally, the works of Nkombe, Ntumba Tshiamalenga, I. P. Leleye, John Kinyongo, and others Mudimbe includes in the subgroup of writings which share a concern for philosophical hermeneutics.[30]

African American Philosophy

The crucible for New World Africans has been (and continues to be) the complex of factors involving various forms of racial oppression and class exploitation, further complicated by matters having to do with sex and gender. In a dialectic of racist imposition and creative response in the process of survival and reproduction, New World African descendants-become-Americans have had to form and perpetuate new ways for getting on with their lives. A recurrent feature of life in the racialized crucible has been the struggle to resolve major tensions infecting identity-formation and all that follows in their wake, the tensions involving the ambiguities and ambivalences of being, in some senses, both "African" and "American." Historically, how these tensions were mediated by particular persons in the forging of an identity was crucial to forming or sharing in agendas and exercising strategies devoted to securing *freedom*, for the person and the "race." For this and other important reasons, differences have always existed among thinkers of African descent in the United States which have resulted from and led to distinct foci, strategies, and objectives of discursive traditions and practices. A brief rehearsal of several complexes of socially engaged thinking will provide examples of what today is being claimed as instances of African American philosophy that, in the words of Leonard Harris, was, indeed, "philosophy born of struggle."[31]

From the earliest presence of Africans as slaves in the portion of the New World that was later to become the United States of America, militant antislavery agitation was a prominent endeavor among "free" persons of color in the North and East (less so from the early 1850s to the Civil War). Frederick Douglass was one of the most well-known participants in the movement to abolish slavery. (The movement had its foundations in the efforts of black folk, though white abolitionists came to play dominant, controlling roles.) Two decades of post-Reconstruction separatist and emigrationist activity (mid-1860s–1880s) followed the Civil War but were soon eclipsed by a period (1880–1915) during which the accommodationist strategy of Booker T. Washington was predominant, though not without "radical" challenges from W. E. B. DuBois and others who initiated the Niagara movement to counter the effects of Washington's agenda and to press for full citizenship rights for African Americans. The National Association for the Advancement of Colored People (NAACP), which grew out of the Niagara movement, and the National Urban League were organized toward the end of this period (in 1909 and 1910, respectively) and would play major roles in promoting the melioration of racial apartheid by utilizing legal attacks and organized protests to attack invidious racial discrimination in schools, workplaces, and public accommodations.

Booker T. Washington's death in 1915 resulted in the declining significance of his accommodationist strategy. Major transformations in the American and world economies including industrialization in the North and Northeast; world war; the pull of jobs; the hope for less restricted social life; and the push of agricultural transformations in the South all led to significantly increased migration of African Americans to the American industrial heartland and the development of conditions which were nurturing soil in which various forms of nationalism flowered (again) among people of African descent (during the period 1916–30). The organizational activities and achievements of Marcus Garvey and the Harlem Renaissance were two of the most significant nationalist developments. Further, recovery from the Depression and its attendant dislocations, spurred by a second world war and, later, the Korean war, conditioned several decades of economic expansion which led to rising prosperity for urban industrial workers in particular. Among these were a significant minority of black persons who ushered in the rise of the modern black middle class and who were to champion, after the decline of nationalist groups and projects as significant forces, "civil rights" and "integration" as objectives of black struggle (1940s–mid-1960s). This period was followed, and momentarily eclipsed, by yet another resurgence of black nationalism, the black power movement of the mid-1960s to the early 1970s.[32]

Assimilation is the name for projects which would have one racial and/or ethnic group absorbed, physically and/or culturally, by another, the former taking on the defining characteristics of the latter and relinquishing its own racial and/or ethnic distinctiveness. For African American assimilationists, the "official" cultural, social, political, and economic ideals of the American republic have been sufficient and appropriate goals for African American life, and people of African descent should pursue these ends "without regard to race, creed, or color." Frederick Douglass is one of the most well-known of African American assimilationists.

Accommodation was the prevailing agenda and strategy during the period when the influence of Booker T. Washington, its most successful purveyor, was dominant. For Washington, the economic and political hegemony of white folks was not to be challenged directly but was to be finessed by subtle strategies of seeming accommodation while black folks prepared themselves for economic self-reliance and eventual full political citizenship "earned" by forming and exercising good character and responsibility through education for and the practice of honest work.

Washington's strategy was fervently opposed by the likes of W. E. B. DuBois.[33] One of the foremost intellectuals in American history, DuBois was a proponent of what I term *pluralist integration*: that is, the commitment to achieving a society that is integrated socially, politically, and economically though made up of a plurality of racial and ethnic groups which maintain and perpetuate their racial and ethnic distinctivenesses to the extent that doing so does not threaten the integration of the social whole.[34] DuBois was thus something of a *nationalist* in being committed to the proposition that black folk should articulate and appropriate a racial identity based, in part, on biologically-based shared characteristics, but including, as well, shared history and culture. In this respect he might best be classed as a cultural nationalist. Other forms of nationalism include economic (capitalist or socialist) and political nationalism (democratic, socialist, or dictatorial) either form of which might – but need not – promote varying degrees of racial and/or ethnic integration or separatism.[35]

In contrast to those who have been called "Left nationalists" (i.e., nationalists committed, as well, to socialist or communist agendas and strategies, such as C. L. R. James and Grace and James Boggs[36]), there are those African American thinkers who have been committed socialists or communists for whom "race" is at best an epiphenomenon secondary to the primary contradictions of class-conflicted capitalist societies. For such persons racial (or ethnic) distinctions will disappear with the transformation of capitalist social formations into self-managing socialist or communist societies in which neither race nor ethnicity will be of any social significance.

Such thought/praxis complexes are among some of the most ready candidates for being regarded as instances of African American philosophy. Of course, organizing, examining, and representing the articulations of these persons and movements as "philosophy" involves positioning them in ways and contexts not intended by the "authors" themselves. W. E. B. DuBois was one of the very few to study philosophy formally, and even considered pursuing it professionally. Alain

Leroy Locke was one of the first persons of African descent in America to earn a doctoral degree in philosophy (Harvard University, 1918). Over the last half-century, a small number of African Americans joined the ranks of professional philosophers. And the need and desire to identify and/or forge distinctive philosophical traditions, literatures, and practices were given major impetus by the modern black power movement. Early in the 1970s, a number of attempts were made to articulate a "Black," or "Afro-American," and later "African American" philosophy.[37] Over the years a number of American Philosophical Association (APA) sessions have been devoted to these discussions, organized by the APA's Committee on Blacks in Philosophy (APA recognition of these efforts as having opened a legitimate discursive field was accorded in 1987 with the decision to list "Africana Philosophy" as a specialty in the discipline.)

Leonard Harris's edited *Philosophy Born of Struggle: Anthology of Afro-American Philosophy from 1917* remains the only widely available, somewhat historically organized collection of writings by African American philosophers. An important earlier collection is Percy E. Johnston's *Afro-American Philosophers*.[38] However, for the most part writings devoted to the formation of African American philosophy as a discursive context so named remain largely unpublished. A significant number of these writings were presented during the special APA sessions and during conferences held, for the most part, at historically black colleges and universities (e.g., Tuskegee and Morgan State Universities) during the 1970s and early 1980s. Of particular note are the following essays: "Value and Religion in Africana Philosophy: The African-American Case" by Robert C. Williams (deceased); George Garrison's "Afro-American Philosophical Thought: The Early Beginnings and the Afro-Centric Substratum"; and Cornel West's insightful critical survey "Black Philosophers and Textual Practice" in which he examines what he terms the "ideological character" of the textual practices ("academic dovetailing," "professional criticism", and "counterhegemonic praxis") of black philosophers in the twentieth century.[39] Other texts in the genre include a continuously expanding corpus of writings by Cornel West; Charles A. Frey's *From Egypt to Don Juan: The Anatomy of Black Studies* and *Level Three: A Black Philosophy Reader*[40]; and endeavors by others that are now bearing fruit and must be noted, among them the presentations and discussions of the writings of such persons as Alain Locke by Johnny Washington[41] and Leonard Harris[42]; and writings in ethics and social and political philosophy by Laurence Thomas, Adrian Piper, Michele Moody-Adams, William Lawson, Howard McGary, Jr., Bernard Boxill, Robert Birt, and others.

Nonetheless, there is a striking aspect to the recent work of African American philosophers: namely, for the most part this work is conducted with little or no knowledge of, or attention to, the history of philosophical activity on the African continent or elsewhere in the African diaspora. At the very least, this lack of awareness and attention may well contribute to deficiencies in our historically informed self-understandings and, to that extent, will have important implications for the work we do whether or not we take our work to be distinguished, or at least conditioned in significant ways, by our being persons of African descent. African philosophers have generally been much more successful in advancing the enterprise of philosophy, theoretically and practically, as a venture conditioned by explicit commitments and linkages to the histories and historical situations and to the interests of African peoples. It is my judgment that the development of traditions of thought by African American philosophers has been seriously curtailed by the absence of more refined, explicit, and shared agendas, conditioned by a sense of shared identities and shared histories. Further, a comparison of instances and traditions of philosophizing of African philosophers in various African countries to the work of particular African American thinkers or traditions highlights sharp differences in the degrees of institutionalization of philosophical praxes and legacies distinctively conditioned by what was called the "black consciousness movement." African and African-descended philosophers in America are perhaps long overdue for coming together for a sustained, systematic, critical reconstruction of our intellectual histories. However, the historical connections and more or less similar experiences of persons of African descent in the United States, in the African diaspora generally, and on continental Africa, do not warrant uncritical appropriations and celebrations of our racial connectedness, nor of the glories of philosophical insight from the African "Motherland" to which we should all turn to be shown the way to the primordial "ancient wisdom" that simply waits to be reclaimed.

Africana Philosophy

Have the all too brief and incomplete surveys of some of the trends and traditions of thought and praxis in African and African American philosophy provided even a glimpse of what would be required in the way of commonalities to support grouping them all under the same heading and, further, support efforts to articulate distinctive agendas, practices, ends, and norms characteristic of the philosophizing of African and African-descended thinkers? In the first instance, the range of universality of the term "Africana," its boundaries and "contents," coincide with the experiences and situated practices of a dispersed *geographic race*[43]: that is, not a genetically homogeneous group but persons and peoples who, through shared lines of descent and ancestry, share a relatively permanent geographical site of origin and development from which descendents were dispersed, and, thereby, who share a relatively distinctive gene pool that determines the relative frequencies of various physical characteristics, even in the diaspora; and persons who share – more or less – evolved social and cultural elements of life-worlds that are, in part, traceable to those of the "ancestors." In turn, geographical, cultural, social, and natural-selection factors influence the shared gene pool and cultural practices to condition *raciation*: that is, the formation and evolution of the biological and cultural factors collectively characterizing the "race."

But, this first instance provides only an initial circumscription of the primary distinguishing feature of some practitioners, and the "objects" or subjects, of the discursive practices of Africana philosophy: i.e., "African" and "African-descended" peoples. The strategy of circumscription is so far at best a point of departure. To avoid undue simplicity – or, worse still, biological or racial essentialism – more is required: namely, to identify the features that make certain intellectual practices and legacies of persons who are situated in geographically and historically-socially diverse societies "philosophy," features characteristic of – though not necessarily *unique* to – these persons *as members of a dispersed race*.

While I have offered a sketch of several forms of thought as possible candidates for inclusion under the heading of Africana philosophy, a key commitment influencing my discussion is the belief that there is no timeless essence shared by any and all forms of thought called "philosophy" that is a function of, say, logical or epistemological characteristics. A serious study of the writings of persons included in canons of western philosophy will disclose thinkings that are the same only in the most general sense of being reflections on . . . thinking, ethics, politics, etc. However, the agendas (motivations), strategies, and achievements involved are extremely diverse. Philosophizing is inherently grounded in socially shared practices, not in transcendental rules. When we view philosophical practices historically, sociologically, and comparatively, we are led inescapably to conclude that "philosophical practice is inherently pluralistic," and "[a]ll philosophical ideals are local" to communities of thinkers.[44] We mislead ourselves if we require that there be something more than "family resemblances" common to all the instances we recognize as instances of "philosophy," where the common feature is more or less systematic *reflection* on various aspects, in various areas, of experience to the end of facilitating ordered, meaningful existence. There are no transcendental rules *a priori* that are the essential, thus defining, feature of "philosophy."

Likewise for "Africana philosophy." To the extent that this phrase identifies a discursive venture or "field" with determinate contours and subregions, it does so, in large part, by constructing the field *ex post facto*: that is to say, through discursive strategies – mine, in the present case – which seek to organize "data" (i.e., instances of reflection and/or accounts of the same) in particular ways including, in important cases, practices and traditions of discourse which were not themselves conditioned by an explicit sense on the part of those involved that they were engaged in something called "philosophy" or "Africana philosophy."

Further, since African peoples are ethnically – hence culturally – diverse and geographically dispersed, very important aspects of these ethnic and geographical diversities were fueled, in significant part, by the incursions of Europeans and others into Africa. Even before the incursions and subsequent related dispersals, however, there were diversities among the peoples of Africa which were manifest even as the herding of slaves began. Thus, the practices, traditions, and literatures comprising "Africana philosophy," because they are tied, in the first instance, to the life-worlds of numerous African peoples, have diverse histories, sites, and conditions of emergence. Africana philosophy is constituted by diversity.

How, then, to speak of "commonalities" or

"unity" in Africana philosophy? The unifying commonality sought for to provide both boundaries and coherence is provided initially through third-order organizing, classificatory strategies: to the discursive practices that are the focus of discussion, practices which are themselves second-order reflections on the first-order lived experiences of various African and African-descended persons and peoples. Further, the presentation of commonalities sufficient to support gathering the practices of dispersed persons under a single heading proceeds by disregarding other factors of difference. The presentation of commonality is a function of my discursive agenda. But not mine alone. It is an agenda for others, as well – indicated, for example, in the efforts of others to develop African American philosophy or African philosophy as disciplinary fields. In the case of African philosophy, Kwame Gyekye's posture is worthy of review:

> I believe that in many areas of thought we can discern features of the traditional life and thought of African peoples sufficiently common to constitute a legitimate and reasonable basis for the construction (or reconstruction) of a philosophical system that may properly be called African – African not in the sense that every African adheres to it, but in the sense that philosophical system arises from, and hence is essentially related to, African life and thought. Such a basis would justify a discourse in terms of "African philosophy" . . .[45]

This search for "unity" is also a political project of long standing, as in that complex tradition of endeavors known as Pan-Africanism. However, is the search for "unity" in African, African American, or Africana philosophy but an instance of a romanticism that distorts the enterprise of philosophy? That remains to be seen. Each case of an appeal to, or purported demonstration of, unity or commonality in the discursive practices of philosophy of African and African-descended persons requires an appraisal on its own merits. What allows initially for the grouping of diverse intellectual endeavors of diverse persons under a single heading is, as indicated, the identity (in part) of the persons that are the subjects-objects of the endeavors as either African or African-descended, thus sharing socially and culturally conditioned biological characteristics, cultural traditions, and historical experiences more or less distinctive of the race. Yet,

these characteristics are sufficient only for providing an *initial* distinguishing that groups persons by race. Doing so, however, provides no immediate and/or necessary insight into the forms, agendas, strategies, or ends of their discursive traditions and practices. It is to these traditions and practices, along with the agendas and strategies structuring their formation and deployment, situated in the context of the cultural life-worlds of those who practice and mediate them, that we must turn to answer questions regarding commonalities and differences. Only there are to be found life-world conditions and practices with shared "unities" sufficient to support a notion of a comprehending, encompassing disciplinary "field." We must take care to avoid conflating calls for unity among African peoples as a function of political mobilization with unity among the subjects-objects – and thereby the discursive norms and practices – of disciplines.

For Kwame Gyekye, the commonalities identified in comparative studies of "traditional" African thought are to be found in the customs, beliefs, traditions, values, sociopolitical institutions, and historical experiences of African societies.[46] The rupture of "traditional" experiences came when millions of heretofore relatively distinct groups of African peoples were thrown together in the crucible of the system of colonization, enslavement, and dispersion fashioned by that unstable racial and ethnic cultural complexity referred to as "European civilization." These mediators were themselves generally unified in the oppression of African peoples and in the shared sense that "they," contrary to African "others," constituted (or were the harbingers of) "civilization." Hence, the emergence of "philosophy" in Africa and the diaspora as a posttraditional discursive enterprise bearing that name is conditioned by the historical circumstances of domination of Africans and people of African descent by "Europeans" and European descendants.

While what is referred to as "Africana philosophy" is initially constituted through a third-order surveying and arranging of discursive practices and literatures according to an agenda exercised through the arranging and naming, the practices named do not require this arranging and naming as security for their meaningfulness or integrity, nor for their validity. Their meaning, integrity, and validity are local to the contexts within which they emerged and are (or were) exercised, not to my naming. This naming is conditioning only of those practices –

mine and others' – that are deployed under this name self-consciously. It is not decisive that many (if not all) of the discursive traditions and practices that might be included under "Africana philosophy" were not so named by those involved in them, or in important cases were not even called "philosophy." That we call the overall "family" of such practices and traditions "philosophy" is a matter of historical, cultural, social, and political circumstance. I wish those of us involved in this enterprise to be free of the pernicious ordering and privileging that has been involved too often in the guardianship and administration of the word "philosophy" as an honorific term reserved for certain practices of certain persons of certain racial/ethnic groups.

Still, what, beyond the race and ethnicity of the thinker, if anything, is common to the endeavors I have included under the "Africana philosophy" heading? In general, for posttraditional thinkers it is the effort to forge and articulate new identities and life-agendas – to survive, and then to flourish – in the face of the limit-situations of racialized oppression and New World relocations; it is, as well, the effort to recover or reconstruct life-defining meaning-connections to lands and cultures of the African continent, to its peoples and their histories.

These efforts have given rise to reconstructions of the history of western philosophy and its relations to peoples on the African continent, to endeavors to recover and rehabilitate African-descended thinkers from earlier periods as precursor and pioneer black philosophers, and to significant moves to deconstruct and revise narratives of the histories of philosophical enterprises in the west and particular aspects of their agendas. The recent vintage of these efforts notwithstanding, they have been of major significance for the self-understandings and identities of African, African-descendant, and, even, non-African thinkers. When considered against the context of the history of western philosophy as narrated and practiced by some of the dominant figures, and against the explicit derogations of African peoples by a number of these figures, the advent of discussions about African and African American philosophy is *necessarily* "deconstructive." Thus, for example, each instance of an attempt to identify and/or articulate a philosophizing effort as distinctively African or African American is, at the outset at least, an important challenge that decenters the very idea, as well as the discursive practices, of "philosophy" into the history of their construction and maintenance, into the historicity of the philo-

sophical anthropology that informs them via the valorized and racialized notion of "rational man." Furthermore, efforts to articulate the norms and boundaries of a distinctly "African" or "African American" philosophy expose the agendas of the persons who constructed and articulated that philosophical anthropology, and the practices through which it was institutionalized, in service to interests and objectives that were more than simply "philosophical" in some restricted, academic sense, but were intimately connected to sociopolitical projects, whether real, anticipated, or desired. Here the reconstructive efforts of a number of persons, and the issues raised in and by their work, demand serious attention: George G. M. James,[47] Henry Olela,[48] Lancinay Keita,[49] and the work of a number of persons in the Association for the Study of Classical African Civilizations, especially Maulana Karenga's and Jacob H. Carruthers' collection, *Kemet and the African World-view: Research, Rescue and Restoration*,[50] and Carruthers' own *Essays in Ancient Egyptian Studies*[51]; and more recently Martin Bernal's multivolume *Black Athena: The Afroasiatic Roots of Classical Civilization*.[52] Along with the earlier work of William Leo Hansberry[53] and Frank M. Snowden, Jr.,[54] all of these efforts deserve serious attention.

Still, the discussion so far has focused on the objects of Africana philosophy, that is, on the articulated reflections of various African and African-descended peoples. But what about Africana philosophy *as a disciplinary venture*? There are major challenges to be met in the further articulation of its discursive norms and practices, as well as its agenda. One of the striking developments over the past few decades, in the United States in particular, is the extent to which these challenges – with all too few exceptions, to my knowledge – have *not* been taken up by professional philosophers of African descent, but have been by scholars and theoreticians in other fields (literary theory, sociology, history, art, music), especially those contributing to efforts in Black and/or African Studies. The proposals of Molefi Asante, the leading proponent of an "Afrocentric" approach to an "Africalogical" disciplinary agenda and practices (his attempted recasting of Black or African American Studies), is one of the most prominent and contested current attempts to take up these challenges.[55]

Asante's proposal centers on the concept of "Afrocentricity," which, along with its dialectical corollary "Eurocentricity," has come to have a pervasive life of its own in discussions regarding intellectual ventures that focus on black folks. "Afrocentricity" is the name for the principle that instructs us, when pursuing or articulating knowledge of (or about) African peoples, to always "center" our perspectives on norms drawn from the "African Cultural System" in which, Asante has claimed, *all* African people participate "although it [this cultural system] is modified according to specific histories and nations."[56] The core of Afrocentricity, he has said, is *Njia*: ". . . the collective expression of the Afro-centric worldview based in the historical experience of African people. . . . Incorporating Njia into our lives, we become essentially ruled by our own values and principles. Dispensing with alien views at our center, Njia puts us in and on our own center."[57] With Njia, we become "Africa-centered" in our objective and normative commitments and, thereby, in practices structured and guided by them. Thus, "Afrocentric" or "Afrocentricity."

When oriented and guided by Afrocentricity, Asante argues, a new criticism emerges. "It introduces relevant values, denounces non-Afrocentric behavior, and promotes analysis . . . the Afrocentric critical methods start with the primary measure! Does it place Africans in the center?"[58] For the present, the primary task of this new criticism is the "recapturing of our own collective consciousness. . . . It is reclaiming Egypt, deciphering the ancient writing of Nubia, circulating the histories and geographies of Ibn Khaldun and Ibn Battuta, and examining records of Africans in Mexico and other places in the new world."[59] On the way to this collective consciousness there are five levels of awareness:

1 *skin recognition* – "when a person recognizes that his or her skin is black and or her heritage is black but cannot grasp any further reality";
2 *environmental recognition* – seeing the environment "as indicating his or her blackness through discrimination and abuse";
3 *personality awareness* – "It occurs when a persons [*sic*] says 'I like music, or dance or chitterlings'. . . ." Even if the person speaks truthfully, this is not Afrocentricity;
4 *interest-concern* – "demonstrates interest and concern in the problems of blacks and tries to deal intelligently with the issues of the African people." This level is also not Afrocentricity since "it does not consume the life and spirit of the person";

5 *Afrocentricity* – is achieved "when the person becomes totally changed to a conscious level of involvement in the struggle for his or her own mind liberation."[60]

Once achieved, Afrocentricity allows one to predict the actions of whites and non-Afrocentric persons "with certainty." Further, one does not refuse to "condemn mediocrity and reactionary attitudes among Africans for the sake of false unity."

What does this mean for disciplinary practices devoted to studies "centered" on Africans and peoples of African descent? For Asante it means that such studies ("Afrology" in an earlier formulation, "Africalogy" in *Kemet, Afrocentricity and Knowledge*) must be guided by norms that are "rooted in the social, political and economic values of our people." Asante offers two "theoretical propositions" which will "set the tone" for an analysis of the emerging discipline of Afrology with its Afrocentric core:

> Afrology is primarily pan-Africanist in its treatment of the creative, political and geographic dimensions of our collective will to liberty. . . . A second proposition is that the Afrologist, by virtue of his perspective, participates in the coming to be of new concepts and directions. His perceptions of reality, political and social, allow him to initiate novel approaches to problems and issues. Not being encapsulated by the Western point of view he is a person who is mentally as free as possible. . . . In fact, the Afrologist . . . is a person who is capable of participating in both the African and the Western point of view; however, as a practicing Afrologist he must act Afrocentrically. What he has learned is the value of every viewpoint.[61]

The future of Afrology?

> Since Afrology is based upon an Afrocentric interpretation and a particular conception of society, the results of our work will alter previous perceptions and set standards for future studies of African peoples. It is here that Afrology comes into its own as an organizing methodology, and a reflective philosophy, able to open the door to a more assertive, and therefore proper, consciousness of cultural and historical data. Such a

proper consciousness is founded upon the genuine acceptance of our African past, without which there is no Afrological discourse or basis for peculiar analysis.[62]

In *The Afrocentric Idea* Asante continued his articulation of Afrocentricity.[63] In this text Afrocentricity is further defined and deployed as "a critique that propounds a cultural theory of society by the very act of criticism" and proposes "a cultural reconstruction that incorporates the African perspective as a part of an entire human transformation." The object of critique: "Eurocentricism," that is, "the preponderant . . . myths of universalism, objectivity, and classical traditions [that retain] a provincial European cast." Afrocentric analysis will "reestablish . . . the centrality of the ancient Kemetic (Egyptian) civilization and the Nile Valley cultural complex as points of reference for an African perspective in much the same way as Greece and Rome serve as reference points for the European world." Afrocentricity, as the foundation of the discipline of Afrology, will "expand . . . the repertoire of human perspectives on knowledge."[64] The goal: "a post-Eurocentric idea where true transcultural analyses become possible"[65]:

> Sustained by new information and innovative methodologies, Afrology will transform community and social sciences, as well as arts and humanities, and assist in constructing a new, perhaps more engaging, way to analyze and synthesize reality. Perhaps what is needed is a post-Western or meta-Western metatheory to disentangle us from the consuming monopoly of a limited intellectual framework . . .[66]

In his more recent *Kemet, Afrocentricity and Knowledge*, Asante has more to say about the adoption of an "Afrocentric" perspective and its importance:

> one steps outside one's history with great difficulty. In fact, the act itself is highly improbable from true historical consciousness. There is no antiplace, since we are all consumers of space and time. . . . Our place is the constantly presenting and re-presenting context, the evolving presentation context, the perspective – that is, history to us. The Afrocentrist sees knowledge of this

"place" perspective as a fundamental rule of intellectual inquiry because its content is a self-conscious obliteration of the subject/object duality and the enthronement of an African wholism. A rigorous discipline is necessary to advance the intellectual movement toward a meaningful concept of place. In saying this I am challenging the Afrocentrist to maintain inquiry rooted in a strict interpretation of place in order to betray all naive racial theories and establish Afrocentricity as a legitimate response to the human conditions. All knowledge results from an occasion of encounter in place. But the place remains a rightly shaped perspective that allows the Afrocentrist to put African ideals and values at the center of inquiry. If this does not happen then Afrocentricity does not exist. . . . The Afrocentrist seeks to uncover and use codes, paradigms, symbols, motifs, myths, and circles of discussion that reinforce the centrality of African ideals and values as a valid frame of reference for acquiring and examining data. Such a method appears to go beyond western [*sic*] history in order to re-valorize the African place in the interpretation of Africans, continental and diasporan.[67]

Asante's project is of a kind with established efforts in the sociology of knowledge and ideology critique. Further, I take seriously Asante's concern to contribute to the opening of democratically informed intellectual spaces to accommodate the creative and constructive play of a plurality of knowledge formations in which norms and agendas from the cultural life-worlds of European peoples – or of any particular people – are no longer hegemonic. To this extent Asante is on to something very important; and he has taken up and furthered an agenda with a long history among African and African-descended (and other) thinkers.

Asante's efforts have their source in a complex of endeavors that comprise modern Black Studies, which has been radically and consistently historicist. A major portion of his programmatic efforts have involved the critique of, and struggle against, institutionalizations of the histories of peoples of Europe and Euro-America as the supposed evolutionary flow of reason embodied, simultaneously, in the discursive practices of persons of European descent and those socialized by them into disciplinary enterprises. Black Studies emerged in the space opened by this historicist, relativizing critique, and in its cultural-nationalist orientations remains firmly wedded to this position. Asante's program continues this line of development.

From a critical antifoundationalist perspective, a close reading of Asante's agenda reveals that it involves a critique of, and opposition to, claims by some that "Eurocentric" styles of rationality[68] are, in fact, the telos of all of humankind. However, Asante then moves to substitute an equally originary "African" foundation by way of reclaiming, rehabilitating narratives offering reassurance of our "Afrocentricity" through identification with forms of Africanness or Africanity seemingly preserved in their essence across all spaces and times. The discontinuities resulting from the spatial and temporal disruptions of historical, geographical, cultural, and sociological dispersions do not seem to be taken seriously.

Likewise the "ready-made syntheses" such as *the* "spirit" or "value system" of all African peoples (e.g., Njia), or "African history" involve attempts to satisfy our need to secure and reclaim originary "truths" established "at the beginning" (during the times of ancient Kemetic and Nubian civilizations, the original "African" civilizations for Asante) which escape historical determination and discontinuities. As noted by Foucault, the consequences of such efforts for historiography are not insignificant:

> history, in its traditional form, undertook to "memorize" the *monuments* of the past, transform them into *documents*, and lend speech to those traces which, in themselves, are often not verbal, or which say in silence something other than what they actually say; in our time, history is that which transforms *documents* into *monuments*. In that area where, in the past, history deciphered the traces left by men, it now deploys a mass of elements that have to be grouped, made relevant, placed in relation to one another to form totalities. There was a time when archaeology, as a discipline devoted to silent monuments, inert traces, objects without context, and things left by the past, aspired to the condition of history, and attained meaning only through the restitution of a historical discourse; it might be said, to play on words a little, that in our time history aspires to the condition of archaeology, to the intrinsic description of the monument.[69]

From the context of the critique of historiography as the raising of monuments the theme and possibility of a "total" history begin to disappear and those of a "general" history emerge. The difference between the two is that a total history seeks to provide a *complete* description that "draws all phenomena around a single centre – a principle, a meaning, a spirit, a world-view, an overall shape." The aim is to "reconstitute the overall form" of a civilization or society in the identification of its material or spiritual principle, and, thereby, to fix "the significance common to all the phenomena of a period, the law that accounts for their cohesion." A general history, on the other hand, would "deploy the space of a dispersion";[70] that is, would be sensitive to the possible *discontinuities* constitutive of a field of discourse.[70]

At issue in the distinction between these two approaches to history is the question whether the lived history of the civilization, society, or people under study can be properly thought to cohere around a material or spiritual principle, or set of norms, that fixes the significance common to all phenomena of the period. In the context of a consideration of Africology or Africalogy, the force of this question opens us to a serious concern for *discontinuity* without the overextended presumptions of unity involved in seeking the total history of all African peoples, across all times and spaces, as is invoked, perhaps, in claims regarding the "cultural unity" of all African peoples, both on the continent and throughout the diaspora. We may be required, then, to reconsider our understandable commitment to historiography as a form of archaeology, in something of the old sense noted by Foucault: as an effort to raise *monuments* that glorify African pasts in correction to the disparaging lies and distortions of racist European and Euro-American historiography.

Certainly we must question the veracity of attempted reclamations and rehabilitations as "total history" given that they are executed from the platform of, and in service to, agendas constructed in the present. Further, such efforts are conditioned by anticipated, desired, or hoped-for futures the likes of which our ancestors did not live. Nor, for that matter, are the presents and anticipated futures the same in all their important particulars for *all* African peoples. The *similarities* of experiences of African peoples as a function of the global political economy of racialized capitalism notwithstanding, at the level of lived experience and its perpetuation as tradition there are significant *differences* among us.

We can speak of such "cultural unity" among African peoples only by disregarding very important dissimilarities. But is the cost of that disregard at times too high for serious, self-critical scholarship that aspires to reasonableness and "truthfulness" with regard to the totalities that are involved? The unifying power of "African" ("Black" or "*African* American" "civilization") will have to be reconsidered: "unity" can no longer be presumed to be pregiven and automatically recovered with the deployment of "African," as though the term has the unifying power of a trans-historical, transgeographical *essence*.

In light of these considerations, we are left to consider Africana philosophy as a discursive venture. What we speak about, *who* speaks *how*, using what *concepts*, for what *purposes* – all of these are determined by the *rules of discourse* at work in the constitution of the venture. And if Foucault is right, these rules do not define "the dumb existence of a reality, nor the canonical use of a vocabulary" but, instead, involve "the ordering of objects."[71] The greater the historical distance from the "objects" we order, the more it is distinctively *our* rules of ordering that are in force.

We need only remember just how recent is our (re-) embracing of "Black" and "African" as definitively constitutive of our identity for evidence of our need to take seriously the historicity of our rules of discourse. First, in regard to *what* we speak about: the terms "Africa," "African," "African peoples," etc., are, in part, backward-looking, second-order constructions that have emerged from historical encounters with Europe and America; in part forward-looking notions in the context of projects seeking the achievement of shared identities and shared historical endeavors. Second, the rules governing *who* speaks are made by those of us involved in the reclaiming, rehabilitative efforts *we* take to be necessitated by the disruptive encounters with Europe. We have authorized ourselves to speak, and seek to justify our doing so persuasively: that is to say, by giving arguments that seek to link our praxis and its justification with the needs and interests of those in behalf of whom we speak. Third, with respect to *how* we speak: in part as persons who have come to identify ourselves as "Africans" or persons of "African descent"; in part as "persuasive ideologues" not initially authorized by those in whose interest we claim to speak; often from organizational or institutional contexts not of our own making (e.g., historically and predominantly "white" institutions). Fourth, via *concepts*

shot through with the experience of discontinuity brought on by violent disruptions (forced relocation and enslavement in the "New World"), concepts forged in a language often not the same as the language of those of whom we speak – whom we reconstruct *as* we speak – concepts (e.g., "Afrocentricity," "Africana philosophy") created in service to contemporary needs and projects. For what *purpose*? Precisely to overcome *discontinuity* and the absence of unity; to promote *reconstructions* that we hope will lead to psychic wholeness and health, and to social and political empowerment, through which will come historical integrity.

But these are items on an agenda of the *present* that is conditioned by the lived experiences of disruption and marginalization. The rules of our discourse have thus been formed in the crucible of struggle: contemporary concerns leading to the development of Afrocentricity and Africana philosophy emerged in part from the historical contexts of the modern civil rights and black power movements. The connection between the historicity and dimensions of those struggles and our African "origins" is anything but simple continuity.

To the degree that Africalogy is intended as a *discipline*, for which the most constitutive medium and form of praxis is discourse, it cannot be the case that its governing norms will *inherently* be available only to persons of African descent, even though the discipline emerges out of the life-worlds of African peoples. Discourse is possible, and proceeds successfully, only if participants abide by shared governing rules. And, given the committed *social* imperatives conditioning Africalogy, the rules must be available to those to whom we wish to speak, in whose behalf we speak: in short, the rules of discourse must be *public*.

This is true, as well, for our discursive efforts addressed to others who, by virtue of race and/or ethnicity (or, even, class position), are not members of "our group" but to whom we feel compelled to speak. Our critiques of "Eurocentrism," for example, must be expressed in terms to which these "others" of European descent, among others, will have access *if* we would have them understand the limitations of their perspectives and practices, and come to regard and treat us in ways that are more respectful of our integrity. Thus, "we" and "they" must share a norm-structured discursive context that transcends the bounds of our own racial/ethnic life-worlds. At a deeper level, the basis for this sharing is provided by historical circumstances. When we have proper regard for the discontinuities, as well as the continuities, conditioning the existences of African peoples, we are compelled to realize that the "Africanity" of those of us of African descent in the "New World" is in no way purely "African": we are African *and* American (Caribbean, Cuban, Brazilian, etc.). To that extent, we share, in some instances, to some degrees, important aspects of our being with peoples of European descent. Consequently, a stringently relativist cultural nationalism as a platform for Africalogy would be inconsistent even with our most quotidian praxis: ordinary speech expressed in "American" English and addressed to *both* black and non-black audiences.

More fundamentally, such a cultural nationalism would certainly be inconsistent with intellectual praxis conducted in institutional settings and by way of the disciplinary practices of the modern academy with its "European" legacies. For these legacies provide much of the context within which, and the rules by which, modern Black or African American Studies emerged and was shaped into a "discipline" – the importance and truth of the claims that it was to be a radically *different* discipline notwithstanding. Subsequently, if Africalogy is to involve practices of *systematic* knowledge development, acquisition, refinement, and distribution, and, as part of these efforts, is to contribute to the articulation and institutionalization of appropriate norms for peoples of African descent, its structuring norms must satisfy rules which, among other things, promote such activities as critical and *self*-critical endeavors. Furthermore, since a discipline is an inherently *social* enterprise in which some degree of consensus – at the very least – is necessary, that in itself requires shared rules. Without them there can be no agreement, even among ourselves. The rules – the norms – for obtaining such agreement are not provided by melanin.

These rules are not *necessarily* and *irrevocably* restricted to the particular cultural, historical life-worlds of particular racial/ethnic – or gender – groups. It is possible to have norms that transcend particular groups such that they cover the "intellectual" and "social" life-praxes of different groups in ways, even, that make it *possible* to resolve what otherwise might be "fundamental" disagreements. Norms governing "ways of life" in general, systematic intellectual praxis in particular, are *strategies* serving *choices*, ultimately choices about life "in general," in service to which research enterprises have their ground and being. But these are choices

not only about *our* intellectual praxis, but about the world we would co-make and share with others *even as we do so with uncompromising commitment to insuring, as best we can, "our" survival and "our" flourishing, now and in the foreseeable future.*

Thus, a crucial and complex question is: how shall we shape the intellectual praxes of Africana philosophy to serve the best interests of African peoples, first and foremost, and thereby provide practitioners with normative guidance while, at the same time, we preserve norms that secure "truthfulness" and appropriate "objectivity" in larger sociohistorical contexts within which our praxes are situated?

The answer to this question cannot be provided by "us" alone. Even if we would have that sharing based on consensus regarding the rules – a consensus arrived at through *open, free,* and *democratic* discussion – it is also a question whether "others" will abide by these same rules. Still, as an enterprise of the modern academy that seeks to speak authoritatively to black folk and to others for and about black folk, the rules of discourse for Africana philosophy will have to satisfy institutionalized rules governing scholarly practices, even as we continue to refine institutionalized rules. We have helped to change the rules of discourse in the contemporary academy. However, as long as we consent to share in such institutional settings and to participate in national and international publics – whether academic or nonacademic – our discourse cannot proceed by private rules.

But the same questions have to be faced when we are talking just about "us." Some black cultural nationalists continue to argue that the values and norms that should ground and structure the study of black folks exist in the "way of life," the "collective worldview and belief system," the "African cultural system" of *all* African peoples worldwide and throughout history. The rhetorical force of these notions has a great deal to do. I think, with the emotional, even psychological, rehabilitation and satisfaction they provide in the cultivation of an identity that is still crucial to our struggles against racialized domination and hegemony. And deliberately so. But at what price to serious critical thought? Some critics have reaped large harvests challenging the abstract naiveté and romanticism often involved in such declarations, which tend to disregard factors such as class stratifications, gender (black women's experiences, for example), and the subsequent serious disparities in values and practices among groups of African peoples. Such declarations also disregard the fact that no "African" of ancient Egypt or Nubia shares our historical world, nor we theirs.

Further, there are important ways in which the very notion "African" is problematic when we move to apply it to concrete persons, as is always the case with general terms. Asante, for example, in *Kemet, Afrocentricity and Knowledge*, takes the following approach: "By 'African' I mean clearly a 'composite African' not a specific discrete African orientation which would rather mean ethnic identification, i.e. Yoruba, Zulu, Nuba, etc."[72] What is a "composite African"? The unity such a concept harbors is gained at the price of abstracting from many vital aspects and details of historical and daily existence of living African peoples, an abstraction accomplished by we intellectuals who do so, supposedly, in the interest of others who have little or no recall on our efforts. In fact, we appropriate to ourselves the power, the right, the responsibility for doing so. Can real, living persons and peoples called "African," from all over the globe, find themselves in our concepts, in our prescriptions for their futures? Are reconstructions of "Africans" and prescriptions for their future justified simply by claiming solidarity with "the people"? Have we, in rightfully criticizing the racism and ethnocentrism that have historically conditioned many of the norms and justificatory strategies of Europeans and Americans, gone too far, at times, in discarding such strategies completely, in doing so without having fashioned new ones to replace them?

A critical stance toward our own disciplinary endeavors requires that we review the presuppositions and requirements too often invested in totalizing deployments of the notions of "African" and/or "black" as names for identity-formations which, it seems, as in the case of Asante's notion of Afrocentricity, often presume a single, shared subjective position for all persons African and African-descended. Such a presumption follows, I think, from a too easy conflation – or explicit identification – of knowledge production and articulation with psychic rehabilitation and political mobilization: for example, taking cultural *commonalities* shared by diverse African and African-descended peoples as *prima facie* evidence of an immediate *cultural* unity that can be a foundation for *political* unity. "All knowledge is political," we critics of modernity have often said. And I take this to be a fundamental truth in terms of the situatedness of the production and distribution of what passes for "knowledge" in the complexities of historically

specific social formations. Still, the truism says nothing about the variety of forms and ends of politics, or about the variety of ways in which the production and distribution of knowledge stands toward and is related to the complex social formations in which these processes take place. Modern Black and African Studies, the Afrocentric approach in particular, emerged in service to particular political agendas and have sought to fashion identity-formations thought to be appropriate to the politics.

However, Stuart Hall is correct in stating that we must recognize

> the extraordinary diversity of subjective positions, social experiences and cultural identities which compose the category "black": that is, the recognition that "black" is essentially a politically and culturally *constructed* category, which cannot be grounded in a set of fixed trans-cultural or transcendental racial categories and which therefore has no guarantees in Nature. . . . This inevitably entails a weakening or fading of the notion that "race" or some composite notion of race around the term black will either guarantee the effectivity of any cultural practice or determine in any final sense its aesthetic value.[73]

Neither politics more generally, nor scholarship, can be properly conducted, as Hall notes, by the simple reversal of replacing "the bad old essential white subject" with "the new essentially good black subject."

Of course, personal and social culturally-informed identities are vital to the well-being of individuals and peoples. How such identities are formed, revised, maintained, or overthrown is always a matter of importance, especially in historical situations conditioned by racialized domination and hegemony. Afrocentrists continue centuries-old traditions of African and African-descended "race-men" and "race-women" – taking up the critical tasks of marshalling meanings into articulate configurations meant to provide rehabilitative and mobilizing identity-formations in and through which black folks would fashion social worlds that provide for flourishing, liberated existences. Stuart Hall is especially insightful and helpful in thinking about how we might approach the business of cultural identity-formation: on the one hand, as a function of a shared ancestry, history, and culture that provide continuous and unchanging frames of reference and meaning out of which is formed a collective "one true self" shared by all; or, on the other, as a matter of recurrent, historicized "becoming": "Far from being grounded in a mere 'recovery' of the past, which is waiting to be found, and which, when found, will secure our sense of ourselves into eternity, identities are the names we give to the different ways we are positioned by, and position ourselves within, the narratives of the past."[74] I would add, identities are the names we give to the different ways we are positioned by/position ourselves, *recurrently*, within narrations of the past, the present, and anticipated or desired futures – since no identity-formation is permanent, individually or socially. Hence the need for critical intellectuals, Asante included, to review the legacies and practices shaping any people's reproduction of themselves, and to mediate the results of the reviews as "knowledge" meant to assist reproduction. And Asante, along with the "race-men" and "race-women" who were his predecessors, as well as those who are his contemporaries, is right to focus on the matter of the self-identifications of the thinkers and scholars involved in, and the normative, informing relation of their identities to, knowledge production and distribution as part of cultural reproduction and the formation of cultural identities more generally.

In light of the "untruth" racking the embodiment of the mainstream narratives of the history of philosophy, the advent of Africana philosophy is of very real importance to this reproductive and formative work. We are required to give greater respect to racial, ethnic, and gender "differences" as conditioners of philosophical praxis in various ways without necessarily invalidating reconstructed notions of "reasoning." This prospect cuts to the very core of mainstream western philosophy – one of the central endeavors of which continues to be to provide the definitive characterizations of what it is to be human. And, in general, the terms in which the characterizations have been articulated are void of explicit references to race, ethnicity, or gender. Certainly the modern enlightenment was a triumph of precisely this mode of characterizing humans. And it was a triumph that made possible substantive progressive achievements without which we would have a world not much to the liking of many of us.

But the victory has meant that attention to the unique, dissimilar, individual, and particular human groups has often been lacking in the exclusive focus on "the universal" that, in truth, has all too often been but the norms of particular Europeans in disguise. Further, the aspirations of universalist philosophy notwithstanding, where race, ethnicity, gender, etc., were supposedly irrelevant to the formulations of key notions, critical reviews are disclosing ethnocentricism and racism, sexism, and class biases at the very heart of the classical western philosophical enterprise.

Does this signal the complete inadequacy of the achievements of ancient and modern "European" Enlightenments? Not necessarily. But the recognition and acknowledgment of inadequacies in basic notions, and of histories of invidious appropriations and applications of them, open us to challenging possibilities for further revising our philosophical practices. Africana philosophy as an enterprise can contribute to a critical review of the "universalist" liberal agenda that has dominated so much of philosophical praxis in the west since the modern Enlightenment.

We are in the midst of a historical conjuncture that is relatively new, one highly charged by efforts to achieve democracy in multi-"ethnic," multi-"racial" societies in which "group thinking" is a decisive feature of social and political life. I join others in calling for a serious revision of our philosophical agenda and praxes. It is my sincere hope that the expansion of the recognized arenas of discourse in philosophy to include Africana philosophy is indicative of a movement in this direction, and that, as a result, philosophy will come to be practiced without pernicious racism and ethnocentrism.

It is also a sincere hope that Africana philosophy, conditioned by concerns some of which are taken up in Asante's Afrocentric Africalogy, will not only take root and grow, but will be nurtured in this revised context to which it will continue to make substantial contributions. All who have and might contribute to the formation and work of the enterprise need not be African or of African descent. The similarities and commonalities in the experiences of the dispersed race of African peoples in their varied ethnicities are one thing (their differences another); the coherence of an intellectual enterprise yet another. We must not confuse the former with the latter. Racial identity and common experiences, cultural commonalities and shared site of origin, *do not*, automatically and necessarily, provide the essential unifying coherence of a disciplinary enterprise, its norms, agenda, and strategies. "Africana philosophy" is indeed a "gathering notion," not a proxy for an immutable essence shared by all African peoples. Gathering together various traditions and practices, various literatures, identified as "philosophy," is just an initial, though important, step. Then real labor begins: interrogating works, learning from them, comparing and contrasting them (with endeavors by African and other peoples) as part of a larger, ongoing effort to catalog and study the many creations of African peoples, the contributions of African peoples to the treasure houses of human civilization.

Notes

1 Important examples are Placide Tempels, *Bantu Philosophy*, tr. Colin King (Paris: Présence Africaine, 1959) and Marcel Griaule's *Conversations with Ogotemmêli* (New York: Oxford University Press, 1965).

2 An important contribution to these efforts is H. Odera Oruka's *Sage Philosophy: Indigenous Thinkers and Modern Debate on African Philosophy* (Leiden, Netherlands: E. J. Brill, 1990).

3 A very rich collection of texts is available (though not presented as "philosophy") in Howard Brotz (ed.), *African-American Social and Political Thought, 1850–1920*, 2nd edn (New Brunswick, N.J.: Transaction Publishers, 1992).

4 For examples of these recent endeavors, see Leonard Harris (ed.), *Philosophy Born of Struggle: Anthology of Afro-American Philosophy from 1917* (Dubuque, Iowa: Kendall/Hunt, 1983).

5 The following discussion is based on my "African 'Philosophy': Deconstructive and Reconstructive Challenges," in *Contemporary Philosophy: A New Survey*, vol. 5: *African Philosophy*, ed Guttorm Fløistad (Boston: Martinus Nijhoff, 1987), pp. 19–26.

6 Tempels, *Bantu Philosophy*. One finds in the literature of this discussion references to the following works of earlier dates, though they are not concerned exclusively with Africa, if at all: V. Brelsford, *Primitive Philosophy* (1935) and *The Philosophy of the Savage* (1938); R. Allier, *The Mind of the Savage* (no date); and P. Radin, *Primitive Man as Philosopher* (1927).

7 See Marcel Griaule's "Introduction" to his *Conversations with Ogotemmêli*.

8 Franz Crahay, "Conceptual Take-off Conditions for a Bantu Philosophy." *Diogenes*, 52 (Winter 1965), pp. 55–78.

9 Crahay, "Bantu Philosophy," pp. 55–8.

10 Ibid., pp. 69–71.

11 Certainly one of the most poignant critiques of European encounters leading to the "invention" of Africa and one of the most informed discussions of African philosophy is V. Y. Mudimbe's *The Invention of Africa: Gnosis, Philosophy, and the Order of Knowledge* (Bloomington: Indiana University Press, 1988). I am deeply indebted to Mudimbe's great learning, and to his active participation in the formation of contemporary African philosophy as a discursive formation.

12 H. Odera Oruka, "Four Trends in Current African Philosophy," in Oruka, *Trends In Contemporary African Philosophy* (Nairobi, Kenya: Shirikon Publishers, 1990), pp. 13–22.

13 A. J. Smet, *Histoire de la Philosophie Africaine Contemporaine: Courants et Problèmes* (Kinshasa-Limete, Zaire: Departement de Philosophie et Religions Africaines, Faculté de Théologie Catholique, 1980).

14 O. Nkombe and A. J. Smet, "Panorama de la Philosophie Africaine contemporaine." *Recherches Philosophiques Africaines*, vol. 3: *Mélanges de Philosophie Africaine* (Kinshasa, Zaïre: Faculté de Théologie Catholique, 1978), pp. 263–82.

15 This discussion of the classifications of Smet and Nkombe is aided significantly by the insightful discussion of Valentine Mudimbe in his "African Philosophy as an Ideological Practice: The Case of French-Speaking Africa," in *African Studies Review*, 26, nos. 3/4 (September/December 1983), pp. 133–54.

16 The phrase is taken from a complex of arguments the principal source of which are the speeches and writings of Edward Wilmot Blyden, who attempted to articulate the difference between Africans and Europeans in terms of the former's "personality." Blyden's works include: *Africa and Africans* (1903); *Selected Letters of Edward Wilmot Blyden*, ed. Hollis R. Lynch (New York: KTO Press, 1978); *Liberia's Offering* (1862); *Liberia: Past, Present, and Future* (1869); *The Negro in Ancient History* (1869); *Christianity, Islam and the Negro Race* (London, 1888; new edition: Edinburgh: Edinburgh University Press, 1967). For additional readings see Kwame Nkrumah, "The African Personality," and Alex Quaison-Sakey, "The African Personality," in *Readings in African Political Thought*, eds Gideon-Cyrus M. Mutiso and S. W. Rohio (London: Heinemann, 1975).

17 Pan-Africanism was an organized ideological and political tradition and movement that emerged in the late 1800s, at the instigation of Henry Sylvester Williams, a Trinidadian lawyer, and, later, W. E. B. DuBois, African-American activist scholar and champion *par excellence* of the interests of Africans and people of African descent. The principal manifestations of the tradition were a series of conferences (London, 1900) and congresses (Paris, 1919; London-

Brussels, 1921; London-Lisbon, 1923; New York, 1927; Manchester, 1945; and Dar es Salaam, Tanzania, 1974 – the first Pan-African congress to be held on the continent of Africa), which called upon Africans and peoples of African descent world wide (hence *pan*-African) to join together in an organized struggle to liberate the continent of Africa from European colonialism, and to free African peoples everywhere from domination and the invidious discrimination of racism. See Immanuel Geiss, *The Pan-African Movement* (New York: Africana Publishing Co., 1974).

18 The "Négritude Movement," as it has come to be called, takes its name from the central concept which, like Blyden's "African personality," attempts to distinguish Africans from Europeans by defining the African in terms of the complex of character traits, dispositions, capabilities, natural endowments, etc., in their relative predominance and overall organizational arrangements, which form the negro *essence*, i.e., our *Négritude*. Originating in literary circles, at the instigation of Aimé Césaire, Léon Damas, and Léopold Sédar Senghor, the Négritude Movement quickly exploded the boundaries of these circles as the powerful political forces contained in its arguments played themselves out and took root in the fertile soil of the discontent of colonized Africa. See "What is Négritude?" (pp. 83–4) by Léopold Sédar Senghor and "Remarks on African Personality and Négritude" (pp. 67–70) by Alioune Diop, in Mutiso & Rohio, *African Political Thought*.

19 "African humanism" is another recurrent theme in discussions of the past quarter century that have attempted to identify values and life-practices indigenous to African peoples which distinguish them, in non-trivial ways, from peoples of European descent. In the words of M. Gatsha Buthelezi: "Long before Europeans settled in South Africa little more than three centuries ago, indigenous African peoples had well-developed philosophical views about the worth of human beings and about desirable community relationships. A spirit of humanism – called *ubuntu* (humanness) in the Zulu language and *botho* in the Sotho language – shaped the thoughts and daily lives of our peoples. Humanism and communal traditions together encouraged harmonious social relations." "The Legacy of African Humanism," in *Natural History*, 12 (1984), p. 2.

20 In some cases, discussions of African socialism are quite similar to arguments regarding African "humanism" to the extent that the claim is made that "traditional" Africa (i.e., Africa before its colonization by Europeans) was indigenously "socialist," prior to the discussions of Marx and other Europeans, in view of Africa's "communal traditions" (as Buthelezi puts it in the passage quoted above). In other discussions, the objective is to fashion a particularly *African* form of socialism, one more in keeping with the historical

and cultural realities of black Africa. See, for example, Léopold Sédar Senghor, *Nationhood and the African Road to Socialism*, tr. Mercer Cook (Paris; Présence Africaine, 1962).

21 An expressly political/ideological venture that, in service to its conception of the goal of African liberation, involves the importation of the Engels–Lenin scientization of "Marxism" and its consolidation and institutionalization in highly centralized, authoritarian, revolutionary political parties and movements.

22 The title of a book by Kwame Nkrumah, first president of the postcolonial independent state of Ghana. In this work Nkrumah offers what he terms "philosophy and ideology for decolonization": "conscienicism is the map in intellectual terms of the disposition of forces which will enable African society to digest the Western and the Islamic and the Euro-Christian elements in Africa, and develop them in such a way that they fit into the African personality. The African personality is itself defined by the cluster of humanist principles which underlie the traditional African society. Philosophical conscienicism is that philosophical standpoint which, taking its start from the present content of the African conscience, indicates the way in which progress is forged out of the conflict in that conscience." Kwame Nkrumah, *Conscienicism* (New York: Monthly Review Press, 1970), p. 79.

23 This the name for yet another cultural nationalist program which emerged during the period of anticolonial struggles in Africa. Here again the objective is to argue in behalf of a complex of indigenous and/or reconstructed values, practices, and social arrangements which, supposedly, will best serve contemporary Africa. The chief proponent of this program has been President Mobutu of Zaire.

24 Important examples of works in this group are Alexis Kagame's *La Philosophie Bantu-Rwandaise de I'Etre* (Brussels: Académie Royale des Sciences Coloniales, 1956), Kwame Gyekye's *An Essay on African Philosophical Thought: The Akan Conceptual Scheme* (New York: Cambridge University Press, 1988); and Segun Gbadegesin's *African Philosophy: Traditional Yoruba Philosophy and Contemporary African Realities* (New York: Peter Lang, 1991).

25 Mudimbe, "African Philosophy as Ideological Practice," p. 138.

26 See, for example, Theophilus Okere, *African Philosophy: A Historico-Hermeneutical Investigation of the Conditions of its Possibility* (Lanham, Md.: University Press of America, 1983).

27 Paulin Hountondji offers one such characterization: "In its popular meaning the word 'philosophy' designates not only the theoretical discipline that goes by the same name, but, more generally, all visions of the world, all systems of virtually stable representation that lie deep beneath the behavior of an individual or a group of people. . . . 'Philosophy', in that sense, appears as something which is held on to, a minimum

system of creeds more deep-rooted in the self than any other systems . . . 'philosophy', in that sense, is more a matter of assumption than of observation. . . . It matters little whether the individual or society concerned are conscious or not of their own 'philosophy'; in strict terms, spontaneous 'philosophy' is necessarily unconscious . . . all told, it constitutes a testimony to the intellectual identity of the person or the group." Paulin Hountondji, "The Myth of Spontaneous Philosophy," *Consequence*, 1 (January–June 1974), pp. 11–12.

28 Mudimbe takes care to note that, contrary to other African scholars (notably Paulin Hountondji and Marcin Towa), he does *not* employ "ethno-philosophy" as a pejorative characterization: "I am using the term in its etymological value: ethnos-philosophia or weltanschauung of a community." "African Philosophy," p. 149. note 7.

29 Mudimbe, "African Philosophy," p. 142.

30 Mudimbe, "African Philosophy," p. 142. Mudimbe has provided a more elaborate, subtle, nuanced discussion and critique of the nature and production of knowledge about Africa generally, African philosophy in particular, in his *The Invention of Africa*. A recently published work, *Parables & Fables: Exegesis, Textuality, and Politics in Central Africa* (Madison: University of Wisconsin Press, 1991), is described as a confrontation with "the philosophical problems of otherness and identity through readings of the parables and fables" of the Luba, a colonized people of Zaire. Discussion of this most recent text must await a completed reading.

31 This review will be based on my "African-American Philosophy: Social and Political Case Studies," published in *Social Science Information* (London: Sage) 26, 1 (1987): 75–97.

32 For discussions of these historical periods and their guiding ideas/ideals, see, for example, Robert H. Brisbane, *Black Activism* (Valley Forge, Penn.: Judson Press, 1974); and August Meier, *Negro Thought in America, 1880–1915* (Ann Arbor: University of Michigan Press, 1966).

33 See W. E. B. DuBois, "Of Mr. Booker T. Washington and Others," in *The Souls of Black Folk* (1903): reprinted in Brotz, *African American Social and Political Thought*, pp. 509–18.

34 See, in particular, DuBois "The Conservation of Races," in Brotz, *African American Social and Political Thought*, pp. 483–92.

35 For discussions of black nationalism see, among others, John Bracey, August Meier, & Eliott Rudwick (eds), *Black Nationalism in America* (New York: Bobbs-Merrill, 1970), and A. Pinkney, *Red, Black, and Green: Black Nationalism in The United States* (New York: Cambridge University Press, 1976).

36 C. L. R. James, *The Independence of Black Struggle* (Washington. D.C.: All African Peoples Revolutionary Party, 1975); James Boggs & Grace Lee Boggs,

Revolution and Evolution in the Twentieth Century (New York: Monthly Review Press, 1974).

37 For a survey of African American philosophy, see Leonard Harris, "Philosophy Born of Struggle: Afro-American Philosophy from 1917," in Gerald McWorter (ed.), *Philosophical Perspectives in Black Studies* (Urbana: Afro-American Studies and Research Program, University of Illinois, 1982). For representative essays from the period, see the special issue of the *Philosophical Forum* devoted to "Philosophy and the Black Experience," vol. IX (winter–spring 1977–78), especially William Jones, "The Legitimacy and Necessity of Black Philosophy: Some Preliminary Considerations."

38 Montclair, N.J.: Montclair State College Press, 1970.

39 These three essays were presented during the Africana Philosophy International Research Conference held at Haverford College during the summer of 1982.

40 Lanham, Md.: University Press of America, 1988; and Lanham, Md.: University Press of America, 1980, respectively.

41 *Alain Locke and Philosophy: A Quest For Cultural Pluralism* (Westport, Conn.: Greenwood Press, 1986).

42 Leonard Harris (ed.), *The Philosophy of Alain Locke: Harlem Renaissance and Beyond* (Philadelphia: Temple University Press, 1989).

43 The notion of a "geographic race" makes use, in the first instance, of geographic categories to group peoples who share distinctive biologically-based characteristics but who are not thereby regarded as constituting a "pure" biological type. Hence, I speak of African and African-descended peoples as a geographical, biological, and cultural "race." See Michael Banton & Jonathan Harwood, *The Race Concept* (New York: Praeger, 1975), p. 62.

44 A. J. Mandt, "The Inevitability of Pluralism: Philosophical Practice and Philosophical Excellence," in Avner Cohen & Marcelo Dascal (eds), *The Institution of Philosophy: A Discipline in Crisis* (La Salle, Ill.: Open Court, 1989), p. 100.

45 Kwame Gyekye, "On the Idea of African Philosophy," in *An Essay on African Philosophical Thought*, p. 191. For arguments in behalf of the "cultural unity" of Africa, see especially, Cheikh Anta Diop, *The Cultural Unity of Black Africa* (Chicago: Third World Press, 1978); and Jacques Maquet, *Africanity: The Cultural Unity of Black Africa*, tr. Joan R. Rayfield (New York: Oxford University Press, 1972).

46 Gyekye, *African Philosophical Thought*, p. 191. For presentations and discussions of African thought and life along these lines, one might note, for example: Griaule, *Conversations with Ogotemmêli*; M. Fortes & G. Dieterlen (eds), *African Systems of Thought* (New York: Oxford University Press, 1965); Ivan Karp & Charles S. Bird (eds), *Explorations in African Systems of Thought* (Bloomington: Indiana University Press, 1980); Daryll Forde (ed.), *African Worlds: Studies in the Cosmological Ideas and Social Values of African*

Peoples (New York: Oxford University Press, 1954).

47 *Stolen Legacy* (New York: Philosophical Library, 1954).

48 "The African Foundations of Greek Philosophy," in Richard A. Wright (ed.), *African Philosophy: An Introduction*, third edn (Lanham, Md.: University Press of America, 1984), pp. 77–92, and *From Ancient Africa to Ancient Greece* (Atlanta, Ga.: Select Publishing Co., 1981).

49 "The African Philosophical Tradition," in Wright, *African Philosophy*, pp. 57–76.

50 Los Angeles: University of Sankore Press, 1986. Essays in this text were selected from presentations during two Association for the Study of Classical African Civilizations conferences held in February 1984 (Los Angeles) and March 1985 (Chicago).

51 Los Angeles: University of Sankore Press, 1984.

52 *Black Athena: The Afroasiatic Roots of Classical Civilization*, vol. 1: *The Fabrication of Ancient Greece 1785–1985* (New Brunswick, N. J.: Rutgers University Press, 1987).

53 *Africa and Africans as Seen by Classical Writers: African History Notebook*, vol. 2 (Washington, DC: Howard University Press, 1981).

54 *Blacks in Antiquity* (Cambridge, Mass.: Belknap Press, 1970).

55 See Molefi Kete Asante, *Kemet, Afrocentricity and Knowledge* (Trenton, N.J.: Africa World Press, 1990), especially "Part I. Interiors," in which he sets out a revised version of his theory and method for an Afrocentric approach to proper knowledge about African peoples which, together (i.e., the approach and the knowledge obtained through it), constitute the field of "Africalogy."

56 Molefi Kete Asante, *Afrocentricity: The Theory of Social Change* (Buffalo: Amulefi Publishing Co., 1980), p. 5.

57 Ibid., p. 26.

58 Ibid., p. 52.

59 Ibid., p. 55.

60 Ibid., pp. 55–6.

61 Ibid., pp. 68–71.

62 Ibid., p. 73.

63 Philadelphia: Temple University Press, 1987.

64 Asante, *The Afrocentric Idea*, pp. 6, 8–9, 16.

65 Ibid., p. 8. "Most of the so-called universal concepts fail transculturally, and without transcultural validity there is not universality." *The Afrocentric Idea*, p. 56.

66 Asante, *The Afrocentric Idea*, p. 34.

67 Asante, *Kemet, Afrocentricity and Knowledge*, pp. 5–6.

68 For a discussion of "cognitive style" see Alfred Schutz & Thomas Luckmann, *Structures of the Life-World* (Evanston, Ill.: Northwestern University Press, 1973).

69 Michel Foucault, *The Archaeology of Knowledge and the Discourse on Language*, tr. A. M. Sheridan Smith (New York: Harper and Row, 1972), p. 7.

70 Ibid., pp. 9–10.

71 Ibid., p. 48.

72 Asante, *Kemet, Afrocentricity and Knowledge*, p. 9.

73 Stuart Hall, "New Ethnicities," *ICA Documents: Black Film British Cinema* (ICA Conference, February 1988), p. 28 (emphasis in original).

74 Stuart Hall, "Cultural Identity and Diaspora," pp. 223, 225.

4

The African Foundations of Greek Philosophy

Henry Olela

Introduction

The following discussion will attempt to justify the legitimacy of a Black philosophy from its historical African background. We further intend to demonstrate that such a philosophy also serves as the basis of Ancient Greek Philosophy. This latter claim is evidenced when one undertakes to examine the nature of the intellectual influence on specific Greek philosophers of merit by the Ancient African World-View.

Many sources have now dispelled the dogma of the "compulsive originality" of the Greek mind. Any claims concerning the lack of precedence for Greek philosophy overlook its historical development, although this insistence on the "purity" of Western philosophy has successfully forged a place in academic circles. The argument has been that the African mind is in no way capable of any systematic philosophy. But if we agree that basic assumptions about the Universe are points beyond which one can say nothing; if we further agree that basic assumptions about a world-view are by nature theoretical and Universal, then it would be quite difficult to deny such assumptions in regard to either Ancient Africans (Egyptians) or modern Africa. The elements of these basic assumptions are, as it were, those regarding the structure of reality, the nature of the origin of things, problems of justice, etc.

From *African Philosophy: An Introduction*, ed. Richard Wright (1984); by kind permission of University Press America, Inc.

The question which we must perhaps settle before proceeding with our investigation is: Are basic assumptions in essence distinguishable from philosophical assumptions? It seems that if one were to insist in distinguishing between the two, such a distinction would not be that one is metaphysical and the other is empirical. The distinction would, furthermore, not lie in the fact that one is held by philosophers and the other held by laymen. The only distinction which may be rationally made would be the tradition in which the assumptions are made. Thus we are here forced to recognize the impact of culture on philosophy: philosophy was not and is not immune to the universal human process of sharing and assimilating of culture traits; philosophy was not, is not, culture free.

We are, in this essay, making a fundamental claim; the historical foundation of the Modern African World-View as well as that of the Greeks and Romans, came from Ancient Africans (Egyptians). Secondly, the most obvious claim, that the authentic theoretical foundation of African diaspora's experience is African, need not posit a difficulty.

In dealing with our topical subject matter, we will adopt a methodology which is familiar but has received little attention – to the genetic approach. It may behoove us to give some attention to Theodore Gomperz's analysis of the origin of the intellectual tradition in societies of antiquity; of special attention is his discussion of geographical determining. Gomperz believes that knowledge about geographical factors and influences are necessary conditions for the understanding of a people's philosophy.[1] The location of Greece was ideal for cultural influences from neighboring states and civilizations, thereby becoming an "apprentice of older civilizations."

The genetic approach, therefore, can establish some correlations between types of cultures; it presupposes that contiguity of either cultures or persons is important. The major problem with establishing such a thesis is the unfortunate situation professional philosophers themselves have created. There are very few philosophical texts devoted to the problem of the origin of philosophy. But a small number of these philosophical texts written on this issue have not received approval by Western philosophers. An example of such a work which has been regarded as non-philosophical (in the eyes of many philosophers) is George G. M. James' book, *The Stolen Legacy*. In fact the book is quite rare, almost to the point of being out of print. We may outrightly suggest that this book should be a required text for courses in History of Ancient Philosophy.

A better understanding of Greek theology or philosophy must be preceded first by considering the "mystery of Crete, where primary Hellenic culture was born."[2] Crete is an island standing on the southern part of the Aegean Sea and the Archipelago. It is also the largest of the islands on the Mediterranean Sea. The question we must ask then is: Who were the Creteans? Various reliable sources do confirm that "the ancestors of Creteans were natives of Africa, a branch of the Western Ethiopians."[3] Long before the Sahara became a desert, these people were living on the grassland areas of North Africa. But by about 2500 BC when drought plagued the Sahara, they were scattered around, some of them moving toward the Mediterranean Sea. They became the most skilled seamen and established a powerful maritime culture in Crete. They carried on a flourishing trade with other Africans then living in Sais (the land which the Greeks later renamed Egypt), Sicily, and southern Italy. This prosperity lived on to see its destruction by 1400 BC by the "semi-barbarous Greeks from the North."[4] Along with this position is the implication that the questions of the Phoenicians or Canaanites were initially from Punt, situated in East Africa (what is now known as Somali and extending to Kenya). The ancient Greeks also knew them as Ethiopians. According to Leonard Cottrel, *Lost Worlds*, it is safe "to assume that Minoan Civilization throughout its development

gathered ideas and techniques from both African and Asian sources."[5] But a slightly stronger position is taken by Willis N. Huggins, *Introduction to African Civilization*. He asserts that "No evidence exists to show that they were influenced from any other source other than African. Everything so far unearthed in Crete and the Sudan apparently indicate that in the Mediterranean area, there was a common race of men."[6] Thus far we have allowed ourselves to use Egyptian and Ethiopian civilization interchangeably. In ancient times all black men were called Ethiopian or Egyptian by others, also Ethiopians had a tremendous impact on Egyptian religion. We have noted that Egypt was originally called Sais. If we add the Egyptian prefix Ma (Ma simply means "of") to Sais we would have the Ma-Sais. Indeed, the ancient Egyptians were the descendants of the Gallas Somalians and the Masais (who today live in Kenya and Tanzania).

Modern philosophical speculation, however, has generated a tendency toward the neglect of truth in regard to many aspects of the foundation of philosophy. This is particularly indicative of the Hegelian idealism, which tended to underestimate African civilization. Hegel's dictum was basically that Africa was outside history because it had not achieved the "German" consciousness. Indeed, like most modern and contemporary Western philosophers, Hegel had consciously attempted to subscribe to the argument of the European or Asian origin of any cultural traits of merit found in Africa.[7] This ignored the fact that even the ancient Greeks themselves often credited Africa with being the source of foundations of philosophical knowledge.

There is one historical and archaeological note to which we must address ourselves – the relationship of Ancient Africa and Asia. Most Western philosophers who are liberal enough to admit to the Eastern origin of Greek philosophy, hold that it was a "trival" influence, and it came from Babylonia. But according to historical, as well as archaeological findings, there was an African presence in Southern Mesopotamia (Babylonia and Sumer). These same Africans were also responsible for the construction of the Tower of Babel. Albert Churchward's position seems plausible when he claims that all that the Babylonians knew and speculated about was borrowed from the Africans. According to him, "The Babylonians copied and obtained all their knowledge from the Egyptians . . . what the Babylonians knew they borrowed either directly from the Egyptians or Sumerians – the latter obtained it from Egypt."[8]

The Elements of the Ancient African World-View

The Ancient Africans were well known for their tight cosmological views; Sais (Egypt) was the intellectual center of the world. Their speculation covered the whole realm of human knowledge including pure metaphysics, ethics, astronomy, mathematicians, science, and medicine. Because of the small space allotted in this volume we can only briefly outline their systematic philosophy.

Mathematics

One of the ancient African mathematical texts which has survived to the present is the *Rhind Mathematical Papyrus*. This work became a property of the British Museum upon Henry Rhind's death, but it became known to modern scholars in 1858 when Rhind secured the rights to it. The Mathematical Papyrus was written during the reign of King A–User–Re, 1650 BC and copies of this work were made roughly about 1800 BC by the Scribe A'hmose. The entire papyrus contains eight sections of arithmetical problems dealing with forty problems. We also find in this work four sections of pure geometry containing nineteen problems.

Arithmetical problems were of varied nature – but most solutions partook fractional and decimal processes. The Ancient Africans were, therefore, the first to discover the use of both decimal points and fractions. To this day we use their method, with only slight changes. To say that the mathematical problems solved in the *Rhind Papyrus* are simple algebra and fractions is to fail to recognize that during the days that this was written, man was *Inventing* such problems and their solutions – not *just* copying them out of textbooks. Besides fractions and decimal points, the Ancient Africans discovered methods of solving problems pertaining to volumes of pyramids and areas of cylinders. Their methods in these two cases are directly adopted by modern mathematicians.

The greatest achievements in the areas of mathematics was geometry. Without going into details, we may do well to state the basic African's geometrical maxims or theorems which were later directly adopted by the Greeks. There are at least five such basic propositions which found their way to Greece after the voyages of Thales, Pythagoras, and Euclid (the latter being the basis of Keat's philosophy) in Egypt, and their lessons from the Egyptian seers.

Proposition 1
The square of the hypotenuse of a right angled triangle is equal to the sum of the squares on the sides containing the right angle.

The ancient Africans had a knowledge of possible combinations, in definite ratios, of the square of 3 and 4 which when added make 5. The acquisition of such knowledge made it possible, then, to construct a right angled triangle with sides of 3, 4, and 5. There were various versions of this theorem regarding strategies for the construction of the great pyramids. Problems of this type presupposed the knowledge of isosceles triangles.

Proposition 2
The three angles of a triangle are together equal to two right angles.

According to Charles Tylor, the "positive part of it must have been observed by the Egyptians, who must therefore have known that the three angles of an equilateral triangle are together equal to two right angles."[9]

Proposition 3
The diameter of any circle bisects that circle.

It is worth noting that the ancient Africans gave pi the value 3 and 13/18. They calculated that if a diameter is marked or divided into 9 units, the circle drawn around it was equal to the square on a line with 8 units.

Proposition 4
The vertical angles of two straight lines cutting each other are equal.

The proof of this theorem is found in any of today's standard texts of elementary geometry.

Because of their mathematical knowledge, the Ancient Africans of Sais were able to calculate the height of a pyramid as well as the distance of a ship in the ocean from a given point on land. But in the history of philosophy written by Western philosophers, these two discoveries have been falsely attributed to Thales. Euclid adopted the ancient African method of determining the distance of a ship at sea (Euclid Theorem 1.26).

The most common observation made by Western scholars about the nature of the Egyptian mathematical activities is that theirs was more of a practical inclination than a speculative endeavor. But contrary to this attitude the ancient people of Sais were also concerned with the theoretical demand of the acquisition of knowledge. They considered mathematical knowledge to be sacred and it was taught only to the intellectuals who were also the priests. The distinction between the intellectual and practical was rigidly enforced. The priests told laymen how to use this knowledge for their activities, but the actual theorems and proofs remained a sacred trust.

Science

The next discipline for which ancient Egyptians laid the foundation is science. We can rightly claim that they marked the foundation of modern science in the sense that modern science is a spin-off from the medieval scientific outlook which, in turn, took its direction from the ancient Greeks. The Greek science is a continuation of African science. There has been a tendency in Western scholarship to label African science as mere technical knowledge and not pure science. At any rate we may only point out that knowledge of whatever form does have an aspect pursued for its own sake – which would make it theoretical. Even if the distinction between *technique* and *pure science* was legitimate, there still is one phenomenon which is common to both; they are based on empirical observation. We may say that the pre-occupation of the laymen of Ancient Africa with solutions of problems of immediate concerns may appear to have dominated the thorough-going theoretical considerations of the priestly class. We must remember, however, that we are talking about a period far removed from our own – 5000 BC to 2000 BC. In our own times, scientists do not bother developing all their findings for laymen who may or may not be interested. Further, they are in disagreement over whether or not the scientists of the middle ages were *really* scientists or technicians; whether astronomy is science or magic; and what the cut-off point is between "pure" and "applied" science. It would not be surprising if, in a matter of a few generations, our so-called "pure

science" of today would be considered "technique"!

The text which contains one aspect of Ancient African science – mainly a medical treatise – is what is known as *Edwin Papyrus*. The observations made in this work form the core of natural sciences. As Brested has pointed out, the authors of the text "were the earliest known natural scientists."[10] It would be incorrect, however, to say that African science was limited to the practice of medicine. In the other natural sciences – chemistry and physics – we find that as early as 4000 BC the discovery of metals in Egypt had already been made; glass-making was a major industry; and, the Egyptians had a definite knowledge of the ratios of elements, one of which was used to make bronze (a ratio of 12 per cent tin makes the alloy harden).

Now if we agree that the exact sciences are theoretical by virtue of their basis in mathematical knowledge, then the Africans had mathematical capabilities of a far-reaching nature which they definitely used to formulate working scientific theories.

Philosophical Systems (Schools) in Ancient Africa

We need to distinguish about four distinct schools of thought in Ancient Africa or Sais. These were:

a) School at Heliopolis
b) School at Hermopolis
c) School at Thebes
d) School at Memphis

Of these systems, the one which fashioned the basis of Greek philosophy was that at Memphis. However, in this brief account we will only point out some of the important concepts which later became the concern of most Greek philosophers.

What is common to all these schools of thought was their consistent theory of Creation and the nature of basic elements. At Heliopolis, the account was that above everything else was Atum-Ra, the Sun-God or Fire-God. Atum-Ra was basic to all natures. It was self-created – thus we hear echoes from the *Pyramid Text* that: "O Atum, when you came into being you rose up as a high hill." Besides Atum-Ra, we also find four major gods or elements: Shu, Air-God. Shu was the spirit of life and eternity – "I am the eternity the Creator of the millions . . ." The ancient African theologians conceived a Universe of opposites; the opposite of Shu now became Tefnut – the living female. Tefnut is responsible for World Order. In the *Coffin Text* we read: "Order is her name . . . Life reposed with my daughter Order." The other major elements were Geb – the Earth and Nut, the Sky. While Shu and Tefnut were children of Atum-Ra, Geb and Nut were his grandchildren. Thus we can arrange these elements in order of their priorities. We must add here that before anything else was created there was nothing but a Primordial abyss of Water (Nun).

Now we must hasten to see the consistency of thought between the Memphite School and that of the Heliopolis. According to the former, Ptah, the God of Gods, was actually the God of Creation. He first of all emerged from Nun (water) as a Primeval Hill. But while the Heliopolis school does not make mention of Ptah as the High God, the Memphite theology clearly states that after Ptah had posited himself as a Hill, Atum-Ra appeared from the Primoridal water and sat upon the Hill. The emergence of Atum was necessary because it was he who completed the creative process already started by Ptah. Atum was responsible for the being of World Order through his daughter Tefnut.

The Memphite Schools also posited a series of opposite gods – males and females:

Nun and Naunet (Water and Heavens)
Huk and Hauhet (Boundless and its opposite – limited)
Amum and Amaumet (the invisible and the visible)
Kuk and Kauket (Darkness and Light)

In the creative process Ptah merely uttered the *Word* for creation to take place. R. T. Rundle Clark writes that:

> The Memphite author has built his theory on the analogy of the *mind* controlling the motions of the body. This is the unique contribution of this text to cosmology. Whereas later philosophers – from the Ionians down to Hegel – retreated into tautologies before the problem of how the Word or the Idea actualized itself, the Egyptian constructed his theory on the model of mind and body.[11]

There was already a thoroughgoing sense of metaphysical idealism. Ptah, therefore, was both Mind and Word. We may also remind ourselves here of Clark's further assertion that:

> When Kant looked upon the movements of the starry sky and then into the moral order

within himself and recognized the two as the signs of one and the same God, he was closely following the thought of an anonymous Memphite more than four thousand years before.[12]

Creation was therefore done out of thought and command of Ptah. We can therefore summarize this discussion by stating that the Ancient Africans had already identified the following elements:

1 Water (Nun)
2 Boundless (Huk)
3 Air (Shu)
4 Fire (Atum)
5 The Mind
6 Chaos and Order the latter in the form of Tefnut.

The Doctrine of Immortality of the Soul

We now need to say something about the nature of the human soul. Again because of the limited space, we can only list a few of the concepts which are relevant to our thesis. The Egyptian word for soul in general is *Ba*. But Ba has human characteristics and is distinguishable from *Ka*, which is a *double*. The other major concepts connected with the general theory of the soul are: *Khu*, the shining part of man which bridges the gap between human (man) and superhuman (God) beings; and the Body, *Khat*. Khat was subject to complete destruction upon the phenomenon of death. Ba does have some visible characteristics. In most African societies we find that it is to the Ba (soul of the ancestor) that libation is poured and food offered, in the hope that he will eat, drink, and rejoice. Ka is not identical with Ba; it is more conceptual. Ka is the double of anything man can think of, of any conceivable object. In short, Ka is the conceptual replica of physical reality – created by Ptah, the *unmoved mover*, and completed by Atum, residing in the world of intellect.

A. H. Sayce believes that the notion of Ka was directly adopted by Plato in his theory of ideas. According to Sayce's interpretation,

> The ideas of Plato were the last development of the Egyptian doctrine of Ka. They were the archetype after which all things have been made.[13]

Plato believed that the real world is the world of ideas or forms. This borrowing of the sense of Ka is understandable since Plato went to study in Egypt when he was about 27 years old.

According to the Egyptians, when a person dies, what remains is his real self – the Ka, but within the Ka there resides Khu which is the intellect or pure intelligence. The term "Khu" could be rendered as meaning "mind." Khu is the divine part of man; it makes the linkage between man and God possible. The Egyptians believed that the soul, being imprisoned in the body, found it difficult to achieve or attain pure intelligence. It is only upon death that man can grasp the nature of reality, because then he is pure intelligence. The salvation of man, which is the highest God, is the separation of Khat from Ka.

The Ancient Greek Philosophers Influenced by Ancient African World-View

In this section, I will merely list Greek Philosophers who are identified with elements borrowed from the ancient African cosmology.

1. *Thales* – After studying in Egypt for a considerable number of years, he came to believe that water was the fundamental stuff underlying the Universe. Thales was influenced by Egyptian theory that water (Nun) was the origin of all things – even the Gods.

2. *Anaximander* – A student of Thales thought that the basic element was the *boundless*. This was an adoption of the Egyptian Huk (boundless).

3. *Anaximenes* – Held that air was the basic stuff. The Egyptian teachers taught that Shu – Air God – was the life force. Shu was life giving spirit.

4. *Hericlitus* – Believed that fire is the basic element – taking the notion from the Egyptian *Atum*, Fire.

5. *Pythagoras* – Believed that the Universe is basically mathematical. He also taught the theory of transmigration of the soul, which was generally known as Orphic doctrine. Orpheus, like Pythagoras, had been to Egypt, where he learned from the Egyptian priests: Pythagoras studied in Egypt for about 22 years – learning mathematics and the mystery systems of the Egyptians.

6. *Xenophanes* – the first Greek to teach the doctrine of the One God. His monism was of Egyptian origin. The ancient Egyptians as well as other Africans had a thoroughgoing doctrine of the One God, Ptah, who sways all things by the thought of his mind.

7. *Parmenides* – The founder of the Eleatic School, believed in the One Being. He furthered the doctrine of the One, which Xenophanes theologically developed. Influenced by Pythagoras, from whom he learned his philosophy, he inherited the Egyptian belief that the Earth was spherical. According to Josef ben Jochannan, "Xenophenes, Parmenides, Zeno and Melissus (all of them natives of Ionia) migrated to Elea, Italy, after completing their education in Egypt."[14]

8. *Anaxagoras* – He believed that the initiator of motion in the Universe was the mind (Nous). Mind was identified with the soul. We earlier noted that the Egyptian identified Khu with the mind. He also believed that air was the most pervasive of all the elements. He is also known to have gone to study in Egypt.

9. *Democritus* – Taught that the atoms are the ultimate constituents of the Universe. He was widely traveled – went to Egypt and Ethiopia, where he is reported to have stayed for five years learning both astronomy and geometry. He is supposed to have brought back to Greece the atomic theory from the East – mainly for the Nyaya school, of India. According to George James, in *The Stolen Legacy*, "The original source of this doctrine, however, is the philosophy of the Mystery System of Egypt ... under the circumstances and in consequence of those facts, the Egyptian Mystery System was the source of the doctrines a) of the atom, b) of opposites. Leucippus and Democritus taught nothing new and must have obtained their knowledge of the doctrines from the Egyptians, directly or indirectly."[15]

10. *Plato* – He traveled to Egypt where he studied under Egyptian priests. He picked up from Egypt some of the doctrines found in the *Republic*; that is to say, the three levels of society

a) the philosophers – kings
b) the soldiers
c) artisans

These doctrines were well established in the Egyptian social system. But before Plato, Pythagoras had identified these levels, which he called:

a) the Spectators – philosophers
b) Athletes – soldiers
c) Pedlers – laborers, artisans

Secondly, Plato adopted the Egyptian view of immortality of the soul. Thirdly, he adopted the

Egyptian view of Creation – Atum is Demiurge God of Creation. Fourthly, Plato's theory of ideas was influenced by the Egyptian concept of Ka. Fifth, the doctrine of the Good – this is the further development of the Egyptian theory of Salvation. The release of the soul from the body was the highest good.

11. *Aristotle* – He went to Egypt with Alexander the Great. He had access to Priestly material in the Temples – he freely acquired books from the Library at Alexandria. He adopted the Egyptian notion of the *unmoved mover*. Creative process developed from disorder (chaos) to order. This process was performed through mind and word – or pure intelligence. He also adopted the doctrine of the soul as discussed in the *Book of the Dead*.

Conclusion

The preceding discussion has attempted to do three things. One most important supposition is that any discussion of "Black Philosophy" is reducible to African Philosophy. Any philosophy must be evaluated from the context of its history. Contemporary Black Philosophy is moribund if it does not take as its starting point an African World-View – which is the basis of the Black experience. Similarly, the contemporary African philosophy is moribund if it does not take into account the "history of African philosophy" which takes us back to ancient Africa (Ancient Egypt, Ethiopia, etc.). Once the Black scholars have done this, their admiration of the

Western philosophy will take a new dimension; the monopoly of philosophy by the Greeks will have a turn.

At this point we may do well to take James' recommendation:

> Now that it has been shown that philosophy, arts, and sciences were bequeathed to civilization by the people of North Africa and not by the people of Greece; the pendulum of praise and honor is due to shift from the people of Greece to the people of the African continent who were the rightful heirs of such a praise and honor.
>
> This is going to mean a tremendous change in world opinion and attitude for all people and races who accept the new philosophy of African redemption, i.e. the truth that the Greeks were not the authors of Greek philosophy; but the people of North Africa . . .[16]

What this position suggests is that systematic African/Black Philosophy does not need to start from scratch. African philosophy or Black philosophy does not have to collapse into ideology – it has its legitimate basis. Similarly the newly developed "Black Theology" must have its basis on an African World-View to provide a history for it. Failure to recognize this demand merely reduces it to ideology – in which case, after Black Liberation is done with, the Black Theology (we may say the same thing for Black philosophy) will have no relevance.

Notes

1 Theodore Gomperz, *Greek Thinkers*, trans. L. Magnus and G. Berry (London: J. Murray, 1920), pp. 3–42.
2 Dibinger Wa Said, *Theosophies of Plato, Aristotle, and Plotinus* (New York: Philosophical Library, 1970), p. 1.
3 Willis Huggis and John G. Jackson, *Introduction to African Civilization* (New York: Negro University Press, 1969), p. 77.
4 Ibid.
5 Leonard Cottrel, *The Penguin Book of Lost Worlds* (Hamondsworth, Eng.: Penguin, 1966), p. 24.
6 Huggins and Jackson, p. 4.
7 G. W. F. Hegel, *Philosophy of History*, passim.
8 Albert Churchward, *The Signs and Symbols of Primordial Man* (London: Sonnenschein, 1910), pp. 212–213.
9 Charles Taylor, *An Introduction to the Ancient and Modern Geometry of Conics* (Cambridge: Deighton, Bell & Co., 1881), p. xxxiv.
10 Edwin Brested, *The Edwin Smith Surgical Papyrus*, vol. 1, p. 12.
11 R. T. Rundle Clark, *Myth and Symbol in Ancient Egypt* (London: Thames and Hudson, 1959), p. 64.
12 Ibid., p. 66.
13 A. H. Sayce, *The Religions of Ancient Egypt and Babylonia* (Edinburgh: T & T Clark, 1902), pp. 48–9.
14 Yosef ben Jochannan, *The African of the Nile* (New York: Alkebu-Lan Books, 1970), p. 193.
15 George James, *The Stolen Legacy* (New York: Philosophical Library, 1954), pp. 75–6.
16 Ibid., p. 171.

5

Contemporary Moslem Philosophies in North Africa

Mourad Wahba

For thirty years an international symposium has been held in Bordeaux on "Classicism and Cultural Decadence in the History of Islam." It is well known that this decadence began in the thirteenth century with the death of Ibn Rushd who played an active role in shaping the European philosophical conscience in the transition from the Middle Ages to the Enlightenment across the Renaissance, whereas he has been totally alienated from Islamic culture. Being alienated implies that the Islamic world lacks two essential periods, that is, Renaissance and Enlightenment, which are a prelude to the liberation of human reason from any authority save that of reason itself.

Consequently, in modern times Islam has been challenged by a bewildering array of forces, from outside and inside. From outside, a large part of the Islamic world from North Africa to Indonesia came under Western colonial rule just at the time when the scientific and technological revolutions in the West were making strides forward, reinforcing the colonialist sense of superiority. Moreover, the most rigorous force challenging Islam has been socialist ideology both Marxist and non-Marxist. Muslim response from inside, to the outside forces, has given rise to two outlooks: traditionalism and abortive modernism. Traditionalism is to be viewed as a negative attitude toward Western civilization and toward any futuristic outlook on the grounds

that the locus of Golden Age was the past and not the future. Abortive modernism is to be understood as a positive attitude toward the West but at the same time tradition-bound. It is not much more than enlightened traditionalism. And that is why the abortive modernism, in its fundamental premises and ultimate conclusions, opposes secularization elements of social modernization more effectively than traditionalism ever does precisely because it is more rational.

The two most influential figures in the traditionalist movement were Gamal al-Din al-Afghani and Muhammad Abdu. It must be stressed from the start that this movement spearheaded by these two Muslim philosophers did not question the dogma. The primary impulse had its source in the challenge which the West posed to Muslim society. Its aim was to reinstitute and strengthen the Islamic dogma, but not to expose it to rational criticism.

Afghani put the issue of the decadence of Islam in a clear short-cut, "Every Muslim is sick, and his only remedy is in the Qur'an."[1] Thus, the task of muslim countries is not how to be strong, but how to understand religion and live in accordance with its teachings. Emphasizing this theme, Afghani published a book entitled *The Refutation of the Materialists*[2] which became the model for traditionalist thought in dealing with materialist philosophy. Those whom he attacked under the name of the materialists included all, from Democritus to Darwin with their counterparts in Islam, who gave an explanation of the world not involving the existence of a transcendent God. Afghani's preoccupation with the Western materialism reflected a general

From *Philosophy in Africa: Trends and Perspectives*, ed. P. O. Bodunrin, University of Ife Press (1985); reproduced by kind permission of P. O. Bodunrin.

Muslim bias against science, which was regarded as responsible for the disintegration of traditional Christianity, and which was now threatening Islam. It is, therefore, not surprising if this stand blocked logical discourse and contributed to deflecting interest in rational criticism.

Thus, Afghani formulated the general direction traditionalism was to take, but it was Abdu who, using Afghani's teachings as a springboard, gave this direction its precise formulation. The task he set himself involved two things: first, a restatement of what Islam really was; second, a consideration of its implications for modern society. As for the first point, Abdu is of the opinion that reason must accept everything that is in the Qur'an without hesitation; once it acknowledges that Muhammed was a prophet, it must accept the entire content of his prophetic message. The second point proceeds from the first, for as long as reason is controlled by the Qur'an, so the ideal society is that which submits to God's commandments, for these commandments are also the principles of human society. The behaviour which the Qur'an teaches to be pleasing to God is also that which modern social thought teaches to be the key to progress. Islam is the true sociology, the science of happiness in this world as well as the next. So when Islamic law is fully obeyed society flourishes; when it is rejected society decays.[3]

This is ideal society but for Abdu it is also a society which once existed. His imagination is fixed on the golden age of Islam. And that is why Abdu was against the secular society. As an evidence of this fact, the dispute between Abdu and Antum Farah on the occasion of a book on the life and philosophy of Ibn Rushd published by the latter. In his dedication Antum declares that the book is meant for "the new shoots of the east".[4]

> Those men of sense in every community and every religion of the east who have seen the danger of mingling the world with religion in an age like ours, and have come to demand that their religion be placed on one side in a sacred and honoured place, so that they will be able really to unite, and to flow with the tide of the European civilization, in order to be able to compete with those who belong to it, for otherwise it will sweep them all away and make them the subject of others.[5]

A little further on he explains why he is writing about Ibn Rushd: it is to separate the temporal from the religious authorities. There are five reasons why this is necessary. The most important is the third one in which he states that the religious authorities legislate with a view to the next world, and therefore their control would interfere with the purpose of government, which is to legislate for this world. Abdu protested on the grounds that the separation of religion and state was not only undesirable, it was also impossible, for the ruler must belong to a specific religion. Along with this traditionalist movement came Moslem Brotherhood, headed by Hassan al-Banna and influenced by Rashid Rida, the most important disciple of Abdu.

Now, we come to the second movement, that is, abortive modernism. The most influential figures are: Osman Amin, Zaki Naguib Mahmoud, Ben Nabi, Lahbabi, and Loraui. Osman Amin is the advocate of the "Philosophy of Inwardness" (al-Gouwaniya). It is a philosophy which tries to see people and things from a spiritual angle. In other words, it tries to see the invisible world by not being limited to the visible. It seeks the inward being, not stopping at the outward. Many traditions, attributed to the Prophet, emphasize this opposition between the invisible and the visible. For example: "God does not look at your faces and wealth, but He looks at your hearts and your actions."[6] In this religious sense, al-Gouwaniya is a synonym for freedom. For freedom must not be sought in the possession of objects, like wealth and honours, but in our soul, that is, in something of absolute autonomy, namely, faith in God and attachment to the dignity of man. In this context, Amin thinks that he combines Western philosophy with the framework of Islamic tradition. He says:

> I now go back to the philosophical explanation of Al-Gouwaniya. In this respect Maine de Biran is of great help. He says that there is much difference between knowing a truth through our intelligence and having it always present in our soul.[7]

Further on he states that the philosophy of al-Gouwaniya adopts the distinction made by Bergson between two different ways of knowledge:

> the one being the way of inward vision, penetration by the spirit, by intellectual sympathy; the other being the way of exterior vision, effected by using the testimony of the sense or by applying logical analysis alone.[8]

Concerning his concept of freedom, Amin assumes that it is found in the Cartesian ethics which aims at establishing the mastery of the soul over the passions, and in Kant's idea of the moral law which is wholly inward and *a priori*, that is to say, preceding and conditioning all experience, not being derived from the exterior world.

Due to this interiorized idealist tendency, Osman Amin is against logical positivism and historical materialism. He is against logical positivism because it stops at the limits of senses and experiment and denies authenticity of reason. He is also against historical materialism because it uses science to abolish man and, consequently, religion, since man according to Amin's definition is a religious animal.

The inevitable consequence of this is the confrontation of social issues, not only in an idealist manner, but in a religious manner. Amin adopts the question of socialism as an example of this double confrontation. For the idealist confrontation regards the notion of socialism, above all, as an absolute truth that exists in the mind, an impersonal existence that is unlimited either by time or by space.

According to religious confrontation, the non-temporal, non-spatial cannot serve as a theory or ideology nor can it be subject to any law, but can only serve as a subject of religious faith. Consequently, socialism is Islamic socialism and its pioneers are Gamal al-Din al-Afghani, Muhammad Abdu, al-Kawakibi, and Muhammed Iqbal, because they have awakened the socialist consciousness of the individual society.

The purpose of such a philosophic system – according to its advocator – is the attempt to restore to our atomic age, the age of historical materialism and logical positivism, faith in God and allegiance to man. However, in all his lectures which he delivered at the university, Amin harshly criticized logical positivism rather than historical materialism. This can be explained by the fact that Zaki Naguib Mahmoud, who is a professor of philosophy at the same department, adopts logical positivism.

Zaki Naguib Mahmoud adopts the attitude of logical positivism towards science. Science, for him, is the natural experimental science, and the means of scientific knowledge are the senses which are the only source of knowledge. The scientific outlook obliges us not to transcend the *status quo*. Since placing the issues within reality is the only field of scientific research, the scientific outlook is called logical positivism. If the *status quo* which

preoccupies the researcher is a linguistic statement, positivism in this case becomes "logical." Hence, the label "logical positivism," denotes a group of thinkers who do not transcend reality and who concern themselves with a reality which becomes the language in which scientists formulate their diverse subjects. Hence, philosophy should be limited to the linguistic analysis of scientific statements.

Zaki Naguib Mahmoud reaches two important conclusions through his linguistic analysis: The first conclusion is that the logical analysis of a mathematical sentence indicates its tautology, and that its certainty is due to the fact that it says nothing. He writes: "The strange discovery about the nature of the mathematical sentence justifies the fact that there is only one source of knowledge for man, namely, his sense and that nothing can justify an element beyond the senses, independent from them, namely, "the mind." The second conclusion is that value "is purely a subjective expression which has nothing to do with the external world." The significance of that is, if two people disagree about a value judgment "the only alternative would be to resort to an external criterion to decide who is wrong and who is right."

The question now is: What is Zaki Naguib Mahmoud's motive behind adopting this interpretation of science? The motive is a social one. In one of his later books,[3] he says that his aim is to reconcile Arab tradition with modernism. What is meant by Arab tradition? According to Zaki Naguib Mahmoud, Arab tradition is the technique used by our ancestors for living. Our task is to choose the techniques that can help us in improving our living. Hence, Arab tradition is not a matter of ideology but technology. What is meant by modernism? To Zaki Naguib Mahmoud, "Logical positivism" represents the spirit of modernism. That is why it is an essential part of Naguib Mahmoud's philosophy to affirm a legitimate distinction between factual judgment and value judgment. One is scientific, the other is not. As a consequence, one cannot advocate a scientific approach to the study of social change. Hence, ideology also is non-scientific, and what we call ideological struggle is nonsense. That is why, according to Mahmoud, those terms "capitalist or socialist society" have been replaced by "technological or post-industrial society."

This trend has become the main theme of modern bourgeois ideology, and it has received the name of "de-ideologization" which is an attempt to implant an apolitical state of mind that does not care either for social change or for society. That is why Naguib Mahmoud is consistent with his philosophy when he writes: "Owing to my philosophical trend I approve of anything that could strengthen the individuality of the individual and that could destroy society in case solidarity is to grow up at my own expense. There is no real fact except my own being and everything else is but an instrument for strengthening this being."[10] This statement confirms our point of view: de-ideologization is an ideological weapon used against social change.

Abdel-Rahman Badawi comes to the same conclusion but through atheistic Existentialism. According to him, existence and time are synonymous. In his book titled *Existential Time*, he writes: "We clearly and frankly declare that any existence that is not temporalized is an absolute falsehood."[11] Since time, for Badawi, is divided into physical and subjective time, there is, likewise, physical and subjective existence. Physical existence is the existence of objects in the world in which man exists while subjective existence is the existence of the self, an independent and quite isolated existence. Consequently, communication between selves is totally absent. However, this schism may be overcome by means of a leap. This leap, however, cannot be explained rationally, according to Badawi, because nothingness is an essential factor in the structure of existence, and the irrational is the intellectual expression of existential nothingness, and modern physics corroborates the notion of the irrational. Non-causality stated in modern physics in the Quantum theory and wave mechanics is quite irrational in the sense that it cannot be reduced to pure rational elements.

In this respect, Badawi relies upon Louis de Broglie's assumption that physics should reject the idea of continuity and limit itself to deducing laws which are necessarily of a statistical nature. Consequently, self-knowledge cannot be attained by reason but by another faculty, namely, intuition. The logic of intuition is tense. This tension means the inability to supersede the contradiction. This is the meaning of the dialectic which is placed only within the self and not outside the self.

Badawi considers his system as an appropriate ideology for the Arab society. He justifies this appropriateness – in an article published in 1967 – by Islamic legacy as represented in Sufism. He finds a close connection between Sufism and

Existentialism. Both start from subjectivism and place subjective existence above physical existence. The purpose of abstraction in Sufism is to release the self from the other so that the self is kept alone. The notion of the perfect man for the Sufis means a polarization of existence in man alone. In this way, humanity becomes a substitute for God. But such humanity, however, is a subjective, rather than an objective, humanity.

The main theme of the Algerian philosopher Malek Ben Nabi is to reconstruct an Islamic society free from exploitation, imperialism, and coping with modern civilization. But this is impossible unless the Islamic idea becomes efficient. Ben Nabi means, by efficiency, the ability to change the world radically, to create history. He says that this kind of efficiency was realized during the Prophet's time, that is creating the Islamic empire and deepening the Islamic truth. One could object saying that truth was not identified with one point of view but with many. This objection could be acceptable, but no one can deny efficiency at that time.

What does this mean, according to Ben Nabi? It means that truth is subjective, while efficiency is objective. Hence, objective factors are required for the realization of efficiency. Unfortunately, these conditions are absent nowadays and their absence is due to two reasons:

1　Presence of imperialism
2　Absence of ideas

The first reason is obvious but the second one is obscure and has to be explained in detail.

According to Ben Nabi's ideology, there are three worlds which are necessary for any civilization:

1　World of ideas
2　World of persons
3　World of things

The leading world is the world of ideas because man is distinguished from animal by reason, and this means that our idea of a thing precedes its realization in reality. Therefore, ideas have this ability of changing world of persons and world of things. Here, a question is to be raised: What is the matter with the world of ideas in the Islamic world at the present time? Ben Nabi's answer is that the world of ideas is absent, and its absence is due to two factors: objective factor and subjective factor. Imperialism represents the objective factor. It negates man from his creative powers by involving him in the world of things instead of the world of ideas. In this way, man retreats to the infantile period which is characterized by handling things without knowing what they are. That is why imperialism is always keen to sell us things and not ideas, and even if it accepts to sell us ideas, it sells them after distorting and falsifying them. But, imperialism as an objective factor is valueless without the subjective factor which designates the "ability towards imperialism," that is, the refusal of utilizing one's potentialities to raise the standard of living.

Ben Nabi, in his book *Vocation of Islam* says that liberation from imperialism – implies liberation from ability towards capitalism. Hence, any revolution neglecting this subjective factor, condemns itself to failure.[12] How could a revolution avoid such a failure? Through cultural revolution, but such revolution is not sufficient, though it is necessary. It is in need of "explosive economic policy" to liberate productive forces, and in this way the Islamic idea retains its efficiency. But what is the definition of this technical term "explosive economic policy"? Ben Nabi's definition is that it is neither the capitalist pattern nor the Marxist pattern. What is it, then? We get no answer from Ben Nabi, and that is his dilemma, because one cannot control and orientate social change if one lacks a clear idea about what is required for such a change.

As for Lahbabi, he resorts to the radical questioning of the decadence of the muslim world in the light of the original fountains of Islam, that is, the Qur'an and the *Sunna* (the biography of the Prophet as it shows his historical conduct) as a call for a sweeping transformation of the *status quo* and the attitudes allied to it, which are extremely backward. A call to go back to original Islam and shed the idea of the fixity of "taqlid" (blind belief in holy texts), and attempt to perform "ijtihad" that is, to rethink for oneself the meaning of the original message. In the light of these characteristics which are attributed to Salafiyya (revivalists), Lahbabi enlists the radical difference between the Salafiyya and the Western Renaissance.

Western Renaissance is a rupture in the continuity of civilization. One was freed from medieval-style thinking to enslave oneself to antiquity (one step forward, two steps backward). On the contrary, the Salafiyya go back to the sources of Islam without rejecting the cultural acquisitions, whether Islamic or not, and going back to the Qur'an and *Sunna* to liberate the dogma and the laws from superstition, sufism, and "taqlid." The Salafiyya is

a search for the original force of Islam. The Salafiyya is a creative going back, whereas the Renaissance was a movement against the Middle Ages, and Protestantism against the Church. A paradox phenomenon, progress is realized through reaction, through imitation of what the Greeks and Romans had thought of. On the contrary, the Middle Ages, for muslims, were ages of creativity, of free interpretation in all fields. In this sense, a marriage was held between the sacred and the secular. The classics of Greek antiquity, especially philosophy and science, were taken, not as perfect models, as they were during the Renaissance, but as something that could be adopted and could be adapted to.[13]

But in my own opinion, Lahbabi's theme suffers two weaknesses: the first weakness is that he does not fully elaborate a specific method; the second weakness is that he does not tackle the social implications of his theme. Thus, we can see that Lahbabi has not been able to transcend positively the ever-haunting ghost of the West. It is certain that the medieval religious output of muslims cannot give any comprehensible guidance either for today or for the future even though there is much that is highly valuable in this medieval thought.

And that is why Laroui is right when he assumes that the weakness of the Arab intellectuals is their confinement to two rationales, the traditionalist rationale (*Salafi*) and the eclectic rationale. Together, these tendencies succeed in abolishing the historical dimension. Consequently, a historical thinking has but one consequence: failure to see the real. The only way to do away with these two modes of thought consists in strict submission to the discipline of historical thought and acceptance of all its assumptions; the existence of laws of historical development, the unicity of the meaning of history, and the effectiveness of the political role of the philosopher. Nevertheless, these assumptions are not accepted. The *Salafi* believe in Providence and the eclectics are at the mercy of every passing fashion.[14]

But, in my own opinion, it is not easy to adopt the historical thinking, which requires a certain stage of civilizational development, that is the enlightenment, or the liberation of human reason from any authority save reason itself. Thus, without passing through enlightenment, being looked at not as an outcome of accidental civilization but of human civilization, historical thinking is impossible.

Notes

1 Afghani, quoted in Muhammad al-Makhzumi, *Kharitat Jamal al-Din Afghani al-Husayni* ("Thoughts of Jamal al-Din al-Afghani al-Husayni"), Beirut, 1931, p. 88.
2 Translated from Persian by M. Abdu, 2nd edn, Cairo, 1955.
3 Abdu, *Risalat al-tawhid*, p. 214.
4 Antum Farah, *Ibn Rushd*, Cairo, 1903, p. 23.
5 Ibid.
6 Osman Amin, "*Al-Gouwaniya* or the Philosophy of Inwardness", in *Al-Hikmat*, Lahore, 1973, pp. 4–6.
7 Ibid.
8 Ibid.
9 Zaki Naguib Mahmoud, *Revival of Arab Thought*, Beirut, 1971, p. 207.
10 Zaki Naguib Mahmoud, *Days in America*, Cairo, 1955.
11 Abdel-Rahman Badawi, *Existential Time*.
12 Malek Ben Nabi, *Vocation of Islam*, Beirut, 1970, p. 105.
13 Lahbabi, *Le Personalisme Musulman*, Paris, PUF, 1967, pp. 88–99.
14 A. Laroui, *The Crisis of the Arab Intellectuals*, London, 1976, pp. 153–77.

PART II

Human Nature: Mind, Body, and Self-identity

6

The Relation of Ōkra (Soul) and Honam (Body): An Akan Conception

Kwame Gyekye

What is a person? Is a person just the bag of flesh and bones that we see with our eyes, or is there something additional to the body that we do not see? A conception[1] of the nature of a human being in Akan philosophy is the subject of this chapter.

Ōkra (Soul)

We are given to understand from a number of often quoted, though mistaken, anthropological accounts that the Akan people consider a human being to be constituted of three elements: *ōkra, sunsum*, and *honam* (or *nipadua*: body).

The *ōkra* is said to be that which constitutes the innermost self, the essence, of the individual person. *Ōkra* is the individual's life, for which reason it is usually referred to as *ōkrateasefo*, that is, the living soul, a seeming tautology that yet is significant. The expression is intended to emphasize that *ōkra* is identical with life. The *ōkra* is the embodiment and transmitter of the individual's destiny (fate: *nkrabea*). It is explained as a spark of the Supreme Being (Onyame) in man. It is thus described as divine and as having an antemundane existence with the Supreme Being. The presence of this divine essence in a human being may have been the basis of the Akan proverb, "All men are the children of God; no one is a child of the earth"

From Kwame Gyekye, *An Essay on African Philosophical Thought* (1995), copyright © 1995 by Kwame Gyekye; reproduced by kind permission of Temple University Press.

(*nnipa nyinaa yē Onyame mma, obiara nnyē asase ba*). So conceived, the *ōkra* can be considered as the equivalent of the concept of the soul in other metaphysical systems. Hence, it is correct to translate *ōkra* into English as soul.

. . . The conception of the *ōkra* as constituting the individual's life, the life force, is linked very closely with another concept, *honhom*. *Honhom* means "breath"; it is the noun form of *home*, to breathe. When a person is dead, it is said "His breath is gone" (*ne honhom kō*) or "His soul has withdrawn from his body" (*ne 'kra afi ne ho*). These two sentences, one with *honhom* as subject and the other with *ōkra*, do, in fact, say the same thing; they express the same thought, the death-of-the-person. The departure of the soul from the body means the death of the person, and so does the cessation of breath. Yet this does not mean that the *honhom* (breath) is identical with the *ōkra* (soul). It is the *ōkra* that "causes" the breathing. Thus, the *honhom* is the tangible manifestation or evidence of the presence of the *ōkra*. [In some dialects of the Akan language, however, *honhom* has come to be used interchangeably with *sunsum* ("spirit"), so that the phrase *honhom bōne* has come to mean the same thing as *sunsum bōne*, that is, evil spirit. The identification of the *honhom* with the *sunsum* seems to me to be a recent idea, and may have resulted from the translation of the Bible into the various Akan dialects; *honhom* must have been used to translate the Greek *pneuma* (breath, spirit).] The clarification of the concepts of *ōkra, honhom, sunsum* and others bearing on the Akan conception of the nature of a person is the concern of this chapter.

Sunsum (Spirit)

Sunsum is another of the constituent elements of the person. It has usually been rendered in English as "spirit." It has already been observed that *sunsum* is used both generically to refer to all unperceivable, mystical beings and forces in Akan ontology, and specifically to refer to the activating principle in the person. It appears from the anthropological accounts that even when it is used specifically, "spirit" (*sunsum*) is not identical with soul (*ōkra*), as they do not refer to the same thing. However, the anthropological accounts of the *sunsum* involve some conceptual blunders, as I shall show. As for the *mind* – when it is not identified with the soul – it may be rendered also by *sunsum*, judging from the functions that are attributed by the Akan thinkers to the latter.

On the surface it might appear that "spirit" is not an appropriate rendition for *sunsum*, but after clearing away misconceptions engendered by some anthropological writings, I shall show that it is appropriate but that it requires clarification. Anthropologists and sociologists have held (1) that the *sunsum* derives from the father,[2] (2) that it is not divine,[3] and (3) that it perishes with the disintegration of the *honam*,[4] that is, the material component of a person. It seems to me, however, that all these characterizations of the *sunsum* are incorrect.[5]

Let us first take up the third characterization, namely, as something that perishes with the body. Now, if the *sunsum* perishes along with the body, a physical object, then it follows that the *sunsum* also is something physical or material. Danquah's philosophical analysis concludes that "*sunsum* is, in fact, the matter or the physical basis of the ultimate ideal of which *ōkra* (soul) is the form and the spiritual or mental basis."[6] Elsewhere he speaks of an "interaction of the material mechanism (*sunsum*) with the soul," and assimilates the *sunsum* to the "sensible form" of Aristotle's metaphysics of substance and the *ōkra* to the "intelligible form."[7] One might conclude from these statements that Danquah also conceived the *sunsum* as material, although some of his other statements would seem to contradict this conclusion. The relation between the *honam* (body) and the *sunsum* (supposedly bodily), however, is left unexplained. Thus, philosophical, sociological, and anthropological accounts of the nature of the person give the impression of a tripartite conception of a human being in Akan philosophy:

Ōkra (soul)	immaterial
Sunsum ("spirit")	material (?)
Honam (body)	material

As we shall see, however, this account or analysis of a person, particularly the characterization of the *sunsum* ("spirit") as something material, is not satisfactory. I must admit, however, that the real nature of the *sunsum* presents perhaps the greatest difficulty in the Akan metaphysics of a person and has been a source of confusion for many. The difficulty, however, is not insoluble.

. . . The explanation given by most Akans of the phenomenon of dreaming also indicates, it seems to me, that *sunsum* must be immaterial. In Akan thought, as in Freud's, dreams are not somatic but psychical phenomena. It is held that in a dream it is the person's *sunsum* that is the "actor." As an informant told Rattray decades ago, "When you sleep your 'Kra (soul) does not leave you, as your *sunsum* may."[8] In sleep the *sunsum* is said to be released from the fetters of the body. As it were, it fashions for itself a new world of forms with the materials of its waking experience. Thus, although one is deeply asleep, yet one may "see" oneself standing atop a mountain or driving a car or fighting with someone or pursuing a desire like sexual intercourse; also, during sleep (that is, in dreams) a person's *sunsum* may talk with other *sunsum*. The actor in any of these "actions" is thought to be the *sunsum*, which thus can leave the body and return to it. The idea of the psychical part of a person leaving the body in sleep appears to be widespread in Africa. The Azande, for instance, maintain "that in sleep the soul is released from the body and can roam about at will and meet other spirits and have other adventures, though they admit something mysterious about its experiences. . . . During sleep a man's soul wanders everywhere."[9]

The idea that some part of the soul leaves the body in sleep is not completely absent from the history of Western thought, even though, as Parrinder says, "the notion of a wandering soul is foreign to the modern European mind."[10] The idea occurs, for instance, in Plato. In the *Republic* Plato refers to "the wild beast in us" that in pursuit of desires and pleasures bestirs itself "in *dreams* when the *gentler part of the soul* slumbers and the control of reason is withdrawn; then the wild beast in us, full-fed with meat and drink, becomes rampant and shakes off sleep to go in quest of what will gratify its own instincts."[11] The context is a discussion of tyranny. But Plato prefaces his discussion with remarks on the *psychological* foundation of the tyrannical man, and says that desire (Greek: *epithumia*) is the basis of his behavior.

It is not surprising that both scholars of Plato and modern psychologists have noted the relevance of the above passage to the analysis of the nature of the human psyche. On this passage the classical scholar James Adam wrote: "The theory is that in dreams the part of the soul concerned is not asleep, but awake and goes out to seek the object of its desire."[12] The classicist Paul Shorey observed that "The Freudians have at least discovered Plato's anticipation of their main thesis."[13] The relevance of the Platonic passage to Freud has been noted also by other scholars of Plato such as Renford Bambrough[14] and Thomas Gould,[15] and by psychologists. Valentine, a psychologist, observed: "The germ of several aspects of the Freudian view of dreams, including the characteristic doctrine of the censor, was to be found in Plato."[16]

It is clear that the passage in Plato indicates a link between dreams and (the gratification of) desires.[17] In Akan psychology the *sunsum* appears not only as unconscious but also as that which pursues and experiences desires. (In Akan dreams are also considered predictive.) But the really interesting part of Plato's thesis for our purposes relates to *the idea of some part of the human soul leaving the body in dreams.* "The wild beast in us" in Plato's passage is not necessarily equivalent to the Akan *sunsum*, but one may say that just as Plato's "wild beast" (which, like the *sunsum*, experiences dreams) is a *part* of the soul and thus not a physical object, so is *sunsum*.

It might be supposed that if the *sunsum* can engage in activity, such as traveling through space or occupying a physical location – like standing on the top of a mountain – then it can hardly be said not to be a physical object. The problem here is obviously complex. Let us assume, for the moment, that the *sunsum* is a physical object. One question that would immediately arise is: How can a purely physical object leave the person when he or she is asleep? Dreaming is of course different from imagining or thinking. The latter occurs during waking life, whereas the former occurs only during sleep: *wōnda a wōnso dae*, that is, "Unless you are asleep you do not dream" is a well-known Akan saying. The fact that dreaming occurs only in sleep makes it a unique sort of mental activity and its subject, namely *sunsum*, a different sort of subject. A purely physical object cannot be in two places at the same time: A body lying in bed cannot at the same time be on the top of a mountain. Whatever is on the top of the mountain, then, must be something nonphysical, nonbodily, and yet somehow connected to a physical thing – in this case, the body. This argument constitutes a *reductio ad absurdum* of the view that *sunsum* can be a physical object.

But, then, how can the *sunsum*, qua nonphysical, extrasensory object, travel in physical space and have a physical location? This question must be answered within the broad context of the African belief in the activities of the supernatural (spiritual) beings in the physical world. The spiritual beings are said to be insensible and intangible, but they are also said to make themselves felt in the physical world. They can thus interact with the physical world. But from this it cannot be inferred that they are physical or quasi-physical or have permanent physical properties. It means that a spiritual being can, when it so desires, take on physical properties. That is, even though a spiritual being is nonspatial in essence, it can, by the sheer operation of its power, assume spatial properties. Debrunner speaks of "temporary 'materializations,' i.e., as spirits having taken on the body of a person which afterwards suddenly vanish."[18] Mbiti observed that "Spirits are invisible, but may make themselves visible to human beings."[19] We should view the "physical" activities of the *sunsum* in dreaming from the standpoint of the activities of the spiritual beings in the physical world. As a microcosm of the world spirit, the *sunsum* can also interact with the external world. So much then for the defense of the psychical, nonphysical nature of *sunsum*, the subject of experiences in dreaming.

As the basis of personality, as the co-performer of some of the functions of the *ōkra* (soul) – undoubtedly held as a spiritual entity – and as the subject of the psychical activity of dreaming, the *sunsum* must be something spiritual (immaterial). This is the reason for my earlier assertion that "spirit" might not be an inappropriate translation for *sunsum*. On my analysis, then, we have the following picture:

Ōkra (soul) ⎫	immaterial (spiritual)
Sunsum ("spirit") ⎭	
Honam (body)	material (physical)

Relation of *Ōkra* and *Sunsum*

Having shown that the *sunsum* is in fact something spiritual (and for this reason I shall henceforth translate *sunsum* as "spirit"), we must examine whether the expressions *sunsum* and *ōkra* are identical in terms of their referent. In the course of my field research some discussants stated that the *sunsum*, *ōkra*, and *honhom* (breath) are identical; they denote the same object; it is one and the same object that goes under three names. I have already shown that although there is a close link between *ōkra* and *honhom*, the two cannot be identified; likewise the identification of *honhom* and *sunsum* is incorrect. What about the *sunsum* and *ōkra*? Are they identical?

The relation between the *sunsum* and *ōkra* is a difficult knot to untie. The anthropologist Rattray, perhaps the most perceptive and analytical researcher into the Ashanti culture, wrote: "It is very difficult sometimes to distinguish between the *'kra* and the next kind of soul, the *sunsum*, and sometimes the words seem synonymous, but I cannot help thinking this is a loose use of the terms."[20] Rattray was, I think, more inclined to believe that the two terms are not identical. Such a supposition, in my view, would be correct, for to say that the two are identical would logically mean that whatever can be asserted of one can or must be asserted of the other. Yet there are some things the Akans say of the *sunsum* which are not said of the *ōkra*, and vice versa; the attributes or predicates of the two are different. The Akans say:

A(1) "His *'kra* is sad" (*ne 'kra di awerēhow*); never, "His *sunsum* is sad."
(2) "His *'kra* is worried or disturbed" (*ne 'kra teetee*).
(3) "His *'kra* has run away" (*ne 'kra adwane*), to denote someone who is scared to death.
(4) "His *'kra* is good" (*ne 'kra ye*), referring to a person who is lucky or fortunate. [The negative of this statement is "His *'kra* is not good." If you used *sunsum* in lieu of *'kra*, and made the statement "His *sunsum* is not good" (*ne sunsum nnyē*), the meaning would be quite different; it would mean that his *sunsum* is evil, that is to say, he is an evil spirit, a witch.]
(5) "His *'kra* has withdrawn from his body" (*ne 'kra afi ne ho*).
(6) "But for his *'kra* that followed him, he would have died" (*ne 'kra dii n'akyi, anka owui*).
(7) "His *'kra* is happy" (*ne 'kra aniagye*).

In all such statements the attributions are made to the *ōkra* (soul), never to the *sunsum*. On the other hand, the Akans say:

B(1) "He has *sunsum*" (*ōwōo sunsum*), an expression they use when they want to refer to someone as dignified and as having a commanding presence. Here they never say, "He has *ōkra*," soul, for it is believed that it is the nature of the *sunsum* (not the *ōkra*) that differs from person to person; hence they speak of "gentle *sunsum*," "forceful *sunsum*," "weak or strong *sunsum*," etc.
(2) "His *sunsum* is heavy or weighty" (*ne sunsum yē duru*), that is, he has a strong personality.
(3) "His *sunsum* overshadows mine" (*ne sunsum hyē me so*).
(4) "Someone's *sunsum* is bigger or greater than another's" (*obi sunsum so kyēn obi deē*). To say "someone"s *'kra* is greater than another's" would be meaningless.
(5) "He has a good *sunsum*" (*ōwō sunsum pa*), that is, he is a generous person.

In all such statements the attributions are made to the *sunsum* (spirit), never to the *ōkra* (soul). Rattray also pointed out correctly that "an Ashanti would never talk of washing his *sunsum*."[21] It is the *ōkra* that is washed (*okraguare*). In the terminology of the modern linguist, sentences containing *ōkra* and *sunsum* differ, according to my analysis, not only in their surface structures but also in their deep structures.

It is pretty clear from this semantic analysis that *ōkra* and *sunsum* are not intersubstitutable in predications. Intersubstitution of the terms, as we saw above, leads either to nonsense as in B(4) or to change of meaning as in A(4) and B(1). Semantic analysis suggests a nonidentity relation between *sunsum* and *ōkra*. One might reject this conclusion by treating these distinctions as merely idiomatic and not, therefore, as evidence for considering *ōkra* and *sunsum* as distinct. Let us call this the "idiomatic thesis." In the English language, for instance, it is idiomatic to say "He's a sad soul" rather than "He's a sad spirit," without implying that soul and spirit are distinct. But in English the substitution of one for the other of the two terms – even if unidiomatic – will not lead to nonsense and would not change the *meaning*; in Akan it would.

. . . It may be the easiest way out of an interpretative labyrinth to identify *ōkra* and *sunsum*,[22] but I do not think it is the most satisfactory way out. There are, I believe, other considerations for rejecting the "identity theory."

First, most Akans agree that in dreaming it is the

sunsum, not the *ōkra*, that leaves the body. The departure of the *ōkra* (soul) from the body means the death of the person, whereas the *sunsum* can leave the body, as in dreaming, without causing the death of the person. Second, moral predicates are generally applied to the *sunsum*. Rattray wrote: "Perhaps the *sunsum* is the more volatile part of the whole '*kra*," and " . . . but the '*kra* is not volatile in life, as the *sunsum* undoubtedly is."[23] Moreover, the *ōkra* and *sunsum* appear to be different in terms of their functions or activities. The *ōkra*, as mentioned before, is the principle of life of a person and the embodiment and transmitter of his or her destiny (*nkrabea*). Personality and character dispositions of a person are the function of the *sunsum*. The *sunsum* appears to be the source of dynamism[24] of a person, the *active* part or force of the human psychological system; its energy is the ground for its interaction with the external world. It is said to have extrasensory powers; it is that which thinks, desires, feels, etc. It is in no way identical with the brain, which is a physical organ. Rather it acts upon the brain (*amene, hon*). In short, people believe that it is upon the *sunsum* that one's health, worldly power, position, influence, success, etc. would depend. The attributes and activities of the *sunsum* are therefore not ascribable to the *ōkra*. Lystad was wrong when he stated: "In many respects the *sunsum* or spirit is so identical with the *ōkra* or soul in its functions that it is difficult to distinguish between them."[25]

Now, given x and y, if whatever is asserted of x can be asserted of y, then x can be said to be identical with y. If there is at least one characteristic that x has but y does not, then x and y are not identical. On this showing, insofar as things asserted of the *ōkra* are not assertable of the *sunsum*, the two cannot logically be identified. However, although they are logically distinct, they are not *ontologically* distinct. That is to say, they are not independent existents held together in an accidental way by an external bond. They are a unity in duality, a duality in unity. The distinction is not a relation between two separate entities. The *sunsum* may, more accurately, be characterized as a *part* – the active part – of the *ōkra* (soul).

I once thought that the *sunsum* might be characterized as a state,[26] an epiphenomenon, of the *ōkra*. I now think that characterization is wrong, for it would subvert the entitative nature of *sunsum*. The fact that we can speak of the inherence of the *sunsum* in natural objects as their activating principle means that in some contexts reference can be made to the *sunsum* independently of the *ōkra*. This, however,

is not so in the context of the human psyche: In man *sunsum* is part of the *ōkra* (soul). Plato held a tripartite conception of the human soul, deriving that conception from his view of the functions said to be performed by the various parts of the soul. So did Freud. There is nothing inappropriate or illogical or irrational for some Akan thinkers to hold and argue for a bipartite conception of the human soul. Neither a tripartite nor a bipartite conception of the soul subverts its *ontic unity*. As already stated, the *ōkra* and *sunsum* are constitutive of a spiritual unity, which survives after death. Therefore the soul (that is, *ōkra* plus *sunsum*) does not lose its individuality after death. It survives individually. Beliefs in reincarnation (which I do not intend to explore now) and in the existence of the ancestors in the world of spirits (*asamando*) undoubtedly presuppose – and would be logically impossible without – the survival of each individual soul.

Relation of *Ōkra* (Soul) and *Honam* (Body)

Understanding the *sunsum* and *ōkra* to constitute a spiritual unity, one may say that Akan philosophy maintains a dualistic, not a tripartite, conception of the person: A person is made up of two principal entities or substances, one spiritual (immaterial: *ōkra*) and the other material (*honam*: body).

But Akans sometimes speak as if the relation between the soul (that is, *ōkra* plus *sunsum*) and the body is so close that they comprise an indissoluble or indivisible unity, and that, consequently, a person is a homogeneous entity. The basis for this observation is the assertion by some discussants that "*ōkra* is blood" (*mogya*),[27] or "*ōkra* is in the blood." They mean by this, I think, that there is some connection between the soul and the blood, and that ordinarily the former is integrated or fused with the latter. I think the supposition here is that the blood is the physical or rather physiological "medium" for the soul. However difficult it is to understand this doctrine, it serves as a basis for a theory of the unity of soul and body. But Akan thinkers cannot strictly or unreservedly maintain such a theory, for it logically involves the impossibility of the doctrine of disembodied survival or life after death, which they tenaciously and firmly hold. The doctrine of the indivisible unity of soul and body is a doctrine that eliminates the notion of life after death, inasmuch as both soul and body are held to disintegrate together. The doctrine that the souls of the dead have some form of existence or life therefore cannot be maintained together with a doctrine of the indivisible unity of soul and body. The former doctrine implies an independent existence for the soul. I think their postulation of some kind of connection between the soul and blood is a response to the legitimate, and indeed fundamental, question as to how an entity (that is, the soul), supposed to be immaterial and separate, can "enter" the body. Though their response certainly bristles with difficulties and may be regarded as inadequate, like most theses on the soul, Akan thinkers had sufficient awareness to focus philosophical attention also on the intractable question regarding the beginnings of the connection of the soul to the body, of the immaterial to the material. Other philosophies attempt to demonstrate that man consists of soul and body, but they do not, to my knowledge, speculate on the manner of the soul's "entry" into the body.

In the Akan conception, the soul is held to be a spiritual entity (substance). It is not a bundle of qualities or perceptions, as it is held to be in some Western systems. The basis of this assertion is the Akan belief in disembodied survival. A bundle theory of substance implies the elimination of the notion of substance, for if a substance is held to be a bundle or collection of qualities or perceptions, when the qualities or perceptions are removed, nothing would be left. That is, there would then be no substance, that is, a substratum or an "owner" of those qualities.[28] Thus, if the soul is held to be a bundle of perceptions, as it is in the writings of David Hume, it would be impossible to talk of disembodied survival in the form of a soul or self since the bundle itself is an abstraction. One Akan maxim, expressed epigrammatically, is that "when a man dies he is not (really) dead" (*onipa wu a na onwui*). What is implied by this is that there is something in a human being that is eternal, indestructible, and that continues to exist in the world of spirits (*asamando*). An Akan motif expresses the following thought: "Could God die, I will die" (*Onyame bewu na m'awu*). In Akan metaphysics, God is held to be eternal, immortal (*Odomankoma*). The above saying therefore means that since God will not die, a person, that is, his or her *'kra* (soul), conceived as an indwelling spark of God, will not die either. That is, the soul of man is immortal. The attributes of immortality make sense if, and only if, the soul is held to be a substance, an entity, and not a bundle of qualities or perceptions (experiences).

But where in a human being is this spiritual substance located? Descartes thought that the soul was in the pineal gland. The Akans also seem to hold that the soul is lodged in the head, although they do not specify exactly where. But "although it is in the head you cannot see it with your natural eyes," as they would put it, since it is immaterial. That the soul is "in the head (*ti*)" may be inferred from the following expressions: When they want to say that a person is lucky or fortunate they say: "His head is well (good)" (*ne ti ye*), or "His soul is well (good)" (*ne 'kra ye*). From such expressions one may infer some connection between the head and the soul. And although they cannot point to a specific part of the head as the "residence" of the soul, it may be conjectured that it is in the region of the brain which, as observed earlier, receives its energy from the *sunsum* (spirit), a part of the soul. That is, the soul acts on the brain in a specific locality, but it is itself not actually localized.

The Akan conception of a person, in my analysis, is dualistic, not tripartite, although the spiritual component of a person is highly complex. Such dualistic conception does not necessarily imply a belief in a causal relation or interaction between the two parts, the soul and body. For instance, some dualistic philosophers in the West maintain a doctrine of psychophysical parallelism, which completely denies interaction between soul and body. Other dualists advance a doctrine of epiphenomenalism, which, while not completely rejecting causal interaction, holds that the causality goes in one direction only, namely, from the body to the soul; such a doctrine, too, is thus not interactionist. Akan thinkers, however, are thoroughly interactionist on the relation between soul and body. They hold that not only does the body have a causal influence on the soul but also that the soul has a casual influence on the body (*honam*). What happens to the soul takes effect or reflects on the condition of the body. Thus, writing on Akan culture, Busia stated:

> They [that is, Akans] believed also that spiritual uncleanness was an element of ill-health and that the cleansing of the soul was necessary for health. When, for example, a patient was made to stand on a broom while being treated, it was to symbolize this cleansing. The broom sweeps filth away from the home and keeps it healthy; so the soul must be swept of filth to keep the body healthy.[29]

Similarly, what happens to the body reflects on the conditions of the soul. It is the actual bodily or physical behavior of a person that gives an idea of the condition of the soul. Thus, if the physical behavior of a man suggests that he is happy they would say, "His soul is happy" (*ne 'kra aniagye*); if unhappy or morose they would say, "His soul is sorrowful" (*ne 'kra di awerēhow*). When the soul is enfeebled or injured by evil spirits, ill health results; the poor conditions of the body affect the condition of the soul. The condition of the soul depends upon the condition of the body. The belief in psychophysical causal interaction is the whole basis of spiritual or psychical healing in Akan communities. There are certain diseases that are believed to be "spiritual diseases" (*sunsum yare*) and cannot be healed by the application of physical therapy. In such diseases attention must be paid to both physiological and spiritual aspects of the person. Unless the soul is healed, the body will not respond to physical treatment. The removal of a disease of the soul is the activity of the diviners or the traditional healers (*adunsifo*).

Conclusion

The Akan conception of the person, on my analysis, is both dualistic and interactionist. It seems to me that an interactionist psychophysical dualism is a realistic doctrine. Even apart from the prospects for disembodied survival that this doctrine holds out – prospects that profoundly affect the moral orientation of some people – it has had significant pragmatic consequences in Akan communities, as evidenced in the application of psychophysical therapies. There are countless testimonies of people who have been subjected to physical treatment for months or years in modern hospitals without being cured, but who have been healed by traditional healers applying both physical and psychical (spiritual) methods. In such cases the diseases are believed not to be purely physical, affecting only the body (*honam*). They are believed rather to have been inflicted on the *sunsum* through mystical or spiritual powers, and in time the body also gets affected. When Western-trained doctors pay attention only to the physical aspects of such diseases, they almost invariably fail to heal them. The fact that traditional healers, operating at both the physical and psychical levels, cope successfully with such diseases does seem to suggest a close relationship between the body and the soul.

From the point of view of the Akan metaphysics of the person and of the world in general, all this seems to imply that a human being is not just an assemblage of flesh and bone, that he or she is a complex being who cannot completely be explained by the same laws of physics used to explain inanimate things, and that our world cannot simply be reduced to physics.

Notes

1 I say "a conception" because I believe there are other conceptions of the person held or discernible in that philosophy.
2 K. A. Busia, "The Ashanti of the Gold Coast," in Daryll Forde (ed.), *African Worlds* (Oxford University Press, Oxford, 1954), p. 197; M. Fortes, *Kinship and the Social Order* (University of Chicago Press, Chicago, 1969), p. 199, n. 14; Robert A. Lystad, *The Ashanti, A Proud People* (Rutgers University Press, New Brunswick, N.J., 1958), p. 155; Peter K. Sarpong, *Ghana in Retrospect: Some Aspects of the Ghanaian Culture* (Ghana Publishing Corp., Accra. 1974), p. 37.
3 Busia, p. 197; Lystad, p. 155; E. L. R. Meyerowitz, *The Sacred State of the Akan* (Faber and Faber, London, 1951), p. 86; and "Concepts of the Soul among the Akan," *Africa*, vol. 21, no. 1, Jan. 1951, p. 26.
4 Busia, p. 197; Lystad, p. 155; P. A. Twumasi, *Medical Systems in Ghana* (Ghana Publishing Corp., Accra, 1975), p. 22.

5 Here the views of W. E. Abraham are excepted, for he maintains, like I do, that the *sunsum* is not "inheritable" and that it "appears to have been a spiritual substance." W. E. Abraham, *The Mind of Africa* (University of Chicago Press, Chicago, 1962), p. 60.
6 J. B. Danquah, *The Akan Doctrine of God* (Lutterworth Press, London, 1944), p. 115.
7 Ibid., p. 116.
8 R. S. Rattray, *Religion and Art in Ashanti* (Oxford University Press, Oxford, 1927), p. 154.
9 E. E. Evans-Pritchard, *Witchcraft, Oracles and Magic among the Azande* (Clarendon Press, Oxford, 1937), p. 136; also E. G. Parrinder, *West African Religion* (Epworth Press, London, 1961), p. 197.
10 Parrinder, *West African Religion*, p. 197.
11 Plato, *The Republic*, 571c, beginning of Book IX.
12 James Adam (ed.), *The Republic of Plato*, 2d ed. (Cambridge University Press, Cambridge, 1975), vol. 2, p. 320.

13 Plato, *The Republic*, ed. and trans. by Paul Shorey (Loeb Classical Library, Harvard University Press, Cambridge, Mass., 1935), p. 335.

14 Plato, *The Republic*, trans. by A. D. Lindsay (J. M. Dent, London, 1976), p. 346.

15 Thomas Gould, *Platonic Love* (Routledge and Kegan Paul, London, 1963), p. 108ff and p. 174ff.

16 Charles W. Valentine, *Dreams and the Unconscious* (Methuen, London, 1921), p. 93; also his *The New Psychology of the Unconscious* (Macmillan, New York, 1929), p. 95.

17 Wilfred Trotter, *Instincts of the Herd in Peace and War* (T. F. Unwin, London, 1916), p. 74.

18 H. Debrunner, *Witchcraft in Ghana* (Waterville Publishing House, Accra, 1959), p. 17.

19 Mbiti, *African Religions and Philosophy* (Doubleday, New York, 1970), p. 102.

20 Rattray, *Religion and Art*, p. 154.

21 Ibid., p. 318. Soul-washing is a symbolic religious rite meant to cleanse and purify the soul from defilement. "This cult," wrote Mrs. Meyerowitz, "adjures the person to lead a good and decent life." *Sacred State*, p. 117; also p. 88.

22 Incidentally, the "identity theory" immediately subverts any physical conception of the *sunsum*, since the *ōkra* (soul), with which it is being identified, is generally agreed to be a spiritual, not a physical, entity.

23 Rattray, *Religion and Art*, p. 154.

24 The dynamic and active character of the *sunsum* has given rise to metaphorical use as in the sentences, "there is 'spirit' in the game" (*agoro yi sunsum wɔ mu*), "the arrival of the chief brought 'spirit' into the festival celebration." Not long ago the dynamism, action and energy of a late Ghanaian army general earned him the by-name of "Sunsum!" among his soldiers.

25 Lystad, p. 158.

26 See Kwame Gyekye, "The Akan Concept of a Person," *International Philosophical Quarterly*, vol. 18, no. 3, Sept. 1978, p. 284.

27 This view was expressed also to Meyerowitz, *Sacred State*, p. 84.

28 See Kwame Gyekye, "An Examination of the Bundle Theory of Substance," *Philosophy and Phenomenological Research*, vol. 34, no. 1, Sept. 1973.

29 Busia, *The Challenge of Africa* (Praeger, New York, 1962), p. 19.

7

"Chi" in Igbo Cosmology

Chinua Achebe

There are two clearly distinct meanings of the word *chi* in Igbo.[1] The first is often translated as god, guardian angel, personal spirit, soul, spirit double, etc. The second meaning is day, or daylight, but is most commonly used for those transitional periods between day and night or night and day. Thus we speak of *chi ofufo* meaning day-break and *chi ojiji*, nightfall. We also have the word *mgbachi* for that most potent hour of noon that splits the day in two, a time favored in folklore by itinerant spirits and feared by children.

I am chiefly concerned here with the first meaning of chi, a concept so central in Igbo psychology and yet so elusive and enigmatic. The great variety of words and phrases which has been put forward at different times by different people as translations of this concept attests to its great complexity and lends additional force to the famous plea of Dr. J. B. Danquah that we pay one another's gods the compliment of calling them by their proper name.

In a general way we may visualize a person's chi as his other identity in spiritland – his *spirit being* complementing his terrestrial *human being*; for nothing can stand alone, there must always be another thing standing beside it.

Without an understanding of the nature of chi one could not begin to make sense of the Igbo world-view; and yet no study of it exists that could even be called preliminary. What I am attempting here is not

From Chinua Achebe, *Morning Yet On Creation Day* (1975). Copyright © 1975 Chinua Achebe. Reproduced by kind permission of David Bolt Associates on behalf of the author and Doubleday, a division of Bantam Doubleday Dell Publishing Group.

to fill that gap but to draw attention to it in a manner appropriate to one whose primary love is literature and not religion, philosophy, or linguistics. I will not even touch upon such tantalizing speculations as what happens to a person's chi when the person dies and its shrine is destroyed. Does it retreat completely back to its old home? And finally what happens at the man's reincarnation?

But before we embark on a consideration of the nature and implication of this concept which is so powerful in Igbo religion and thought, let us examine briefly what connection there may be between it and the other meaning of chi. For a long time I was convinced that there couldn't possibly be any relationship between chi (spirit being) and chi (daylight) except as two words that just happened to sound alike. But one day I stumbled on the very important information that among the Igbo of Awka a man who has arrived at the point in his life when he needs to set up a shrine to his chi will invite a priest to perform a ritual of bringing down the spirit from the face of the sun at daybreak. Thereafter it is represented physically in the man's compound until the day of his death when the shrine must be destroyed.

The implication of this is that a person's chi normally resides with the sun, bringer of daylight, or at least passes through it to visit the world. Which itself may have an even profounder implication, for it is well known in Igbo cosmology that the Supreme Deity, Chukwu Himself, is in close communion with the sun. But more on that later.

Since Igbo people did not construct a rigid and closely argued system of thought to explain the universe and the place of man in it, preferring the metaphor of myth and poetry, anyone seeking an insight into their world must seek it along their own way. Some of these ways are folk tales, proverbs, proper names, rituals, and festivals. There is of course the "scientific" way as well – the tape-recorded interview with old people. Unfortunately it is often more impressive than useful. The old people who have the information we seek will not often bare their hearts to any passer-by. They will give answers, and true answers too. But there is truth and there is truth. To get to the inner truth will often require more time than the recording interviewer can give – it may require a whole lifetime. In any case no one talks naturally into a strange box of tricks!

It is important to stress what I said earlier: the central place in Igbo thought of the notion of duality. Wherever Something stands, Something Else will stand beside it. Nothing is absolute. *I am the truth, the way, and the life* would be called blasphemous or simply absurd, for is it not well known that a man may worship Ogwugwu to perfection and yet be killed by Udo? The world in which we live has its double and counterpart in the realm of spirits. A man lives here and his chi there. Indeed the human being is only one half (and the weaker half at that) of a person. There is a complementary spirit being, chi. (The word *spirit*, though useful, does create serious problems of its own, however, for it is used to describe many different orders of non-human being.) Thus the abode of chi may be confused with *ani mmo* where the dead who encounter no obstacles in their passage go to live. But ani mmo is thought to be not above, like the realm of chi, but below, inside the earth. Considerable confusion and obscurity darken the picture at this point because there is a sense in which the two supernatural worlds are both seen as parallel to the land of the living. In an early anthropological study of the Igbo, Major A. G. Leonard at the opening of this century reported the following account from one of his Igbo informants:

We Igbo look forward to the next world as being much the same as this . . . we picture life there to be exactly as it is in this world. The ground there is just the same as it is here; the earth is similar. There are forests and hills and valleys with rivers flowing and roads leading from one town to another. . . . People in spiritland have their ordinary occupations, the farmer his farm.[2]

This "spiritland" where dead ancestors recreate a life comparable to their earthly existence is not only parallel to the human world but is also similar and physically contiguous with it, for there is constant coming and going between them in the endless traffic of life, death, and reincarnation. The masked spirits who often grace human rituals and ceremonies with their presence are representative visitors from this underworld and are said to emerge from their subterranean home through ant holes. At least that is the story as told to the uninitiated. To those who know, however, the masked "spirits" are only *symbolic* ancestors. But this knowledge does not in any way diminish their validity or the awesomeness of their presence.

These ancestral spirits which may be personified by man are, however, of a very different order from chi and so is their place of abode. There is a story of how a proud wrestler, having thrown every challenger in the world, decides to go and wrestle in the world of spirits. There he also throws challenger after challenger, including many multiple-headed ones – so great was his prowess. At last there is no one left to fight. But the wrestler refuses to leave. The spirits beg him to go; his companion praise-singer on the flute pleads with him. But it is all in vain. *There must be somebody left; surely the famed land of spirits can do better than this,* he said. Again everyone begs him to collect his laurels and go, but again he refuses. Finally his own chi appears, reluctant, thin as a rope. The wrestler laughs at this miserable-looking contender and moves forward contemptuously to knock him down, whereupon the other lifts him clear off the ground with his little finger and smashes him to death.

This cautionary tale is concerned mainly, I think, with setting a limit to man's aspirations. The limit is not the sky; it is somewhere much closer to earth. A sensible man will turn round at the frontiers of absolutism and head for home again. There is, however, around the story as well a vague intimation that the place where chi inhabits is forbidden to man in a way that ani mmo, the abode of his dead fathers, does not appear to be. For we have, at least, a description of the landscape of ani mmo; nothing comparable exists for the territory of chi.

There is another cautionary tale about chi, this time involving the little bird, *nza*, who ate and drank somewhat more than was good for him and in a fit of recklessness, which inebriation alone would explain, taunted his chi to come and get him if he could. Whereupon a hawk swooped down from the clear sky and carried him away. Which shows the foolishness of counting on chi's remoteness, for chi need not come in person or act directly but may use one's enemy who is close by.

The story of the headstrong wrestler, in addition to all the other things it tells us, makes also the important point that a man's chi does have a special hold over him such as no other powers can muster. This is why, for instance, it can dispense with the physical endowments and terrors of the multiple-headed spirits. This special power that chi has over its man (or the man's special vulnerability to his chi) is further exemplified in a proverb: *No matter how many divinities sit together to plot a man's ruin, it will come to nothing unless his chi is there among them.* Clearly chi has unprecedented veto powers over a man's destiny.

But power so complete, even in the hands of chi, is abhorrent to the Igbo imagination. Therefore the makers of proverbs went to work again, as it were, to create others that would set a limit to its exercise. Hence the well-known *Onye kwe chie ekwe.* (If a man agrees, his chi agrees.) And so the initiative, or some of it at least, is returned to man.

If you want to know how life has treated an Igbo man, a good place to look is the names his children bear. His hopes, his fears, his joys and sorrows; his grievances against his fellows, or complaints about the way he has been used by fortune; even straight historical records are all there. And because chi is so central to Igbo thought, we will also find much about it in proper names – more I think than from any other single source.

Chika (chi is supreme); Chibuzo (chi is in front); Nebechi (look to chi) are only a few examples of the large number of names that show the general primacy of chi over mankind. Chinwuba asserts chi's special responsibility for increase and prosperity; Chinwendu, its power over life; and Chikadibia, over health. A man who suffers from false accusations or calumnies heaped on him by his fellows may call his child Chiebonam (may chi not accuse me) meaning that the moral justification which chi can give is what counts in the end. It is, however, unusual to link chi in this way with moral sanction, a responsibility that belongs normally to Ani, the earth goddess and proper source of moral law – a fact recognized in the name Aniebonam which is analogous to Chiebonam.

The Igbo believe that a man receives his gifts or talents, his character – indeed his portion in life generally – before he comes into the world. It seems there is an element of choice available to him at that point, and that his chi presides over the bargaining. Hence the saying *Obu etu nya na chie si kwu,* which

we often hear when a man's misfortune is somehow beyond comprehension and so can only be attributable to an agreement he himself must have entered into, at the beginning, alone with his chi; for there is a fundamental justice in the universe and nothing so terrible can happen to a person for which he is not somehow responsible. A few other names suggest this role of chi as the great dealer out of gifts: Nkechinyelu and Chijioke, for example.

Although, as we have seen, the Igbo believe that when a man says yes his chi will also agree; but not always. Sometimes a man may struggle with all his power and say yes most emphatically and yet nothing he attempts will succeed. Quite simply the Igbo say of such a man: *Chie ekwero.* (His chi does not agree). Now, this could mean one of two things; either the man has a particularly intransigent chi or else it is the man himself attempting too late to alter that primordial bargain he had willingly struck with his chi, saying yes now when his first unalterable word had been no, forgetting that "the first word gets to Chukwu's house."

But of course the idea of an intransigent chi does exist in Igbo: *ajo chi,* literally *bad chi.* We must remember, however, when we hear that a man has a bad chi that we are talking about his fortune rather than his character. A man of impeccable character may yet have a bad chi so that nothing he puts his hand to will work out right. Chi is therefore more concerned with success or failure than with righteousness and wickedness. Which is not to say that it is totally indifferent to morality. For we should know by now that nothing is *totally* anything in Igbo thinking; everything is a question of measure and degree. We have already seen in the name Chiebonam that chi shares a little of the moral concerns of Ani, the earth goddess. But in addition there is a hint of moral attribution to chi in the way the Igbo sometimes explain differences in human character. For maximum dramatization they pick two brothers who are dissimilar in character: one good, the other bad. And they say: *Ofu nne n'amu, ma ofu chi adeke,* a very neat and tight statement which can only be approximately interpreted as: one mother gives birth, different chi create.

This statement apart from reiterating the idea of "one man, one chi" goes further to introduce the fundamental notion of chi as creator which is of the utmost importance: a man does not only have his own chi but is created by it and no two people, not even blood brothers, it seems, are created by the same chi. What we know of chi can thus be summed up as follows: every person has an individual chi who created him; its natural home is somewhere in the region of the sun, but it may be induced to visit an earthly shrine; a person's fortunes in life are controlled more or less completely by his chi. (Perhaps this is a good place to point out that there are many minor, and occasionally even major, divergences of perception about chi from different parts of Igbo land so that one can at best only follow what appears to be the dominant and persistent concepts. For example, although communities exist which assert categorically that chi lives with Chukwu, in most places such closeness can only be deduced indirectly.)

There are many names and sayings in Igbo which confirm the creative role of chi. When we name a child Chiekezie, we imply that chi has restored a certain balance by that particular creation, or has at last apportioned shares equitably. Of a man unattractive or deficient in character, we might say: *Chi ya kegbulu ya ekegbu*. Here again there are two possible interpretations to our statement: either the man in question was created badly or else was cheated of his full share of things. Or both interpretations may even be intended, for what else is creation but the imparting of distinguishing characteristics and bestowing of gifts? Certainly the Igbo language by having the same root word *ke* for *create* and *share* does encourage this notion.

The idea of individualism is sometimes traced to the Christian principle that God created all men and consequently every one of them is presumed worthy in His sight. The Igbo do better than that. They postulate the concept of every man as both a unique creation and the work of a unique creator. Which is as far as individualism and uniqueness can possibly go! And we should naturally expect such a cosmogony to have far-reaching consequences in the psychology and institutions of the people. This is not the place, however, to go into that. But we should at least notice in passing the fierce egalitarianism (less charitable people would have other names for it, of course) which was such a marked feature of Igbo political organization and may justifiably speculate on its possible derivation from this concept of every man's original and absolute uniqueness. An American anthropologist who studied the Igbo community of Onitsha in recent years called his book *The King in Every Man*.[3]

All this might lead one to think that among the Igbo the individual would be supreme, totally free, and existentially alone. But the Igbo are unlikely to concede to the individual an absolutism they deny even to chi. The obvious curtailment of a man's power to walk alone and do as he will is provided by another potent force – the will of his community. For wherever Something stands, no matter what, Something Else will stand beside it. No man, however great, can win judgment against all the people.

We must now turn to the all-important relationship between chi and Chi Ukwu, one of the names by which the Supreme Deity is known in Igbo. Chi Ukwu (or simply, Chukwu) means literally Great Chi. Thus whatever chi may be it does seem to partake of the nature of the Supreme God. Another link is provided by the sun, bringer of daylight. As we saw earlier, among the Igbo of Awka, a man's chi may be invoked to descend from the solar realm. As it happens, the Igbo also see the sun as an agent of Chukwu to whom it is said to bear those rare sacrifices offered as man's last desperate resort. It would seem then that wherever the abode of Chukwu happens to be in the heavens it cannot be distant from the place of chi.

In Yoruba[4] cosmology the Supreme God, Olodumare (one of whose titles is, incidentally, Owner of the Sun), sent the god, Obatala, on a mission of creation to make man. The Igbo are not so specific about Chukwu's role in the creation of man but may be suggesting a similar delegation of power by the Supreme Overlord to a lesser divinity except that in their case every act of creation is the work of a separate and individual agent, chi, a personified and unique manifestation of the creative essence.

Still farther west, the Akan of Ghana believe in a moon goddess whom they call Ngame, Mother of the World, who gives a "soul" to every human being at birth by shooting lunar rays into him. The Igbo, seemingly more reticent about such profound events, may yet be hinting at a comparable cosmic relationship between their chi and solar rays. This would explain the invocation of chi from the face of the sun at the consecration of its shrine and account also for the second meaning of the word: daylight. And, of course, the Igbo being patrilineal (as anthropologists tell us) where the Akan are matrilineal, a preference by them for the sun over the moon would be completely in character!

The significance of the sun in Igbo religion though subtle and unobtrusive is nonetheless undeniable and may even be called pervasive. If we are to believe the *New Larousse Encyclopaedia of Mythology*, it seems that two-times-two-times-two is everywhere the sun's mystical figure (just as three-times-three is the moon's). Certainly the Igbo have a lot of use for fours and eights. The basic unit of their calendar is the four-day "small" week and an eight-day "great" week; the circumcision of their male child takes place on the eighth day after which it is accounted a human being; they compute largeness in units of four hundred, *nnu*, etc., etc.

The exact relationship between the Supreme God (Chukwu), the sun, and chi in Igbo cosmology will probably never be (and perhaps was intended not to be) unraveled. But if Chukwu means literally Great Chi, one is almost tempted to borrow the words of Christian dogma and speak of chi as being of the same "substance" as, and "proceeding" from, Chukwu. Or is chi an infinitesimal manifestation of Chukwu's infinite essence given to each of us separately and uniquely, a single ray from the sun's boundless radiance? Or does Chukwu have a separate existence as ruler over a community of chi, countless as the stars and as endless in their disparate identities, holding anarchy at bay with His will?

One last word about Chineke which we have come to interpret as *God who creates* and use as an alternative name for Chukwu. If our interpretation and use were supported by Igbo language and religious tradition, the role of Chukwu as *the* Creator would be established and the activity of chi in their multiplicity relegated to the status of mere figure of speech. Unfortunately the early missionaries who appropriated Chineke as the Creator-God of Christianity acted a little hastily, unaware that the Igbo language was capable of treachery to hasty users on account of its tonality. (The story of the white preacher who kept saying that God had great buttocks when he meant great strength may be apocryphal, but it makes an important point.)

Chineke consists of three words: chi na eke. In assigning a meaning to it the crucial word is *na*, which itself has three possible meanings. Let us examine each meaning in turn and see what it does to Chineke:

a) said with a high tone, na means *who* or *which*. Chineke will then mean *chi which creates*;
b) said with a low tone, na can mean the auxiliary verb *does*, in which case Chineke will mean *chi does create*; and finally
c) again said with a low tone, na can mean the conjunctive *and*. Here something fundamental changes because eke is no longer a verb but a noun. Chineke then becomes chi and eke. And that, in my opinion, is the correct version.

Chineke which we have come to interpret as *chi who creates* is nothing of the sort, but rather is a dual deity, chi and eke. The early missionaries by putting the wrong tone on that little word na escorted a two-headed, pagan god into their holy of holies!

Now what are the grounds for making such a terrible assertion? Quite simply I have looked at traditional Igbo usage. But before I give the examples that will make this clear let us take a quick look at eke, this mysterious second member of the duality. What is it? I do not know for certain, but it does seem to have more or less the same attributes as chi; also it is sometimes called *aka*.

We have already referred to the common name Chinwuba (chi has increase) earlier on. Another version of this name is Ekejiuba (eke holds increase). We have also mentioned the name Nebechi (look to chi). Now, there is also Lemeke (Leweke) which would appear to be exactly the same name except that eke occurs instead of chi. It is interesting to note that the chi versions of these names occur more in the northern and western parts of Igbo land while the eke names tend to occur more in the southern and eastern parts.

Let us turn for a moment from proper names to other sayings in which chi and eke are yoked together. If you want to curse a man in the most thorough fashion, you curse his chi and his eke (or aka). That really takes care of him!

There is also the well-known little anecdote about the hen. Someone once asked her why it was that from day-break to sunset she was always scratching the ground for food; was she never satisfied? To which she replied: "You see, my dear fellow, when I wake up in the morning I begin to look for food for my chi. When I am through with that I must then find some for my eke. By the time I finish with that too it is already sunset and I haven't catered for myself!"

From the foregoing it would appear that chi and eke are very closely related deities, perhaps the same god in a twofold manifestation, such as male and female; or the duality may have come into being for the purpose of bringing two dialectal tributaries of Igbo into liturgical union. This last is particularly attractive because there exists a small number of similar "double-headed" phrases, each comprising two words and the conjunctive, both words being of identical meaning but drawn from two basic dialectal areas. Used in this conjunction the words immediately introduce the element of totality into their ordinary meaning. Thus *ikwu na ibe* stands for the entire community of kinsmen and women; *ogbo na uke* for the militant and aggressive band of spirit adversaries; *okwu na uka* for endless wranglings; *nta na imo* for odds and ends, etc. If indeed *chi na eke* should turn out to belong to this group of phrases, the idea of using it to curse a man absolutely would then make a lot of sense! Which might be bad news indeed for the Christian church in Igbo land. But it may surely draw consolation from the fact that the Book of the Old Testament itself, in all its glory and dignity, ends "with a curse"!

Far be it from me, however, to suggest that Chineke should be dropped at this late hour as an alternative name for Chukwu. That would be futile pedantry; for whatever doubts we may entertain about its antecedents, it has certainly served generations of Christians and non-Christians in Igbo land in contemplating the nature of the all-distant Supreme Deity, whose role in the world is shrouded in mystery and metaphor. The attraction of Chineke for the early evangelists must have been its seeming lack of ambiguity on the all-important question of creation. They needed a "God who creates" and Chineke stood ready at hand. But Igbo traditional thought in its own way and style did recognize Chukwu as the Supreme Creator, speculating only on the modalities, on *how* He accomplished the work and through what agencies and intermediaries. As we have seen He appears to work through chi to create man. Similarly there are numerous suggestions in Igbo lore of Him working with man to make the world – or rather to enhance its habitability, for the work of creation was not ended in one monumental effort but goes on still, Chukwu and man talking things over at critical moments, sometimes agreeing, sometimes not. Two examples will suffice:

When Death first came into the world, men sent a messenger to Chukwu to beg Him to remove the terrible scourge. Although He was disposed to consider the matter, the first request that actually got through to Him from mankind was the wrong one and once He had granted it there was no way it could be altered.

In a study of Igbo people published in 1913, Northcote Thomas recorded the following story about Ezenri, that fascinating priest/king whose spiritual pre-eminence was acknowledged over considerable parts of Igbo land:

Ezenri and Ezadama came from heaven and rested on an ant heap; all was water. Cuku (Chukwu) asked who was sitting there and they answered "We are the kings of Nri and Adama," thereupon Cuku gave them each a piece of yam; yams were at that time unknown to man, for human beings walked in the bush like animals. . . .[5]

Later on Chukwu tells Ezenri how to plant and tend the yam, but Ezenri complains that the ground is too wet; and Chukwu advises him to send for Awka people – workers in iron – to blow on the earth with their bellows and make it dry.

There is a very strong suggestion here, and also in the story about the coming of death, that at crucial cosmological moments Chukwu will discuss His universe with man. The moment of man's first awareness of the implications of death was such a time; but so also was the great turning point when man ceased wandering in the bush and became a settled agriculturist calling upon the craft of the blacksmith to effect this momentous transition.

And finally, at the root of it all lies that very belief we have already seen: a belief in the fundamental worth and independence of every man and of his right to speak on matters of concern to him and, flowing from it, a rejection of any form of absolutism which might endanger those values. It is not surprising that the Igbo held discussion and consensus as the highest ideals of the political process. This made them "argumentative" and difficult to rule. But how could they suspend, for the convenience of a ruler, limitations which they impose even on their gods? For as we have seen, a man may talk and bargain even with his chi at the moment of his creation. And what was more, Chukwu Himself in all His power and glory did not make the world by fiat. He held conversations with mankind; he talked with those archetypal men of Nri and Adama and even enlisted their good offices to make the earth firm and productive.

Notes

1 The Igbo people (called Ibo by the English) inhabit southeastern Nigeria. They caught world attention for a while as chief protagonists of the Biafran tragedy. Igbo is both the people (about ten million) and their language.

2 A. C. Leonard, *The Lower Niger and Its Tribes*. London: Cass, pp. 185–6.

3 Richard Henderson, *The King in Every Man*. New Haven: Yale University Press, 1971.

4 The Yoruba of Western Nigeria are, in size and achievement, among the great peoples of Africa.

5 Northcote W. Thomas, *Igbo-speaking Peoples of Nigeria*. London: Harrison & Sons, 1913, vol. I; reprinted Negro Universities Press, New York, 1969, p. 50.

8

The Sociality of Self

Okot p'Bitek

There is a false and misleading assumption that on the one end, there is some notion called "philosophy" and on the other, some things and actions named "culture." Culture is philosophy as lived and celebrated in a society. Human beings do not behave like dry leaves, smoke or clouds which are blown here and there by winds. Men live in organizations called institutions: the family and clan, a chiefdom or kingdom or age-set system. He has a religion, an army, legal and other institutions. And all these institutions are formed by or built around the central issue of a people, what they believe, what life is all about, their social philosophy, their world view.

• • •

The bourgeois believe that liberty consists in absence of social organization; that liberty is a negative quality, a deprivation of existing obstacles to it: and not a positive quality, the reward of endeavour and wisdom. . . . Because of this basic fallacy this type of intellectual always *tries to cure positive social evils, such as wars, by negative individual actions, such as non-cooperation, passive resistance or conscientious objection.* This is because he cannot rid himself of the assumption that the individual is free. But we have shown that the individual is *never free.* He can only

From Okot p'Bitek, *The Artist as Ruler*, Heinemann (1985); by kind permission of East African Educational Publishers Ltd.

obtain freedom by *social cooperation.* He can only do what he wants by *using social forces.* But in order to use social relations he must understand them. He must become conscious of the laws of society, just as if he wants to lever up a stone, he must know the laws of levers – *Christopher Caudwell*

The French philosopher Jean-Jacques Rousseau (1712–1778) was quite wrong when he declared "Man is born free. . . ." Man is not born free. At birth he is firmly tied to his mother through the umbilical cord. He is physically cut free from her. But *this cutting free* is not merely a biological act. It is symbolic and most significant. Henceforth, he is an individual, who through upbringing is prepared to play his full role as a member of society.

Rousseau was not correct when he added, "and everywhere he is in chains." Man is not born free. He cannot be free. He is incapable of being free. For only by being in *chains* can he be and remain "human." What constitute these chains? Man has a bundle of *rights* and *privileges* that society owes him. In African belief, even death does not free him. If he had been an important member of society while he lived, his ghost continues to be revered and fed: and he in turn is expected to guide and protect the living. This is the essence of what is wrongly called "ancestor worship." Should he die a shameful death, his haunting ghost has to be laid. In some cases his ghost has to be "killed." "Till death do us part," the Christian vow made between man and woman at the wedding ritual, sounds hollow, in that at the death of the man, the woman does not walk out of the "home." She is *inherited* by one of the brothers of the dead man. Should the woman die her death does not extinguish the bonds between the man and his in-laws.

Man has always asked the most terrifying questions: What am I? What is the purpose of life? Why do people suffer? What is happiness? What is death? Is it the end? etc. etc. And, according to the "answers" provided by the "wise men," and have been accepted, society is then organized to achieve these ends. It is these fundamental ideas, the philosophy of life, which constitute the pillars, the foundations, on which the social institutions are erected.

Some have called these *myths* or *world-views*: others refer to them as ideologies (which, as in the case of socialism, is even described as scientific): fanatics refer to them as *Truth*, as if these ideas are about verifiable or indisputable facts, or about the actual state of the matter. These fundamental ideas are concerned with *meaning*. The meaning of being alive in this world. And meaning is wider in scope than is truth. As John Dewey has put it, " . . . truths are but one class of meanings, namely, those in which a claim to verifiability by their consequences is an intrinsic part of the meaning. Beyond this island of meanings, which in their own nature are true or false, lies the ocean of meanings to which truth or falsity are irrelevant."

Man cannot, and must not be free. "Son," "Mother," "Daughter," "Father," "Uncle," "Husband," "Grandfather," "Wife," "Clansman," "Mother-in-law," "Grandfather," "Chief," "Medicineman," and many other such terms, are the stamps of man's unfreedom. It is by such complex titles that a person is defined and identified. They order and determine human behaviour in society. The central question "Who am I?" cannot be answered in any meaningful way unless the relationship in question is known. Because "I" is not only one relationship, but numerous relationships: "I" has a clan, and a shrine, a country, a job. "I" may or may not be married, may or may not have children. Is "I" a chief? Then he has subjects or followers, etc. etc.

Permanent bondage seems to be man's fate. Because he cannot escape, he cannot be liberated, freed. The so-called "outcast" is not a free agent. Being "cast out" from society, for a while, does not sever the chains that bind him to society.

The act is a judgment, punishment and a lesson, not only for the victim, but for all members of the society. But the outcast, the refugee, the exile, soon joins another society and becomes a subscribed member of the group.

Even the hermit who pretends to withdraw to a solitary place for a life of religious seclusion, is not free. He peoples his cave, forest, mountain top, oasis, riverside, or whatever abode, with gods and spirits, devils and angels, etc.; and, as has been reported of one St Francis of Asisi, these cowards (hermits), who exile themselves from human society, enter into communion with these non-existent, imaginary creations as well as with Nature: birds, flowers, animals, reptiles, trees, fruits, rocks and rivers, etc.

PART III

Philosophy, Politics, and Society

9

Leaders must not be Masters

Julius Nyerere

. . . My aim is to say goodbye to you. But before I do that, I wish to use this opportunity to tell you a few things which may be of benefit to you in days to come. During this visit I have tried to go to almost every part of this island. It is true that I have been here before, but on those past occasions I did not visit as many parts of the island as I have done on this visit. It is also true that when I came here in 1959, I visited Mbweni. But there is a marked difference between the Mbweni I saw in 1959, and the Mbweni I visited on this occasion. Mbweni has changed; there has been some progress, which is the result of the efforts of the inhabitants of Mbweni. In 1959 there was no school there; yesterday I saw some few schools. Their roads are still as bad as they were in 1959. I do not know who is to blame in this matter – whether the Government or the residents at Mbweni. I was shown a big rice farm in the same area and, although it is not yet a good farm, it will be good after some time. This is because nothing has a perfect beginning; time is required for anything to be perfect. The people at Mbweni have already cleared their farm, and have planted it with rice which shows signs of germinating well.

We visited many other farms of this island and

saw good progress there. My hope is that this progressive development will continue to improve and become better and better. But I did not give a speech at any of the places I visited. Instead, I encouraged people to ask me questions, or to tell me their problems. This means that this is my first speech since I arrived on this island. I did not make a speech even when I met with your leaders of TANU, UWT, NUTA, and Government departments this morning in that office. I told them to ask me questions about Government and development. From the questions which were asked, I was able to learn a lot of things. Among the questions asked was one on ujamaa. One woman asked me to explain to her the meaning of ujamaa because she did not understand what ujamaa meant, although she had occasionally used the word or had heard other people use it. I tried to answer her question, and I wish to repeat that answer here in public.

I was the first to use the word ujamaa in order to explain the kind of life we wish to live in our country. The word ujamaa denotes the kind of life lived by a man and his family – father, mother, children and near relatives. Our Africa was a poor country before it was invaded and ruled by foreigners. There were no rich people in Africa. There was no person or group of persons who had exclusive claim to the ownership of the land. Land was the property of all the people, and those who used it did not do so because it was their property. They used it because they needed it, and it was their responsibility to use it carefully and hand it over in good condition for use by future generations. Life was easy. It was possible for a man to live with his wife,

<hr>

In February 1966, President Nyerere spent some days on Mafia Island in the course of one of his frequent tours of his country. Before leaving the area, he gave an extempore public speech, in Swahili, which was typical of the kind of teaching which the President always undertakes during his meet-the-people journeys. This translation was made from the tape-recorded text of the speech.

his children, and other close relatives. Wealth belonged to the family as a whole; and every member of a family had the right to the use of family property. No one used wealth for the purpose of dominating others. This is how we want to live as a nation. We want the whole nation to live as one family.

This is the basis of socialism. Yet we say we want socialism and want to build a socialist state. What do we mean by this? We mean two things. First, that we do not already have what we are looking for. Secondly, we believe that the thing we want is good. If you know that something is bad, you will not waste time trying to get it: it will not benefit you. This means that if we want socialism and aim at developing our country on the basis of socialist principles, it is because we believe that socialism is good.

Let me first explain that many countries are not socialist. Many countries in the world want to be socialist, and different people give different names to this concept of socialism. I have said I chose the word 'ujamaa' to explain socialism. I shall now try to explain why I chose the word ujamaa.

Normally a country is divided into two sections. Some people are called 'masters' and others are called 'servants'. We accept this division of people into classes of 'masters' and 'slaves'. Sometimes we are even content to live with these divisions and to accept them as they are. I will tell you an example which one old man told me. During the German administration a group of people were told to do a certain job. They did not do it. Then they were called to a meeting where their German master told them to divide themselves between 'masters' and 'slaves'. Some of the slaves joined the masters' group, hoping that they would escape punishment if the slaves were going to be punished. After the division, the German master allowed the slaves to go home, but immediately ordered the masters to be caned because they were lazy, and also because they were inducing the slaves to be lazy too. Those slaves who had joined the group of masters regretted their decision.

. . . Yet it is true that even in countries where such divisions between masters (who cannot be bought like sheep) and servants (who are bought like sheep) are absent, the people are divided into classes. This division exists even though there are no slaves in a country. In such a case the masters have the habit of being served by other people. The wives of masters do not work; they do not cook, or wash clothes, or make their beds. These things are done for them by other people. The masters have cars, but they do not drive them; they are driven. Masters can eat without working despite the fact that a man normally works in order to eat, except if he is ill, crippled, a child, or mad. What these masters are capable of doing is to give instructions to their servants. Sometimes, however, they employ other people to instruct servants on their behalf. The master does not have to do any work; other people will work for him and report to him month after month. They will report to him about the total harvest from one of his farms, and also about the total income obtained through the sale of his crops. These masters live comfortable lives, despite the fact that they do not work.

But this does not mean that all masters are equal; some are more equal than others. There are two groups of masters – the big masters and the little masters. Then there is the group of workers and servants who are often oppressed by the masters. Our aim is to abolish this division of people between masters and servants, and to make every person a master – not a master who oppresses others, but one who serves himself. A person who serves himself is a true master. He has no worries, he has confidence in himself and is confident of his own actions. He dislikes being pushed around and being told what to do. Why should a person who is his own master be pushed into doing work which will not benefit him?

Let me go back to what I said earlier in order to explain what I mean. I said that I did not make speeches at any of the places I had visited on my current tour of this island. Instead, I told the people I met to ask me questions, or to tell me the problems which face them in their everyday lives. It was difficult to get people to ask me questions. They told me they had no problems and that all was well. They were afraid to speak, probably thinking they would be punished. Why should they be punished? In the past years and centuries, we were greatly intimidated and harassed by the colonialists. If you stood before a colonial leader to speak or to ask him a question, you would be harassed by his juniors, who would ask you why you spoke or asked questions. This practice instilled fear in the minds of many citizens. The people did not respect their seniors; they simply feared them. This practice has not ended yet, and it explains why people did not want to tell me their problems when I asked them to. They refused to speak not because they had no problems, but because they were afraid to speak.

This is a bad habit. This is your country. We tell you every day that this is your country and that you have the freedom of speech. If you do not accept your responsibility for this country, I shall claim ownership of it! Any country must be looked after by people. If you do not like to accept the responsibility for looking after this country, I shall get a few clever people, and together we will declare this country to be our property. If we are asked why we are taking it, we shall say you do not want it. But this habit of evading responsibility has been inherited. We have been led to accept the division of men into masters and slaves. Sometimes you hear people talk about themselves as being simply ordinary men. They think their leaders know everything. When you talk to them and explain an issue to them, they will simply say, 'What can we say? You leaders know everything.'

This is a bad habit. You have been brought up badly. We have been treated as slaves and we have accepted that status. This is bad. What is the meaning of leadership? When you are selected to lead your fellow men, it does not mean that you know everything better than they do. It does not even mean that you are more intelligent than they are – especially the elders. Sometimes my own mother calls me and gives me some advice. She tells me not to do this or that. She advises me even in matters of Government. Why must she not advise me? She is a parent and parents are not afraid of their children. She advises me even though she has no formal school education. Why? Does it mean that a person who does not have formal education is a fool? What does education mean? An uneducated man has a brain – given to him by God. Does a man become a goat because he is uneducated? No! Such a person understands the nature of his children; he will know when one of them goes astray. It may be true that I am educated; but how can this mean that I am more intelligent than my mother?

At the moment our aim is to remove fear from the minds of our people. The fear which our people have can be removed from their minds. It was instilled in us by the Portuguese, the Germans, the Arabs, and the British. We have been told that we are not capable of doing this or that, and we have accepted this verdict. We are not even sure where to live. We fear to take decisions. This is why some people tell me to decide things for them on the grounds that we know better. This is not true. You must not fear your leaders. Our aim is to hand over responsibility to the people to make their own

decisions. Our leaders are not leaders by birth; they are elected by the people. For why should a person be a leader by birth? Our leaders must be chosen by us. There is no need to have hereditary leaders.

This Area Commissioner is your son. He is not a District Commissioner. If he behaves like a District Commissioner we shall terminate his services. He is not supposed to act like a District Commissioner. He will be making a mistake if he acted as if he were a District Commissioner. We did not want to replace a white DC by a black DC. The Area Commissioner is the servant of the people. He is here to listen to the problems of the people, and to report to us about those problems or the progress being made to remove the problems. I shall keep on urging Tanzanians not to fear their leaders. If we do not remove fear from our people, and if we do not abolish the two classes of masters and servants from our society, clever people will emerge from among us to take the place of the Europeans, Indians and Arabs. These clever people will continue to exploit our fear for their own benefit. And we leaders can become the clever people. If this happens – that leaders aspire to the positions and privileges enjoyed by colonial leaders – we shall not develop the country on the basis of the equality of all men. Instead, we shall be endangering this country. It will mean that the money we paid to help in the work of removing colonialism will be used to maintain other cleverer Africans capable of oppressing the people more than the colonialists.

This is what is going to happen if you do not remove fear from your minds. You will even lose your property; it will be taken by those who are clever among you. Suddenly you will discover that your Area Commissioner has a farm of 3,000 acres. You will be surprised to hear that even Julius has a 3,000 acre farm. You will be surprised how Julius and the Area Commissioner obtained the farms. And before long you will hear that Regional Commissioner Kitundu has also 3,000 acres of land. This will surprise you more. These farms need not be of the same size because the leaders who own them differ in their status as leaders.

We do not want such a situation to arise. We have stopped TANU leaders from owning farms. We have taken similar steps with other leaders. If we discover that these leaders have farms, we shall ask them. Yesterday we were all poor. If we hear you have a big farm, we shall ask you how you got it. If a person owns a farm of 3,000 acres, he must be aspiring to be a 'master'. What is more, such a person, owning a big farm of 3,000 acres, cannot have time to fulfil effectively the duties of Area Commissioner. If an Area Commissioner has such a large farm, it means he is prepared to employ workers to work on his farm and pay them wages. Where will he get people to work on his farm, and how will he get the money to pay them wages? But even if the money is there, and the workers are there, will there be sufficient land for each of us to have 3,000 acres? I agree that Tanzania is a large country with a small population. But is it true that our country is big enough for each of us to own 3,000 acres of land? The answer is no. And if the answer is no, and we allow a few of us to acquire large farms of 3,000 acres, we are in fact admitting that those who cannot get land will be servants of those who have land. By doing this, are we not dividing people into two classes – masters and slaves? By this action we will not be building socialism. If we give 3,000 acres of land to one man, and fail to give land to another, we shall in effect be making the former person the master and the latter a slave. But why should we do this? If a person says he wants to work for you, why can he not work on his own farm? Does he need to work for you on your farm? That is not socialism. We are going to teach all the people to be their own masters. If we give to one of you a big farm, where will he get the servants to work on it?

Socialism means that no person uses his wealth to exploit others. Just as a father does not use his status to dominate and exploit his wife, children and other relatives, so in a nation the leaders or the fortunate people must not use their positions or their wealth to exploit others. In a small family, the father was respected. He was not feared. Similarly, in a nation it is better to respect leaders than to fear them. Yet respect is a two-way process. Two or more people can respect each other. If one of them ceases to respect the other, they also withdraw their respect for him.

Also, socialism requires all the people to work. The fruits of the labour of the people who lead a socialist life are shared by all on the basis of equality. But everybody must work. It is a shame to be lazy, and those who are lazy are despised by the rest of the community. This means that no man can expect help from his colleagues if he is not willing to help them. It is even true that in order to eat, a man must be willing to work. The rule is that if you work you will eat, but if you do not work you will not eat. Even the old father who appears to eat without doing any work is not exploiting his family. He worked hard during his younger days. He does not work now because he had his turn, and also because the youth respect him for his service when he was young. . . .

10

Consciencism

Kwame Nkrumah

Practice without thought is blind; thought without practice is empty. The three segments of African society, the traditional, the Western and the Islamic, co-exist uneasily; the principles animating them are often in conflict with one another. I have in illustration tried to show how the principles which inform capitalism are in conflict with the socialist egalitarianism of the traditional African society.

What is to be done then? I have stressed that the two other segments, in order to be rightly seen, must be accommodated only as experiences of the traditional African society. If we fail to do this our society will be racked by the most malignant schizophrenia.

Our attitude to the Western and the Islamic experience must be purposeful. It must also be guided by thought, for practice without thought is blind. What is called for as a first step is a body of connected thought which will determine the general nature of our action in unifying the society which we have inherited, this unification to take account, at all times, of the elevated ideals underlying the traditional African society. Social revolution must therefore have, standing firmly behind it, an intellectual revolution, a revolution in which our thinking and philosophy are directed towards the redemption of our society. Our philosophy must find its weapons in the environment and living

Kwame Nkrumah, *Consciencism: Philosophy and Ideology for De-Colonization* (1964), copyright © 1970 by Monthly Review Press; by kind permission of Zed Books Ltd and Monthly review press.

conditions of the African people. It is from those conditions that the intellectual content of our philosophy must be created. The emancipation of the African continent is the emancipation of man. This requires two aims: first, the restitution of the egalitarianism of human society, and, second, the logistic mobilization of all our resources towards the attainment of that restitution.

The philosophy that must stand behind this social revolution is that which I have once referred to as philosophical consciencism; consciencism is the map in intellectual terms of the disposition of forces which will enable African society to digest the Western and the Islamic and the Euro-Christian elements in Africa, and develop them in such a way that they fit into the African personality. The African personality is itself defined by the cluster of humanist principles which underlie the traditional African society. Philosophical consciencism is that philosophical standpoint which, taking its start from the present content of the African conscience, indicates the way in which progress is forged out of the conflict in that conscience.

Its basis is in materialism. The minimum assertion of materialism is the absolute and independent existence of matter. Matter, however, is also a plenum of forces which are in antithesis to one another. The philosophical point of saying this is that matter is thus endowed with powers of self-motion.

Of course, there are diverse sorts of motion. Philosophers have accepted different kinds of phenomena as illustrating motion. There is the obvious case of change of place. If one object changes its position in relation to objects in a locality, it is said to move. Against this, it might be thought at first that the whole universe could revolve asymmetrically around an object, in which case it could in absolute terms be fancied that the object had not moved. If this happened it would be indistinguishable from the first situation in which the object itself changes its position relative to the rest of the universe; it does not signify a difference. And if these putative two states do not signify a difference, the latter cannot constitute an objection to the former.

The statement that an object moves is a significant one. And when two significant statements fail in the above way to indicate a difference they must signify the same thing. What I am enunciating here is quite other than the Verification Principle. The Verification Principle, as is well known, has two parts. In the first place, it asserts a proposition to be significant only if it is subject to empirical verification; and in the second place, it asserts that the meaning of a significant proposition is yielded by its method of verification. The principle which I am on the other hand anxious to defend states no condition for meaningfulness, but only establishes a sufficient condition for identity of meaning. The central idea is as follows: if there are two expressions such that precisely the same consequences follow from the conjunction of the first with any other proposition as follow from the conjunction of the second with the same proposition, then the two expressions are identical in meaning.

It will be seen that this Principle of Identity of Meaning is akin to Leibniz's Principle of Identity of Meaning and to Frege's Principle of Identity of Meaning. I have described one kind of motion which philosophers accept. They also distinguish rotary motion, which Plato illustrated with the movement of a top. There is however a third kind of motion, which consists in alteration of property. If properties can be distinguished from relations, it can be said that there are two broad categories of motion, such that one introduces a change in relation while the other introduces a change in property, seeing that linear as well as rotary motion involves change of relation. If there are these two kinds of motion, one resulting in a change of relation, the other in a change of property, then when it is said that matter has an original power of self-motion, neither kind is necessarily implied, nor are both together.

It is fashionable, in particular among philosophers who eschew dialectics, to say that matter is inert. What this means must be distinguished from what the inertia of matter means in Newton. Newton defined inertia axiomatically as, for example, in his first law of motion. According to this law, a body, except in so far as it is impressed upon by an external force, continues in its state of uniform motion in a straight line. The position of rest is easily accommodated as a limiting case of motion in a straight line. Now it is quite proper, instead of giving a direct definition of an introduced term, to elucidate its meaning by means of axioms. The axioms will in fact set out what one is to gather from the use of the introduced term. In the case of Newton's first law of motion, we see that here too a body's power of linear self-motion is denied. Indeed, Newton would also deny a body's power of rotary self-motion. To borrow a word invented by Whitehead, the inertia of matter corresponds to its pushiness.

When it is enquired what the philosophers mean by the inertness of matter, something different transpires. In reality the philosophers seek an intellectual parallel to physical motion, and deny this of matter. Hence, we find them harping incontinently on the 'stupidity' of matter. They mean by this that matter is incapable of intellectual action, neither thinking, perceiving nor feeling. Of course, they are grateful for Newton's denial of the physical activity of matter. They take this up and increase it with a further denial of the intellectual activity of matter. Hence, when a philosopher says that matter is 'stupid', he does not mean that it is slow-witted, but that it has no wit at all. In this denial of activity, both physical and mental, of matter, it is however not unusual for philosophers to contradict themselves. If one looks through Locke's magnum opus, *The Essay on Human Understanding*, one quickly comes upon such contradictions.

There Locke denies that matter is active, attributing all activity to spirit. Nevertheless, in his theory of perception, he says that corpuscles *travel* from a *perceived object* to our appropriate organ of sense in order that we should be able to perceive it. These corpuscles are said by him to be parts of the perceived object which detach themselves and subject us to a kind of radiative bombardment. Here, Locke patently contradicts himself. For this activity of matter is not said by him to be induced, but original, natural.

But even the theory of gravity, while it does explain the current motion of bodies (including rest), is properly silent over the question of antecedents. It does not face the question why bodies move at all, how it is that the heavenly bodies, for example, come to be moving, but only how they keep moving and why they keep moving as they do.

And yet, all those who conceive the universe in terms of an original super-atom which multiplied internal stresses to such a pitch as to burst asunder, thereby imply that matter has powers of self-motion, for they do not conceive this primordial building-up of internal stresses in terms of *externally* impressed forces.

Both the phenomenon of radiation and the wave mechanics of quantum theory indubitably presuppose that body has original powers of self-motion even in that sense which requires something other than change of property. If matter perpetrates a spontaneous emission, then to the extent that there is an emission of particles there is motion; to the extent that this emission is spontaneous, there is self-motion.

The classical philosophers have in fact been over-impressed by at least two considerations. The first is that we do not discern a direct phenomenon of radiation or corpuscular motion by any of our celebrated five senses. But we do see apples thrown to go up. And we observe feathers blown to make them air-borne. By contrast, even though we know of cases where humans and animals are pushed, we witness day after day the more overt and directly obtrusive phenomenon of spontaneous motion in living things. Our classical philosophers have then without much ado closed the dossier, pleasantly identifying the limits of their own knowledge with the limits of what can be.

Now, if one wishes to maintain the philosophical inertness of matter, one must ascribe the phenomenal self-motion of bodies to some non-material principle, usually a soul or a spirit. This soul or spirit may of course be said to inhere in matter or to be external to it. But even when it is said that there is a spirit or a soul in matter which is responsible for its spontaneous motion, it will not have been said that in *every* case of phenomenal spontaneous motion of a body there must be presumed a spirit concealed in the body, a ghost lurking in the machine. Hence the philosophical inertness of matter is not achieved by the mere postulate of spirit or soul. It is in fact made a defining characteristic of matter that it is philosophically inert.

In the postulate of a soul or spirit, vitalism and diverse forms of occultism could easily be provided sustenance and defence. But in this also, we find the second consideration which has over-impressed philosophers. This is the idea of intention. It was thought that spontaneous motion could only be deliberate or purposeful, subsuming the idea of intention in any case. Deliberateness, purpose, intention was at the same time exclusively attributed only to living things, and not even to all living things at that. Matter, in itself non-living, was therefore held to be incapable of deliberateness, purpose or intention. Spontaneity of any sort could not therefore be ascribed to it. This is in fact at the heart of philosophical inertness which is quaintly called 'stupidity'!

In a way, it is not the philosophers of today but the natural scientists who are the successors of the ancient philosophers. Attentive to the phenomenon of radiation, that of spontaneous emission of particles of matter, and Newton's silence over the source of the original motion of bodies, one can, if an 'inert' philosopher, embrace a thorough-going animism, and infuse non-living matter with a plethora of spirits, or one can correctly abandon the now groundless denial of the capacity of matter for self-motion.

Indeed, the philosophical ancestor of all Western philosophers, Thales, was stared in the face by both alternatives. He had said that the world was not to be explained in terms of super-nature, and had accordingly said that everything was water. It now fell upon him to explain why hosts of things were not 'watery'. The minimum he could do was to put a principle of change in water itself, so that by the operation of that principle, a transmutation from the state we know as water to other things would be possible. But if he was not to abandon his first statement that everything is water, the principle must permit only geometrical changes in water, that is, in its operation, it must be limited to the rarefaction and condensation of water. For this, the principle needed to be a principle of motion. Hence, he said that things were full of gods. Though this smells unpleasantly of animism, he only meant, through asserting the capacity of matter for spontaneous self-motion, to reject its inertness. In saying things were full of gods, he did not mean that every object was the locus of some god, for his whole philosophical revolution consisted in his neutralizing of the gods, his rendering them irrelevant for purposes of explanation of the objects and processes of the world. It is his idiom, not his thought, which was picturesque. Just as Aristotle was later to recover the forms from Plato's heaven and restore them to matter, so Thales was now retrieving the source of motion and the cause of processes from the priests' heaven for matter.

Matter is not inert in the sense of the philosophers. It is capable of self-motion both in the sense of change of relation, and in the sense of change of property. But matter has inertia. Inertia and inertness have been sufficiently distinguished, and while inertness implies inertia, inertia does not imply inertness.

The initial assertions of what I put forward as philosophical consciencism are therefore twofold. First, there is the assertion of the absolute and independent existence of matter; second, there is the assertion of the capacity of matter for spontaneous self-motion. To the extent of these two initial assertions, philosophical consciencism is deeply materialist.

There is a supreme need to distinguish here between the materialism which is involved in philosophical consciencism and that materialism which implies the sole existence of matter. I pointed out in the first chapter that a materialist philosophy which accepts the primary reality of matter must either deny other categories of being, or else claim that they are one and all reducible without leftovers to matter. If this does not present a dilemma, at least the choice is often painful. In a materialist philosophy admitting the primary reality of matter, if spirit is accepted as a category of being, non-residual reduction to matter must be claimed. Furthermore, the phenomenon of consciousness, like that of self-consciousness, must be held to be in the ultimate analysis nothing but an aspect of matter.

Strictly speaking, the assertion of the sole reality of matter is atheistic, for pantheism, too, is a species of atheism. Philosophical consciencism, even though deeply rooted in materialism, is not necessarily atheistic.

According to philosophical consciencism, certain activities possessing all the syndromes of purpose may still be the direct activity of matter. Such activity is widespread and is characterized by a non-apperceptive response to stimulus; that is to say, it is characterized by a response to stimulus emptied of all self-awareness, a response devoid of any cognition beyond the reaction to that which is for the time being acting as stimulus. Instinctive response is this kind of activity, for in instinctive response there is a non-apperceptive response to stimulus, a response which is not conditioned by any realization of a possible relation of purpose between the stimulus and the stimulated. On the other hand, apperceptive response is deliberate. Here, there is a self-awareness and an appraisal of the situation involving stimulus and response.

The suspicion that living things exhibit non-apperceptive response is not new. Indeed, Descartes thought that the response of all non-human animals was non-apperceptive. He therefore denied that non-human animals possessed souls, remaining content to believe that all the actions of such animals could be given a mechanical explanation which is complete. But even humans are not entirely above non-apperceptive response. Indeed a response that starts by being apperceptive could in time be rendered non-apperceptive by the technique of producing a conditioned reflex.

Aristotle had, before Descartes, maintained a similar opinion, that only humans were capable of a self-conscious, apperceptive response. This opinion of Aristotle's was confirmed in his invention of the vegetable and the animal souls, as distinct from the rational soul.

It might seem that a philosophical position which accepts a duality of the Cartesian type cannot comfortably treat all the actions of animals as purely mechanical. For this kind of duality, there should ensue a nagging doubt, the doubt whether spirit as a category should not really be excised with Occam's razor. According to Occam's razor, entities should not be multiplied without logical need.

But according to Cartesian duality, there are two irreducible types of substance. There is spiritual substance which is purely active, thinks and is non-extended. Then there is matter which is purely extended and is inert in the philosopher's sense. Now a great many of the actions of animals are, as outward marks, quite similar to those of men. It is therefore a kind of special pleading to hold that these actions are spirit-produced in the one case and not in the other, especially since Descartes makes an issue of the existence of minds other than his own and God's.

In order to remove this feeling that Occam's razor might be applied to shave off spirit, it is necessary to show, as distinct from claiming, that actions which have syndromes of being mind-inspired can result from mere matter. To do this is to show how some mind-language is reducible without residue to body-language. That is, to show how expressions which might be used in describing spirit-directed operations can be shown to be completely apt in describing mechanical action; almost to show, indeed, that rudimentary minds are nothing but active matter. That this is so was in fact explicitly claimed by Leibniz, who said that matter was rudimentary mind, thereby breaking the categorical ice between matter and mind.

In the first chapter, I discussed at some length how categorial conversion or reduction is possible, making free reference in the course of the discussion to the work of logicians. If spiritual phenomena are in fact the outcome of material phenomena, then it is hardly surprising that environment, which is but a disposition of matter, can enhance, intensify, even develop the consciousness. Furthermore, the mind–body problem is solved. This solution of the mind–body problem has sometimes taken the form of cutting the Gordian knot. The mind–body problem arises in the following manner. If one says that there are only two types of substances, matter and mind, and furthermore allows interaction between them, then the question arises how there can be interaction between substances which are so disparate. Mind is purely active, thinks, and is unextended; matter is passive, extended and is without awareness. If one asserts the sole reality of matter, as extreme materialists do, or if one asserts the sole reality of spirit as Leibniz must be deemed to have done, then the mind–body problem is solved by removing the conditions in which the perplexity arises. This is to cut the Gordian knot, for now mind and body will not be disparate, but will either both be forms of matter or both be forms of spirit.

In philosophical consciencism, however, the interaction of mind and body is accepted as a fact. The philosophical perplexity which darkens this interaction is removed by the demonstration of the possibility of categorial conversion. Categorial conversion must be distinguished from parallelism. Descartes himself tried to solve the mind–body problem by resorting to a kind of parallelism. He instituted parallel occurrences, and thus explained pain as that grief which the soul felt at the damage to its body. On this point, as on several others, Descartes was assailed by the critical acumen of the Ghanian philosopher Anthony William Amo. According to Amo, all that the soul could do on Descartes's terms is to take cognizance of the fact that there is a hole in its body or a contusion on it, and unless knowledge is itself painful, the mind could not be said to grieve thereat. Of course, if the mind could be said to grieve in this way, on bare knowledge of the state of the body, then one *might* say that the body could affect the mind. But not so necessarily, for, strictly speaking, according to Descartes the body does not affect the mind, but the mind *commiserates* with the body.

Philosophical consciencism has no room for a mere parallelism on the mind–body problem. For philosophical consciencism *retains* the two categories of mind and body, *recognizes* the problem by accepting the fact of interaction, but offers a solution thereto. Parallelism, while recognizing the two categories, in fact denies interaction. The solution offered by philosophical consciencism is by way of categorial conversion.

According to philosophical consciencism, qualities are generated by matter. Behind any qualitative appearance, there stands a quantitative disposition of matter, such that the qualitative appearance is a surrogate of the quantitative disposition. I do not mean by this that qualities are the quantities themselves. I am not, for example, saying that a colour is the same thing as a certain wave-length. Of course the wave-length is not the colour, though we do know, thanks to the physicists, that individual colours are tied to characteristic wave-lengths. What I am however saying is that the colour is precisely the visual surrogate of a wave-length. A colour is the eye's mode of impression of a wave with certain mathematical properties; it is the visual surrogate of a quantitative disposition of matter. Sounds, similarly, are the ear's mode of impression of waves with certain properties. In general, sensations and perceptions are sensory surrogates of quantitative dispositions of matter. All natural properties, whatever property is discernible by medium of one sense or more, are nothing but sensory surrogates of quantitative dispositions of matter.

In the first chapter, I refuted the claim that Einstein's Theory of Relativity was incompatible with materialism. The gravamen of the objection was that philosophical materialism requires the absolute and independent existence of space and time as necessary receptacles for matter. At that point, I explained that there was no conflict with the Theory of Relativity, and also that materialism was itself inconsistent with the absolute and independent existence of space or time.

If the sole existence of matter is asserted, then space and time, in so far as they are not matter, must be unreal. Philosophical consciencism does not assert the sole reality of matter. Rather it asserts the primary reality of matter. Here again, if space were absolute and independent, matter could not with respect to it be primary. Therefore philosophical consciencism, in asserting the primary existence of matter, also maintains that space must, to the extent that it is real, derive its properties from those of matter through a categorial conversion. And since the properties of space are geometrical, it then follows from philosophical consciencism that the geometry of space is determined by the properties of matter.

When one now turns to Einstein's General Theory of Relativity, one finds exactly the same conclusion there. For in his Theory, Einstein relies on a principle of Mach's about the conditions of significance to affirm that the properties of space are fixed by the masses of bodies in a gravitational field. This principle of Einstein's, like philosophical consciencism, rejects the absolute and independent existence of space. With regard to space, relativity and philosophical consciencism are mutually consistent.

In discussing the possibility of categorial conversion, I said that two approaches were available to philosophy. First, the possibility of categorial conversion could be demonstrated in conceptual terms. This has been achieved by modern logic. Second, models fulfilling the conditions of categorial conversion might be cited. Such models are offered by modern science.

Philosophical consciencism claims the reality of categorial conversion. But if the conversion from one category to another category is not to represent a mere apparition, a philosophical will-o'-the-wisp, then such a conversion must represent a variation in the mass of its initial matter. The conversion is produced by a dialectical process, and if it is from a lower logical type to a higher logical type, it involves loss of mass.

Here again, that loss of mass actually takes place is deducible from Einstein's General Theory of Relativity. It follows from this Theory that every chemical change from simpler substances to more complex substances, in so far as it entails the emergence of new properties, represents a loss of mass. Indeed, it represents a conversion of part of the mass of matter. In Einstein's Theory, the loss is calculable according to the general formulae $e = mc^2$ where e represents ergs of energy, m mass, and c the velocity of light. If, for example, one gram of mass were substituted for m, the equivalence in ergs of energy will be 9×20^{10} ergs, for in this case e will be equal to c^2. According to philosophical consciencism, however, though the whole of this amount of mass is converted, it is not all of it which is converted to the emergent properties. In actual chemical changes, some of it transpires as heat.

It is this reality of categorial conversion which prompts philosophical consciencism to assert not

the sole reality of matter, but its primary reality. If higher categories are only surrogates of quantitative processes of matter, they are still not empty apparitions, but are quite real.

It follows from this that in philosophical consciencism, matter is capable of dialectic change, for if natural properties are nothing but surrogates of quantitative dispositions of matter, then since natural properties change, matter must change in quantitative disposition. And matter, in being a plenum of forces in *tension*, already contains the incipient change in disposition which is necessary to bring about a change in quality or property. Force itself is the way in which particles of matter exist; it is their mathematical or quantitative constitution. Force is not a description of a particle of matter; it is not something which particles of matter wear on their face. Rather, it is internal to them.

Since matter is a plenum of forces in tension, and since tension implies incipient change, matter must have the power of self-motion original to it. Without self-motion, dialectical change would be impossible.

By a dialectical change, I mean the emergence of a third factor of a higher logical type from the tension between two factors or two sets of factors of a lower logical type. Matter belongs to one logical type, properties and qualities of matter to a higher logical type, properties of properties to an even higher logical type.

This appropriately raises questions of an epistemological nature about consciencism. Epistemological problems are those which concern the nature of knowledge, and its types, and also the avenues to them which are open to the mind. Consciencism, by avoiding the assertion of the sole reality of matter, prepares itself for the painless recognition of the objectivity of different types of being. Indeed, the conception of dialectic is itself connected with a recognition of different types of being. Types of being are logical types. If they form a scale of being, it is not to be inferred that this scale is correlated with a scale of value. The types are logical types, such that material objects form one logical type; those general terms, which can be applied in description only to material objects, form a higher logical type; those general terms which can be applied in description to general terms of the first group form another logical type which is even higher.

Material objects and their properties belong to different logical types, and so do material objects and mind. It is these differences in type which make categorial absurdity possible. By a categorial absurdity, I mean that special absurdity which arises from coupling types of terms which should not be coupled. Terms can be coupled only when they belong to the same type or belong to proximate types. Thus 'people' and 'independence' belong to proximate types, and may therefore be coupled as in the proposition 'we are an independent people'. But the number two and 'red' neither belong to the same type nor belong to proximate types; hence, not unexpectedly, the proposition 'the number two is red', which couples them, does commit a categorial absurdity.

In the same way, terms which can be coupled with philosophical surrogates in description of the latter cannot be coupled with the items which give rise to the surrogates, though there is nothing which is incapable of translation, without residue, to propositions about these items whose surrogates they are.

Terms which can be coupled with philosophical surrogates in description of them cannot be coupled with the items which give rise to the surrogates, because if a term can be coupled with a philosophical surrogate, it must be of the same logical type as the philosophical surrogate, or, if it is in description of it, must be of a type higher than and proximate to that to which the surrogate belongs. Terms which can be coupled in description with a philosophical surrogate must be one logical type higher than the surrogate, since such terms are always one type higher than their subjects. As such these terms are at least two types higher than the items which give rise to the surrogate. They cannot therefore be ascribed even by way of complement. One cannot say that the number two is a red thing (complement) any more than one can say that the number two is red (description).

This epistemological consequence of philosophical consciencism provides an antecedent philosophical justification for such pursuits as the investigation of the nature of mind by the exclusive means of the investigation of the nature and functioning of brain. This is a great advantage, for as the mind is not subject to experimental exposure, if all propositions about mind are in principle translatable without residue to propositions about the nervous system, *which is* subject to experimental exposure, then a great deal of mental research can be done in terms of neural research. In general, philosophical consciencism narrows down the extent of academic hermitage. It does this by making research into the nature of one category possible in terms of another category.

There is a growing tendency among some philosophers who hold the view that when materialism has triumphed and has won victory over idealism, it must, like its victim, disappear or 'wither away' as a philosophy. It is envisaged that this will take place when the classless society is achieved. Marx and Engels regarded materialism as the true form of science and, indeed, held that with the final overthrow of idealism, materialism must have science for its positive content. What is important is not so much that it may not be necessary to stress materialism as a philosophy when idealism is overthrown, but rather that the importance and correctness of materialism will not in any way be diminished in its hour of victory. Some philosophers expect that materialism will then disappear and give way to a philosophy of mind – and that philosophical theory of the mind which is not explicitly prefaced by philosophical materialism will open the door to a new idealism.

Thought without practice is empty, and philosophical consciencism constantly exhibits areas of practical significance, like the one above. If philosophical consciencism initially affirms the absolute and independent existence of matter, and holds matter to be endowed with its pristine objective laws, then philosophical consciencism builds itself by becoming a reflection of the objectivity, in conceptual terms, of the unfolding of matter. When a philosophy so restricts itself to the reflection of the objective unfolding of matter, it also establishes a direct connection between knowledge and action.

This idea of a philosophy as the conceptual image of nature is also found in Spinoza, and, indeed, it is a tenet of rationalism in general. According to Spinoza, at least, the order and connection of ideas is the same as the order and connection of nature. The mistake of the rationalists regarding the connection between philosophy and nature is in their treating philosophy as the blue-print, the strait-jacket for nature, instead of being content with a mere assertion of mutual reflection. If, however, the order and connection of ideas is the same as the order and connection of nature, then according to Spinoza, knowledge of the one order and connection must be knowledge of the other order and connection. Indeed, it can be said that, according to Spinoza, mind is the idea of that whose body is nature. To the extent that he allows action to be possible, knowledge of the mind can be the direct objective basis of an intervention in nature.

I said earlier on that in spite of the profound cleavage between idealism and materialism, they did not present different inventories of the world. This hardly means, however, that they share the same attitude to the world. They certainly differ in their conception of the nature of the connection between thought and action. In this field, idealism is jejune and grotesquely ineffectual. Materialism is, on the other hand, dynamic and constantly throws up areas of practical significance.

But if philosophical consciencism connects knowledge with action, it is still necessary to inquire whether it conceives this connection as a purely mechanistic one, or whether it makes it susceptible of ethical influence and comment.

It is evident at least that philosophical consciencism cannot issue in a closed set of ethical rules, a set of rules which must apply in any society and at any time. Philosophical consciencism is incapable of this because it is itself based upon a view of matter, as caught in the grip of an inexorable dialectical evolution.

To the extent that materialism issues in egalitarianism on the social plane, it issues in ethics. Egalitarianism is not only political but also ethical; for it implies a certain range of human conduct which is alone acceptable to it. At the same time, because it conceives matter as a plenum of tensions giving rise to dialectical change, it cannot freeze its ethical rules with changelessness. It would be wrong, however, to seek to infer from this that the ethical principles which philosophical consciencism sanctions are at any one time gratuitous and devoid of objective grounding; for even when rules change, they can still be informed, still be governed by the same basic principles in the light of changing social conditions.

It is necessary to understand correctly the relationship between rules and principles. This relationship is similar to that between ideals and institutions and also to that between statutes and by-laws. Statutes, of course, state general principles, they do not make explicit those procedures by means of which they may be carried out and fulfilled. By-laws are an application of such principles. It is obvious that when the conditions in which by-laws operate alter seriously, it could be necessary to amend the by-laws in order that the same statute should continue to be fulfilled. Statutes are not on the same level as by-laws, nor do they imply any *particular* by-laws. It is because they carry no specific implication of particular by-laws, but can be subserved by any one of a whole spectrum of such, that it is possible to amend by-laws, while the statute which they are meant to fulfil suffers no change.

The relationship between ideals and institutions is a similar one. That circumstances change is a truism. For all that, it is significant. For it means that, if ideals must be pursued throughout the changing scenes of life, it may be necessary to modify or replace institutions in order that the same ideals should effectively be served. There are no particular institutions, which, irrespective of local circumstances, are uniquely tied to their ideals. Institutions should be shot through and through with pragmatism.

It is in the same way that principles are related to rules even when they are ethical. The idea that ethical rules can change, and indeed need to change, is one which a little reflection can confirm.

Evidently, even when two societies share the same ethical principles, they may differ in the rules which make the principles effective. Asses were of such overwhelming importance in Israel that God found it necessary to regulate human relations by an ethical rule mentioning them specifically. Thou shalt not covet thy neighbour's ass. If God deigned to give us a similar rule today, he would no doubt forbid us to covet our neighbour's motor-car, hardly his ass. Here God would be giving a new ethical rule, designed at giving effect to an unchanging ethical principle, but taking full account of modern times.

Progress in man's conquest and harnessing of the forces of nature has a profound effect on the content of ethical rules. Some ethical rules fall into abeyance, because the situations in which they take effect lose all likelihood of recurrence; others give way to their opposite, as, for example, when a matriarchal society changes into a patriarchal one, for here many ethical rules arising from the position of the women will have to give way to those arising from the new position of the man. And yet, the principles standing behind these diverse clusters of ethical rules may remain constant, and identical as between society and society.

According to philosophical consciencism, ethical rules are not permanent but depend on the stage reached in the historical evolution of a society, so, however, that cardinal principles of egalitarianism are conserved.

A society does not change its ethics by merely changing its rules. To alter its ethics, its principles must be different. Thus, if a capitalist society can become a socialist society, then a capitalist society will have changed its ethics. Any change of ethics constitutes a revolutionary change.

Nevertheless, many times moral rules have

changed so startlingly as to give the impression of a revolution in ethics. For example, one can take that profound change in our attitude to offenders for which modern psychology is responsible. Modern psychology brings to our notice relevant facts of whose existence we have no inkling in our dreams. When these new facts change our attitude, moral rules have not necessarily changed. But application of them is withheld, for the new considerations provoke a re-classification of the act involved, and, possibly, bring it under a different ethical rule. In that case, a different moral attitude could become relevant.

Investigations into the psychology of delinquency are a case in point. Such investigations tend by their results to attenuate the acrimony of our moral attitude to delinquents, by compelling us, not admittedly to waive moral rules, but to re-classify delinquent acts.

The cardinal ethical principle of philosophical consciencism is to treat each man as an end in himself and not merely as a means. This is fundamental to all socialist or humanist conceptions of man. It is true that Immanuel Kant also identified this as a cardinal principle of ethics, but whereas he regarded it as an immediate command of reason, we derive it from a materialist viewpoint.

This derivation can be made by way of that egalitarianism which, we have seen, is the social reflection of materialism. Egalitarianism is based on the monistic thesis of materialism. Matter is one even in its different manifestations. If matter is one, it follows that there is a route connecting any two manifestations of matter. This does not mean that between any two manifestations of matter there is a route which does not pass through any third form; the route need not be direct, for it may take one back to the primary form of matter. Dialectical processes are not unilinear, they do not follow just one line, but are ramified. There is a route from any twig of a tree to any other twig, such that the route never leaves the tree. But this does not mean that the twigs all have some one point in common, for it may be necessary to pass to the trunk and join another branch in order to pass from one twig to another. Nevertheless there is this route. The different manifestations of matter are all results of dialectical processes unfolding according to objective laws. There is a determinate process through which every manifestation is derived.

In saying, however, that there is a route between any two forms of matter, I do not attach the implication that any one form of matter can in fact

be derived from any other form, for this may involve the reversal of a process which is irreversible. The upshot of what I mean is the continuity of nature: though the dialectical evolution of matter may lead to culs-de-sac (like the vanished plants and animals of pre-historic days), dialectical evolution contains no hiatuses.

It is the basic unity of matter, despite its varying manifestations, which gives rise to egalitarianism. Basically, man is one, for all men have the same basis and arise from the same evolution according to materialism. This is the objective ground of egalitarianism.

David Hume raised the question that ethical philosophies begin with statements of fact and suddenly seek to base statements of appraisal thereon, without explaining the legitimacy of their inference. If man is basically one, then if action is objectively attentive to this fact, it must be guided by principles. The guiding principles can be stated with such generality that they become autonomous. That is to say, first, that if action is to conform to the objectivity of human unity, then it must be guided by general principles which always keep this objectivity in view, principles which would prevent action from proceeding as if men were basically different. Second, these principles, because they relate to fact, can be stated boldly, as though they were autonomous, like the principle that an individual should not be treated by another merely as a means but always as an end.

If ethical principles are founded on egalitarianism, they must be objective. If ethical principles arise from an egalitarian idea of the nature of man, they must be generalizable, for according to such an idea man is basically one in the sense defined. It is to this non-differential generalization that expression is given in the command to treat each man as an end in himself, and not merely as a means. That is, philosophical consciencism, though it has the same cardinal principle of ethics as Kant, differs from Kant in founding ethics on a philosophical idea of the nature of man. This is what Kant describes as ethics based on anthropology. By anthropology Kant means any study of the nature of man, and he forbids ethics to be based on such a study.

It is precisely this that philosophical consciencism does. It also agrees with the traditional African outlook on many points, and thus fulfils one of the conditions which it sets for itself. In particular, it agrees with the traditional African idea of the absolute and independent existence of matter, the idea of its powers of self-motion in the sense explained, the idea of categorial convertibility, and the idea of the grounding of cardinal principles of ethics in the nature of man.

The traditional African standpoint, of course, accepts the absolute and independent idea of matter. If one takes the philosophy of the African, one finds that in it the absolute and independent existence of matter is accepted. Further, matter is not just dead weight, but alive with forces in tension. Indeed, for the African, everything that exists, exists as a complex of forces in tension. In holding force in tension to be essential to whatever exists, he is, like Thales and like philosophical consciencists, endowing matter with an original power of self-motion, they were endowing it with what matter would need to initiate qualitative and substantial changes.

When a plurality of men exist in society, and it is accepted that each man needs to be treated as an end in himself, not merely as a means, there transpires a transition from ethics to politics. Politics become actual, for institutions need to be created to regulate the behaviour and actions of the plurality of men in society in such a way as to conserve the fundamental ethical principle of the initial worthiness of each individual. Philosophical consciencism consequently adumbrates a political theory and a social-political practice which together seek to ensure that the cardinal principles of ethics are effective.

The social-political practice is directed at preventing the emergence or the solidifying of classes, for in the Marxist conception of class structure, there is exploitation and the subjection of class to class. Exploitation and class-subjection are alike contrary to consciencism. By reason of its egalitarian tenet, philosophical consciencism seeks to promote individual development, but in such a way that the conditions for the development of all become the conditions for the development of each; that is, in such a way that the individual development does not introduce such diversities as to destroy the egalitarian basis. The social-political practice also seeks to coordinate social forces in such a way as to mobilize them logistically for the maximum development of society along true egalitarian lines. For this, planned development is essential.

In its political aspect, philosophical consciencism is faced with the realities of colonialism, imperialism, disunity and lack of development. Singly and collectively these four militate against the realization of a social justice based on ideas of true equality.

The first step is to liquidate colonialism wherever it is. In *Towards Colonial Freedom* I stated that it is the aim of colonial governments to treat their colonies as producers of raw materials, and at the same time as the dumping-ground of the manufactured goods of foreign industrialists and foreign capitalists. I have always believed that the basis of colonialism is economic, but the solution of the colonial problem lies in political action, in a fierce and constant struggle for emancipation as an indispensable first step towards securing economic independence and integrity.

I said earlier on that consciencism regards matter as a plenum of forces in tension; and that in its dialectical aspect, it holds categorial conversion to be possible by a critical disposition of matter. This gives us a clue how to analyse the fact of colonialism, not only in Africa, but indeed everywhere. It also gives us a clue how to defeat it.

In a colonial situation, there are forces which tend to promote colonialism, to promote those political ties by means of which a colonialist country binds its colonies to itself with the primary object of furthering her economic advantages. Colonialism requires exertion, and much of that exertion is taken up by the combat of progressive forces, forces which seek to negate this oppressive enterprise of greedy individuals and classes by means of which an egotistical imposition of the strong is made upon the weak.

Just as the placid appearance of matter only disguises the tension of forces underlying that appearance, like the bow of Heraclitus, so in a colonial territory, an opposition of reactionary and revolutionary forces can nevertheless give an impression of final and acquiescent subjugation. But just as a quality can be changed by quantitative (measurable) changes of a critical nature in matter, so this acquiescent impression can be obliterated by a change in the relation of the social forces. These opposing sets of forces are dynamic, in the sense that they seek and tend to establish some social condition. One may therefore refer to them by the name of action in order to make their dynamic nature explicit. In that case, one may say that in a colonial situation positive action and negative action can be discerned. Positive action will represent the sum of those forces seeking social justice in terms of the destruction of oligarchic exploitation and oppression. Negative action will correspondingly represent the sum of those forces tending to prolong colonial subjugation and exploitation. Positive action is revolutionary and negative action is reactionary.

It ought to be recognized at the outset that the introduced terms of positive and negative action are abstractions. But the ground for them is in social reality. It is quite possible by means of statistical analysis to discover the ways in which positive action and negative action are related in any given society. The statistical analysis will be of such facts as production, distribution, income, etc. Any such analysis must reveal one of three possible situations. Positive action may exceed negative action, or negative action may exceed positive action, or they may form an unstable equilibrium.

In a colonial situation, negative action undoubtedly outweighs positive action. In order that true independence should be won, it is necessary that positive action should come to overwhelm negative action. Admittedly, a semblance of true independence is possible without this specific relation. When this happens, we say that neocolonialism has set in, for neo-colonialism is a guise adopted by negative action in order to give the impression that it has been overcome by positive action. Neo-colonialism is negative action playing possum.

In order to forestall this, it is necessary for positive action to be backed by a mass party, and qualitatively to improve this mass so that by education and an increase in its degree of consciousness, its aptitude for positive action becomes heightened. We can therefore say that in a colonial territory, positive action must be backed by a mass party, complete with its instruments of education. This was why the Convention People's Party of Ghana developed from an early stage its education wing, workers' wing, farmers' wing, youth wing, women's wing, etc. In this way, the people received constant political education, their self-awareness was increased and such a self-image was formed as ruthlessly excluded colonialism in all its guises. It is also in the backing of millions of members and supporters, united by a common radical purpose, that the revolutionary character of the Convention People's Party consists, and not merely in the piquancy of its programmes. Its mass and national support made it possible to think in realistic terms of instituting changes of a fundamental nature in the social hotch-potch bequeathed by colonialism.

A people's parliamentary democracy with a one-party system is better able to express and satisfy the common aspirations of a nation as a whole, than a multiple-party parliamentary system, which is in fact only a ruse for perpetuating, and covers up, the inherent struggle between the 'haves' and the 'have-nots'.

In order that a territory should acquire the nominal attributes of independence, it is of course not necessary that positive action should exceed negative action. When a colonialist country sees the advance of positive action, it unfailingly develops a policy of containment, a policy whereby it seeks to check this advance and limit it. This policy often takes the form of conferences and protracted constitutional reforms.

Containment is, however, accepted by the colonialist country only as a second best. What it would really like to do is to roll back positive action. It is when it is assured of the impossibility of rolling back the billows of history that it applies the policy of containment, that it tries to limit the achievement of progress by devising frivolous reforms. The colonialist country seeks to divert positive action into channels which are harmless to it.

To do this it resorts to diverse subtle means. Having abandoned direct violence, the colonialist country imparts a deceptive orientation to the negative forces in its subject territory. These negative forces become the political wolf masquerading in sheep's clothing, they join the clamour for independence, and are accepted in good faith by the people. It is then that like a wasting disease they seek from the inside to infest, corrupt, pervert and thwart the aspirations of the people.

The people, the body and the soul of the nation, the final sanction of political decisions, and the inheritors of sovereignty, cannot be fooled for long. Quick on the scent, they ferret out these Janus-faced politicians who run with the hare and hunt with the hounds. They turn away from them. Once this colonialist subterfuge is exposed, and the minion accomplices discredited, the colonial power has no option but to acknowledge the independence of the people. By its very next act, however, it seeks without grace to neutralize this same independence by fomenting discontent and disunity; and, finally, by arrant ingratiation and wheedling it attempts to disinherit the people and constitute itself their conscience and their will, if not their voice and their arm. Political decisions, just as they were before independence was won, lose their reference to the welfare of the people, and serve once again the well-being and security of the erstwhile colonial power and the clique of self-centred politicians.

Any oblique attempt of a foreign power to thwart, balk, corrupt or otherwise pervert the true independence of a sovereign people is neo-colonialist. It is neo-colonialist because it seeks, notwithstanding the acknowledged sovereignty of a people, to subordinate their interests to those of a foreign power.

A colonialist country can in fact offer independence to a people, not with the intention which such an act might be thought to imply, but in the hope that the positive and progressive forces thus appeased and quietened, the people might be exploited with greater serenity and comfort.

Neo-colonialism is a greater danger to independent countries than is colonialism. Colonialism is crude, essentially overt, and apt to be overcome by a purposeful concert of national effort. In neo-colonialism, however, the people are divided from their leaders and, instead of providing true leadership and guidance which is informed at every point by the ideal of the general welfare, leaders come to neglect the very people who put them in power and incautiously become instruments of suppression on behalf of the neo-colonialists.

It is far easier for the proverbial camel to pass through the needle's eye, hump and all, than for an erstwhile colonial administration to give sound and honest counsel of a *political* nature to its liberated territory. To allow a foreign country, especially one which is loaded with economic interests in our continent, to tell us what *political* decisions to take, what *political* courses to follow, is indeed for us to hand back our independence to the oppressor on a silver platter.

Likewise, since the motivation of colonialism, whatever protean forms it may take, is well and truly economic, colonialism itself being but the institution of political bonds fastening colonies to a colonialist country, with the primary object of the metropolitan economic advantages, it is essential that a liberated territory should not bind her economy to that of the ousted rulers. The liberation of a people institutes principles which enjoin the recognition and destruction of imperialistic domination, whether it is political, economic, social or cultural. To destroy imperialistic domination in these forms, political, economic, social and cultural action must always have reference to the needs and nature of the liberated territory, and it is from these needs and nature that the action must derive authenticity. Unless this self-reference is religiously maintained, a liberated territory will welcome with open arms the very foe which it has sought to destroy at cost of terrible suffering.

The true welfare of a people does not admit of compromise. If we compromise on the true interest of our people, the people must one day judge us, for it is with their effort and their sacrifice, with their forbearance and their denial, that independence is won. Independence once won, it is possible to rule against the erstwhile colonial power, but it is not really possible to rule against the wish and interest of the people.

The people are the backbone of positive action. It is by the people's effort that colonialism is routed, it is by the sweat of the people's brow that nations are built. The people are the reality of national greatness. It is the people who suffer the depredations and indignities of colonialism, and the people must not be insulted by dangerous flirtations with neo-colonialism.

There is a fundamental law of the evolution of matter to higher forms. This evolution is dialectical. And it is also the fundamental law of society. It is out of tension that being is born. Becoming is a tension, and being is the child of that tension of opposed forces and tendencies.

Just as in the physical universe, since the moving object is always impressed upon by external forces, any motion is in fact a resultant, so in society every development, every progressive motion, is a resultant of unharmonious forces, a resultant, a triumph of positive action over negative action.

This triumph must be accompanied by knowledge. For in the way that the process of natural evolution can be aided by human intervention based upon knowledge, so social evolution can be helped along by political intervention based upon knowledge of the laws of social development. Political action aimed at speeding up social evolution is of the nature of a catalyst.

The need for such a catalyst is created by the fact that natural evolution is always wasteful. It takes place at the cost of massive loss of life and at the cost of extreme anguish. Evolution speeded by scientific knowledge is prompter, and represents an economy of material. In the same way, the catalysis which political action introduces into social evolution represents an economy of time, life and talent.

Without positive action, a colonial territory cannot be truly liberated. It is doomed to creep in its petty pace from day to day towards the attainment of a sham independence that turns to dust, independence which is shot through and through with the supreme interest of an alien power. To achieve true liberation, positive action must begin with an objective analysis of the situation which it seeks to change. Such an analysis I attempted in *Towards Colonial Freedom*. Positive action must, furthermore, seek an alignment of all the forces of progress and, by marshalling them confront the negative forces. It must at the same time anticipate and contain its own inner contradictions, for, though positive action unites those forces of a situation which are, in regard to a specific purpose, progressive, many of these forces will contain tendencies which are in other respects reactionary.

Hence, when positive action resorts to an alignment of forces, it creates in itself seams at which this alignment might fall apart. It is essential that positive action should in its dialectical evolution anticipate this seminal disintegration and discover a way of containing the future schismatic tendencies, a way of nipping fragmentation in the bud as colonialism begins to reel and totter under the frontal onslaught of positive action.

But even with colonialism worsted, positive action cannot relent, for it is at about this time that the schismatic tendencies referred to ripen. Besides, political independence, though worthwhile in itself, is still only a means to the fuller redemption and realization of a people. When independence has been gained, positive action requires a new orientation away from the sheer destruction of colonialism and towards national reconstruction.

It is indeed in this address to national reconstruction that positive action faces its gravest dangers. The cajolement, the wheedlings, the seductions and the Trojan horses of neo-colonialism must be stoutly resisted, for neo-colonialism is a latter-day harpy, a monster which entices its victims with sweet music.

In order to be able to carry out this resistance to neo-colonialism at every point, positive action requires to be armed with an ideology, an ideology which, vitalizing it and operating through a mass party shall equip it with a regenerative concept of the world and life, forge for it a strong continuing link with our past and offer to it an assured bond with our future. Under the searchlight of an ideology, every fact affecting the life of a people can be assessed and judged, and neo-colonialism's detrimental aspirations and sleights of hand will constantly stand exposed.

In order that this ideology should be comprehensive, in order that it should light up every aspect of the life of our people, in order that it should affect the total interest of our society, establishing a continuity with our past, it must be socialist in form and in content and be embraced by a mass party.

And yet, socialism in Africa today tends to lose its objective content in favour of a distracting terminology and in favour of a general confusion. Discussion centres more on the various conceivable types of socialism than upon the need for socialist development. More is surely required than a mere reaction against a policy of domination. Independence is of the people; it is won by the people for the people. That independence is of the people is admitted by every enlightened theory of sovereignty. That it is won by the people is to be seen in the successes of mass movements everywhere. That it is won for the people follows from their ownership of sovereignty. The people have not mastered their independence until it has been given a national and social content and purpose that will generate their well-being and uplift.

The socialism of a liberated territory is subject to a number of principles if independence is not to be alienated from the people. When socialism is true to its purpose, it seeks a connection with the egalitarian and humanist past of the people before their social evolution was ravaged by colonialism; it seeks from the results of colonialism those elements (like new methods of industrial production and economic organization) which can be adapted to serve the interest of the people; it seeks to contain and prevent the spread of those anomalies and domineering interests created by the capitalist habit of colonialism; it reclaims the psychology of the people, erasing the 'colonial mentality' from it; and it resolutely defends the independence and security of the people. In short, socialism recognizes dialectic, the possibility of creation from forces which are opposed to one another; it recognizes the creativity of struggle, and, indeed, the necessity of the operation of forces to any change. It also embraces materialism and translates this into social terms of equality.

11

Two Traditions in African American Political Philosophy

Bernard Boxill

The history of African American political thought can be divided into two great traditions – the assimilationist and the separatist. The assimilationist tradion maintains that a society in which racial differences have no moral, political, or economic significance – that is, a color-blind society – is both possible and desirable in America.[1] The separatist tradition denies this, some separatists maintaining that a color-blind society in America is not possible, others maintaining that it is not desirable.

Sometimes the differences between the traditions are only strategic, as, for example, where an ostensibly separatist theory recommends self-segregation as a means to eventual assimilation. Sometimes, however, the differences are profound, stemming from conflicting philosophical views about morality and human nature. I will illustrate this thesis by comparing the theories of the separatist Martin Delany, and the assimilationist Frederick Douglass, both of the nineteenth century.

Delany

Delany's separatism depends on his explanation of the enslavement of Africans by Europeans in America, and on his account of the consequences of that enslavement.

Delany's explanation of African enslavement is set out in his book, *The Condition, Elevation,*

Emigration and Destiny of the Colored People of The United States, and can be summarized as follows: the Europeans who first arrived in America were "not of the common people, seeking in a distant land the means of livelihood, but moneyed capitalists, the grandees and nobles."[2] To take full advantage of the opportunities America offered, they decided to enslave another class. Two obvious alternatives occurred to them, the Indians they found in America, and their own subservient class in Europe. But neither class was satisfactory. On the one hand, while the Indians were sufficiently "foreign" to their "sympathies"[3] to be exploited harshly without undue psychological penalty, they were "wholly unaccustomed to labor," and being "unable to withstand the hardships,"[4] died in great numbers. Besides, they had such meager skills in mining and agriculture that enslaving them was often hardly profitable.[5] On the other hand, while European workers had the requisite skills, they were not sufficiently foreign to the sympathies of their masters to be exploited with the severity which conditions in the New World demanded. Finally the Europeans decided to enslave Africans. Africans were an "industrious people, cultivators of the soil,"[6] and had "long been known to Europeans . . . as a long-lived, hardy race, subject to toil and labor of various kinds, subsisting mainly by traffic, trade, and industry." Moreover, they also possessed "distinctive characteristics" like "color" and "character of hair" which strongly marked them off from Europeans and made them "as foreign to the sympathies" of the Europeans as Indians."[7] This combination of characteristics

Reproduced by kind permission of *Philosophical Forum,* Inc.

sealed their fate. From the point of view of the Europeans they were "the very best class that could be selected" for enslavement in America,[8] and they were accordingly captured and brought there for this purpose.

The most striking aspect of this argument is the omission of any mention of morality as a possible constraint on the Europeans' desire to enslave Africans. Delany never even suggests that Europeans had to overcome their moral inhibitions against slavery in order to make slaves of Africans. This was not because he thought that Europeans were especially immoral; it was because he thought that most people were little restrained by moral considerations when they were dealing with those weaker than themselves. Thus he denounced moral suasion as a way for blacks to win their liberty, and disparaged black claims of moral equality as "useless," "nonsense," and "pitiable mockery," "*until*" black men and women attained "to a position" above doing the "drudgery" and "menial" work of whites.[9] In taking this stance Delany knew that he was swimming against the stream. The dominant school of abolitionists led by William Lloyd Garrison, and including Delany's friend Frederick Douglass, emphasized moral suasion. And this emphasis seemed good strategy. Europeans had long discontinued the practice of slavery among themselves, and their philosophers condemned it as the crowning injustice; in the words of John Locke, it was a "vile and miserable estate."[10] But evidently relying on his own observations of the way Europeans treated Africans, Delany remained skeptical of the constraints of morality.

Delany thought that when the strong can profit from mistreating the weak, the only hope for the weak is the sympathy of the strong. But sympathy spared only some of the weak. According to Delany sympathy moves the strong to select as the objects of exploitation and oppression those who "differed as much as possible, in some particulars, from themselves. This is to ensure the greater success, because it engenders the greater prejudice, or in other words, elicits less interest on the part of the oppressing class, in their favor."[11]

Two points about Delany's account of sympathy are especially important. First the absence of sympathetic ties is not in itself a motive for aggression. It only removes the constraints on aggression when aggression serves self-interest. Thus Delany specifically denied that it was "on account of hatred to his color, that the African was selected as the subject of oppression."[12] He insisted

that Africans were enslaved because this served the self-interest of Europeans; the difference in color between Africans and Europeans only dampened European sympathy for Africans. He even believed that the powerful would help the weak who were foreign to their sympathies when doing so served their self-interest. Thus he argued that both England and France would support his project for creating an African state and developing the resources of the continent because "they would have everything to gain from such an adventure, the opening of an immense trade being the consequence."[13]

The second important point about Delany's account of sympathy concerns those apt to be bound by sympathetic ties. David Hume thought that these ties mainly depended on the degree of contiguity and familiarity between the persons involved; thus he wrote in the *Enquiry* that "sympathy with persons remote from us [is] much fainter than that with persons near and contiguous," and in the *Treatise* that, concerning the attention we give to others, "'tis only the weakest which reaches to strangers and indifferent persons."[14] In particular, he did not remark that the strength of sympathetic ties also seemed to depend on the degree of resemblance between the persons involved, although his cruel and dismissive disparagement of "negroes" suggests that this dependence may not be insignificant.[15] Delany could not have failed to appreciate this fact about how our sympathies run. He saw every day that white sympathy for black misfortune was faint and weak, though the races were, by that time, no longer strangers to, nor remote from, one another. The explanation for this poor showing of sympathy, he maintained, lay in the obvious physical differences in appearance between whites and blacks. "Being distinguished by our complexion," he wrote, "we are still singled out – although having merged in the habits and customs of our oppressors."[16]

Faced with this overwhelming and recalcitrant prejudice. Delany recommended the complete emigration of blacks from America. "A new country and a new beginning," he declared "is the only true rational, politic remedy for our disadvantageous position."[17]

This recommendation was based on the assumptions about morality and human motivation that he had used to explain African enslavement. These assumptions not only explain why Europeans enslaved Africans, they also severely limit the options for black elevation. For example, his view that the moral demands the weak make against the strong are "pitiable mockery" clearly rules our moral suasion as a means of black elevation. Similarly, while his argument that Europeans enslaved Africans partly because Africans had economically valuable skills and were markedly different from them in physical appearance implies that Europeans would stop enslaving Africans if Africans became similar in appearance to Europeans, or lost the skills and qualities that made enslaving them profitable, neither of these possibilities offered any basis for hope. The first was evidently unachievable. As Delany noted, blacks could dress like whites and acquire their habits, but they could not become physically similar to whites. The second failed for a different reason. While it was achievable, it would end in disaster. It would put Africans in America in danger of genocide.[18] The fate of the Indians attested to this. But Delany's assumptions left at least one possibility for black salvation. If it was in the nature of things that Africans would always be liable to abuse of one sort or other by Europeans, they could nevertheless avoid abuse by going beyond the reach of Europeans.

Unfortunately this alternative also suffered from fatal drawbacks. The first was obvious. Slaves could not emigrate; their masters were not prepared to let them out of their clutches. The second was less obvious, and in a way more disturbing. Free blacks, those who could emigrate if they wanted to, did not want to emigrate. As Delany admitted, his proposals for emigration to Mexico, California, and South America were "always hooted at, and various objections raised: one on account of distance, and another that of climate."[19] He could not have been surprised. His theory of the consequences of slavery suggested that it was predictable that his proposals would meet with this response.

According to that theory, the major consequence of slavery was that many blacks became reconciled to their condition, and even came to love their masters. "The slave," Delany wrote, "may become a lover of his master, and learn to forgive him for continual deeds of maltreatment and abuse."[20] Because he placed the highest value on freedom ('We had rather be a Heathen freeman, than a Christian slave," he declared[21]) Delany deplored and mourned this consequence of slavery, and called it "degradation."[22] Delany explained that this consequence of slavery was a result of the mind's adaptability. "A continuance in any position," he wrote, "becomes what is termed "Second Nature";

it begets an adaptation and reconciliation of mind to such position."[23] Delany evidently believed that this principle held true for animal nature in general, explaining why both the "lofty-soaring Eagle" and the slave may be tamed to their confinement and learn to love it."[24] Delany also believed that this adaptation of mind went deep, and was passed on from parent to child. "The degradation of the slave parent," he observed grimly, "has been entailed upon the child, induced by the subtle policy of the oppressor . . . until it has become almost a physiological function of our system, an actual condition of our nature."[25] Indeed, he believed that this degradation persisted among free blacks driving them to seek the domination and authority of whites although this invariably meant accepting positions as menials and servants. "We have dwelt much upon the menial position of our people in this country," he lamented, "because there is a seeming satisfaction and seeking after such positions manifested on their part."[26]

But if his theory of the consequences of slavery implied that free blacks would not want to stray far from whites, it also implied that they would balk at emigration. Delany understood this. He pointed out that many of those who objected to emigration to Mexico and South America, complaining that these regions were too hot and too far away, had apparently no objection to going to either place if they could go as servants to whites. They "engage themselves to their white American oppressors – officers in the war against Mexico," he observed, where "in the capacity of servants," they endured not only the climate of that country, but risked also the "dangers of the battlefield."[27] Had the Americans "taken Mexico," Delany concluded ruefully, "no people would have flocked there faster than the colored people of the United States."[28]

Delany had evidently arrived at an impasse. On the one hand, emigration was one clear path to black salvation; on the other hand blacks either could not or would not take this path to their salvation. Somehow Delany had to find a way around this impasse. His solution is in his revised strategy in the appendix to his book.

While emigration was still the most important part of the revised strategy, there were three important changes. First, the revised strategy called on only a section of the people to emigrate, instead of all freemen, only "enlightened freemen,"[29] or "colored adventurers."[30] Second, the revised strategy urged the selected emigrés to go to a different place, instead of Central and South America, the "Eastern Coast of

Africa."[31] Finally the revised strategy set them a different task once they reached their destination: instead of merely becoming useful and prosperous citizens of already existing nations, they were to create a great and powerful black nation.

It is tempting to suppose that Delany's revised strategy called on only "enlightened freemen" and "colored adventurers" to emigrate because he had given up on the majority of the freemen as too degraded to see that the only path to their elevation was emigration. But this would not explain the other two innovations in the revised strategy, the new destination and the new task. The change of destination is especially puzzling. In the body of the book, Delany had argued at length, and with every show of conviction, that Central and South America were far better places for black Americans to emigrate to than was Africa. Answering his own question, "Where shall we go?", he answered, "We must not leave this continent: America is our destination and our home",[32] and again, "Upon the American continent we are determined to stay, in spite of every odds against us."[33] Why then the sudden change to Africa?

The answer to this question is that Delany had shifted to a second strategy to secure black elevation. This strategy was also based on the fundamental assumptions of his philosophy. As we have seen, these assumptions imply that the weak who are foreign to the sympathies of the strong can avoid exploitation by the strong if they can get beyond the reach of the strong. But they also imply that these same weak can avoid exploitation by the strong if they become strong.

Consistently with this strategy, Delany was an early advocate of black power. More particularly, perceiving wealth as a source of power, and capitalist development as a means to wealth, he was also an early advocate of black capitalism. But he saw too that the odds did not favor the success of black capitalism in America. As he put it, "To compete now with the mighty odds of wealth, social and religious preferences, and political influences of this country, at this advanced stage of its national existence, we may never expect."[34] It was the hopelessness of the strategy of acquiring power in the US which drove Delany unwillingly to the strategy of mass emigration. When that strategy also showed every prospect of failing, Delany returned to the strategy of black power, but with a twist. Seeing that the odds were against black power in the US, he concluded logically that it had to be developed outside the US. This left two questions:

Where was black power to be developed, and how was it to be developed? Black power could not be developed just anywhere; a suitable place had to have the necessary economic potentialities, and, of course, an overwhelmingly black population. And, however black power was to be developed, it could not require mass black emigration from the US, for as we have seen Delany knew that this was not in the offing.

After surveying the options, Delany decided that the best place to develop black power was Africa. He came to this decision without any sentimental appeal to the idea of Africa as the fatherland of black people. The facts he appealed to were all directly related to the aim of finding a place where black power could be secured – Africa's vast size, and its agricultural, mining, and commercial possibilities. Delany also believed that Africa's climate discouraged white settlement, making it a special reserve for black people. In his opinion it was a "physiological fact" that black people could "bear more different climates than the white race," and in particular that they could work and flourish in the warm climate of Africa where the white race became "perfectly indolent, requiring somebody to work for them."[35] Finally the choice of Africa as the place to develop black power also made mass black emigration from the US unnecessary, for Africa's population was overwhelmingly black.

Douglass

The most conspicuous disagreement between Delany and Douglass was on the issue of emigration as a strategy for black elevation. Douglass rejected that strategy.[36] His main objection was that it falsely assumed that, "there is no hope for the Negro here."[37] Part of the reason for his optimism was that, unlike Delany, he was convinced of the efficacy of moral suasion.

Douglass thought that morality was justified by certain facts about human nature. In particular, he believed that people have human rights because of their human nature. This was a crucial move. Since all people equally have human nature, it enabled Douglass to conclude that all people – blacks included – equally have human rights. Here is how he put it:

> Human rights stand upon a common basis;
> and by all the reason that they are supported,
> maintained and defended, for one variety of

the human family, they are supported, maintained and defended for all the human family; because all mankind have the same wants, arising out of a common nature.[38]

Douglass also maintained that human nature was plainly or self-evidently possessed by all people – blacks pointedly not excepted. That was the point he was making when he wrote that "common sense itself is scarcely needed to detect the absence of manhood in a monkey, or to recognize its presence in a Negro."[39] This too was a crucial move. It enabled Douglass to conclude that, once the case for human rights was made, there was no need for independent argument to claim that blacks had human rights. As he put it, the Negro is "at once self-evidently a man, and therefore entitled to all the rights and privileges which belong to human nature."[40]

Douglass's claims on the self-evidence of human nature and human rights indicate that he had been deeply affected by the Declaration of Independence. The opening words of the Declaration read, "We hold these truths to be self-evident, that all men are created equal; that they are endowed by their Creator with certain inalienable rights." Given the influence of John Locke on the writers of the Declaration of Independence, it is not surprising that Douglass's claims about the self-evidence of human nature and human rights bear a striking resemblance to claims advanced by Locke. Locke not only maintained that the law of nature is "evident" or "plain,"[41] he also suggested that this was because human beings plainly shared a common humanity. Thus Locke argued that nothing is "more evident, than that creatures of the same species and rank promiscuously born to all the advantages of Nature, and the use of the same faculties, should also be equal one among the other with subordination or subjection."[42] And, even more unmistakenly, citing the "judicious Hooker" with approval, he wrote "This equality of men by nature the judicious Hooker looks upon as so evident in itself . . . that he makes it the foundation of that obligation to mutual love amongst men, on which he builds the Duties they owe one another, and from whence he derives the great Maxims of Justice and Charity."[43] As I shall suggest, it was the influence of Lockean moral theory on Douglass that determined in large measure his confidence in moral suasion and consequently his hope for blacks in the United States. But Douglass was no pedestrian Lockean. His politics is more egalitarian and

democratic than Locke's, and his account of oppression or tyranny more subtle and sophisticated. In addition, Douglass's conception of human nature was different from Locke's, and this put him in a position to provide an account of revolt and rebellion that Locke's theory of politics needed, but which Locke himself never attempted to produce.

Douglass's conviction that all persons, including blacks, self-evidently have human rights put him in a position to reject Delany's view that moral appeals by the weak to the strong are pointless, out-of-place, and probably nonsensical and delusive. If blacks self-evidently possess human rights, it can hardly be out-of-place or nonsensical or delusive for them to protest the violation of these rights. It may also not be pointless. For if blacks self-evidently possess human rights, appealing to the world to help stop the violation of these rights will not fall on deaf ears, and is likely even to shame the violators into desisting.[44]

Douglass's view that all persons self-evidently have human rights also gave him reason to reject Delany's suggestion that the slave and the oppressed readily become reconciled to their positions, and consequently degraded. For Douglass's view not only claims that everyone equally has human rights, it also suggests that everyone – the oppressed and the enslaved included – is likely to see that everyone equally has human rights. But if the oppressed and the enslaved see that everyone equally has human rights, they will see that they themselves have human rights. Assuming that human rights include rights not to be enslaved or oppressed, it follows that the oppressed and enslaved will hardly believe that they suffer no wrong in being enslaved and oppressed. But if they do not believe that they suffer no wrong in being enslaved and oppressed, they will hardly be reconciled to being enslaved and oppressed.

This result is significant enough, but it has important consequences that Douglass used to further strengthen his case for the efficacy of moral suasion. Given that the enslaved and oppressed are very likely to feel wronged by, and therefore resentful of, their enslavement and oppression, it follows that they will have a tendency to resist those who enslave and oppress them. This implies that successful enslavers and oppressors must have devised strategies for crushing that tendency. As Douglass knew for the case of black slavery these strategies involved the infliction of pain or violent death when the slaves showed any sign of dissatisfaction with their condition. To his mind this proved that slavery was not only cruel, but that it was necessarily cruel. Thus, after detailing the cruelties of slavery he concluded that, "it is necessary to resort to these cruelties, in order to make the slave a slave, and to keep him a slave. . . . The slaveholder feels this necessity. I admit this necessity."[45] And he used slavery's unavoidable cruelties to strengthen his moral campaign against it, displaying and recounting them in order to engage the sympathies of an otherwise disinterested world, and to impel it thereby to see that slavery violated self-evident human rights, and therefore should be abolished.

Quite early in his career, however, Douglass began to have doubts about the efficacy of this campaign. The immediate cause of these doubts was probably that the campaign was making little headway against slavery. But they also reflected Douglass's growing awareness that the idea that everyone self-evidently has human rights may not have all the consequences it seemed to have promised. If the sympathies of the world have to be engaged in order to make it see that slavery violated self-evident human rights, then it seems that the mere self-evidence of these rights does not guarantee that a great many people will not ignore their known violation. And an even more sobering limitation should have been evident from the first. The recalcitrance of the slavemasters, their self-righteous denials of wrongdoing, and most of all, the apparent equanimity many of them displayed when confronted with their wickedness, suggests that even if it is self-evident that everyone has human rights, some people may still fail to see, or at least may still refuse to see, that some other people have human rights.

These sobering reflections could have moved Douglass to abandon the idea that everyone self-evidently has human rights. Instead he argued that people could be blind to, or uncaring of, others' human rights, despite the fact that it is self-evident that everyone has human rights. This was Locke's position too. Locke maintained that the plainness of the "law of nature" was consistent with people being ignorant and disrespectful of it. According to Locke, "though the Law of Nature be plain and intelligible to all rational creatures; yet men being biassed by their interest, as well as ignorant of study for it, are not apt to allow of it as a Law binding to them in the application of it to their particular cases."[46]

Locke drew egalitarian consequences from his view. He argued that it helped to protect people against those who affected to be "Masters." According to Locke, "those who affected to be Masters" tended to claim that "general propositions that could not be doubted of, as soon understood" were "innate"; since innate propositions were supposed to be stamped on the mind, and known without any effort or study, the object was to take subjects "off from the use of their own reason and judgment, and put them upon believing and taking" things on trust. "In which posture of blind credulity," Locke continued, "they might be more easily governed by, and made useful to some sort of men, who had the skill and office to principle and guide them."[47] Locke thought that his view saved people from such blind credulity because it insisted that they have to "study" the law of nature in order not to be "ignorant" of it, and consequently encouraged them to use their reason.

But the idea that people have to study and apply their faculties in order to know the law of nature, though that law is plain, offers obvious opportunities for the elitist. Locke seized these opportunities. Thus, in his *Questions Concerning the Law of Nature*, after maintaining that "there exists a law of nature knowable by reason," and that "reason is granted to all by nature," he allowed that "it does not follow necessarily from this that it is known to each and all," concluding eventually that on the question of morality "we must consult not the majority of mankind, but the sounder and more perceptive part."[48]

Locke was aware that governments often deliberately tried to keep people ignorant. In certain countries, he notes, even those with enough money and leisure to discover the truth are prevented from doing so because they are "cooped in close, by the Laws of their countries, and the strict guard of those, whose interest is to keep them ignorant."[49] But he did not extend this excuse for ignorance to the laboring classes generally or to slaves. Thus he maintained that "'Tis not to be expected that a Man, who drudges on, all his life, in a laborious trade, should be . . . knowing in the variety of things done in the world," and that a "great part of Mankind," is confined to this drudgery "by the natural and unalterable state of things in this world."[50]

Douglass describes similar causes of moral ignorance in the slave institution. "To enslave men," he noted, "it is necessary to have their minds occupied with thoughts and aspirations short of the liberty of which they are deprived"[51]; if a slave ever ventures "to vindicate his conduct when harshly and unjustly accused," or suggests "a better way of doing a thing, no matter what," then he must be whipped for being "impudent" and "officious."[52] Slaves were "trained from the cradle up, to think and feel that their masters are superior, and invested with a sort of sacredness," so that "there are few who can outgrow or rise above the control which that sentiment exercises."[53] The moral outrage that imbues these remarks contrasts strikingly with Locke's cool discussion and suggests that Douglass was making more egalitarian use of Locke's theory than Locke himself did.

And Douglass noticed a cause of moral ignorance that Locke never dreamed of. While Douglass maintained that greed and selfishness were the first causes of the slavemasters' moral blindness, he suggested that they found another excuse to remain blind if their slaves submitted. According to Douglass, "the very submission of the slave to his chains is held as evidence of his fitness to be a slave; it is regarded as one of the strongest proofs of the divinity of slavery, that the Negro tamely submits to his fetters."[54]

These considerations indicate that although Douglass never ceased to insist on the moral equality of oppressor and oppressed, he also came to concede that greed, selfishness, exhaustion, fear, a preoccupation with other things, and the responses of the oppressor and oppressed to their relative positions could blind them to that equality. This may seem to imply that the mature Douglass would have to endorse Delany's view that moral suasion is ineffective and irrelevant to the abolition of slavery. Nothing could be further from the truth. Although Douglass did begin to supplement moral suasion with appeals for slave rebellion, he did so mainly because he believed that resistance was a form of moral suasion.

This belief follows logically from his view that the slave who submitted provided his enslavers with a "proof" that he was fit to be a slave. Douglass was clear that this "proof" was bogus. He believed that the right to liberty that slavery violated was self-evident because it was based on self-evident facts of human nature. As he declared, "The existence of this right [the right to liberty] is self-evident. It is written upon all the powers and faculties of man."[55] Now one of these powers and faculties was the desire for liberty. Although Douglass denied that the slave ever lost this desire, or consequently his right to liberty, he allowed that punishment for seeking liberty could persuade the slave not to seek liberty, and that the unremitting

harassment, pain, and exhaustion the slave was subjected to could distract him from the very thought of liberty. "When I was looking for the blow about to be inflicted on my head," Douglass confessed, "I was not thinking of my liberty; it was my life."[56] Thus the constant cruelty heaped on the slave served a purpose that was deeper than merely frightening him into submission. It also distracted him from the main desire that would otherwise move him to resist. Moreover, because the submissive or distracted slave failed to display the desire for liberty that was the basis of the right to liberty, his behavior gave his masters the semblance of an argument that they were justified in enslaving him. But it was only the semblance of an argument, and the slavemasters were dishonest and self-deceived in seizing on it. They knew very well why the slave failed to display a desire for liberty, and that it did not mean that he did not desire liberty. Still Douglass allowed that the argument was psychologically compelling especially to those who wanted to believe that it was sound – at one point he said it was "human nature"[57] to be persuaded by it – and consequently that the best response to it was for the slave to resist. "Resistance," he concluded, "is, therefore wise as well as just."[58]

The crucial point in the above discussion is that Douglass recommends resistance not simply because it may force the slavemasters to give up slavery, but because it denies them the semblance of a rational justification for slavery, and therefore moves them to give up slavery because they have less excuse to question the moral equality of the slave. Consequently, for Douglass, resistance can be a means to the moral regeneration of enslavers and so a form of moral suasion. And Douglass believed that slave resistance would help to make the slavemasters acknowledge the slave's moral equality in another way, viz., through arousing his fear. As he put it, "something must be done to make the slaveholders feel the injustice of their course. We must . . . as John Brown, Jr., has taught us this evening, reach the slaveholders' conscience through his fear of personal danger."[59]

But if the slave's submission could seduce the slavemaster into believing that the slave was his moral inferior, it could also seduce the slave into believing the same thing. Douglass understood this. That is why he thought that resistance was a particularly valuable kind of moral suasion. For he believed that just as it could help clear the slavemaster's moral vision, it could also help clear the slave's moral vision. The view is graphically presented in his account of the results of his fight with Covey, the slavebreaker. Covey, Douglass relates, had succeeded in breaking his spirit through whippings, starvation, and overwork. Finally, in desperation, Douglass fought back. He recalled that this produced a profound moral change in him. "It rekindled in my breast the smouldering embers of liberty. It . . . revived a sense of my own manhood. I was a changed being after that fight. I was nothing before – I was a man now. It recalled to life my crushed self-respect, and my self-confidence, and inspired me with a renewed determination to be a free man."[60]

Whatever their force, these views would have only a theoretical significance if the slave was unlikely to resist. But Douglass's assumptions about human nature suggested that slave resistance could not be put off indefinitely.

The crucial assumption has already been noted. Douglass believed that the human desire for liberty that was the basis of the right to liberty was powerful and almost ineradicable.[61] In his view this desire persisted even if the slave failed to see the self-evident fact that he had a right to liberty. Thus although Douglass yielded to the possibility of the degraded slave, he utterly rejected the possibility of the happy slave.[62] Further he was also clear that cruelty could only distract people from their desire for liberty, not extinguish it. As he put it, "as soon as the blow was not to be feared, then came the longing for liberty."[63] Douglass believed that the cruelty necessary to distract the slave from his desire to be free would eventually combine with his unhappiness for the loss of his freedom and overcome his fear of the only escape – death. At this point, having nothing to lose, the slave would fight back, and in fighting back, would, if Douglass's claims about the morally regenerative nature of resistance are true, regain the sense of his moral equality. This indeed was the route of Douglass's own moral rebirth. As he put it, citing the cause of the fight with Covey, "I had reached the point at which I was not afraid to die."[64]

Assessments

In this essay I have tried to show by a discussion of the views of Delany and Douglass that the disagreement between separatism and assimilationism need not be only over strategies, but may also stem from profoundly different views about morality and human nature. Delany emphasized the enduring role of self-interest and sympathy in human affairs, and deemphasized the role of morality. Douglass on the other hand allowed the salience of self-interest and sympathy in human affairs, but also gave a potentially decisive role to morality because he believed that human beings all had the rational insight to see their self-evident moral equality. In this concluding section I comment on the relative merits of these competing views by considering how they deal with the bane of blacks in America – racism.

Racism presupposes a definition of race. According to that definition a race is a group of people who resemble each other with respect to several conspicuous, normally invariant, not readily disguised, physical, and biologically inherited features such as hair type, facial features, and especially skin color.

Some well-meaning people have tried to refute racism by arguing that there are no races. Usually their arguments simply substitute racism's definition of race with a new definition so designed that no group of people could be a race. This is not refuting racism, it is changing the subject.

Usually these same well-meaning people also argue that racism's definition of race is not scientifically useful. They are right because racists tend to make false claims about the races, typically that racially different people inherit different psychological traits and mental abilities. But these false claims are not essential to racism. They usually would not justify the racist's behavior even if they were true. For example, during the period of slavery, Europeans said that Africans were inherently slow-witted and servile. These claims were false, but even if they were true, they would not have justified the "middle passage," and the routine brutality of plantation slavery, notwithstanding the harsh standards of that harsh period. A contemporary example concerns the race/IQ dispute. Some authors affirm that the difference between the average IQ of blacks and whites is biologically determined. The evidence hardly justifies their confidence, but even if it did, discrimination on the basis of race would not be justified. Justice and fairness would still demand that individuals be judged on their merits.

It is illuminating to compare racism to egoism. The egoist often has false beliefs about himself and others which, were they true, would sometimes justify the partiality he shows to himself. But even if he is disabused of these false beliefs, he usually does not stop being unfairly partial to himself. He usually persists in this however clearly he sees himself and others. The racist tends to behave in a somewhat similar fashion. He often has false beliefs about the races, but he tends to persist in being unfairly partial to his race even if he is forced to give up these beliefs.

This suggests that the real reason the racist makes false claims about the races is not to justify his behavior. My suggestion is that it is to express his contempt and distrust of races other than his own, to encourage the members of his own race to share that contempt and distrust, and to tighten the bonds between them. Thus the false claims associated with racism should not be thought of as parts of racism, but rather as among its causes; and not as informative but rather as expressive.

This point is worth emphasizing because the view that the false claims associated with racism are part of racism implies that racism would vanish if people stopped believing these false claims. This mistaken idea underestimates the persistence of racism. Persuading people of the truth about the races is the easy part in the fight against racism. The hard part is to persuade them not to be unfairly partial to members of their own race.

The importance Delany gives to sympathy in human affairs helps to explain why this is so. Sympathy moves us to identify with others, to be gladdened at their good fortune, and saddened at their misfortune. But, as Delany warned, sympathy is selective. It tends to move us to identify with those we think are most like us; that is, those in whom we notice a considerable resemblance. What this resemblance will be varies. It may be subtle, and it may not even be literally noticed, for it may exist only in the imagination of the beholder. But it is usually a real resemblance, and one that is not only real but also conspicuous, inborn, and invariant. This is so for the fairly obvious reason that, all

else equal, average people will notice resemblances rather than imagine them; and, almost by definition, will more easily notice resemblances that are conspicuous, invariant and not readily disguised, rather than those that are subtle, variable, and readily disguised. But, as we have seen, the resemblances between those of the same race are conspicuous, invariant, and not readily disguised. Consequently, all else equal, most people will tend to identify with those of their own race, or will be more easily persuaded to identify with those of their own race rather than with those of other races.

Delany's theory therefore implies that people tend to be racists or that they are easily persuaded to be racists, and suggests what must be done to prevent this tendency from leading to their degradation, given the force of self-interest. Like Thomas Hobbes, that other great realist, who accepted the overwhelming egoism of human beings and tried to show how they could nevertheless have peace, Delany accepted the marked liability to racism among human beings, and tried to show how they could nevertheless avoid degradation. Where Hobbes recommended a sovereign, Delany recommended an equality of racial groups. The people who object to Hobbes will object to Delany too. They will protest that he takes too cynical, and indeed, too pessimistic a view of human nature. They find it far more agreeable to maintain with Frederick Douglass that human nature has a higher side, rationality, which can be used to expand our imaginations, and enable us to identify with the whole human race. They are right, of course. We are morally equal, we can eventually come to see this, and the best society would rest on that shared insight. The question is whether it is in the offing. Delany warns us that the incredible proclivity of the human race to racism suggests that it is not.

Notes

1 Obviously I am following Richard Wasserstrom's famous account of color-blindness in "On Racism and Sexism," in *Today's Moral Problems* (New York: Macmillan, 1979).

2 *The Condition, Elevation, Emigration and Destiny of the Colored People of the United States* (Salem, Mass.: Ayer Publishing Company, 1988), p. 51.

3 Delany, *Colored People of the United States*, p. 22.

4 Delany, *Colored People of the United States*, p. 20.

5 Delany, *Colored People of the United States*, p. 62.

6 Delany, *Colored People of the United States*, p. 53.

7 Delany, *Colored People of the United States*, p. 22.

8 Delany, *Colored People of the United States*, p. 22.

9 Delany, *Colored People of the United States*, p. 43.

10 John Locke, *Two Treatises of Government* (Cambridge: Cambridge University Press, 1988), Bk. 1, ch. 1, p. 142.

11 Delany, *Colored People of the United States*, p. 22.

12 Delany, *Colored People of the United States*, p. 22.

13 Delany, *Colored People of the United States*, p. 212.

14 David Hume, *Enquiries concerning Human Understanding and concerning the Principles of Morals* (Oxford: Clarendon Press, 1975), p. 229; *A Treatise of Human Nature* (Oxford: Clarendon Press 1978), Bk. II,. Pt. II, p. 488.

15 See his "Of National Characters," in *David Hume: Essays, Moral, Political and Literary* (Indianapolis: Liberty Press, 1985), p. 208.

16 Delany, *Colored People of the United States*, p. 209.

17 Delany, *Colored People of the United States*, p. 205.

18 Some contemporary authors fear that the danger exists today. See William A. Darity, "The Managerial Class and Surplus Population," *Society* 21:1, (Nov./Dec. 1983), 54–62.

19 Delany, *Colored People of the United States*, p. 184.

20 Delany, *Colored People of the United States*, p. 207.

21 Delany, *Colored People of the United States*, p. 181.

22 Delany, *Colored People of the United States*, p. 207.

23 Delany, *Colored People of the United States*, p. 207.

24 Delany, *Colored People of the United States*, p. 207. Compare Rousseau; according to him, "Slaves lose everything in their chains, even the desire to be rid of them. They lose their servitude." J.-J. Rousseau, *On the Social Contract*, ed. Judith R. Masters (New York: Saint Martin's Press, 1978), Bk. I, ch. II, p. 48. The more easily a writer thinks degradation occurs the more radical are his proposals for reform. Delany is no exception.

25 Delany, *Colored People of the United States*, p. 48.

26 Delany, *Colored People of the United States*, p. 197.

27 Delany, *Colored People of the United States*, pp. 184–5.

28 Delany, *Colored People of the United States*, p. 185.

29 Delany, *Colored People of the United States*, p. 213.

30 Delany, *Colored People of the United States*, p. 211.

31 Delany, *Colored People of the United States*, p. 211.

32 Delany, *Colored People of the United States*, p. 171.

33 Delany, *Colored People of the United States*, p. 173.

34 Delany, *Colored People of the United States*, p. 205.

35 Delany, *Colored People of the United States*, p. 214.

36 Only once, in 1861, did Douglass ever seriously entertain the possibility that emigration was a means to black elevation, when he planned to visit Haiti to see whether it was a suitable destination. *Douglass' Monthly*, Jan. 1861. This should be distinguished from his endorsement of emigration out of the South to "other parts of the country" in 1886. See *The Life and Writings of Frederick Douglass*, ed. Philip S. Foner, vol. 4 (New York: International Publishers, 1975), pp. 437–8.

37 Howard Brotz (ed.), *Negro Social and Political Thought 1850–1920* (New York: Basic Books, 1966), p. 329.

38 Brotz, *Negro Social and Political Thought*, p. 307.

39 Brotz, *Negro Social and Political Thought*, p. 291.

40 Brotz, *Negro Social and Political Thought*, p. 130. I have explored the implications of this in "Dignity, Slavery and the 13th Amendment," in Michael Myer and William Parent (eds), *Human Dignity, the Bill of Rights and Constitutional Values* (Ithaca: Cornell University Press, 1992).

41 Locke, *Two Treatises*, Bk. II, ch. II, Sects. 4, 5, 6, 11, 12, etc.

42 Locke, *Two Treatises*, Bk. II, ch. II, Sect. 4.

43 Locke, *Two Treatises*.

44 *Life and Writings of Frederick Douglass*, vol. 1, pp. 136, 147, 162–4.

45 *Life and Writings of Frederick Douglass*, vol. 1, p. 157.

46 Locke, *Two Treatises*, Bk. II, ch. IX, Sect. 124, p. 351.

47 John Locke, *An Essay Concerning Human Understanding* (Oxford: Oxford University Press, 1975), Bk. I, ch. IV, Sect. 24, pp. 101–2.

48 John Locke, *Questions concerning the Law of Nature*, eds Robert Horwitz, Jenny Strauss Clay, Diskin Clay (Ithaca: Cornell University Press, 1990), pp. 109, 111. See also page 119 where Locke maintains that we know the law of nature by the "light of nature," which means that the Law of Nature is a "truth whose knowledge man can, by the right use of those faculties with which he is provided by nature . . . obtain by himself and without the help of another." On pages 135 and 137, however, he notes that the law of nature is "not so easily apprehended" and "very few" know it.

49 Locke, *Essay concerning Human Understanding*, Bk. IV, ch. XX, p. 708.

50 Locke, *Essay concerning Human Understanding*, pp. 707–8. No doubt this was supported by his theory of property which justified vast inequalities.

51 Frederick Douglass, *My Bondage and My Freedom* (New York: Dover, 1969), p. 253.

52 Douglass, *My Bondage and My Freedom*, p. 260.

53 Douglass, *My Bondage and My Freedom*, p. 251.

54 *Life and Writings of Frederick Douglass*, vol. 2, p. 534. See also p. 287 where he wrote that the slave's submission "becomes an argument in the mouths of the community, that Negroes are, by Nature, only fit for slavery; that slavery is their normal condition."

55 *Life and Writings of Frederick Douglass*, p. 140.

56 *Life and Writings of Frederick Douglass*, vol. 1, p. 157.

57 *Life and Writings of Frederick Douglass*, p. 157.

58 *Life and Writings of Frederick Douglass*, vol. 2, p. 534.

59 *Life and Writings of Frederick Douglass*, pp. 534–5.

60 *Life and Times of Frederick Douglass: The Complete Autobiography* (New York: Collier Books, 1962), p. 143. See also *Life and Writings of Frederick Douglass*, vol. 3, pp. 342–3. I have tried to assess the force of this argument and given a more thorough account of the relationship between Locke and Douglass in "Radical Implications of Lockean Moral Theory: The Case of Frederick Douglass," read at the American Philosophical Association, Pacific Division Meeting, San Francisco, April 1991.

61 *Life and Writings of Frederick Douglass*, vol. 2, p. 140.

62 *Life and Writings of Frederick Douglass*, vol. 2, p. 140.

63 *Life and Writings of Frederick Douglass*, vol. 1, p. 157.

64 *Life and Times of Frederick Douglass*, p. 143.

12

Universal Dimensions of Black Struggle I: Black Revolution

Malcolm X

Friends and enemies: Tonight I hope that we can have a little fireside chat with as few sparks as possible being tossed around. Especially because of the very explosive condition that the world is in today. Sometimes, when a person's house is on fire and someone comes in yelling fire, instead of the person who is awakened by the yell being thankful, he makes the mistake of charging the one who awakened him with having set the fire. I hope that this little conversation tonight about the black revolution won't cause many of you to accuse us of igniting it when you find it at your doorstep. . . .

During recent years there has been much talk about a population explosion. Whenever they are speaking of the population explosion, in my opinion

---

On April 8, 1964, Malcolm X gave a speech on "The Black Revolution" at a meeting sponsored by the Militant Labor Forum at Palm Gardens in New York. This forum is connected with *The Militant*, a socialist weekly, which Malcolm considered "one of the best newspapers any-where." The audience was around three-quarters white. Most of it responded favorably to the talk. There were some sharp exchanges during the discussion period between the speaker and white liberals who resented his attacks on liberalism and the Democratic Party and tried to pin the label of hatemonger on him.

The talk gave Malcolm an opportunity for a fuller presentation of his arguments for internationalizing the black struggle by indicting the United States government before the United Nations for racism. It is notable also for his statement that a "bloodless revolution" was still possible in the United States under certain circumstances.

From Malcolm X, *Malcolm X Speaks* (1965), copyright © 1965, 1989 by Betty Shabazz and Pathfinder Press; reproduced by kind permission of Pathfinder Press.

they are referring primarily to the people in Asia or in Africa – the black, brown, red, and yellow people. It is seen by people of the West that, as soon as the standard of living is raised in Africa and Asia, automatically the people begin to reproduce abundantly. And there has been a great deal of fear engendered by this in the minds of the people of the West, who happen to be, on this earth, a very small minority.

In fact, in most of the thinking and planning of whites in the West today, it's easy to see the fear in their minds, conscious minds and subconscious minds, that the masses of dark people in the East, who already outnumber them, will continue to increase and multiply and grow until they eventually overrun the people of the West like a human sea, a human tide, a human flood. And the fear of this can be seen in the minds, in the actions, of most of the people here in the West in practically everything that they do. It governs their political views and it governs their economic views and it governs most of their attitudes toward the present society.

I was listening to Dirksen, the senator from Illinois, in Washington, DC, filibustering the civil-rights bill; and one thing that he kept stressing over and over and over was that if this bill is passed, it will change the social structure of America. Well, I know what he's getting at, and I think that most other people today, and especially our people, know what is meant when these whites, who filibuster these bills, express fears of changes in the social structure. Our people are beginning to realize what they mean.

Just as we can see that all over the world one of the main problems facing the West is race, likewise here in America today, most of your Negro leaders as well as the whites agree that 1964 itself appears to be one of the most explosive years yet in the history of America on the racial front, on the racial scene. Not only is this racial explosion probably to take place in America, but all of the ingredients for this racial explosion in America to blossom into a world-wide racial explosion present themselves right here in front of us. America's racial powder keg, in short, can actually fuse or ignite a world-wide powder keg.

There are whites in this country who are still complacent when they see the possibilities of racial strife getting out of hand. You are complacent simply because you think you outnumber the racial minority in this country; what you have to bear in mind is wherein you might outnumber us in this country, you don't outnumber us all over the earth.

Any kind of racial explosion that takes place in this country today, in 1964, is not a racial explosion that can be confined to the shores of America. It is a racial explosion that can ignite the racial powder keg that exists all over the planet that we call earth. I think that nobody would disagree that the dark masses of Africa and Asia and Latin America are already seething with bitterness, animosity, hostility, unrest, and impatience with the racial intolerance that they themselves have experienced at the hands of the white West.

And just as they have the ingredients of hostility toward the West in general, here we also have 22 million African-Americans, black, brown, red, and yellow people, in this country who are also seething with bitterness and impatience and hostility and animosity at the racial intolerance not only of the white West but of white America in particular.

And by the hundreds of thousands today we find our own people have become impatient, turning away from your white nationalism, which you call democracy, toward the militant, uncompromising policy of black nationalism. I point out right here that as soon as we announced we were going to start a black nationalist party in this country, we received mail from coast to coast, especially from young people at the college level, the university level, who expressed complete sympathy and support and a desire to take an active part in any kind of political action based on black nationalism, designed to correct or eliminate immediately evils that our people have suffered here for 400 years.

The black nationalists to many of you may represent only a minority in the community. And therefore you might have a tendency to classify them as something insignificant. But just as the fuse is the smallest part or the smallest piece in the powder keg, it is yet that little fuse that ignites the entire powder keg. The black nationalists to you may represent a small minority in the so-called Negro community. But they just happen to be composed of the type of ingredient necessary to fuse or ignite the entire black community.

And this is one thing that whites – whether you call yourselves liberals or conservatives or racists or whatever else you might choose to be – one thing that you have to realize is, where the black community is concerned, although the large majority you come in contact with may impress you as being moderate and patient and loving and long-suffering and all that kind of stuff, the minority who you consider to be Muslims or nationalists happen to be made of the type of ingredient that can easily spark the black community. This should be understood. Because to me a powder keg is nothing without a fuse.

1964 will be America's hottest year; her hottest year yet; a year of much racial violence and much racial bloodshed. But it won't be blood that's going to flow only on one side. The new generation of black people that have grown up in this country during recent years are already forming the opinion, and it's a just opinion, that if there is to be bleeding, it should be reciprocal – bleeding on both sides.

It should also be understood that the racial sparks that are ignited here in America today could easily turn into a flaming fire abroad, which means it could engulf all the people of this earth into a giant race war. You cannot confine it to one little neighborhood, or one little community, or one little country. What happens to a black man in America today happens to the black man in Africa. What happens to a black man in America and Africa happens to the black man in Asia and to the man down in Latin America. What happens to one of us today happens to all of us. And when this is realized, I think that the whites – who are intelligent even if they aren't moral or aren't just or aren't impressed by legalities – those who are intelligent will realize that when they touch this one, they are touching all of them, and this in itself will have a tendency to be a checking factor.

The seriousness of this situation must be faced up to. I was in Cleveland last night, Cleveland, Ohio. In fact I was there Friday, Saturday and yesterday. Last Friday the warning was given that this is a year of bloodshed, that the black man has ceased to turn the other cheek, that he has ceased to be nonviolent, that he has ceased to feel that he must be confined by all these restraints that are put upon him by white society in struggling for what white society says he was supposed to have had a hundred years ago.

So today, when the black man starts reaching out for what America says are his rights, the black man feels that he is within his rights – when he becomes the victim of brutality by those who are depriving him of his rights – to do whatever is necessary to protect himself. An example of this was taking place last night at this same time in Cleveland, where the police were putting water hoses on our people there and also throwing tear gas at them – and they met a hail of stones, a hail of rocks, a hail of bricks. A couple of weeks ago in Jacksonville, Florida, a young teen-age Negro was throwing Molotov cocktails.

Well, Negroes didn't do this ten years ago. But what you should learn from this is that they are waking up. It was stones yesterday, Molotov cocktails today; it will be hand grenades tomorrow and whatever else is available the next day. The seriousness of this situation must be faced up to. You should not feel that I am inciting someone to violence. I'm only warning of a powder-keg situation. You can take it or leave it. If you take the warning, perhaps you can still save yourself. But if you ignore it or ridicule it, well, death is already at your doorstep. There are 22 million African-Americans who are ready to fight for independence right here. When I say fight for independence right here, I don't mean any nonviolent fight, or turn-the-other-cheek fight. Those days are gone. Those days are over.

If George Washington didn't get independence for this country nonviolently, and if Patrick Henry didn't come up with a nonviolent statement, and you taught me to look upon them as patriots and heroes, then it's time for you to realize that I have studied your books well. . . .

1964 will see the Negro revolt evolve and merge into the world-wide black revolution that has been taking place on this earth since 1945. The so-called revolt will become a real black revolution. Now the black revolution has been taking place in Africa and Asia and Latin America; when I say black, I mean non-white – black, brown, red or yellow. Our brothers and sisters in Asia, who were colonized by the Europeans, our brothers and sisters in Africa, who were colonized by the Europeans, and in Latin America, the peasants, who were colonized by the Europeans, have been involved in a struggle since 1945 to get the colonialists, or the colonizing powers, the Europeans, off their land, out of their country.

This is a real revolution. Revolution is always based on land. Revolution is never based on begging somebody for an integrated cup of coffee. Revolutions are never fought by turning the other cheek. Revolutions are never based upon love-your-enemy and pray-for-those-who-spitefully-use-you. And revolutions are never waged singing "We Shall Overcome." Revolutions are based upon bloodshed. Revolutions are never compromising. Revolutions are never based upon negotiations. Revolutions are never based upon any kind of tokenism whatsoever. Revolutions are never even based upon that which is begging a corrupt society or a corrupt system to accept us into it. Revolutions overturn systems. And there is no system on this earth which has proven itself more corrupt, more criminal, than this system that in 1964 still colonizes 22 million African-Americans, still enslaves 22 million Afro-Americans.

There is no system more corrupt than a system that represents itself as the example of freedom, the example of democracy, and can go all over this earth telling other people how to straighten out their house, when you have citizens of this country who have to use bullets if they want to cast a ballot.

The greatest weapon the colonial powers have used in the past against our people has always been divide-and-conquer. America is a colonial power. She has colonized 22 million Afro-Americans by depriving us of first-class citizenship, by depriving us of civil rights, actually by depriving us of human rights. She has not only deprived us of the right to be a citizen, she has deprived us of the right to be human beings, the right to be recognized and respected as men and women. In this country the black can be fifty years old and he is still a "boy."

I grew up with white people. I was integrated before they even invented the word and I have never met white people yet – if you are around them long enough – who won't refer to you as a "boy" or a "gal," no matter how old you are or what school you came out of, no matter what your intellectual or professional level is. In this society we remain "boys."

So America's strategy is the same strategy as that which was used in the past by the colonial powers: divide and conquer. She plays one Negro leader against the other. She plays one Negro organization against the other. She makes us think we have different objectives, different goals. As soon as one Negro says something, she runs to this Negro and asks him, "What do you think about what he said?" Why, anybody can see through that today – except some of the Negro leaders.

All of our people have the same goals, the same objective. That objective is freedom, justice, equality. All of us want recognition and respect as human beings. We don't want to be integrationists. Nor do we want to be separationists. We want to be human beings. Integration is only a method that is used by some groups to obtain freedom, justice, equality and respect as human beings. Separation is only a method that is used by other groups to obtain freedom, justice, equality or human dignity.

Our people have made the mistake of confusing the methods with the objectives. As long as we agree on objectives, we should never fall out with each other just because we believe in different methods or tactics or strategy to reach a common objective.

We have to keep in mind at all times that we are not fighting for integration, nor are we fighting for separation. We are fighting for recognition as human beings. We are fighting for the right to live as free humans in this society. In fact, we are actually fighting for rights that are even greater than civil rights and that is human rights. . . .

Among the so-called Negroes in this country, as a rule the civil-rights groups, those who believe in civil rights, spend most of their time trying to prove they are Americans. Their thinking is usually domestic, confined to the boundaries of America, and they always look upon themselves as a minority. When they look upon themselves upon the American stage, the American stage is a white stage. So a black man standing on that stage in America automatically is in the minority. He is the underdog, and in his struggle he always uses an approach that is a begging, hat-in-hand, compromising approach.

Whereas the other segment or section in America, known as the black nationalists, are more interested in human rights than they are in civil rights. And they place more stress on human rights than they do on civil rights. The difference between the thinking and the scope of the Negroes who are involved in the human-rights struggle and those who are involved in the civil-rights struggle is that those so-called Negroes involved in the human-rights struggle don't look upon themselves as Americans.

They look upon themselves as a part of dark mankind. They see the whole struggle not within the confines of the American stage, but they look upon the struggle on the world stage. And, in the world context, they see that the dark man outnumbers the white man. On the world stage the white man is just a microscopic minority.

So in this country you find two different types of Afro-Americans – the type who looks upon himself as a minority and you as the majority, because his scope is limited to the American scene; and then you have the type who looks upon himself as part of the majority and you as part of a microscopic minority. And this one uses a different approach in trying to struggle for his rights. He doesn't beg. He doesn't thank you for what you give him, because you are only giving him what he should have had a hundred years ago. He doesn't think you are doing him any favors.

He doesn't see any progress that he has made since the Civil War. He sees not one iota of progress because, number one, if the Civil War had freed him, he wouldn't need civil-rights legislation today. If the Emancipation Proclamation, issued by that great shining liberal called Lincoln, had freed him, he wouldn't be singing "We Shall Overcome" today. If the amendments to the Constitution had solved his problem, his problem wouldn't still be here today. And if the Supreme Court desegregation decision of 1954 was genuinely and sincerely designed to solve his problem, his problem wouldn't be with us today.

So this kind of black man is thinking. He can see where every maneuver that America has made, supposedly to solve this problem, has been nothing but political trickery and treachery of the worst order. Today he doesn't have any confidence in these so-called liberals. (I know that all that have come in here tonight don't call yourselves liberals. Because that's a nasty name today. It represents hypocrisy.) So these two different types of black people exist in the so-called Negro community and they are beginning to wake up and their awakening is producing a very dangerous situation.

You have whites in the community who express sincerity when they say they want to help. Well, how can they help? How can a white person help the black man solve his problem? Number one, you can't solve it for him. You can help him solve it, but you can't solve it for him today. One of the best ways that you can help him solve it is to let the so-called Negro, who has been involved in the civil-rights struggle, see that the civil-rights struggle must be expanded beyond the level of civil rights to human rights. Once it is expanded beyond the level of civil rights to the level of human rights, it opens the door for all of our brothers and sisters in Africa and Asia, who have their independence, to come to our rescue.

When you go to Washington, DC, expecting those crooks down there – and that's what they are – to pass some kind of civil-rights legislation to correct a very criminal situation, what you are doing is encouraging the black man, who is the victim, to take his case into the court that's controlled by the criminal that made him the victim. It will never be solved in that way. . . .

The civil-rights struggle involves the black man taking his case to the white man's court. But when he fights it at the human-rights level, it is a different situation. It opens the door to take Uncle Sam to the world court. The black man doesn't have to go to court to be free. Uncle Sam should be taken to court and made to tell why the black man is not free in a so-called free society. Uncle Sam should be taken into the United Nations and charged with violating the UN charter of human rights.

You can forget civil rights. How are you going to get civil rights with men like Eastland and men like Dirksen and men like Johnson? It has to be taken out of their hands and taken into the hands of those whose power and authority exceed theirs. Washington has become too corrupt. Uncle Sam has become bankrupt when it comes to a conscience – it is impossible for Uncle Sam to solve the problem of 22 million black people in this country. It is absolutely impossible to do it in Uncle Sam's courts – whether it is the Supreme Court or any other kind of court that comes under Uncle Sam's jurisdiction.

The only alternative that the black man has in America today is to take it out of Senator Dirksen's and Senator Eastland's and President Johnson's jurisdiction and take it downtown on the East River and place it before that body of men who represent international law, and let them know that the human rights of black people are being violated in a country that professes to be the moral leader of the free world.

Any time you have a filibuster in America, in the Senate, in 1964 over the rights of 22 million black people, over the citizenship of 22 million black people, or that will affect the freedom and justice and equality of 22 million black people, it's time for that government itself to be taken before a world court. How can you condemn South Africa? There are only 11 million of our people in South Africa, there are 22 million of them here. And we are receiving an injustice which is just as criminal as that which is being done to the black people of South Africa.

So today those whites who profess to be liberals – and as far as I am concerned it's just lip-profession – you understand why our people don't have civil rights. You're white. You can go and hang out with another white liberal and see how hypocritical they are. A lot of you sitting right here know that you've seen whites up in a Negro's face with flowery words, and as soon as that Negro walks away you listen to how your white friend talks. We have black people who can pass as white. We know how you talk.

We can see that it is nothing but a governmental conspiracy to continue to deprive the black people in this country of their rights. And the only way we will get these rights restored is by taking it out of Uncle Sam's hands. Take him to court and charge him with genocide, the mass murder of millions of black people in this country – political murder, economic murder, social murder, mental murder. This is the crime that this government has committed, and if you yourself don't do something about it in time, you are going to open the doors for something to be done about it from outside forces.

I read in the paper yesterday where one of the Supreme Court justices, Goldberg, was crying about the violation of human rights of three million Jews in the Soviet Union. Imagine this. I haven't got anything against Jews, but that's their problem. How in the world are you going to cry about problems on the other side of the world when you haven't got the problems straightened out here? How can the plight of three million Jews in Russia be qualified to be taken to the United Nations by a man who is a justice in this Supreme Court, and is supposed to be a liberal, supposed to be a friend of black people, and hasn't opened up his mouth one time about taking the plight of black people down here to the United Nations? . . .

If Negroes could vote south of the – yes, if Negroes could vote south of the Canadian border – south South, if Negroes could vote in the southern part of the South, Ellender wouldn't be the head of the Agricultural and Forestry Committee, Richard Russell wouldn't be head of the Armed Services Committee, Robertson of Virginia wouldn't be head of the Banking and Currency Committee. Imagine that, all of the banking and currency of the government is in the hands of a cracker.

In fact, when you see how many of these committee men are from the South, you can see that we have nothing but a cracker government in

Washington, DC. And their head is a cracker president. I said a cracker president. Texas is just as much a cracker state as Mississippi. . . .

The first thing this man did when he came in office was invite all the big Negroes down for coffee. James Farmer was one of the first ones, the head of CORE. I have nothing against him. He's all right – Farmer, that is. But could that same president have invited James Farmer to Texas for coffee? And if James Farmer went to Texas, could he have taken his white wife with him to have coffee with the president? Any time you have a man who can't straighten out Texas, how can he straighten out the country? No, you're barking up the wrong tree.

If Negroes in the South could vote, the Dixiecrats would lose power. When the Dixiecrats lost power, the Democrats would lose power. A Dixiecrat lost is a Democrat lost. Therefore the two of them have to conspire with each other to stay in power. The Northern Dixiecrat puts all the blame on the Southern Dixiecrat. It's a con game, a giant political con game. The job of the Northern Democrat is to make the Negro think that he is our friend. He is always smiling and wagging his tail and telling us how much he can do for us if we vote for him. But at the same time that he's out in front telling us what he's going to do, behind the door he's in cahoots with the Southern Democrat setting up the machinery to make sure he'll never have to keep his promise.

This is the conspiracy that our people have faced in this country for the past hundred years. And today you have a new generation of black people who have come on the scene, who have become disenchanted with the entire system, who have become disillusioned over the system, and who are ready now and willing to do something about it.

So, in my conclusion, in speaking about the black revolution, America today is at a time or in a day or at an hour where she is the first country on this earth that can actually have a bloodless revolution. In the past, revolutions have been bloody. Historically you just don't have a peaceful revolution. Revolutions are bloody, revolutions are violent, revolutions cause bloodshed and death follows in their paths. America is the only country in history in a position to bring about a revolution without violence and bloodshed. But America is not morally equipped to do so.

Why is America in a position to bring about a bloodless revolution? Because the Negro in this country holds the balance of power, and if the Negro in this country were given what the Constitution says he is supposed to have, the added power of the Negro in this country would sweep all of the racists and the segregationism out of office. It would change the entire political structure of the country. It would wipe out the Southern segregationism that now controls America's foreign policy, as well as America's domestic policy.

And the only way without bloodshed that this can be brought about is that the black man has to be given full use of the ballot in every one of the fifty states. But if the black man doesn't get the ballot, then you are going to be faced with another man who forgets the ballot and starts using the bullet.

Revolutions are fought to get control of land, to remove the absentee landlord and gain control of the land and the institutions that flow from that land. The black man has been in a very low condition because he has had no control whatsoever over any land. He has been a beggar economically, a beggar politically, a beggar socially, a beggar even when it comes to trying to get some education. The past type of mentality, that was developed in this colonial system among our people, today is being overcome. And as the young ones come up, they know what they want. And as they listen to your beautiful preaching about democracy and all those other flowery words, they know what they're supposed to have.

So you have a people today who not only know what they want, but also know what they are supposed to have. And they themselves are creating another generation that is coming up that not only will know what it wants and know what it should have, but also will be ready and willing to do whatever is necessary to see that what they should have materializes immediately. Thank you.

Universal Dimensions of Black Struggle II: Human Rights, Civil Rights

Malcolm X

[INTERVIEWER]

One question that I've wondered about – in several of your lectures you've stressed the idea that the struggle of your people is for human rights rather than civil rights. Can you explain a bit what you mean by that?

MALCOLM X:

Civil rights actually keeps the struggle within the domestic confines of America. It keeps it under the jurisdiction of the American government, which means that as long as our struggle for what we're seeking is labeled civil rights, we can only go to Washington, DC, and then we rely upon either the Supreme Court, the President or the Congress or the senators. These senators – many of them are racists. Many of the congressmen are racists. Many of the judges are racists and oftentimes the president himself is a very shrewdly camouflaged racist. And so we really can't get meaningful redress for our grievances when we are depending upon these grievances being redressed just within the jurisdiction of the United States government.

On the other hand, human rights go beyond the jurisdiction of this government. Human rights are international. Human rights are something that a man has by dint of his having been born. The

labeling of our struggle in this country under the title civil rights of the past 12 years has actually made it impossible for us to get outside help. Many foreign nations, many of our brothers and sisters on the African continent who have gotten their independence, have restrained themselves, have refrained from becoming vocally or actively involved in our struggle for fear that they would be violating US protocol, that they would be accused of getting involved in America's domestic affairs.

On the other hand, when we label it human rights, it internationalizes the problem and puts it at a level that makes it possible for any nation or any people anywhere on this earth to speak out in behalf of our human rights struggle.

So we feel that by calling it civil rights for the past 12 years, we've actually been barking up the wrong tree, that ours is a problem of *human* rights.

Plus, if we have our human rights, our civil rights are automatic. If we're respected as a human being, we'll be respected as a citizen; and in this country the black man not only is not respected as a citizen, he is not even respected as a human being.

And the proof is that you find in many instances people can come to this country from other countries – they can come to this country from behind the Iron Curtain – and despite the fact that they come here from these other places, they don't have to have civil-rights legislation passed in order for their rights to be safeguarded.

No new legislation is necessary for foreigners who come here to have their rights safeguarded.

The Constitution is sufficient, but when it comes to the black men who were born here – whenever we are asking for our rights, they tell us that new legislation is necessary.

Well, we don't believe that. The Organization of Afro-American Unity feels that as long as our people in this country confine their struggle within the limitations and under the jurisdiction of the United States government, we remain within the confines of the vicious system that has done nothing but exploit and oppress us ever since we've been here. So we feel that our only real hope is to make known that our problem is not a Negro problem or an American problem but rather, it has become a human problem, a world problem, and it has to be attacked at the world level, at a level at which all segments of humanity can intervene in our behalf.

13

Philosophy, Politics, and Power: An Afro-American Perspective

Cornel West

Is it a mere coincidence that the major philosophical thinkers in the modern West – Marx, Kierkegaard, and Nietzsche in the nineteenth century and Wittgenstein, Heidegger, and Derrida in the twentieth century – call for an end to philosophy? What do these post-philosophical voices have to do with Afro-Americans engaged in the philosophical enterprise?

I suggest that the calls for an end to philosophy are symptomatic of fundamental cultural transformations in the modern West. These transformations primarily consist of three salient developments in modern Western culture. First, the demythologizing of the institution of science – still in its rudimentary stage – renders the status of philosophy problematic. This demythologizing is not a discrediting of the achievements of science, but an undermining of its legitimacy regarding its alleged monopoly on truth and reality. Second, the demystifying of the role of authority makes the function of philosophy suspect. This demystifying is not simply a revolt against intellectual, social, and political authority, it calls into question the very notion of and need for authority. Third, the disclosure of a deep sense of impotence tends to support the view that philosophy is superfluous. This disclosure is not only a recognition of dominant ironic forms of thinking and narcissistic forms of living, but a pervasive despair about the present and lack of hope for the future.

These three developments require that philosophy – both as a professional discipline and as a mode of thinking – either redefine itself or bring itself to an end. In this historical moment, Afro-Americans engaged in the philosophical enterprise can contribute to the redefining of philosophy principally by revealing why and showing how philosophy is inextricably linked to politics and power – to structures of domination and mechanisms of control. This important task does not call for an end to philosophy. Rather it situates philosophical activity in the midst of personal and collective struggles in the present.

Revaluations of the Philosophical Past

In order to understand the prevailing crisis of philosophy in the modern West, it is necessary to examine the beginnings of modern Western philosophy. Modern philosophy emerged alongside modern science. The basic aim of modern philosophy was to promote and encourage the legitimacy of modern science. Descartes, the famous mathematician and scientist, was the father of modern philosophy. He tried to show that modern science not merely provides more effective ways of coping with the world, but also yields objective, accurate, value-free copies of the world. Descartes attempted to do this by putting forward rational foundations for knowledge independent of theological grounds and moral concerns. For the first time, epistemological matters became the center around which philosophical reflection evolved. Henceforth, the principal thrust of modern philosophy would be toward the justification of and rationale for belief. Modern philosophy became a disinterested quest for certainty regulated by a conception of truth that stands outside the world of politics and power – a prop that undergirds the claims of modern science.

The emergence of the capitalist mode of production, with its atomistic individualism and profit-oriented dispositions toward nature and people, partly accounts for the way in which Descartes chose to defend modern science. This defense takes the form of a justification of knowledge that starts with the self-consciousness of the individual, the immediate awareness of the subject, the *cogitatio* of the ego. Descartes's methodological doubt, a search for certainty that begins in radical doubt, rests upon the only mental activity that cannot be doubted: the activity of doubt itself. In his view, such doubting presupposes an agent who doubts, that is, a thinking individual, subject, or ego. Only by validly inferring from this indubitable activity of doubting – the only certainty available – can claims about God, the world, and the bodily self be justified. Like the new literary genre of early capitalist culture – the novel – Descartes's viewpoint supports the notion that we have access to, arrive at, and acquire knowledge of the world through the autonomous individual. Therefore, the primacy of the individual, subject, or ego who accurately copies the world or validly makes inferences about the world serves as the foundation of knowledge, the philosophical basis of modern science.

The obsession of the early modern philosophers with science (especially Newton) partly explains the empiricist twist given to Descartes's subjectivist turn in philosophy. For Locke, Berkeley, and Hume, the primacy of the thinking individual, subject, or ego remained, but experience (understood as sensations and perceptions) became the major candidate for the foundation of knowledge. Yet this ambitious project faltered. When Berkeley rejected the substantial self – the subject to which attributes are attached – and called on God to ground it as spirit, philosophical havoc set in. Hume, who had little philosophical use for God, explicitly articulated the skeptical result: the idea that knowledge has no empirical foundation. Instead, knowledge is but the (philosophical, unjustifiable) imaginative constructs enacted by thinking individuals, subjects, or egos. Yet these thinking individuals, subjects, or egos are but themselves bundles of sensations and perceptions. Hence the

subject and object of knowledge is rendered problematic – and modern philosophy found itself in a quandary.

Kant, the first modern professional philosopher in the West, rescued modern philosophy by providing transcendental grounds for knowledge and science. He reenacted the quest for certainty – the situating of the grounds for truth outside of politics and power – by locating the justification of what we know in the conditions for the possibility of knowing. These conditions are neither deductively arrived at nor empirically grounded. Rather they are transcendental in that they consist of the universal and necessary conceptual scheme people employ in order to know and hence have experience. Although Kant rejected the rationalist inference-making activity of Descartes, he deepened Descartes's subjectivist turn by locating the universal and necessary conceptual scheme in the thinking activity of the subject. Although Kant criticized the empiricist perspectives of Locke, Berkeley, and especially Hume, he accepted Hume's skepticism by holding that the universal and necessary conceptual scheme constitutes an objective world, but not the real world. In addition, Kant's architectonic project tried to link science, morals and aesthetics – Truth, Goodness, and Beauty – while arguing for their different foundations.

With the appearance of Hegel, modern philosophy drifted into a deep crisis. This was so primarily because of the emergence of historical consciousness. This consciousness was threatening to modern philosophy because it acknowledged the historical character of philosophy itself. This acknowledgment presented a major challenge to modern philosophy because it implied that the very aim of modern philosophy – the quest for certainty and search for foundations of knowledge – was an ahistorical enterprise. Hegel's historicizing of Kant's universal and necessity conceptual scheme questioned the very content and character of modern philosophy.

It is no accident that the first modern calls for the end of philosophy were made by the two major thinkers who labored under the shadow of Hegel: Kierkegaard and Marx. Both accepted Hegel's historicizing of the subjectivist turn in philosophy, his emphasis on activity, development, and process, his dialectical approach to understanding and transforming the world, and his devastating critiques of Cartesian and Kantian notions of substance, subject, and the self. Kierkegaard rejected Hegel's intellectualist attempt to link thought to concrete, human existence and put forward a profound existential dialectic of the self. Marx discarded Hegel's idealistic project of resolving the dominant form of alienation in the existing order and presented a penetrating materialistic dialectic of capitalist society. Both Kierkegaard and Marx understood philosophy as an antiquated, outmoded form of thinking, a mere fetter that impeded their particular praxis-oriented projects of redemption. Kierkegaard noted that, "philosophy is life's dry nurse, it can stay with us but not give milk." And Marx stated that, "philosophy stands in the same relation to the study of the actual world as masturbation to sexual love."

Afro-American philosophers should take heed of the radical antiphilosophical stances of Kierkegaard and Marx, not because they are right but rather because of the concerns that motivate their viewpoints. Both stress the value-laden character of philosophical reflection; the way in which such reflection not only serves particular class and personal interest, but also how it refuses to see itself as a form of praxis-in-the-world-of-politics-and-power. This refusal conceals the complex linkages of philosophical reflection to politics and power by defining itself as above and outside politics and power. By viewing itself as the queen of the disciplines that oversee the knowledge-claims of other disciplines, modern philosophy elides its this-worldly character, its role and function in the world of politics and power.

Despite Hegel's historicizing efforts, academic philosophers managed to overthrow Hegelianism, ignore Kierkegaard and Marx (both nonacademics!), and replace Hegelianism with the analytical realism of Bertrand Russell and G. E. Moore in England; the diverse forms of returns to Kant (neo-Kantianisms) and Descartes (phenomenology) in Germany; and the various modes of vitalism (Bergson) and religious-motivated conventionalism (Pierre Duhem) in France. The only kind of professional philosophizing that took Hegel seriously was Dewey's version of American pragmatism, yet even Dewey wrote as if Kierkegaard and Marx never lived. In short, the professionalization of modern philosophy in the West shielded the academy from the powerful antiphilosophical perspectives of post-Hegelian figures, especially that of Nietzsche.

Since Nietzsche is first and foremost a philosopher of power – who links philosophy to power, truth to strategic linguistic tropes, and thinking to coping techniques – he has never been welcomed in the philosophical academy. This is so primarily because – like Kierkegaard and Marx – his understanding of the power dimensions of knowledge and

the political aspects of philosophy calls into question the very conception of philosophy that legitimates philosophical reflection in the academy. Ironically, the recent developments in philosophy and literary theory – antirealism in ontology, antifoundationalism in epistemology, and the detranscendentalizing of the subject – were prefigured by Nietzsche.[1] Yet the relation of these developments to politics and power is ignored.

Repetition in the Post-Philosophical Present

The contemporary philosophical scene can be viewed as a repetition of Hegel's historicizing efforts – but with a difference. This crucial difference primarily consists of retranslating Hegel's stress on History as an emphasis on Language. The Hegelian notions of origins and ends of history, of homogeneous continuities in and overarching totalizing frameworks for history, are replaced by beginnings and random play of differences within linguistic systems, heterogeneous discontinuities in and antitotalizing deconstructions of linguistic discourses. This repetition of Hegel – the replacement of history with language – is mediated by three central-European processes in this century: the nihilistic Death-of-God perspective conjoined with Saussurean linguistics, which radically questions the meaning and value of human life (best portrayed in contemporary literature); the rise of fascism and totalitarianism, which tempers efforts for social change; and the sexual revolution, which unleashes hedonistic and narcissistic sensibilities on an unprecedented scale. These three processes circumscribe the repetition of Hegel within the perimeters of philosophical nihilism, political impotence, and hedonistic fanfare. Professional philosophy finds itself either radically historicized and linguisticized hence vanishing or holding on to the Kantian tradition for dear life.[2]

On a philosophical plane, the repetition of Hegel takes the form of an antirealism in ontology, antifoundationalism in epistemology, and a detranscendentalizing of the Kantian subject. The antirealism in ontology leaves us with changing descriptions and versions of the world, which come from various communities as responses to problematics, as fallible attempts to overcome specific situations and as means to satisfy particular needs and interests. The antifoundationalism in epistemology precludes notions of privileged representations that correctly correspond to the world, hence ground our knowledge; it leaves us with sets of transient social practices that facilitate our survival as individuals and members of society. The detranscendentalizing of the Kantian subject – the historical and linguistic situating of ourselves as knowers and doers – focuses our attention no longer on the mental activity of thinking individuals, but rather on the values and norms of historical and linguistic groups. Kierkegaard and Marx, like their master Hegel, held such antirealist, antifoundationalist, detranscendentalist views, but they did so with a sense of engagement in the present and hope for the future. The repetition of Hegel holds similar post-philosophical views yet despairs of the present and has little hope, if any, for the future.

This post-philosophical despair and hopelessness – with its concomitant forms of ironic and apocalyptic thinking and narcissistic living – is inextricably linked to the fundamental cultural transformations I noted earlier: the demythologizing of the institution of science, the demystifying of the role of authority, and the disclosure of a deep sense of impotence. Since modern philosophy at its inception was the handmaiden to modern science, it is not surprising that the demythologizing of science occurs alongside the vanishing of modern philosophy. Just as the Enlightenment era witnessed the slow replacement of the authority of the church with that of science, so we are witnessing a displacement of science, but there is no replacement as of yet. The *philosophes* of the Enlightenment – the propagandists for science and ideologues for laissez-faire capitalism – had a vision of the future; whereas the professional avant-gardists – propagandists against "bourgeois" science and ideologues against monopoly capitalism – rarely present a project for the future. The neo-Marxist Frankfurt School, including Max Horkheimer, Theodor Adorno, and Herbert Marcuse, along with creative followers like Stanley Aronowitz and Michel Foucault, are pioneers of this novel perspective of philosophy.[3] Yet, with the exception of Aronowitz and Marcuse at times, the hopelessness for the future is overwhelming. Nevertheless, these figures are much further along than their contemporaries, as illustrated by Quine's outdated neo-positivist veneration of physics or Rorty's nostalgic longing for pre-professional humanistic "conversation" among men and women of letters.

The demystifying of the role of authority – promoted by the "hermeneutics of suspicion" of Marx, Nietzsche, and Freud and encouraged by the antifoundationalism in contemporary philosophy – can be traced to the more general problem of the deep crisis of legitimacy in post-modern capitalist civilization. Of course, the breakdown of scientific, technocratic culture also affects the socialist world, but the crisis of legitimacy is in many ways a phenomenon rooted in the processes of monopoly capitalist societies. By undermining traditional forms of authority – church, family, school – owing to the profit-motivated promotion of hedonistic sensibilities, capitalist societies can legitimate themselves principally by satisfying the very needs they help activate. These societies keep the populace loyal to their authority primarily by "delivering the goods," often luxury consumer goods that are rendered attractive by means of ingenious advertising. These goods do not merely pacify the populace; they also come to be viewed as the basic reason, in contrast to moral, religious or political reasons, that people have for acquiescence to capitalist authority. Hence, the crisis of legitimacy – the undermining of the work ethic, the collapse of the family, anarchy in public schools, and the proliferation of sexually oriented advertisements, commercials, movies, and television shows – becomes part and parcel of the very legitimizing processes of monopoly capitalist societies.

The disclosure of a deep sense of impotence sits at the center of the post-philosophical present: the sense of reaching an historical dead end with no foreseeable way out and no discernible liberating projects or even credible visions in the near future. This disclosure is related to the detranscendentalizing of the Kantian subject in the sense that the emergence of the transcendental subject – the creative and conquering romantic hero – signifies the sense of optimistic triumph of early modern capitalist civilization. The detranscendentalizing of the subject portrays the sense of pessimistic tragedy of post-modern capitalist civilization, with the primary redemptive hope for this civilization, Marx's collective subject, the proletariat, remaining relatively dormant and muted.

The dominant forms of intellectual activity, especially philosophical reflection, enact this sense of impotence: analytical philosophy makes a fetish of technical virtuosity and uses it as a measure to regulate the intense careerism in the profession; antiacademic professional avant-gardists fiercely assault fellow colleagues and fervently attack notions of epistemological privilege yet remain relatively silent about racial, sexual, and class privilege in society at large; and poststructuralists perennially decenter prevailing discourses and dismantle philosophical and literary texts yet valorize a barren, ironic disposition by deconstructing, hence disarming and discarding, any serious talk about praxis. In this way, the repetition of Hegel is, from an Afro-American perspective, meretricious: attractive on a first glance but much less substantive after careful examination.

Recommendations for a Revolutionary Future

The principal task of the Afro-American philosopher is to keep alive the idea of a revolutionary future, a better future different from the deplorable present, a state of affairs in which the multifaceted oppression of Afro-Americans (and others) is, if not eliminated, alleviated. Therefore the Afro-American philosopher must preserve the crucial Hegelian (and deeply Christian) notions of negation and transformation of what is in light of a revolutionary not-yet.[4] The notions of negation and transformation – the pillars of the Hegelian process of *Aufhebung* – promote the activity of resistance to what is and elevate the praxis of struggle against existing realities. In this way, Afro-American philosophers must wage an intense intellectual battle in the form of recovering the revolutionary potential of Hegel against the ironic repetition of Hegel, which dilutes and downplays this potential. The revolutionary potential of Hegel – indigenously grounded in the prophetic religious and progressive secular practices of Afro-Americans – can be promoted by a serious confrontation with the Marxist tradition and, among others, the recent work of Michel Foucault.

Foucault's exorbitant reaction to his former vulgar Marxism and past Communist allegiances often leads him to embody the worst of the repetition of Hegel: precluding any talk about a better future and downplaying the activity of resistance and struggle in the present. Despite these limitations, certain aspects of Foucault's work can contribute to a revolutionary future, notably his attempt to construct "a new politics of truth." For Foucault, the Western will to truth has not been truthful about itself. Only with the appearance of Hegel and later Kierkegaard, Marx, and Nietzsche, has the this-worldly character of truth – its rootedness in politics and power – been disclosed and dissected. Foucault, who views his own work as

"philosophical fragments put to work in a historical field of problems," beings his philosophical reflections with two basic questions: How are the conditions for the possibility of knowledges – the rules, conventions, and operations that circumscribe fields of discourse wherein notions, metaphors, categories, and ideas are rendered intelligible and comprehensible – ensconced in particular sets of power-relations? How are these conditions articulated in discursive practices and elaborated (in the sense in which Antonio Gramsci defines this crucial term) in nondiscursive formations? These questions are answered neither by abstract philosophical arguments nor by systematic theoretical treatises, but rather by detailed analytical descriptions – containing arguments and explanations – that constitute a genealogy of moral and political technologies, a genealogy that lays bare the workings of structures of domination and mechanisms of control over human bodies. Foucault's genealogical approach eschews the philosophical past and shuns the ironic repetition of Hegel in the present; he writes a subversive history of this past and present by discerning and detaching "the power of truth from the forms of hegemony, social, economic, and cultural, within which it operates."[5]

Foucault's perspective can be valuable for Afro-American philosophers whose allegiance is to a revolutionary future. With the indispensable aid of sophisticated neo-Marxist analysis, Foucault's viewpoint can be creatively transformed and rendered fruitful for a genealogy of modern racism, in both its ideational and material forms. This genealogy would take the form of detailed, analytical descriptions of the battery of notions, categories, metaphors, and concepts that regulate the inception of modern discourse, a discourse that constituted the idea of white supremacy in a particular way (e.g. inaugurated the category of "race") and excluded the idea of black equality in beauty, culture, and character from its discursive field.[6] Unlike Foucault, this Afro-American genealogical approach also would put forward an Afro-American counter-discourse, in all its complexity and diversity, to the modern European racist discourse and examine and evaluate how the Afro-American response promotes or precludes a revolutionary future.[7] In addition, a more refined effort would even delve into the political content of Afro-American everyday life and disclose the multivarious Afro-American cultural elements that debilitate or facilitate an Afro-American revolutionary future.

If Afro-American philosophers are to make a

substantive contribution to the struggle for Afro-American freedom, it is imperative that we critically revaluate the grand achievements of the past philosophical figures in the West and avoid falling into their alluring ahistorical traps, traps that disarm Afro-American philosophers and render us mere colorful presences in the glass menagerie of the academy in monopoly capitalist USA. Afro-American philosophers must understand the repetition of Hegel in the present time as inescapable yet of highly limited value owing to its nihilistic outlooks; outlooks that implicitly presuppose luxury and explicitly preclude any serious talk about a future better than the inferno-like present. Lastly, Afro-American philosophers must articulate and elaborate recommendations for a revolutionary future. This articulation and elaboration requires a recovery of the revolutionary potential of Hegel, a deepening of the Marxist tradition, and a concrete grounding in the indigenous prophetic and progressive practices of Afro-Americans. This calling of Afro-American philosophers – this vocation of service – permits us to take our place alongside, not above, other committed Afro-Americans who continue to hold up the blood-stained banner, a banner that signifies the Afro-American struggle for freedom.

Notes

1 Cornel West, "Nietzsche's Prefiguration of Post-modern American Philosophy," *Boundary 2: A Journal of Postmodern Literature*, Special Nietzsche issue, vols. 9, 10, nos. 1, 3 (Fall–Winter 1980–1), pp. 241–70.

2 The most penetrating and provocative examination of these two options for contemporary philosophy is Richard Rorty's *Philosophy and the Mirror of Nature* (Princeton, 1979). For a sympathetic yet biting critique of this book, see my review in *Union Seminary Quarterly Review*, vol. 37, nos. 1, 2 (Fall–Winter 1981–2).

3 The central works on this subject are Max Horkheimer and Theodor Adorno, *Dialectic of Enlightenment* (New York, 1972); Herbert Marcuse, *One-Dimensional Man: Studies in the Ideology of Advanced Industrial Society* (Boston, 1964); Stanley Aronowitz, *The Crisis in Historical Materialism: Class, Politics and Culture in Marxist Theory* (New York, 1981); Michel Foucault, *Discipline and Punish: The Birth of the Prison*, trans.

Alan Sheridan (New York, 1977).

4 For a brief treatment of these two basic notions as a basis for prophetic Christian and progressive Marxist praxis, see Cornel West, *Prophesy Deliverance! An Afro-American Revolutionary Christianity* (Philadelphia, 1982), "Introduction: The Sources and Tasks of Afro-American Critical Thought."

5 Michel Foucault, *Power/Knowledge: Selected Interviews & Other Writings 1972–1977* (New York, 1980), p. 133.

6 For a rudimentary effort at such a genealogical approach, see Cornel West, *Prophesy Deliverance! An Afro-American Revolutionary Christianity*, chapter 2.

7 For a humble attempt at such a project, see Cornel West, "Philosophy and the Afro-American Experience," *The Philosophical Forum*, vol. IX, nos. 2–3 (Winter–Spring 1977–8), pp. 117–48, and, with additions and revisions, Cornel West, *Prophesy Deliverance! An Afro-American Revolutionary Christianity*, chapter 3.

Recommended Readings

Texts

Best, Steven, and Douglas Kellner. *Postmodern Theory*. New York: The Guilford Press, 1991.

Dreyfus, Hubert, and Paul Rabinow. *Michel Foucault: Beyond Structuralism and Hermeneutics*. Chicago: University of Chicago, 1983.

Foucault, Michel. *The Archaeology of Knowledge*. New York: Pantheon, 1972.

Giddens, A. "Jürgen Habermas." In *The Return of Grand Theory in the Human Sciences*, ed. Q. Skinner, 121–39. Cambridge: Cambridge University Press, 1985.

Ingram, D. *Habermas and the Dialectic of Reason*. New Haven, CT: Yale University Press, 1987.

McCarthy, T. *The Critical Theory of Jürgen Habermas*. Cambridge, MA: MIT Press, 1978.

Rabinow, Paul, ed. *Foucault Reader*. New York: Pantheon Books, 1984.

White, S. K. *The Recent Work of Jürgen Habermas: Reason, Justice, and Modernity*. Cambridge: Cambridge University Press, 1989.

Feminist Perspective

Fraser, N. "What's Critical about Critical Theory?: The Case of Habermas and Gender." In *Feminism as Critique: On the Politics of Gender*, ed. S. Benhabib and D. Cornell. Minneapolis, MN: University of Minnesota Press, 1987.

Sawicki, Jana. "Foucault and Feminism." *Hypatia* (1990).

Cornel West

Multicultural Perspective

Allen Norm, ed. *African-American Humanism*. Buffalo: Prometheus Books, 1991.

Harris, Leonard, ed. *Philosophy Born of Struggle*. Dubuque: Kendall/Hunt, 1983.

PART IV

Ethics

14

"Mutumin Kirki": The Concept of the Good Man in Hausa

Anthony H. M. Kirk-Greene

Not that there is anything new in the idea of defining the good man. Every culture and every century – often every generation, too, though sometimes those of the matinee idol variety are as transient as literally that – has its own concept of the standards of good behaviour, of what is to be admired and what abhorred. Yet by and large, within a single culture the fundamentals of what is decent and decorous possess the elements of continuity. What of an African concept of the good man? Among the Hausa-speakers of Nigeria, what is really meant by the cynosure of *shi mutumin kirki ne*, "he's a good man"? What are the implications of the frequently heard antithesis of *ba shi da kirki*, "he has no *kirki*", *no intrinsic goodness of character*? What, in short, did the Kano poet have in mind, when, in his song to celebrate Nigeria's independence, he described Hausaland as *kasar mutan kirki*, the land of the *kirki* people?"[1]

The Hausa of Nigeria require no introduction.[2] In our delineation of the societal hero in Hausaland, we shall first identify a number of elements in his moral make-up and then seek to illustrate these by searching for outstanding exponents of those virtues down the ages. To do this, we shall be drawing our data from various sources: language and literature, traditions, written and oral, proverbs, and politics, and the records of a thousand years of Hausa history.[3]

From *The Substance of African Philosophy*, ed. C. S. Momoh (1989); reproduced by kind permission of African Philosophy Projects Publications.

In Hausaland the fundamental locus of *kirki*, of a man's intrinsic goodness, rests in the *hali*, his character. *Kirki* is thus an inner quality, or an accumulation of qualities. It is not a physical attribute. The warrior-hero of Hausaland may be seven feet tall, with the heart of a lion and the strength of a bull-elephant, of heroic stature at every turn, and yet never qualify for recognition as *mutumin kirki*. Another man may earn that very admiration, though he be as modest as an ostrich and meeker than a gazelle. Physical stature and the heroic qualities alone are no index to the moral stature nor any warranty of *kirki*, of inner worth. It is in the character that *kirki* reposes, so that *halin mutum*, a man's character, is at once the wellspring of his virtue and the mirror of his moral make-up. It is what the great dramatists of the *grand siècle* explored in their stage-heroes as *la complexion*, a constant pre-occupation with the moral integrity of "human beings realizing their aspiration in action . . . in the idiom of *la solide vertu*.[4] For the Hausa this *hali*, the character, is all-important. "Character is a line drawn on a rock," runs one of the most quoted of Hausa proverbs, "nobody can erase it."[5] In parenthesis let me say that I make no apology for the frequent recourse to proverbs as corroboratory data in the first half of this paper. In Hausa, as elsewhere in Africa, proverbial lore embodies a language group's cultural heritage. More than this, in the absence of a vigorous written literature, proverbs may serve as the guardian and the carrier of a nation's philosophy and genius. They are an exponent of group culture, Sapir's "traditional body of social usage." In Hausaland, proverbs are constantly on the lips of adults, amply fulfiling Professor Ida Ward's definition of its place in West African society:

> In law, it seems to classify a court-case, to provide a precedent, to generalize a particular action; in family life, it regulates the attitude of one member of the family to another; it helps in the education of children; and in social intercourse it smooths out difficulties and adds pith to the well-known accomplishment of the African conversation.[6]

Another popular saying in Hausaland is that character is like a tail: "If the inner character is sound," a tongue-twisting aphorism assures us, "the exterior will be pleasing; but if it is not then the pleasing exterior is nothing but a sham."[7] As the syntax of this last proverb indicates, *hali* without any qualifying epithet presupposes "good" character. With an accompanying epithet, that character may be raised to the excellence of *tana da kyan hali*, "she has a sweet disposition," or to the reprehensible *mugun hali a gare shi*, "he has a nasty nature," and the summary dismissal of *ba shi da hali* for one who has absolutely no "character" at all.

Having established the central position of character in evaluating the *beau ideal* of traditional Hausa society, we may now proceed to isolate the principle distinguishing "characteristics" (*halaye*) that comprise the "character" (hali) of *mutumin kirki*, our "man of approved behavioural qualities." The signals of such *kirki* can be encoded at a number of levels but they all relate to the message of human interacting. If *hali* is restricted to the quality of internal goodness – and proverbial lore implies that it may be innate too – it is always interpreted within an external context. You will note that in this anatomy of *mutumin kirki* I shall frequently emphasize and refer to his social context. Let me explain. First, I am differentiating the national hero from the good man. In Hausaland, I would suggest that the hero need not simultaneously be the good man but that the good man will always be the hero of his community. The framework is exclusively the societal context. Secondly, so ubiquitous has the patron/client structure of traditional Hausa society been that it sometimes seems to me one might justifiably say of it that everyone's client is someone else's patron. Thus when we talk of a man's reputation as *mutumin kirki*, we need to leave ample room for the fact that in the

display of some of the characteristics of the good man in Hausa discussed later he may well be consciously underwriting his status as A's patron or B's client. Whatever the case, in the role of both patron and client, the repute of *mutumin kirki* never comes amiss in Hausaland. It is in social intercourse alone, in relationships with his fellow men, that the accolade of *mutumin kirki* is awarded by the Hausa. It was, I think, Ralph Waldo Emerson who said that men of character were the conscience of the society to which they belong: it is a sentiment equally worthy of a *malam*, the Hausa man of letters.

The first stratum in the concept of the goodman is not a criterion confined to his image in Hausaland. But if the gift of *gaskiya*, "truth", is an item of universal esteem, the frequency of its occurrence in Hausa conversation is noticeably higher than in any equivalent Western situation. Significantly, it was the theme chosen by Alhaji Abubakar Imam, the father of modern Hausa literature, for the title of the first vernacular newspaper in Hausaland: *Gaskiya ta fi kwabo*, literally "truth is worth more than a penny."[8] The priority of truthfulness as the hallmark of the good man has been long sanctioned by Hausa aphoristic lore. Maxims asserting that "truth is stronger than an iron horse" are complemented by those declaring truth to exceed the powers of any known *laya*, the amulet or conventional charm of Hausaland. Equally, the *tatsuniyoyi* or traditional fables of Hausaland emphasize the supremacy of truth. The title of one asserts that "A lie can give more pain than a spear";[9] another declares as the acme of good behaviour the man who is endowed with truth of the purest kind, *yana da salihiyar gaskiya*. In the same vein, a favourite modern Hausa novel assures the readers that nothing can ever harm the man who takes honesty as his tenet. Often the force of this virtue of *gaskiya* shifts from truth to reliability, a nuance that becomes especially clear in the compound form of *bangaskiya*, literally "the giving of truth" and hence the idea of "trustworthiness." Thus a Hausa will commend the best among his fellow men by describing him as *bangaskiya a gare shi kwarai*, "he is utterly reliable", thereby allowing us to read into his judgement a full measure of what the moralists of the Central Victorian era knew as "honesty of character." Indeed, it was that greatest of all nineteenth-century dominoes, Dr Thomas Arnold of Rugby (whose brooding spirit we were perpetually, and proudly, aware of at Tom Brown's a hundred years later), who defined truth as "moral transparency."

But if the possession of truth is not exclusive to

the make-up of the good man in Hausaland, the virtue of *amana* does have peculiar force in Hausa society. *Amana*, in its societal context, goes beyond its original Arabic sense and Hausa surface definition of "friendliness." Its deep-structure meaning of "truth" is hinted at in the vernacular rendering of the United Nations concept of "Trust Territory," *Kasar Amana*. It embraces a notion of the sanctity of something – or indeed someone – given in trust, a belief so strongly perceived among the Hausa that both the giver and the one charged therewith are sensitive to the awesomeness of the responsibility. A whole section of the standard school texts in Hausaland is given over to the solemnity of *rikon amana*, "on keeping one's word." And in it the conclusion is unambiguously spelled out, namely that *gaskiya* and *amana*, truth and trust, must be the standard of children everywhere. They are the fundamental virtues that earn respect in life and reward on the day of resurrection. Elsewhere in the same text the moral is drawn, no less unequivocally, that *rikon amana*, the capacity to be trusted and keep faith, forms the basis of all social behaviours. By extension the sin of *cin amana*, to embezzle or convert something entrusted to one's care (not necessarily cash) ranks as an exceedingly grave blemish of character among the Hausa. It goes beyond the conventional disapproval of one who breaks a promise, and the disgrace is accordingly more dire. For instance, we learn from one of the greatest of Hausa autobiographies how a Zaria man accused of misappropriating a sum of money lent him by a kola-nut seller falsely swore his innocence. Within a week he became raving mad, and in remorse he sang, as he staggered around the market-place.

I am a good-for-nothing.
I have broken trust, I ate it (*na ci amana*)
I am a wanderer.

The narrative goes on:

When they reached the gate of Zaria, he said: "leave me to say my prayers. In thirty days I shall die". *Shi ke nan*, that was that, thirty days later, he died. He used to keep saying "I broke trust, I broke it. I broke faith . . ." Such is the madness of breaking faith.[11]

With the endorsement of our next virtue, that of generosity, we are once more back to the universal requirements of societal esteem; though once again

among the Hausa the expectation of personal bountifulness often seems larger than life. As might be anticipated in a peasant society, where historically the majority of people have been accustomed to the caprices of the seasons' cycle and are resolutely inured to the hazards of subsistence farming dependent thereon, considerable importance attaches to the trait of generosity; and to its antithesis, the social sin of niggardliness. Both terms are loaded in Hausa, commendation of the one being matched by contempt for the other. *Karamci*, open-handed generosity, is contrasted with the tight-fisted miserliness of *rowa*; and both qualities are accentuated when, as is so often the case among the status-conscious Hausa,[12] either is practised by *manya manya*, "the big shots." While the big spender is adulated as *mai-baiwa*, "he who gives freely," and his respect and status are institutionalized in such proverbs as "true greatness is identified by generosity," his opposite member among the big men of a community is searingly anathematized in the eliptical maxim, *laifin baba bowa*, "an important man's sin is avarice." The close-fisted man stands roundly condemned in Hausa. One aphorism warns that it is a waste of breath to beg from a man acknowledged to be a miser; another implies that the man who can make gifts but does not is far more despicable than one who does not because he cannot. The miser, *bahili*, is the butt of Hausa society (with little of the comic relief of the curmudgeonly Scrooge) and is heaped with opprobrium for *rowa*, his stinginess. Characteristically, there exist in Hausa a colourful stigmatic vocabulary for niggardliness, including words for that most despicable of men, he who is barbarous enough to eat a meal without offering to share it with those present, and again for the – *horrible dictu* – furtive act of deliberately eating alone so as to avoid sharing one's food.[13] "Avarice," as the Kano begger ministrels remind us, "is not a trait that calls for honour."

In this context of generosity as part of the concept of the good man in Hausa, I am purposely separating the social expectation of *baiwa*, gifts to the impoverished – in money or in kind – from the religious requirements of *sadaka*, the giving of alms. The latter is *domin Allah*, for God; the former is *sabo da tausayi*, in the name of compassion and humanity. Furthermore, as an indispensable feature of the good man in Hausa, the whole concept of *karama*, generosity, may be said to extend to an intense cordiality of spirit as much as to the physical giving, a warm-heartedness of personality encapsulated perhaps in the English imagery of "My Lady Bountiful"; in Hausa it is more than God that loveth a cheerful giver. Let us leave this supreme virtue of the good man with a picturesque Hausa metaphor; when the Hausa talk of a person possessing, in the context of generosity, his assuaging liberality is being directly compared to the soothing cry of the hornbill.

We have commented on the peasant origin of the strong expectation of generosity in the character of *mutumin kirki*. Another virtue, much prized and much preached, is what the Hausa call *hakuri*, "patience"; and for all its undeniable overlay of Islamic doctrine, with its comfortable dovetailing into the principle of submission to the will of Allah and the uncomplaining acceptance of one's *rabo*, lot or fate, it is not impossible to discern in the importance attached to the exercise of this virtue the same background of an agricultural community contending with the misfortunes of drought and deluge, pest and plague, and so resigned in the face of calamities, inexplicable and uncontrollable, sent presumably by God. Such a reaction of dour doggedness has often characterized peasant communities like the Normands, the Rajputs – or maybe those farmers in Indiana and Idaho. Indeed, today in Hausaland, a ritual greeting involving no response other than one from a set of conventional replies, remains *ina hakuri?* literally "how is the patience?", to ask "how are you?" It is likely that Islam enhanced rather than inaugurated the concept of patience as a virtue in Hausaland, and that the Islamic obligation of alms-giving extended the usage of the term *hakuri* in formalized greetings to the phrase now sanctioned for a beggar – especially the Koranic pupil kind – when one is unable to offer anything more tangible than the invocation *Allah (ya) ba hakuri*, "may God grant you patience." For all the vigorous Islamic content of life in Hausaland today, it is, I think, permissible to suggest a difference between *hakuri*, "patience," in its pre-Islamic application, and the essential Islamic precept of submission to *nufin Allah*, "God's will."

But this is may be little more than a digression into speculation. We are on safer ground again when we examine the frequency rather than the pedigree of this fundamental Hausa concept *hakuri*, patience. In a topic-count of Hausa proverbial lore, *hakuri* is an item that emerges high up the list. The evidence is extensive. "Whatever the trouble, it always has an end", and "whatever you have endured, you will see it come to a finish," "both parallel our sustaining philosophy of every cloud

having a silver lining. One of the most commonly invoked folkloric prescriptions, urging the speaker not to kick against the pricks, is the maxim *hakuri maganin duniya*, "patience is the universal remedy." Yet just because the Hausa is an exceptionally shrewd judge of his fellow men, he is quick to recognize the human frailty of impatience and its dangerous nearness to the surface. Two proverbs, both deriving from the Ur-Hausa agricultural experience, serve to demonstrate that even patience can have its breaking-point. "Patience is corn in the pot; it is soon used up"; the other, "only a donkey shows patience under a heavy load." Of such stuff, of course, are the dreams of a peasants' revolt made. These, and many more like them, illustrate the constant preoccupation – in proverb and poem, in fable and in *hira*, conversation – with patience. In turn, they help to induce that very Hausa attitude of uncomplaining, unemotional acceptance of *rabo*, "fate," be it *masifa*, "adversity" or *sa'a*, "good fortune." This, then, is *hakuri*, that marked feature of daily life in rural Hausaland: the Hausa's immense capacity for patience – a gift that is not yet altogether lost even in the hurly-burly of metropolitan Kano, Zaria and Sokoto.

Our portrait of the good man in Hausa is taking shape. We see him as a man of great integrity, steadfast in truth and trust, displaying a generous spirit and gifted with patience in adversity. These are the virtues of the superior man. Already the paragon begins to emerge. Yet to earn recognition as *mutumin kirki* Hausa society demands further qualities still. The good man in Hausa has to be a man of many parts; and much perfection, too.

No Hausa can aspire to the title of *mutumin kirki* unless he be amply endowed with the quality of *hankali*. Now, the conventional gloss of "sense" is inadequate. True, the laudatory comment *yan a da hankali* can mean that a person has a fair share of that elusive paradox, "common sense." For instance, what better rendering of *mai hankali* can there be than a "sensible person" in the proverb which warns that such indeed is the person who gives water to the hen even in the rainy season? But the man who has *hankali* in his make-up has something more than common sense. He has sound mature judgment. He knows the wrong time as well as the right time to do or say the right thing. He has manners. *Mai hankali* is, in short, the prudent and well-behaved man, sober within the meaning of the Book of Common Prayer. The derogatory *ba shi da hankali* implies that a person not only lacks common sense: he also does not know how to behave. It is, I believe, this essential virtue of *hankali* that the Hausa poet had in mind when, in an oral tradition still found among beggar-minstrels in Kano,[14] he advanced the caution that "it is not fitting that a Muslim should lack sober reflectiveness." May I add a postscript on *hankali*? In another context I am exploring the degree of correlation between *hankali*, considered, polite, and prudent judgment at the personal level, and the Hausa preference for *sannu sannu*, the slow-but-sure, look-before-you-leap[15] approach at the institutional level. Identifiable as "gradualism," this became a marked feature of the Northern Nigerian government's political style in the pre-independence decade of 1950–60.

The quality of *hankali*, the prudence on which good behaviour is built, lead us directly into two related aspects of our *mutumin kirki*: a proper sense of *kunya*, "shame" and the due display of *ladabi*, "good manners." This *ladabi* (the word, like so many abstract terms in Hausa, is an Arabic borrowing: one meets the root in Swaihili, too), this exercise of courtesy, is so influential a factor in the ultimate assessment of the good man in Hausa that it would be no exaggeration to view it as the summation of *hankali* and *kunya* put together: sober behaviour and the due modesty of conduct together form good manners. Let us look a little more closely at these two new dimensions to the character of our *mutumin kirki*.

First, the rendering of *kunya* by its standard dictionary explanation of "shame" is, at least in our social context, incomplete. While there are, of course, occasions when "shame" will suffice, the concept in Hausa carries a far more specific meaning. For those at home in French, the noun *pudeur* admirably conveys the range of nuances identified by the Hausa in *kunya*. While "shame" in its popular sense is certainly one element of *kunya*, there are at the same time implications of that which could, and should, cause shame, so that *kunya* develops overtones of the expected personal reaction to and avoidance of a shame-making action or word. Hence the proposed dimension of "harshfulness," of a due sense of feeling ashamed because of a breach of propriety, either by oneself or by another person. Such a reading is reinforced by the maxim that tells us "the face is the index of shame," literally "shame is to be found in the eyes." Thus while *ya ji kunya* will translate as "he was ashamed" and *da kunya suka tashi* as "they left with their tails between their legs," sentences like the often-heard *kada ka ba mu kunya*, "do not shock

us," requires a concept less limited than that of simply shame, and can be grasped only by a reading into them of some such message as "do not offend our sense of the proprieties." The stigmatic *ba shi da kunya*, frequent and forceful reproof among the Hausa for one who has brashly trespassed against their social code, is better translated not literally as "he has no shame" but as "he is a shameless creature." And to feel shame for a shame-less man is, according to the Hausa, a waste of time. In a favourite passage in Hausa literature, we learn from the praise-song of Dammaliki, one of the sons of the Galadima of Sokoto, responsible for the governance of Katsina in the nineteenth century, that among his supreme attributes were his quality of being "outspoken, fearless, and a stranger to shame." And the oral tradition of Kano tells of the disgrace suffered by the Madawaki Kuma at the command of the Emir, Sarki Mohammad Kukuna, in the middle of the seventeenth century, when he was placed on a donkey (doubtless with his face to the tail, a popular deflation of dignity in Hausaland) and driven through the streets of Kano by a gaggle of young girls. The Madawaki, we learn, died of *kunya* "chargrin."[16] How acutely sensitive to the stigma of *kunya* the Hausa are, can be perceived in the grave choice recommended by the proverbialist in a paronomastic aphorism that defines similar skill in translation "bequeath to your son debt rather than (the) disgrace (of *kunya*)."

If *kunya*, "a proper sense of the proprieties," is the restrictive force in the conduct of the good man, *ladabi* is its essential manifestation. For *ladabi* is all that we understand by courtesy: the public display of personal manners, the oil that lubricates the wheels of social intercourse, the supreme and easy index of what is and what is not good behaviour. To the Hausa, *ladabi* in informal relations is what, in other contexts, the Western world formalized as etiquette or has institutionalized as protocol. The standard, however, expected of *ladabi* is no less uncompromising. Nor is *ladabi* the exclusive prerogative of the peasant; it is admired and awaited in the princeling too. In the narrative of how his brother Shehu dan Fodio undertook his preaching mission in Gobir prior to the Jihad, Abdulahi makes the ubiquitous nature of *ladabi* quite clear: "I saw . . . the common people and the nobles coming to Sheikh Usman, profiting by his admonitions and being influenced by his good manners."[17] *Ladabi* is the courteous behaviour obligatory towards all those who traditionally earn such respect: parents and older folk as much as those in position like *alkali* the judge, *sarki* the chief. To a certain extent, too, *ladabi* can be interpreted as the outward manifestation of that ready obedience which permeated the Hausa attitude to legitimate authority. The motto *addinimmu biyaya ne*, "our religion is one of respect and obedience," for long the mainspring of Hausa behaviour, was raised to the level of a national slogan in *zamanin siyasa*, those heady, wordy days of political competitiveness between the North and South in the 1950s and early 1960s. That the Hausa insistence on respectful behaviour may shade off into *bangirma* or *girmawa*, ritual deference, where customary courtesies demand it, is evidenced by the root form *ladab*, used to describe the submissive position traditionally adopted by the Hausa in the presence of one in authority. *Yi ladab*, "sit up properly," was sometimes heard as the reprimand by the emir's *dogari* or private bodyguard to a litigant seated on the floor in a sloppy manner. The same Abdullahi quoted above also uses the term *ladabi* in what is a somewhat archaic sense, to denote the actual punishment due for showing lack of respect to those in authority. Nowadays, my Hausa friends inform me, such usage is very secondary, and only an older generation would immediately recognize it as a term to indicate the slight physical reproof administered by a superior such as an emir or *mai sarauta*, traditional title-holder, of a slap on the face or the more deflamatory knocking of an offender's turban askew as a warning not to repeat some piece of impudent behaviour. *Rashin ladabi*, to show a lack of proper respect, stands forth as a major mote in the Hausa's social eye. It is behaviour unthinkable in *mutumin kirki*. Any hint of *gidadanci*, uncouth behaviour, is at once the sign of a rough diamond, the very denial of a "gentleman". His, on the contrary, is a conduct signalled by easy and grave courtesy, by good manners, by all the sound savoir-faire subsumed under the quintessential concept of *ladabi*. In Hausaland, the maxim that manners maketh man still remains very much alive. Visiting the Hausa country 120 years ago, Heinrich Barth was struck by how it was that in Katsina,

> just as the Hausa language here attained the greatest richness of form and the most refined pronounciation, so also the manners of Katsina were distinguished by superior politeness.

In their model of *mutumin kirki*, the Hausa firmly endorse the verdict of our English variant of your Oliver Wendell Holmes, the master-conversations list Sydney Smith: "Manners are the shadows of virtues."

There we almost have him, then, our *mutumin kirki*. Truthful and trustworthy; motivated by generosity; patient, his every action inspired by sober judgment and a sense of the proprieties and translated into faultless manners. Such virtues are tested in a single situation: that of human interaction. It is by the way a man treats his fellow men, regardless of their station in society, that the Hausa will finally evaluate him as meeting the criteria of the good man and fulfilling – or not – their concept of *mutumin kirki*. Indeed, our eighth aspect of the good man in Hausa relates exclusively to his capacity for interaction with his fellow man. The term *mutunci* is used to describe the manner of treating others with due respect for their feelings. It differs from *ladabi* in that whereas good manners are largely manifested by outward action or words, *mutunci* is also demonstrated by an inner spirit, it is a psychological humanism, the ability to respect the dignity of Everyman. While *ladabi* is good manners expected above all (though by no means exclusively) in an inferior–superior situation, *mutunci* is at its most visible in the behaviour of a superior towards an inferior. The derivation of the word *mutunci* is significant here. It is the same root as we have in our title, *mutum* in Hausa being a man or human being. Hence literally, *mutunci* refers to a sort of non-physical man-hood, so that we may consider it as human dignity residing in the individual. The full extent of the attribute of *mutunci* is well revealed in its negative sense. The vice of *cin mutunci*, to humiliate a person by depriving him of his self-respect (to treat someone like dirt, literally to "eat his self-esteem") is one of the worst sins in the roll-call of reprehension in Hausa society. The commonest vehicle for this social assault is that of *zage*, of abuse. Frequent are the injunctions against slanderous language, and he with the evil tongue is condemned by society to the point of *zage* ruling out further consideration of eligibility for the role of *mutumin kirki*. Nowhere is the offence of *cin mutunci* more heinous than when it is committed by a superior on an inferior. In many of the humpty-dumpty days of kingship in the Hausaland of the 1950s, one of the commonest and most telling of the allegations was that *sarki ya ci mutuncimmu, ya rena mu*: the Emir has publicly humiliated and scorned us. Such, too, was the bitter complaint of the NPC ministers when they were booed and jeered by the vulgar Lagos mob after the constitutional crisis of 1953: *sun ci mutuncimmu*, "they belittled us."[18] As I have written elsewhere in discussing the far-reaching consequences of that public ridicule on the official mind of the North, to the Hausa *cin mutunci* is such a gross offence that it outweighs in gravity physical assault.[19]

My ninth and tenth categories of behavioural excellence need be touched on but briefly, and are best treated together. They relate to the whole Hausa religious conduct, with all that that implies by way of an all-encompassing Islamic way of life. The strongly Islamized culture-hero of Hausaland is expected to display two more virtues: *hikima* and *adalci*. *Hikima*, "wisdom," presupposes a certain measure of age and so an even more generous one of *ilmi*, Islamic learning and hence, by extension, "education." *Adalci*, "scrupulous behaviours," is likewise an essentially Islamic virtue. Both are particularly sought for in the leader; indeed, without them no one in a position of leadership is likely to be conceded the tribute of *mutumin kirki*. We could safely leave them both thus, as predominantly Islamic traits in the good man in Hausa – and, in general, features at the leadership level – were it not for a gloss that I feel needs to be made in respect of the epithet derived from *Adalci*, "behaving in a just and honest way." Some have seen in this golden opinion of *shi adali ne* no more than a synonym for *kirki*, "he is an upright man." I would beg to differ from these pundits. Instead, let me render this vital virtue of *adali* in another idiom. If we translate *adali* by "he is a God-fearing man," we at once achieve two things. First, it caters for a universal attribute of the admired man in Hausa society: "God-fearing" has enjoyed a high frequency in the vocabulary of Hausa approbation. *Ibada* and *imani*, the path of righteousness and godly fear, have been the prescription for rulers in Hausaland since al-Maghili's code of conduct drawn up for the king of Kano nearly 500 years ago.[20] And was not the motto chosen to embellish the coat of arms of a self-governing Northern Nigeria in 1959 *Aiki da Ibada*, "Work and Worship"? Secondly, it allows us to subsume under this meaning the whole of *addini*, the religion of Islam, with its own manifestations of good conduct, its own criteria as a way of life. That the overlap is a conscious one – inevitably so, given the nature of Hausa society – is reinforced by the prescription for the good man of Hausaland written 150 years ago by Abdullah ibn Muhammad, to whom we have turned before for guidance:

> That which is best, *nay* that which is incumbent on the believer, is that he should think well of his brother and think the best of him in respect of everything . . . The five necessary things [for judging a man's character] are religion, intelligence, propriety, genealogy and honour; if they are contradictory, then religion comes first and the other evil is borne patiently, for it is less serious than an offence against religion.[21]

Thus, while the good man in Hausa society is today, almost by definition, the good man of Islam, our anatomy of his excellence of character consciously excluded separate consideration of the specific criteria of religious conduct by incorporating the whole range of personal Islamic performance within the virtue of *adali* – "the God-fearing man."

For our *mutumin kirki*, then, these are the ten principle obligatory features of his character. With the exception of truth, none of them is a really universal moral virtue. For the Hausa, their value lies in their exercise in the person-to-person situation, as a social emollient. Hence the emphasis on the outward civilities of human relations – patience, propriety, generosity, respect: the paramountcy of humanism. This is not to argue that the Hausa is not a moral man. I think Tremearne is inaccurate in his conclusion that the Hausa have no moral standards and that for them "courage covers a multitude of sins."[22] Their prominent adherence to the tenets of Islam implies the contrary. Our analysis here has been concentrated not on the alternative meaning of moral, ethically "conforming," but on its primary sense of pertaining to the *mores*, the manners and conduct of men. For our purpose of identifying the good man in Hausa, we are concerned with character or disposition, not with the distinction between right and wrong save in social context. What we have before us now are the approbative qualities in a man's disposition. These will be reflected in what the Hausa call *fara'a*, the outward and infective goodwill of the good man, and his *haiba* or *kwarjini*, the radiance of his presence. Together, these virtuous elements will be recognized as *farin jini*, the totality of qualities in a man which are conducive to popular respect. Collectively, they will evoke recognition of the *mutumin kirki*. Translate the *mutumin kirki* to high office in Hausaland, and these are the qualities that put the seal on his *girma*, that aura of respected distinction that emanates from high office properly filled in accordance with the protocol and proprieties expected of its incumbent by the Hausa.[23]

Notes

Edited version of the 3rd Annual Hans Wolff Memorial Lecture, 1973, first published by the African Studies Program, Indiana University Bloomington and published here with the permission of the Program.

1 Na'ibi Sulaiman, *Mara ba'yanci, Zaria 1960.*

2 Two useful summaries have been written by N. G. Smith: his introduction to Mary F. Smith, *Baba of Kano*, London 1954, and his chapter in James L. Gibbs, *Peoples of Africa*, New York 1965. A valuable bibliography on the Hausa, listing over 300 entries, is included in Polly Hill's comprehensive *Rural Hausa: A Village and a Setting*, Cambridge 1972.

3 In proposing glosses for the Hausa terms used, I am aware that total equivalence is not always possible in handling cultural concepts borrowed from a non-Western vernacular. My model remains a political interpretation.

4 Martin Turnell, *The Classical Moment*, London 1947, p. 22.

5 *Hali zanen dutne, ba mai shafawa.* It has been pointed out to me that the usual translation of "Character is like a line on a rock nobody can erase it" suggests a quality of innateness and immutability that would deny the whole purpose of the exhortatory precepts and literature of admonition to which Hausa youth is ceaselessly exposed; and that without a reinterpretation along the lines of "Let your character resemble the appearance of the grinding stone whose impressions cannot be erased whatever pressure is put on them" (Pauline Ryan) it is difficult to reconcile this paramount proverb with *gargadi* and *tarbiyya* (see below).

6 A. H. M. Kirk-Greene, *Hausa ba dabo ba ne: 500 Hausa Proverbs*, Ibadan 1966, pp. xi and xii.

7 *Idan da hali, muni kyau ne: Idan babu hali, kyau muni ne.*

8 Abubakar Imam, novelist and man of letters, has now been awarded the Margaret Wrong Memorial Medal for his contribution to African literature, thereby joining his opposite number for East Africa, the Swahili author, Shaaban Robert.

9 See A. J. N. Tremearne, *Hausa Superstitions and Customs*, 1913, reprinted London 1970, pp. 195–6.

10 Abubakar Tafawa Balewa, *Shaihu Umar*, Zaria 1936, p. 12.

11 Mary F. Smith, *Baba of Kano: the Autobiography of a Hausa Woman*, London 1954, pp. 180–2.

12 The basic analysis of Hausa system of social stratification is M. G. Smith, "The Hausa system of social status," *Africa*, xx–ix, 1959, pp. 239–42. The literature on this aspect of Hausa society grows apace; some twenty references are cited in the author's "The merit principle in an African bureaucracy" in Arnold Rivkin, ed., *Nations by Design*, New York 1968, p. 318, n. 13, and more work has been published since, e.g. by Guy Nicolas for the Hausa of Maradi and Polly Hill for those of Katsina. The study of Hausa society by Hausa sociologists is an event eagerly awaited by Africanists: something may soon be expected from Ibrahim Tahir, who has been working for his doctorate at Cambridge University and is now lecturing at Ahmadu Bello University. Recent exchanges in the correspondence columns of *West Africa*, 1972 *passim*, suggest that sociology in Nigeria has not been able to escape its *damnosum hereditas* of eurocentric undertones and overrule.

13 *Kurulla: kurumusu; mursisi.* The Western tradition of fixed numbers for a formal dinner and the convention of meals for the invited guests alone have been stock subjects for mirth among the Hausa.

14 *Wakar Bagauda.*

15 Proverbial precepts and moralistic fable in Hausa are extensive in illustrating the principle that the tortoise may beat the hare to the finishing post.

16 *Kano Chronicle*, in H. R. Palmer, *Sudanese Memoirs*, Lagos 1928, vol. III, p. 120.

17 Abdulah ibn Muhammad, 1st Emir of Gwandu, *Tazyin al-Waraqat*, translated by M. Hisket, Ibadan 1963, p. 98. Admonition, *garadi*, and even *horo*, disciplinary action, are typically expected from the leader in Hausaland, and may be looked on as a necessary and desirable way of *gyaran hali*, improving a regrettable blemish in one's character. The Hausa primary textbook *Labaru na da da na yanzu*, first published in the 1930s, still carries in its 1968 reissue a section unequivocally headed *Gargad*.

18 Cf. *Ahmadu Bello, My Life*, Cambridge 1962, pp. 133–5, *Report on the Kano Disturbances*, Kaduna 1953, p. 4; *Daily Times* (Lagos), 6 April 1953.

19 See A. H. M. Kirk-Greene, *Crisis and Conflict in Nigeria*, Oxford 1971, vol. I, p. 9. In his award-winning "The Go Between, L.P." Hartley puts this sensitivity to ridicule like this: "In my experience, most people mind being laughed at more than anything else. What causes war, what makes them drag on so interminable but the fear of losing face?" (1953, p. 47).

20 Al-Maghili, *The Obligations of Princes*, trans. T. H. Baldwin, Beirut 1932, p. 6.

21 Abdullah ibn Muhummad, *Tazyin al-Waragat*, Ibadan 1963, pp. 87–8.

22 A. J. M. Tremearne, *Hausa Superstitions and Customs*, Ibadan 1963, repr. London 1970, pp. 47 and 53.

23 Hausa literature tends to favour enumerations of the component parts of the ideal *hali*. For instance, Shehu dan Fodio wrote in *Bayan Wujub*:

Good morals are indeed purified behaviour:
The first is wisdom; second is religion;
Third is learning; fourth is clemency;
Fifth is generosity; sixth is kindness;
Seventh is piety; eighth is patience;
Ninth gratitude; and the tenth is leniency.

Again, the Sultan of Sokoto has listed in *Hali Zanen Dutse* twelve elements in the make-up of the faultless Hausa child, including, additionally, taking advice, keeping a secret, love for one's parents and eschewing conceit.

15

Yoruba Philosophy: Individuality, Community, and the Moral Order

Segun Gbadegesin

The issues of interest to us in this chapter are mainly two: What is the relationship between individuality and the community in a traditional African thought system? Included in this are the value placed on individuality vis-à-vis community, the expectations of the community on its members and the humanist foundations of communalism. Second, the philosophical basis of traditional moral values will be explored. There have been controversies over the alleged religious basis of morality in Africa and this needs to be clarified. In the process we will discuss some of the moral values in the hope that they will throw some light on their foundation.

To better understand the meaning of the individual in relationship to the community, it is worthwhile to trace our steps back to the coming-to-being of the new member of the family and community. The new baby arrives into the waiting hands of the elders of the household. Experienced elderly wives in the household serve as mid-wives, they see that the new baby is delivered safely and the mother is in no danger after delivery. They introduce the baby into the family with cheerfulness, joy and prayers: "*Ayò abara tíntín*" (This is a little thing of great joy). From then on, the new mother may not touch the child except for breast feeding. The baby is safe in the hands of others: co-wives, husband's mother and step-mothers and a whole lot of others, including senior sisters, nieces and cousins.

On the seventh or eighth day, the baby gets his/her names, a ceremony performed by the adult members of the household. Before the actual naming ceremony, the most elderly male member – usually the baby's grandfather – consults the *Ifá* divination oracle to find out the child's portion, the chosen profession and *òrìsà*. The appropriate names that will be given to the baby are then decided upon by looking at a combination of factors, including the household profession (e.g., hunting family will give a name reflecting this – *Odéwálé*), the household *òrìsà* (e.g., *Sàngó* devotees will give a name after *Sàngó* – *Sàngó-fúnmiké*); the day of birth (*Bósèdé*); the significance of the birth (e.g., a reincarnation or a symbol of a recently dead member of the family – *Babáwálé* or *Iyábòdé* – or a symbol of victory over a recent crisis – *Olúségun*). In all these, the importance of the new arrival as a unique individual is reconciled with his or her belonging to an existing family which not only decides his or her name but also have a duty to see his or her birth as a significant episode in its existence. The Yoruba say "*Ilé ni à nwò, kí á tó so omo lórúko*" (We look back at the family traditions before we give names to a new baby). The meaning of this is that the child, as an extension of the family tree, should be given a name that reflects his/her membership therein, and it is expected that the name so given will guide and control the child by being a constant reminder for him/her of his/her membership in the family and the circumstance of his/her birth.

From Segun Gbadegesin, *African Philosophy* (1992); by kind permission of Peter Lang Publishing Inc.

The process of socialization begins right from birth. The mother constantly communicates with the baby by tracing the family tree from the beginning, reminding him/her of the nobility of his/her birth and the uniqueness of the family. Co-wives (step-mothers) are on hand to tease the growing child, chanting the family praise-names and demanding gratifications in return. All these raise the consciousness of the child as a member of a family and he/she begins to internalize its norms.

The structure of the family compound makes the process easy. Members of the extended household of several related extended family belonging to a common ancestor occupy a large compound called *agbo-ilé*. The compound is usually in the form of a circle with one or two main entrances. The various extended families have their own houses joined together (to form the compound or household) and each family member has apartments within the house, with each wife having a room. There is a large covered corridor into which all the wives' rooms lead and there they all sit, play and eat in the daytime with their children, and at night they retire to their rooms. Inside each apartment, the children of co-wives and other elderly members play together and are overseen by the elders. A child who misbehaves is corrected immediately and may be punished by any of the elders. This is the first exposure to socialization. Then in the larger compound, all the children play together and, again, any of them may be punished by any older member of the household for misbehaving. Where there is a misunderstanding among the co-wives, the elderly male or female members intervene, or if they do not succeed, the matter is taken to the head of the compound – *Baálé*, assisted by other male members. In this kind of environment, growing children are able to see themselves as a part of a household and not as atoms. They see their intrinsic relation to others and see the interdependent existence of their lives with others. Here is the limit of individualism. Not that the community forces itself on an unyielding individual; rather the individual, through socialization and the love and concern which the household and community have extended to him/her *cannot* now see himself or herself as anything apart from his/her community. Interest in his/her success is shown by members of the extended family who regard him/her as their "blood" and the community are also able to trace their origin to a common even if mythical ancestor. There is therefore a feeling of solidarity among its members and this is neither forced nor solicited. It develops naturally as a result of the

experience of love and concern which the growing child has been exposed to.

The process of socialization that begins in the family apartment and the household compound finally gets into the larger community where the child is further exposed to the virtues of communal life. Here children of the community are exposed to the display of selfless efforts by others to uplift the community. They have a first-hand experience of how adults are contributing to the welfare of children, how women and men work on the farms and how the warriors risk their lives to save the community. Building on the initial exposure in the family compound they now see themselves as one of those who should carry the banner and, having been prepared for the task, they, severally and collectively, cannot but shun individualism. This is the meaning of the common reference to the typical African as saying "I am because we are; I exist because the community exists." From what we have discussed above, there is the simple truth.

It follows that the usual rendering of this to the effect that the individual in traditional African societies is crushed by the almighty presence of the community is not the whole truth. Of course, individuals are valued in themselves and as potential contributors to communal survival. For why should the new baby be so immersed in love and affection? Further, it is known that many individuals have the wisdom to guide the community and such people are well respected. Emphasis is placed on usefulness for self and community and not on wealth or strength. If individual uniqueness were not recognized, how could we have such powerful figures as *Kúrunmí, Látóòsà, Obòkun, Móremí* becoming charismatic leaders?

The example of *Móremí* is worth recounting here. A native of Ile-Ife, *Móremí* was a woman of great strength, power and communal feeling. At a time when Igbo invaders were troubling the Ife kingdom, *Móremí* decided to do something. She went to ask for permission from the *Oòni*, the king of Ife, to be allowed to pursue the invaders. After some hesitation occasioned by surprise, the king allowed her. She then sought help from the *Ifá* oracle about how she can accomplish the task. She was advised to perform some sacrifice to the Esinminrin river. She did this and a spirit appeared to her with information on the Igbo and how to capture them. Specifically she was informed that they disguised themselves in grass-made costumes which made them look like spirits and she should prepare fire to burn them down. Armed with this information she went back and prepared the warriors against the invaders. They came as usual and they were routed.

Now, before this information was given to *Móremí*, she had promised the spirit of *Esìnmìrìn* river anything it would take if she could succeed in her mission. The spirit demanded the sacrifice of her only son, *Olúorogbo*, in return for the favor. *Móremí* could not go back on her words. She sacrificed her only son for the sake of her community. This is an example *par excellence* of the spirit of community, the voluntary submission of individual happiness to the community. There are common examples like this in African social history as elsewhere. Such cases exemplify the possibility of individuals forgoing their own interests when the interest of the community is at stake, and so the idea of individual right does not, for traditional people, defeat the claim of the community. A high premium is placed on the practical demonstration of oneness and solidarity among the members of a community. Every member is expected to consider him/herself as an integral part of the whole and to play an appropriate role towards the good of all. Cooperation is voluntarily given and is institutionalized in several ways. Wives of the family (co-wives, wives of brothers, wives of cousins, etc.) know that they are expected to cooperate in raising their children as full members of the family. They are free to borrow household items from one another, they feel free to baby-sit for one another, they advise one another and settle any dispute between themselves and their children. A person who watches while children fight or when tension mounts between two adults is not a good person. Also, properties left outside are taken care of by other members around in case there is rain or storm. Everyone is expected to be the keeper and protector of the interests of others which are, by extension, their own too.

All the above point to the value that traditional Yoruba place on community and communal existence with all its emphasis on fellow-feeling, solidarity and selflessness. This leads directly to the social order of communalism. The structure of traditional African society is communal. This means that the organization of socio-economic life is based on the principle of common ownership of land, which is the major means of production in a non-industrial, agrarian subsistence economy. Ownership of land is vested in the community which gives out portions for individual use as required from time to time. Such land reverts to the community when it is no

longer needed by the individual. Some scholars have identified this social practice as an outgrowth of the principles of solidarity and selflessness which pervades the traditional society. This is only partially so. More important is the fact that in traditional society a man is not able to accumulate and appropriate a large area of land because he does not have the machinery and technique to operate it. So the reasonable thing is to have some portion earmarked for each adult. This is with respect to the distribution of land and its communal ownership.

On the other hand, however, the indigenous values of fellow-feeling, solidarity and cooperation feature prominently in the economic activities of individuals. Thus there is the system of *òwè*, a cooperative endeavor in which people help one another on a specific task; for instance, building a new house or clearing a forest for farmland requires help from others. Such is freely given on the basis of reciprocity. Sometimes a male adult with married female children may seize this opportunity to call on his sons-in-law to help with the task. They are only too willing to do this. There is another kind of mutual cooperation known as *àró* in the form of a standing cooperative association. A member may call upon the group to help him harvest or plant or clear the weeds. He only has to feed the participants and later on he may also be called upon to help.[1] In this kind of situation, where commercial labor is not available and not encouraged, it becomes clear that individuality is helped by communality. "I am because we are" becomes an understandable and reasonable expression of dependence which does not thereby mean suppression. For even here the sky is the limit for an enterprising person.

The picture presented thus far should not be interpreted as meaning that there were no conflicts at all in traditional Yoruba societies. Any human society is bound to have cases of conflicts involving individuals who either refuse to conform or who feel offended somehow. Even in such occasions of conflict, there are avenues for resolution in the traditional system. Elders intervene, to reconcile the disputing parties on the basis of the community's accepted moral principles. For instance, a man may be blamed for mistreating his wife and for not considering her interests as a human being. The point here is that appeals are made in such cases to some moral principles or standards which also occur in Western societies. However, in the case in which survival of the community is pitched against an individual's will, it is clear that the community's welfare is more emphasized. The reason for this is not far-fetched. As has been observed earlier, the individual involved also understands and appreciates the meaning of community: "I am because we are." From this it follows that there need not be any tension between individuality and community since it is possible for an individual to freely give up his/her own perceived interest for the survival of the community.[2] But in giving up one's interest thus, one is also sure that the community will not disown one and that one's well-being will be its concern. It is a life of give and take. The idea of individual rights, based on a conception of individuals as atoms, is therefore bound to be foreign to this system. For the community is founded on notions of an intrinsic and enduring relationship among its members.

This same theme of individuality-in-community is prominent in other African social thoughts. For instance, K. A. Busia says of the Akan that

> There is, everywhere, the heavy accent on family – the blood relatives, the group of kinsfolk held together by a common origin and a common obligation to its members, to those who are living and those who are dead . . . The individual is brought up to think of himself in relation to this group and to behave always in such a way as to bring honor and not disgrace to its members. The ideal set before him is that of mutual helpfulness and cooperation within the group of kinsfolk.[3]

Furthermore:

> Cooperation and mutual helpfulness are virtues enjoined as essential; without them, the kingroup cannot long endure. Its survival depends on its solidarity.[4]

And Gyekye recalls an Akan proverb on the same theme: "The prosperity [or well-being] of man depends upon his fellow-man."[5] Such proverbs are numerous in African social thought and they help to point up the wisdom of traditional thinkers concerning matters pertaining to the good of the community.

Foundations of Morality

What is the basis of morality in traditional African thought? There are two opposing views on this question. On the one hand there is the view held by Mbiti and Idowu that religion is the source and foundation of morality. On the other hand, Wiredu is in the forefront of those who oppose this view with his claim that at least for the Akan of Ghana, the moral outlook is "logically independent of religion."[6] The same position (modified in a sense) is held by Gyekye.[7]

Idowu starts off by questioning the positions of two schools of thought regarding the foundation of morality: the social school and the common-sense school. The first traces morality to society: "it is essentially a social phenomenon. Society must keep itself alive and its machinery smooth-running, and to this end it evolves a system of self-preservation."[8] Conscience on this hypothesis is nothing more than "a complex of residual habits, which society implants in him as if it brings him up."[9] The second school of thought sees morality as a product of common sense. In order to live, man must adapt himself to his environment. Experience soon taught him what could be done and what must be avoided. A steady accumulation of this experience over a long period has resulted in a very strong sense of what has come to be popularly known as 'right' and 'wrong'."[10]

Idowu rejected both hypotheses on the ground that they are partial explanations. They "have conveniently overlooked two vital questions. The first school still has to make it explicit why this 'mass' which is called society should be so keen on its own preservation."[11] Idowu's point is that were society a soulless machine, it would not bother about its own breakdown. So someone must be responsible for giving society its sense of its own value. Obviously, God is needed as a basis for society's concern for morality. On the other hand, the second school of thought has not made its case. For it remains to tell us, Idowu argues, "what it is that puts so much 'common sense' in man. Why is it that, like the candle-drawn moth, he does not fly into the flame and be burnt."[12]

I find these arguments interesting but not convincing. But before raising my objection, let us note that Idowu has not here given an account of the Yoruba view of morality. Thus far, it is his own view about the foundation of morality. This view may or may not agree with the Yoruba account; and one may disagree with the view without thereby denying that it is one held by the Yoruba.

Now, the problem with this view is simply that the way Idowu puts it does not help his case. If one says that society creates morality to avoid its own self-destruction, why is that not enough as a reason? Why must we assume that there is some other being responsible for putting the soul in man to think of his survival? This would seem to deny the independent rationality of human beings. The second objection is even less helpful. The denial of the sufficiency of common-sense experience as a basis for correction is something I find rather interesting. So we are being asked to agree with the view that if a child puts his finger in the fire a first time, he cannot on the basis of this experience, refrain from fire next time unless we assume that something other than the pain of the first experience intervenes to convince him to so refrain. Then what prevents a wicked person from claiming that God has not intervened to guide him in his actions?

Idowu's view is that "morality is basically the fruit of religion and that, to begin with, it was dependent upon it. Man's concept of the Deity has everything to do with what is taken to be the norm of morality. God made man, and it is He who implants in him the sense of right and wrong. This is a fact the validity of which does not depend upon whether man realizes and acknowledges it or not."[13] Perhaps one point may be granted here – that human beings are created by the Deity and that the creature endows them with reasoning ability as well as the conscience as source of moral reasoning. However, it does not then follow that given this reasoning ability, human beings cannot, on their own, make moral choices, and determine their ideas of moral rightness and wrongness. The Euthyphro Question is pertinent here.

But as I have observed, this is Idowu's view and we are concerned here with traditional Yoruba account of moral values. On this too, however, Idowu has argued that:

> With the Yoruba, morality is certainly the fruit of religion. They do not make any attempt to separate the two; and it is impossible for them to do so without disastrous consequences.[14]

Idowu then goes on to observe that:

(i) The Yoruba belief in taboo [èèwò – what ought not to be done] took its origin from the people's discernment of certain things that were morally approved or disapproved by the Deity.

(ii) Some scholars have misunderstood Yoruba religion and morality in their assessment of the cruelty of certain Yoruba practices as emanating from their religion.

(iii) But they are wrong because such practices they attack, e.g., human sacrifice, do not originate from religion but rather from the desire of the Yoruba to fulfil an imperative, what they understand as a sacred duty.

(iv) But they [i.e. the Yoruba who sacrifice human beings] are wrong because the Deity's demand is not for physical sacrifice but for one's heart and his demands are purely ethical and spiritual.

What is interesting here is that one would expect Idowu to follow through his original claim that as God is the source of our conscience and therefore of notions of right and wrong, everything is traceable to him. But if, in fact, humans can discern on their own, what is good (even to please God) then the identification of morality with religion is not as tight as first assumed. In other words, since the people are credited with discerning what is good or bad (as in the concept of eewo) they should also be credited with an independent arrival at notions of right and wrong using their reasoning ability which is granted to be God-given. This is clear especially if we examine Idowu's claims (iii) and (iv) above.

Again this seems to be borne out more clearly in Idowu's treatment of covenants in Yoruba ethics. "Person-to-person, and divinity-to-person relations," Idowu observes, "have their basis in covenants."[15] In person-to-person covenants, the parties bind themselves to each other by bilateral obligations. It is like a contract. But while the divinities are called in as witness to the covenant in most cases (e.g., the Earth or Ogún divinities) to give it more force, the essence and purpose of a covenant is to assure the parties of the sincerity of each other. And as Idowu goes on to suggest (rightly, I think):

> Although every covenant has a ritualistic basis, nevertheless, the obligations which are its outcome are ethical. It would seem that the Yoruba have found it necessary in an imperfect society to introduce this element of subtle "coercion" in order to strengthen their weak will in the performance of ethical duties.[16]

This suggests that we have a distinction between rituals and ethics and that therefore the Yoruba may have an independent basis for their ethical duties but bring in the Deity for enforcing such duties in the minds of the not-so-trusted fellow human beings.

Theologians are not the only ones defending the idea of a religious foundation for morality in Africa; philosophers are also into it. Thus Moses Makinde has recently attempted "to defend the religious foundation of an African system of morality and to show that this position is reasonably defensible, in spite of the views of some contemporary Africans to the contrary."[17] His position is that "whatever else anybody may say, religion is surely a competing foundational theory of morals in African societies."[18] In defence of this position, which appears to be a modest one, he gives some arguments and appeals to the authorities of Kant, Mill and Awolowo. I must say, however, unfortunately, that the defence does not succeed because the considerations brought in its support are too weak for the realization of the objective. I would like to examine here six arguments which I have been able to dig out from the clusters of considerations that Makinde has urged us to accept.

The first argument is based on the authority of Mbiti, who has asserted that Africans live in a religious universe. Makinde's argument, based on this, may be reconstructed as follows:

1 Africans live in a religious universe (as confirmed by Mbiti and others).
2 Religion plays a great role in the lives of African peoples (another way of putting the first premise).
3 All their activities must be influenced by one religion or the other (yet another way of putting the first premise).
4 Therefore an African system of morality, based on African cultural beliefs, *must* have a religious foundation.[19]

Spread out in this way, it seems obvious that the conclusion does not follow. Even if we grant that premise 1 is true, and that premises 2 and 3 are just other ways of stating premise 1, premise 4 still does not follow. Religion may influence peoples' activities and play a great role in their lives. This is still a long way from the conclusion that therefore morality must have a religious foundation. At best, we may conclude that religion may (even must) have influence on their morality. But from this, it does not still follow that it is the foundation. To say it is the foundation or must be the foundation is to suggest that without religion, the people cannot have any conception of what is good or bad. Perhaps this is what Makinde wants to establish, but this

argument is too weak to accomplish that task.

2. In his second argument, it seems to me that Makinde's purpose is to establish the meaning of the claim that Africans live in a religious universe by connecting it with their belief in God's existence. However, the argument here even seems to me to be less successful. Makinde notes that:

(a) Some religions are based on a belief in God, Jesus Christ, Prophet Mohammed and in lesser deities.
(b) The existence of God cannot be established empirically, neither can it be established by *a priori* reasoning.
(c) Nonetheless, Africans, like the rest of the universe, do believe in the existence of God and do attempt to establish His existence *a priori* [does this include traditional priests too?]
(d) But the existence of God can be established *a priori* only if that existence is completely independent of experience.
(e) If African systems of morality depend on the existence of the deity, then perhaps morality can be established *a priori* too, since it will be completely independent of what is.
(f) African morality is prescriptive and *a priori*, not descriptive or empirical.
(g) Therefore, because African system of morality is prescriptive and *a priori*, the idea of [the will] of God [which is also established *a priori*] comes in as a ready foundation for it.[20]

The problem with this argument seems easy to identify. To establish that an African system of morality can be established *a priori*, he ties it with the existence of the Deity in premise (e). But premise (g) now uses the same premise that African morality is *a priori* to conclude that therefore it has a religious foundation. In other words, Makinde is urging on us the following:

(i) If African system of morality depends on the existence of the Deity, then morality can be established *a priori*.
(ii) African system of morality can be established *a priori*.
(iii) Therefore, because it is *a priori* and prescriptive, it depends on the existence of the deity. [This can be the only meaning of "the will of God comes in as a ready foundation" in this context].

Spelled out in this way, the problem with the argument seems obvious.

3. The third argument is an appeal to the authority of Idowu and others.[21] If my argument against Idowu's position is sound, Makinde's appeal to it falls with that position. Besides, it is important to note that the idea of taboo among a people is not an adequate proof of their having a religious foundation for their moral system. The wise people of a community have their own well-tried ways of motivating their less cooperative members to perform. If there is an appeal to God or religion, as in some taboos, it is only to influence behavior. But surely the concept of support should not be confused with that of foundation. Consider this. A building has a foundation. When, however, the foundation becomes weak, there is the danger of its collapse. Then the owner is advised either to demolish it and rebuild or provide a support for it. In our traditional villages, it is a common practice to prop up buildings with columns or beams. Furthermore, it cannot be true that the idea of "things not to be eaten" (taboo) is never understood except in connection with religion.[22] And even if it is, it is not quite clear how that could help the case of a religious foundation for morality. *Obàtálá*, the Yoruba deity of creativity, hates palm wine. His devotees are therefore forbidden to take it – perhaps a clear case of a taboo from religion. But *Orúnmìlà*, the deity of wisdom, has no such taboo for his devotees. From Makinde's showing, drinking palm wine (against *Obàtálá*'s injunction) must also be an offence against *Olódùmarè* since any offence against the lesser deities is also an offence against the supreme deity. But are the devotees of *Orúnmìlà* who drink palm wine also committing an offence against *Olódùmarè*? Perhaps not. For we may say that since they are devotees of different deities, what is morally wrong for one (*Obàtálá*) is just not so for the other (*Orúnmìlà*). What is not clear is how this helps the case of a religious foundation for morality. For we now have a relativity of morals in which what is right is determined by particular *òrìsà*'s. Since people serve different gods; how they are expected to organize their social life from a moral perspective is not clear if we deny them an independent source of morality.

4. There is, next, an appeal to the authority of Kant which may be reconstructed as follows:

1 Though Kant argues against our need for God in a moral law, he nevertheless based his moral law on the Golden rule (do unto others as you would wish them do unto you).

2 This is a corollary of the biblical injunction: love thy neighbor as thyself.

3 Since Kant's statement is in every sense similar to that of the Bible, there is the possibility that he actually derived his categorical imperative from the same source and later claimed that morality did not depend or is not based on religion.[23]

There seems to me to be a problem with this argument. Kant insists that the categorical imperative is a principle of reason. Even if there is reference to the golden rule in Kant's theory, does this make it the foundation of the theory? Is there no difference between the golden rule and the categorical imperative even in terms of their logic? Notice that the golden rule takes its cue from what "you would wish others do unto you." Thus if you would wish other people to steal from you, you would presumably be free to steal from them, following the golden rule. But the categorical imperative does not depend on any prior desire, at least in Kant's various formulations of it. It is a formula of reason. Kant's theory, of course, has its problems. But a motive of basing that theory on religion or God is hardly an adequate criticism of it.

Makinde also takes Mill's reference to the golden rule as an evidence that he thereby derives it from the Bible. Mill's point is that *even* Jesus of Nazareth lived by and preached the ideas that make up the content of the utilitarian morality. In other words, Mill would say that more than anything else, Jesus was a utilitarian! Which is to say that the utilitarian ethics was the *basis* of Jesus' injunction as contained in the golden rule. Since there was an historical Jesus, Mill's point is that he (Jesus) understood and utilized the insights that inform the utilitarian theory. Recall here, again, the Euthyphro question. We may well ask why Jesus recommended the golden rule. The answer, for Mill, is that because he knows that the general consequence of following that principle is good. And regarding the appeal to the authority of Chief Awolowo who, according to Makinde "is convinced that virtually all systems of good morality spring from the Bible,"[24] we can only infer that, contrary to what Makinde has deduced from this claim, it must be Awolowo's view that traditional Yoruba, as other Africans, had no (good) morality until the Bible was introduced to them. I am not sure that this view could be attributed to Awolowo. But assume that it is a view that Awolowo may in fact be willing to have attributed to himself. This fact alone does not make the view correct. For there are a number of other people who hold quite contrary views, and we need to weigh the reasons for each of the views. Tai Solarin, for instance, comes from the same home town as Awolowo and he would certainly deny that view. I am sure that if we look close enough there would be at least a few Tai Solarins in the traditional society. Are we to say that such people cannot behave in a morally responsible way? Or that in the traditional society, they are not given due respect if they so behave?

5. A fifth argument is supposedly derived from the Yoruba understanding of the dialectics of good and evil as necessary for a meaningful experience of reality. The following is a reconstruction of a very obscure passage.

1 Moral principles only make sense when we can distinguish between moral and immoral acts, between good and evil.
2 The concept of good and evil [*ire* and *ibi*] are necessary for our understanding of moral concepts and moral principles.
3 God's will is the source of good and evil in man's behavior without which we would never have had the concept of morality.
4 Therefore God must be the source of our concept of morality.
5 Therefore God is the source of our moral ideas.[25]

This reconstruction of the argument should reveal the problem with it: premise 3, which seems to be the crucial one for the conclusion, is asserted without any argument.

Finally, I would like to comment briefly on Makinde's use of the *Ifá* literary corpus. Put simply, I do not think that it helps his case. It is true that the most important religious and moral ideas of the Yoruba are contained in the *Ifá* corpus. But, as is clear to even the traditionalists, *Ifá* is not only a religion. It is, as Abimbola puts it, also "a literary and philosophical system." Furthermore, it is "the store-house of Yoruba culture inside which the Yoruba comprehension of their own historical experiences and understanding of their environment can always be found."[26] Makinde himself refers to it as "the ancient wisdom" of the Yoruba.[27] The *Odù*'s make use of parables to teach moral ideas, in most cases, without reference to Olodumare or the other deities. Makinde also provides a clear illustration of such cases in his first example which deals with the ethic of respect for elders and the

consequences of breaking it as a moral law: "Don't you know that prosperity ever eludes those who assault a *Babaláwo* of high repute, long life will not be within the reach of those who beat up reputable herbalists. Surely a young man who physically assaults a Mallam at his prayer is courting premature death."[28] The point of this *Odù* is to emphasize the undesirable consequence (in this world) of disrespect for elders, not just for experts. Besides, Yoruba proverbs, regarded as signposts in Yoruba ethics, also feature numerous cautionary notes of good behavior and respect for elders. Thus, they say "*omo tó mó ìyá rè lójú, òsì ni yóó ta omo náà pa* (a child who makes an abusive face at his mother will die in abject penury). Or *omo tí kò gbó ti ìyá, tí kò gbó ti baba, òde níí lé'mo wálé* (a child who habitually disobeys his mother and pays no heed to his father's admonitions, will need to seek refuge with the same parents, when chased (from outside) by malevolent strangers).[29] These make no reference to oracles or religion. It is clear, from the foregoing, that Makinde has not succeeded in making a case for the idea of a religious foundation for morality in Yoruba thought.

It is one thing to claim that religion influences peoples' approach to moral behavior; but another thing entirely to argue that religion *must* be the foundation of their morality. To say that religion is the foundation of a people's morality is to say that without it they could not behave in a morally responsible manner. But the questions remain: which comes first, religion or morality? Indeed, is it not plausible to suggest that it is the concern that people have about their moral and social relationships that force religious concerns on them? Second, is it really the case that we do not have people who are not bothered about spiritual issues among the traditional Yoruba? I have myself argued elsewhere[30] that there are evidences for the view that some moral values have a religious *influence* for virtually all Nigerian traditional thinkers, but that this does not mean that morality is founded on religion or that a further ultimate source cannot be found for their moral ideas. I referred to the belief common among the Yoruba that a person who is morally good, who is generous in giving, or respectful to elders, or chaste in words and deeds would find favor with the gods and, barring the evil machinations of the people of the world, he or she would prosper. I then observed that from this last point, it appears that "morality is also justified by reference to its consequences for the individual." It seems now the answer to the question "why be morally good?" is the prudential one: "It will pay you." This appears to be the ultimate appeal for moral goodness in traditional Nigerian world-views.[31] As a Yoruba saying puts it: *Eniti ó se oore, ó seé fún ara rè, eniti ó se ìkà, ó seé fún ara rè. Ati oore àti ìkà, òkan kìi gbé. Ojó àtisùn l'ó sòro.* (The person who performs good deeds does so for him/herself. The person who performs wicked acts does so for him/herself. Neither good deeds nor wicked acts will go unrewarded. The time of death is the hard fact that should be born in mind). Of course, this is not to say that the Yoruba therefore emphasize selfish considerations in moral matters. The question why should I be morally good is not posed by everyone. It is posed by those who have inclinations to do otherwise. They are the selfish ones who need to be motivated for reasons that appeal to themselves. The point, therefore, is that, for those who may, for selfish reasons, not be motivated to do what is right, there are considerations in the system to help them. The important thing is to get people to do what is right. There are several evidences for this contention.[32] In Yoruba world-view, a person is expected to show hospitality and generosity to others since s/he may sometimes be in a position in which s/he would need the hospitality of others, and if s/he has denied it to others sometimes, s/he cannot expect to have it from anyone. For "the calabash which contains poison does not break easily" (*Igbá oró kì í fó*), meaning whatever one sows, one would reap; or on the positive side, "kindness begets kindness" (*oore loore í wó tò*). Even when it cannot be guaranteed that one would reap the fruits of one's character in one's lifetime, moral goodness is still enjoined by appeal to one's moment of death – so that it may be a peaceful one.

A wealthy and powerful person who thinks he or she may afford to be selfish and arrogant should think twice then. On the one hand, no one knows what tomorrow may bring. Today's powerful human being may be the most underprivileged tomorrow. A wise person would therefore be open handed and respectful of others, however poor and wretched they may be. Even when people are sure that they cannot themselves need help from anyone; they should think of their children's fate. For their own seeds of selfishness or, indeed, real wickedness, the Yoruba believe, would be reaped by their children. On the other hand, one of the most valued things in life is a peaceful moment of death. For this is generally regarded as an indication of a pleasant life in the land of the dead. A wicked person, it is believed, would start paying for his or her deeds on

the death-bed by an unusual agony that would be their lot. Far from having a religious foundation, then, we have here a system of morality which, while it makes use of religion as a motivating factor, is clearly pragmatic and this-worldly to the core.

Ìwà: The Primacy of Existence and Character

Ìwà is, for the Yoruba, perhaps the most important moral concept. A person is morally evaluated according to his/her *ìwà* – whether good or bad. A miser (*ahun*) is an *oníwà-burúkú*; a generous person (*òlàwó*) is an *oníwà-rere*. A gentle person is an *oníwà-pèlé*; a short-tempered aggressive person (*onínú fùfù*) is an *oníwà-líle*. It is interesting, though, that each of these evaluations has an adjective attached, suggesting that *ìwà* may be good or bad, gentle or tough, generous or stingy. *Ìwà* as character needs further elaboration.

That elaboration has been provided by Wande Abimbola and Roland Abiodun in two original contributions to the issue. According to Abimbola, the original meaning of *ìwà* is "the fact of being, living or existing." So *ìwà* means existence. *Ìwà* as character is therefore a derivative from this original. In its original meaning, the perfect ideal of *ìwà* is *àìkú* (immortality). Hence the saying "*Aìkú parí ìwà*" (immortality completes existence or immortality is perfect existence).[33] However, *ìwà* (as character) and *ìwà* (as existence) do not just have a homophonous relationship; they are also related by etymology and one appears to be a derivation of the other.[34]

Ìwà as existence has a strong connection with *ìwà* as character. According to a myth recorded in the Ifa Literary Corpus, *Ìwà*, the daughter of *Sùùrù* – the first child of *Olódùmarè*, was married to *Orúnmìlà*. *Ìwà* was extremely beautiful, but lacked good behavior and character. When *Orúnmìlà* could no longer accommodate her bad dispositions, he sent her packing. However, he later discovered a terrible plunge in his fortunes, which had been made possible by *Ìwà*'s presence. He therefore decided to seek out *Ìwà* again, even if it meant selling all his property. He eventually went out looking for *Ìwà*, singing the praise names of *Ìwà* along the way: "*Ìwà, Ìwà l'à nwá, Ìwà. Kámúrágbá tarágbá, Ìwà; Ìwà, l'à nwá, Ìwà*" etc. He got her back finally; but he (not *Ìwà* and her misbehavior) was blamed. The moral is that he is expected to be tolerant; to understand *Ìwà* for what she is: "*Mo ìwà fún oníwà.*"

As Abiodun rightly noted, it is noteworthy that *Iwà* (as the one with bad character) is not blamed, but *Orúnmìlà* (who cannot tolerate her) is blamed.[35] This should point to another element in the emphasis on individuality in the tradition. *Iwà* is the handiwork of the deity; the originator of existence; and her beauty as well as her character are expressions of her existence as an individual being. The fact of existence which *Iwà* illustrates is an endowment of the deity. Her beauty is consistent with that endowment and so *Orúnmìlà* is expected to treat her as an individual expression of *Olódùmarè*'s creativity. Existence is primary, then, and character is derivative, based as it is, on human ideas of morality. Each creature of *Olódùmarè* is thought of as having its beauty (*Iwà l'ewà*) by the fact of its existence, and it is not to be undermined by human valuation. Thus among the Yoruba there are admirers and devotees of such historical figures and deities as *Sàngó* (in spite of his recognition as a strict disciplinarian), *Esù* (trickster god, in spite of his unpredictability), *Sònpònná* (god of smallpox). All these manifest characters which may be inadequate in human terms.[36] And physically deformed persons are also expected to be appreciated and respected in virtue of their special relationship to *Orìsà-nlá*, the creation divinity who is supposed to have made them specially as his devotees. Thus they deserve special protection: *òwò òrìsà làá fíí wo àfin.*

Yet *iwà* as character is given its own place too. Individuality is symbolized by the appeal to *Iwà* (as existence), the wife of *Orúnmìlà*. On the other hand, paradoxically, it is *Sùúrù* (the father of *Iwà*) that symbolizes the idea of *iwà* as character. *Sùúrù* means patience. Patience is therefore symbolically the father (we may say master) of *Iwà* (in both senses). *Iwà* (as existence), wife of *Orúnmìlà* who lacks good character, needs patience to understand her, deal with her and, if possible, transform her. On the other hand, *iwà* (as character) is a child of *Sùúrù* (patience) in the sense that patience is the overall embodiment of good character – *Agbà t'ó ní sùúrù, ohun gbogbo l'óní* – (The elder who has *Sùúrù* has everything). *Sùúrù* is the source of gentle character (or *iwà pèlé*) and good character (*iwà rere*). A demonstration of *iwà pèlé* is to be mindful of the individuality of others, to treat them gently, to be tolerant and accommodating of the peculiarity of others' existence. The Yoruba expression "*Iwà l'ewà*" depicts their understanding of existence itself as constituting beauty, while the cognate expression "*Iwà rere l'èsó èniyàn*" (Good character

– good existence – is the adornment of a human being) depicts the significance attached to good character. An existence, in virtue of its source in the deity, is good and to be appreciated. It is good to exist. Existence itself is beautiful. But however beautiful a thing is, there is always room for improvement. There are degrees of beauty. Thus an original beauty of existence could be improved upon by adorning it with character. The difference between one form of existence and another would then be located in the quality of its adornment, that is, the quality of its character. This is the meaning of *iwà rere l'èsó èniyàn*. But *èsó* (cosmetic) is fleeting; it could fade. Does this mean that *iwà* (character) could fade too? It would appear so. It is not unusual to find a person who has been known to be a very good model of excellent character (*omolúwàbí*) suddenly turn bad. This may be due to several factors: downturn in fortunes, sudden and shocking loss of a loved one, etc. The case of *Efúnsetán Aníwúrà, Iyálóde Ibadan* comes readily to mind here. In the play written by Akinwumi Isola, Efunsetan is presented as a very cheerful and generous woman. Then something happens. Her only daughter dies during childbirth and suddenly Efunsetan turns monstrous, committing all kinds of atrocities. The point that needs to be noted in this is that even in such cases, when the cosmetic of existence suddenly disappears, there still remains the core of existence and its original beauty. The moral that appears to come out of this, therefore, is that to avoid this sudden degeneration of *iwà* (character), there is need for character training from the beginning so that the cosmetic of *iwà* (character) may have time to sink into the core of *iwà* (existence) very early in life. This is what the socialization process is all about, though the limits on how far it can go are also very well appreciated in the pragmatic approach of the people to moral education. Both concepts of *iwà* are therefore important for our understanding Yoruba moral ideas and attention is normally paid to them in traditional patterns of moral education.

Children are appreciated for what they are. Though they are encouraged to be the best they could be, when, for some reason, they do not conform, they are not thrown out because, as they say, "*a kì í fi omo burúkú fún ekùn pa je*" (we do not throw a child to the tiger just because he/she is bad). Indeed, it is recognized, in various idioms, that a child cannot be altogether bad; he/she must have certain traits of goodness or virtues and even if all bad, he/she must have certain useful features even in his/her badness: "*omo burúkú ní ojó tirè*" (a bad child has his/her day of usefulness), and also "*nítorí wèrè ti ìta làá fíí ní wèrè ti ilé*" (since there are rascals outside, we should not mind the rascality of our own kids – because they can stand up to defend us if the rascals from outside should attempt to attack us). These sayings show that the Yoruba have a more or less pragmatic approach to the moral upbringing of children and an attitude of tolerance to adult behavior. While they do not encourage immoral behavior, they know that once in a while people may behave immorally when they are out of sight. (*Kò sí eniti kìi hu ìwà ìbàjé bí ilè bá dá tán; eniti Olódùmarè pa tirè mó ní èniyàn rere.*)

It may be argued by advocates of the claim that religion is the foundation for Yoruba morality that the foregoing reference to *Ìwà* as the primacy of existence and character supports their position and contradicts the point I have made concerning the pragmatic nature of Yoruba ethics. However, it would be a misconception of the whole point. As I have observed above, *Ifá* is not just a religion. It is a source of Yoruba collective wisdom. It is generally acknowledged that *Orúnmìlà* speaks in parables and when traditional thinkers need to drive home a point, they make easy recourse to what appears to be the age-old tradition of speaking in parables. Notice also that in the story *Orúnmìlà*, the oracle himself, is *blamed* for maltreating his wife. This should strike a note: that even the oracle is not spared as far as the moral judgment of actions is concerned. And for a devotee of the *Ifá* oracle, the morality of the society appears to provide a yardstick for even judging the conduct of the oracle. It follows therefore that the Yoruba are very pragmatic in their approach to morality, and though religion may serve them as a motivating force, it is not the ultimate appeal in moral matters.

Notes

1 N. A. Fadipe, *The Sociology of the Yoruba*, ed. with an Introduction by F. Olu Okediji and O. O. Okediji, Ibadan University Press, 1970, p. 150.

2 Recall here the story of Moremi, the Yoruba heroine who sacrificed her only son for the survival of her community.

3 K. A. Busia, *The Challenge of Africa*, New York: Praeger, 1962, p. 33.

4 Busia, p. 34.

5 Kwame Gyekye, *An Essay on African Philosophical Thought: The Akan Conceptual Scheme*, New York: Cambridge, 1987, p. 155.

6 Kwasi Wiredu, "Morality and Religion in Akan Thought" in H. Odera Oruka and D. A. Masolo, eds, *Philosophy and Cultures*, Nairobi: Bookwise, 1983, p. 13.

7 Gyekye, pp. 129–53.

8 Bolaji Idowu, *Olodumare: God in Yoruba Belief*, Lagos: Longmans, 1962, p. 144.

9 Ibid.

10 Idowu, p. 144.

11 Ibid., p. 145.

12 Ibid.

13 Ibid.

14 Ibid., p. 146.

15 Ibid., p. 149.

16 Ibid., p. 150.

17 M. Akin Makinde, "African Culture and Moral Systems: A Philosophical Study," *Second Order: An African Journal of Philosophy* [New Series], Special Issue on Ethics and African Societies, vol. 1, no. 2, July 1988, pp. 1–27.

18 Ibid., p. 2.

19 Makinde, p. 2.

20 Ibid., p. 3.

21 Ibid.

22 Ibid., p. 4.

23 Ibid., p. 6.

24 Ibid.

25 Ibid., p. 10.

26 Wande Abimbola, *Sixteen Great Poems of Ifa*, UNESCO, 1975, p. 32.

27 Ibid., p. 11.

28 Ibid., p. 12.

29 See Niyi Oladeji, "Proverbs as Language Signposts in Yoruba Pragmatic Ethics," *Second Order: An African Journal of Philosophy*, vol. 1, no. 2, July, 1988, p. 49. For a similar emphasis on the pragmatic nature of Yoruba ethics, see Olatunde B. Lawuyi, "The Tortoise and the Snail: Animal Identities and Ethical Issues Concerning Political Behaviors among the Yoruba of Nigeria," *Second Order*, ibid., pp. 29–43.

30 Segun Gbadegesin, "World-view" in Toyin Falola and A. Adediran, eds, *A New History of Nigeria for Colleges*, Lagos: John West, 1986, pp. 227–44.

31 Ibid., p. 242.

32 My discussion here has benefited immensely from a series of taped interviews I had with some traditional thinkers: Pa Joseph Olanrewaju Gbadegesin, Pa Adeojo and Gbenle Ogungbenro.

33 Wande Abimbola, "*Ìwàpèlé*: The Concept of Good Character in *Ifá* Literary Corpus" in Wande Abimbola, ed., *Yoruba Oral Tradition*, Ife African Languages and Literatures Series no. 1, 1975, p. 393; and Roland Abiodun, "Identity and the Artistic Process in Yoruba

Aesthetic Concept of *Iwa*," *Journal of Cultures and Ideas*, vol. 1, no. 1, 1983, pp. 13–30. In the following discussion, I draw on these contributions.

34 Abiodun, p. 14.
35 Ibid.
36 Ibid., p. 15.

16

Concerning Violence

Frantz Fanon

Decolonization, which sets out to change the order of the world, is, obviously, a program of complete disorder. But it cannot come as a result of magical practices, nor of a natural shock, nor of a friendly understanding. Decolonization, as we know, is a historical process: that is to say that it cannot be understood, it cannot become intelligible nor clear to itself except in the exact measure that we can discern the movements which give it historical form and content. Decolonization is the meeting of two forces, opposed to each other by their very nature, which in fact owe their originality to that sort of substantification which results from and is nourished by the situation in the colonies. Their first encounter was marked by violence and their existence together – that is to say the exploitation of the native by the settler – was carried on by dint of a great array of bayonets and cannons. The settler and the native are old acquaintances. In fact, the settler is right when he speaks of knowing "them" well. For it is the settler who has brought the native into existence and who perpetuates his existence. The settler owes the fact of his very existence, that is to say, his property, to the colonial system.

Decolonization never takes place unnoticed, for it influences individuals and modifies them fundamentally. It transforms spectators crushed with their inessentiality into privileged actors, with the grandiose glare of history's floodlights upon them.

It brings a natural rhythm into existence, introduced by new men, and with it a new language and a new humanity. Decolonization is the veritable creation of new men. But this creation owes nothing of its legitimacy to any supernatural power; the "thing" which has been colonized becomes man during the same process by which it frees itself.

In decolonization, there is therefore the need of a complete calling in question of the colonial situation. If we wish to describe it precisely, we might find it in the well-known words: "The last shall be first and the first last." Decolonization is the putting into practice of this sentence. That is why, if we try to describe it, all decolonization is successful.

The naked truth of decolonization evokes for us the searing bullets and bloodstained knives which emanate from it. For if the last shall be first, this will only come to pass after a murderous and decisive struggle between the two protagonists. That affirmed intention to place the last at the head of things, and to make them climb at a pace (too quickly, some say) the well-known steps which characterize an organized society, can only triumph if we use all means to turn the scale, including, of course, that of violence.

You do not turn any society, however primitive it may be, upside down with such a program if you have not decided from the very beginning, that is to say from the actual formulation of that program, to overcome all the obstacles that you will come across in so doing. The native who decides to put the program into practice, and to become its moving force, is ready for violence at all times.

From birth it is clear to him that this narrow world, strewn with prohibitions, can only be called in question by absolute violence.

The colonial world is a world divided into compartments. It is probably unnecessary to recall the existence of native quarters and European quarters, of schools for natives and schools for Europeans; in the same way we need not recall apartheid in South Africa. Yet, if we examine closely this system of compartments, we will at least be able to reveal the lines of force it implies. This approach to the colonial world, its ordering and its geographical layout will allow us to mark out the lines on which a decolonized society will be reorganized.

The colonial world is a world cut in two. The dividing line, the frontiers are shown by barracks and police stations. In the colonies it is the policeman and the soldier who are the official, instituted go-betweens, the spokesmen of the settler and his rule of oppression. In capitalist societies the educational system, whether lay or clerical, the structure of moral reflexes handed down from father to son, the exemplary honesty of workers who are given a medal after fifty years of good and loyal service, and the affection which springs from harmonious relations and good behavior – all these aesthetic expressions of respect for the established order serve to create around the exploited person an atmosphere of submission and of inhibition which lightens the task of policing considerably. In the capitalist countries a multitude of moral teachers, counselors, and "bewilderers" separate the exploited from those in power. In the colonial countries, on the contrary, the policeman and the soldier, by their immediate presence and their frequent and direct action maintain contact with the native and advise him by means of rifle butts and napalm not to budge. It is obvious here that the agents of government speak the language of pure force. The intermediary does not lighten the oppression, nor seek to hide the domination; he shows them up and puts them into practice with the clear conscience of an upholder of the peace; yet he is the bringer of violence into the home and into the mind of the native.

The zone where the natives live is not complementary to the zone inhabited by the settlers. The two zones are opposed, but not in the service of a higher unity. Obedient to the rules of pure Aristotelian logic, they both follow the principle of reciprocal exclusivity. No conciliation is possible, for of the two terms, one is superfluous. The settlers' town is a strongly built town, all made of stone and steel. It is a brightly lit town; the streets are covered with asphalt, and the garbage cans swallow all the leavings, unseen, unknown and hardly thought about. The settler's feet are never visible, except perhaps in the sea; but there you're never close enough to see them. His feet are protected by strong shoes although the streets of his town are clean and even, with no holes or stones. The settler's town is a well-fed town, an easygoing town; its belly is always full of good things. The settlers' town is a town of white people, of foreigners.

The town belonging to the colonized people, or at least the native town, the Negro village, the medina, the reservation, is a place of ill fame, peopled by men of evil repute. They are born there, it matters little where or how; they die there, it matters not where, nor how. It is a world without spaciousness; men live there on top of each other, and their huts are built one on top of the other. The native town is a hungry town, starved of bread, of meat, of shoes, of coal, of light. The native town is a crouching village, a town on its knees, a town wallowing in the mire. It is a town of niggers and dirty Arabs. The look that the native turns on the settler's town is a look of lust, a look of envy; it expresses his dreams of possession – all manner of possession: to sit at the settler's table, to sleep in the settler's bed, with his wife if possible. The colonized man is an envious man. And this the settler knows very well; when their glances meet he ascertains bitterly, always on the defensive, "They want to take our place." It is true, for there is no native who does not dream at least once a day of setting himself up in the settler's place.

This world divided into compartments, this world cut in two is inhabited by two different species. The originality of the colonial context is that economic reality, inequality, and the immense difference of ways of life never come to mask the human realities. When you examine at close quarters the colonial context, it is evident that what parcels out the world is to begin with the fact of belonging to or not belonging to a given race, a given species. In the colonies the economic substructure is also a superstructure. The cause is the consequence; you are rich because you are white, you are white because your are rich. This is why Marxist analysis should always be slightly stretched every time we have to do with the colonial problem. . . .

The violence which has ruled over the ordering

of the colonial world, which has ceaselessly drummed the rhythm for the destruction of native social forms and broken up without reserve the systems of reference of the economy, the customs of dress and external life, that same violence will be claimed and taken over by the native at the moment when, deciding to embody history in his own person, he surges into the forbidden quarters. To wreck the colonial world is henceforward a mental picture of action which is very clear, very easy to understand and which may be assumed by each one of the individuals which constitute the colonized people. To break up the colonial world does not mean that after the frontiers have been abolished lines of communication will be set up between the two zones. The destruction of the colonial world is no more and no less than the abolition of one zone, its burial in the depths of the earth or its expulsion from the country.

The natives' challenge to the colonial world is not a rational confrontation of points of view. It is not a treatise on the universal, but the untidy affirmation of an original idea propounded as an absolute. The colonial world is a Manichean world. It is not enough for the settler to delimit physically, that is to say with the help of the army and the police force, the place of the native. As if to show the totalitarian character of colonial exploitation the settler paints the native as a sort of quintessence of evil. Native society is not simply described as a society lacking in values. It is not enough for the colonist to affirm that those values have disappeared from, or still better never existed in, the colonial world. The native is declared insensible to ethics; he represents not only the absence of values, but also the negation of values. He is, let us dare to admit, the enemy of values, and in this sense he is the absolute evil. He is the corrosive element, destroying all that comes near him; he is the deforming element, disfiguring all that has to do with beauty or morality; he is the depository of maleficent powers, the unconscious and irretrievable instrument of blind forces.

As soon as the native begins to pull on his moorings, and to cause anxiety to the settler, he is handed over to well-meaning souls who in cultural congresses point out to him the specificity and wealth of Western values. But every time Western values are mentioned they produce in the native a sort of stiffening or muscular lockjaw. During the period of decolonization, the native's reason is appealed to. He is offered definite values, he is told frequently that decolonization need not mean regression, and that he must put his trust in qualities which are well-tried, solid, and highly esteemed. But it so happens that when the native hears a speech about Western culture he pulls out his knife – or at least he makes sure it is within reach. The violence with which the supremacy of white values is affirmed and the aggressiveness which has permeated the victory of these values over the ways of life and of thought of the native mean that, in revenge, the native laughs in mockery when Western values are mentioned in front of him. In the colonial context the settler only ends his work of breaking in the native when the latter admits loudly and intelligibly the supremacy of the white man's values. In the period of decolonization the colonized masses mock at these very values, insult them, and vomit them up.... As far as the native is concerned, morality is very concrete; it is to silence the settler's defiance, to break his flaunting violence – in a word, to put him out of the picture. The well-known principle that all men are equal will be illustrated in the colonies from the moment that the native claims that he is the equal of the settler. One step more, and he is ready to fight to be more than the settler. In fact, he has already decided to eject him and to take his place; as we see it, it is a whole material and moral universe which is breaking up. The intellectual who for his part has followed the colonialist with regard to the universal abstract will fight in order that the settler and the native may live together in peace in a new world. But the thing he does not see, precisely because he is permeated by colonialism and all its ways of thinking, is that the settler, from the moment that the colonial context disappears, has no longer any interest in remaining or in co-existing. It is not by chance that, even before any negotiation between the Algerian and French governments had taken place, the European minority which calls itself "liberal" had already made its position clear: it demanded nothing more nor less than twofold citizenship. By setting themselves apart in an abstract manner, the liberals try to force the settler into taking a very concrete jump into the unknown. Let us admit it, the settler knows perfectly well that no phraseology can be a substitute for reality.

Thus the native discovers that his life, his breath, his beating heart are the same as those of the settler. He finds out that the settler's skin is not of any more value than a native's skin; and it must be said that this discovery shakes the world in a very necessary manner. All the new, revolutionary assurance of the native stems from it. For if, in fact, my life is worth as much as the settler's, his glance no longer shrivels me up nor freezes me, and his voice no longer turns me into stone. I am no longer on tenterhooks in his presence; in fact, I don't give a damn for him. Not only does his presence no longer trouble me, but I am already preparing such efficient ambushes for him that soon there will be no way out but that of flight.

We have said that the colonial context is characterized by the dichotomy which it imposes upon the whole people. Decolonization unifies that people by the radical decision to remove from it its heterogeneity, and by unifying it on a national, sometimes a racial, basis. We know the fierce words of the Senegalese patriots, referring to the maneuvers of their president, Senghor: "We have demanded that the higher posts should be given to Africans; and now Senghor is Africanizing the Europeans." That is to say that the native can see clearly and immediately if decolonization has come to pass or not, for his minimum demands are simply that the last shall be first.

17

Morals and the Value of Human Life

M. M. Agrawal

B. What do you call just and unjust?
A. What seems so to the world as a whole.

Voltaire

In the first section of this paper I wish to present and defend the following thesis. A large part of what we call moral discourse is directly concerned with procuring a relevant kind of *justification* for an actual or proposed act of an individual, a group of persons or, indirectly, of an institution. When in actual life we justify our actions morally, use do so by reference to certain values, generally accepted by the members of the society in which the question of justification is raised, and recognized by them as moral values. But to give a moral justification is, in principle, to provide an *ultimate* kind of justification, which presupposes the notion of 'ultimate value'. The moral values of a particular society, therefore, should be seen to interpret to its members, the notion of an ultimate value, which they may or may not consciously recognize. Thus the notion of ultimate value serves as the regulative principle for the determination of moral values and in certain cases it may serve to disqualify an accepted value as a moral value. In a society, as more and more of its members come to regard morality as a rational enterprise, the role of the regulative principle gathers importance. Conversely, in a hide-bound society where morality is simply identified with a strictly prescribed mode of behaviour, the role of the regulative principle awaits a revolution.

In the second part of this paper I contend that the ultimate value, presupposed to a rational morality, is the value of human life.

I

In recent analytical moral philosophy, philosophers have concentrated their attention on the study of the logical character of moral judgments. Through an understanding of the formal features of a moral judgment, which centrally involves answering the question 'what is one doing in making a moral judgment?', one is expected to discover the main burden of moral discourse. To the above question, as we know, the intuitionists, the emotivists, and the prescriptivists have given different answers. But unfortunately their attempts have not met with great successes. One main reason for this seems to rest in their (mistaken) approach, which puts the study of the nature of moral judgments at the centre of ethical studies.

It seems clear that a moral judgment is just the tail-piece to a lot of discussion and reflection on matters of conduct which naturally emerges between human beings, in their predicament characterized by the fact that they have to live together and have to share the resources of their environment and their labour amongst them, and who, unfortunately, find it hard to secure their fair share

From *Philosophy in Africa: Trends and Perspectives*, ed. P. O. Bodunrin, University of Ife Press (1985); reproduced by kind permission of P. O. Bodunrin.

without prejudice to other people's interests. It is in these discussions and reflections, generally referred to as 'moral reasoning' i.e. in the business that is conducted or presumed to have been conducted before a moral judgment is arrived at, that the main features of man's concern with morality are revealed. Thus it is more to the point that we try to understand what kinds of transaction are made during the conduct of the business in question.

This point is completely obscured by the talk in contemporary moral philosophy of 'justifying a moral or a value judgment' itself. For to seek and give a justification of a moral judgment must be a relatively more sophisticated second order activity. In real life, at the first order level of moral discourse, mostly, what we have to justify are our *actions* or decisions to act in x, y manner, which we do, among other things, by *making* moral judgments. So when we are trying to understand the nature of moral discourse the talk of justifying moral judgments, as a primary task, can be very misleading.

What I am saying here can be explained further by analogy to logical reasoning. In a court of law, first there is a case about someone's alleged offense, and the prosecutor cross-examines the witnesses and the accused to establish the facts of the case including the intention of the accused. Then reference to relevant laws is made and a judgment, or a verdict by the jury, is arrived at. So far, what was up for justification was a certain alleged *act* of the offender, and not a legal judgment. It is only if the judgment in question is challenged that the question of justifying it arises and then a higher court, following a somewhat different procedure, may discuss the case as presented in the first court and arrive at their own judgment. Similarly, the question of justification of a moral *judgment* arises only when a disagreement is to be settled. Normally; we discuss a case from the moral point of view to be in a position to pass a moral judgment. Of course a morally aware person has already taken into account the morality of the act he performs just as a law-abiding citizen keeps on the right side of the law, as though he had done the reasoning which might have been conducted in a court if he acted contrary to the law.

Some philosophers who do not follow the judgment approach in ethical studies, turn, on the contrary, their attention on the study of moral practices. But here, they forget that the following of rules such as 'Thou shalt not steal', without, in general, the availability of the backing of moral reasoning will not amount to a *moral* practice; for then there would be no way of distinguishing it from action based upon mere prudence, custom, or religious conditioning etc.

Moral reasoning, as distinct from moral practice, is a self-conscious human activity. As such it must have a definite *purpose*. Further, as a species of reasoning, it is obviously a rational enterprise, while a moral practice can be 'blind'. Thus to understand, in general terms, the nature of the transactions that take place during moral reasoning we must enquire into the aim or the point of such engagement. What is it that we are seeking to establish through such reasoning, not as a social or a psychological consequence of this exercise, but as its objectively intended result? What is it that enables us to close the business by announcing a moral judgment?

When we are trying to discover the aim or the point of moral reasoning it may help us to consider what in actual life prompts us to engage in moral discussions. Especially, is there anything about the human predicament such that at times we could be *required* by the society to participate, even though minimally, in discussion on questions of right and wrong in human conduct?

If, for example, I were a very reserved sort of person, minding mostly, as it were, my own business, it would be unlikely that I would subject other people's behaviour to moral scrutiny. Similarly, if I had the capacity to suffer a great deal of personal loss and injustice, I may never take a stand and go to the extent of condemning other people's attitude towards me. Needless to say that I would not be the right sort of person who would seek to give moral guidance to others, least of all try to influence their feelings and attitudes to turn them into moral creatures. Again if I were a happy-go-lucky sort of person who lived from day to day without much thought and reflection on life as a whole, I may never in fact face a dilemma to compel me to reason with myself. And to this extent I may in fact have no need for *moral* reasoning. Nor to this extent a tolerant society need find my attitude morally repugnant. But supposing, to take an extreme case, a war broke out, and men of my age and fitness were required to fight in defence while I did not wish to do so. Well, in this situation, I could no longer remain a moral recluse short of being classified 'insane'. The least, surely, I will have to do is to give a moral *justification* of my option which will involve me in moral reasoning.

What I am trying to say is this. Given the social

predicament, i.e. given the fact that human beings live *together* and yet are free to pursue the satisfaction of their personal goals, there will always be numerous occasions when the interests of the individuals or groups will clash and people will be called upon to justify their decisions to act in this or that way. In other words, it is a feature of the social situation in which a human being finds himself that other people could always reasonably ask him to justify his actual or proposed conduct, when that is expected to affect the wellbeing of others. That is, unless I am a 'drop-out', my membership of a human society carries with it the assumption that I would normally come forward to justify my actions to others, if need be. There is kind of incoherence in the suggestion that a normal person may, in general, refuse to be accountable for his socially relevant kind of conduct to the society which nurtures him. And the kind of accountability that is required here is what we refer to as 'moral'. And the kind of discussion that produces the required justification is what we call moral reasoning.

We can summarize the point just made as follows. On such occasions when a man can be required to participate in moral reasoning, the context is primarily that of seeking a *justification* for some actual or proposed act. From this it follows that finding the relevant kind of justification, or exposing the lack of it, must be the primary aim or the point of moral reasoning. It is true that, more apparently, moral reasoning is employed not only to seek justification of actions but also to appraise people – their character and motives etc. But it is not difficult to see that our interest in making such appraisals is dependent upon our interest in the nature of what they *do* or what they might possibly do. In recent times many philosophers, notably Mrs Phillippa Foot, have argued that moral argument must have a *point*, and that its point is to determine what relationship a given conduct has to 'human good and harm'. There is no doubt that in moral arguments, questions of human good and harm naturally arise. But that does not explain the point of a *moral* argument as opposed to any other argument, e.g. political, economic, etc. The point of a moral argument, as we have seen, is to seek a relevant kind of justification; it is a further question whether that justification is procured by reference to human good and harm or not.

It may now be objected that my analysis of the situation that requires us to invoke morality does not bear with reality. In many societies the conduct of their members is not judged by reasoning in open public forums. Rather, moral appraisals are made strictly by reference to a prescribed set of standards. In these societies people tend to identify the prescribed practices with the content of morality. They tend to think that acting morally means behaving in the prescribed manner, and no distinction is drawn between customary expectations, such as regarding matters of etiquette, and matters of morality. Moreover, people in these societies tend to think of the dissimilar, although similarly prescribed, practices of other societies as immoral. In these societies the question of seeking justifications by moral reasoning simply does not arise. How then do I say that, typically, moral questions arise when someone's conduct is required to be shown to have a rational justification.

Now, in the kind of social order in question, it is true that the question of justification is not often raised. But this is not because the idea of justification is thought to be irrelevant to moral appraisal but because the procedure of justifying has been over-simplified by setting up absolute standards to which behaviour must conform. And this simplification is achieved by sacrificing the freedom of the rational agent to defend himself if he decides to reject the operative moral standards of his society. It is a feature of an authoritarian society that its people are denied a chance to engage in a rational discussion of the standards of behaviour thrust upon them, to which they can only conform. But the enforcement of a packaged morality does not dissolve the need of rational discussion, it only evades it and consequently brutalizes morality. Conversely, in an open society, it must always be possible to discuss the morality of particular issues rationally. The conduct of moral reasoning seems to be embedded in the very structure of human relationship, where people expect of each other that certain of their actions should be justifiable, and therefore acceptable, to them. In a society of free and rational creatures, it is natural that we demand and offer justification for our actions when such actions seem to threaten or minimize the wellbeing of people, since to seek justification is to follow a rational procedure in determining what ought to be done. So far, then, our contention is that moral reasoning is characteristically a justificatory enterprise. The next crucial question that naturally arises concerns the nature of this justification. More specifically, what is it that justifies actions *morally*? In trying to answer this question we shall not concern ourselves with the substantial principles that might be appealed to in moral justification. Our effort will be limited to determining some of the formal features of whatever may serve to justify actions morally, and to showing why anything to be considered as a standard in moral justification must possess those formal features.

Now, before we can give a straight answer to the above question, it will be necessary to be clear about the following matters. First, we must note certain general points about the notion of justification itself. Among other things, any process of justification involves:

1 following rational procedure, which in turn involves looking for reasons which are relevant to the case in view. (If whatever pleased onself justified one's conduct then there could be no question of justification.)
2 a reference to some principle or characteristics other than those constituting the contents of the conduct to be justified.
3 This external element referred to should be such that it is either already accepted without needing further justification, or else it can be shown to be acceptable by reference to another element of that kind, i.e. a justification is necessarily impersonal and objective or else it could not come to be *required* by other rational creatures.
4 What eventually justifies must be recognized to possess the highest value or worth in the universe of discourse within which the question of justification is raised.

Next, we must be clear about the context in which a moral justification is sought. For this we need to consider: (a) the nature of the conduct for which it is sought, and (b) the nature of the entity to which the justification is offered. Let us take the former first. While ideally a rational being needs to have some sort of justification for all his deeds, it is not always a moral justification that is required. A commander, for example, in a battlefield may have to take a snappy decision and order his force to withdraw from the advanced positions. It is a technical decision, and the justification of this decision will be sought by reference to the norms of good combat tactics. And even though his decision affects the lives of many, unless he is suspected of some non-military motives for his decision, he would not be required to give a moral justification for it. Similarly, many things which we all do in day to day life, which have no foreseeable consequence for others, such as choosing to have tea

rather than coffee, do not need moral justification. By contrast, I think it will suffice us to note that any action when considered in its non-technical and non-personal aspect, and in terms of its possible relevance to the lives of others, *could be* in need of moral justification.

Now let us consider (b) above. At first, this enquiry may strike us as a bit odd, for after all, I may have to offer moral justification to all sorts of entities, my father, the head of my department, the government or the trade union to which I belong, etc. But now let us note the following complexity. The justification which I may offer to my father is supposed to be a moral justification; it is not something such that it has to satisfy him *qua* my father, not even if he happens to be the person who is directly affected by the act which is to be justified. That is, in general, a moral justification is not such that it has necessarily to satisfy the person who is the victim of my misdeed. In fact, I may not have to offer a justification to my father at all, since he may not be bothered about it. But my friends and colleagues may be more concerned about my behaviour towards my father. So I may have to satisfy them rather than the victim. In fact, it could be anyone who feels concerned about my behaviour in question whom I may have to satisfy. Similarly, the justification of my behaviour which I have to offer to the head of my department has nothing to do with its being offered to the *head*. It is offered to the head rather than the cleaner only because he is more directly concerned with hearing my case.

What these observations show is that the entity to which a moral justification is offered is conceived as anyone. When we are giving a moral justification we have to ignore the social status or the personality of the entity to be satisfied. Our moral justifications are not to consist of such reasons which may have a sectarian or idiosyncratic appeal. When we offer a moral justification to anyone – a father, a stranger, the state or church – it has to be to the satisfaction of *anyone*. That is, a moral justification is not restricted to the satisfaction of an individual or to the members of a select group or a sect, etc., but, in principle, it should be able to satisfy the whole mankind.

We can now attempt to answer our main question concerning the formal features of the standard in moral justification. We have seen, one, that the action which needs a moral justification is considered in its non-technical and non-personal aspect, and in terms of its possible relevance to the lives of others. And, two, that the justification offered should be such that, in principle, it could satisfy the whole mankind. So much is implied by the context in which a moral justification is sought. And now, these implications, coupled with the last requirement (see 4 above) for anything to count as a justification at all, lead to the answer we are looking for. They lead to the conclusion that to provide a justification in morals, ultimately, what we appeal to must be a universally *accepted value*. Such a value must necessarily transcend the limitations of creed, race, and culture. It must be a sort of value such that by reference to it the historically determined social values of particular societies might themselves be justified. Such a value, then, rightly deserves the title of 'ultimate human value'.

It is pertinent at this juncture to take note of the position taken by Phillips and Mounce and to compare it with mine. It is true that in actual day-to-day life, actions are morally justified by reference to certain generally accepted values in a given society. Thus Phillips and Mounce point out that 'when we wish to justify our moral judgments or render them intelligible, we make use of such concepts as honesty, truthfulness, generosity, etc.'[1] 'Within our society, it is taken as a matter of course that a man should tell the truth rather than lie, respect life rather than kill, be generous rather than mean, and it is possible for a man on a particular occasion to make a moral judgment or adopt a moral position.'[2] And later they say:

> In order to ask whether something is right or wrong, we must abide by the rules governing the use of these terms. The application of the word 'wrong' to uses of lying is one of our criteria for the use of that term. When we consider lying in a purely descriptive aspect, then for the moment we step outside these criteria. Having done so, however, we can no longer ask whether lying is wrong because in deciding whether an act is wrong we use lying as one of our criteria. One can convince oneself of this simply by trying to imagine the situation in which one would ask whether or not lying is right. One can imagine oneself asking whether a *particular* lie is justified, but if one asks whether lying in general is right, one finds oneself at a loss, not simply to answer the question, but to imagine the kind of consideration that would lead one to answer it.[3]

Now, ignoring the difficulty we discussed ear-

lier, in the talk of justifying moral *judgments*, there seems to be some truth in the positions taken above. But Phillips and Mounce put too much weight on the contingent fact that certain values are taken as a matter of course in a given society which obscures the nature of justification in morals. It is for example true that unless certain moral values were taken as a matter of course there will be no occasion for a moral discussion. But this fact has no tendency to show that for that reason any set of values taken as a matter of course are ambiguous or unquestionable. Nor does it explain why the values taken as a matter of course are *moral* values. Since a prevailing value may not be a true moral value at all but a historical product of prejudice and ignorance. Consider, for example, a society in which a young prince and a princess are executed in public for loving each other of their own free will but against the wishes of the 'elder' of their royalty. In such a society the obedience to the authority of the elder is taken as a matter of course and apparently rated much higher than respect for human life and personal freedom. Are we then going to take it as a true moral value? Phillips and Mounce will naturally retort that it was a true moral value *for that society*, but not in all human societies. But then they have to explain to us why *we* should describe it as a *moral* value at all. It cannot be so simply because that value is in that society taken as a matter of course to justify conduct. For that is not *our* concept of morality or moral value. In the last quotation above, Phillips and Mounce themselves maintain that 'if one asks whether lying in general is right, one finds oneself at a loss, not simply to answer the question, *but to imagine the kind of consideration* that would lead one to answer it' (my italics). If this is true, then indeed, we cannot question the truth of 'lying in general is wrong'. But then this would not be so simply because 'within our society, it is taken as a matter of course that a man should tell the truth rather than lie.' Moreover, we need some explanation of the fact why it is so difficult 'to imagine the kind of consideration that would lead one to answer' if lying in general is right. And if it is impossible to imagine this, then 'lying in general is wrong' must be a universally valid belief, irrespective of whether or not, in any particular society it was actually taken as a matter of course.

The truth, however, is that there is no human society in which lying is preferred to truth, where murder and rape are encouraged, where old and disabled, not useful to the society, are dumped in the sea, where ignorance, poverty, and disease are contemplated as perfections of the human condition. That is, we can separate a nexus of moral values which are universally accepted, from those values which are more or less peculiar to a given society. We can then enquire why there is such a universal nexus of moral values, and whether, in the nature of the human situation, it must be so. The answer to these questions will also reveal the limits of the range of values which a society could possibly uphold as moral values.

Thus it can be argued against Phillips and Mounce that among the values taken as a matter of course in a given society some may turn out to be phoney ones. And often it may be possible to detect them by criteria available from within the axiological resources of that society. The rationale of the distinction between the genuine and non-genuine moral values is, as we have suggested, to be found in their connection with the constitutive principle of the universal nexus of moral values or what we have called the 'ultimate human value'. Thus the values which are taken as a matter of course in a society exhibit the understanding, or the lack of it, of its members of the true nature of morality, since, as we have noted, they constitute their interpretation of the ultimate human value. A value is not a moral value unless, in principle, it could be upheld by all mankind. Moral justification as a concept distinct from other forms of social justifications could not exist without the assumption that there are certain values which *any* human being will accept if only he had the freedom and reason to perceive them.

The role of moral values can be appreciated now. We do not normally justify our actions by reference to ultimate values. Many of us may never have even thought of any such thing. In day-to-day life we justify actions by reference to what are generally accepted as moral values in the society to which we belong. But if my analysis is correct, the validity of this procedure requires us to assume that the moral values in question embody some or other aspect of an ultimate human value. Thus, in effect, moral values mediate between particular actions and an ultimate human value. Theoretically, one can do without the use of moral principles, if one has the intelligence and time to begin, as it were, always from the beginning. For one who perceives the true end of morality and knows how to realize it in actual life, conformity to the ready made moral principles is unnecessary. The sum total of the moral values of a society is its image of humanity, for it constitutes the society's conception of human perfection.

II

We have argued that the concept of moral reasoning primarily signifies a rational enterprise, namely, an undertaking to seek and offer an ultimate kind of justification for human conduct. It is a kind of justification which is *in principle* offered to the whole mankind and can be required of anyone. Although, in day-to-day life, moral justification is sought by reference to certain values which constitute the universal nexus of morality, for such a system to work there must exist an *ultimate* value (or values) by reference to which the ultimate character of moral justifications may be established, if need be. The universal nexus of morality represents the immediate meaning of the ultimate value and thus, in a secondary sense, it may also be regarded as ultimate. Now, in this section, I offer the suggestion that the ultimate value pre-supposed to morality is what has traditionally been recognized as the sanctity of human life, and derivatively, as the supreme worth of the individual person, or simply as the value of human life or humanity. To value human life is to have respect for persons as *ends*, i.e. to care for them for what they are, to care for their existence. Subsequently, to value human life is to value all those things which are necessary for man to develop all his potentialities to live as a truly rational social being. Thus moral values can be defined as those in whose pursuit the ultimate value of human life is best realized.

Many philosophers, often as diverse as Kant and Marx, have from different considerations, reached the conclusion that morality must be universal. Thus, Kant founded morality on human reason, which is universal in mankind and which transcends the limitations of his 'inclinations'. He saw that human beings *qua* rational agents possess intrinsic worth, since they are *ends* in themselves; while other worldly entities, such as seas, hills, forests, and animals, are not objects of values or disvalue until they are considered in terms of human interests, goals and purposes. Human beings, he thought, must also be the ultimate end of man's rational pursuits, since man's practical reason can consider only that as an end which is in some sense necessarily an end, such as an end-in-itself. Thus, since the ultimate end of man's rational pursuit is the same for Kant as the moral end, he gave the fundamental principle of morality, in one of its formulations in the following: 'So act that you treat humanity in your own person and in the person of everyone else always at the same time as an end and never merely as means.'[4]

Similarly Karl Marx, although notoriously a critic of universal morality, was led to a similar position from the considerations of his glorified image of the natural status of man as the bearer of such potentialities which allow him to treat himself truly as an end in himself. Recognizing that in the universe, man is the only subject and thus the highest being for man, Marx held that the truly social man is the supreme *end* of morality, and any situation or action that hinders him to be that is unethical.[5] Implicitly, then, Marx is also advocating the Kantian ethic 'to treat humanity as an end,' and explicitly, he goes beyond Kant to advocate the destruction of all those conditions which hinder man in becoming truly human.

Now, both the positions sketched above suffer from a common malady. Both Kant and Marx (and numerous others), as we have seen, are keen to attribute a certain dignity and worth to man, i.e. to recognize the value of human life, so that man can merit being treated as the true *end* of ethics. But they try, explicitly or implicitly, to *derive* this value from the consideration of certain facts about the nature of the *individual* man, such as his possession of a rational will, in case of Kant, or his potentiality to become the master of nature and himself, in case of Marx. And here they seem to go wrong on two counts. First, it seems clear that from the fact that man is a rational subject, or has extraordinary potentialities as a knowing being, it simply does not follow that he has any intrinsic moral superiority over other creatures that exist in nature. (Why, for example, should man not devote his life to the care of animals?) Second, from the fact that man has such potentialities as Marx claims, or, even from the fact that each individual person is, in some sense, an end in himself, as Kant claims, it cannot be seen to follow that each individual must make the whole humanity the supreme end of his rational or moral pursuit. From the fact, that is, that each individual is an end in himself, it does not follow that we should not *use* him for our individual ends. Kant and others seem to have raised the wrong question: 'what is the distinctive endowment of man by virtue of which he possesses intrinsic worth?' Traditionally it amounts to a search for some natural property of man which distinguishes him from brutes. And then it is claimed that by

virtue of possessing that property, and not for his *unitary being*, man is to be classed as a creature of intrinsic worth. And further, by implication, it is suggested that the claim about the worth of human life is a claim about which we can *decide*, in the light of some criteria. But, from what we go on to say about the value of human life, it will be apparent that the above views are totally mistaken.

The notion of ultimate value, as I am employing it here, carries with it a sort of necessity, implying a deep-rooted and an inalienable consciousness of worth in all mankind. In this sense, whatever is supposed to have ultimate worth is, albeit a *matter of fact*, not just a naturalistic value, i.e. something that just *happens* to be valued and which could easily be imagined to be otherwise. Nor is the ultimate value a non-naturalistic value, in the sense of being absolute and transcendental. Ethical systems based on both types of values have often been proposed, but none have stood the test of time. Further, an ultimate value could not be founded upon personal decision or belief or some kind of authority. For all these could easily be challenged. Nor, obviously, could the ultimate value derive its worth from anything extrinsic to it. In the sense which I am proposing, then, it will be seen that the ultimate value draws its necessity from the fact that given the human situation, the object of ultimate value must be so valued if human beings are to *be* what they are and act as they do. Thus, if, for human beings, human life must necessarily be an object of ultimate value, it should not, strictly speaking, require us to prove that it is so; rather we should expect, it to be manifest in the human situation. We should expect, that is, that when we open our eyes and look, we would see that the value of human life was already recognized to be ultimate. Let us then resist the temptation to ask, 'what gives him intrinsic worth?', and simply acknowledge the facts as they are.

In a society of persons, the attitude of one human being towards another *is* such that they regard each other as creatures of intrinsic worth. To say this is to take note of an inalienable element in human nature. It is to make what Wittgenstein calls 'remark on the natural history of man.'[6] This attitude is clearly manifest in the fact that one constantly expects of others to treat oneself in a manner which shows respect for one's person, since this expectation is not due to the fact that one thinks of oneself as a special case, rather, it is present irrespective of the considerations of one's social status. That is to say, that we constantly expect of others to treat us in a manner which shows that they have respect for persons generally. And this we expect as an exercise of their *freedom*, and not as an expression of their self-interest or some kind of coercion or fear of God etc. Needless to say that this expectation can be natural to us only if we ourselves recognize the value of human life.

Further, the attitude in question is manifest in our readiness to expect the other to behave as if he valued his own life, and also, in our preparedness to accept the other's expectation from us to honour his human status. This would not be the case if we did not, in general, attribute that dignity and value to human existence, which we find, in the human situation, so natural to do.

Moreover, it is not that we decide not to manipulate others like household objects because of moral reasons, or, as some philosophers think,[7] because we need others in other ways than we need household objects, i.e., because it is profitable not to manipulate them. Rather, to manifest this attitude is a part of what constitutes being a human person. To paraphrase an epithem of Wittgenstein's: 'My attitude towards human life is an attitude towards what is of ultimate worth. I am not of the *opinion* that human life has value.'[8]

We can understand a person who did not show respect for human life in his dealings with certain class of people or in certain special circumstances, such with a people of a different race or in the situation of war. For then we can explain his behaviour by reference to his conditioned upbringing in a philistine culture, or by reference to his role as a soldier which requires him to adopt a rough attitude towards his enemy. But we cannot understand a person who showed no respect for human life *generally*, who always showed contempt and disregard for other people's existence. I think it is certain that we will be led to think of such a person as somewhat subhuman.

And further, if we try to imagine a whole people who are totally devoid of the consciousness of the worth of human life, we find it even more difficult to understand what forms of life could exist in their society, or for that matter, if they could exist as a society of persons at all. For, in the human situation, a person exists in constant interaction with others. It is in this interaction that man reveals his 'personhood' to others and realizes his 'personhood' for himself. That is, the interaction between human beings is not like the interaction between mere objects or animals, rather, it is of the nature of *inter-personal relationship*. But could there be meaningful inter-personal relationship between people who are naturally disposed to attach no value to each other's existence? The following considerations make it difficult to imagine that it could be.

The ideal *form* of inter-personal relationship is manifest in communal activity, in which people cooperate with each other for common ends, with an understanding of the point or purpose of their pursuit. And in the choices exercised in communal activity comprising intentional actions of free and rational agents, we clearly *assert* the characteristic human attitude towards each other, viz., the attitude of treating each other with the natural presupposition of the worth or value of human life. In the human situation, we are all for each other, paradigms of existing beings who have intrinsic worth, unless in particular cases we can produce reasons to under-value someone's life. Clearly, without this attitude human beings could not relate to each other on the level of rational communal activity, and consequently could not realize a society of persons. I conclude then that the recognition of the value of human life is a necessary feature in the human situation. Indeed, it is possible in many circumstances and in many different ways to oppose or disregard this attitude, to the extent that we tend not to realize that it is so deep-rooted in human nature. If we wish to understand what it is in the nature of things that makes it intelligible why we have the attitude of value in question, we should consider the fact that in order to *become* a person from the very beginning, one has to be submerged in human life.

It is through such immersion that one comes to acquire the characteristically human conceptual framework of thought. A being who did not have the attitude of value towards the life of *others*, could actually imbibe, in their fellowship, this framework which is completely essential for his 'personhood'. A man's being is a *being-in* in the web of human relationships. One cannot choose to get in and get out of the web of life. To attain the consciousness of selfhood as a person requires one, choicelessly, to have submitted oneself to the personifying process of human relationships. And to have done so is to have recognized the value of human life, that is, the recognition of the value of human life is a necessary presupposition to that form of thought in which we think of ourselves in relationship with others. The existence of the whole web of inter-relatedness is a necessary precondition of the continuing realization of one's 'personhood'. Thus if I am going to attain the characteristically human aspirations, I, surely, could not regard humanity merely as a field for personal exploits. I could not regard my being in the human situation like being in a shop: Nor can I conceive of an alternative human situation.

We grow up to 'personhood' getting woven in the web of life around us. From the very beginning our mode of being in relation to others is characterized by our unconditional and unreasoned *acceptance* of the existence of others and of the whole web of life around them as the only intelligible reality. There is no question of *choosing* our mode of being in relation to that which presents itself as the original form of existence, within which we ourselves are being constituted. It is not surprising then that human life appears to us necessarily as a thing of ultimate worth.

In sum, what I have tried to say is that for human beings human life is unquestionably a reality of ultimate worth. Moral reasoning, concerned with ultimate justification, is possible because man is naturally disposed to uphold the value of human life. The moral values of a rational morality must reflect what we conceive to be the perfection of the human condition, since that is what, in the human situation, we must always value most.

Notes

1 Phillips and Mounce, *Moral Practices*, Routledge and Kegan Paul, 1969, p. 7.
2 Ibid., p. 8.
3 Ibid., p. 11.
4 See *Groundwork of the Metaphysics of Morals*.
5 Cf. E. Kamenka, *Marxism and Ethics*, Macmillan, 1969, p. 11.
6 See *Remarks on the Foundation of Mathematics*.
7 See Phillipa Foot, 'Moral Beliefs', *Aristotle Society Proceedings*, 1958.
8 See *Philosophical Investigations*, II, iv.

18

Moral Reasoning versus Racial Reasoning

Cornel West

The most depressing feature of the Clarence Thomas/Anita Hill hearings was neither the mean-spirited attacks of the Republicans nor the spineless silences of the Democrats – both reveal the predictable inability of most white politicians to talk candidly about race and gender. Rather, what most disturbed me was the low level of political discussion in black America about these hearings – a crude discourse about race and gender that bespeaks a failure of nerve of black leadership.

This failure of nerve was already manifest in the selection and confirmation process of Clarence Thomas. Bush's choice of Thomas caught most black leaders off guard. Few had the courage to say publicly that this was an act of cynical tokenism concealed by outright lies about Thomas being the most qualified candidate regardless of race. The fact that Thomas was simply unqualified for the Court – a claim warranted by his undistinguished record as a student (mere graduation from Yale Law School does not qualify one of the Supreme Court!); his turbulent 8 years at the EEOC, where he left thirteen thousand age-discrimination cases dying on the vine for lack of investigation; and his mediocre performance during a short 15 months as an appellate court judge – was not even mentioned. The very fact that no black leader could utter publicly that a black appointee for the Supreme Court was *unqualified* shows how captive they are to white-racist stereotypes about black intellectual talent. The point here is not simply that if Thomas were white they would have no trouble uttering this

fact from the rooftops, but also that their silence reveals that they may entertain the possibility that the racist stereotype is true. Hence their attempt to cover Thomas's mediocrity with silence. Of course, some privately admit his mediocrity then point out the mediocrity of Judge Souter and other Court judges – as if white mediocrity is a justification for black mediocrity. No double standards here, this argument goes, if a black man is unqualified, one can defend and excuse him by appealing to other unqualified white judges. This chimes well with a cynical tokenism of the lowest common demoninator – with little concern about shattering the racist stereotype or furthering the public interest in the nation. It also renders invisible highly qualified black judges who deserve serious consideration for selection to the Court.

How did much of black leadership get in this bind? Why did so many of them capitulate to Bush's cynical strategy? Three reasons loom large. First, Thomas's claim to racial authenticity – his birth in Jim Crow Georgia, his childhood spent as the grandson of a black sharecropper, his undeniably black phenotype degraded by racist ideals of beauty, and his gallant black struggle for achievement in racist America. Second, the complex relation of this claim to racial authenticity to the increasing closing-ranks mentality in black America. Escalating black-nationalist sentiments – the notion that America's will to racial justice is weak and therefore black people must close ranks for survival in a hostile country – rests principally upon claims to racial authenticity. Third, the way in which black-nationalist sentiments promote and encourage black cultural conservatism, especially black patriarchal (and homophobic) power. The idea of black people closing ranks against hostile white Americans reinforces black male power exercised over black women (e.g., to protect, regulate, subordinate, and hence usually, though not always, use and abuse women) in order to preserve black social order under circumstances of white-literal attack and symbolic assault.

Most black leaders got lost in their thicket of reasoning and thus got caught in a vulgar form of racial reasoning: *black authenticity – black closing-ranks mentality – black male subordination of black women in the interests of the black community in a hostile white-racist country*. This line of racial reasoning leads to such questions as 'Is Thomas really black?'; 'Is he black enough to be defended?'; 'Is he just black on the outside?' *et al*. In fact, these kind of questions were asked, debated, and answered throughout black America in barber shops, beauty salons, living rooms, churches, mosques, and schoolrooms.

Unfortunately, the very framework of this line of racial reasoning was not called into question. Yet as long as racial reasoning regulates black thought and action, Clarence Thomases will continue to haunt black America – as Bush and his ilk sit back, watch, and prosper. How does one undermine the framework of racial reasoning? By dismantling each pillar slowly and systematically. The fundamental aim of this undermining and dismantling is to replace racial reasoning with moral reasoning, to understand the black-freedom struggle not as an affair of skin pigmentation and racial phenotype but rather as a matter of ethical principles and wise politics, and to combat black-nationalist views of subordinating the issues and interests of black women by linking mature black self-love and self-respect to egalitarian relations within and outside black communities. The failure of nerve of black leadership is to refuse to undermine and dismantle the framework of racial reasoning.

Let us begin with the claim to racial authenticity – a claim Bush made about Thomas, Thomas made about himself in the hearings, and black nationalists make about themselves. What is black authenticity? Who is really black? First, blackness has no meaning outside of a system of race-conscious people and practices. After centuries of racist degradation, exploitation, and oppression in America, blackness

means being minimally subject to white supremacist abuse and being part of a rich culture and community that has struggled against such abuse. All people with black skin and African phenotype are subject to potential white-supremacist abuse. Hence, all black Americans have some interest in resisting racism – even if their interest is confined solely to themselves as individuals rather than to larger black communities. Yet how this 'interest' is defined and how individuals and communities are understood vary. So any claim to black authenticity – beyond being the potential object of racist abuse and heir to a grand tradition of black struggle – is contingent on one's political definition of black interest and one's ethical understanding of how this interest relates to individuals and communities in and outside black America. In short, blackness is a political and ethical construct. Appeals to black authenticity ignore this fact; such appeals hide and conceal the political and ethical dimension of blackness. This is why claims to racial authenticity trump political and ethical argument – and why racial reasoning discourages moral reasoning. Every claim to racial authenticity presupposes elaborate conceptions of political and ethical relations of interests, individuals, and communities. Racial reasoning conceals these presuppositions behind a deceptive cloak of racial consensus – yet racial reasoning is seductive because it invokes an undeniable history of racial abuse and racial struggle. This is why Bush's claims to Thomas's black authenticity, Thomas's claims about his own black authenticity, and black-nationalist claims about black authenticity all highlight histories of black abuse and black struggle.

But if claims to black authenticity are political and ethical conceptions of the relation of black interests, individuals, and communities, then any attempt to confine black authenticity to black-nationalist politics or black male interests warrants suspicion. For example, black leaders failed to highlight the problematic claims Clarence Thomas made about his sister, Emma Mae, regarding her experience with the welfare system. In front of a conservative audience in San Francisco, Thomas made her out to be a welfare scrounger dependent on state support. Yet, like most black women in American history, Emma Mae is a hardworking person, sensitive enough to take care of her sick aunt, and she was unable to work for a short period of time. After she got off welfare, she worked two jobs – until three in the morning! This episode reveals not only a lack of integrity and character on

Thomas's part; failure to highlight it by black leaders discloses a conception of black authenticity confined to black male interests, individuals, and communities. In short, the refusal to give weight to the interests of black women by most black leaders was already apparent before Anita Hill appeared on the scene.

The claims to black authenticity that feed on the closing-ranks mentality of black people are dangerous precisely because this closing of ranks is usually done at the expense of black women. It also tends to ignore the divisions of class and sexual orientation in black America – divisions that require attention if *all* black interests, individuals, and communities are to be taken into consideration. Thomas's conservative Republican politics does not promote a closing-ranks mentality; instead, his claim to black authenticity is for the purpose of self-promotion, to gain power and prestige. All his professional life he has championed individual achievement and race-free standards. Yet when he saw his ship sinking, he played the racial card of black victimization and black solidarity at the expense of Anita Hill. Like his sister Emma Mae, Anita Hill could be used and abused for his own self-interested conception of black authenticity and racial solidarity.

Thomas played this racial card with success – first with appeals to his victimization in Jim Crow Georgia and later to his victimization by a 'high-tech lynching' – primarily because of the deep cultural conservatism in white and black America. In white America this cultural conservatism takes the form of a chronic racism, sexism, and homophobia. Hence, only certain kinds of black people deserve high positions, that is, those who accept the rules of the game played by white America. In black America, this cultural conservatism takes the form of an inchoate xenophobia (e.g., against whites, Jews, and Asian Americans), systemic sexism, and homophobia. Like all conservatisms rooted in a quest for order, the pervasive disorder in white and, especially, black America fans and fuels the channeling of rage toward the most vulnerable and degraded members of the community. For white America this means primarily scapegoating black people, women, gays, and lesbians. For black America the targets are principally black women and black gays and lesbians. In this way black-nationalist and black-male-centered claims to black authenticity reinforce black cultural conservatism. The support of Louis Farrakhan's Nation of Islam for Clarence Thomas

– despite Farrakhan's critique of Republican Party racist and conservative policies – highlights this fact. It also shows how racial reasoning leads disparate viewpoints in black America to the same dead end – with substantive ethical principles and savvy, wise politics left out.

The undermining and dismantling of the framework of racial reasoning – especially the basic notions of black authenticity, the closing-ranks mentality, and black cultural conservatism – leads toward a new framework for black thought and method. This new framework should be a *prophetic* one of moral reasoning, with its fundamental ideas of a mature black identity, coalition strategy, and black cultural democracy. Instead of cathartic appeals to black authenticity, a prophetic viewpoint bases mature black self-love and self-respect on the moral quality of black responses to undeniable racist degradation in the American past and present. These responses assume neither a black essence that all black people share nor one black perspective to which all black people should adhere. Rather, a prophetic framework encourages *moral* assessment of the variety of perspectives held by black people and selects those views based on black dignity and decency that eschew putting any group of people or culture on a pedestal or in the gutter. Instead, blackness is understood to be either the perennial possibility of white-supremacist abuse or the distinct styles and dominant modes of expression found in black cultures and communities. These styles and modes are diverse – yet they do stand apart from those of other groups (even as they are shaped by and shape those of other groups). And all such styles and modes stand in need of ethical evaluation. Mature black identity results from an acknowledgment of the specific black responses to white-supremacist abuses and a moral assessment of these responses such that the humanity of black people does not rest on deifying or demonizing others.

Instead of a closing-ranks mentality, a prophetic framework encourages a coalition strategy that solicits genuine solidarity with those deeply committed to antiracist struggle. This strategy is neither naive nor opportunistic; black suspicion of whites, Latinos, Jews, and Asian Americans runs deep for historical reasons. Yet there are slight though significant antiracist traditions among whites, Asian Americans, and especially Latinos, Jews, and indigenous people that must not be cast aside. Such coalitions are important precisely because they not only enhance the plight of black people but also because they enrich the quality of life in the country.

Lastly, a prophetic framework replaces black cultural conservatism with black cultural democracy. Instead of authoritarian sensibilities that subordinate women or degrade gays and lesbians, black cultural democracy promotes the equality of black women and men and the humanity of black gays and lesbians. In short, black cultural democracy rejects the pervasive patriarchy and homophobia in black American life.

If most black leaders had adopted a prophetic framework of moral reasoning rather than a narrow framework of racial reasoning, the debate over the Thomas–Hill hearings would have proceeded in a quite different manner in black America. For example, both Thomas and Hill would be viewed as two black conservative supporters of some of the most vicious policies to besiege black working and poor communities since Jim and Jane Crow segregation. Both Thomas and Hill supported an unprecedented redistribution of wealth from working people to well-to-do people in the form of regressive taxation, deregulation policies, cutbacks and slowdowns in public service programs, takebacks at the negotiation table between workers and management, and military build-ups at the Pentagon. Both Thomas and Hill supported the unleashing of unbridled capitalist market forces on a level never witnessed before in this country that have devastated black working and poor communities. These market forces took the form principally of unregulated corporative and financial expansion and intense entrepreneurial activity. This tremendous ferment in big and small businesses – including enormous bonanzas in speculation, leveraged buyouts and mergers, as well as high levels of corruption and graft – contributed to a new kind of culture of consumption in white and black America. Never before has the seductive market way of life held such sway in nearly every sphere of American life. This market way of life promotes addictions to stimulation and obsessions with comfort and convenience. These addictions and obsessions – centered primarily around bodily pleasures and status rankings – constitute market moralities of various sorts. The common denominator is a rugged and ragged individualism and rapacious hedonism in quest of a perennial 'high' in body and mind.

In the hearings Clarence Thomas emerged as the exemplary hedonist, addicted to pornography and captive to a stereotypical self-image of the powerful black man who revels in sexual prowess in a racist society. Anita Hill appears as the exemplary careerist addicted to job promotion and captive to the stereotypical self-image of the sacrificial black woman who suffers silently and alone. There should be little doubt that Thomas's claims are suspect – those about his sister, his 18-year silence about *Roe* v. *Wade*, his intentions in the Heritage Foundation speech praising the antiabortion essay by Lewis Lehrman, and the contours of his conservative political philosophy. Furthermore, his obdurate stonewalling in regard to his private life was symptomatic of all addicts – passionate denial and irrational cover-up. There also should be little doubt that Anita Hill's truth-telling was a break from her careerist ambitions. On the one hand, she strikes me as a person of integrity and honesty. On the other hand, she indeed put a premium on job advancement – even at painful personal cost. Yet her speaking out disrupted this pattern of behavior and she found herself supported only by people who opposed the very conservative policies she otherwise championed, namely, progressive feminists, liberals, and some black folk. How strange she must feel being a hero to her former foes. One wonders whether Judge Bork supported her as fervently as she did him a few years ago.

A prophetic framework of moral reasoning would have liberated black leaders from the racial guilt of opposing a black man for the highest court in the land and feeling as if one had to choose between a black woman and a black man. Like the Congressional Black Caucus (minus one?), black people could simply oppose Thomas based on qualifications and principle. And one could choose between two black conservatives based on their sworn testimonies in light of the patterns of their behavior in the recent past. Similarly, black leaders could avoid being duped by Thomas's desperate and vulgar appeals to racial victimization by a white male Senate committee who handled him gently (no questions about his private life, no queries about his problematic claims). Like Senator Hollings, who knows racial intimidation when he sees it (given his past experiences with it), black leaders could see through this rhetorical charade and call a moral spade a moral spade.

Unfortunately, most of black leadership remained caught in a framework of racial reasoning – even when they opposed Thomas and/or supported Hill. Rarely did we have a black leader highlight the moral content of a mature black identity, accent the crucial role of coalition strategy in the struggle for justice, or promote the ideal of black cultural democracy. Instead, the debate evolved around glib formulations of a black 'role model' based on mere pigmentation, an atavistic defense of blackness that mirrors the increasing xenophobia in American life and a silence about the ugly authoritarian practices in black America that range from sexual harassment to indescribable violence against women. Hence, a grand opportunity for substantive discussion and struggle over race and gender was missed in black America and the larger society. And black leadership must share some of the blame. As long as black leaders remain caught in a framework of racial reasoning, they will not rise above the manipulative language of Bush and Thomas – just as the state of siege (the death, disease, and destruction) raging in much of black America creates more wastelands and combat zones. Where there is no vision, the people perish; where there is no framework of moral reasoning, the people close ranks in a war of all against all. The growing gangsterization of America results in part from a market-driven racial reasoning prevalent from the White House to the projects. In this sense, George Bush, David Duke, and gangster rap artists speak the same language from different social locations – only racial reasoning can save us. Yet I hear a cloud of witnesses from afar – Sojourner Truth, Wendell Phillips, Emma Goldman, A. Philip Randolph, Ella Baker, Fannie Lou Hamer, Michael Harrington, Abraham Joshua Heschel, Tom Hayden, Harvey Milk, Robert Moses, Barbara Ehrenreich, Martin Luther King, Jr., and many anonymous others – who championed the struggle for freedom and justice in a prophetic framework of moral reasoning. They understood that the pitfalls of racial reasoning are too costly in mind, body, and soul – especially for a downtrodden and despised people like black Americans. The best of our leadership have recognized this valuable truth – and more must do so in the future if America is to survive with any moral sense.

PART V

On Knowledge and Science

19

Elements of Physics in Yoruba Culture – I

Supo Ogunbunmi and Henry M. Olaitan

1 Introduction

A large number of what the early Yorubas did, observed and believed had a strong scientific basis. This basis had never been recognized because there had been no thorough inquiry into their scientific implications. This does not imply that the Yorubas lacked the experimental, theoretical and technical know-how, born of empirical knowledge. We would like to suggest, however, that this know-how does not reasonably reflect the process of the scientific thinking which necessarily leads to the detection of the general laws underlying the variety of natural phenomena.

In a bid to understand the world in which they lived, the early Yorubas built up some models (religious or otherwise) to express their scientific ideas, thus creating a link between their scientific and cultural backgrounds. Despite the superstitious outlook of some of these models, they embody some basic elements of physics, which can readily be explained within the framework of contemporary physics.

The practice of physics and the interpretation of physical phenomena certainly depends upon the structure of the society. In highly sophisticated societies physics is almost wholly carried on in institutions of higher learning and in industries. However in the early Yoruba societies, their scien-

tists were also the leaders or even priests of the then Yoruba traditional religions. This is why in Yorubaland the scientific interpretation of nature was closely linked with religious beliefs and cultural practices. The limitation of the effectiveness of such empirical knowledge should now however be recognized. As such the practice of physics among the early Yorubas cannot be seen in the same sense as the highly generalized science of modern physics.

In what follows we shall seek to discuss the elements of physics in some of the ideas and models built by the early Yorubas to explain their observations of nature.

2.1 The Electrostatic Trap

The early Yoruba tradition forbade the carrying of pointed metallic objects (usually manufactured by our blacksmiths), during a rainfall. It also discouraged the stretching of fingers out in the rain. It is our intention to discuss the elements of physics embodied in such a traditional practice.

The early Yorubas built up a model to explain this traditional practice. According to them (Adekogbe (1)) the metal is the symbol of Ogun, "the god of iron," who was regarded to be powerful. Equally powerful was Sango, "the god of thunder and lightning." Obviously Sango would be furious at the sight of the bearer of the symbol of Ogun in his (i.e. Sango's) domain when it is raining or about to rain. As such he would use the symbol of his strength (i.e. thunder and lightning) to strike down the bearer and deter other possible violators of his domain.

From the *Journal of African Philosophy and Studies*, 1/1–2 (1988); reproduced by kind permission of African Philosophy Projects Publications.

A thunderstorm is rain or hail accompanied by thunder and lightning. The main condition for its occurrence is great atmospheric instability, giving rise to rapid convection of a mass of very moist air, to great heights. The thunderstorm is marked by towering anvil-shaped cumulonimbus cloud with a dark turbulent base. In the turbulent conditions inside the cloud, the raindrops are broken down; the smaller droplets are carried to the top of the cloud, the larger ones remaining at lower levels. This process of separation leads to the separation of electric charges. When the insulation of the air breaks down, a lightning stroke results, sometimes entirely within the cloud, but sometimes from cloud to earth. The lightning travels along thin channels usually branched. At a distance it is often obscured by the clouds and only seen as a flash of diffuse light. On passing through the air the lightning momentarily gives rise to great heat. The resulting sudden expansion and contraction of the air sets up sound waves, which are heard as thunder. The sound from the different parts of the lightning is not all heard at the same time and this with echoes gives the reverberation characteristic of thunder. This finds expression in Yoruba traditional saying "Enito mule ti'gbo ni 'se ore arira" (Arira being the angry voice of Sango).

The basis of the element of physics involved in the above-mentioned model by the early Yorubas is the phenomenon of the "point-discharge." A pointed metallic object has a curvature which increases strongly over the surface and becomes maximum at the pointed end. When charged, the surface charge density increases rapidly over the surface and also becomes maximum at the pointed end, thus producing a very strong electric field strength just outside the point. This may be sufficiently high to cause the dielectric breakdown of the surrounding air. The strong field accelerates the few free electrons or charged atoms (naturally present in the surrounding air) to such an energy that they can produce further ionization by bombardment.

The necessarily charged cloud in a thunderstorm induces opposite charges on the earth. The pointed metallic object and the human carrier now form a conducting system through which charges from the earth escape (via a point-discharge) to neutralize the charges in the cloud before a stroke occurs. If a lightning stroke occurs before neutralization of cloud charges, the conducting system offers a path through which electric charges from the cloud flow into the earth (analogous to the operation of a lightning conductor). In both cases the passage of

electric charges through the human body adversely affects the composition and physiology of the body of the carrier, leading to sudden shock or subsequent death.

The above analysis is also valid even if pointed metallic objects are not carried, but fingers are stretched out in a thunderstorm. This is because the human body then becomes a pointed "conductor." Hence the Yoruba farmers in those days always warned children to lie flat in the farm any time there is a thunderstorm. The element of physics in this warning is based on the fact that by lying flat on the farm, no part of the body acts as a pointed conductor.

The practice of lying flat when in a thunderstorm, is regarded by the early Yorubas as an act of worship of Sango (the god of thunder and lightning) who becomes appeased and consequently spares the life of the worshiper. To Sango, a tall tree in the field during a thunderstorm refuses to worship. Hence he strikes it down in annoyance. This is why according to the early Yorubas, branches of trees are cut down through Sango's wrath. According to contemporary physics, however, Sango's wrath is identical to lightning since the tall tree now behaves as a pointed conductor. This is the case with Oak tree (Araba) which is essentially a big tree with hard and rough bark unable to bend in a storm and hence gets the lightning stroke. In contrast Asorin, a smooth barked big tree, hardly even gets hit by lightning. This fact is reflected in the Yoruba traditional saying:

> "Bi Sango n'paraba bon pa roko, bii ti gi nla ko."
> (Igi nla = Asorin)   (1)

Another similar saying is:

> "Arira (ara) ki i pa igi osè"
> (Igi ose is smooth-barked)   (2)

If a tree is uniformly wet, the current descends through the water sheath and leaves the tree unharmed, because the tree provides an electrical path to ground. If not the current may enter the tree to descend through the sap. The rapid heating and expansion of the sap then blows the tree apart. Oak (Araba) is more susceptible to explosions than many other trees because it has rough bark. If the lightning stroke occurs early in the rainstorm, it may find only the top part of an Oak tree wet, whereas a smooth bark tree would be wet to the ground. The Oak would be blown apart, and the smooth bark tree left untouched.

Another observation of the early Yorubas is the fact that lightning never strikes a blacksmith's workshop as indicated in the traditional Yoruba saying:

"Ara ki i ja ko wole Arọ, iji kii ja ko patorin"
(Arọ – Blacksmith) (3)

This is because there are many pointed metallic objects in a blacksmith's shop, such that in a thunderstorm, a lightning stroke is always prevented before it occurs, by heavy neutralization, due to the multiplicity of escape paths for electrical charges from the earth. According to the early Yorubas the blacksmith's workshop is the canopy of Ogun, the god of metallic structures. Ogun was a friend of Sango (they had common favourite food "ipẹtẹ" (boiled beans) as indicated in the Yoruba traditional saying:

"Onisango d'ewa nu, bo'he, o he'nmo" and
"Ipete jinna ara Ogun gbekan" (4)

Surely Sango will never strike at his friend's canopy. Also another Yoruba traditional saying:

"Ko si orisa ti i se bi Ogun l'agbede a fi arira oba onina lenu" (5)
(Here arira is used for Sango himself rather than his angry voice).

(*Note*: In a blacksmith's shop one finds metals and fire, the symbols of Ogun and Sango respectively. One also finds water only to temper the erratic nature of Sango).

The near-simultaneity of lightning and thunder was also recognized by the early Yorubas who also observed the order of occurrence of the two events. The knowledge was embodied in the Yoruba traditional saying:

"Monamona laja arira, ati arira ati monamona, gbogbo won ni ise eru oba onina lenu" (6)

(*Note*: The hunting dog always goes in front of the hunter in a hunting expedition).

2.2 Gravity Concept in Yoruba Culture

What we know as gravity is a field of force first demonstrated by Newton's falling apple. Gravity as a field of force has found many expressions in Yoruba culture and cultural thoughts. Yoruba mythology has it (Ogunbunmi (2), 1979) that God (Olodumare) had a duel with Obaluaye, a less powerful Yoruba god at the beginning of time. Olodumare won the duel and decided to punish Obaluaye rather than destroy him. Obaluaye was to carry for all times the earth and all it contains on his head. Olodumare will not allow anything to lighten the burden on Obaluaye. As such anything that leaves the surfaces of the earth has the tendency of reducing the burden on Obaluaye and Olodumare (God) will return it immediately to the earth. This means that as long as there exists the earth and the heavens there will always be a force returning anything that leaves the earth's surface to the earth the magnitude of the force depending on the "amount" of that which leaves the surface. This is why the Yorubas say that "anything that goes up [i.e. leaves the earth's surface] must return to the earth's surface." This is expressed in the Yoruba traditional saying:

"Lala to t'oke, ile lo nbo" and (7)
"Irawe'ki'i dajo ile ko sun oke" (8)

Anything that stands on the earth like a tree that grows, a house or any other structure that is built on the earth, is in Olodumare's concept part of the earth. Once the connection is removed (a man trying to jump up, a tree that is cut through, etc.), this now tends to lighten the burden and must then return to the earth. Anything which is not directly earth connected must connect itself to an earth connected object to evade the repulsive geotropic force of Olodumare. This shows up in Yoruba tradition. If a climber wants to climb a tree, he uses both hands and thighs as connections to the tree. A palm-wine tapper or a palm-kernel harvester uses what the Yorubas call "Igba" or "elekere" as connecting devices.

That this geotropic force acts through a point in any object was also known to the Yorubas and finds expression in the Yoruba culture. The human head was the means of transporting loads in Yoruba culture. A Yoruba woman normally puts "osuka," a disc-shaped piece of folded cloth, on the head before carrying a heavy load on it. The physics of the "osuka" is twofold. Apart from the fact that it presents a larger surface area to the load than the skull, and hence reduces pressure due to the load on the head, it also helps to ensure that the point through which the "geotropic force" (gravity) due to the load acts (i.e. its centre of gravity) is located somewhere on the head, otherwise the load will fall off.

The knowledge of potential in a gravitational field also manifests itself in some of the orginal Yoruba animal traps such as "ebiti" which consists of a heavy load suspended in a way that when the animal for which it is designed is well under the load, it bites the bait on a chord, thus destroying the suspension, and the geotropic force makes the heavy load fall on the animal. This and many other types of Yoruba animal traps employ not only the physics of gravitational fields but also simple machines (levers, pulleys, etc. and tension in strings and cords).

When a Yoruba man or woman wants to carry a log of wood or some firewood but cannot lift it against the gravitational force up to his or her head, a trial is made to find the centre of gravity of the load by slanting it at an angle to the horizontal. The head is then moved along the length until a balance point is found. This is the centre of gravity. The load is then easily lifted from the ground and carried.

Gravity concept is not unconnected with the early Yoruba concept of rain ("opa teere kan' le o kan' run") as a slender whip from heaven into the earth and the unusefulness of the vulture (igun). The early Yorubas believed that after Olodumare's conquest of duel with Obaluaye, Olodumare promised that in addition to carrying the earth, Obaluaye would be whipped (to increase his agony) at regular intervals of time. The whip is the rain that falls at intervals. During raining season, plants become heavy, rivers have more water, the soil becomes heavier etc. – all these serve to increase the load on Obaluaye.

Obaluaye proposed a sacrifice to appease Olodumare in order to obtain a pardon for part (if only) of the sentence. Obaluaye would probably have appeased Olodumare if the vulture, the carrier of the sacrifice to heaven, was not enticed by some sweet preparations of Olokun (goddess of the sea); eventually the vulture (igun) arrived in Olodumare's heaven late. On account of this, Olodumare got annoyed, sent the vulture back, and started to whip Obaluaye and the vulture. The vulture arriving at the earth, bald in the head; could find no place of abode and became hated by the people. All these are indicated in the Yoruba traditional saying:

"A kii pa igun bo'ri" (Vulture will not take one's wishes to his "ori" or "Eleda")   (10)
"Eko ila gba'ra re l'owo obe, igun bo l'owo apeyeje   (11)
(Vulture is unsuitable for human consumption and hence useless).
"Igun omo abelebo se'gusi, abelebo ja bi ko s'ebore, a k'owo ebo ko mo lo le"   (12)
(The Vulture feed mainly on sacrificial preparations).

3 Conclusion

We have, in the above, discussed the physics relevant to some traditional beliefs and practices of the early Yorubas. We have demonstrated beyond doubt that the supposed striking down of a person by Sango (god of thunder and lightning) is in fact a physical phenomenon of lightning and thunder. We have also demonstrated that the existence of gravity as a field of force was known to the early Yorubas. Some of their traditional practices therefore were conditioned by an unexpressed knowledge of this concept.

Elements of Physics in Yoruba Culture – II

Supo Ogunbunmi and Henry M. Olaitan

1 Introduction

In our earlier paper, "Elements of Physics in Yoruba Culture, I," we discussed the scientific basis of the early Yorubas' concept and observation of some natural phenomena. We have shown that the early Yorubas have demonstrated a clear understanding of the principle of physics involved in the phenomenon of electrostatics and gravity. Results of their logical deductions from a series of observational experiments were unfortunately not written in scientific journals but are unambiguously embodied in some of the Yoruba traditional sayings. In this paper we are reporting the scientific basis of the early Yorubas' beliefs about rain and rain prediction. We have not included the Physics of traditional rain making in this paper because our investigation on this is not yet complete.

2 Types and Nature of Rain

The early Yorubas studied the art of rainfall and made observations about the phenomena associated with it. This is not surprising because in the early Yoruba societies, indoor crafts were developed only as past-time hobbies, and hence the early Yoruba men were mostly farmers or hunters while the women were mainly farm workers, hawkers of agricultural consumables, etc. They were mainly "outdoor" people. The early Yorubas studied, *inter alia*, not only rain prediction, but also types and

nature of rainfall as indicated in the saying:

"Mo de werewere bi eji ale,
mo de warawara bi eji aro,
mo de papa pa bi eji iyaleta" (1)

Mostly their studies were observational and results, although not written, were unambiguously expressed in what is now called the traditional sayings.

In Yoruba philosophy as evident in Ifa literacy corpus, things such as rain, rivers, trees, lower animals were given the status of human beings and endowed with the characteristic human properties such as power of expression, show of strength, exercise of will power etc. In this context the power of rain and fire was usually compared as indicated in the following sayings:

"Eji ja nile Ara, o yo'ke lehin alara, o ja l'ode ajero, o d'oko ogulutu" (2)
"Eji o jaja f'ese ha'para o ba sango ja ni Koso, o gba'na l'enu oba onina le'nu" (3)
"Sigidi ti yoo we l'odo, ere ete ni o fe se" (4)
"Ojo ba 'gba gunnugun nibi won gbe nd'ifa aiku o da won ru; O ba 'gba agba merindilogun nibi won gbe nd'ifa ainirorun, gbogbo won lo tu yetuyele" (5)

These show the power of rain over many things including sigidi, a "powerful harbinger" of evils and evil doings; and fire, which is supposed to have power over everything. The confrontation between rain and fire always leads to battle, as noticed by the early Yorubas who concluded:

"Ina omo aje werewere Ojo omo aja warawara, Eniti yoo woran ija agba meji, ko ni sai rubo ayalu" (6)

This means that anybody who wants to witness the battle between fire and rain must protect himself from a sort of "sudden attack" on himself. This conclusion has a strong physical basis. When rain falls on fire or on a very hot object some of the rain water is evaporated. 1 gram of steam has a volume of the order of 2000 cm³ at NTP whereas 1 gram of water from which the steam is made has a volume of about 1.0 cm^3. Thus steam is an "expanding" system. If somebody is very near the point at which this happens, some of the steam will condense on his face and he will suffer a severe scald (Ayalu) due to the very high specific thermal content of steam. A way of preventing this disaster is not to move near the point.

This sudden evaporation and eventual condensation form the physical basis of the conclusion drawn from the observation and physical explanation of some of the Yoruba culture in this respect, i.e.

"A ki i sinto sinna (never spit into a burning fire)" (7)
"Omo ina laa ran sina, a ki i fi omi pana adi" (8)
(Never attempt to extinguish fire from burning oil with water, rather use the fire produced to fight the fire).

When strongly heated oil catches fire, the Yorubas do not pour water on it. Rather, since the usual container (a clay pot) does not burn, the lid of the pot containing the burning oil is just used to cover it and the fire will be extinguished after a short time. Contemporary physics now confirms the scientific nature of the practice and indicates that the fire is extinguished because of lack of oxygen. If water were poured onto the burning oil, the water will not cool the oil below the ignition temperature, since water will evaporate; a mixture of the oil vapour and steam forms an expanding burning system and the fire will expand vigorously.

3 Rain Prediction

One of the research topics to which the early Yorubas addressed themselves was the prediction of rainfall. In this field they scored a series of success in that they could predict the occurrence of rain to within the tolerance allowed by the statistical nature of their observations. Some simple experiments usually performed by the early Yoruba farmers were the following:

3.1 Dry dust experiment

The farmer picks up some of the dry earth under a tree, throws it upwards and notices the scatter of the light particles of the dust. From the scatter and its rapidity, the imminence of rain or otherwise is predicted.

3.2 The hand–saliva hygrometer

The farmer spits on the back of his palm and notices the time taken for the saliva to dry off. If the saliva dries up quickly the chance of rain falling at that time is put as negligible. But if the saliva dries up slowly (not fast enough) the imminence of rain is confirmed.

These two predictive experiments have strong physical basis. The early Yorubas recognized that high wind and presence of water vapour in the air were two conditions of rainfall. The second experiment was designed to measure in effect relative humidity (which must be high for rain to fall). If the saliva dried very quickly, the early Yorubas recognized the very low water content in air (and hence low relative humidity); otherwise slow drying of the saliva indicated to them high water content in the air (high relative humidity) and hence the imminence of rainfall. The hand–saliva system thus constitutes a hygrometer. The first experiment predicts rainfall from the existence and speed of wind. If the light particles of dust were scattered fast, then there is a fast wind blowing and one of the conditions for rainfall is thus satisfied. In fact, experienced Yoruba farmers could look at the leaves on a tree and predict fairly accurately the imminence of rain. If the leaves appear still, there is no wind and hence the chance of having rain is small. This result finds expression in the traditional saying:

"E fufu ti ko se'we igbo lalolalo ki i ro'jo" (a wind that does not disturb the leaves of the forest can't lead to rain)   (a)

3.3 The hand-thermometer

The early Yoruba also predicted the imminence of rain by dipping his hand in a deep stream or river and noticing the variation of temperature with depth as he withdraws his hand. If he feels uniformly warm or cold in the hand as he withdraws, then the probability of rainfall is small.

These observations have sound physical background. If the surface of water in the deep stream or river is cooled either by cloud or evaporation due to strong wind (both are required for rainfall) the surface is then cooler than the layers below; hence a negative temperature gradient exists from lower layers to upper layers. He then feels cooler and cooler as he withdraws his hand. Conversely, a positive temperature gradient will exist from lower layer to the upper layer in the absence of wind or cloud, indicating vanishingly small probability of rainfall. However, if zero temperature gradient exists in the surface layer (i.e. absence of wind, cloud or any cooling agent on the surface) he feels uniformly hot or cold as he withdraws his hand and the probability of rainfall then is small.

3.4 Rainbow and the thermo-optical critical point

The early Yorubas, after a series of prolonged careful observations, asserted that "whatever the degree of cloudiness in the sky, whenever a rainbow appears in the sky, there exists a very high probability that the rain will not fall" (Adekoya (3), 1979). This is embodied in the Yoruba traditional saying:

"Osumare ni yio jare ojo yi i"   (10)
(It is the rainbow that will win over this imminent rain).

This observation has a strong scientific basis and we shall now seek to examine the elements of physics involved.

Cloud formation in the sky is a process which follows simply from the thermodynamics of the atmosphere. Rising cloud is cooled by adiabatic expansion (although the atmosphere is an open system the cooling is fast enough to be adiabatic). An adiabatic process is one in which no heat enters or leaves the system during the process. The first law of thermodynamics implies that the external work done by such system is done at the expense of its internal energy, which is a function of its temperature, and as such cooling results. The lapse rate in still air is about 0.6k to every 100m, but the adiabatic gradient is about 0.96k to every 100m. Rising air may cool below its dew point after which condensation may occur, depending on the availability of condensation-nuclei. The droplets will at first be minute, perhaps about 0.02 millimetres in diameter, but these will rapidly grow if cooling continues. However, before precipitation is possible much larger drops with diameters of at least 0.1 millimetres must be formed. The minute droplets of about 0.02 mm diameter gradually grow until they attain diameters just below 0.1 mm. If at this point the location of the sun is just right for the sun rays incident on these droplets to suffer appropriate refraction and reflection, a rainbow occurs.

The droplets absorb radiant energy from the sun converting it into thermal energy. This absorption continues until the droplets have gained enough heat equal to the latent thermal energy required for vapourization. At this stage, the thermo-optical energy balance on the droplets sets in. The

$$Eab = Nh\upsilon = mL + \mathcal{E}$$

where Eab is the absorbed radiant energy.

υ is the mean frequency of the incident light.

N   is the number of photons absorbed.

$\mathcal{E}$ is the thermal energy required to raise the temperature of the drops to the boiling point characteristic of the atmosphere.

m   is the total mass of the droplets (at the critical diameter).

L   is the specific latent heat of vapourization.

h   is the Planck's constant.

At the thermo-optical energy balance, the droplets have gained enough energy for eventual evaporation. Hence they start decreasing in diameters. The result is that the rainbow starts to fade away until it eventually disappears. It is now obvious that the appearance of the rainbow is simultaneous with the absorption of radiant energy and ipso facto with the evaporation of the droplets. The diameters of the droplets then decrease below the critical diameter required for precipitation, thus leading to a high probability of rain not falling.

Although the appearance of the rainbow may be accompanied by a light shower of rainfall, yet light showering is within the tolerance inherent in the experimental deduction of a theoretical fact from statistical observations. It only means that a few of the droplets still possess critical diameters required for precipitation, even during evaporation. It is obvious from the above that the occurrence of a rainbow is closely associated.

This assertion can be at best statistical, because the formation of showers of rainfall depends on a delicate balance between large-scale and small-scale atmospheric properties. This balance is affected by a number of factors which includes, *inter alia* the size, speed and distribution of cloud updraughts, the cloud-base temperature, the degree of mixing between the cloud and its surroundings, the distribution of humidity, temperature and wind in the environment, the concentration and nature of the atmospheric aerosol, which are important and which are subject to great natural variation.

4 Conclusion

The above discussions have demonstrated clearly that the early Yorubas were versed in elementary meteorology and the physics of the lower atmosphere. By careful observation they discovered that strong wind and relative humidity are factors (among others) that affect the probability of rainfall. It is noteworthy that the tolerance range involved in the early Yoruba's rain prediction is comparable to that of Nigeria's weather forecasting services today.

References

1. Chief T. A. Adekogbe – personal interview (1979)
2. Chief O. Ogunbunmi – personal interview (1979)
3. Chief A. O. Adekoya – personal interview (1979)

20

"Divination": A Way of Knowing?

Philip M. Peek

Every human community recognizes a need for the special knowledge gained through divination. While this need is hardly of the same order as the need for food and shelter, it is nonetheless universal. Murdock, for instance, includes divination among the features found "in every culture known to history or ethnography" (1945: 124).

Prometheus's gift of fire to humankind is well known, but his gift of the arts of divination has almost been forgotten, even though his name, meaning "forethought," reflects the importance of this contribution to Greek culture (Oswalt 1969: 249–51). Other great civilizations have granted similar prominence to divination. Anthologies by Caquot and Leibovici (1968) and Loewe and Blacker (1981) include contributions on divination's critical role not only in the classical world but also in the Americas, India, Tibet, Japan and China, Africa, ancient Egypt and the Middle East, Judaism and Islam, and the Germanic world.

Although divination practices continue worldwide, remarkably little research has been done on these systems of knowledge, including those in Africa, the focus of this collection. Mbiti's observation remains valid: "With few exceptions, African systems of divination have not been carefully studied, though diviners are found in almost every community" (1970: 232).

From *African Divination Systems*, ed. Philip M. Peek (1991); by kind permission of Indiana University Press.

Ways of Knowing

. . . [G]iven the pivotal role of divination in African cultures, the study of divination systems must assume a central position in our attempts to better understand African peoples today. . . . The sheer volume of information gained from recent thorough investigations of these systems reveals how much knowledge we lost as a result of earlier prejudices against divination. Throughout Africa – whether in the city or in the country, no matter the religion, sex, or status of the individual – questions, problems, and choices arise for which everyday knowledge is insufficient and yet action must be taken. The information necessary to respond effectively is available, but often only through a diviner. That is why divination continues to provide a trusted means of decision making, a basic source of vital knowledge.

A divination system is a standardized process deriving from a learned discipline based on an extensive body of knowledge. This knowledge may or may not be literally expressed during the interpretation of the oracular message. The diviner may utilize a fixed corpus, such as the Yoruba Ifa Odu verses, or a more diffuse body of esoteric knowledge. Divining processes are diverse, but all follow set routines by which otherwise inaccessible information is obtained. Some type of device usually is employed, from a simple sliding object to the myriad symbolic items shaken in diviners' baskets. Sometimes the diviner's body becomes the vehicle of communication through spirit possession. Some diviners operate self-explanatory

Philip M. Peek

mechanisms that reveal answers; other systems require the diviner to interpret cryptic metaphoric messages. The final diagnosis and plan for action are rendered collectively by the diviner and the client(s).

Divination sessions are not instances of arbitrary, idiosyncratic behavior by diviners. A divination system is often the primary institutional means of articulating the epistemology of a people. Much as the classroom and the courtroom are primary sites for the presentation of cultural truths in the United States, so the diviner in other cultures is central to the expression and enactment of his or her cultural truths as they are reviewed in the context of contemporary realities. The situating of a divination session in time and space, the cultural artifacts utilized (objects, words, behaviors), the process of social interaction, and the uses made of oracular knowledge all demonstrate the foundations of a people's world view and social harmony. Divination systems do not simply reflect other aspects of a culture; they are the means (as well as the premise) of knowing which underpin and validate all else. Contemporary Africans in both urban and rural environments continue to rely on divination, and diviners play a crucial role as mediators, especially for cultures in rapid transition.

References

Caquot, André, and Marcel Leibovici. 1968. *La Divination*. 2 vols. Paris Presses Universitaires de France.

Loewe, Michael, and Carmen Blacker, eds. 1981. *Oracles and Divination*. Boulder, Colo.: Shambhala.

Mbiti, John. 1970. *African Religions and Philosophy*. New York: Doubleday Anchor.

Murdock, George P. 1945. "The Common Denominator of Cultures." In *The Science of Man in the World Crisis*, ed. Ralph Linton. New York: Columbia University Press.

Oswalt, Sabine G. 1969. *Concise Encyclopedia of Greek and Roman Mythology*. Glasgow: Collins.

21

The Problem of Knowledge in "Divination": The Example of Ifa

E. Chukwudi Eze

Whether it is the Divine Command theory, the Natural Law theory, the Utilitarian theory or Kant's Categorical Imperative, the quest among philosophers has been to find objective criteria with which actions or conduct can be established as right or wrong.

The difficulty in establishing such objective criteria has become compounded by the current crisis in the conception of the nature of reason, and consequently, of truth. When the nature of reason and of truth is questioned, the nature of moral knowledge becomes a major philosophical issue. Now let us look at moral thought from the perspective of *Ifa*, a system – or rather a "way" – of interpretation and understanding inscribed in the religious-hermeneutic tradition of the Yorubas as well as of many other African peoples – such as the Igbo where it is called "Afa."

Ifa: The Ontological Background

The starting point of thought in *Ifa* is not Idea in the abstract, but rather a fundamental experience – the experience of life itself. Within the Yoruba tradition, thought has its origin in *ashé*. And what is *ashé*?

Ashé, often translated as "power," is a concept that designates the dynamism of being and the very vitality of life. *Ashé* is the creative source of all that is; it is the power-to-be, the principle in things that enables them to be.

Scholars like Henry Louis Gates (in his *The Signifying Monkey: A Theory of Afro-American Literary Criticism*, New York, Oxford University Press, 1988) often emphasize this creative role of *ashé* (i.e., its nature as the primal "stuff" of being and of the universe). This emphasis leads to the now canonical translation of *ashé* as the word – the "creative Word," or "logos."

According to Professor Gates,

> We can translate *ase* in many ways, but the *ase* used to create the universe I translate as "logos," as the word as understanding, the word as the audible, and later the visible, sign of reason. (Gates 1988, p. 7)

Ashé, then, can be understood as the principle of intelligibility in the universe and in humans, or as rationality itself. It is creative power, the word, reason, the logos which "holds" reality. More specifically, *ashé* is that principle which accounts for the uniqueness of humans; it is a rational and spiritual principle which confers upon humans their identity and destiny. It endows individuals with *ori* or *akara-aka*, the Yoruba or Igbo word for destiny.

But what is destiny? *Ori*, or *akara-aka*, understood as destiny, is the defining character of the individual. It is that sense of being an existential project, a *homo viator*, which comes from the spiritual and the rational character of the human person. Destiny comes from/as an awareness of being and at the same time being-yet-to-fully-become. Destiny as a projective course of self is a characteristic unique to the spiritual and rational being that is the human. Life fully alive is a life on course, i.e., a life fully on course towards its historical self-actualization. The Igbo, for example, measures achievement in terms of how successful a rational course of has been achieved in the "journey" of life, and success is measured in terms of growth in wisdom, sociality, and wealth.

Ifa is a process of pursuit of knowledge about destiny, i.e., about the course of life. It is a quest for greater and greater individual and social self-understanding, especially in order to determine the right course of action for life. Because destiny is the sense of becoming endowed the individual by the human spiritual and rational nature, *Ifa* is, in fact, a process of attempting to understand the nature of *ashé*, for *ashé* is that quality in the human which makes him/her characteristically *destined*. *Ashé* is that which, so to speak, places the demand on the human to realize concretely the fullness of being and of thought.

Ifa is a framework for the quest for answers to the questions such as: What is the meaning of being? What is the goal of my life? What is my destiny? What does reason demand that one do in this particular circumstance? and so on. In short, how can the spiritual and the rational character of humans be more and more made manifest in a particular situation of action?

Ifa: Reason in Tradition?

Ifa-work is, therefore, a quest for discovery of meaning and direction in life, personal or communal, through rational discernment and liberation. I want to argue that, from a theoretical point of view, *Ifa* should be understood as a practice of "deep understanding" (*uche omimi*). This search for deep understanding, I believe, is of philosophic nature, because it is a reflective process of seeking knowledge about human life and action – by way of established discernment and epistemological processes.

The self-consciously epistemological nature of *Ifa* may not be obvious to us, because historically, philosophic thought in traditional Africa seems to have developed a protective tendency – partly because (perhaps, as in medieval scholasticism?) – philosophical activity was very closely allied with theology and soteriology. For example, among the Yoruba, the guardians of the *Ifa* text were priests, called the *Babalawo*, a word which literally means "Fathers of Secrets." Works of philosophical nature in this and similar African traditions are often neglected or misunderstood when they are completely confused with the religious or the theological environment. . . .

The core of the *Ifa* corpus is the literary text, *Odu*. *Odu* is a collection of thousands of aphorisms, poems, and riddles passed on from generation to generation of *babalawos*. Every *babalawo*, during and after the mandatory several years of training, is required to have memorized as much of this text as possible. *Odu*, however, is not a dead document merely repeated from one generation to the next. It contains elaborate exegesis on the text, but more importantly, it contains theories about how to read (the text) – i.e., theories about how to do the work of interpretation. It is this unique theoretical potential in/of *Ifa* that Professor Gates noted when he pointed out that *Ifa* is a particular kind of "discourse upon text."

> Indeed *Ifa* consists of the sacred texts of the Yoruba people, as does the Bible for the Christians, but it also contains the commentaries on these texts, as does the Midrash. (Gates 1988, p. 10)

The commentaries that Professor Gates talks about are not just interpretations but also reflections on the nature of meaning. What is truth? How do we come to truth? and so on. The Commentaries contain implicit theories of reading and understanding, as well as ideas about the nature of truth, knowledge and human understanding. There is, therefore, in the structure of interpretation in *Ifa*, an autochthonous, theoretical consciousness which is relevant to theories of truth and reason – and especially of moral knowledge.

For example, central to the interpretation and understanding of *Odu* is *Esu*, *Odu* is *ashé* conceived of as revealed yet hidden in the *Ifa* text. In fact, the *Odu* is regarded as praise songs to *Esu* – *Esu* being a mythological figure considered to be the way as well as barrier to *ashé*. *Esu* – as figura – makes understanding possible (or impossible!), and therefore mediates between text and reader.

In fact, in Yoruba language, *Esu* is called *Onitumo*, "one who loosens knowledge," i.e. the interpreter.

The nature of the activity of interpretation that goes on in the processes of *Ifa* is clearly of philosophical interest, since it may constitute one way of gaining a fresh and unusual perspective on the serious philosophical issue of how we obtain knowledge, especially moral knowledge.

For example, the nature of *Esu* as "figure" of the activity of interpretation would lead us to ask: What is the nature of human understanding in the *Ifa* practice? What kind of "truth" is that sought after or generated by the inquirer? And how does one, through/in *Ifa* process, distinguish between the true and the false, the right and the wrong – course of action, direction of life, and so on?

22

The Concept of Truth in the Akan Language

Kwasi Wiredu

Ask any ordinary Akan who speaks English what the Akan word for truth is and, unless he has made a special study of the matter, the chances are that he will answer: *nokware*. In a certain sense he would be right. A little reflection however discloses a complication. The opposite of *nokware* is *nkontompo* which means lies. But the opposite of truth is falsity, not lies.

What seems to have happened is that the Akan has correlated the word 'truth' with a primarily moral, rather than cognitive concept of truth in the Akan language. But why should he do this? There are three reasons. First, the main preoccupation with truth in the traditional Akan society was moral. Second, the moral concept of truth presupposes the cognitive concept of truth, and third, the English word 'truth' itself is ambiguous. When high-minded publicists wax eloquent in praise of the eternal verities of Truth, Beauty and Goodness, what they have in mind in this reference to truth is truthfulness rather than truth as just what is the case. And it is not only in particularly high-minded contexts that 'truth' is used as a synonym for truthfulness; it is quite a common usage. So we have to say that our non-too-sophisticated Akan had some excuse for his translation.

It emerges, then, that *nokware* translates 'truthfulness' rather than truth in the cognitive sense. Naturally we must go on to show how the latter i.e.

the cognitive concept of truth translates into Akan. But before then let us note one or two things about *nokware*. This word is made up of two words *ano*, meaning literally mouth and *koro*, meaning one.[1] *Nokware*, then, means literally being of one mouth. Less literally, it means being of one voice. It is sometimes suggested that this oneness of voice refers to communal unanimity; so that the truth is that which is agreed to by the community. Obviously, the authors of this suggestion have failed to distinguish between *nokware* and the purely cognitive concept of truth. It is intelligible, though extremely implausible, to suggest that truth in the cognitive sense is constituted by communal agreement, but it is not intelligible at all to make the same suggestion about truthfulness. Truthfulness has to do with the relation between what a person thinks and what he says. To be truthful is to let your speech reflect your thoughts. In this, what others think or say has no particular role to play. And this was not lost upon the traditional Akan. One can conceive of thinking as a kind of talking to oneself without embracing behaviourism; all that is needed is a little flight of metaphor. It then becomes possible to see truthfulness as saying unto others what one would say unto oneself. This is the oneness of voice that is etymologically involved in the word *nokware*.

The idea that truth (cognitive truth) consists in agreement among the members of a community is, in fact, far from the traditional Akan mind, for there is a sharp awareness of the disparity in the cognitive capabilities of the wise men of the community (the *anyansafo*) and the populace (*akwasafo*).[2] No elitist

From *Philosophy in Africa: Trends and Perspectives*, ed. P. O. Bodunrin, University of Ife Press (1985); reproduced by kind permission of P. O. Bodunrin.

contempt for the populace is implied here. The Akan are a communally oriented people, and consensus is one of their most prized values. Nevertheless, to make communal agreement the essence of truth[3] is an epistemological aberration that cannot be imputed to the Akan.

Of course, truth has something to do with agreement, which is evident in the fact that to say of something someone has said that it is true implies agreeing with him. This is agreement between two points of view which does not necessarily involve a whole community. But community-wide or not, agreement cannot be the essence of truth in the primary sense, for when there is agreement in cognition it is about something being so; the agreement is that something is so, i.e., is the case. It is this notion of something being so that connects agreement with truth at all. It is a notion that will loom large in our discussion of the concept of truth in Akan.

It is important to note that *nokware* (truthfulness) involves the concept of truth. To say that somebody is speaking truthfully is to say that he genuinely believes what he is saying to be *true*. Moreover, it also implies that it is in fact true. Apparent counter-examples are easily accommodated. If, for example, a man speaking sincerely, says that there is a cat on the mat when there is, in fact, no cat on the mat, there is a sense in which he speaks truthfully. Certainly, we would not say that he was telling lies. But it would be misleading to say simply that he spoke truthfully when he said that there was a cat on the mat. The most that can be said is that he was being truthful in conveying the impression that he believed that the cat was on the mat.

It is the connection between truthfulness and truth which makes the ambiguity of the English word 'truth' so confusing when it comes to translating into Akan. To say that an *asem* (statement) is *nokware* implies that it is true (cognitively). And so long as one is preoccupied with the affirmative, one might be tempted to think that this is all it means.[4] As soon, however, as one considers the negative, i.e., the case in which we say that something someone has said is not *nokware*, it becomes clear that there is also an element of moral comment in the use of *nokware*. There are a couple of words in Akan which have the same significance as *nokware*. There are *ampa* and *ewom*. *Ampa* implies truth but it has the same excess of meaning over 'truth' that 'truthfulness' has. The word is a unification of the phrase *eye asem pa*, literally 'it is a good piece of

discourse'. *Ewom* literally means 'it is in it'.

It is now time to consider the Akan rendition of truth in its purely cognitive sense. And here we meet with a remarkable fact, which is that there is no one word in Akan for truth. To say that something is true, the Akan say simply that it is so, and truth is rendered as what is so. No undue sophistication is required to understand that although the Akan do not have a single word for truth, they do have the concept of truth. This concept they express by the phrase *nea ete saa*, 'a proposition which is so'. The word *nea* means 'that which'; *ete* which is a form of 'to', which is the verb 'to be' in Akan, means 'is'; and *saa* means 'so'. *Asem* is an all-purpose word which means, in the present context, statement or proposition.

Notice that in the case of the adjective 'true', the Akan have a single word *saa* which provides a simple translation. (*Saa*, you will recall, means 'so'). But in English one has both 'is true' and 'is so', whereas in Akan one has only *te saa* ('is so'). This obviously does not indicate any insufficiency in the Akan language, for if 'is true' means the same as 'is so' then one can get along as well with any one of them as with both, as far as the making of truth-claims (i.e. 'is-so' claims) is concerned.

Another linguistic contrast between Akan and English is that there is no word in Akan for the English word 'fact'. A fact in Akan is simply that which is so (*nea ete saa*). Again no insufficiency is indicated; whatever can be said about the world in English using the word 'fact' can be said in Akan using the notion of what is so.

These linguistic contrasts have some very interesting consequences for the theory of truth. Consider the correspondence theory of truth. This is supposed to assert something like this: ' "p" is true' means ' "p" corresponds to a fact'. What does this come to in Akan? Simply that ' "p" *te saa*' which in truth is nothing more than saying that ' "p" *te saa*' means ' "p" *te saa*'. In other words, the correspondence definition amounts to a tautology in Akan. In a certain sense, this might be taken as a verification of the correspondence theory, for it might be said that being a tautology is a specially splendid way of being true. Be that as it may, one thing that cannot be pretended in Akan is that the correspondence theory offers any enlightenment about the notion of being so.

This comes out even more clearly in connection with the following variant of the correspondence theory. Some proponents of the theory sometimes formulate it by saying that a proposition is true if and only if things are as they are said to be in the proposition. Now, as pointed out above, in Akan ' "p" *te saa*' translates as ' "p" is so', and this obviously is an abbreviation for 'what the proposition "p" says things are is as they are'. Accordingly, the theory reduces to tautology that things are as a proposition says they are if and only if things are as they are said to be in the proposition.

Aristotle's famous dictum about truth and falsity which provided Tarski's intuitive motivation in his semantic conception of truth is a close approximation to the formulation commented upon in the last paragraph. Aristotle says in his *Metaphysics*, 'To say of what is that it is not, or of what is not that it is, is false, while to say of what is that it is, or of what is not that it is not, is true.'

This is very compressed phrasing, indeed. 'What is' in Aristotle's context, is of course, short for 'what is so'. Translating into Akan then yields: 'To say of what is so that it is not so, or of what is not so that it is so, is (to say what is) not so, while to say of what is so that it is so, or of what is not so that it is not so, is (to say what is) so.' One can, perhaps, derive some lesson about double negation from this piece of discourse, but certainly no insight into the notion of something being so.

It seems, then, that there are some apparently important issues that can be formulated in English but not in Akan. Such, for example, is the question 'How are true propositions related to facts?' Since this is not because of any insufficiency in the Akan language it might be tempting, at least to an Akan philosopher, to suggest that the issues in question are not really philosophical issues but narrowly linguistic ones due to the character of the vocabulary of English. Now, although it is, I think, correct to say that a problem like the one about the relation between truth and fact arises out of the nature of the vocabulary of English, it does not follow that it is not a genuine philosophical issue in English. The concepts of truth and fact are among the most fundamental concepts of human thought. Without the notion of something being a fact or of a proposition being true, thinking is inconceivable unless it be a mere succession of ideas, and even that can be doubted. It seems obvious then, that the relation between the terms 'truth' and 'fact' is a philosophical issue; for, of course, one cannot give a fundamental clarification of any of these foundational concepts in English without relating them one to the other. Yet, since these terms need not be both present in all natural languages, as the case of Akan shows, this task is not inescapable for

the human mind. From which it follows that some philosophical problems are not universal. Of course, there must be others that are universal. It must, for example, be apparent from a remark just made that the clarification of the notion of something being so is a universal philosophical problem.

As the point that a problem may be genuinely philosophical and yet dependent on some contingent features of a particular natural language may possibly be controversial, I shall endeavour to reinforce it by analogy with a simple illustration still involving a linguistic contrast between English and Akan. In the English language there occur both the statement forms 'p is equivalent to q' and 'p if and only if q'. It seems obvious that any natural language should have the means of expressing the idea of equivalence; and, indeed, in Akan we have a way of doing so, albeit somewhat circuitously. We say of two equivalent statements that they have the same destination: *ne nyinaa kosi faako* – more literally, 'they both reach the same place'. Since equivalence is distinct from identity of meaning, we might note, parenthetically that we have a different way of expressing the latter. We say *nsem no mienu ye baako*, the two pieces of discourse are one. The point now is that in Akan we have no such statement form as might be rendered as 'p if and only if q'. We can, of course, assert 'if p then q' (*se p a ende* q) and 'only if p then q' (*se p nkoara a na* q"), and the conjunction of these two forms is equivalent to 'p if and only if q'. But the conjunction is not the same form as the biconditional. If we now assert that the statement form 'p if and only if q' is equivalent to '(if p then q) and (if q then p)', we are obviously asserting a logical truth in English, but no such logical truth exists in Akan. There is nothing necessary about the form 'p if and only if q', so that it might be thought obligatory that the Akan should have a phrase literally corresponding to it. Whatever can be expressed by means of that form can be expressed by the Akan way of expressing equivalence as indicated above. It follows that the question whether the relation between 'p if and only if q' and '[(if p then q) and (if q then p)]' is really one of equivalence is a genuine logical issue in English which is, nevertheless, not universal.

The analogy with the question of the relation between truth and fact is quite complete. Just as the relation between 'p if and only if q' and '[(if p then q) and (if q then p)]' is a genuinely logical question which is dependent on a contingent feature of English vocabulary (and that of any similar language), so is the relation between truth and fact a genuine philosophical issue dependent on the English language. And just as any reasoner in English, whether he be a native speaker or not, will have to be conversant with the logic of the two statement forms, so anybody essaying a theory of truth in the medium of the English language will have to give some attention to the relation between truth and fact. It may well be that there are – indeed, I am sure that there are – ontological pitfalls into which native as well as non-native speakers of English are liable to fall in their thought about this relation.

There is a fairly obvious lesson that can be drawn from the foregoing observations. If some philosophical and logical problems – actually logical problems are philosophical problems – are relative to particular natural languages, then they cannot be as fundamental as those that are universal to all natural languages. Take, for example, the concept of implication. Any natural language will have to be capable of expressing this concept. Furthermore, if we use the term 'entailment' to refer to the relation between the premises and conclusion of a valid argument, then we can raise the question whether and how entailment can be defined in terms of implication. Such a question would be universal to all natural languages in the sense that it can be posed for any intuitively workable logic that may be constructed in any natural language. In comparison with this, the question of the relation between 'p if and only if q' and '[(if p then q) and (if q then p)]' is of very much less moment for the analysis of human reasoning.

Consider now the issue of the relation between fact and truth, on the one hand, and the problem of clarifying the notion of something being so, on the other. Since, as I have suggested above, no cogent thinking is possible without the notion of something being so, but one can reason to one's heart's content in Akan without any recourse to any word or phrase separately standing for *fact* (that is, in addition to the term expressing the idea of being so), it follows that the second problem (that is, concerning being so) is more fundamental than the first (that is, as to the relation to truth of fact).

Suppose the problem of relating truth to fact is solved in the English language. Still, if there is a problem of truth in the Akan Language at all – and there surely is – the position would be that the question has not even begun to be raised. In Akan the question would correspond to: 'What is meant by saying that a statement is so, that is, what is meant by saying that things are as a statement says

they are?' It is here obvious that certain versions of the correspondence theory of truth can at best only be part of the fundamental problem of truth, not part of its solution. The correspondence theory begins to shape up as an attempted solution at all when a certain account of the nature of facts is offered. Some accounts, whether correct or incorrect, will not satisfy this requirement. For example, defining 'fact' simply as 'true proposition' may be correct, but it would leave us exactly where we started in the matter of the more fundamental problem of truth. On the other hand, an ontological interpretation of 'fact' may take us somewhere, though not necessarily in a desirable direction. Suppose, for example, that facts are construed as interconnected objects of a certain sort, then to say that a statement corresponds to fact would mean claiming a certain relation between the statement and the interconnected objects in question. From the point of view of the Akan language this could be interpreted as saying that being so is a relation between a statement and a certain configuration of objects.

In the following passage taken from Bertrand Russell's *Philosophical Essays* he seems to me to be advancing a theory of this sort:

> When we judge that Charles I died on the scaffold, we have before us (not one object but) several objects, namely, Charles I and dying and the scaffold. Similarly, when we judge that Charles I died in his bed, we have before us Charles I, dying and his bed . . . Thus in this view judgement is a relation of the mind to several other terms: when these other terms have *inter se* a 'corresponding' relation, the judgement is true; when not, it is false.

(Note that since Charles I died many years ago, the objects which one is supposed to have before one's mind when one makes a judgment now to that effect must be of a rather unearthly nature.) Russell gave a somewhat more refined formulation of the correspondence theory in later life.[5] However, refined or not, it seems to me that when the correspondence theory is given meat in an ontological fashion it becomes open to fatal objections.

But it is not my intention to discuss the merits or demerits of the correspondence theory. I merely wish to make a meta-doctrinal point which reflection on the Akan language enables us to see, which is that a theory of truth is not of any real universal significance unless it offers some account of the notion of being so. This some correspondence theories fail to do.

Let me in this connection make one or two comments about Tarski's semantic conception of truth, since it is closely related to the correspondence theory of truth and is, besides, of great independent interest. The apparent intuition which motivates Tarski's theory is the same as that which underlies the correspondence theory at the level at which, as I have tried to show, it has a philosophical interest only relatively to the English Language and kindred languages. (Recall, in this connection, our comment on Aristotle's dictum.) Still, Tarski's theory, or a part of it, has the merit of providing a logically precise formulation of the idea of a statement being so, that is, the idea of things being as a statement says they are. A Tarskian 'T' sentence to the effect that 'Snow is white' is true if and only if 'snow is white' may be taken as a logically precise instantiation of the idea that to say that a statement is true is to say that things are as they are said to be in the statement. In Akan, since 'is true' is *te saa*, which means 'is so', that is, 'is how things are', the Tarski sentence becomes ' "snow is white" is as things are if and only if snow is white'.

In this form the sentence sounds trivially truistic, and is indeed so, if it is intended even as a partial theory of truth. But it can acquire a more substantial significance if it is made the starting point of an inquiry into the status of the second 'snow is white' in the Tarski equivalence. This component gives a 'concrete' instantiation of the idea of something being so. If, as I suggest, the puzzle about truth is a puzzle about the notion of something being so, then the use of Tarski's equivalence (in this connection) can only be to provide us in its second component with a vivid instantiation of our abstract notion of something being so. Such presentations can concentrate the mind and possibly lead to an illuminating elucidation. However, in itself, Tarski's 'T' sentence, even as completed by the rest of the theory, can only provide a possible starting point in the solution of the problem of truth.[6]

The other main theories of truth, namely, the pragmatic and coherence theories, do not suffer any trivialization on being translated into Akan, but they take on a new look if they are measured against the task of elucidating the notion of something being so, which reflection on the concept of truth in the Akan language presses on our mind.

Notes

1 A different etymology is sometimes suggested for *nokware*. It is sometimes said that the word consists of *ano* which, as we have seen, literally means 'mouth', and *kwa* which means, metaphorically, 'to polish into', 'make good', 'to protect'. Adopting this etymology would not make any essential difference to our main thesis since the 'polishing', 'protecting' would have to be construed morally.

2 There is a close relation between *nyansa* (wisdom) and *nimdee* (knowledge) (*nim* means know, *ade* means thing; so that *nimdee* means the knowing of things). One can, of course, know many things without being wise (Heraclitus) but one cannot be wise without knowing quite some things. When the things at issue are principles and philosophical notions, *nyansa* (wisdom) coincides with *nimdee* (knowledge) in Akan thought. Thus for many purposes the *anyansafo* will be the same as the people who are said to have *nimdee*.

3 I shall henceforward normally use 'truth' to render the cognitive concept of truth.

4 Another circumstance that might tempt one to suppose that *nokware* or *ewom* or *ampa* means 'true' is that in concessive contexts it is correct to translate any of these words by 'true'. Thus the phrase 'Although it is true that . . . yet . . .', where no moral component is present in 'true', is correctly translated as *Eve nokware se . . . nanso, Ampa se . . . nanso*. Here it seems that we are content to exploit only that part of the meaning of these words that is relevant in the context.

5 See for example *Human Knowledge, its Scope and Limits*, Allen and Unwin, 1948, p. 170.

6 The great elaborateness of Tarski's theory arises from his supposition that the scheme ' "p" is true if and only if p' cannot be universally quantified into a general definition of the form '(p) "p" is true if and only if p' because the 'p' in quotes in the first component is only a name and one cannot quantify over a mere name. But I do not believe this.

23

African Traditional Thought and Western Science

Robin Horton

From Tradition to Science

Social anthropologists have often failed to understand traditional religious thought for two main
reasons. First, many of them have been unfamiliar
with the theoretical thinking of their own culture.
This has deprived them of a vital key to understanding. For certain aspects of such thinking are
the counterparts of those very features of traditional
thought which they have tended to find most
puzzling. Secondly, even those familiar with theoretical thinking in their own culture have failed to
recognize its African equivalents, simply because
they have been blinded by a difference of idiom.
Like Consul Hutchinson wandering among the
Bubis of Fernando Po, they have taken a language
very remote from their own to be no language at all.

My approach is also guided by the conviction
that an exhaustive exploration of features common
to modern Western and traditional African thought
should come before the enumeration of differences.
By taking things in this order, we shall be less likely
to mistake differences of idiom for differences of
substance, and more likely to end up identifying
those features which really do distinguish one kind
of thought from the other.

Not surprisingly, perhaps, this approach has
frequently been misunderstood. Several critics
have objected that it tends to blur the undeniable

From Robin Horton, *Patterns of Thought in Africa and the
West* (1993); reproduced by kind permission of Cambridge University Press.

distinction between traditional and scientific thinking; that indeed it presents traditional thinking as
a species of science.[1] In order to clear up such
misunderstandings, I propose to devote the second
part of this paper to enumerating what I take to be
the salient differences between traditional and
scientific thinking and to suggesting a tentative
explanation of these differences.

In consonance with this programme, I shall start
by setting out a number of general propositions on
the nature and functions of theoretical thinking.
These propositions are derived, in the first instance, from my own training in biology, chemistry,
and philosophy of science. But, as I shall show, they
are highly relevant to traditional African religious
thinking. Indeed, they make sense of just those
features of such thinking that anthropologists have
often found most incomprehensible.

*1. The quest for explanatory theory is basically the
quest for unity underlying apparent diversity; for
simplicity underlying apparent complexity; for order
underlying apparent disorder; for regularity
underlying apparent anomaly*

Typically, this quest involves the elaboration of a
scheme of entities or forces operating 'behind' or
'within' the world of common-sense observations.
These entities must be of a limited number of kinds
and their behaviour must be governed by a limited
number of general principles. Such a theoretical
scheme is linked to the world of everyday experience by statements identifying happenings within
it with happenings in the everyday world. In the
language of philosophy of science, such identifica-

tion statements are known as Correspondence Rules. Explanations of observed happenings are generated from statements about the behaviour of entities in the theoretical scheme, plus Correspondence-Rule statements. In the sciences, well-known explanatory theories of this kind include the kinetic theory of gases, the planetary-atom theory of matter, the wave theory of light, and the cell theory of living organisms.

One of the perennial philosophical puzzles posed by explanations in terms of such theories derives from the Correspondence-Rule statements. In what sense can we really say that an increase of pressure in a gas 'is' an increase in the velocity of a myriad tiny particles moving in an otherwise empty space? How can we say that a thing is at once itself and something quite different? A great variety of solutions has been proposed to this puzzle. The modern positivists have taken the view that it is the things of common sense that are real, while the 'things' of theory are mere fictions useful in ordering the world of common sense. Locke, Planck, and others have taken the line that it is the 'things' of theory that are real, while the things of the everyday world are mere appearances. Perhaps the most up-to-date line is that there are good reasons for conceding the reality both of common-sense things and of theoretical entities. Taking this line implies an admission that the 'is' of Correspondence-Rule statements is neither the 'is' of identity nor the 'is' of class-membership. Rather, it stands for a unity-in-duality uniquely characteristic of the relation between the world of common sense and the world of theory.

What has all this got to do with the gods and spirits of traditional African religious thinking? Not very much, it may appear at first glance. Indeed, some modern writers deny that traditional religious thinking is in any serious sense theoretical thinking. In support of their denial they contrast the simplicity, regularity, and elegance of the theoretical schemes of the sciences with the unruly complexity and caprice of the world of gods and spirits.[2]

But this antithesis does not really accord with modern field-work data. It is true that, in a very superficial sense, African cosmologies tend towards proliferation. From the point of view of sheer number, the spirits of some cosmologies are virtually countless. But in this superficial sense we can point to the same tendency in Western cosmology, which for every common-sense unitary object gives us a myriad molecules. If, however, we recognize that the aim of theory is the demonstration of a limited number of *kinds* of entity or process underlying the diversity of experience, then the picture becomes very different. Indeed, one of the lessons of such recent studies of African cosmologies as Middleton's *Lugbara Religion*, Lienhardt's *Divinity and Experience*, Fortes's *Oedipus and Job*, and my own articles on Kalabari, is precisely that the gods of a given culture do form a scheme which interprets the vast diversity of everyday experience in terms of the action of a relatively few *kinds* of forces. Thus in Middleton's book, we see how all the various oppositions and conflicts in Lugbara experience are interpreted as so many manifestations of the single underlying opposition between ancestors and *adro* spirits. Again, in my own work, I have shown how nearly everything that happens in Kalabari life can be interpreted in terms of a scheme which postulates three basic *kinds* of forces: ancestors, heroes, and water-spirits.

The same body of modern work gives the lie to the old stereotype of the gods as capricious and irregular in their behaviour. For it shows that each category of beings has its appointed functions in relation to the world of observable happenings. The gods may sometimes appear capricious to the unreflective ordinary man. But for the religious expert charged with the diagnosis of spiritual agencies at work behind observed events, a basic modicum of regularity in their behaviour is the major premiss on which his work depends. Like atoms, molecules, and waves, then, the gods serve to introduce unity into diversity, simplicity into complexity, order into disorder, regularity into anomaly.

Once we have grasped that this is their intellectual function, many of the puzzles formerly posed by 'mystical thinking' disappear. Take the exasperated, wondering puzzlements of Lévy-Bruhl over his 'primitive mentality'. How could primitives believe that a visible, tangible object was at once its solid self and the manifestation of an immaterial being? How could a man literally see a spirit in a stone? These puzzles, raised so vividly by Lévy-Bruhl, have never been satisfactorily solved by anthropologists. 'Mystical thinking' has remained uncomfortably, indigestibly *sui generis*. And yet these questions of Lévy-Bruhl's have a very familiar ring in the context of European philosophy. Indeed, if we substitute atoms and molecules for gods and spirits, these turn out to be the very questions posed by modern scientific theory in the minds of Berkeley, Locke, Quine, and a whole host of European philosophers from Newton's time onwards.

Why is it that anthropologists have been unable to see this? One reason is that many of them move only in the common-sense world of Western culture, and are unfamiliar with its various theoretical worlds. But perhaps familiarity with Western theoretical thinking is not by itself enough. For a thoroughly unfamiliar idiom can still blind a man to a familiar form of thought. Because it prevents one from taking anything for granted, an unfamiliar idiom can help to show up all sorts of puzzles and problems inherent in an intellectual process which normally seems puzzle-free. But this very unfamiliarity can equally prevent us from seeing that the puzzles and problems are ones which crop up on our own doorstep. Thus it took a 'mystical' theorist like Bishop Berkeley to see the problems posed by the materialistic theories of Newton and his successors; but he was never able to see that the same problems were raised by his own theoretical framework. Again, it takes materialistically inclined modern social anthropologists to see the problems posed by the 'mystical' theories of traditional Africa; but, for the same reasons, such people can hardly be brought to see these very problems arising within their own theoretical framework.

2. Theory places things in a causal context wider than that provided by common sense

When we say that theory displays the order and regularity underlying apparent disorder and irregularity, one of the things we mean is that it provides a causal context for apparently 'wild' events. Putting things in a causal context is, of course, one of the jobs of common sense. But although it does this job well at a certain level, it seems to have limitations. Thus the principal tool of common sense is induction or 'putting two and two together', the process of inference so beloved of the positivist philosophers. But a man can only 'put two and two together' if he is looking in the right direction. And common sense furnishes him with a pair of horse-blinkers which severely limits the directions in which he can look. Thus common-sense thought looks for the antecedents of any happening amongst events adjacent in space and time: it abhors action at a distance. Again, common sense looks for the antecedents of a happening amongst events that are in some way commensurable with it. Common sense is at the root of the hard-dying dictum 'like cause, like effect'. Gross incommensurability defeats it.

Now one of the essential functions of theory is to help the mind transcend these limitations. And

one of the most obvious achievements of modern scientific theory is its revelation of a whole array of causal connections which are quite staggering to the eye of common sense. Think for instance of the connection between two lumps of a rather ordinary looking metal, rushing towards each other with a certain acceleration, and a vast explosion capable of destroying thousands of people. Or think again of the connection between small, innocuous water-snails and the disease of bilharziasis which can render whole populations lazy and inept.

Once again, we may ask what relevance all this has to traditional African religious thinking. And once again the stock answer may be 'precious little'. For a widely current view of such thinking still asserts that it is more interested in the supernatural causes of things than it is in their natural causes. This is a misinterpretation closely connected with the one we discussed in the previous section. Perhaps the best way to get rid of it is to consider the commonest case of the search for causes in traditional Africa – the diagnosis of disease. Through the length and breadth of the African continent, sick or afflicted people go to consult diviners as to the causes of their troubles. Usually, the answer they receive involves a god or other spiritual agency, and the remedy prescribed involves the propitiation or calling-off of this being. But this is very seldom the whole story. For the diviner who diagnoses the intervention of a spiritual agency is also expected to give some acceptable account of what moved the agency in question to intervene. And this account very commonly involves reference to some event in the world of visible, tangible happenings. Thus if a diviner diagnoses the action of witchcraft influence or lethal medicine spirits, it is usual for him to add something about the human hatreds, jealousies, and misdeeds, that have brought such agencies into play. Or, if he diagnoses the wrath of an ancestor, it is usual for him to point to the human breach of kinship morality which has called down this wrath.

The situation here is not very different from that in which a puzzled American layman, seeing a large mushroom cloud on the horizon, consults a friend who happens to be a physicist. On the one hand, the physicist may refer him to theoretical entities. 'Why this cloud?' 'Well, a massive fusion of hydrogen nuclei has just taken place.' Pushed further, however, the physicist is likely to refer to the assemblage and dropping of a bomb containing certain special substances. Substitute 'disease' for 'mushroom cloud', 'spirit anger' for 'massive fusion of hydrogen nuclei', and 'breach of kinship morality' for 'assemblage and dropping of a bomb', and we are back again with the diviner. In both cases reference to theoretical entities is used to link events in the visible, tangible world (natural effects) to their antecedents in the same world (natural causes).

To say of the traditional African thinker that he is interested in supernatural rather than natural causes makes little more sense, therefore, than to say of the physicist that he is interested in nuclear rather than natural causes. Both are making the same use of theory to transcend the limited vision of natural causes provided by common sense.

Granted this common preoccupation with natural causes, the fact remains that the causal link between disturbed social relations and disease or misfortune, so frequently postulated by traditional religious thought, is one which seems somewhat strange and alien to many Western medical scientists. Following the normal practice of historians of Western ideas, we can approach the problem of trying to understand this strange causal notion from two angles. First of all, we can inquire what influence a particular theoretical idiom has in moulding this and similar traditional notions. Secondly, we can inquire whether the range of experience available to members of traditional societies has influenced causal notions by throwing particular conjunctions of events into special prominence.

Theory, as I have said, places events in a wider causal context than that provided by common sense. But once a particular theoretical idiom has been adopted, it tends to direct people's attention towards certain kinds of causal linkage and away from others. Now most traditional African cultures have adopted a personal idiom as the basis of their attempt to understand the world. And once one has adopted such an idiom, it is a natural step to suppose that personal beings underpin, amongst other things, the life and strength of social groups. Now it is in the nature of a personal being who has his designs thwarted to visit retribution on those who thwart him: Where the designs involve maintaining the strength and unity of a social group, members of the group who disturb this unity are thwarters, and hence are ripe for punishment. Disease and misfortune are the punishment. Once a personal idiom has been adopted, then, those who use it become heavily predisposed towards seeing a nexus between social disturbance and individual affliction.

Are these traditional notions of cause merely artefacts of the prevailing theoretical idiom, fanta-sies with no basis in reality? Or are they responses to features of people's experience which in some sense are 'really there'? My own feeling is that, although these notions are ones to which people are predisposed by the prevailing theoretical idiom, they also register certain important features of the objective situation.

Let us remind ourselves at this point that modern medical men, though long blinded to such things by the fantastic success of the germ theory of disease, are once more beginning to toy with the idea that disturbances in a person's social life can in fact contribute to a whole series of sicknesses, ranging from those commonly thought of as mental to many more commonly thought of as bodily. In making this rediscovery, however, the medical men have tended to associate it with the so-called 'pressures of modern living'. They have tended to imagine traditional societies as psychological paradises in which disease-producing mental stresses are at a minimum.

If life in modern industrial society contains sources of mental stress adequate to causing or exacerbating a wide range of sicknesses, so too does life in traditional village communities. Hence the need to approach traditional religious theories of the social causation of sickness with respect. Such respect and readiness to learn is, I suggest, particularly appropriate with regard to what is commonly known as mental disease. I say this because the grand theories of Western psychiatry have a notoriously insecure empirical base and are probably culture-bound to a high degree.

Even of those diseases in which the key factor is definitely an infecting micro-organism, I suggest, traditional religious theory has something to say which is worth listening to.

Over much of traditional Africa, let me repeat, we are dealing with small-scale, relatively self-contained communities. These are the sort of social units that, as my friend Dr Oruwariye puts it, 'have achieved equilibrium with their disease's'. A given population and a given set of diseases have been co-existing over many generations. Natural selection has played a considerable part in developing human resistance to diseases such as malaria, typhoid, small-pox, dysentery, etc. In addition, those who survive the very high peri-natal mortality have probably acquired an extra resistance by the very fact of having lived through one of these diseases just after birth. In such circumstances, an adult who catches one of these (for Europeans) killer diseases has good chances both of life and of death. In the absence of antimalarials or antibiotics, what happens to him will depend very largely on other factors that add to or subtract from his considerable natural resistance. In these circumstances the traditional healer's efforts to cope with the situation by ferreting out and attempting to remedy stress-producing disturbances in the patient's social field is probably very relevant. Such efforts may seem to have a ludicrously marginal importance to a hospital doctor wielding a nivaquine bottle and treating a non-resistant European malaria patient. But they may be crucial where there is no nivaquine bottle and a considerable natural resistance to malaria.

After reflecting on these things the modern doctor may well take some of these traditional causal notions seriously enough to put them to the test. If the difficulties of testing can be overcome, and if the notions pass the test, he will end up by taking them over into his own body of beliefs. At the same time, however, he will be likely to reject the theoretical framework that enabled the traditional mind to form these notions in the first place.

This is fair enough; for although, as I have shown, the gods and spirits do perform an important theoretical job in pointing to certain interesting forms of causal connection, they are probably not very useful as the basis of a wider view of the world. Nevertheless, there do seem to be few cases in which the theoretical framework of which they are the basis may have something to contribute to the theoretical framework of modern medicine. To take an example, there are several points at which Western psycho-analytic theory, with its apparatus of personalized mental entities, resembles traditional West African religious theory. More specifically, as I have suggested elsewhere,[3] there are striking resemblances between psycho-analytic ideas about the individual mind as a congeries of warring entities, and West African ideas, about the body as a meeting place of multiple souls. In both systems of belief, one personal entity is identified with the stream of consciousness, whilst the others operate as an 'unconscious', sometimes co-operating with consciousness and sometimes at war with it. Now the more flexible psycho-analysts have long suspected that Freud's allocation of particular desires and fears to particular agencies of the mind may well be appropriate to certain cultures only. Thus his allocation of a great load of sexual desires and fears to the unconscious may well have been appropriate to the Viennese subculture he so largely dealt with, but it may not be appropriate to many other cultures. A study of West African soul theories, and of their allocation of particular desires and emotions to particular agencies of the mind, may well help the psycho-analyst to reformulate his theories in terms more appropriate to the local scene.

Modern Western medical scientists have long been distracted from noting the causal connection between social disturbance and disease by the success of the germ theory. It would seem, indeed, that a conjunction of the germ theory, of the discovery of potent antibiotics and immunization techniques, and of conditions militating against the build-up of natural resistance to many killer infections, for long made it very difficult for scientists to see the importance of this connection. Conversely, perhaps, a conjunction of no germ theory, no potent antibiotics, no immunization techniques, with conditions favouring the build-up of considerable natural resistance to killer infections, served to throw this same causal connection into relief in the mind of the traditional healer. If one were asked to choose between germ theory innocent of psychosomatic insight and traditional psychosomatic theory innocent of ideas about infection, one would almost certainly choose the germ theory. For in terms of quantitative results it is clearly the more vital to human well-being. But it is salutary to remember that not all the profits are on one side.

From what has been said in this section, it should be clear that one commonly accepted way of contrasting traditional religious thought with scientific thought is misleading. I am thinking here of the contrast between traditional religious thought as 'non-empirical' with scientific thought as 'empirical'. In the first place, the contrast is misleading because traditional religious thought is no more nor less interested in the natural causes of things than is the theoretical thought of the sciences. Indeed, the intellectual function of its supernatural beings (as, too, that of atoms, waves, etc.) *is* the extension of people's vision of natural causes. In the second place, the contrast is misleading because traditional religious theory clearly does more than postulate causal connections that bear no relation to experience. Some of the connections it postulates are, by the standards of modern medical science, almost certainly real ones. To some extent, then, it successfully grasps reality.

I am not claiming traditional thought as a variety of scientific thought. In certain crucial respects, the two kinds of thought are related to experience in quite different ways, but it is not only where scientific method is in use that we find theories which both aim at grasping causal connections and to some extent succeed in this aim. Scientific method is undoubtedly the surest and most efficient tool for arriving at beliefs that are successful in this respect; but it is not the only way of arriving at such beliefs. Given the basic process of theory-making, and an environmental stability which gives theory plenty of time to adjust to experience, a people's belief system may come, even in the absence of scientific method, to grasp at least some significant causal connections which lie beyond the range of common sense. It is because traditional African religious beliefs demonstrate the truth of this that it seems apt to extend to them the label 'empirical'.

3. Common sense and theory have complementary roles in everyday life

In the history of European thought there has often been opposition to a new theory on the ground that it threatens to break up and destroy the old, familiar world of common sense. Such was the eighteenth-century opposition to Newtonian corpuscular theory, which, so many people thought, was all set to 'reduce' the warm, colourful beautiful world to a lifeless, colourless, wilderness of rapidly moving little balls. Not surprisingly, this eighteenth-century attack was led by people like Goethe and Blake – poets whose job was precisely to celebrate the glories of the world of common sense. Such, again, is the twentieth-century opposition to behaviour theory, which many people see as a threat to 'reduce' human beings to animals or even to machines. Much recent Western philosophy is a monotonous and poorly reasoned attempt to bludgeon us into believing that behaviour theory cannot possibly work. But just as the common-sense world of things and people remained remarkably unscathed by the Newtonian revolution, so there is reason to think it will not be too seriously touched by the behaviour-theory revolution. Indeed, a lesson of the history of European thought is that, while theories come and theories go, the world of common sense remains very little changed.

One reason for this is perhaps that all theories take their departure from the world of things and people, and ultimately return us to it. In this context, to say that a good theory 'reduces' something to something else is misleading. Ideally, a process of deduction from the premises of a theory should lead us back to statements which portray the common-sense world in its full richness. In so far as this richness is not restored, by so much does

theory fail. Another reason for the persistence of the world of common sense is probably that, within the limits discussed in the last section, common-sense thinking is handier and more economical than theoretical thinking. It is only when one needs to transcend the limited causal vision of common sense that one resorts to theory.

Take the example of an industrial chemist and his relationships with common salt. When he uses it in the house, his relationships with it are governed entirely by common sense. Invoking chemical theory to guide him in its domestic use would be like bringing up a pile-driver to hammer in a nail. Such theory may well lend no more colour to the chemist's domestic view of salt than it lends to the chemically uneducated rustic's view of the substance. When he uses it in his chemical factory, however, common sense no longer suffices. The things he wants to do with it force him to place it in a wider causal context than common sense provides; and he can only do this by viewing it in the light of atomic theory. At this point, someone may ask: 'And which does he think is the real salt; the salt of common sense or the salt of theory?' The answer, perhaps, is that both are equally real to him. For whatever the philosophers say, people develop a sense of reality about something to the extent that they use and act on language which implies that this something exists.

This discussion of common sense and theory in Western thought is very relevant to the understanding of traditional African religions. Early accounts of such religions stressed the ever-presence of the spirit world in the minds of men. Later on, fieldwork experience in African societies convinced most reporters that members of such societies attended to the spirit world rather intermittently.[4] Many modern criticisms of Lévy-Bruhl and other early theorists hinge on this observation. For the modern generation of social anthropologists, the big question has now become: 'On what kinds of occasion do people ignore the spirit world, and on what kinds of occasion do they attend to it?'

In answer we need to recognize the essentially theoretical character of traditional religious thinking. And here our discussion of common sense and theory in European thought becomes relevant.

I suggest that in traditional Africa relations between common sense and theory are essentially the same as they are in Europe. That is, common sense is the handier and more economical tool for coping with a wide range of circumstances in everyday life. Nevertheless, there are certain circumstances that can only be coped with in terms of a wider causal vision than common sense provides. And in these circumstances there is a jump to theoretical thinking.

Let me give an example drawn from my own fieldwork among the Kalabari people of the Niger Delta. Kalabari recognize many different kinds of diseases, and have an array of herbal specifics with which to treat them. Sometimes a sick person will be treated by ordinary members of his family who recognize the disease and know the specifics. Sometimes the treatment will be carried out on the instructions of a native doctor. When sickness and treatment follow these lines the atmosphere is basically commonsensical. Often, there is little or no reference to spiritual agencies.

Sometimes, however, the sickness does not respond to treatment, and it becomes evident that the herbal specific used does not provide the whole answer. The native doctor may rediagnose and try another specific. But if this produces no result the suspicion will arise that 'there is something else in this sickness'. In other words, the perspective provided by common sense is too limited. It is at this stage that a diviner is likely to be called in (it may be the native doctor who started the treatment). Using ideas about various spiritual agencies, he will relate the sickness to a wider range of circumstances – often to disturbances in the sick man's general social life.

What we are describing here is generally referred to as a jump from common sense to mystical thinking. But, as we have seen, it is also, more significantly, a jump from common sense to theory. And here, as in Europe, the jump occurs at the point where the limited causal vision of common sense curtails its usefulness in dealing with the situation on hand.

4. Level of theory varies with context
A person seeking to place some event in a wider causal context often has a choice of theories. Like the initial choice between common sense and theory, this choice too will depend on just how wide a context he wishes to bring into consideration. Where he is content to place the event in a relatively modest context, he will be content to use what is generally called a low-level theory – i.e. one that covers a relatively limited area of experience. Where he is more ambitious about context, he will make use of a higher-level theory – i.e. one that covers a larger area of experience. As the area

covered by the lower-level theory is part of the area covered by the higher-level scheme, so too the entities postulated by the lower-level theory are seen as special manifestations of those postulated at the higher level. Hence they pose all the old problems of things which are at once themselves and at the same time manifestations of other quite different things.

It is typical of traditional African religious systems that they include, on the one hand, ideas about a multiplicity of spirits, and on the other hand, ideas about a single supreme being. Though the spirits are thought of as independent beings, they are also considered as so many manifestations of dependants of the supreme being. This conjunction of the many and the one has given rise to much discussion among students of comparative religion, and has evoked many ingenious theories. Most of these have boggled at the idea that polytheism and monotheism could coexist stably in a single system of thought. They have therefore tried to resolve the problem by supposing that the belief-systems in question are in transition from one type to the other. It is only recently, with the Nilotic studies of Evans-Pritchard and Lienhardt,[5] that the discussion has got anywhere near the point – which is that the many spirits and the one God play complementary roles in people's thinking. As Evans-Pritchard says: 'A theistic religion need be neither monotheistic nor polytheistic. It may be both. It is the question of the level, or situation, of thought, rather than of exclusive types of thought.'[6]

On the basis of material from the Nilotic peoples, and on that of material from such West African societies as Kalabari, Ibo, and Tallensi,[7] one can make a tentative suggestion about the respective roles of the many and the one in traditional African thought generally. In such thought, I suggest, the spirits provide the means of setting an event within a relatively limited causal context. They are the basis of a theoretical scheme which typically covers the thinker's own community and immediate environment. The supreme being, on the other hand, provides the means of setting an event within the widest possible context. For it is the basis of a theory of the origin and life course of the world seen as a whole.

In many (though by no means all) traditional African belief-systems, ideas about the spirits and actions based on such ideas are far more richly developed than ideas about the supreme being and actions based on them. In these cases, the idea of God seems more the pointer to a potential theory than the core of a seriously operative one. This perhaps is because social life in the communities involved is so parochial that their members seldom have to place events in the wider context that the idea of the supreme being purports to deal with. Nevertheless, the different levels of thinking are there in all these systems. It seems clear that they are related to one another in much the same way as are the different levels of theoretical thinking in the sciences. At this point the relation between the many spirits and the one God loses much of its aura of mystery. Indeed there turns out to be nothing peculiarly religious or 'mystical' about it. For it is essentially the same as the relation between the homogeneous atoms and planetary systems of fundamental particles in the thinking of a chemist. It is a by-product of certain very general features of the way theories are used in explanation.

5. All theory breaks up the unitary objects of common sense into aspects, then places the resulting elements in a wider causal context. That is, it first abstracts and analyses, then re-integrates

Commentators on scientific method have familiarized us with the way in which the theoretical schemas of the sciences break up the world of common-sense things in order to achieve a causal understanding which surpasses that of common sense. But it is only from the more recent studies of African cosmologies, where religious beliefs are shown in the context of the various everyday contingencies they are invoked to explain, that we have begun to see how traditional religious thought also operates by a similar process of abstraction, analysis, and reintegration. A good example is provided by Fortes's recent work on West African theories of the individual and his relation to society. Old-fashioned West African ethnographers showed the wide distribution of beliefs in what they called 'multiple souls'. They found that many West African belief-systems invested the individual with a multiplicity of spiritual agencies. The general impression they gave was one of an unruly fantasy at work. In his recent book,[8] however, Forests takes the 'multiple soul' beliefs of a single West African people (the Tallensi) and places them in the context of everyday thought and behaviour. His exposition dispels much of the aura of fantasy.

Fortes describes three categories of spiritual agency especially concerned with the Tale individual. First comes the *segr*, which presides over the individual as a biological entity – over his sickness and health, his life and death. Then comes the *nuor*

yin, a personification of the wishes expressed by the individual before his arrival on earth. The *nuor yin* appears specifically concerned with whether or not the individual has the personality traits necessary if he is to become an adequate member of Tale society. As Fortes puts it, evil *nuor yin* 'serves to identify the fact of irremediable failure in the development of the individual to full social capacity'. Good *nuor yin*, on the other hand, 'identifies the fact of successful individual development along the road to full incorporation in society'. Finally, in this trio of spiritual agencies, we have what Fortes calls the '*yin* ancestors'. These are two or three out of the individual's total heritage of ancestors, who have been delegated to preside over his personal fortunes. *Yin* ancestors only attach themselves to an individual who has a good *nuor yin*. They are concerned with the fortunes of the person who has already proved himself to have the basic equipment for fitting into Tale society. Here we have a theoretical scheme which, in order to produce a deeper understanding of the varying fortunes of individuals in their society, breaks them down into three aspects by a simple but typical operation of abstraction and analysis.

Perhaps the most significant comment on Fortes's work in this field was pronounced, albeit involuntarily, by a reviewer of 'Oeidipus and Job'.[9] 'If any criticism of the presentation is to be made it is that Professor Fortes sometimes seems to achieve an almost mystical identification with the Tallensi world-view and leaves the unassimilated reader in some doubt about where to draw the line between Tallensi notions and Cambridge concepts!' Now the anthropologist has to find *some* concepts in his own language roughly appropriate to translating the 'notions' of the people he studies. And in the case in question, perhaps only the lofty analytic 'Cambridge' concepts did come anywhere near to congruence with Tallensi notions. This parallel between traditional African religious 'notions' and Western sociological 'abstractions' is by no means an isolated phenomenon. Think for instance of individual guardian spirits and group spirits – two very general categories of traditional African religious thought. Then think of those hardy Parsonian abstractions – psychological imperatives and sociological imperatives. It takes no great brilliance to see the resemblance.[10]

6. In evolving a theoretical scheme, the human mind seems constrained to draw inspiration from analogy between the puzzling observations to be

explained and certain already familiar phenomena
In the genesis of a typical theory, the drawing of an analogy between the unfamiliar and the familiar is followed by the making of a model in which something akin to the familiar is postulated as the reality underlying the unfamiliar. Both modern Western and traditional African thought-products amply demonstrate the truth of this. Whether we look amongst atoms, electrons, and waves, or amongst gods, spirits, and entelechies, we find that theoretical notions nearly always have their roots in relatively homely everyday experiences, in analogies with the familiar.

What do we mean here by 'familiar phenomena'? Above all, I suggest, we mean phenomena strongly associated in the mind of the observer with order and regularity. That theory should depend on analogy with things familiar in this sense follows from the very nature of explanation. Since the overriding aim of explanation is to disclose order and regularity underlying apparent chaos, the search for explanatory analogies must tend towards those areas of experience most closely associated with such qualities. Here, I think, we have a basis for indicating why explanations in modern Western culture tend to be couched in an impersonal idiom, while explanations in traditional African society tend to be couched in a personal idiom.

In complex, rapidly changing industrial societies the human scene is in flux. Order, regularity, predictability, simplicity, all these seem lamentably absent. It is in the world of inanimate things that such qualities are most readily seen. This is why many people can find themselves less at home with their fellow men than with things. And this too, I suggest, is why the mind in quest of explanatory analogies turns most readily to the inanimate. In the traditional societies of Africa, we find the situation reversed. The human scene is the locus *par excellence* of order, predictability, regularity. In the world of the inanimate, these qualities are far less evident. Here, being less at home with people than with things is unimaginable. And here, the mind in quest of explanatory analogies turns naturally to people and their relations.

7. Where theory is founded on analogy between puzzling observations and familiar phenomena, it is generally only a limited aspect of such phenomena that is incorporated into the resulting model
Philosophers of science have often used the molecular (kinetic) theory of gases as an illustration of this feature of model-building. The molecular theory, of course, is based on an analogy with the behaviour of fast-moving, spherical balls in various kinds of space. And the philosophers have pointed out that although many important properties of such balls have been incorporated into the definition of a molecule, other important properties such as colour and temperature have been omitted. They have been omitted because they have no explanatory function in relation to the observations that originally evoked the theory. Here, of course, we have another sense in which physical theory is based upon abstraction and abstract ideas. For concepts such as 'molecule', 'atom', 'electron', 'wave' are the result of a process in which the relevant features of certain prototype phenomena have been abstracted from the irrelevant features.

Many writers have considered this sort of abstraction to be one of the distinctive features of scientific thinking. But this, like so many other such distinctions, is a false one; for just the same process is at work in traditional African thought. Thus when traditional thought draws upon people and their social relations as the raw material of its theoretical models, it makes use of some dimensions of human life and neglects others. The definition of a god may omit any reference to his physical appearance, his diet, his mode of lodging, his children, his relations with his wives, and so on. Asking questions about such attributes is as inappropriate as asking questions about the colour of a molecule or the temperature of an electron. It is this omission of many dimensions of human life from the definition of the gods which gives them that rarefied, attenuated aura which we call 'spiritual'. But there is nothing peculiarly religious, mystical, or traditional about this 'spirituality'. It is the result of the same process of abstraction as the one we see at work in Western theoretical models: the process whereby features of the prototype phenomena which have explanatory relevance are incorporated into a theoretical schema, while features which lack such relevance are omitted.

8. A theoretical model, once built, is developed in ways which sometimes obscure the analogy on which it was founded
In its raw, initial state, a model may come up quite quickly against data for which it cannot provide any explanatory coverage. Rather than scrap it out of hand, however, its users will tend to give it successive modifications in order to enlarge its coverage. Sometimes, such modifications will involve the drawing of further analogies with

Robin Horton

phenomena rather different from those which provided the initial inspiration for the model. Sometimes, they will merely involve 'tinkering' with the model until it comes to fit the new observations. By comparison with the phenomena which provided its original inspiration, such a developed model not unnaturally seems to have a bizarre, hybrid air about it.

Examples of the development of theoretical models abound in the history of science. One of the best documented of these is provided by the modern atomic theory of matter. The foundations of this theory were laid by Rutherford, who based his original model upon an analogy between the passage of ray-beams through metal foil and the passage of comets through our planetary system. Rutherford's planetary model of the basic constituents of matter proved extremely useful in explanation. When it came up against recalcitrant data, therefore, the consensus of scientists was in favour of developing it rather than scrapping it. Each of several modifications of the model was a response to the demand for increased explanatory coverage. Each, however, removed the theoretical model one step further away from the familiar phenomena which had furnished its original inspiration.

In studying traditional African thought, alas, we scarcely ever have the historical depth available to the student of European thought. So we can make few direct observations on the development of its theoretical models. Nevertheless, these models often show just the same kinds of bizarre, hybrid features as the models of the scientists. Since they resemble the latter in so many other ways, it seems reasonable to suppose that these features are the result of a similar process of development in response to demands for further explanatory coverage. The validity of such a supposition is strengthened when we consider detailed instances: for these show how the bizarre features of particular models are indeed closely related to the nature of the observations that demand explanation.

Let me draw one example from my own fieldwork on Kalabari religious thought which I have outlined in earlier publications. Basic Kalabari religious beliefs involve three main categories of spirits: ancestors, heroes, and water-people. On the one hand, all three categories of spirits show many familiar features: emotions of pleasure and anger, friendships, enmities, marriages. Such features betray the fact that, up to a point, the spirits are fashioned in the image of ordinary Kalabari people. Beyond this point, however, they are bizarre in

many ways. The ancestors, perhaps, remain closest to the image of ordinary people. But the heroes are decidedly odd. They are defined as having left no descendants, as having disappeared rather than died, and as having come in the first instance from outside the community. The water-spirits are still odder. They are said to be 'like men, and also like pythons'. To make sense of these oddities, let us start by sketching the relations of the various kinds of spirits to the world of everyday experience.

First, the ancestors. These are postulated as the forces underpinning the life and strength of the lineages, bringing misfortune to those who betray lineage values and fortune to those who promote them. Second, the heroes. These are the forces underpinning the life and strength of the community and its various institutions. They are also the forces underpinning human skill and maintaining its efficacy in the struggle against nature. Third, the water-spirits. On the one hand, these are the 'owners' of the creeks and swamps, the guardians of the fish harvest, the forces of nature. On the other hand, they are the patrons of human individualism – in both its creative and its destructive forms. In short, they are the forces underpinning all that lies beyond the confines of the established social order.

We can look on ancestors, heroes, and water-spirits as the members of a triangle of forces. In this triangle, the relation of each member to the other two contains elements of separation and opposition as well as of co-operation. Thus by supporting lineages in rivalry against one another, the ancestors can work against the heroes in sapping the strength of the community; but in other contexts, by strengthening their several lineages, they can work with the heroes in contributing to village strength. Again, when they bring up storms, rough water, and sharks, the water-spirits work against the heroes by hampering the exercise of the village's productive skills; but when they produce calm water and an abundance of fish, they work just as powerfully with the heroes. Yet again, by fostering anti-social activity, the water-spirits can work against both heroes and ancestors; or, by supporting creativity and invention, they can enrich village life and so work with them.

In this triangle, then, we have a theoretical scheme in terms of which Kalabari can grasp and comprehend most of the many vicissitudes of their daily lives. Now it is at this point that the bizarre, paradoxical attributes of heroes and water-spirits begin to make sense: for a little inspection shows that such attributes serve to define each category of spirits in a way appropriate to its place in the total scheme. This is true, for example, of such attributes of the heroes as having left no human descendants, having disappeared instead of undergoing death and burial, and having come from outside the community. All these serve effectively to define the heroes as forces quite separate from the ancestors with their kinship involvements. Lack of descendants does this in an obvious way. Disappearance rather than death and burial performs the same function, especially when, as in Kalabari, lack of burial is almost synonymous with lack of kin. And arrival from outside the community again makes it clear that they cannot be placed in any lineage or kinship context. These attributes, in short, are integral to the definition of the heroes as forces contrasted with and potentially opposed to the ancestors. Again, the water-spirits are said to be 'like men, and also like pythons'; and here too the paradoxical characterization is essential to defining their place in the triangle. The python is regarded as the most powerful of all the animals in the creeks, and is often said to be their father. But its power is seen as something very different from that of human beings – something 'fearful' and 'astonishing'. The combination of human and python elements in the characterization of the water-people fits the latter perfectly for their own place in the triangle – as forces of the extra-social contrasted with and potentially opposed to both heroes and ancestors.

Another illuminating example of the theoretical significance of oddity is provided by Middleton's account of traditional Lugbara religious concepts.[11] According to Middleton, Lugbara belief features two main categories of spiritual agency – the ancestors and the *adro* spirits. Like the Kalabari ancestors, those of the Lugbara remain close to the image of ordinary people. The *adro*, however, are very odd indeed. They are cannibalistic and incestuous, and almost everything else that Lugbara ordinarily consider repulsive. They are commonly said to walk upside down – a graphic expression of their general perversity. Once again, these oddities fall into place when we look at the relations of the two categories of spirits to the world of experience. The ancestors, on the one hand, account for the settled world of human habitation and with the established social order organized on the basis of small lineages. The *adro*, on the other hand, are concerned with the uncultivated bush, and with all human activities which run counter to the estab-

lished order of things. Like the Kalabari water-spirits, they are forces of the extra-social, whether in its natural or its human form. The contrast and opposition between ancestors and *adro* thus provides Lugbara with a theoretical schema in terms of which they can comprehend a whole series of oppositions and conflicts manifest in the world of their everyday experiences. Like the oddities of the Kalabari gods, those of the *adro* begin to make sense at this point. For it is the bizarre, perverse features of these spirits that serve to define their position in the theory – as forces contrasted with and opposed to the ancestors.

In both of these cases the demands of explanation result in a model whose structure is hybrid between that of the human social phenomena which provided its original inspiration, and that of the field of experience to which it is applied. In both cases, oddity is essential to explanatory function. Even in the absence of more direct historical evidence, these examples suggest that the theoretical models of traditional African thought are the products of developmental processes comparable to those affecting the models of the sciences.

In treating traditional African religious systems as theoretical models akin to those of the sciences, I have really done little more than take them at their face value. Although this approach may seem naïve and platitudinous compared to the sophisticated 'things-are-never-what-they-seem' attitude more characteristic of the social anthropologist, it has certainly produced some surprising results. Above all, it has cast doubt on most of the well-worn dichotomies used to conceptualize the difference between scientific and traditional religious thought. Intellectual versus emotional; rational versus mystical; reality-oriented versus fantasy-oriented; causally oriented versus supernaturally oriented; empirical versus non-empirical; abstract versus concrete; analytical versus non-analytical: all of these are shown to be more or less inappropriate. If the reader is disturbed by this casting away of established distinctions, he will, I hope, accept it when he sees how far it can pave the way towards making sense of so much that previously appeared senseless.

One thing that may well continue to bother the reader is my playing down of the difference between non-personal and personal theory. For while I have provided what seems to me an adequate explanation of this difference, I have treated it as a surface difference concealing an underlying similarity of intellectual process. I must confess that I have used brevity of treatment here as a device to play down the gulf between the two kinds of theory. But I think this is amply justifiable in reaction to the more usual state of affairs, in which the difference is allowed to dominate all other features of the situation. Even familiarity with theoretical thinking in their own culture cannot help anthropologists who are dominated by this difference. For once so blinded, they can only see traditional religious thought as wholly other. With the bridge from their own thought-patterns to those of traditional Africa blocked, it is little wonder they can make no further headway.

The aim of my exposition has been to reopen this bridge. The point I have sought to make is that the difference between non-personal and personalized theories is more than anything else a difference in the idiom of the explanatory quest. Grasping this point is an essential preliminary to realizing how far the various established dichotomies used in this field are simply obstacles to understanding. Once it is grasped, a whole series of seemingly bizarre and senseless features of traditional thinking becomes immediately comprehensible. Until it is grasped, they remain essentially mysterious. Making the business of personal versus impersonal entities the crux of the difference between tradition and science not only blocks the understanding of tradition. It also draws a red herring across the path to an understanding of science.

All this is not to deny that science has progressed greatly through working in a non-personal theoretical idiom. Indeed, as one who has hankerings after behaviourism, I am inclined to believe that it is this idiom, and this idiom only, which will eventually lead to the triumph of science in the sphere of human affairs. What I am saying, however, is that this is more a reflection of the nature of reality than a clue to the essence of scientific method. For the progressive acquisition of knowledge, man needs both the right kind of theories *and* the right attitude to them. But it is only the latter which we call science. Indeed, as we shall see, any attempt to define science in terms of a particular kind of theory runs contrary to its very essence. Now, at last, I hope it will be evident why, in comparing African traditional thought with Western scientific thought, I have chosen to start with a review of continuities rather than with a statement of crucial differences. For although this order of procedure carries the risk of one's being understood to mean that traditional thought is a kind of science, it also carries the advantage of having the path clear of red herrings when one comes to tackle the question of differences.

Notes

This paper first appeared in a rather longer form in *Africa* XXXVII, nos. 1 and 2 (Jan. and April, 1967), pp. 50–71 and 155–87.

1 See, for instance, John Beattie, 'Ritual and Social Change', *Journal of the Royal Anthropological Institute*, 1966, vol. 1, no. 1.

2 See Beattie.

3 Robin Horton, 'Destiny and the Unconscious in West Africa', *Africa* XXXI, 2, 1961, pp. 110–16.

4 See for instance E. E. Evans-Pritchard, *Theories of Primitive Religion*, Oxford, 1995, p. 88.

5 E. E. Evans-Pritchard, *Nuer Religion*, Oxford, 1956; Godfrey Lienhardt, *Divinity and Experience: The Religion of the Dinka*, London, 1961.

6 Evans-Pritchard, *Nuer Religion*, p. 316.

7 Robin Horton, 'The Kalabari World-View: An Outline and Interpretation', *Africa*, XXXII, 3, 1962, pp. 197–220; 'A Hundred Years of Change in Kalabari Religion' (unpublished paper for the University of Ife Conference on 'The High God in Africa', Dec. 1964); 'God, Man and the Land in a Northern Ibo Village Group', *Africa*, XXVI, I, 1956, pp. 17–28; M. Fortes, *The Web of Kinship among the Tallensi*, London, 1949, esp. pp. 21–2 and 219.

8 Fortes, *Web of Kinship*.

9 R. E. Bradbury in *Man* Sept. 1959.

10 Such parallels arouse the more uncomfortable thought that in all the theorizing we sociologists have done about the working of traditional African societies, we may often have done little more than translate indigenous African theories about such workings.

11 John Middleton, *Lugbara Religion: Ritual and Authority among an East African People*, London, 1960.

24

How Not to Compare African Thought with Western Thought

Kwasi Wiredu

Many western anthropologists and even non-anthropologists have often been puzzled by the virtual ubiquity of references to gods and all sorts of spirits in traditional African explanations of things. One western anthropologist, Robin Horton, has suggested that this failure of understanding is partly attributable to the fact that many western anthropologists "have been unfamiliar with the theoretical thinking of their own culture."[1] I suggest that a very much more crucial reason is that they have also apparently been unfamiliar with the folk thought of their own culture.

Western societies too have passed through a stage of addiction to spiritistic explanations of phenomena. What is more, significant residues of this tradition remain a basic part of the mental make-up of a large mass of the not-so-sophisticated sections of western populations. More importantly still, elements of the spiritistic outlook are, in fact, deeply embedded in the philosophical thought of many contemporary westerners – philosophers and even scientists.

Obviously it is a matter of first rate philosophical importance to distinguish between traditional, i.e., pre-scientific, spiritistic thought and modern scientific thought by means of a clearly articulated criterion (or set of criteria). Indeed, one of the most influential and fruitful movements in recent Western philosophy, namely the logical positivist movement, may be said to have been motivated by the quest for just such a criterion. Also anthropologically and psychologically it is of interest to try to

understand how traditional modes of thought function in the total context of life in a traditional society. Since African societies are among the closest approximations in the modern world to societies in the pre-scientific stage of intellectual development, the interest which anthropologists have shown in African thought is largely understandable.

Unfortunately instead of seeing the basic non-scientific characteristics of African traditional thought as typifying traditional thought in general, western anthropologists and others besides have tended to take them as defining a peculiarly African way of thinking. The ill-effects of this mistake have been not a few.

One such effect is that the really interesting cross-cultural comparisons of modes of thought have tended not to be made. If one starts with the recognition that all peoples have some background of traditional thought – and remember by *traditional* thought here I mean pre-scientific thought of the type that tends to construct explanations of natural phenomena in terms of the activities of gods and kindred spirits – then the interesting and anthropologically illuminating comparison will be to see in what different ways spiritistic categories are employed by various peoples in the attempt to achieve a coherent view of the world. In such specific differences will consist the real peculiarities of, say, African tradition thought in contradistinction from, say, western traditional thought. Such comparisons may well turn out to hold less exotic excitement for the western anthropologist than present practice would seem to suggest. In the absence of any such realization, what has generally happened is that not only the genuine distinguishing features of African traditional thought but also its basic non-scientific, spiritistic, tendencies have been taken as a basis for contrasting Africans from western peoples. One consequence is that many westerners have gone about with an exaggerated notion of the differences in nature between Africans and the peoples of the west. I do not imply that this has necessarily led to anti-African racism. Nevertheless, since in some obvious and important respects, traditional thought is inferior to modern, science-oriented thought, some western liberals have apparently had to think hard in order to protect themselves against conceptions of the intellectual inferiority of Africans as a people.

Another ill-effect relates to the self-images of Africans themselves. Partly through the influence of western anthropology and partly through insufficient critical reflection on the contemporary African situation, many very well placed Africans are apt to identify African thought with *traditional* African thought. The result has not been beneficial to the movement for modernization, usually championed by the very same class of Africans. The mechanics of this interplay of attitudes is somewhat subtle. To begin with, these Africans have been in the habit of calling loudly, even stridently, for the cultivation of an African authenticity or personality. True, when such a call is not merely a political slogan, it is motivated by a genuine desire to preserve the indigenous culture of peoples whose confidence in themselves has been undermined by colonialism. But it was a certain pervasive trait of this same culture that enabled sparse groups of Europeans to subjugate large masses of African populations and keep them in colonial subjection for many long years and which even now makes them a prey to neo-colonialism. I refer to the *traditional* and non-literate character of the culture, with its associated technological underdevelopment. Being traditional is, of course, not synonymous with being non-literate. A culture can be literate and yet remain traditional i.e., non-scientific, as the case of India, for example, proves. India has a long tradition of written literature, yet it was not until comparatively recent times that the scientific spirit made any appreciable inroads into the Indian way of life. But, of course, a culture cannot be both scientific and non-literate, for the scientific method can only flourish where there can

be recordings of precise measurements, calculations and, generally, of observational data. If a culture is both non-scientific and non-literate, then in some important respects it may be said to be backward in a rather deep sense. We shall in due course note the bearing of the non-literate nature of the traditional African culture on the question of just what African philosophy is.

What is immediately pertinent is to remark that unanalyzed exhortations to Africans to preserve their indigenous culture are not particularly useful – indeed, they can be counter-productive. There is an urgent need in Africa today for the kind of analysis that would identify and separate the backward aspects of our culture – I speak as an anxious African – from those aspects that are worth keeping. That such desirable aspects exist is beyond question, and undoubtedly many African political and intellectual leaders are deeply impregnated by this consideration. Yet the analytical dimension seems to be lacking in their enthusiasm. So we have, among other distressing things, the frequent spectacle of otherwise enlightened Africans assiduously participating in the pouring of libation to the spirits of our ancestors on ceremonial occasions, or frantically applauding imitation of the frenzied dancing of "possessed" fetish priests – all this under the impression that in so doing they are demonstrating their faith in African culture.

In fact, many traditional African institutions and cultural practices, such as the ones just mentioned, are based on superstition. By "superstition" I mean a rationally unsupported belief in entities of any sort. The attribute of being superstitious attaches not to the content of a belief but to its mode of entertainment. Purely in respect of content the belief, for example, in abstract entities in semantic analysis common among many logistic ontologists in the west is not any more brainy then the traditional African belief in ancestor spirits. But logisticians are given to arguing for their ontology. I happen to think their arguments for abstract entities wrong-headed;[2] but it is not open to me to accuse them of superstition. When, however, we come to the traditional African belief in ancestor spirits – and this, I would contend, applies to traditional spiritistic beliefs everywhere – the position is different. That our departed ancestors continue to hover around in some rarefied from ready now and then to take a sip of the ceremonial schnapps is a proposition that I have never known to be rationally defended. Indeed, if one were to ask a traditional elder, "unspoilt" by the scientific orientation, for the rational justification of such a belief, one's curiosity would be quickly put down to intellectual arrogance acquired through western education.

Yet the principle that one is not entitled to accept a proposition as true in the absence of any evidential support is not western in any but an episodic sense. The western world happens to be the place where, as of now, this principle has received its most sustained and successful application in certain spheres of thought, notably in the natural and mathematical sciences. But even in the western world there are some important areas of belief wherein the principle does not hold sway. In the west just as anywhere else the realms of religion, morals and politics remain strongholds of irrationality. It is not uncommon, for example, to see a western scientist, fully apprised of the universal reign of law in natural phenomena, praying to God, a spirit, to grant rain and a good harvest and other things besides. Those who are tempted to see in such a thing as witchcraft the key to specifically *African* thought – there is no lack of such people among foreigners as well as Africans themselves – ought to be reminded that there are numbers of white men in today's London who proudly proclaim themselves to be witches. Moreover, if they would but read, for example, Trevor-Roper's historical essay on "Witches and Witchcraft,"[3] they might conceivably come to doubt whether witchcraft in Africa has ever attained the heights to which it reached in Europe in the sixteenth and seventeenth centuries.

It should be noted, conversely, that the principle of rational evidence is not entirely inoperative in the thinking of the traditional African. Indeed, no society could survive for any length of time without conducting a large part of their daily activities by the principle of belief according to the evidence. You cannot farm without some rationally based knowledge of soils and seeds and of meteorology; and no society can achieve any reasonable degree of harmony in human relations without a *basic* tendency to assess claims and allegations by the method of objective investigation. The truth, then, is that rational knowledge is not the preserve of the modern west[4] nor is superstition a peculiarity of the African peoples.

Nevertheless, it is a fact that Africa lags behind the west in the cultivation of rational inquiry. One illuminating (because fundamental) way of approaching the concept of "development" is to measure it by the degree to which rational methods have penetrated thought habits. In this sense, of course, one cannot compare the development of peoples in absolute terms. The western world is "developed," but only relatively. Technological sophistication is only an aspect, and that not the core, of development. The conquest of the religious, moral and political spheres by the spirit of rational inquiry remains, as noted earlier, a thing of the future even in the west. From this point of view the west may be said to be still underdeveloped. The quest for development, then, should be viewed as a continuing world-historical process in which all peoples, western and non-western alike, are engaged.

There are at least two important advantages in looking at development in this way. The first is that it becomes possible to see the movement towards modernization in Africa not as essentially a process in which Africans are unthinkingly jettisoning their own heritage of thought in the pursuit of western ways of life, but rather as one in which Africans in common with all other peoples seek to attain a specifically *human* destiny – a thought that should assuage the qualms of those among thoughtful Africans who are wont to see modernization as a foreign invasion. The relation between the concepts of development and modernization ought to be obvious. Modernization is the application of the results of modern science for the improvement of the conditions of human life. It is only the more visible side of development; it is the side that is more immediately associated with the use of advanced technology and novel techniques in various areas of life such as agriculture, health education and recreation. Because modernization is not the whole of development there is a need to view it always in a wider human perspective. Man should link the modernization of the conditions of his life with the modernization of all aspects of his thinking. It is just the failure to do this that is responsible for the more unlovable features of life in the West. Moreover, the same failure bedevils attempts at development in Africa. Rulers and leaders of opinion in Africa have tended to think of development in terms of the visible aspects of modernization – in terms of large buildings and complex machines, to the relative neglect of the more intellectual foundations of modernity. It is true that African nations spend every year huge sums of money on institutional education. But it has not been appreciated that education ought to lead to the cultivation of a rational[5] outlook on the world on the part of the educated and, through them, in the traditional folk at large. Thus it is that even while calling for modernization, influential Africans can still be seen to encourage superstitious practices such as the pouring of libation to spirits in the belief that in this kind of way they can achieve development without losing their Africanness. The second advantage of seeing development in the way suggested above is that the futility of any such approach becomes evident. To develop in any serious sense, we in African must break with our old uncritical habits of thought; that is we must advance past the stage of traditional thinking.

Lest these remarks appear rather abstract, let us consider a concrete situation. Take the institution of funerals in Ghana, for example. Owing to all sorts of superstitions about the supposed career of the spirits of departed relatives, the mourning of the dead takes the form of elaborate, and, consequently expensive and time consuming social ceremonies. When a person dies there has first to be a burial ceremony on the third day; then on the eighth day there is a funeral celebration at which customary rites are performed; then forty days afterwards there is a fortieth day celebration (*adaduanan*). Strictly, that is not the end. There are such occasions as the eightieth day and first anniversary celebrations. All these involve large alcohol-quaffing gatherings. Contrary to what one might be tempted to think, the embracing of Christianity by large sections of Ghanaian population has not simplified funeral celebration; on the contrary, it has brought new complications. Christianity too teaches of a whole hierarchy of spirits, starting from the Supreme Threefold Spirit down to the angels both good and refractory down further to the lesser spirits of deceased mortals. Besides, conversion to Christianity in our lands has generally not meant the exchange of the indigenous religion for the new one, but rather an amalgamation of both, which is made more possible by their common spiritistic orientation. Thus, in addition to all the traditional celebrations, there is nowadays the neo-Christian Memorial Service, replete with church services and extended refreshments, a particularly expensive phase of the funeral process. The upshot is that if a close relation of a man, say his father, dies, then unless he happens to be rich, he is in for very hard financial times indeed. He has to take several days off work, and he has to borrow respectable sums of money to defray the inevitable expenses.

The extent of the havoc that these funeral habits have wrought on the national economy of Ghana has not been exactly calculated, but it has become obvious to public leaders that it is enormous and that something needs urgently to be done about it. However, the best that these leaders have seemed capable of doing so far has been to exhort the people to reform their traditional institutions in general and cut down on funeral expenses in particular. These appeals have gone unheeded; which is not surprising, if one recalls that these leaders themselves are often to be seen ostentatiously taking part in ceremonies, such as the pouring of libation, which are based on the same sort of beliefs as those which lie behind the funeral practices. It has so far apparently been lost upon our influential men that while the underlying beliefs retain their hold, any verbal appeals are wasted on the populace.

The ideal way to reform backward customs in Africa must, surely, be to undermine their superstitious belief-foundations by fostering in the people – at all events, in the new generation of educated Africans – the spirit of rational inquiry in all spheres of thought and belief. Even if the backward beliefs in question were *peculiarly* African, it would be necessary to work for their eradication. But my point is that they are not African in any intrinsic, inseparable sense; and the least that African philosophers and foreign well-wishers can do in this connection is to refrain, in this day and age, from serving up the usual congeries of unargued conception about gods, ghosts, and witches in the name of *African philosophy*. Such a description is highly unfortunate. If at all deserving of the name "philosophy," these ideas should be regarded not as a part of African philosophy simply, but rather as a part of *traditional* philosophy in Africa.

This is not verbal cavilling. The habit of talking of African philosophy as if all African philosophy is *traditional* carries the implication, probably not always intended, that modern Africans have not been trying, or worse still, ought not to try, to philosophize in a manner that takes account of present day development in human knowledge, logical, mathematical, scientific, literary, etc: Various causes have combined to motivate this attitude. African nationalists in search of an African identity, Afro-Americans in search of their African roots and western foreigners in search of exotic diversion – all demand an African philosophy that shall be fundamentally different from western philosophy, even if it means the familiar witches brew. Obviously, the work of contemporary African philosophers trying to grapple with the modern philosophical situation cannot satisfy such a demand.

The African philosopher writing today has no tradition of written philosophy in his continent[6] to draw upon. In this respect, his plight is very much unlike that of say, the contemporary Indian philosopher. The latter can advert his mind to any insights that might be contained in a long-standing Indian heritage of written philosophical meditations; he has what he might legitimately call *classical* Indian philosophers to investigate and profit by. And if he is broad-minded, he will also study western philosophy and try in his own philosophizing to take cognizance of the intellectual developments that have shaped the modern world. Besides all this, he has, as every people have, a background of unwritten folk philosophy which he might examine for whatever it may be worth. Notice that we have here three levels of philosophy: we have spoken of a folk philosophy, a written traditional[7] philosophy and a modern philosophy. Where long-standing written sources are available folk philosophy tends not to be made much of. It remains in the background as a sort of diffused, immanent, component of community thought habits whose effects on the thinking of the working philosopher is largely unconscious.[8] Such a fund of community thought is not the creation of any specifiable set of philosophers; it is the common property of all and sundry, thinker and non-thinker alike, and it is called a *philosophy* at all only by a quite liberal acceptation of the term. Folk thought, as a rule, consists of bald assertions without argumentative justification, but philosophy in the narrower sense must contain not just theses. Without argumentation and clarification, there is, strictly, no philosophy.

Of course, folk thought can be comprehensive and interesting on its own account. Still its non-discursiveness remains a drawback. For example, according to the conception of a person found among the Akans of Ghana (the ethnic group to which the present writer belongs), a person is constituted by *nipakua* (a body) and a combination of the following entities conceived as spiritual substances:[9] (1) *okra* (soul, approximately), that whose departure from a man means death, (2) *Sunsum*, that which gives rise to a man's character, (3) *ntoro*, something passed on from the father which is the basis of inherited characteristics and, finally, (4) *mogya*, something passed on from the mother which determines a man's clan identity and which at death becomes the *saman* (ghost). This last entity seems to be the one that is closest to the material aspect of a person; literally, *mogya* means blood. Now, in the abstract, all this sounds more interesting, certainly more imaginative, than the thesis of some western philosophers that a person consists of a soul and body. The crucial difference, however, is that the western philosopher tries to argue for his thesis, clarifying his meaning and answering objections, known or anticipated; whereas the transmitter of folk conceptions merely says: "This is what our ancestors said."[10] For this reason folk conceptions tend not to develop with time. Please note that this is as true in the west and elsewhere as it is in Africa.

But in Africa, where we do not have even a written traditional philosophy, anthropologists have fastened on our folk world-views and elevated them to the status of a continental philosophy. They have then compared this "philosophy" with western (written) philosophy. In other, better placed, parts of the world, if you want to know the philosophy of the given people, you do not go to aged peasants or fetish priests or court personalities; you go to the individual thinkers, in flesh, if possible, and in print. And as any set of individuals trying to think for themselves are bound to differ among themselves, you would invariably find a variety of theories and doctrines, possibly but not necessarily, sharing substantial affinities. Since the reverse procedure has been the only one that has seemed possible to anthropologists, it is not surprising that misleading comparisons between African traditional thought and western scientific thought have resulted. My contention, which I have earlier hinted at, is that African traditional thought should in the first place only be compared with western folk thought. For this purpose, of course, western anthropologists will first have to learn in detail about the folk thought of their own peoples. African folk thought may be compared with western philosophy only in the same spirit in which western folk thought may be compared also with western philosophy, that is, only in order to find out the marks which distinguish folk thought in general from individualized philosophizing. Then, if there be any who are anxious to compare African philosophy with western philosophy, they will have to look at the philosophy that Africans are producing today.

Naturally western anthropologists are not generally interested in contemporary African philosophy. Present day African philosophers have been trained in the western tradition, in the continental or Anglo-American style, depending on their colonial history. Their thinking, therefore, is unlikely to hold many peculiarly African novelties for anyone knowledgeable in western philosophy. For this very same reason, African militants and our Afro-American brothers are often disappointed with the sort of philosophy syllabus that is taught at a typical modern department of philosophy in Africa. They find such a department mainly immersed in the study of logic, epistemology, metaphysics, ethics, political philosophy, etc., as these have been developed in the west, and they question why Africans should be so engrossed in the philosophy of their erstwhile colonial oppressors.

The attentive reader of this discussion should know the answer by now: The African philosopher has no choice but to conduct his philosophical inquiries in relation to the philosophical writings of other peoples, for his own ancestors left him no heritage of philosophical writings. He need not – to be sure, he must not – restrict himself to the philosophical works of his particular former colonial oppressors, but he must of necessity study the written philosophies of other lands, because it would be extremely injudicious for him to try to philosophize in self-imposed isolation from all modern currents of thought, not to talk of longer-standing nourishment for the mind. In the ideal, he must acquaint himself with the philosophies of all the peoples of the world, compare, contrast, critically assess them and make use of whatever of value he may find in them. In this way it can be hoped that a tradition of philosophy as a discursive discipline will eventually come to be established in Africa which future Africans and others too can utilize. In practice the contemporary African philosopher will find that it is the philosophies of the west that will occupy him the most, for it is in that part of the world that modern developments in human knowledge have gone farthest and where, consequently, philosophy is in closest touch with the conditions of the modernization which he urgently desires for his continent. In my opinion, the march of modernization is destined to lead to the universalization of philosophy everywhere in the world.

The African philosopher cannot, of course, take the sort of cultural pride in the philosophical achievements of Aristotle or Hume or Kant or Frege or Husserl of which the western student of philosophy may permit himself. Indeed an African needs a certain level-headedness to touch some of these thinkers at all. Hume,[11] for example, had

absolutely no respect for black men. Nor was Marx,[12] for another instance, particularly progressive in this respect. Thus any partiality the African philosopher may develop for these thinkers must rest mostly on considerations of truth-value.

As regards his own background of folk thought, there is a good reason why the African philosopher should pay more attention to it than would seem warranted in other places. Africans are a much oppressed and disparaged people. Some foreigners there have been who were not even willing to concede that Africans as a traditional people were capable of any sort of coherent[13] world-view. Those who had the good sense and the patience and industry to settle down and study traditional African thought were often, especially in the nineteenth and early twentieth centuries, colonial anthropologists who sought to render the actions and attitudes of our forefathers intelligible to the colonial rulers so as to facilitate their governance. Although some brilliant insights were obtained, there were also misinterpretations and straightforward errors. Africans cannot leave the task of correction to foreign researchers alone. Besides, particularly in the field of morality, there are non-superstition-based conceptions from which the modern westerner may well have something to learn. The exposition of such aspects of African traditional thought specially befits the contemporary African philosopher.

Still, in treating of their traditional thought, African philosophers should be careful not to make hasty comparisons.[14] Also they should approach their material critically; this last suggestion is particularly important since all peoples who have made any breakthrough in the quest for modernization have done so by going beyond folk thinking. It is unlikely to be otherwise in Africa. I should like to repeat, however, that the process of sifting the elements of our traditional thought and culture calls for a good measure of analytical circumspection lest we exchange the good as well as the bad in our traditional ways of life for dubious cultural imports.

It should be clear from the foregoing discussion that the question of how African thought may appropriately be compared with western thought is not just an important academic issue but also one of great existential urgency.

Notes

1 Robin Horton, "African Traditional Thought and Western Science," in *Rationality*, ed. Bryan Wilson (Oxford: Basil Blackwell). Originally published in *Africa* 37, nos. 1 & 2 (1967).

2 My reasons for this remark will be found in my series of articles on "Logic and Ontology," *Second Order: an African Journal of Philosophy* 2, no. 1 (Jan. 1973) and no. 2 (July 1973); 3, no. 2 (July 1974); 4, no. 1 (Jan. 1975).

3 *Encounter* 28, no. 5 (May 1967) and no. 6 (June 1967).

4 Note that "the west" and "western" are used in a cultural, rather than ideological sense in this discussion.

5 I am aware that my insistence on the overriding value of rationality will be found jarring by those westerners who feel that the claims of rationality have been pushed too far in their countries and that the time is overdue for a return to "Nature" and the exultation in feeling, intuition and immediacy. No doubt the harsh individualism of western living might seem to lend support to this point of view. But in my opinion the trouble is due to too little rather than too much rationality in social organization. This, however, is too large a topic to enter into here.

6 The Arab portions of Africa are of course, an exception, though even there what we have is the result of the interaction between indigenous thought and Greek influences.

7 "Traditional" here still has the pre-scientific connotation. Of course, if one should speak of *traditional* British empiricism, for example, that connotation would be absent.

8 Since such effects do, in fact, occur, this threefold stratification should not be taken as watertight.

9 See, for example, W. E. Abraham, *The Mind of Africa* (Chicago: University of Chicago Press, 1967).

10 However, the circumstance that in Africa, for example, our traditional thought tends not to be elaborately argumentative should be attributed not to any intrinsic lack of the discursive spirit in our ancestors but rather to the fact that their thoughts were not written down.

11 Hume was able to say in his *Essays* (London: George Routledge & Sons, Ltd), footnote on pages 152 and 153 in the course of the essay on "National Characters": "I am apt to suspect the Negroes to be naturally inferior to the Whites. There scarcely ever was a civilized nation of that complexion, nor any individual, eminent either in action or speculation. . . . In Jamaica, indeed they talk of one Negro as a man of parts and learning; but it is likely that he is admired for slender accomplishments, like a parrot who speaks a few words plainly." Obviously considerable maturity is required in the African to be able to contemplate impartially Hume's disrespect for Negroes and his philosophical insights, deploring the former and acknowledging and assimilating the latter. A British philosopher, Michael Dummett, was recently placed in a not altogether dissimilar situation when, himself a passionate opponent of racialism, he discovered in the course of writing a monumental work on Frege (*Frege: Philosophy of Language*, Duckworth, London, 1973) – a work which he had, indeed, suspended for quite some time in order to throw himself heart and soul into the fight against racial discrimination in his own country, Britain – that his subject was a racialist of some sort. (See his own remarks in his preface to the above-mentioned book.) It would have argued a lack of balance in him if he had scrapped the project on the discovery. In the event he went ahead to complete the work and put all students of the philosophy of logic in his debt.

12 Marx is known once, in a burst of personal abuse of Lassalle, in a letter to Engels, to have animadverted: "This combination of Jewry and Germany with a fundamental Negro streak . . . The fellow's self assertiveness is Negro too." Quoted in J. Hampden Jackson, *Marx, Proudhon and European Socialism* (London: English Universities Press, 1951), p. 144. It is sometimes understandable for a man to chide his own origins, but to condemn a downtrodden people like this is more serious. Would that black men everywhere had more of the self-assertiveness which Marx here deprecates. The Akans of Ghana have a proverb which says: "If the truth happens to lie in the most private part of your own mother's anatomy, it is no sin to extract it with your corresponding organ." African enthusiasts of Marx (or of Hume, for that matter) may perhaps console themselves with the following less delicate adaptation of this proverb. "If the truth happens to lie in the mouth of your racial traducer it is no pusillanimity to take it from there."

13 Coherent thought is not necessarily scientific thought. Traditional thought can display a high degree of coherence; and certainly African traditional thought is not lacking in coherence.

14 I ought perhaps to point out that the kind of comparison between African thought and western thought that has been criticized in this discussion is the sort which seeks to characterize the given varieties of thinking as wholes. My remarks do not necessarily affect the comparison of isolated propositions.

25

Literacy, Criticism, and the Growth of Knowledge

Jack Goody

The Word was made flesh, and dwelt among us.

John, i. 14

[T]he division of societies or modes of thought into advanced and primitive, domesticated or savage, open or closed, [makes] use of a folk-taxonomy by which we bring order and understanding into a complex universe. But the order is illusory, the meaning superficial. As in the case of other binary systems, the categorization is often value-laden and ethnocentric.

I certainly do not find that any such simple design provides an adequate framework for the examination of human interaction and development. Yet neither is it possible to accept the opposing tendency, adopted by many social scientists heavily committed to cultural relativism, which leads them to treat all societies as if their intellectual processes were essentially the same. Similar, yes; the same, no. And once one allows this, the specification of difference is not in itself enough; one needs also to point to mechanisms, to causal factors.

Towards this end I want to pursue further an argument that has been outlined elsewhere,[1] and points to the role of changes in the mode of communication in the development of cognitive structures and processes, and to illustrate the thesis by reference to developments in the growth of

From Jack Goody, *The Domestication of the Savage Mind* (1977); reproduced by kind permission of Cambridge University Press.

human knowledge and in the growth of man's capacity to store and to augment that knowledge. For some, at least, of the differences in intellectual processes that are indicated in a very general way by means of terms like 'open' and 'closed' can be related not so much to differences in 'mind' but to differences in systems of communication.

In using the words 'thought' and 'mind', I am referring to what might more technically be described as the content and processes of cognition. I take it as axiomatic that these two aspects are very closely intertwined, so that a change in one is likely to effect a change in the other. In other words, we are dealing with what Cole and Scribner, following Luria, describe as 'functional cognitive systems' (1974: 194). I am interested here in certain general dimensions of such systems that are related to what historians of culture perceive as 'the growth of knowledge'. While this has to do with 'content', it also presupposes certain processes which are related, I argue, to the modes of communication by which man interacts with man and, more especially, transmits his culture, his learned behaviour, from generation to generation.

Culture, after all, is a series of communicative acts, and differences in the mode of communication are often as important as differences in the mode of production, for they involve developments in the storing, analysis, and creation of human knowledge, as well as the relationships between the individuals involved. The specific proposition is that writing, and more especially alphabetic literacy, made it possible to scrutinize discourse in a different kind of way by giving oral communication a semipermanent form; this scrutiny favoured the increase in scope of critical activity, and hence of rationality, scepticism, and logic to resurrect memories of those questionable dichotomies. It increased the potentialities of criticism because writing laid out discourse before one's eyes in a different kind of way; at the same time increased the potentiality for cumulative knowledge, especially knowledge of an abstract kind, because it changed the nature of communication beyond that of face-to-face contact as well as the system for the storage of information; in this way a wider range of 'thought' was made available to the reading public. No longer did the problem of memory storage dominate man's intellectual life; the human mind was freed to study static 'text' (rather than be limited by participation in the dynamic 'utterance'), a process that enabled man to stand back from his creation and examine it in a more abstract, generalized, and 'rational' way.[2] By making it possible to scan the communications of mankind over a much wider time span, literacy encouraged, at the very same time, criticism and commentary on the one hand and the orthodoxy of the book on the other.

To argue this way is not to subscribe to a 'great divide' theory; it is an attempt to get away from the non-developmental perspective of much thinking about human thought and, at the same time, to link the discussion to the history of scientific endeavour in its broadest context – an undertaking that involves modifying certain categories of most historical and philosophical approaches to the subject.

It might be argued that there is all the difference in the world between the scientific attitude towards the control of nature that is adopted by the modern world and the mystical attitude seen as characteristic of pre-literate societies. But is this difference as radical as it appears? Robin Horton, who has given us the most intelligent of the available accounts of African traditional thought and its relationship to Western science, denies that this is so. He attempts to treat African traditional religious beliefs as 'theoretical models akin to those of the sciences' and argues that, if we recognize the aim of theory to be the demonstration of a limited number of *kinds* of entity or process underlying the diversity of experience (1967: 51), then recent analyses of African cosmologies make it clear that 'the gods of a given culture do form a scheme which interprets the vast diversity of everyday experience in terms of the action of a relatively few *kinds* of force' (1967: 52). The gods are not capricious; spiritual agencies are at work behind observed

events, and there is a basic modicum of regularity in their behaviour. Like 'atoms, molecules, and waves, then, the gods serve to introduce unity into diversity, simplicity into complexity, order into disorder, regularity into anomaly' (1967: 52).

While I would argue towards the same conclusion, I would do so along different lines. For in stressing resemblances, the author has laid himself open to the criticism directed at earlier comparisons or contrasts of this kind (e.g. by Evans-Pritchard 1934, and Beattie 1970: 260), namely, that he has compared the religious thought of simple societies with the scientific thought of complex ones instead of comparing the latter with the technical thinking of traditional societies. It was on this technical aspect, what one might call proto-scientific rather than pre-scientific thought, that Malinowski, and after him Lévi-Strauss, laid much stress. Note also that by 'science' Horton usually refers to modes of thought rather than to an activity, an organization, or a body of knowledge. The semantic leeway that surrounds the concept 'science' allows considerable latitude in many discussions about its growth.

I would suggest that we may compare entities of the modern scientific kind not only with specifically religious concepts but also with a more generalized kind of element (air, fire, water, etc.) based upon perceived objects or processes but also used more generally to break down the surface structure of the physical world. The generalization of these elements, which is a way of analysing the nature of the world in its spiritual as well as its physical aspects, takes elaborate forms in early literate civilizations. [Such] elaborations are clearly based upon simpler forerunners. Take, for example, the account of creation (or procreation) found in the Bagre myth of the LoDagaa of West Africa. In the second part of the Black Bagre, the first man goes to the sky to visit God.

> When he arrives there,
> God says that our ancestor
> should come forward.
> When he came,
> [God] took some earth,
> and pressed it together.
> When this was done,
> he spoke again
> and called a young girl,
> a slender girl,
> to come there too.
> She came over,
> and when she had done so,

he told her
to take a pot.
She took it,
and stood up with it.
Then he told her
to look for okra
to bring to him.
He chose a piece,
put it in his mouth,
chewed it to bits,
spat them out
into the pot. (Goody 1972: 230–1)

Here we have a 'symbolic' representation of procreation, the sap of the okra being sticky and white like semen and the pot being a receptacle resembling the vagina. As a result of this bringing together of the elements that go to make up human-kind, a child is born, and the man and woman who observed the act of creation quarrel over the owner-ship of the child. But this is not the only part of the narrative which gives an account of procreation. Later on the girl goes into the woods and sees snakes at play. She then goes back to tell her husband how pleasurable intercourse can be. In a sense a difference is being pointed out between the (first) spiritual act of creation and the (continuing) animal act of procreation, the first having to do with the super-natural, the latter with the natural. However, I am not primarily concerned with the interpretation of these processes but with the fact that the human body is seen as compounded of elements, of earth and water (or semen) and (elsewhere) of blood. So, in this society (and in its verbal constructs) we find the world analysed not only in terms of supernatural entities but also, at least in an embryonic way, in terms of natural elements, including fire and air, blood and water. It did not need the elaborations of Taoist, Mohist, or Greek to introduce us to these basic notions. In all probability, such elementary ideas, like the kernel of the wave theories, which Joseph Needham links with developments in Chi-nese science, and the essence of those atomistic ideas developed in the West, are universally present.[3] The bases for such general notions of science exist much more widely in human societies than many of our current dichotomies allow, whether these dichoto-mies are viewed in a developmental way (*from* magic *to* science) or not.

Indeed, what lies behind Joseph Needham's idea of these developments in human thought turns out to be a more sophisticated version of the simple dichotomy between primitive and advanced that we

have been trying to qualify. He sees two kinds of thinking emerging from 'primitive thought',[4] namely, the causal account of natural phenomena associated with the Greeks and the 'co-ordinative or associa-tive thinking' typical of the Chinese, which at-tempts 'to systematise the universe of things and events into a pattern of structure, by which all the mutual influences of its parts were conditioned' (1956: 285). In the scientific or proto-scientific ideas of the Chinese, this conceptualization de-pended upon two fundamental principles or forces in the universe, first, the Yin and the Yang, the negative and positive projections of man's own sexual experience, and, second, the five 'elements' of which all process and all substance were com-posed (1956: 279). For, he concludes, 'once a system of categorisations such as the five-element system is established then anything can by no means be the cause of anything else' (1956: 284).

In writing of the concept of Yin and Yang, Needham himself suggests that we could be dealing with ideas of such simplicity that 'they might easily have arisen independently in several civilizations' (1956: 277). Such 'independent invention' must surely have occurred, both with the dualistic divisions and with the concept of elements; indeed, in their most general form such ideas seem intrinsic to human thought, to the use of language itself. I have already suggested that the notion of elements is present in embryonic form in LoDagaa mythol-ogy and in similar verbal forms. Other writers have found, indeed pursued, dualisms in many parts of the globe among a variety of peoples, where they have invariably succeeded in discovering at least some 'opposition' between right and left, male and female; while, even for purely oral societies, some authors have erected much more elaborate schemes, which appear to display all the features of the 'co-ordinative or associative thinking' said to be char-acteristic of the Chinese.

I would therefore extend Horton's analysis fur-ther than he does himself; for the comparison between science and religion overlooks the com-parison between science and proto-science (or simple technology), and this starting point tends in turn to distort the differences between simple and complex societies. The result is seen in the second part of Horton's discussion, where he deals with the differences rather than the similarities. Here he adopts Popper's distinction between what he calls the 'closed' and 'open' predicaments, which are defined in the following words: 'in traditional cultures there is no developed awareness of alternatives and anxiety about threats to the system; with scientifically oriented cultures, such an awareness is highly developed' (1967: 155); it is 'the awareness of alternatives which is crucial for the take-off into science'. Closure is associated with lack of awareness of alternatives and anxiety about threats to the system; openness, with the opposite.

Horton attempts to link these general characteristics with the more specific features of traditional thought. While I would accept most of these statements as pointing to certain differences between two broad groups of societies, the West and the rest, the dichotomies need to be treated as variables, both as regards the societies and as regards their characteristics. A dichotomization of this kind is often a useful preliminary for descriptive purposes,[5] once we accept it as such, we can go further and attempt to elucidate the possible mechanisms that bring about the differences, a step that usually involves modifying or even rejecting the original dichotomy. Without in any way insisting upon a single-factor theory, I want to try to show how these differences can be partly explained (rather than simply described) by looking at the possible effects of changes in the mode of communication.

Horton isolates two major features of the difference between closed and open systems, the first of which has four aspects, the second three. These characteristics can be summarized as follows:

1. The absence of alternatives, which is indicated by:

(a) a magical versus non-magical attitude to words. In traditional thought, words, ideas, and reality are intrinsically bound up; in science, words and reality vary independently.

(b) ideas-bound-to-occasions against ideas-bound-to-ideas. In the scientific situation, the thinker can 'get outside' his own system, because it is not bound to occasions, but to reality.

(c) unreflective versus reflective thinking. In traditional thought there is no reflection upon the rules of thinking, hence there can be no Logic (rules) or Epistemology (grounds for knowing) in the limited sense.

(d) mixed versus segregated motives. While traditional thought deals with explanation and prediction, it is also influenced by other factors, e.g. emotional needs, especially for personal relations of a surrogate kind. This personalization of theory gets eliminated only with the application of the rules of the game.

2. Anxiety about threats to the system, which is indicated by:

(a) protective versus destructive attitudes towards established theory. In traditional thought, failures are excused by processes of 'secondary elaboration' which protect beliefs; the questioning of basic beliefs, on divination, for example, is a blocked path 'because the thinkers are victims of the closed predicament' (1967: 168). Contrast the scientific attitude. It is above all his '*essential scepticism* towards established beliefs' that distinguishes the scientist from the traditional thinker (1967: 168, my italics). Having said this, Horton introduces a caveat by referring not only to Kuhn's discussion of normal science but also to the 'magical' attitude of the modern layman towards theories invented by scientists.

(b) protective versus destructive attitudes to the category system. Following Douglas' analysis, he sees 'taboo' as related to events and actions which seriously defy the established lines of classification in the particular culture. Taboo is the equivalent of secondary elaboration, a defensive measure.

(c) the passage of time: bad or good? Horton relates the 'widespread attempt to annul the passage of time' (1967: 178) to the closed predicament; for scientists, the future is in their bones, but traditional societies lack any idea of Progress.

Let us examine these features from a different angle and ask what it is that lies behind the closed situation. Is the absence of awareness of alternatives due simply to the fact that traditional societies were not presented with other choices until Europe intervened? Or are we dealing with closure of a more inherent sort, a feature of the traditional mind? I doubt whether Horton would ask us to accept the latter proposition, which is essentially circular. What about the first? Here we seem to be offered a view of African societies which ignores historical complexity. The Kalabari, of whom he writes, have, after all, been in contact with Europeans for a number of centuries, and many other African societies have been influenced by Islam for a much longer period. Quite apart from these northern imports, there was certainly much traffic in ritual, much exchange of religious ideas and theories, among the 'indigenous' societies themselves. Some might claim that central beliefs in the efficacy of witchcraft and the powers of diviners remained unquestioned by such contact, being common to all these societies; but even this very general statement is open to query; certainly the forms of divination and the intensity of witchcraft changed under both internal and external pressures.[6] The religious systems of simple societies are indeed open and very far from closed. The well-established mobility of cult is incompatible with the complete closure of thought, closure and openness being in any case variables rather than binary oppositions. Horton has himself pointed to the true situation in non-literate societies: if traditional cultures see ideas as bound to occasions – if, for example, general statements arise in the context of healing rather than as abstract programmes about what we believe – then, when the contexts change (because of famine, invasion, or disease) or when individual attitudes change (because of the recognition that the remedy has not worked), the ideas and practices will themselves change. They seem more likely to do so here than in societies where ideas, religious or scientific, are written down in scholarly treatises or in Holy Writ.

This observation raises the question of the relationship between modes of thought and modes for the production and reproduction of thought that lies at the heart of the unexplained but not inexplicable differences that so many writers have noted. As I have said, Horton argues that traditional and scientific thought differ in the 'essential scepticism' of the latter towards established beliefs. However, we saw in the previous chapter that many observers have described Africans as being sceptical, especially about witchcraft, divination, and similar matters. What seems to be the *essential* difference, however, is not so much the sceptical attitude in itself but the accumulation (or reproduction) of scepticism. Members of oral (i.e. 'traditional') societies find it difficult to develop a line of sceptical thinking about, say, the nature of matter or man's relationship to God simply because a continuing critical tradition can hardly exist when sceptical thoughts are *not* written down, *not* communicated across time and space, *not* made available for men to contemplate in privacy as well as to hear in performance.

In many cases it is 'oral' and 'literate' that need to be opposed rather than 'traditional' and 'modern'. Awareness of alternatives is clearly more likely to characterize literate societies, where books and libraries give an individual access to knowledge from different cultures and from different ages, either in the form of descriptive accounts or of utopian schemes. But it is not simply the awareness of being exposed to a wider range of influences. Such openness would be largely mechanical and would be available to the inhabitants of a city like Kano, with its variety of trans-Saharan travellers, as much as to the inhabitants of eighteenth-century Boston or Birmingham. It is rather that the *form* in which the alternatives are presented makes one aware of the differences, forces one to consider contradiction, makes one conscious of the 'rules' of argument, forces one to develop such 'logic'. And the form is determined by the literary or written mode. Why? Because when an utterance is put in writing it can be inspected in much greater detail, in its parts as well as in its whole, backwards as well as forwards, out of context as well as in its setting; in other words, it can be subjected to a quite different type of scrutiny and critique than is possible with purely verbal communication. Speech is no longer tied to an 'occasion'; it becomes timeless. Nor is it attached to a person; on paper, it becomes more abstract, more depersonalized.

In giving this summary account of some of the implications of writing or, at any rate, of extensive literacy, I have deliberately used words with which others have spelled out the traditional–modern dichotomy. Horton speaks of the differences between personal and impersonal theories; and while he is referring to a rather different aspect of the problem (personal gods as against impersonal forces), the points are related. Again he speaks of thought being tied to occasions (hence in a sense less abstract or less abstracted), an idea which can also be discussed more concretely in terms of systems for communicating signs and symbols. Writing makes speech 'objective' by turning it into an object of visual as well as aural inspection; it is the shift of the receptor from ear to eye, of the producer from voice to hand.

Here, I suggest, lies the answer, in part at least, to the emergence of Logic and Philosophy. In the opening chapter it was noted that Logic, in its formal sense, is closely tied to writing: the formalization of propositions, abstracted from the flow of speech and given letters (or numbers), leads to the syllogism. Symbolic logic and algebra, let alone the calculus, are inconceivable without the prior existence of writing. More generally, a concern with the rules of argument or the grounds for knowledge seems to arise, though less directly, out of the formalization of communication (and hence of 'statement' and 'belief') which is intrinsic to writing. Philosophic discourse is a formalization of just the kind one would expect with literacy. 'Traditional' societies are marked not so much by the absence of reflective thinking as by the absence of the proper tools for constructive rumination.

Let me now turn to the second category of contrasting aspects, those related to anxiety about threats to the system. As Horton appreciates, traditional thinkers are not the only people who find change threatening; so too, Kuhn claims, does 'normal science' (1962: 81). It is certainly true that growth, progress, change is more characteristic of 'modern' societies, but it is not absent from other cultures. Nor, as we have seen, is scepticism. With regard to concepts of time, we find a difference of emphasis which can reasonably be related to differences in technology, in procedures for the measurement of time (Goody 1968). Indeed, too much weight is often placed upon differences between cyclical and linear approaches. For example, the concept of chronology is linear rather than circular; it needs numbered series starting with a fixed base, which means that some form of graphic record is a prerequisite.

Note that in talking of anxiety about change, Horton is not referring to observed reactions to threats but rather what are hypothesized as possible defences against such threats. My own experience has not revealed major difficulties of this kind on the individual level; people accommodate the aeroplane flying overhead into some classificatory scheme, as Worsley (1955) pointed out in the context of Groote Eyland totemism, without finding themselves threatened because it cuts across their distinction between birds that fly in the air and machines that move on the ground. I make this point because Horton sees one of the main distinguishing features of African thought as the 'closure' of the systems of classification and follows Mary Douglas' discussion of taboo as a reaction to events that seriously defy the established lines of classification.

In support of this theory, incest is seen as flagrantly defying the established category system because it treats the mother, for example, as a wife and is therefore subject to taboo. Equally, twins are dangerous because multiple births confuse the animal and the human world; the human corpse is polluting because it falls between the living and the dead, just as faeces and menstrual blood occupy the no-man's-land between animate and inanimate. But what does this mean?

Let us take incest. The argument is difficult to follow, for several reasons. Societies in West Africa often classify potential wives as 'sisters' (this is indeed a feature of permitted cousin marriage and a Hawaiian terminology); nevertheless, men find no difficulty in sleeping with some and not others. Equally, some 'mothers' are accessible as sexual partners, just as, in our society, some 'mothers' are 'superior' to childbirth. If we look at systems of classification from the actor's standpoint, there is little problem in coping with overlapping categories; the Venn diagram is as relevant a model as the Table. Moreover, the whole discussion seems to rest upon a simplistic view of the relationship between linguistic acts and other social behaviour. What is at issue here is the question of 'taboo' as a category requiring explanation, either in the terms of Douglas or Horton. Neither classificatory closure nor taboo seems very satisfactory as defining characteristics of traditional thought.

Another aspect on which Horton comments is the contrast between the magical and non-magical use of the word.[7] The author himself points out – for he is very sensitive to questions of similarity and difference – that the outlook behind magic (at least in the sense of the dominance of the word, its entailment with ideas and action) is an intellectual possibility even in scientifically oriented cultures (e.g. in the dominance of mind over matter). I would go further and say that even the problem of classification (a mode of bringing data under control which is intrinsic to the whole range of sciences) is not far removed from the magical use of words in spells. Today the magic of the printed word has in a sense replaced the magic of the spoken one. Nevertheless, there certainly is some truth in Horton's contention concerning the shift away from word magic. What truth there is, I suggest, turns once again on the effect of separation, of objectification, which writing has on words; for words assume a different relationship to action and to object when they are on paper than when they are spoken. They are no longer bound up directly with 'reality'; the written word becomes a separate 'thing', abstracted to some extent from the flow of speech, shedding its close entailment with action, with power over matter.

Many of the differences that Horton characterizes as distinctive of open and closed systems of thought can be related to differences in the systems of communication and, specifically, to the presence or absence of writing. But this does not mean that we are dealing with a simple dichotomy, for systems of communication differ in many particular respects (for example, ideographic from phonetic scripts). There is no single 'opposition' but rather a succession of changes over time, each influencing the system of thought in specific ways. I do not maintain that this process is unidirectional let alone monocausal; thought feeds back on communication; creed and class influence the kind and extent of literacy that prevails; only to a limited extent can the means of communication, to use Marx's terminology from a different context, be separated from the relations of communication, which together form the mode of communication. In drawing attention to the significance of this factor, I attempt to avoid the conceptual slush into which one flounders when such differences are attributed either to 'culture' (who denies it, but what does it mean?) or to vague, descriptive divisions such as open and closed, which themselves need explaining rather than serve to explain.

The above discussion has attempted to show that it is not so much scepticism itself that distinguishes post-scientific thought as the accumulated scepticism that writing makes possible; it is a question of establishing a cumulative tradition of critical discussion. It is now possible to see why science, in the sense we usually think of this activity, occurs only when writing made its appearance and why it made its most striking advances when literacy became widespread. In one of his essays (1963, chap. 5, esp. pp. 148–52), Karl Popper traces the origin of 'the tradition of critical discussion [which] represents the only practical way of expanding our knowledge' to the Greek philosophers between Thales and Plato, the men who, as he sees it, encouraged critical discussion both between schools and within individual schools. Kuhn, on the other hand, sees these forms of activity as having no resemblance to science.

Rather it is the tradition of claims, counter-claims, and debates over fundamentals which, except perhaps during the Middle Ages, have characterised philosophy and much of social science ever since. Already by the Hellenistic period mathematics, astronomy, statics and the geometric parts of optics had abandoned this mode of discourse in favour of puzzle solving. Other sciences, in increasing numbers, have undergone the same transition since. In a sense . . . it is precisely the abandonment of critical discourse that marks the transition to a science. Once a field has made that transition, critical discourse recurs only at moments of crisis when the bases of the field are again in jeopardy (1970: 6–7).

Let us leave aside the discussion about the distinction between critical discourse and puzzle-solving, between innovative and normal science, with Kuhn's implication of incompatibility (an implication Popper would strenuously deny). Thales' thought is not science as we know it, rather an essential preliminary to the kind of problem-solving involved in science, and it is significant that this kind of critical discourse is seen as emerging in one of the first widely literate societies.

This point relates to another of the concepts that have been much discussed by philosophers and anthropologists as a critical feature in cultural development, namely, rationality (see, e.g. Wilson 1970). As with scepticism, rationality is often seen as one of the differentiating features of the 'modern mind', of the scientific view. This is not a debate I find very promising. For, as with logicality, the argument is conducted in terms of an opposition between rationality and irrationality (with the occasional introduction of the non-rational as a third term), and rationality is seen as characterizing certain operations rather than others. The usual way of avoiding the radical dichotomy is by resort to diffuse relativism (all societies are rational). However, if we look more closely, a third possibility emerges. Take as a starting point Wartofsky's definition of rationality. Science is 'concept-ordered', but the use of concepts is intelligent, not yet rational: 'rational practice entails . . . the self-conscious or reflective use of concepts; i.e. the critical attitude towards scientific practice and thought, which constitutes not simply scientific knowledge alone (which is its necessary condition), but the *self-knowledge* of science, the critical examination of its own conceptual foundations' (1967: 151). Rationality in this sense implies metaphysics which is 'the practice of rationality in its most theoretical form' (1967: 153); 'a rational theoretical science is continuous with the tradition of metaphysical theory-construction' (1967: 154); metaphysics is a 'heuristic for science'. Whether or not we agree with Wartofsky, it seems clear that the kind of reflective use of concepts required by his definition of rationality is greatly facilitated by the process of giving speech some permanent embodiment and thus creating the conditions for an extension of reflective examination.

Since my theme has been the relationship between processes of communication, the development of a critical tradition, and the growth of knowledge (including the emergence of science), I want to conclude by offering an illustration of the way in which literate techniques operate as an analytic tool, promoting criticism leading to the growth of knowledge. My example is taken from a book on this subject, edited by Lakatos and Musgrave (1970), which discusses Thomas Kuhn's *The Structure of Scientific Revolutions* (1962). For Kuhn, a scientific revolution consists of a change in paradigm, a gestalt-switch, from one set of assumptions and models to another. Otherwise, science (normal science) proceeds to work within one paradigm by solving the puzzles offered by it. The very boundaries of a paradigm are a condition of growth of a subject, a development from a pre-paradigmatic stage, since, by limiting the scope of enquiry, they create specialist areas of concentration, based on positive results. Contrast this approach to that of Popper, who sees criticism as lying at the heart of the scientific enterprise, which is a state of 'revolution in permanence'. The difference between the two views is essentially between science as a closed community and as an open society.

For any discussion of Kuhn's contribution to the history of science, some agreement on the word 'paradigm' is essential. Yet in his book, as Margaret Masterman points out in a favourable essay, he has used the word in some 21 different ways, which she attempts to reduce to three major clusters of meaning (1970: 65):

1 *metaphysical paradigms*, associated with a set of beliefs;
2 *sociological paradigms*, a universally recognized scientific achievement; and
3 *artefact or construct paradigms*, which turn problems into puzzles.

In his reply to criticisms, Kuhn acknowledges the ambiguity of his usage and suggests a substitution of disciplinary matrix for cluster (2) above (1970: 271), and *exemplars* or *problem-solution paradigms* for (3), though he sees (3) as contained in (2) (1970: 272). In other words, the author explicitly qualifies his earlier use of the term paradigm and hence can no longer talk of a pre- or post-paradigm period when describing the maturation of a scientific speciality. His footnote on p. 272 explains this somewhat radical modification, which waters down the whole concept in the process of clarifying it.

Let us suppose (I will complicate the assumption

later) that Kuhn's reformulation, which makes a 'revolutionary' statement seem to fall well within the bounds of 'normal' science, was due to Masterman's criticism. How, from the standpoint of technique, was that criticism developed? Her first footnote explains the circumstances of the composition of her chapter.

> This paper is a later version of an earlier paper which I had been asked to read when there was to have been a panel discussion of T. S. Kuhn's work in this Colloquium; and which I was prevented from writing by getting severe infective hepatitis. This new version is therefore dedicated to the doctors, nurses and staff of Block 8, Norwich Hospital, who allowed a Kuhn subject index to be made on a hospital bed. (1970: 59)

In other words, the detection of ambiguity or inconsistency leading to a reformulation of the argument was effected by reference to a box of filing cards which kept track of different usages of one key word in the author's argument. It was effected by a purely graphic technique, which permitted a more systematic exploration of a written text than was possible by the more casual techniques of visual inspection usually undertaken by critics of a written text and which form the basis of the kind of criticism offered by Watkins or Feyerabend in the same volume.

My point here is that, by putting speech down on to paper, one creates the possibility of what is almost a different kind of critical examination. Imagine (though it is a fanciful task) Kuhn's book as an oral discourse. No listener, I suggest, could ever spot the 21 different usages of the word 'paradigm'. The argument would flow from one usage to another without anyone being able to perceive any discrepancy. Inconsistency, even contradiction, tends to get swallowed up in the flow of speech (*parole*), the spate of words, the flood of argument, from which it is virtually impossible for even the most acute mind to make his mental card-index of different usages and then compare them one with another.

I am not suggesting that the differences (or shades) of usage were deliberately manipulated to confuse the reader and to carry the argument. Kuhn's acceptance of the criticism shows that he recognizes what he did not earlier perceive, that his new concept (new in this context) was largely unanalysed. It was a kind of self-deception. My point is that the oral mode makes this kind of self-deception easier to carry out and less easy to detect. The process of (constructive) criticism, whether by the speaker or by another, is inhibited, made more difficult.

Equally, the more deliberate deception of the orator is perhaps less easy to overcome than the unintentional ambiguities of the writer, whose inconsistencies stand out by themselves. By means of rhetoric, through the gift of the gab, the 'tricks' of the demagogue are able to sway an audience in a more direct way than the written word. What is at issue here is in part the *immediacy* of the face-to-face contact, the visual gesture and tones of voice, that marks oral communication. It is the play seen, the symphony heard, rather than the drama read, the score studied. But, more than this, the oral form is intrinsically more persuasive because it is less open to criticism (though not, of course, immune from it).

The balance of my argument continues to be a delicate one. In the first place, I have attempted to set aside radical dichotomies; in the second, I reject diffuse relativism. The third course involves a more difficult task, that of specifying particular mechanisms. I have tried to analyse some aspects of the processes of communication in order to try to elucidate what others have tried to explain by means of those dichotomies. This is not a great-divide theory. It sees some changes as more important than others, but it attempts to relate specific differences to specific changes.

The effort to compare and contrast the thought ways of 'traditional' and 'modern', literate and pre-literate, societies may seem of marginal interest to the more recent history of human knowledge. So it is, from many standpoints. But from the most general of these, it serves to define the problem we are dealing with. For example, the development of science in Western Europe in the seventeenth century is sometimes seen as resting upon views about (1) the lawfulness of nature, which permits comprehension, and (2) man and nature as antagonists, and the outcome of the ideology of the control of nature as 'growth'. If we are to understand the particular contributions of Western (or any other) science to the development of human thought, then we must be a good deal more precise about the matrix from which it was emerging, about the pre-existing conditions and the nature of 'pre-scientific thought'. Thus the attempt to gain precision leads us inevitably into an examination of the ways of thinking of earlier times and of other cultures, as well as of the manner in which these ways of thinking were related to particular modes of communication between man and man, man and God, man and nature. All of these were influenced by major changes in the means, such as the development of scripts, the shift to alphabetic literacy, and the invention of the printing press. I repeat that I am not proposing a single-factor theory; the social structure behind the communicative acts is often of prime importance. Nevertheless, it is not accidental that major steps in the development of what we now call 'science' followed the introduction of major changes in the channels of communication in Babylonia (writing), in Ancient Greece (the alphabet), and in Western Europe (printing).

Notes

1 See, specifically, J. Goody and I. P. Watt, 'The consequences of literacy', *Comparative Studies in Society and History* (1963: 304–45).

2 I am indebted to E. A. Havelock, *Preface to Plato*, Cambridge, Mass, 1963, and to David Olsen, 'The bias of language in speech and writing', in H. Fisher and R. Diez-Gurerro (eds), *Language and Logic in Personality and Society*, New York, 1976.

3 I am much indebted to discussions with D. Gjertsen, Department of Philosophy, University of Ghana.

4 Joseph Needham's view of primitive thought owes much to Lévy-Bruhl, a fact that influences his interpretation of the Chinese achievement: 'The selection of "causes" at random from this undifferentiated magma of phenomena was called by Lévy-Bruhl the "law of participation" in that the whole of the environment experienced by the primitive mind is laid under contribution, i.e. participates, in its explanations, without regard either for true causal connection or for the principle of contradiction' (Needham 1956: 284).

5 I do not myself see how the suggestions that Watt and I put forward concerning the consequences of literacy can be considered a 'great-divide theory', since we treat 'literacy' as a variable. Moreover, it is clearly only one of many changes in the *mode of* communication which might influence the *content* of communication. Since I am referring to Ruth Finnegan's article in the volume on *Modes of Thought* (1973) that she edited with Robin Horton, I should add that Horton's article takes a somewhat different position than the one I have commented upon here.

6 See my 'Religion, social change and the sociology of conversion' in *Changing Social Structure in Ghana* (London, 1975).

7 For a more recent discussion see S. J. Tambiah (1968) and T. Todorov (1973).

References

Cole, M. and Scribner, S. (1974), *Culture and Thought*. New York.

Douglas, M. (1966), *Purity and Danger*. London.

Goody, J. (1968), 'Time: social organisation', in *International Encyclopedia of Social Sciences*, 16: 30–42. New York.

Goody, J. (1972), *The Myth of the Bagre*. Oxford.

Horton, R. (1967), 'African traditional thought and Western science', *Africa*, 37: 50–71, 155–87.

Horton, R. and Finnegan, R. eds (1973), *Modes of Thought*. London.

Kuhn, T. (1962), *The Structure of Scientific Revolutions*. Chicago.

Kuhn, T. (1970), 'Logic of discovery or psychology of research?', in I. Lakatos and A. Musgrave, eds, *Criticism and the Growth of Knowledge*. Cambridge.

Lakatos, I. and Musgrave, A. eds (1970), *Criticism and the Growth of Knowledge*. Cambridge.

Needham, J. (1956), *Science and Civilisation in China*, vol. 2, *History of Scientific Thought*. Cambridge.

Popper, K. (1963), *Conjectures and Refutations*. London.

Tambiah, S. J. (1968), 'The magical power of words', *Man*, 3: 175–208.

Todorov, T. (1973), 'Le discours de la magie', *L'Homme*, 13: 38–65.

Wartofsky, M. W. (1967), 'Metaphysics as a heuristic for science', in R. S. Cohen and Wartofsky, eds, *Boston Studies in the Philosophy of Science* III. New York.

Wilson, B. R. ed. (1970), *Rationality*. Oxford.

Worsley, P. M. (1955), 'Totemism in a changing society', *American Anthropology*, 57: 851–61.

PART VI

Philosophy and Colonial Encounter

26

Modern Western Philosophy and African Colonialism

E. Chukwudi Eze

By "colonialism" we should understand the indescribable crisis disproportionately suffered and
endured by the African peoples in their tragic
encounter with the European world, from the
beginning of the fifteenth century through the end
of the nineteenth into the first half of the twentieth.
This is a period marked by the horror and violence
of the transatlantic slave trade, the imperial occupation of most parts of Africa and the forced
administrations of its peoples, and the resilient and
enduring ideologies and practices of European
cultural superiority (ethnocentrism) and "racial"
supremacy (racism). In vain do we seek to limit the
colonial period to the "brief" 70 years between the
1884 Berlin Conference that partitioned and legitimized European occupation of Africa and the early
1960s when most African countries attained constitutional decolonization.[1]

The beginnings of colonialism need to be traced
to both the sporadic and the systematic maritime
commercial incursions into Africa by European
fortune seekers which began in the mid-fifteenth
century. These commercial interests, individual as
well as institutional, were aimed at the extraction
and trading of gold, ivory, and other natural
resources and raw materials, but it quickly expanded into the exportation of able-bodied Africans
and their children as slaves to the Americas and
other parts of the world. It was the wealth and
capital, accumulated by European merchants and

institutions (Barclays, Lloyds, etc.) in the Triangular Trade that financed technological innovations in
arms and other sailing equipment. These, in turn,
made possible subsequent large-scale military expeditions that eventually "pacified" African kingdoms. Most of these trading companies kept
salaried armies, or financed, through taxes, the
(European) governmental administrations of the
conquered territories. Aijaz Ahmad's observation
about Britain, in this regard, is accurate:

> *commercial developers and adventurers* like
> Cecil Rhodes in Southern Africa, Frederick
> Luggard in Nigeria, and Hugh Cholmondeley
> Delamere in Kenya, *played important roles in
> later British colonization* on the African
> continent. Although the British government
> initially kept a safe distance from these
> adventurers and their questionable aims and
> practices, it later adopted many of their early
> dreams and ambitions to justify colonial
> expansion . . . And the English government
> in most cases provided the companies with
> protection to ensure free trading rights.
> Eventually the government took the natural
> step of establishing administrative, colonial
> control over those areas in which British
> trading companies were involved.[2]

With respect to Africa, then, I use the term
"colonialism" as a clustered concept to designate
the historical realities of: (a) the European imperial
incursions into Africa, which began in the late
fifteenth and early sixteenth centuries and grew

From *Postcolonial African Philosophy*, ed. E. Chukwudi
Eze, Blackwell Publishers (1997).

into the massive transatlantic slave trade; (b) the violent conquest and occupation of the various parts of the continent by diverse European powers which took place in the late nineteenth and early twentieth centuries; (c) the forced administration of African lands and peoples which followed this conquest, and lasted into the years of independence in the 1950s and 1960s and – in case of Zimbabwe and South Africa – into the 1980s and the 1990s. Slave trade, conquest, occupation, and forced administration of peoples, in that order, were all part of an unfolding history of colonialism.

Philosophy, Modernity, and Colonialism

The "colonial period," in a larger sense, should then be understood to cover, roughly, what Cornel West has correctly characterized as "the Age of Europe." This, according to West, is the period "[b]etween 1492 and 1945," a period that was marked by "European breakthroughs in oceanic transportation, agricultural production, state consolidation, bureaucratization, industrialization, urbanization and *imperial dominion* [that] shaped the makings of the modern world."[3] And since the imperial and the colonial domination of Africa were, at root, constitutive elements in the historical formation of the economic, political, and cultural expressions of the Age of Europe, including the Enlightenment, it is imperative that when we study the nature and the dynamic of European modernity, we examine the intellectual and the philosophical productions of the time in order to understand how, in too many cases, they justified imperialism and colonialism. Significant aspects of the philosophies produced by Hume, Kant, Hegel, and Marx have been shown to originate in, and to be intelligible only when understood as, an organic development within larger socio-historical contexts of European colonialism and the ethnocentric idea: Europe is *the* model of humanity, culture, and history in itself. It is precisely this critical (re)examination of the colonial intentions organic to Western modern philosophy that animates at least one wing of contemporary African/a Philosophy. It is a philosophical project aptly captured by Serequeberhan's phrase, "the critique of Eurocentrism."

Basil Davidson, in *Africa: History of a Continent* and in his recent *The African Genius* (as well as in his other numerous publications on African hist-

ory), points out that the earliest recorded encounters between Europeans and African kingdoms in the beginning of the fifteenth century reveal remarkable accounts of relationships between equals: the exchange of diplomatic counsels was routine, and glowing European accounts of the thriving and vibrant nations of Bini, Dahomey, Ashanti, etc. whose organizational powers and influence were constantly favorably compared by the Europeans to that of the Roman papacy. However, as the plantations in the Americas developed and Afro-European trade demands shifted from raw material to human labor, there was also a shift in the European literary, artistic, and philosophical characterizations of Africans. Specifically within philosophy, Africans became identified as a sub-human "race" and speculations about the "savage" and "inferior" nature of "the African" and "the African mind" became widespread and intertextually entrenched within the *univers de discours* of the French, British, and German Enlightenment thinkers. David Hume, for example, who at one time served in the British colonial office, wrote in the famous footnote to his essay, "On National Character":

> I am apt to suspect the Negroes to be naturally inferior to the whites. There scarcely ever was a civilized nation of that complexion, nor even any individual eminent in action or speculation. No ingenious manufacturers amongst them, no arts, no sciences. On the other hand, the most rude and barbarous of the whites, such as the ancient GERMANS, the present TARTARS, have still something eminent about them . . . Such a uniform and constant difference could not happen . . . if nature had not made original distinction betwixt these breeds of men.[4]

What is philosophically significant here, I think, is Hume's casting of the "difference" between Europeans and Africans, "white" and "negroes" (*negre*, black), as a "constant" (read: permanent) and "original distinction" established by "nature." It is this form of "natural" philosophical casting of racial differences that framed the African outside of "proper" (read: European) humanity. And since, for the Enlightenment philosophers, European humanity was not only universal but was the embodiment of, and coincident with, humanity *as such*, the framing of the African as being of a

different, sub-human, species therefore philosophically and anthropologically sanctioned the exploitation of Africans in barbaric ways that were not
allowed for Europeans.

Such formulations of philosophical prejudices
against Africa and Africans (and other non-European peoples generally) were easily circulated and
recycled among modern European philosophers –
with little originality. In his essay "On the Varieties
of the Different Races of Man," Immanuel Kant
amplified and completed the remarks he had made
about "the Negro" elsewhere (*Observations On the
Feeling of the Beautiful and Sublime*) with the
following hierarchical chart on the different "races."

STEM GENUS: *white brunette*
First race, very blond (northern Europe)
Second race, Copper-Red (America)
Third race, Black (Senegambia)
Fourth race, Olive-Yellow (Indians)[5]

As in Hume, the assumption behind this arrangement and this order is precisely skin color: white,
black, red, yellow; and the ideal skin tone is the
"white" – the *white brunette* – to which others are
superior or inferior as they approximate the "white."
It is therefore not unfair to point once again to
Kant's statement: "This man was black from head
to toe, *a clear proof* that what he said was stupid"
as clear proof that Kant ascribed to skin color (white
or black) the evidence of rational (and therefore,
human) capacity – or the lack of it. But when he
needs to justify his statement and his positions on
this issue, Kant directly appealed to Hume's
footnote, already cited.[6]

If the trade and practices of transatlantic slavery
were carefully philosophically constructed on the
alleged sub-humanity of the African "race," the
practice of colonialism was parallely predicated on
a metaphysical denial of the historicity of African
existence. Nowhere is this line of modern European
thought as evident as in Hegel's twin treatise:
Lectures on Philosophy of History and *Lectures on
the Philosophy of Right*. In the former, Hegel
positions Africa *outside* of History, as the absolute,
non-historical beginning of the movement of Spirit.
Accordingly, Africans are depicted as incapable of
rational thought or ethical conduct. They therefore
have no laws, religion, and political order. Africa,
in human terms, is, for Hegel a wasteland filled with
"lawlessness," "fetishism," and "cannibalism" –
waiting for European soldiers and missionaries to
conquer it and impose "order" and "morality."[7] For
Hegel, the African *deserved* to be enslaved. Besides,

slavery to Europeans, Hegel argued, benefited *the
African*, as it provided him/her with moral "education"! Accordingly, colonialism was also a benefit
to Africa because Europe inseminated it with its
reason, ethic, culture, and mores, and thereby
historicized it.

Although he is already quite aware of the colonial
phenomenon in the *Philosophy of History*,[8] it is not
until the *Philosophy of Right* that Hegel elaborately
lays out the theoretical structures that at once
directly justify and explain colonialism – as the
inevitable logic of the unfolding of Spirit in
(European) history. Building upon the metaphysical schemes laid out in the *Logic* and in the
Philosophy of History, Hegel in the *Philosophy of
Right* accurately and painstakingly explains why
and how the modern capitalist organization of state
and economy in Europe necessarily leads to imperialism and colonialism.

For Hegel, the imperial and the colonial expansion of Europe is the necessary and *logical* outlet for
resolving the problem of poverty inherent to
capitalism. When the capitalist division of labor and
trade that was meant to satisfy the "system of
wants" of a civil society generates at the same time
a class of paupers and disenfranchised segments of
the population, there are, for Hegel, only two ways
of resolving this contradiction. The first option is
welfare, while the second is more jobs. The
consequences of both options, however, violate
what Hegel considered the basic tenets of the civil
society. Welfare deprives the individual [the poor]
of initiative and self-respect and independence,
while the second – the creation of more jobs –
according to Hegel, would cause over-production
of goods and services in proportion to available
market. This is how Hegel stages the scenario:

> When the masses begin to decline into
> poverty, (a) the burden of maintaining them
> at their ordinary standards of living might be
> directly laid on the wealthier class [higher
> taxes, for example], or they might receive the
> means of livelihood directly from other
> public sources of wealth . . . In either case,
> however, the needy would receive subsist-
> ence directly, not by means of their work,
> and this would violate the principle of civil
> society and the feeling of individual inde-
> pendence and self-respect . . . (b) As an
> alternative, they might be given subsistence
> indirectly through being given work, i.e.,
> opportunity to work. In this event the

volume of production would be increased, but the evil consists precisely in an excess of production and in the lack of a proportionate number of consumers . . . It hence becomes apparent that despite an excess of wealth civil society is not rich enough, i.e., its own resources are insufficient to check excessive poverty and the creation of a penurious rabble.[9]

In order, then, to resolve the problem of the poverty of the "penurious rabble" which results from the unequal distribution of wealth inherent to modern European capitalist societies, the solution, Hegel recommends, is the generation of more wealth for Europe from outside of Europe, through expansion of the market for European goods as well as through colonist and colonialist expansions. Poverty and the need for market, Hegel says,

> drives it [the capitalistically "mature" European society] to push beyond its own limits and seek markets and so its necessary means of subsistence, in other lands which are either deficient in the goods it overproduced, or else generally backward in industry.[10]

Colonial and capitalist expansions are therefore a logical necessity for the realization of the obviously universal European Idea, and by labeling the non-European territories and people as "backward" in "industry," they become legitimate prey for colonial and colonialist activities. According to Hegel: "All great peoples . . . press onward to the sea," because

> the sea *affords the means for the colonizing activity* – sporadic or systematic – to which the mature civil society is driven and by which it supplies to part of its population a return to life on the family basis in a new land and so also supplies itself with a new demand and field for its industry.[11]

In this articulation of Europe's rush for wealth and for territory in other lands, Hegel does not raise any ethical questions or moral consideration precisely because, in addition to Hume and Kant, Hegel himself had declared the African sub-human: the African lacked reason and therefore moral and ethical content. This philosophically articulated "natural" status of the African automatically precludes the possibility that the relationship between Europe and Africa, the European and the African, the colonizer and the colonized, may be governed or regulated by any sort of law or ethics. In Hegel's words (*Philosophy of Right*):

> The civilized nation [Europe] is conscious that the rights of the barbarians [Africans, for example] are unequal to its own and treats their autonomy as only a formality.[12]

It is clear, then, that nowhere is the *direct* conjunction/intersection of the philosophical and the political and economic interests in the European denigration and exploitation of Africans so evident and shameless as in Hegel. Since Africa, for Hegel, "Is the Gold-land compressed within itself," the continent *and* its peoples become, all at once, a treasure island and a *terra nulla*, a virgin territory brimming with natural and human raw-material passively waiting for Europe to exploit and turn it into mini-European territories.[13]

It is for good reasons then that "the critique of Eurocentrism" has become a significant, if "negative," moment in the practice of African Philosophy.[14] For it is with the authorities of Hume, Kant, Hegel, and Marx behind them, and with the enduring image of "the African" as "black," "savage," "primitive," and so forth, in conjunction with clearly articulated political and economic colonial interests, that nineteenth- and twentieth-century European anthropologists descended upon Africa. And *quelle surprise*!: the Lévy-Bruhls and the Evans-Pritchards report that the "African mind" is "pre-logical," "mystical," and "irrational." These anthropological productions, often commissioned after military invasion of an African territory or after a rebellion against occupying European powers,[15] were intended to provide the European administrations and missionary-cultural workers with information about the "primitive" to guarantee both efficient administration as well as provide knowledge of the "African mentality" so that, while demonizing and repressing African practices, the "superior" European values and attitudes could be effectively inculcated into the African conscience. From the transformations in the African economies and politics to religion and the educational institutions, the goal was to maximize European profit, secure the total domination and subjection of the colonial territory to the metropole, and reproduce Europe and European values not only in the material lives but also in the cultural and spiritual lives and expressions of the African.

African Philosophy as Counter-Colonial Practice

(a) It is within the colonial context that we must explore the significance of a book which, more than any other, influenced, at the continental level, the development and self-understanding of twentieth-century history of African philosophy. I am speaking of Father Placide Tempels' *Bantu Philosophy* (1945). As stated by the author, the aim of the book is to serve the European colonialist as a handbook on indigenous African "philosophy." According to the argument of the book, the European needed to understand the African worldviews and belief systems so that the missionary message and "civilizationary" projects could be implanted in the vital nodes of the structures of faith and the existential interiority of the African. Thus, colonization could succeed, and succeed in a self-sustaining manner. Tempels' work is therefore predominantly an exposition of the ontological systems of the Baluba, an ethnic group in Zaire where Tempels, a Belgian missionary, worked for many years. Tempels believed that the Baluba ontology grounded and regulated the daily ethical, political, and economic existence of the African. In order to elevate the "pagan" existence of the African to "civilization," one must work through this onto-logical system which grounds the subjectivity of the Bantu.

But the volcanic historical significance of Tempels' work is not necessarily located in its intentions. It is located elsewhere – in the title of the book; specifically the author's explicit use of the term "philosophy" to characterize an intellectual product associated with the African. Whereas the anthropologist spoke of "savage mentality," or "primitive thought," Tempels spoke of *philosophy*; and because philosophy, to the Western mind, is the honorific term symbolizing the highest exercise of the faculty of reason, the book's title amounted to an admission of the existence of an African philosophy, the existence of African reason, and hence – following this logocentric European logic – African humanity. This notion flew in the face of the entire intellectual edifice of slavery and colonialism which was built precisely on the negation of this possibility.

Tempels' book, then, became inadvertently fruitfully ambiguous. The author intended it as a "handbook" for the missionary-cultural worker: a plea to the European colonialist administrator or missionary that the African's "philosophy" and culture ought to be understood and respected in order for the "civilizing" mission to succeed. But the ambiguous conjunction of "philosophy" as an implicit ontological system which underlies and sustains an African communal worldview, and the honorific notion of "philosophy" in the West as the highest rational (human) achievement was not lost on the African intelligentsia engaged in anti-colonial projects. Tempels' book, for them had collapsed the ideological scaffold that had supported and sustained racism and colonialism, and the book became for these Africans a manual for cultural and political revolt.[16]

With the "discovery" of Bantu philosophy in Africa and the emergence in the United States of the Harlem Renaissance – with its philosophers and intellectuals: Alain Locke, Claude McKay, W. E. B. Dubois and others – where Africans in the Diaspora were already engaged in the critique of African colonialism and the racism of the New World, a third moment in the history of African philosophy was born: Négritude.[17] As a literary, artistic, and philosophical movement originated in Paris by African and Afro-Caribbean students, Négritude, through Aimé Césaire and Leopold Sedar Senghor, found in *Bantu Philosophy* and in the pluralist anthropologies of Frobenius, Herskovits, and Delafosse, and in the cultural movements of the Harlem Renaissance, renewed energy and resources for a continuing struggle against European denigration and depravation of Africans, on the continent and in Europe. The idea of "African philosophy" as a field of inquiry thus has its contemporary roots in the effort of African thinkers to combat political and economic exploitations, and to examine, question, and contest identities imposed upon them by Europeans. The claims and counter-claims, justifications and alienations that characterize such historical and conceptual protests and contestations indelibly mark the discipline of African philosophy.

(b) A major and continuing dilemma for African philosophy, then, is its attempt to understand and articulate Africa's experience of the "Age of Europe." How, it is asked, could the same European modernity and Enlightenment that promoted "precious ideals like the dignity of persons" and "democracy" also be so intimately and inextricably implicated in slavery and the colonial projects?

Confronted with this duplicity at the heart of European modernity – the subscription to the ideals of universal humanity and democracy on the one hand, and the imperial and colonial subjugation of non-European peoples and racism on the other, some critics are satisfied to attribute the contradictions, as Cornel West suggests, to an inevitable "discrepancy between sterling rhetoric and lived reality," between "glowing principles and actual practices."[18] Abiola Irele, for example, while recognizing that "many have been betrayed by . . . the Enlightenment ideals of universal reason and universal equality . . . by the difference between word and deed," recommends that we "separate" the ideal from the real, holding on to one while rejecting the other. According to Irele:

> Africans have suffered greatly from the derogatory insults of the Enlightenment. I believe we must separate the ideals of universal reason and equality from their historical implementation. We must, as it were, trust the tale and not the teller, for though the messenger be tainted, the message need not be.[19]

But how does one, even conceptually, nicely and neatly separate the "ideals" of European modernity, the Age of Europe, from its concreteness or "historical implementation"? Were the European philosophers' ideas about "humanity" and "freedom" pure and "sterling" and perfect as this argument presumes – in which case it is only in the "implementation" that imperfections (racism, colonialism, etc.) arose? Is it not evident that these "imperfections" were conceptualized as integral and as constitutive of the logic of capitalist and ethnocentric and racist modernity?

Irele's exhortation that "we must separate the [European] ideals of universal reason" from the imperfect "historical implementation" operates a false dichotomy that may mislead one to believe that we can clearly separate the "ideal" from the "real" (the tale from the teller, the message from the messenger, etc.) How do we know what constitutes "ideal" except in/through the way it was and has been practiced? Furthermore, to speak of ideals or ideas as universally neutral schemes or models which we historically perfectly or imperfectly implement obscures the fact that these ideals and ideas and models are always already part and parcel of, i.e., always already infused with historical practices and intentions out of which ideals are, in the first place, constituted as such – and judged worthy of pursuit. Ideals do not have meaning in a historical vacuum.

It is more appropriate I think, to consider Africa's experience of the "Age of Europe" as the *cost* of Occidental modernity. This idea of "cost," introduced but left undeveloped by the West, is to be understood literally, as that which had to be *sacrificed* in order to purchase, or pursue, European modernity's "order," "progress," "culture," "civilization," etc. By *negating* Africa, Europe was able to posit and represent itself and its contingent historicity as the ideal culture, the ideal humanity, and ideal history. While "reason" and "humanity" and "light" remained in Europe, "irrationality" and "savagery," and "darkness" were conveniently – and perhaps unconsciously – projected unto Africa, the Big, Bad, Primeval Evil, the "Dark Continent." The very condition of the possibility of European modernity as an Idea was the explicit metaphysical negation and theoretical exclusion of Africa and the African, archetypally frozen as "savage" and "primitive."

To gain a general understanding of the historical scope of this "Africa" in the European imaginary, one has only to carefully study V. Y. Mudimbe's most recent works: *The Invention of Africa* and the sequel, *The Idea of Africa*.[20] But to appreciate its continuing depth and endurance within professional European philosophy, one could easily point to the works of those who claim to be the most radical critics of modernity, for example, Martin Heidegger or the critical-reformist philosopher of European modernity, Jürgen Habermas. Consider Heidegger's very recent comments, to this effect: "Nature has its history. But then *Negroes* would also have history. Or does nature then have no history? It can enter into the past as something transitory, but not everything that fades away enters into history."[21] Or Habermas' willful typologies of Africa and the African worldview in his two-volume *Theory of Communicative Action*.[22] The aims and intentions, the questions and the problems, that preoccupy twentieth-century African philosophy are stalked by a singular and incisive Occidental model of man.

When Western philosophy speaks of "reason," it is not just speaking of "science" and "knowledge" and "method," and "critique," or even "thought." In and through these codes it is more fundamentally the question of the "anthropos," of the human, that is at stake, for questions of knowledge and identity, logos and anthropos, always hang together. It is within this background of *anthropos* as *logikos*, the interlacing of human understanding and the understanding of the human, that Europeans originally introduced the notion of a *difference in kind* between themselves and Africans as a way of justifying unspeakable exploitation and denigration of Africans.

Philosophy and the (Post)colonial

African Philosophy labors under this yet-to-end exploitation and denigration of African humanity. It challenges the long-standing exclusion of Africa, or more accurately, its inclusion as the negative "other" of reason and of the western world in the major traditions of modern Western philosophy. And because this is an ongoing task, as well as in light of many other factors not unconnected with the colonial and neo-colonial nature of Africa's relationship with the West, the "post" of the "postcolonial" African philosophy has to be written under erasure, or – more conveniently – in brackets. Scribing the "post" of the postcolonial under erasure or brackets serves as signal and pointer to the unfulfilled dreams of the independence achievements of the 1960s.

It also highlights the paradoxical – and productively "deconstructive" – nature of a self-conscious (post)colonial critical philosophical work. For, to borrow an eloquent passage from Gayatri Spivak:

> Postcoloniality – the heritage of imperialism in the rest of the globe – is a deconstructive case. As follows: Those of us from formerly colonized countries are able to communicate with each other and with the metropolis to exchange and to establish sociality and transnationality, because we have had access to the culture of imperialism. Shall we then assign to that culture, in the words of the ethical philosopher Bernard Williams, a measure of "moral luck"? I think there can be no question that the answer is "no". This impossible "no" to a structure which one critiques, yet inhabits intimately, is the deconstructive philosophical position, and the everyday here and now of "postcoloniality" is a case of it.[23]

Spivak's "impossible 'no'" confirms what I have always known from an enduring truth of the Igbo proverb: *Okuko bere na ngugu na-azo isi, na-azokwa odu*. Like this Igbo proverbial hen, on a rope minding both its head and tale, distrustful of one-

dimensional vision, the "(post)colonial" in philosophy, historically, is also a place of dangerous potency, and as critical project, it must necessarily remain a project in double-gesture.[24]

We know that the earliest Africans in America and Europe were largely forcefully brought there through slavery, and that the succeeding generation who came after the abolition of slave trade came largely to learn the ways of the West in preparation for the revolutions that would crystallize in constitutional de-colonization (Kwame Nkrumah, Nnamdi Azikiwe, Senghor, etc.). Today, however, for the first time in known history, Africans come to Europe and America to find – ironically – a place of refuge, a refuge always precarious because of racism and discriminatory immigration laws. This sad and ironic recent development results from the fact that Africa's transition from colony to nation-states has failed to translate into freedom. A commentator recently stated:

> The oppressive class configuration which colonialism epitomized, in essence, remains intact, as direct colonial presence was effectively replaced with indigenous clones. Not only did strife ensue, thanks in part to the conceited manner of colonial withdrawal, repression returned and [political] opposition was once more anathematized, often with a crudity and brutality equaling the barbarism of colonialism.[25]

With migration and instability as chronic elements in modern history of African, African/a philosophy must find ways to make sense, and speak of, the multiplicities and the pluralisms of these historical "African" experiences.

"The African experience," however, has never really been a monolith, on the continent or abroad. From Amo to Nkrumah to Du Bois; from Equiano to Locke to Senghor; continental and Diaspora modern Africans found a "language" – largely based upon their awareness of a collective entanglement with the history of the modern West, their objectification and "thingfication" by this West, and so have also always individually and collectively struggled in multi-faceted and pluralistic ways against the oppressive tendencies within European capitalist cultures, and the illegitimate colonial structures that crush African initiatives on the continent.

Notes

1 Ali Mazrui refers to this point of view as the "episodic" theory of African colonialism. This theory "asserts that the European [occupation] of Africa has been shallow rather than deep, transitional rather than long-lasting." As proof, the theorists argue: "It is not often realized how brief the colonial period was," and offer, as examples, "When Jomo Kenyatta was born, Kenya was not yet a crown colony. Kenyatta lived right through the period of British rule and outlasted British rule by fifteen years." Conclusion: "if the entire period of colonialism could be compressed into the life-span of a single individual, how deep was the impact?" See: Mazrui, *The African: A Triple Heritage* (Boston: Little, Brown and Company, 1986), p. 14. The position I take, and my arguments, are against this "theory".

2 "The Politics of Literary Postcoloniality," *Race and Class*, vol. 36, no. 3, 1995, p. 7. Italics are mine.

3 Cornel West, *Keeping Faith: Philosophy and Race in America* (New York: Routledge, 1993), p. 5; my emphasis.

4 I am quoting from a later version of this statement which incorporated corrections Hume had made to it in response to criticisms and objections raised against the original by James Beatie (*An Essay on the Nature and Immutability of Truth in Opposition to Sophistry and Skepticism* 1770). For a detailed discussion of the differences between the earlier and the later versions, see my editorial notes in *Racist Enlightenment* (forthcoming from Blackwell); or my essay, "The Idea of 'Race' in Hume's Social Philosophy and Its Impact on Eighteen-Century America," included in Dorothy Coleman, ed. *Hume and Eighteenth-Century America*, forthcoming.

5 The most extensive discussion of the role the idea of "race" plays in Kant's thought is probably my essay, "The Color of Reason: The Idea of 'race' in Kant's Anthropology," in *Anthropology and the German Enlightenment*, ed. Katherine Faull (London: Bucknell and Associated University Presses, 1994), pp. 201–41. (Partially reprinted in SAPINA: *Bulletin of Society for African Philosophy in North America*, vol. 8, nos. 1–2, Jan.–July, 1995, pp. 53–78. Other valuable sources are: Christian Neugebauer, "The Racism of Kant and Hegel," in Odera Oruka, ed., *Sage Philosophy: Indigenous Thinkers and Modern Debate on African Philosophy* (New York: Brill, 1990), pp. 259–72; Ronald Judy, "Kant and the Negro," SAPINA, Jan.–July, 1991.

6 According to Kant: "Mr Hume challenges anyone to cite a simple example in which a Negro has shown talents, and asserts that among the hundreds of thousands of black . . . not a single one was ever found who presented anything great in art or science . . . So fundamental is the difference between the two races of man, and it appears to be great in regard to mental capacities as in color." *Observations*, trans. John T. Goldthwait (Berkeley: University of California Press, 1960), pp. 110–11.

7 Within a few pages of *Philosophy of History*, Hegel has used the following terms to describe African peoples: "barbarism and savagery," "barbarous ferocity," "terrible hordes," "barbarity," "animal man," "savagery and lawlessness," "primitive," "animality," "the most terrible manifestation of human nature," "wild confusion," and "Unhistorical, Undeveloped Spirit." A first-year Bucknell student, Sean Gray, who researched this language as part of an assignment for my course, "Hegel, Modernity and the African World," had this to say: "This [Hegel's] language is argumentative in nature, attempting to shock the reader into following what he said. These words show up way before Hegel provides specific accounts of any historical African peoples. By formulating such steep language ahead of time, the reader is psychologically set to look for the worst and so won't be shocked by whatever fantasies or exaggerations about Africa Hegel chooses to provide." (Sean Gray: "The Notions of Barbarism and Savagery in Hegel's Treatment of Africa.") Critical literature on Hegel's ideas about Africa include Serequeberhan, "The Idea of Colonialism in Hegel's Philosophy of Right," in *International Philosophical Quarterly*, vol no. 3, Sept. 29, 1989, pp. 302–18; Robert Bernasconi, "Hegel at the Court of the Ashanti," forthcoming. I also examined Hegel's *Philosophy of History* and *Philosophy of Right* in the second chapter of my 1993 dissertation, "Rationality and the Debates about African Philosophy," and will expand this study in a volume, *Racist Enlightenment*, under preparation for Blackwell Publishers.

8 Hegel, for example, writes in this volume that "the North American states . . . were entirely *colonized* [emphasis in the original] by the Europeans." *Lectures on the Philosophy of World History*, trans. H. B. Nisbet (Cambridge: Cambridge University Press, 1993), p. 167

9 Hegel, *Philosophy of Right*, trans. T. M. Knox (Oxford: Oxford University Press, 1967) p. 150.

10 Hegel, *The Essential Writings*, ed. F. Weiss (New York: Harper Books, 1974), pp. 282–3.

11 Ibid. Italics are mine.

12 Knox trans., par. 351, p. 219.

13 As we know, subsequent major European philosophers re-inscribed these Hegelian colonialist intentions on Africa into their own philosophical systems. Edward Said pointed out in *Orientalism* that although Marx may have "turned Hegel on his head," his views on European colonization of India and Africa were no different.

14 It is, however, only a "negative" moment in a qualified sense. Positively, it is a way of de-blocking African

philosophical consciousness clouded over by Eurocentric and racist writings, a way of critiquing in order to reject the pernicious parts of the philosophical traditions we ambiguously inherit from European modernity, because we recognize human and humane elements in them that may also speak cross-culturally and with less exploitation, less racism, and less ethnocentrism.

15 See the excellent volume edited by Tala Asad: *Anthropology and the Colonial Encounter* (London: Ithaca Press, 1973); also some choice essays in Chinua Achebe, *Hopes and Impediments* (New York: Doubleday, 1988).

16 It was not until much later that African philosophers such as Aimé Césaire (*Discourse on Colonialism*, trans. J. Pinkham (New York: Monthly Review Press, 1972)) and Frantz Fanon started to focus negative-critical attention explicitly and publicly on the colonialist and ideological intentions of Tempels' *Bantu Philosophy*. The more widespread immediate response was similar to that of Aléxis Kagamé and a host of others now identified in the "ethno-philosophy" schools: they revised and expanded but continued Tempels' major methodological orientation, namely, the documentation and analysis of evidence of philosophical thought in African languages and in the unwritten traditions of various African peoples.

17 I do not intend to make Tempels, or the three "moments" I discuss here, the absolute beginning for African philosophical practice. In addition to philosophical works in the "oral" traditions (for example, the "Ifa" [or "Afa"] Corpus among the Yorubas and the Igbos of West Africa), there are bodies of written anti-slavery and anti-colonial philosophical works that date back to the sixteenth century. On the continent, the rational hermeneutics of the Abyssinian Zera Yecob (1599–1692), for example, was concerned with the question of the nature of reason and faith in the context of the acute crisis of Abyssinian cultural, and political integrity, "In confrontation with the subversive work of Jesuit missionaries and aggressive Catholicism" (Tsenay Serequeberhan, *The Hermeneutics of African Philosophy*, New York: Routledge, 1994, p. 18). In the Diaspora, in 1732, William Amo, a native of a little town in present Ghana, at age 27 received what is today called a doctorate degree in Philosophy from the University of Wittenberg. He taught at the universities of Halle and Jena, and, in addition to extant works on epistemology and philosophical psychology, also wrote and, perhaps, published a lost work entitled *On the Freedom of Africans in Europe*. Amo returned to Ghana in 1747 and lived there as a hermit for the rest of his life (his date of death is unknown). Likewise, the autobiography of the Igbo gentleman Olaudah Equiano, although written from the point of view of his involvement in abolitionist movements in eighteenth- and nineteenth-century England, is an excellent document of the racist and colonialist social and political thinking of Europeans on Africa in modern Europe. The examples of Amo and Equiano only alert us to Leonard Harris's landmark collection, *Philosophy Born of Struggle* (Dubuque, Iowa: Kendall/Hunt, 1983) which chronicles the enormous wide-ranging philosophical productivity in Afro-America from the beginning of our century. Today, as we know, African and African-Diasporic men and women of letters: Chinua Achebe, Wole Soyinka, Toni Morrison, Cheikh Amidou-Kane, etc. – in addition to the efforts of those whose professional vocation is more strictly "Philosophy" – are producing literary resources of unsurpassed philosophical depths that powerfully articulate and chronicles our contemporary experiences. Finally, we should specifically mention the numerous successful attempts by Osabutey (1936), G. James (1954), Diop (1974), Henry Olela (1980) Onyenwuenyi (1994), Th. Obenga (1973; 1990), and Martin Bernal (1991) to (re)write the history of the African origins of Greek and European philosophy. Regardless of the admittedly ideological functions of *some* of these works, others are needed antidotes to racist inanities that have been spouted for too long about a supposedly a-historical "Greek miracle," as a way of marginalizing or suppressing African and Semitic contributions to ancient philosophy.

18 *Keeping Faith*, p. 6.

19 Abiola Irele, "Contemporary Thought in French Speaking Africa," in Albert Moseley, ed., *African Philosophy: Selected Readings* (Englewood Cliffs, NJ: Prentice Hall, 1995), p. 296.

20 Both published by Indiana University Press, 1988 and 1994.

21 Heidegger went on to illustrate his assertion with the following example: "When an airplane's propeller turns, then nothing actually 'occurs.' Conversely, when the same airplane takes the Führer to Mussolini, then history occurs." We wish this plane would make a return trip for Abacha and Mobutu and Idi Amin and Emperor Bokassa – so that "history" will truly fully "occur"!

22 See especially the first chapters of volume I subtitled *Reason and the Rationalization of Society*, trans. Thomas McCarthy (Boston: Beacon Press, 1984).

23 *Outside in the Teaching Machine* (London: Routledge, 1993).

24 Outlaw's "African Philosophy: Deconstructive and Reconstructive Challenges" is an elaborate case of this; Serequeberhan's *The Hermeneutics of African Philosophy* and Amilcar Cabral's *Return to the Source* are exemplary in terms of working with colonial "tools" to dismantle the house that colonialism built – for the sake of a (re)new(ed) sense of humanity and values in the social order.

25 Olu Oguibe, ed., *Sojourners: New Writings by Africans in Britain* (London: Africa Refugee Publishing Collective, 1994) pp. xiv–xv.

27

Discourse on Colonialism

Aimé Césaire

A civilization that proves incapable of solving the problems it creates is a decadent civilization.

A civilization that chooses to close its eyes to its most crucial problems is a stricken civilization.

A civilization that uses its principles for trickery and deceit is a dying civilization.

The fact is that the so-called European civilization – "Western" civilization – as it has been shaped by two centuries of bourgeois rule, is incapable of solving the two major problems to which its existence has given rise: the problem of the proletariat and the colonial problem; that Europe is unable to justify itself either before the bar of "reason" or before the bar of "conscience"; and that, increasingly, it takes refuge in a hypocrisy which is all the more odious because it is less and less likely to deceive.

Europe is indefensible.

Apparently that is what the American strategists are whispering to each other.

That in itself is not serious.

What is serious is that "Europe" is morally, spiritually indefensible.

And today the indictment is brought against it not by the European masses alone, but on a world scale, by tens and tens of millions of men who, from the depths of slavery, set themselves up as judges.

The colonialists may kill in Indochina, torture in Madagascar, imprison in Black Africa, crack down

in the West Indies. Henceforth the colonized know that they have an advantage over them. They know that their temporary "masters" are lying.

Therefore that their masters are weak.

And since I have been asked to speak about colonization and civilization, let us go straight to the principal lie which is the source of all the others.

Colonization and civilization?

In dealing with this subject, the commonest curse is to be the dupe in good faith of a collective hypocrisy that cleverly misrepresents problems, the better to legitimize the hateful solutions provided for them.

In other words, the essential thing here is to see clearly, to think clearly – that is, dangerously – and to answer clearly the innocent first question: what, fundamentally, is colonization? To agree on what it is not: neither evangelization, nor a philanthropic enterprise, nor a desire to push back the frontiers of ignorance, disease, and tyranny, nor a project undertaken for the greater glory of God, nor an attempt to extend the rule of law. To admit once for all, without flinching at the consequences, that the decisive actors here are the adventurer and the pirate, the wholesale grocer and the ship owner, the gold digger and the merchant, appetite and force, and behind them, the baleful projected shadow of a form of civilization which, at a certain point in its history, finds itself obliged, for internal reasons, to extend to a world scale the competition of its antagonistic economies.

Pursuing my analysis, I find that hypocrisy is of recent date; that neither Cortez discovering Mexico from the top of the great teocalli, nor Pizzaro before

From Aimé Césaire, *Discourse on Colonialism* (*Discours sur le colonialisme*) (1989); by kind permission of Présence Africaine.

Cuzco (much less Marco Polo before Cambaluc), claims that he is the harbinger of a superior order; that they kill; that they plunder; that they have helmets, lances, cupidities; that the slavering apologists came later; that the chief culprit in this domain is Christian pedantry, which laid down the dishonest equations *Christianity = civilization, paganism = savagery*, from which there could not but ensue abominable colonialist and racist consequences, whose victims were to be the Indians, the yellow peoples, and the Negroes.

That being settled, I admit that it is a good thing to place different civilizations in contact with each other; that it is an excellent thing to blend different worlds; that whatever its own particular genius may be, a civilization that withdraws into itself atrophies; that for civilizations, exchange is oxygen; that the great good fortune of Europe is to have been a crossroads, and that because it was the locus of all ideas, the receptacle of all philosophies, the meeting place of all sentiments, it was the best center for the redistribution of energy.

But then I ask the following question: has colonization really *placed civilization in contact*? Or, if you prefer, of all the ways of *establishing contact*, was it the best?

I answer *no*.

And I say that between *colonization* and *civilization* there is an infinite distance; that out of all the colonial expeditions that have been undertaken, out of all the colonial statutes that have been drawn up, out of all the memoranda that have been dispatched by all the ministries, there could not come a single human value.

First we must study how colonization works to *decivilize* the colonizer, to *brutalize* him in the true sense of the word, to degrade him, to awaken him to buried instincts, to covetousness, violence, race hatred, and moral relativism; and we must show that each time a head is cut off or an eye put out in Vietnam and in France they accept the fact, each time a little girl is raped and in France they accept the fact, each time a Madagascan is tortured and in France they accept the fact, civilization acquires another dead weight, a universal regression takes place, a gangrene sets in, a center of infection begins to spread; and that at the end of all these treaties that have been violated, all these lies that have been propagated, all these punitive expeditions that have been tolerated, all these prisoners who have been tied up and "interrogated," all these patriots who have been tortured, at the end of all the racial pride that has been encouraged, all the boast-fulness that has been displayed, a poison has been instilled into the veins of Europe and, slowly but surely, the continent proceeds toward *savagery*.

And then one fine day the bourgeoisie is awakened by a terrific reverse shock: the gestapos are busy, the prisons fill up, the torturers around the racks invent, refine, discuss.

People are surprised, they become indignant. They say: "How strange! But never mind – it's Nazism, it will pass!" And they wait, and they hope; and they hide the truth from themselves, that it is barbarism, but the supreme barbarism, the crowning barbarism that sums up all the daily barbarisms; that it is Nazism, yes, but that before they were its victims, they were its accomplices; that they tolerated that Nazism before it was inflicted on them, that they absolved it, shut their eyes to it, legitimized it, because, until then, it had been applied only to non-European peoples; that they have cultivated that Nazism, that they are responsible for it, and that before engulfing the whole of Western, Christian civilization in its reddened waters, it oozes, seeps, and trickles from every crack.

Yes, it would be worthwhile to study clinically, in detail, the steps taken by Hitler and Hitlerism and to reveal to the very distinguished, very humanistic, very Christian bourgeois of the twentieth century that without his being aware of it, he has a Hitler inside him, that Hitler *inhabits* him, that Hitler is his *demon*, that if he rails against him, he is being inconsistent and that, at bottom, what he cannot forgive Hitler for is not *crime* in itself, *the crime against man*, it is not *the humiliation of man as such*, it is the crime against the white man, the humiliation of the white man, and the fact that he applied to Europe colonialist procedures which until then had been reserved exclusively for the Arabs of Algeria, the coolies of India, and the blacks of Africa.

And that is the great thing I hold against pseudo-humanism: that for too long it has diminished the rights of man, that its concept of those rights has been – and still is – narrow and fragmentary, incomplete and biased and, all things considered, sordidly racist.

I have talked a good deal about Hitler. Because he deserves it: he makes it possible to see things on a large scale and to grasp the fact that capitalist society, at its present stage, is incapable of establishing a concept of the rights of all men, just as it has proved incapable of establishing a system of individual ethics. Whether one likes it or not, at the end of the blind alley that is Europe, I mean the Europe of Adenauer, Schuman, Bidault, and a few others, there is Hitler. At the end of capitalism, which is eager to outlive its day, there is Hitler. At the end of formal humanism and philosophic renunciation, there is Hitler.

And this being so, I cannot help thinking of one of his statements: "We aspire not to equality but to domination. The country of a foreign race must become once again a country of serfs, of agricultural laborers, or industrial workers. It is not a question of eliminating the inequalities among men but of widening them and making them into a law."

That rings clear, haughty, and brutal and plants us squarely in the middle of howling savagery. But let us come down a step.

Who is speaking? I am ashamed to say it: it is the Western *humanist*, the "idealist" philosopher. That his name is Renan is an accident. That the passage is taken from a book entitled *La Réforme intellectuelle et morale*, that it was written in France just after a war which France had represented as a war of right against might, tells us a great deal about bourgeois morals.

The regeneration of the inferior or degenerate races by the superior races is part of the providential order of things for humanity. With us, the common man is nearly always a déclassé nobleman, his heavy hand is better suited to handling the sword than the menial tool. Rather than work, he chooses to fight, that is, he returns to his first estate. *Regere imperio populos*, that is our vocation. Pour forth this all-consuming activity onto countries which, like China, are crying aloud for foreign conquest. Turn the adventurers who disturb European society into a *ver sacrum*, a horde like those of the Franks, the Lombards, or the Normans, and every man will be in his right role. Nature has made a race of workers, the Chinese race, who have wonderful manual dexterity and almost no sense of honor; govern them with justice, levying from them, in return for the blessing of such a government, an ample allowance for the conquering race, and they will be satisfied; a race of tillers of the soil, the Negro; treat him with kindness and humanity, and all will be as it should; a race of masters and soldiers, the European race. Reduce this noble race to working in the *ergastulum* like Negroes and Chinese, and

they rebel. In Europe, every rebel is, more or less, a soldier who has missed his calling, a creature made for the heroic life, before whom you are setting *a task that is contrary to his race* – a poor worker, too good a soldier. But the life at which our workers rebel would make a Chinese or a fellah happy, as they are not military creatures in the least. *Let each one do what he is made for, and all will be well.*

Hitler? Rosenberg? No, Renan.

But let us come down one step further. And it is the long-winded politician. Who protests? No one, so far as I know, when M. Albert Sarraut, the former governor-general of Indochina, holding forth to the students at the Ecole Coloniale, teaches them that it would be puerile to object to the European colonial enterprises in the name of "an alleged right to possess the land one occupies, and some sort of right to remain in fierce isolation, which would leave unutilized resources to lie forever idle in the hands of incompetents."

And who is roused to indignation when a certain Rev. Barde assures us that if the goods of this world "remained divided up indefinitely, as they would be without colonization, they would answer neither the purposes of God nor the just demands of the human collectivity"?

Since, as his fellow Christian, the Rev. Muller, declares: "Humanity must not, cannot allow the incompetence, negligence, and laziness of the uncivilized peoples to leave idle indefinitely the wealth which God has confided to them, charging them to make it serve the good of all."

No one.

I mean not one established writer, not one academician, not one preacher, not one crusader for the right and for religion, not one "defender of the human person."

And yet, through the mouths of the Sarrauts and the Bardes, the Mullers and the Renans, through the mouths of all those who considered – and consider – it lawful to apply to non-European peoples "a kind of expropriation for public purposes" for the benefit of nations that were stronger and better equipped, it was already Hitler speaking!

What am I driving at? At this idea: that no one colonizes innocently, that no one colonizes with impunity either; that a nation which colonizes, that a civilization which justifies colonization – and therefore force – is already a sick civilization, a civilization that is morally diseased, that irresistibly, progressing from one consequence to another, one repudiation to another, calls for its Hitler, I mean its punishment.

Colonization: bridgehead in a campaign to civilize barbarism, from which there may emerge at any moment the negation of civilization, pure and simple.

Elsewhere I have cited at length a few incidents culled from the history of colonial expeditions.

Unfortunately, this did not find favor with everyone. It seems that I was pulling old skeletons out of the closet. Indeed!

Was there no point in quoting Colonel de Montagnac, one of the conquerors of Algeria: "In order to banish the thoughts that sometimes besiege me, I have some heads cut off, not the heads of artichokes but the heads of men."

Would it have been more advisable to refuse the floor to Count d'Hérisson: "It is true that we are bringing back a whole barrelful of ears collected, pair by pair, from prisoners, friendly or enemy."

Should I have refused Saint-Arnaud the right to profess his barbarous faith: "We lay waste, we burn, we plunder, we destroy the houses and the trees."

Should I have prevented Marshal Bugeaud from systematizing all that in a daring theory and invoking the precedent of famous ancestors: "We must have a great invasion of Africa, like the invasions of the Franks and the Goths."

Lastly, should I have cast back into the shadows of oblivion the memorable feat of arms of General Gérard and kept silent about the capture of Ambike, a city which, to tell the truth, had never dreamed of defending itself: "The native riflemen had orders to kill only the men, but no one restrained them; intoxicated by the smell of blood, they spared not one woman, not one child. . . . At the end of the afternoon, the heat caused a light mist to arise: it was the blood of the five thousand victims, the ghost of the city, evaporating in the setting sun."

Yes or no, are these things true? And the sadistic pleasures, the nameless delights that send voluptuous shivers and quivers through Loti's carcass when he focuses his field glasses on a good massacre of the Annamese? True or not true?[1] And if these things are true, as no one can deny, will it be said, in order to minimize them, that these corpses don't prove anything?

For my part, if I have recalled a few details of these hideous butcheries, it is by no means because I take a morbid delight in them, but because I think that these heads of men, these collections of ears, these burned houses, these Gothic invasions, this steaming blood, these cities that evaporate at the edge of the sword, are not to be so easily disposed of. They prove that colonization, I repeat, dehumanizes even the most civilized man; that colonial activity, colonial enterprise, colonial conquest, which is based on contempt for the native and justified by that contempt, inevitably tends to change him who undertakes it; that the colonizer, who in order to ease his conscience gets into the habit of seeing the other man as *an animal*, accustoms himself to treating him like an animal, and tends objectively to transform *himself* into an animal. It is this result, this boomerang effect of colonization, that I wanted to point out.

Unfair? No. There was a time when these same facts were a source of pride, and when, sure of the morrow, people did not mince words. One last quotation; it is from a certain Carl Siger, author of an *Essai sur la colonisation* (Paris, 1907):

> The new countries offer a vast field for individual, violent activities which, in the metropolitan countries, would run up against certain prejudices, against a sober and orderly conception of life, and which, in the colonies, have greater freedom to develop and, consequently, to affirm their worth. Thus to a certain extent the colonies can serve as a safety valve for modern society. Even if this were their only value, it would be immense.

Truly, there are stains that it is beyond the power of man to wipe out and that can never be fully expiated.

But let us speak about the colonized.

I see clearly what colonization has destroyed: the wonderful Indian civilizations – and neither Deterding nor Royal Dutch nor Standard Oil will ever console me for the Aztecs and the Incas.

I see clearly the civilizations, condemned to perish at a future date, into which it has introduced a principle of ruin: the South Sea islands, Nigeria, Nyasaland. I see less clearly the contributions it has made.

Security? Culture? The rule of law? In the meantime, I look around and wherever there are colonizers and colonized face to face, I see force, brutality, cruelty, sadism, conflict, and, in a parody of education, the hasty manufacture of a few thousand subordinate functionaries, "boys," artisans, office clerks, and interpreters necessary for the smooth operation of business.

I spoke of contact.

Between colonizer and colonized there is room only for forced labor, intimidation, pressure, the police, taxation, theft, rape, compulsory crops, contempt, mistrust, arrogance, self-complacency, swinishness, brainless elites, degraded masses.

No human contact, but relations of domination and submission which turn the colonizing man into a classroom monitor, an army sergeant, a prison guard, a slave driver, and the indigenous man into an instrument of production.

My turn to state an equation: colonization = "thingification."

I hear the storm. They talk to me about progress, about "achievements," diseases cured, improved standards of living.

I am talking about societies drained of their essence, cultures trampled underfoot, institutions undermined, lands confiscated, religions smashed, magnificent artistic creations destroyed, extraordinary *possibilities* wiped out.

They throw facts at my head, statistics, mileages of roads, canals, and railroad tracks.

I am talking about thousands of men sacrificed to the Congo-Océan.[2] I am talking about those who, as I write this, are digging the harbor of Abidjan by hand. I am talking about millions of men torn from their gods, their land, their habits, their life – from life, from the dance, from wisdom.

I am talking about millions of men in whom fear has been cunningly instilled, who have been taught to have an inferiority complex, to tremble, kneel, despair, and behave like flunkeys.

They dazzle me with the tonnage of cotton or cocoa that has been exported, the acreage that has been planted with olive trees or grapevines.

I am talking about natural *economies* that have been disrupted – harmonious and viable *economies* adapted to the indigenous population – about food crops destroyed, malnutrition permanently introduced, agricultural development oriented solely toward the benefit of the metropolitan countries, about the looting of products, the looting of raw materials.

They pride themselves on abuses eliminated.

I too talk about abuses, but what I say is that on the old ones – very real – they have superimposed others – very detestable. They talk to me about local tyrants brought to reason; but I note that in general the old tyrants get on very well with the new ones, and that there has been established between them, to the detriment of the people, a circuit of mutual services and complicity.

They talk to me about civilization, I talk about proletarianization and mystification.

For my part, I make a systematic defense of the non-European civilizations.

Every day that passes, every denial of justice, every beating by the police, every demand of the workers that is drowned in blood, every scandal that is hushed up, every punitive expedition, every police van, every gendarme and every militiaman, brings home to us the value of our old societies.

They were communal societies, never societies of the many for the few.

They were societies that were not only ante-capitalist, as has been said, but also *anti-capitalist*.

They were democratic societies, always.

They were cooperative societies, fraternal societies.

I make a systematic defense of the societies destroyed by imperialism.

They were the fact, they did not pretend to be the idea; despite their faults, they were neither to be hated nor condemned. They were content to be. In them, neither the word *failure* nor the word *avatar* had any meaning. They kept hope intact.

Whereas those are the only words that can, in all honesty, be applied to the European enterprises outside Europe. My only consolation is that periods of colonization pass, that nations sleep only for a time, and that peoples remain.

This being said, it seems that in certain circles they pretend to have discovered in me an "enemy of Europe" and a prophet of the return to the ante-European past.

For my part, I search in vain for the place where I could have expressed such views; where I ever underestimated the importance of Europe in the history of human thought; where I ever preached a *return* of any kind; where I ever claimed that there could be a *return*.

The truth is that I have said something very different: to wit, that the great historical tragedy of Africa has been not so much that it was too late in making contact with the rest of the world, as the manner in which that contact was brought about; that Europe began to "propagate" at a time when it had fallen into the hands of the most unscrupulous financiers and captains of industry; that it was our misfortune to encounter that particular Europe on our path, and that Europe is responsible before the human community for the highest heap of corpses in history.

In another connection, in judging colonization, I have added that Europe has gotten on very well indeed with all the local feudal lords who agreed to serve, woven a villainous complicity with them, rendered their tyranny more effective and more efficient, and that it has actually tended to prolong artificially the survival of local pasts in their most pernicious aspects.

I have said – and this is something very different – that colonialist Europe has grafted modern abuse onto ancient injustice, hateful racism onto old inequality.

That if I am attacked on the grounds of intent, I maintain that colonialist Europe is dishonest in trying to justify its colonizing activity *a posteriori* by the obvious material progress that has been achieved in certain fields under the colonial regime – since *sudden change* is always possible, in history as elsewhere; since no one knows at what stage of material development these same countries would have been if Europe had not intervened; since

the technical outfitting of Africa and Asia, their administrative reorganization, in a word, their "Europeanization," was (as is proved by the example of Japan) in no way tied to the European *occupation*; since the Europeanization of the non-European continents could have been accomplished otherwise than under the heel of Europe; since this movement of Europeanization *was in progress*; since it was even slowed down; since in any case it was distorted by the European takeover.

The proof is that at present it is the indigenous peoples of Africa and Asia who are demanding schools, and colonialist Europe which refuses them; that it is the African who is asking for ports and roads, and colonialist Europe which is niggardly on this score; that it is the colonized man who wants to move forward, and the colonizer who holds things back.

Notes

1 This is a reference to the account of the taking of Thuan-An which appeared in *Le Figaro* in September 1883 and is quoted in N. Serban's book, *Loti, sa vie, son oeuvre*. "Then the great slaughter had begun. They had fired in double-salvos! and it was a pleasure to see these sprays of bullets, that were so easy to aim, come down on them twice a minute, surely and methodically, on command . . . We saw some who were quite

mad and stood up seized with a dizzy desire to run . . . They zigzagged, running every which way in this race with death, holding their garments up around their waists in a comical way . . . and then we amused ourselves counting the dead, etc."

2 A railroad line connecting Brazzaville with the port of Pointe-Noire. (Trans.)

28

The Wretched of the Earth

Frantz Fanon

We see that the primary Manicheism which governed colonial society is preserved intact during the period of decolonization; that is to say that the settler never ceases to be the enemy, the opponent, the foe that must be overthrown. The oppressor, in his own sphere, starts the process, a process of domination, of exploitation and of pillage, and in the other sphere the coiled, plundered creature which is the native provides fodder for the process as best he can, the process which moves uninterruptedly from the banks of the colonial territory to the palaces and the docks of the mother country. In this becalmed zone the sea has a smooth surface, the palm tree stirs gently in the breeze, the waves lap against the pebbles, and raw materials are ceaselessly transported, justifying the presence of the settler: and all the while the native, bent double, more dead than alive, exists interminably in an unchanging dream. The settler makes history; his life is an epoch, an Odyssey. He is the absolute beginning: "This land was created by us"; he is the unceasing cause: "If we leave, all is lost, and the country will go back to the Middle Ages." Over against him torpid creatures, wasted by fevers, obsessed by ancestral customs, form an almost inorganic background for the innovating dynamism of colonial mercantilism.

The settler makes history and is conscious of making it. And because he constantly refers to the history of his mother country, he clearly indicates that he himself is the extension of that mother country. Thus the history which he writes is not the history of the country which he plunders but the history of his own nation in regard to all that she skims off, all that she violates and starves.

The immobility to which the native is condemned can only be called in question if the native decides to put an end to the history of colonization – the history of pillage – and to bring into existence the history of the nation – the history of decolonization.

A world divided into compartments, a motionless, Manicheistic world, a world of statues: the statue of the general who carried out the conquest, the statue of the engineer who built the bridge; a world which is sure of itself, which crushes with its stones the backs flayed by whips: this is the colonial world. The native is a being hemmed in; apartheid is simply one form of the division into compartments of the colonial world. The first thing which the native learns is to stay in his place, and not to go beyond certain limits. This is why the dreams of the native are always of muscular prowess; his dreams are of action and of aggression. I dream I am jumping, swimming, running, climbing; I dream that I burst out laughing, that I span a river in one stride, or that I am followed by a flood of motorcars which never catch up with me. During the period of colonization, the native never stops achieving his freedom from nine in the evening until six in the morning.

The colonized man will first manifest this aggressiveness which has been deposited in his

From Frantz Fanon, *The Wretched of the Earth*, trans. Constance Farrington (1967), copyright © 1963 by Présence Africaine; by kind permission of HarperCollins Publishers and Grove/Atlantic Inc.

bones against his own people. This is the period when the niggers beat each other up, and the police and magistrates do not know which way to turn when faced with the astonishing waves of crime in North Africa. . . . When the native is confronted with the colonial order of things, he finds he is in a state of permanent tension. The settler's world is a hostile world, which spurns the native, but at the same time it is a world of which he is envious. We have seen that the native never ceases to dream of putting himself in the place of the settler – not of becoming the settler but of substituting himself for the settler. This hostile world, ponderous and aggressive because it fends off the colonized masses with all the harshness it is capable of, represents not merely a hell from which the swiftest flight possible is desirable, but also a paradise close at hand which is guarded by terrible watchdogs.

The native is always on the alert, for since he can only make out with difficulty the many symbols of the colonial world, he is never sure whether or not he has crossed the frontier. Confronted with a world ruled by the settler, the native is always presumed guilty. But the native's guilt is never a guilt which he accepts; it is rather a kind of curse, a sort of sword of Damocles, for, in his innermost spirit, the native admits no accusation. He is overpowered but not tamed; he is treated as an inferior but he is not convinced of his inferiority. He is patiently waiting until the settler is off his guard to fly at him. The native's muscles are always tensed. You can't say that he is terrorized, or even apprehensive. He is in fact ready at a moment's notice to exchange the role of the quarry for that of the hunter. The native is an oppressed person whose permanent dream is to become the persecutor. The symbols of social order – the police, the bugle calls in the barracks, military parades, and the waving flags – are at one and the same time inhibitory and stimulating: for they do not convey the message "Don't dare to budge"; rather, they cry out "Get ready to attack." And, in fact, if the native had any tendency to fall asleep and to forget, the settler's hauteur and the settler's anxiety to test the strength of the colonial system would remind him at every turn that the great showdown cannot be put off indefinitely. That impulse to take the settler's place implies a tonicity of muscles the whole time; and in fact we know that in certain emotional conditions the presence of an obstacle accentuates the tendency toward motion.

The settler–native relationship is a mass relationship. The settler pits brute force against the weight of numbers. He is an exhibitionist. His preoccupation with security makes him remind the native out loud that there he alone is master. The settler keeps alive in the native an anger which he deprives of outlet; the native is trapped in the tight links of the chains of colonialism. But we have seen that inwardly the settler can only achieve a pseudo petrification. The native's muscular tension finds outlet regularly in bloodthirsty explosions – in tribal warfare, in feuds between sects, and in quarrels between individuals.

Where individuals are concerned, a positive negation of common sense is evident. While the settler or the policeman has the right the livelong day to strike the native, to insult him and to make him crawl to them, you will see the native reaching for his knife at the slightest hostile or aggressive glance cast on him by another native; for the last resort of the native is to defend his personality vis-à-vis his brother. Tribal feuds only serve to perpetuate old grudges buried deep in the memory. By throwing himself with all his force into the vendetta, the native tries to persuade himself that colonialism does not exist, that everything is going on as before, that history continues. Here on the level of communal organizations we clearly discern the well-known behavior patterns of avoidance. It is as if plunging into a fraternal blood-bath allowed them to ignore the obstacle, and to put off till later the choice, nevertheless inevitable, which opens up the question of armed resistance to colonialism. Thus collective autodestruction in a very concrete form is one of the ways in which the native's muscular tension is set free. All these patterns of conduct are those of the death reflex when faced with danger, a suicidal behavior which proves to the settler (whose existence and domination is by them all the more justified) that these men are not reasonable human beings. In the same way the native manages to by-pass the settler. A belief in fatality removes all blame from the oppressor; the cause of misfortunes and of poverty is attributed to God: He is Fate. In this way the individual accepts the disintegration ordained by God, bows down before the settler and his lot, and by a kind of interior restabilization acquires a stony calm.

Meanwhile, however, life goes on, and the native will strengthen the inhibitions which contain his aggressiveness by drawing on the terrifying myths which are so frequently found in underdeveloped communities. There are maleficent spirits which intervene every time a step is taken in the wrong direction, leopard-men, serpent-men, six-legged dogs, zombies – a whole series of tiny animals or giants which create around the native a world of prohibitions, of barriers and of inhibitions far more terrifying than the world of the settler. This magical superstructure which permeates native society fulfills certain well-defined functions in the dynamism of the libido. One of the characteristics of underdeveloped societies is in fact that the libido is first and foremost the concern of a group, or of the family. The feature of communities whereby a man who dreams that he has sexual relations with a woman other than his own must confess it in public and pay a fine in kind or in working days to the injured husband or family is fully described by ethnologists. We may note in passing that this proves that the so-called prehistoric societies attach great importance to the unconscious.

The atmosphere of myth and magic frightens me and so takes on an undoubted reality. By terrifying me, it integrates me in the traditions and the history of my district or of my tribe, and at the same time it reassures me, it gives me a status, as it were an identification paper. In underdeveloped countries the occult sphere is a sphere belonging to the community which is entirely under magical jurisdiction. By entangling myself in this inextricable network where actions are repeated with crystalline inevitability, I find the everlasting world which belongs to me, and the perenniality which is thereby affirmed of the world belonging to us. Believe me, the zombies are more terrifying than the settlers; and in consequence the problem is no longer that of keeping oneself right with the colonial world and its barbed-wire entanglements, but of considering three times before urinating, spitting, or going out into the night.

The supernatural, magical powers reveal themselves as essentially personal; the settler's powers are infinitely shrunken, stamped with their alien origin. We no longer really need to fight against them since what counts is the frightening enemy created by myths. We perceive that all is settled by a permanent confrontation on the phantasmic plane.

It has always happened in the struggle for freedom that such a people, formerly lost in an imaginary maze, a prey to unspeakable terrors yet happy to lose themselves in a dreamlike torment, such a people becomes unhinged, reorganizes itself, and in blood and tears gives birth to very real and immediate action. Feeding the *moudjahidines*,[1] posting sentinels, coming to the help of families which lack the bare necessities, or taking the place of a husband who has been killed or imprisoned: such are the concrete tasks to which the people is called during the struggle for freedom.

In the colonial world, the emotional sensitivity of the native is kept on the surface of his skin like an open sore which flinches from the caustic agent; and the psyche shrinks back, obliterates itself and finds outlet in muscular demonstrations which have caused certain very wise men to say that the native is a hysterical type. This sensitive emotionalism, watched by invisible keepers who are however in unbroken contact with the core of the personality, will find its fulfillment through eroticism in the driving forces behind the crisis's dissolution.

On another level we see the native's emotional sensibility exhausting itself in dances which are more or less ecstatic. This is why any study of the colonial world should take into consideration the phenomena of the dance and of possession. The native's relaxation takes precisely the form of a muscular orgy in which the most acute aggressivity and the most impelling violence are canalized, transformed, and conjured away. The circle of the dance is a permissive circle: it protects and permits. At certain times on certain days, men and women come together at a given place, and there, under the solemn eye of the tribe, fling themselves into a seemingly unorganized pantomime, which is in reality extremely systematic, in which by various means – shakes of the head, bending of the spinal column, throwing of the whole body backward – may be deciphered as in an open book the huge effort of a community to exorcise itself, to liberate itself, to explain itself. There are no limits – inside the circle. The hillock up which you have toiled as if to be nearer to the moon; the river bank down which you slip as if to show the connection between the dance and ablutions, cleansing and purification – these are sacred places. There are no limits – for in reality your purpose in coming together is to allow the accumulated libido, the hampered aggressivity, to dissolve as in a volcanic eruption. Symbolical killings, fantastic rides, imaginary mass murders – all must be brought out. The evil humors are undammed, and flow away with a din as of molten lava.

One step further and you are completely possessed. In fact, these are actually organized séances of possession and exorcism; they include vampirism, possession by djinns, by zombies, and by Legba, the famous god of the voodoo. This disintegrating of the personality, this splitting and dissolution, all this fulfills a primordial function in the organism of the colonial world. When they set out, the men and women were impatient, stamping their feet in a state of nervous excitement; when they return, peace has been restored to the village; it is once more calm and unmoved.

During the struggle for freedom, a marked alienation from these practices is observed. The native's back is to the wall, the knife is at his throat (or, more precisely, the electrode at his genitals): he will have no more call for his fancies. After centuries of unreality, after having wallowed in the most outlandish phantoms, at long last the native, gun in hand, stands face to face with the only forces which contend for his life – the forces of colonialism. And the youth of a colonized country, growing up in an atmosphere of shot and fire, may well make a mock of, and does not hesitate to pour scorn upon the zombies of his ancestors, the horses with two heads, the dead who rise again, and the djinns who rush into your body while you yawn. The native discovers reality and transforms it into the pattern of his customs, into the practice of violence and into his plan for freedom. . . . A colonized people is not alone. In spite of all that colonialism can do, its frontiers remain open to new ideas and echoes from the world outside. It discovers that violence is in the atmosphere, that it here and there bursts out, and here and there sweeps away the colonial regime – that same violence which fulfills for the native a role that is not simply informatory, but also operative. The great victory of the Vietnamese people at Dien Bien Phu is no longer, strictly speaking, a Vietnamese victory. Since July, 1954, the question which the colonized peoples have asked themselves has been, "What must be done to bring about another Dien Bien Phu? How can we manage it?" Not a single colonized individual could ever again doubt the possibility of a Dien Bien Phu; the only problem was how best to use the forces at their disposal, how to organize them, and when to bring them into action. This encompassing violence does not work upon the colonized people only; it modifies the attitude of the colonialists who become aware of manifold Dien Bien Phus. This is why a veritable panic takes hold of the colonialist governments in turn. Their purpose is to capture the vanguard, to turn the movement of liberation toward the right, and to disarm the people: quick, quick, let's decolonize. Decolonize the Congo before it turns into another Algeria. Vote the constitutional framework for all Africa, create the French *Communauté*, renovate that same *Communauté*, but for God's sake let's decolonize quick. . . . And they decolonize at such a rate that they impose independence on Houphouët-Boigny. To the strategy of Dien Bien Phu, defined by the colonized peoples, the colonialist replies by the strategy of encirclement – based on the respect of the sovereignty of states.

But let us return to that atmosphere of violence, that violence which is just under the skin. We have seen that in its process toward maturity many leads are attached to it, to control it and show it the way out. Yet in spite of the metamorphoses which the colonial regime imposes upon it in the way of tribal or regional quarrels, that violence makes its way forward, and the native identifies his enemy and recognizes all his misfortunes, throwing all the exacerbated might of his hate and anger into this new channel. But how do we pass from the atmosphere of violence to violence in action? What makes the lid blow off? There is first of all the fact that this development does not leave the settler's blissful existence intact. The settler who "understands" the natives is made aware by several straws in the wind showing that something is afoot. "Good" natives become scarce; silence falls when the oppressor approaches; sometimes looks are black, and attitudes and remarks openly aggressive. The nationalist parties are astir, they hold a great many meetings, the police are increased and reinforcements of soldiers are brought in. The settlers, above all the farmers isolated on their land, are the first to become alarmed. They call for energetic measures.

The authorities do in fact take some spectacular measures. They arrest one or two leaders, they organize military parades and maneuvers, and air force displays. But the demonstrations and warlike exercises, the smell of gunpowder which now fills the atmosphere, these things do not make the people draw back. Those bayonets and cannonades only serve to reinforce their aggressiveness. The atmosphere becomes dramatic, and everyone wishes to show that he is ready for anything. And it is in these circumstances that the guns go off by themselves, for nerves are jangled, fear reigns and everyone is trigger-happy. A single commonplace incident is enough to start the machine-gunning: Sétif in Algeria, the Central Quarries in Morocco, Moramanga in Madagascar.

The repressions, far from calling a halt to the forward rush of national consciousness, urge it on. Mass slaughter in the colonies at a certain stage of the embryonic development of consciousness increases that consciousness, for the hecatombs are an indication that between oppressors and oppressed everything can be solved by force. It must be remarked here that the political parties have not called for armed insurrection, and have made no preparations for such an insurrection. All these repressive measures, all those actions which are a result of fear are not within the leaders' intentions: they are overtaken by events. At this moment, then, colonialism may decide to arrest the nationalist leaders. But today the governments of colonized countries know very well that it is extremely dangerous to deprive the masses of their leaders; for then the people, unbridled, fling themselves into *jacqueries*, mutinies, and "brutish murders." The masses give free rein to their "bloodthirsty instincts" and force colonialism to free their leaders, to whom falls the difficult task of bringing them back to order. The colonized people, who have spontaneously brought their violence to the colossal task of destroying the colonial system, will very soon find themselves with the barren, inert slogan "Release X or Y."[2] Then colonialism will release these men, and hold discussions with them. The time for dancing in the streets has come.

In certain circumstances, the party political machine may remain intact. But as a result of the colonialist repression and of the spontaneous reaction of the people the parties find themselves outdistanced by their militants. The violence of the masses is vigorously pitted against the military forces of the occupying power, and the situation deteriorates and comes to a head. Those leaders who are free remain, therefore, on the touchline. They have suddenly become useless, with their bureaucracy and their reasonable demands; yet we see them, far removed from events, attempting the crowning imposture – that of "speaking in the name of the silenced nation." As a general rule, colonialism welcomes this godsend with open arms, transforms these "blind mouths" into spokesmen, and in two minutes endows them with independence, on condition that they restore order.

So we see that all parties are aware of the power of such violence and that the question is not always to reply to it by a greater violence, but rather to see how to relax the tension.

What is the real nature of this violence? We have seen that it is the intuition of the colonized masses that their liberation must, and can only, be achieved by force . . .

The violence of the colonial regime and the counter-violence of the native balance each other and respond to each other in an extraordinary reciprocal homogeneity. This reign of violence will be the more terrible in proportion to the size of the implantation from the mother country. The development of violence among the colonized people will be proportionate to the violence exercised by the threatened colonial regime. In the first phase of this insurrectional period, the home governments are the slaves of the settlers, and these settlers seek to intimidate the natives and their home governments at one and the same time. They use the same methods against both of them. The assassination of the Mayor of Evian, in its method and motivation, is identifiable with the assassination of Ali Boumendjel. For the settlers, the alternative is not between *Algérie algérienne* and *Algérie française* but between an independent Algeria and a colonial Algeria, and anything else is mere talk or attempts at treason. The settler's logic is implacable and one is only staggered by the counter-logic visible in the behavior of the native insofar as one has not clearly understood beforehand the mechanisms of the settler's ideas. From the moment that the native has chosen the methods of counter-violence, police reprisals automatically call forth reprisals on the side of the nationalists. However, the results are not equivalent, for machine-gunning from airplanes and bombardments from the fleet go far beyond in horror and magnitude any answer the natives can make. This recurring terror de-mystifies once and for all the most estranged members of the colonized race. They find out on the spot that all the piles of speeches on the equality of human beings do not hide the commonplace fact that the seven Frenchmen killed or wounded at the Col de Sakamody kindles the indignation of all civilized consciences, whereas the sack of the douars of Guergour and of the dechras of Djerah and the massacre of whole populations – which had merely called forth the Sakamody ambush as a reprisal – all this is of not the slightest importance. Terror, counter-terror, violence, counter-violence: that is what observers bitterly record when they describe the circle of hate, which is so tenacious and so evident in Algeria. . . .

The mobilization of the masses, when it arises out of the war of liberation, introduces into each man's consciousness the ideas of a common cause, of a national destiny, and of a collective history. In the same way the second phase, that of the building-up of the nation, is helped on by the existence of this cement which has been mixed with blood and anger. Thus we come to a fuller appreciation of the originality of the words used in these underdeveloped countries. During the colonial period the people are called upon to fight against oppression;

after national liberation, they are called upon to fight against poverty, illiteracy, and underdevelopment. The struggle, they say, goes on. The people realize that life is an unending contest.

We have said that the native's violence unifies the people. By its very structure, colonialism is separatist and regionalist. Colonialism does not simply state the existence of tribes; it also reinforces it and separates them. The colonial system encourages chieftaincies and keeps alive the old Marabout confraternities. Violence is in action all-inclusive inclusive and national. It follows that it is closely involved in the liquidation of regionalism and of tribalism. Thus the national parties show no pity at all toward the caids and the customary chiefs. Their destruction is the preliminary to the unification of the people.

At the level of individuals, violence is a cleansing force. It frees the native from his inferiority complex and from his despair and inaction; it makes him fearless and restores his self-respect. Even if the armed struggle has been symbolic and the nation is demobilized through a rapid movement of decolonization, the people have the time to see that the liberation has been the business of each and all and that the leader has no special merit. From thence comes that type of aggressive reticence with regard to the machinery of protocol which young governments quickly show. When the people have taken violent part in the national liberation they will allow no one to set themselves up as "liberators." They show themselves to be jealous of the results of their action and take good care not to place their future, their destiny, or the fate of their country in the hands of a living god. Yesterday they were completely irresponsible; today they mean to understand everything and make all decisions. Illuminated by violence, the consciousness of the people rebels against any pacification. From now on the demagogues, the opportunists, and the magicians have a difficult task. The action which has thrown them into a hand-to-hand struggle confers upon the masses a voracious taste for the concrete. The attempt at mystification becomes, in the long run, practically impossible.

Notes

1 Highly-trained soldiers who are completely dedicated to the Moslem cause. (Trans.)

2 It may happen that the arrested leader is in fact the authentic mouthpiece of the colonized masses. In this case colonialism will make use of his period of detention to try to launch new leaders.

29

Colonialism and the Colonized: Violence and Counter-violence

Tsenay Serequeberhan

Tribes living exclusively on hunting or fishing are beyond the boundary line from which real [historical] development begins.

> Karl Marx, from *Introduction to a Critique of Political Economy*, 1857–8

I say, listen to my words and mark them. We have fought for a year. I wish to rule my country and protect my religion. We have both suffered considerably in battle with one another. I have no forts, no houses. I have no cultivated fields, no silver or gold for you to take. If the country was cultivated or contained houses or property, it would be worth your while to fight. The country is all jungle, and that is no use to you. If you want wood and stone you can get them in plenty. There are also ant-heaps. The sun is very hot. All you can get from me is war, nothing else.

> Sayyid Mohamed Abdille Hassen, Somali anti-colonialist leader 1899–1920, from an "Open Letter to the English People"

Given the violence of Africa's encounter with Europe through which the "dark" continent was introduced into the modern world, the question of violence should have a central importance for the discourse of contemporary African philosophy. And yet, to date, African philosophers have not properly dealt with or even engaged the question. To my knowledge the only texts in Anglophone

From Tsenay Serequeberhan, *The Hermeneutics of African Philosophy* (1994), by kind permission of Routledge, New York and London.

Africa that directly address this issue are: a short paper by Kwasi Wiredu titled, "The Question of Violence in Contemporary African Political Thought" (1986); and a slender booklet by Henry Odera Oruka titled, *Punishment and Terrorism in Africa* (1976).[1] Both of these texts are rather formalistic tracts that do not engage, let alone properly explore, the question of violence in the context of the historicity out of which it arises.

Wiredu's paper is a concise tactical discussion of the utility and value of violence, as contrasted to nonviolent methods, in the context of the anticolonial struggle. But does the question of violence historically pose itself in this way? Oruka's booklet, on the other hand, is an analytic discussion of crime and punishment that advocates leniency and a curative pedagogical approach to villainy. But can the question of punishment be queried without looking at the grounds – political and historical – for the legitimacy of the punishing authority?

In both cases the historicity out of which the question of violence arises in contemporary Africa is silently ignored. This chapter is an attempt to redress this deficiency. Based on Frantz Fanon's seminal reflections on violence, it hopes to engage the question in and out of the historicity of Africa's encounter with Europe.[2] Why so? Precisely because this encounter was, in its very nature inherently violent and had, for the actuality of contemporary Africa, a transfiguring and defining impact.

The importance of this historically attentive approach lies in the fact that it takes its point of departure from a grounding and necessary fact of our contemporary African historicity. This concrete situatedness of our present is the origin of its reflective engagement. In other words, it starts from and grounds itself on the violent inception of its own present enigmatic condition.

In view of the above this chapter will be composed of three sections. The first section will place the question of violence within the historicity of Africa's encounter of Europe. The second section will explore this encounter by utilizing, for this purpose, Fanon's originative discussion of violence in the first section of *The Wretched of the Earth*. The third section will conclude by suggesting the prospect of negating the enduring violence of colonialism and neocolonialism in the consolidation of the concrete possibilities of the African liberation struggle.

I

Aimé Césaire opens his *Discourse on Colonialism* (1955) by noting that interior to the essential constitution of European modernity is the relation with its Other – the colonized non-European world. Césaire observes that

> Europe is unable to justify itself either before the bar of "reason" or before the bar of "conscience"; and that, increasingly it takes refuge in a hypocrisy which is all the more odious because it is less and less likely to deceive.[3]

In referring to "reason" and "conscience" Césaire indicates that he is engaged in an internal and immanent critique. Europe is found wanting on its own terms, by the very criteria it uses to externally evaluate and condemn the humanity of the non-European as uncivilized and primitive.

For Césaire, colonialism and the hypocrisy that is needed to justify it are predicated on "internal reasons" that impel European modernity to "extend to a world scale the competition of its antagonistic economies."[4] In pointing to internal economic reasons, Césaire makes clear that he presupposes a classical Marxist-Leninist analysis of imperialism and colonialism. As is well known, a year later, in conjunction with his resignation from the French Communist Party, he gives us, in addition to the above, a much more substantial and non-Eurocentric reading of the relationship of the colonized to Europe.

In his *Letter to Maurice Thorez* (1956) he asserts, against the universalizing and hegemonic politics of the European Left, that the fundamental concern of the colonized is to retake the initiative of history: to again become historical Being. It is to *negate the negation* of its lived historicalness and overcome the violence of merely being an object in the historicity of European existence that the colonized fights.

Thus, it is the inter-implicative dialectic of this primordial violence, and the counter-violence it evokes, that we need to concretely grasp. For this is the lived historicity out of which the actuality of violence presents itself in the non-European world and thus in contemporary Africa. As Edward Said insightfully observes:

> Imperialism was the theory, colonialism the practice of changing the uselessly unoccupied territories of the world into useful new versions of the European metropolitan society. Everything in those territories that suggested [difference] waste, disorder, uncounted resources, was to be converted into productivity. . . . You get rid of most of the offending human and animal blight . . . you confine the rest to reservations, compounds, native homelands, where you can count, tax, use them profitably, and you build a new society on the vacated space. Thus was Europe reconstituted abroad its "multiplication in space" successfully projected and managed. The result was a widely varied group of little Europes throughout Asia, Africa, and the Americas, each reflecting the circumstances, the specific instrumentalities of the parent culture, its pioneers, its vanguard settlers. All of them were similar in one other major respect – despite the differences, which were considerable – and that was that their life was carried on with an air of *normality*.[5]

The first act of freedom that the colonized engages in is the attempt to *violently* disrupt the "normality" which European colonial society presupposes. The tranquil existence of the colonizer is grounded on the chaotic, abnormal, and subhuman existence of the colonized. The "new societies" that replicate Europe in the non-European world are built on "vacated space" which hitherto was the uncontested *terra firma* of different and differing peoples and histories.

The dawn and normalcy of colonial society – i.e.,

the birth and establishment of the modern Europe-anized world, as Karl Marx approvingly points out in the first few pages of the *Communist Manifesto* – is grounded on the negation of the cultural difference and specificity that constitutes the historicity and thus humanity of the non-European world.[6] Euro-pean modernity establishes itself globally by vio-lently negating indigenous cultures. This violence in replication, furthermore, accentuates the regressive and despotic/aristocratic aspects internal to the histories of the colonizing European societies.

In imposing itself Europe cannot keep faith with the central tenets of its own bourgeois democratic heritage. In fact, paradoxically, the colonies are the negation of this heritage in the very act of "dupli-cating" it. European democracy in the colonies is unabashed fascism.[7] Apartheid South Africa, Brit-ish Kenya, and French Algeria are paradigmatic examples of this contradiction. In order to verify this observation, all one needs to do is compare the life of the colonized African under European democracies and avowed fascist dictatorships. French Algeria and the Portuguese colonies, British Kenya and Italian Eritrea, despite their many differences and in differing ways, are identical in their respec-tive disparagement of the indigenous historicity.

In all of this, it has to be noted that Europe – fascist or democratic – undertook the domination of the world and Africa not in the explicit and cynical recognition of its economic-colonialist interest, but in the delusion that it was spreading civilization and beneficially Christianizing the globe. For the colonialist consciousness, colonialism is an altruis-tic and generous self-sacrificing project. At least, as Albert Memmi tells us, this is the image the colonialist wants to believe and wants others to believe about him.[8]

In fact, as Mudimbe has correctly pointed out, the colonizing venture of Europe in Africa has always been and cannot but be a twofold mission of spiritual and earthly dominion disguised, even to itself, as an evangelic and civilizing mission to the world.[9] In other words:

> Missionary speech is always predetermined, preregulated, let us say *colonized*. . . . This is God's desire for the conversion of the world. . . . This means, at least, that the missionary does not enter into dialogue with the pagans . . . but must impose the law of God that he incarnates. . . . God is rightly entitled to the use of all possible means, even violence, to achieve his objectives.[10]

Conveniently, European colonial consciousness saw itself in the image of fulfilling both the demands of God and the requirements of civilized human existence. In colonizing, the missionary – or gener-ally speaking the Christian European – is not violating or transgressing on non-European cul-tures. Rather, he is realizing divine providence, the mission bestowed on the twelve apostles by Christ: to spread the faith to the four corners of the globe.

Thus, colonial consciousness, in the very act of conquest is itself spellbound by its own spiritual and earthly myths. In Rudyard Kipling's poignant words:

> Take up the white Man's burden –
> Send forth the best ye breed –
> Go bind your sons to exile
> To serve your captives' need;
> To wait in heavy harness
> On fluttered folk and wild –
> Your new-caught, sullen peoples,
> Half devil and half child.[11]

As Mudimbe's account indicates, and as the above shows, the European takes himself as the norm of human existence *per se* and imposes his own particularity as universal on the non-European who is viewed as "half devil and half child." Notice the clear and clean concurrence of God's work and the exigencies of European expansion. Given this "coincidence," European colonial consciousness, in contrast to the rest of us, cannot but see itself as the vicar of the true revealed faith. The epistemic untenability of this blind belief is the metaphysical ground on which the colonialist project, both in its sacred and secular manifestations, rests. Indeed, it goes without saying, the "devil" has to be exorcized and the "child" has to mature![12]

Elaborating a secular variant of the above from within the engaged discourse of the "materialist conception of history," Karl Marx wrote in 1853:

> England, it is true, in causing a social revolution in Hindustan, was actuated only by the vilest interests, and was stupid in her manner of enforcing them. But that is not the question. The question is, can mankind [in the singular] fulfill its *destiny* [in the singular] without a fundamental revolution in the social state of Asia? If not, whatever may have been the *crimes* of England she was the *unconscious tool of history* in bringing about that revolution. Then, whatever bit-

terness the spectacle of the crumbling of an ancient world may have for our personal feelings, we have the right, *in point of history*, to exclaim with Goethe:

> Should this torture then torment us
> Since it brings us greater pleasure?
> Were not through the rule of Timur
> Souls devoured without measure?[13]

What has to be noted in these lines – which applies not only to India but to the rest of the non-European world as a whole – is that Marx is not blind to the hypocrisy and brutality of British or European rule. In fact he recognizes in detail, in his articles on India, as well as in chapters 26 and 31 of *Capital*, vol. 1, the violence upon which European expansion is grounded. In point of "history," however, and in terms of the singular "destiny" of "mankind," the destructive violence of European conquest and expansion are exonerated. This is so precisely because the violence of colonial conquest makes possible a "fundamental revolution in the social state" of the non-European world, i.e., it brings about the forced but necessary and propitious globalization of Europe.[14]

In like manner, reflecting on the socio-economic dialectic internal to European modernity, G. W. F. Hegel wrote in 1821:

> This inner dialectic of civil society [i.e., of European modernity] thus drives it – or at any rate a specific civil society – to push beyond its own limits and seek markets, and so its *necessary* means of subsistence, in other lands which are either deficient in the goods it has overproduced, or else generally backward in industry.[15]

Colonialist expansion is presented by Hegel as the ideal solution to the internal and inherent (i.e., "necessary") contradictions of European modernity. Thus, territories which do not suffer from the peculiarly modern European problem of "overproduction" are labeled "generally backward in industry" and thereby become the legitimate prey of colonialist conquest. Expansion and "systematic colonization"[16] directed by the state are, in this scenario, the process by which culture and civilization are spread. What is silently left out of this picture is the fact that this globalization of European civilization presupposes and is grounded on the systemic destruction of non-European civilizations.

Like Marx – who is himself, in this respect, Hegel's faithful disciple – but focused on the self-unfolding of *Weltgeist* (world-spirit), Hegel also thinks of humanity and history (in the singular) as the phenomenal manifestation of *Geist* (spirit), and European culture and historicity as the proper and highest illustration of this world-historical process.[17] For Kipling, Marx, and Hegel, in keeping with the critical self-consciousness and self-conception of European modernity, colonialism is seen as a required and necessary step in the unfolding of world history.[18] In this regard the opinions of David Hume and Immanuel Kant, the pivotal precursors of nineteenth-century European thought, are of cardinal importance. For as Hume puts it:

> I am apt to suspect the negroes, and in general all the other species of men (for there are four or five different kinds) to be naturally inferior to whites. There never was a civilized nation of any complexion than white.

In categorical agreement with the above, Kant asserts that

> so fundamental is the difference between the two races of men, and it appears to be as great in regard to mental capacities as in color.[19]

In view of the above, as Father Placide Temples puts it, "our civilizing mission alone can justify our occupation of the lands of uncivilized peoples."[20] Notice the correlation between "occupation" – i.e., unmitigated violence – and Europe's "civilizing mission." Colonial violence sees itself as character-forming chastisement and in this unequivocally adheres to Aristotle's self-serving dictum that "slaves stand even more in need of admonition than children."[21]

Just as for the Greeks the barbarian was the legitimate object of enslavement,[22] in like manner European modernity sees itself as the *Hellas* of the modern age. Colonialist violence justifies itself in its own eyes by its "progressive," "civilizing," and "christianizing" "mission" to the world. As Alan Ryan correctly points out:

> Greek and Roman philosophers thought history was cyclical and repetitive just like any other natural process. . . . The Judeo-Christian tradition was anti-classical in thinking that history had a definite dramatic

shape, with a beginning, a middle, and a conclusion. It was the Christian image of history as a three-act play – Fall, Suffering, Redemption – that found its way into Kant's philosophy of history, into Hegel's and eventually into Marx's supposedly empirical and sociological "materialist conception of history."[23]

Non-European cultures are saved from their "fallen" condition of heathenism through the "suffering" of colonialism and can, through this suffering, look forward to a distant future of possible "redemption." In both its secular and religious manifestations, this view does nothing more than universalize the singular historico-cultural particularity of Europe in the name of a metaphysical – earthly or divine – *telos*.

Thus, in the very act of violent conquest, paradoxically, Europe sees itself as serving its "captive's need." Or, not so enigmatically, as Said puts it:

> Images of blacks, of women, of primitives that occur in the nineteenth century are . . . part of the production of these beings as inferior, and hence as dominated [and justifiably so] by the wielders of the . . . discourse about blacks, women, primitives.[24]

This then is the duplicity that Césaire accuses Europe of. For the image of the "primitive" is interior and necessary to Europe's own gratuitous self-conception. This same "image" is, however, also used to justify the violent destruction of the specific humanity of aboriginal peoples which it supposedly describes.

This violence, furthermore – the violence of the "civilizing mission" – is not a violence of mere destruction. Rather, as Césaire reminds us, it is a duplicitous violence that ranks human societies in subordination. Now, beyond this strange deceit, to the non-European, the expansion of Europe is experienced as the unabashed dawn of systematic and organized global violence. This is a violence that closes off the different and differing cultural and historical totalities within which the non-European exists. The "little Europes" throughout Asia, Africa, and the Americas arose out of this primordial colonizing violence.[25]

The un-freedom in which Africa is presently entangled is thus directly rooted in European dominance. This is what Césaire refers to as the

"peculiarity of our history, laced with terrible misfortunes which belong to no other history."[26] We need now to ask: How was this violent dawn experienced by the colonized?

In order to properly grasp the sense of this question let us look at two well-known texts of African imaginative production; Chinua Achebe's *Things Fall Apart* (1959) and Cheikh Hamidou Kane's *Ambiguous Adventure* (1962). These texts concisely articulate – from within Anglophone and Francophone Africa, respectively – the existential anguish suffered by those of us who, as part of our cultural and historical heritage, have a colonized past. Beyond the colonizer's self-serving and delusory self-perception, we need now to look at the colonized.

As Achebe puts it, with the advent of European colonialism "things fell apart." The African's mode of life, his indigenous habitat of human existence, was displaced by the violence of the "civilizing mission." Things African were devalued and the African was reduced to slavery. In the fictional recreation of the demise of the Igbo at the hands of the British, Achebe concisely depicts the truth of this tragic moment of our modern African historicity.

Things Fall Apart ends with the suicide of Okonkwo the warrior chief and main character of the novel, and the reduction of the wise Obierika – the respected and prudent elder in this circumstance – to the status of an informant explaining to the Colonial District Commissioner the abominable character of his worthy friend's appalling end.

> 'That man [Okonkwo] was one of the greatest men in Umuofia. You drove him to kill himself; and now he will be buried like a dog. . . .' He could not say any more. His voice trembled and choked his words.[27]

The wise Obierika explains what, up to that point, had been clear and in need of no explanation or interpretation. He is both the witness and incarnation of the estrangement in African existence inaugurated by colonial conquest. From within an Africa overwhelmed by Europe he laments, and by his political impotence manifests, the agonized primordial moment of Africa's mortifying enslavement.

Standing at the feet of Okonkwo's dangling cadaver, which represents defeated but unconquered Africa, the District Commissioner contemplates the writing of a book.

The story of this man who had killed a messenger and hanged himself would make interesting reading. One could almost write a whole chapter on him. Perhaps not a whole chapter but a reasonable paragraph. . . . There was so much else to include, and one must be firm in cutting out details. He had already chosen the title of the book, after much thought: *The Pacification of the Primitive Tribes of the Lower Niger.*[28]

The unbending Okonkwo is the "jungle savage,"[29] to borrow Fanon's sarcastic phrase; he exists beyond the pale of "humanity" proper, i.e., the historicity of European conquest. He is the one who refuses the designation "the Primitive Tribes of the Lower Niger," a colonialist designation which presupposes the negation, as primitive, of the indigenous historicity. Or, in Hegelian terms, Okonkwo symbolizes the rejection of the dialectic of colonial enslavement. In being the concrete personification of its own freedom, this consciousness cannot even conceive of the possibility of being the bondsman in Hegel's dialectic of "lordship and bondage." It chooses demise over bondage.

Okonkwo is the consciousness that refuses to barter, or even contemplate the possibility of bartering, its concrete ethical life – i.e., its freedom – for biological existence.[30] Obierika, obversely, is the spiritual forefather of the *assimilado* and the *évolué* – the enslaved.[31] His wisdom is a prudent knowledge, a skill at bartering self-preservation and the default of freedom. On the other hand, in Obierika's remorse for proud Okonkwo's tragic end, we see the demised remains of self-standing Africa inaugurating the moment of reflective thought out of colonial estrangement in the historicity of our present.[32]

In *Ambiguous Adventure*, Kane recounts the story of Samba Diallo, a young Diallobe boy, from French Senegal, who finds himself in a spiritual-cultural *imbroglio* between his traditional Islamic ambience and the imposed materialistic world of the West, which he has partially internalized. The spiritual–cultural crisis that Samba feels and fails to resolve is the conflict around which the narrative is structured. Utilizing this quandary as a metaphor, Kane engages the lived and systemic enigma of colonized existence.

Again the story ends with the death of the central character. The conclusion strongly suggests that the failure to reconcile the imposed modernity of Europe with the enduring traditions of Africa –

which kills Samba – will also, ultimately, be the demise of the continent. In all this, the central moment is the moment of conquest and violence. Let us read Kane.

Strange dawn! The morning of the Occident in black Africa was spangled with smiles, with cannon shots, with shining glass beads. Those who had no history were encountering those who carried the world on their shoulders. It was a morning of accouchement: the known world was enriching itself by a birth that took place in mire and blood.

From shock, the one side made no resistance. They were a people without a past, therefore without memory. The men who were landing on their shores were white, and mad. Nothing like them had ever been known. The deed was accomplished before the people were even conscious of what had happened.

Some among the Africans, such as the Diallobe, brandished their shields, pointed their lances, and aimed their guns. They were allowed to come close, then the cannons were fired. The vanquished did not understand. . . .

Others wanted to parley. They were given a choice: friendship or war. Very sensibly, they chose friendship. They had no experience at all.

The result was the same. . . . Those who had shown fight and those who had surrendered . . . they all found themselves . . . checked by census, divided up, classified, labeled, conscripted, administrated.

For the newcomers did not know only how to fight. They were strange people. . . . Where they had brought disorder, they established a new order. They destroyed and they constructed.

Thus, behind the gunboats [stood] . . . the new school.[33]

Behind the "gunboats" stands the "new school": the institutional/cultural weapon which will permanently scar and violate the indigenous culture. The sarcasm of Kane's prose illustrates well the sense of terror and bewilderment with which European modernity dawned on Africa.

This "Strange dawn! The morning of the Occident in black Africa" is the primeval violence on which is grounded the quotidian normalcy of colonialism and neocolonialism, of being "checked by census, divided up, classified, labeled, conscripted, administrated." Or as Said puts it:

> You get rid of most of the offending human and animal blight . . . confine the rest to reservations . . . where you can count, tax, use them profitably, and you build a new society on the vacated space.[34]

Europe experienced the dawn of modernity as the age of Enlightenment. In the words of Immanuel Kant, this was the age in which "man's release from his self-incurred tutelage"[35] was to be actualized. A century later Africa experienced its entry into this modern *European* world, not as liberation or enlightenment, but as the painful process of colonial subjugation. This is how Fanon puts it:

> Conquest, it is affirmed, creates historic links. The new time inaugurated by the conquest, which is a colonialist time because occupied by colonialist values, because deriving its *raison d'être* from the negation of the national time, will be endowed with an absolute coefficient. The history of the conquest, the historic development of the colonization and of the national spoliation will be substituted for the real time of the exploited. . . . And what is affirmed by the colonized at the time of the struggle for national liberation as the will to break with exploitation and contempt will be rejected by the colonialist power as a symbol of barbarism and of regression.
>
> The colonialist, by a process of thinking which is after all fairly commonplace, reaches the point of no longer being able to imagine a time occurring without him. His irruption into the history of the colonized people is deified, transformed into absolute necessity. Now a "historic look at history" requires, on the contrary, that the French colonialist retire, for it has become historically necessary for the national time in Algeria to exist.[36]

I have quoted extensively from Fanon and earlier from Kane precisely because they articulate concisely the moments of primordial conflict of the two contending forces in the colonial encounter. Kane tells us that where the colonizers "had brought disorder, they established a new order." They end

one order of time and inaugurate a new colonial order of time.

Using the example of the French in Algeria, Fanon articulates the obverse of the colonial conquest. Just as the "irruption" of colonialism "into the history of the colonized" interrupts the historicity of the indigenous culture, in like manner the reclaiming of the "national time" is possible only on the demise of colonial temporality. The clash is thus a conflict of contending and radically noncommensurable cultural-historical totalities. As Patrick Taylor correctly points out, for Fanon, the demise or destruction of "the colonizer means the beginning of the possibility of a new history for the colonized."[37] The actualization of this possibility is the reclaiming of human existence for both the former colonizer and the colonized. In Hegelian terms, this is the moment of recognition and freedom.

Let us now with Fanon look in greater detail at the nature and phenomenal character of this violent confrontation and its possible resolution. In so doing we will not be using "Fanon as a global theorist *in vacuo*" as Henry Louis Gates, Jr., accuses Edward Said of doing.[38] Rather, our deployment of this violent text, on violence, stems from the actuality and the ferocity of conflict in colonized and neocolonized Africa. This is the concretely situated – historically and politically originative – context out of which Fanon's reflections on violence were first produced.

II

In the opening pages of his seminal work, *The Wretched of the Earth*, Fanon observes that:

> The colonial world is a world cut in two. The dividing line, the frontiers are shown by barracks and police stations. In the colonies it is the policeman and the soldier who are the official, instituted go-between, the spokesmen of the settler and his rule of oppression.[39]

Fanon is describing the colonial situation as it existed and still exists in Africa. In the colonies things are clear-cut, especially in avowedly colonial times, but also in their neocolonial prolongations. The difference is not only one of pigmentation but also of indigenized colonialist methods. Neocolonialism replicates colonial violence – by proxy – between Westernized and non-Westernized natives. Or, as Fanon puts it

> [This] is the antagonism which exists between the native who is excluded from the advantages of colonialism and his counterpart who manages to turn colonial exploitation to his account.[40]

Thus, what is said of the colonial situation *mutatis mutandis* applies with equal force to neocolonial Africa.

On the one hand, you have the colonizer; on the other, the colonized. These two groups – one of human beings in the process of extending and globalizing their cultural and historical actuality, and the other of *thingified*[41] entities frozen in time and degraded beyond belief – exist as an organic whole in subordination. The colonizer and the colonized each constitute the Other for one another and determine themselves in terms of the Other.

In the metropolis, the socio-economic relations of civil society and the hierarchical structure of the state – i.e., society as an organic and differentiated whole – are maintained in place by a variety of intersecting socio-historical institutions. The national educational system, the heritage of a common history, norms, and modes of behavior and moral conduct implicitly accepted by all muffle class conflicts and institute a reality in which the lower classes' antagonism to those in power is channeled through peaceful avenues. Even the militant communist parties of the European working classes are accepted and represent a respectable political position within the confines of European modernity. All these conflicting, and potentially lethal, political perspectives are held in check by the hegemonic power of a common modern European historicity.

As Fanon points out, the "serf is in essence different from the knight but a reference to divine right is necessary to legitimate this statutory difference."[42] Indeed, in Europe social contradictions are mediated. In the medieval age religion served this purpose, and in modern capitalist Europe the liberal abstract discourse of rights and the ideals of "liberty, equality and fraternity," which animated the French Revolution, still fulfill this task. In the colonies, on the other hand, the dialectic of social existence has no middle term, or, to be more precise, the dialectic is mediated by violence. The relation of the colonizer and the colonized is based on brute force.

Colonialism, as Hegel approvingly observes, originates in the violent contradictions of "civil society" and is a desirable way of institutionally externalizing this violence, which is internal and endemic to European modernity.[43] From the inception of the colonial situation – the time of the colonial conquest – the settler and the colonial society in which he exists are established and maintained by force and violence. The colonized is constantly reminded of his place; in this divided world no one can breach the boundaries with impunity. Be it in the presence of the colonialist police, the wealth of the European farms, or the innumerable statues to the heroes of the period of conquest, the colonized is reminded that he is a "native," an outcast in his own land, a conquered person – a *thing* of service in the historicity of the colonizer.

The "native" is maintained – or held down – in his designated inferior position by the tremendous material and intellectual force exerted against him by the settler and the "mother" country. As Fanon observes:

> Their first encounter was marked by violence and their existence together – that is to say the exploitation of the native by the settler – was carried on by dint of a great array of bayonets and cannons. The settler and the native are old acquaintances. In fact . . . it is the settler who has brought the native into existence and who perpetuates his existence.[44]

One has to grasp the force of Fanon's words. The "settler and the native are old acquaintances." The settler maintains and constitutes – brings "into existence" – the "native" as an inferior being. As the embodiment of his own inferiority, and as long as he remains in this position, the native upholds and endures – as if by choice! – the supremacy of the settler. In this mutual relation one is the complement and the ground of the other. The opposite moments of this inter-implicative bond necessarily stand or fall together. Master implies slave and slave implies master.

The colonized is the member of a defeated history. But he also knows that his forefathers – those who confronted the original conquest – fought the aggressor and were defeated not because they lacked courage or wisdom but because they lacked cunning and shrewdness. He knows that his history, the process of his communal becoming, was violently interrupted not because it was impotent, but because it failed – as Cheikh Hamidou Kane tells us – to organize and call forth the requisite violence against the original intruders. The colonized is aware at some level that the socio-human habitat – the *ethos* (i.e., the social-historical space) in which his forefathers lived and acted out their historicity, his peculiar experience of Being or existence – was suppressed, not for lack of wisdom, but because of violence and military strength. In this awareness, the colonized sees the colonizer as a brute with nothing to his merit save his strength. This – the colonizer's strength, his violence – he envies.

The settler and the learned experts from the "mother" country – or the elite of the Westernized native ruling class in a neocolonial context – see things differently. As Fanon points out, they speak of brown, yellow, and black multitudes, or of a backward peasantry in a neocolonial setup. They speak of the colonized or of the subjects of neocolonial exploitation in biological terms and declare them to be the antagonist of history. The native, or the neocolonized peasantry, is said to be inferior and to have no appreciation of values. It is in short, "the negation of values" and of all that humanity claims for itself as human.[45] Thus the settler, or the neocolonial elite, has no regrets or qualms of conscience, for he does violence not to human beings, but to strange entities located between humanity and undifferentiated nature.[46]

For the settler, the "native" – just as for the neocolonial elite, the peasant – is a *thing*, a beast of burden. Just as the flora and fauna of the conquered territory or the neocolonial state, the "native," or the neocolonized peasant, as the case may be, is a more or less useful resource, an object of calculative exploitation. In a neocolonial setup this manifests itself as the defensive and reactive animosity of the elite toward the indigenous peasantry. This rancor, furthermore, is much more pronounced and accentuated to the extent that the neocolonial elite, unlike the former colonizers, has to actively and desperately maintain its difference from the indigenous and indigent folk. This is a case of being more Catholic than the Pope! Thus, the neocolonial elite "does not hesitate to assert that 'they [the peasants] need the thick end of the stick if this country is to get out of the Middle Ages.'"[47] To progress or "get out of the Middle Ages" here means to replicate and perpetuate the technological *Ge-stell* of European dominance.[48]

The settler recognizes in his own person the indispensable agent of history. The "settler makes

history and is conscious of making it."[49] His constant point of reference, furthermore, is European history and it is in terms of this past that he projects a future. Indeed, it is in light of this duplicity that Césaire's critical remarks, with which we opened this chapter, make sense. Césaire, as we noted, charges colonialist Europe with dissimulation precisely because in the name of the universality of values Europe universalizes its own singular particularity. In the colonies, the paradox of this situation manifests itself in the fact that Europe subjugates the native in order to "civilize" and "liberate" or "save" his soul from barbarism. Thus, in the name of democracy, in the non-European world, Europe institutes colonial fascism.

The colonized, on the other hand, knows that he is human and the incarnation of a distinctive civilization. He knows that the values and culture the settler speaks of were established by force and violence. He is aware, and is made aware by the very structure of colonialist society, of:

> The violence with which the supremacy of white values is affirmed and the aggressiveness which has permeated the victory of these values over the ways of life and of thought of the native:[50]

The colonized is not only a defeated person, he is also resentful, since he is forced to accept the illegitimate power of the colonizer. The colonialist is everything, and the native is forced to accept this in silent terror. Thus:

> The immobility to which the native is condemned can only be called in question if the native decides to put an end to the *history of colonization* – the history of the pillage – and to bring into existence the *history of the nation* – the history of decolonization.[51]

This is possible only through the explicit confrontation of the colonizer and the colonized. It is only when the colonized appropriates the violence of the colonizer and puts forth his own concrete counter-violence that he reenters the realm of history and human historical becoming. Out of bitter experience, the colonized learns the truth of the words with which Jean-Jacques Rousseau opens *The Social Contract*: Force has no moral sanction and thus what is taken by violence can, by the same means, legitimately be regained.[52]

It is at this point that the colonized actively

realizes, beyond the inertness of resentment, the viability of his own suppressed indigenous historicity. The very possibility of appropriating a liberating violence has thus a therapeutic effect on the consciousness of the colonized. It is at these moments, as Fanon tells us, that

> We must notice in this *ripening process* the role played by the history of the resistance at the time of the conquest. The great figures of the colonized people are always those who led the national resistance to invasion . . . [they] all spring [at these moments] again to life with peculiar intensity in the period which comes directly before action. This is the proof that the people are getting ready to begin to go forward again, to put an end to the *static period begun by colonization* and to *make history*.[53]

The organic metaphor – "ripening" – that Fanon uses is insightful. Just as the seed or fruit in ripening brings out of itself what it inherently is, in like manner the colonized in resisting makes itself what it inherently is – a community of human beings – by effectively negating its thingification and bringing out of itself the historicity that accentuates its thus far thwarted humanity. It is only in the struggle to contest its subjugation that the colonized concretely reactivates its Being as human. The conflict is between stasis (death) and activity (life).

To exist as a human being is to temporalize, but the colonized as colonized only passively *does* time and subsists in a history of which he is not a participant. As Memmi observes, at times even the citizens of free countries feel helpless in the face of the modern machinery of states and governments. They are like pawns in the hands of the politicians, their elected "civil servants." Yet in principle the citizen is a free member of the body politic. Thus in spite of their apathy and skepticism, the free citizens periodically rise up – for example, May 1968, France – and "upset the politicians' little calculations." On the other hand, the colonized

> Feels neither responsible nor guilty nor skeptical, for he is out of the *game*. He is in no way a subject of history *any more*. Of course, he carries its burden, often more cruelly than others, but always as an object. He has *forgotten* how to participate actively in history and no longer even asks to do so.[54]

So far as he is colonized and remains so, he is nothing more than a *thingified* biological organism with specific life functions. These life functions – eating, breathing, defecating, procreating – are secured at the heavy coast of freedom, namely, human existence. The "native" strictly speaking exists only in the realm of nature. In the realm of history he is a nonperson – his master's zombie.

In order to remember and reenter the realm of human historicity, the colonized has to put his situation as a whole in question. This question, furthermore, assumes the character of violent confrontation precisely because the colonized not only wants to be in the "game" but wants to be the author of the rules as well. In confrontation, the colonized reclaims and asserts the humanity of his existence. This is the particularity of his specific historico–cultural experience of existence/Being. It is in this way that the colonized claims his autonomy and freedom, his Being as history.

As Oliva Blanchette puts it:

> man enters into society [history] as he begins to form his own projects in consort with others or, put another way, society [history] in the concrete is constituted by a community of projects.[55]

But colonialism is precisely the complete negation of the "community of projects" which constitute the historicity of the colonized. The colonized, the "native," is forcefully barred from and does not historicize. Rather he endures as a subordinate *thing* in the historicity of the colonizer. The colonized's Being or humanity – the specific cultural, political, and historical difference that constitutes his existence – begins to unfold only in the act of confrontation. This is so precisely because in this violent engagement he affirms his existence by opening up its concrete possibilities.

In struggle and conflict the colonized passes beyond himself – his thingified status of "native" – and claims the freedom to be the being which opens existence out of itself, through and by its engagement with the world.[56] Conflict and violence are not a choice, they are an existential need negatively arising out of the colonial situation which serves as a prelude to the rehumanization of the colonized. As Fanon points out:

> The settler makes history; his life is an epoch, an Odyssey. He is the absolute beginning: "This land was created by us"; he

is the unceasing cause: "If we leave, all is lost, and the country will go back to the middle ages." Over against him torpid creatures, wasted by fevers, obsessed by ancestral customs, form an almost inorganic background for the innovating dynamism of colonial mercantilism.

The other side of this divide the

coiled, plundered creature which is the native provides fodder for the process as best he can . . . and all the while the native, bent double, more dead than alive, exists interminably in an unchanging dream.[57]

In all this what has to be taken note of is the fact that the violence of the colonized is a reactive violence aimed at the primordial violence incarnated in the colonial situation. It is in a desperate attempt to overcome the delirium of the "unchanging dream" that the colonized is forced to live in the confines of a dehumanized existence.

In this regard, the paradigm *par excellence* of the colonized is the domestic servant. The domestic exists as a "domestic" only to the extent that he does not exist as a human being and is implicated in his own non-existence. As Memmi puts it, the domestic is "his master's respectful shadow."[58] He is the act of executing another's will. He does not have a will of his own. The domestic "acts when he is ordered to, he does not speak of himself, he is never anything but a reflection of his master."[59] The domestic is the embodiment of debasement, "a debasement to which he consents" and in this is implicated in forsaking his own humanity.[60]

The situation of the domestic and the colonized is thus inherently – in its very nature – not open to compromises and half-measures. For what is at stake in this inter-implicative dialectic on the level of ontological description is the humanity of the colonized and of the domesticated nonperson. The being of the master necessarily presupposes the nonbeing of the domestic. The only alternative to the above is the violence of resistance. In this context a "nonviolent" resistance is a contradiction in terms precisely because any self-assertive act of the colonized is bound to violate – hence do violence to – the rule and standard or norm of subjugation and domination on which the colonial relation is grounded.

In Marx's famous words, "violence is the midwife" of social change and historical transforma-

tion. In the colonial context, violence is a great deal more: it is the avenue through which humanity is reclaimed.

Decolonization is the veritable creation of new men [i.e., of a new humanity]. But this creation owes nothing of its legitimacy to any supernatural power; the "thing" which has been colonized becomes man during the same process by which it frees itself.[61]

Through and out of this historical process, which is necessarily violent, the "thing" (i.e., the native) reclaims its own humanity. This is a self-reflexive process from which, if exhaustively consummated, the colonized emerges as human. Borrowing a phrase from Hegel, one can say that decolonization, properly speaking, is "the process of its own becoming . . . and only by being worked out to its [very] end is it actual."[62] Fanon's French properly captures and conveys this self-reflexive Hegelian nuance; "*la 'chose' colonisée deviant homme dans le processus même par lequel elle se libère.*"[63] The process of liberation – *le processus même* – is the avenue through which the concept of humanity is adequated to the lived actuality of the decolonized.

Fanon emphasizes the term "thing" (*chose*) precisely because, just as a domesticated animal, the "native" has lost the sense of life and living. The colonized "native" is a thingified entity, just as the domesticated animal is an agricultural resource – a beast of burden. It is only in the process of violent confrontation that life is reappropriated and the colonized reinstitute their humanity.

In this regard, as Patrick Taylor points out, it should be noted that, "[u]nderneath the roles into which they are forced, the colonized preserve a human identity and temporal being."[64] This is so, however, only to the extent that the silent resignation of the colonized is itself a form of passive resistance to colonial thingification. To be sure, the humanity of the colonized can be concretely reclaimed only in an explicit historico-political confrontation, since the half-measure of resistance as silent resignation is itself prone to the temptation of dissolving and diluting the struggle in the imaginary world of arcane phantasmic myth.[65] Hidden under "the roles" forced on the colonized, one finds the smoldering tension of a subjugated and humiliated existence that needs to explode into open resistance if it is not to implode into an interior world of torpid and mystical self-mortification.

In what has been said thus far we have been

expounding Fanon's views on violence in the colonial and the neocolonial situation. To be sure, all Fanon does is to articulate a prevalent theme of European philosophy in the context of Africa's experience of the modern Europeanized world. In other words: In Thomas Hobbes's conception of society, it is through the possibility of the uncompromising violence of the political state (i.e., the Leviathan) that order and stability are maintained.[66] In Hegel's famous dialectic of "lordship and bondage," it is through labor and in fear of death, the ultimate violence, and "the sovereign master" that the dialectic of "the master" and "the slave" unfolds. In Marx's idea of the class struggle it is through violent class conflict that the new is born out of the dying old society. In Heidegger's conception of the primordial *Polemos*, which is a violent "conflict that prevailed prior to everything divine and human," it is this primeval violence – as in Hesiod's *Theogony* – that "first projects and develops what had hitherto been unheard of, unsaid and unthought."[67]

In differing ways, what is being articulated is a conception of violence which is fundamental to the varied problematics of the above thinkers and thus to the socio-political thinking of European philosophy. In this respect, it could be said that the whole contractarian perspective of modern political philosophy is grounded on a prolonged discourse on how to avert as well as to use violence for socially beneficial ends. Rousseau opens *The Social Contract* with a discussion of how force does not, of itself, have moral sanction. Hobbes, on the other hand, in the *Leviathan*, overcomes civil strife by instituting the state as the ultimate guarantor and embodiment of legitimate violence.

In talking about violence as he does, Fanon's novelty lies in the fact that his problematic is the concrete question of colonialism. Fanon describes the violence of colonial confrontation and in so doing shows us how "what had hitherto been unheard of, unsaid and unthought" – namely, the freedom of the colonized people of Africa – could come to pass. In this, Fanon does nothing more than specify within the colonial context what Heidegger articulates as the *"apolis"*[68] of human existence in the context of ancient Greek history and tragedy. This is the first emergence, the inauguration of a new order or "beginning" which "is the strangest and mightiest."[69] It is the originative violence with which Hesoid begins the *Theogony*. It is the foundational opening or origin that first institutes human existence in society – the *polis* (or community).

In Hegelian terms, Fanon's meditation on violence is an attempt to situate the dialectic of "lordship and bondage" within the colonial context, while being true to the historicity of Africa's encounter of Europe. In the section of *Black Skin, White Masks* (1952), titled "The Negro and Recognition" (section B of chapter 7), Fanon explicitly makes this the object of his deliberations. In fact, as Taylor puts it, "Fanon draws from the Hegelian-Marxist tradition" but in so doing reinterprets this tradition "in terms of the concrete specificity of the colonial situation."[70] Indeed, as Jean-Paul Sartre has astutely observed, in all of this, Fanon "acts as the interpreter of the [violent colonial] situation, that's all."[71]

The above notwithstanding, Hannah Arendt – an erudite scholar of the Occidental tradition – criticizes Fanon for glorifying violence in and for itself. In fact, Fanon is for Arendt one of the few thinkers who "glorified violence for violence's sake."[72] Nothing could be further from the truth. What Fanon does is to accurately depict the situation of conflict in the colonial context. In fact, as Arendt has observed, in the context of inter-European conflicts, the generation which lived under Nazi occupation found its freedom and salvation in "the resistance" – the *organized counter-violence* with which Europe defended itself against the brutality of Hitler's Germany.

In the midst of unsparing conflict, open and hidden, one does not philosophize. Violence understands only the language of violence. In Arendt's sagacious observation, the generation that lived the Nazi occupation found its "treasure" in violent confrontation. But what was this "treasure"?

As they themselves understood it, it seems to have consisted, as it were, of two interconnected parts: they had discovered that he who "joined the resistance, found himself," that he ceased to be "in quest of [himself] without mastery, in naked unsatisfaction," that he no longer suspected himself of "insincerity" of being "a carping, suspicious actor of life," that he could afford "to go naked." In this nakedness, stripped of all masks – of those which society assigns to its members as well as those which the individual fabricates for himself in his psychological reactions against society – they had been visited for the first time in their lives by *an apparition of freedom*, not, to be sure, because they acted against tyranny and things worse than tyranny – this was true for every soldier in the allied armies – but because they had become "*challengers*," had taken the initiative upon themselves and therefore, without knowing or even noticing it, had begun to create that public space between themselves where *freedom could appear*.[73]

It is important to note that the character of Arendt's observation is impeccable. Those who fought the occupation found freedom. In confronting domination, they created and held open the "public space" in which "freedom could appear," not because they fought an odious tyranny, or because "they acted," but because "they took the initiative upon themselves" and in so doing became "challengers." In other words, it is the character of their actions that counts.

In joining the resistance one "found himself" precisely because one renounced passive submission to subjugation and engaged life. Those in the resistance made history by concretely reclaiming themselves, in the act of resisting, as human beings and thus "freedom could appear." Arendt understands all too well the existential import of *organized counter-violence* in the context of oppression and domination. Yet, what she recognizes in the European she fails to see in the non-European. The fact that Arendt does not see this can, at best, be attributed to her lack of sympathy for or understanding of colonized non-European peoples, or at worst, it could be taken as the symptom of a latent Eurocentric double standard at work in her thought.[74]

The colonized non-European, just like the generation of Europeans who lived under Nazi occupation, finds freedom and liberation in the resolved confrontation with the colonial apparatus. The colonized, in so doing, takes the initiative and carves out the "space" in which freedom can appear, thus overcoming colonial thingification. But why is this the case? It is precisely because colonialism – just as the Nazi occupation in respect to non-Aryans – is the complete negation of the historicity of the colonized. The very fact of conquest is taken by the colonizer as a metaphysical proof of the unhistoricity (i.e., the nonhumanness) of the colonized.

Colonialism is the blatant denial of the humanity of the colonized which serves as its own proof. It is the affirmation that the colonized have no history and are introduced into the human community by European conquest.[75] It is the violent claim that the colonized stand on the other side of the *difference* that constitutes humanity as human. Only by unleashing a self-redeeming counterclaim – and given the reality of colonialism and neocolonialism this can only be a counter-violence – can the colonized establish categorically to himself and to the colonizer the fact of his humanity.[76] As Fanon astutely points out in *A Dying Colonialism*:

> Before the rebellion there was the life, the movement, the existence of the settler, and on the other side the continued agony of the colonized. Since 1954 [the inception of the Algerian Revolution], the European has discovered that another life parallel to his own has *begun to stir*, and that is Algerian society.[77]

In this respect it has to be emphasized that the colonized does not choose violence. Violence is not a choice. It is the condition of existence imposed on the colonized by the colonizer, which enforces the colonized's status of being a "native," a *thing*, a historical being forcefully barred from history. In other words, the direct confrontation between the colonizer and the colonized is not the beginning of violence in the colonial situation. The "continued agony of the colonized" is in fact the historically grounding violence of colonialism.

In view of the above, any attempt to avert the violent conflict between the antagonists of colonial society – the moment the colonized begin to "stir" – is suspect, on the political level, for it is concretely implicated in the defense of colonialism. The feared "blood bath" will not commence with the awakening of the colonized. This hemorrhage is of long standing. This profuse loss of vitality, on the part of the colonized, is as old as the colonial settlement itself. This is what Albert Camus, an Algerian-born French citizen, fails to understand in all of his comments on the Algerian resistance in *Resistance, Rebellion and Death* (1960).[78] In like manner, all those who talk about violence in South Africa should ask themselves which violence they mean: that of the colonizer or of the colonized?

The counter-violence of the colonized is a *de-thingifying*, life-enhancing project of human liberation. The settler, a European migrant, originates in the systematic violence of colonization and expansion. The colony and the settler are the exteriorization of the dialectic of violence (i.e., poverty) internal to European modernity. As Memmi tells us, writing in 1957: "Today, the economic motives of colonial undertakings are revealed by every historian of colonialism."[79] The settler, in order to avoid the violence of poverty in Europe, where he is the victim of the socio-economic dialectic of modern European society, migrates to a foreign land and by force and violence makes others victims. The sheer egoism and inhumanity of this position is astounding. The more so because, as we noted earlier, the colonizer is duped by his own myths to such a point that he sees himself as the benefactor of those he victimizes.

In observing the settler's inhuman conduct and demeanor, the colonized learns that he can recover his freedom only by unleashing a counter-violence of his own. As Cabral emphatically and categorically points out,

> We are not defending the armed fight. . . . It is a violence against even our own people. But it is not our invention – it is not our cool decision; it is the *requirement of history*.[80]

For the colonized, violence is the avenue through which freedom and humanity are reclaimed. Violence is the "requirement of history" precisely because through it the colonized reclaims the possibility of human existence. This violence, furthermore, in being life-enhancing is also a violence that affects and fundamentally uproots the colonized.

The continual risking of life, the perpetual tension of confrontation against an odious enemy, the anxiety and intensity of a prolonged war, in short, the discipline and regimen of conflict purge the colonized of servility, dependence, cowardice, and similar vices that constitute the stunted existence of the colonized under colonialist conditions. In other words, the colonized

> formerly . . . a prey to unspeakable terrors yet happy to lose themselves in a dreamlike torment, such a people becomes unhinged, reorganizes itself, and in blood and tears gives birth to very real and immediate action.[81]

It is important to grasp the organic poise and poetry of Fanon's words. Just as a new being comes forth out of its mother's womb in "blood and tears" thus terminating the abnormal state of pregnancy, in like manner, the colonized in "blood and tears gives birth to" itself out of the lived historicity of the liberation struggle. The "very real and immediate

action" of the struggle is thus the reverse of the static passivity of colonized existence. The colonizer makes history or historicizes by subjugating the "native" and replicating European society in a distorted manner.[82] The colonized, on the other hand, historicizes or enters the realm of human historical becoming in the determined confrontation with the colonial apparatus.

Colonialism literally freezes the internal dynamic of the subjugated society. In this situation, and in a futile attempt to diminish their wretchedness, the colonized produce out of their stagnant existence a fantastic magical world of sorcery and witchcraft. This is a realm of phantasms inhabited by "the dead who rise again, and the djinns who rush into your body while you yawn."[83] The ferocious unreality of this fantastic world is the ineffectual attempt by the colonized to displace – in the realm of the imaginary – the effective violence and terror of colonialism. This stunted "creativity," produced out of the native's lifeless and antiquated past, inadvertently adds to the stagnant and enigmatic reality of colonized "existence."

A noncolonized society grows, transforms, and, in all of this, constantly evaluates and re-evaluates its past in light of the future exigencies of its existence. As Nietzsche and Heidegger tell us, it is only in view of a future that a past is fruitfully appropriated. Colonized society, on the other hand, is not free to evaluate its past in terms of a possible future. It is a society without a future precisely because this is what colonialism negates and grounds itself on.

The violent confrontation with the colonial apparatus is the process through which this stagnant situation is eradicated. As Fanon puts it,

> the youth of a colonized country, growing up in an atmosphere of shot and fire . . . does not hesitate to pour scorn upon the zombies of his ancestors.[84]

In *A Dying Colonialism* (1959), taking the Algerian Revolution as his example, Fanon discusses in great detail how the struggle is a concrete process of historical self-creation. He does so in terms of the traditional attire (i.e., the veil), the relation of modern technology and medicine to the indigenous society, and the structure of subordination in the Algerian family. In all of this, Fanon shows how the struggle has a revitalizing and dynamic effect that puts into question the inert and superfluous dregs of the indigenous culture.

In confronting colonialism, the colonized projects a future and claims, for the vitality of the present, the effective heritage of the past. What he "jects" or throws ahead, in this emancipatory project, is his own effective and enduring heritage. This is what Aimé Césaire celebrates in his play *The Tragedy of King Christophe*, when he has his tragic hero say,

> Freedom yes, but not an easy freedom. Which means that they need a state. Yes, my philosopher friend, something that will enable this transplanted people to strike roots, to burgeon and flower, to fling the fruits and perfumes of its flowering into the face of the world, something which, to speak plainly, will oblige our people, by force if need be, to be born to itself, to surpass itself.[85]

The freedom Césaire advocates is a freedom which is constituted by the colonized's rebirth to "itself" in the fullness of its humanity. But why must the colonized "surpass itself"? Precisely because it does not suffice merely to expel the colonizer in order to effectively decolonize. It is further necessary to destroy the parasitic and ossified inert and residual Being-in-the-world of the colonized and to institute "the practices of freedom"[86] within the cultural and historical context of the decolonizing society, in the process of self-formation.

In decolonizing, the decolonized has to open up and claim its historical existence, its Being as history, closed off by colonial conquest. In so doing it reestablishes its political actuality in appropriating and living/practicing its existence in freedom. As Césaire's tragic hero, Christophe, forcefully asserts:

> This people's enemy is its indolence, its effrontery, its hatred of discipline, its self-indulgence, its lethargy. Gentlemen, for the honor and survival of this nation, I don't want it ever to be said, I won't have the world so much as suspect, that ten years of black freedom, ten years of black slovenliness and indifference, have sufficed to squander the patrimony that our martyred people has amassed in a hundred years of labor under the whip. You may as well get it through your heads this minute that with me you won't have the right to be tired.[87]

For Césaire what has to be reclaimed is not the "whip" or the multitude of social vices bred by slavery and freedom, but the "patrimony ... amassed in a hundred years of labor." The "patrimony" of endurance, fortitude, resistance, and creativity which, as Hegel tells us, constitutes the existential character of the slave in the dialectic of surmounting the master. This is the slave whose life experience is tempered by the immanent and ever-present possibility of death and the transfiguring creativity of productive labor. For Césaire "black freedom" is the effort of transcending enslavement aimed at instituting the historicity of the decolonized as decolonized.

Thus the violence of the colonized is also self-directed against the petrified forms of existence, whose actuality was the stagnant situation of external domination. In the struggle, the dying forms of existence in which the native found recourse and was forced to live as a "native" are thus challenged and *possibly* overcome. What concerns us here is the actualization, or failure thereof, of a definite historic *possibility*. Of course, in a very real way, if this does not happen – as Fanon tells us and as is concretely evinced by the actuality of neocolonial Africa – then:

> There's nothing save a minimum of readaptation, a few reforms at the top, a flag waving: and down there at the bottom an undivided mass, still living in the middle ages, endlessly marking time.[88]

As we noted in the beginning of this section, this is the stagnant actuality of neocolonialism. It is nothing more than the *de facto* renegotiation of the colonial status. That is why, as we noted earlier, all that is said of colonialism also holds true, in every essential, of neocolonial Africa.

Thus far, relying on Fanon, we have described the dialectic of violence and counter-violence that constituted, until very recently, colonial Africa and, by extension, constitutes our neocolonial present. Let us now briefly look at each aspect of the colonial and neocolonial situation.

III

The society of the settler is a cohesive and homogeneous community. The class distinctions internal to it are maintained, but in a friendly manner. The worker, the priest, the merchant are first and foremost settlers and only secondly members of this or that class or profession. The cohesiveness of the settler community is maintained against and in reference to the colonized, whose existence is fixed and frozen as the permanent underclass of this setup. The colony is the settler's own lived self-image. He foregrounds his individuality against the background of this collective. It is his domain, that in which his will and Being are embodied: the land that gave him his social and economic stability, the status he lacked in Europe.[89]

For the settler the colony is his salvation. He is, nonetheless, always a Frenchman or an Englishman in Algeria or Kenya, never an Algerian or a Kenyan. The settler cannot indigenize and remain a settler. His existence is innately parasitic. He is dependent on the mother country for his spiritual and historic legitimacy as a colonizer, and on the colony for his socio-economic existence and preeminence. The duplicity of this situation, as noted earlier, is the grounding source of colonial fascism.[90]

On the other hand, the colonized's existence is not cohesive but split in two. Within the colonized part of the colonial structure we have the *urban* and the *rural* native: in other words, those who have been Westernized and who, as Fanon puts it, "profit – at a discount, to be sure – from the colonial setup"[91] and the rural peasant/nomad masses who experience colonialism only or mostly as an external control and imposition.

At this point, it is important to note that this split is the originative ground of neocolonialism. In creating and maintaining this fracture among the colonized, colonial conquest establishes the material and cultural conditions in which the self-aggrandizing metaphysical delusions of Europe can be institutionally established, by being embodied in the consciousness and the physical actuality of "independent" Africa.[92]

The actuality of conquest confirms, after the fact, the servility of the colonized. Subjugation is thus historicized into and as the historicity of African existence.[93] This requires and presupposes the cultural negation of Westernized (i.e., modernized) Africans, whose very existence, as a section of the colonized society, was predicated on the rupture of African existence in the face of European conquest. Non-Europeanized Africa, on the other hand, was forced to submit to a stagnant petrification of its cultural, economic, historical, and political actuality. The peoples of the continent – in all the wealth of their diverse traditions – were thus reduced to a frozen existence as a subaltern and passive element in the historical eventuation of European modernity. Under the guise of the African's oneness with nature, it is this subordinate passivity of African existence under European dominance that Senghor celebrates as *Africanité*.

Thus the inheritance and actuality of post-colonial Africa manifests itself and is basically grounded on the schizoid existence of two complementary and yet violently contradictory modes of African (non)-Being-in-the-world: the Westernized dominating and the indigenous dominated native. Encased between these two forms of estranged existence one finds the presence of the present. These two paradoxical types replicate and constantly reproduce by proxy the colonizing historicalness of Europe and the historical stasis of present-day Africa. It is from within this situation, as we saw in the preceding chapter, that Nkrumah and Hountondji advocate an abstract and "universalistic" Marxism Leninism instead of concretely submitting this stagnant situation to scrutiny.

As graphically depicted by Sembene Ousmane in his 1968 film *Mandabi*, it is the estranging dialectic of these two broad segments of society that constitutes the contemporary crisis of the continent.[94] These two segments of African society parrot the estranged and estranging violent dialectic of the colonizer and the colonized, described so well by Memmi. But, in this case, the roles of colonizer and colonized are played by the native, cast on both sides of this antagonistic and complementary divide by reference to the culture and "know-how" (i.e., political and economic managerial skills, technology, science, etc.) of the former colonial power.[95] The Westernized African, in this context, is "Caliban become Prospero."[96]

Insofar as the anti-colonial struggle is aimed at overcoming colonialism and neocolonialism, it is an attempt to end the fissure in African existence between Westernized dominating and indigenous dominated Africa. It is in overcoming this split and in the positive union or fusion of these two broad segments of African society that the counter-violence of the colonized acquires a political form and becomes a project for a possible future of freedom. In fact, demographically and sociologically speaking, African liberation movements are born out of the "fusion of horizons" of these two broad segments of African society.[97]

Each manifests, in itself, what the other does not have and is estranged from. The Westernized native is acquainted with the world beyond the colony or neocolony and the struggles of other peoples. The rural non-Westernized native, on the other hand, is steeped in the broken heritage of his own particular African past. In the fusion of these two fractured "worlds" the possibility of African freedom is concretized or made tangible in the form of specific historical movements.

The struggle is a historically pedagogical and a concretely self-formative process. Its success is measured by the extent to which it overcomes the "Manichean world"[98] of colonialism and neo-colonialism. In other words, "the settler is not simply the man who must be killed" and "not every Negro or Moslem is issued automatically a hallmark of genuineness." The struggle is successful to the extent that it breaks down the "barriers of blood and race-prejudice ... on both sides."[99] Unthinking prejudices are thus displaced by the prejudgements cultivated out of the lived experience of the struggle. It is thus that "the practices of freedom" are established in the context of the African liberation struggle.

In like manner, in a neocolonial context, it is when the Westernized native puts "at the people's disposal the intellectual and technical capital that it has snatched when going through the colonial universities"[100] that the dialectic of violence and counter-violence is sublated in the reconstitution of a new ethical whole, of a new *ethos*. This is the process that appropriates the possibilities of a specific tradition from within the lived confines and concrete possibilities of that tradition itself.

Tempered by and produced out of the lived exigencies of the struggle, and grounded on the concrete experiencing – with all its limitations and creative possibilities – of its own mortal existence, a very practical and pragmatic rationality dominates and directs the development of this *praxis* of concrete communal self-creation. This is the lived quotidian self-formative *ethos* of the liberation struggle – "the practices of freedom." It is what Marx refers to as the dialectical process through which the educators are themselves educated.[101]

In view of all of the above then, and beyond the initial moment of counter-violence, the African liberation struggle is an originative process through which the historicity of the colonized is reclaimed and appropriated anew.

Thus, in contradistinction to Senghor and Ethnophilosophy, on the one hand, and Nkrumah, Hountondji, and Professional Philosophy, on the other, this will be our hermeneutical response to the question: What are the people of Africa trying to free themselves from and what are they trying to establish?

Notes

All emphasis in the original unless otherwise indicated.

1 Kwasi Wiredu, "The Question of Violence in Contemporary African Political Thought," *Praxis International*, vol. 6, no. 3 (Oct. 1986); and Henry Odera Oruka, *Punishment and Terrorism in Africa* (Nairobi, Kenya: East African Literature Bureau, 1976).
2 As Jean-Paul Sartre has observed, since Sorel, Fanon is the one thinker who has seriously engaged and examined the internal dialectic of violence and counter-violence, in the specific context of an oppressive setup. (See the preface to *The Wretched of the Earth* [New York: Grove Press, 1968], p. 14.) In this respect, Kenneth David Kaunda's book, *The Riddle of Violence* (New York: Harper & Row, 1980), is not useful for our present discussion, precisely because it is not a systemic study of a violent setup, but the conscientious musings of a Christian nonviolent politician in the face of the all-pervasive presence of violence in politics.
3 Aimé Césaire, *Discourse on Colonialism* (New York: Monthly Review Press, 1972), p. 9. In this respect see also Cornelius Castoriadis, "The Crises of Western Societies," *Telos*, no. 53 (Fall 1982), pp. 26–8. In "Defending the West," *Partisan Review*, no. 3 (1984), Castoriadis argues that South Africa cannot be considered part of the Western world because it violates the basic premises of the European heritage. He fails to note, however, that the West as a whole is responsible for the present existence of South Africa, and furthermore the West has never acted in accordance with its heritage (i.e., its self-conception) in its relations with non-European peoples.
4 Césaire, ibid., p. 11.
5 Edward Said, *The Question of Palestine* (New York: Vintage Books, 1980), p. 78. For a similar description of the colonial experience in its dehumanization of the colonized see Fanon, *The Wretched of the Earth*, p. 250.
6 Karl Marx and Frederick Engels, *The Communist Manifesto* (New York: International Publishers, 1983), pp. 9–13. The relevant passages are: "The discovery of America, the rounding of the Cape, opened up fresh ground [*sic*] for the rising bourgeoisie. The East Indian and Chinese markets, the colonization of America, trade with the colonies, the increase in the means of exchange and in commodities generally, gave to commerce, to navigation, to industry, an impulse never before known" (pp. 9–10). In other words:

"Modern industry has established the world market, for which the discovery [i.e., the colonization] of America paved the way. This market has given an immense development to commerce, to navigation, to communication" (p. 10). Thus: "In a word, it [i.e., the European bourgeoisie] creates a world after its own image" (p. 13). In everything that the bourgeoisie does to globalize Europe it is the "tool of History" and it has Marx's unconditional support. In other words, in the above passages Marx, like a good colonialist, is celebrating the globalization of European temporality. This is the temporality grounded on, as Said tells us, "the conversion into productivity" of the human and natural resources of the non-European world (see note 5).

7 On the theme of colonial fascism see, Albert Memmi, *The Colonizer and the Colonized* (Boston: Beacon Press, 1967), p. 55, and also pp. 62–5.

8 Memmi, ibid., p. 3.

9 V. Y. Mudimbe, "African Gnosis: Philosophy and the Order of Knowledge," *African Studies Review*, vol. 28, nos. 2–3 (June–Sept. 1985), p. 154.

10 V. Y. Mudimbe, *The Invention of Africa* (Bloomington: Indiana University Press, 1988), pp. 47–8.

11 T. S. Eliot, A *Choice of Kipling's Verse* (New York: Anchor Books, 1962), p. 143.

12 It should be noted that, to this day, the language of economic "development" and political "maturity" or lack thereof, with which United Nations and World Food experts assess the economic and political situation of non-European territories is internal to this colonialist conception of human existence.

13 Karl Marx, "British Rule in India," in Karl Marx and Frederick Engels, *On Colonialism* (New York: International Publishers, 1972), p. 41.

14 For a detailed exposition of the colonialist orientation of Marx's "materialist conception of history" see my paper, "Karl Marx and African Emancipatory Thought: A Critique of Marx's Euro-Centric Metaphysics," *Praxis International*, vol. 10, nos. 1/2 (April/July 1990).

15 *Hegel's Philosophy of Right*, trans. T. M. Knox (New York: Oxford University Press, 1973), p. 151, para. no. 246, emphasis added.

16 Ibid., pp. 151–2, paras no. 246–9.

17 For a detailed discussion of the colonialist orientation of Hegel's thought please see my paper, "The Idea of Colonialism In Hegel's *Philosophy of Right*," *International Philosophical Quarterly*, vol. 29, no. 3, issue no. 115 (Sept. 1989).

18 On this point see Loren Eisely, *Darwin's Century* (New York: Anchor Books, 1961), *passim*; Cornel West, *Prophesy Deliverance!* (Philadelphia: Westminster Press, 1982), chap. 2, "A Genealogy of Modern Racism"; and Edward W. Said, "Representing the Colonized: Anthropology's Interlocutors," *Critical Inquiry*, vol. 15, no. 2 (Winter 1989).

19 As quoted by Richard H. Popkin, "Hume's Racism,"

The Philosophical Forum, vol. 9, nos. 2–3 (Winter–Spring 1977–8); for Hume's remarks, see p. 213; for Kant's remarks, see p. 218.

20 Placide Temples, *Bantu Philosophy* (Paris: Présence Africaine, 1969), pp. 171–2.

21 Aristotle, *Politics*, ed. Stephen Everson (New York: Cambridge University Press, 1989), 1260b6–7, p. 20.

22 On this point see H. D. F. Kitto, *The Greeks* (New York: Penguin Books, 1979). See also, Aristotle, *Politics*, 1252b5–9, p. 2.

23 Alan Ryan, "Professor Hegel Goes to Washington," a review of Francis Fukuyama's *The End of History and the Last Man* (New York: Free Press, 1989), in *The New York Review of Books*, vol. 39, no. 6, March 26, 1992, p. 10.

24 Edward Said, "The Burdens of Interpretation and the Question of Palestine," *Journal of Palestine Studies*, vol. 16, no. 1, issue 61 (Autumn 1986), pp. 29–30.

25 In chapter 26 of *Capital*, vol. 1, Marx explicates in great detail this whole development, which he refers to as "primitive accumulation." As a true nineteenth-century European, however, Marx's concern is much more focused on the economic mechanisms of accumulation and not on the extirpation of aboriginal populations, which is just mentioned in passing.

26 Aimé Césaire, *Letter to Maurice Thorez* (1956), English translation by *Présence Africaine* (Paris: Présence Africaine, 1957), p. 6.

27 Chinua Achebe, *Things Fall Apart* (New York: A Faucett Premier Book, 1959), p. 191.

28 Ibid.

29 Fanon, *Black Skin, White Masks* (New York: Grove Press, 1967), p. 12.

30 *Hegel's Phenomenology of Spirit*, trans. A. V. Miller (New York: Clarendon Press, 1977), paras 187 and 188.

31 In this regard, as Kwame Anthony Appiah points out (*In My Father's House* [Oxford University Press, 1992], p. 4) the European colonial attitude toward the colonized was not uniform or homogeneous. For example, the French practiced a policy of assimilation the British did not. This, however, does not invalidate my point that the character of Obierika is the spiritual ancestor of the subjugated *évolué* or Westernized African. My point is not that the British and the French had similar policies or results, but that different as their polices might be they both presuppose the cultural, historical, and political subjugation and subservience of the colonized. In this regard then Obierika symbolizes, in Achebe's narrative, that initial moment of humiliation and subordination that is the necessary point of origin for the consciousness of the Westernized African. In other words – whether it was so intended by the colonizer and whether or not it was accepted on these terms by the colonized – the process of Westernization necessarily presupposes the subjugation and deprecation of the indigenous culture and historicity. This is so precisely because, on epistemic

grounds, it is the act of surreptitiously privileging, on a metaphysical level, a particular culture and historicity as being coterminous with Being or existence as such.

32 For an interesting but fundamentally different reading of this text, see Rhonda Cobham, "Problems of Gender and History in the Teaching of *Things Fall Apart*," in *Matatu*, no. 7 (1990).

33 Cheikh Hamidou Kane, *Ambiguous Adventure* (Portsmouth, N.H.: Heinemann Educational Books, 1989), pp. 48–9.

34 For this reference see note 5.

35 *Kant on History*, ed. Lewis White Beck (Indianapolis: Bobbs-Merrill Educational Publishing, 1963), p. 3.

36 Frantz Fanon, *Towards the African Revolution* (New York: Grove Press, 1988), pp. 158–9.

37 Patrick Taylor, *The Narrative of Liberation* (Ithaca: Cornell University Press, 1989), p. 74.

38 Henry Louis Gates, Jr., "Critical Fanonism," *Critical Inquiry*, vol. 17, no 3 (Spring 1991), p. 459. Gates's charge against Said rests on projecting the singular situation of minorities in the USA as the norm in the non-European world as a whole. It should be noted that the historic-political conflicts that engaged and produced the texts of Fanon are, on the whole, the lived actuality in which we – of the non-Euro-American world – still find ourselves.

39 Fanon, *The Wretched of the Earth*, p. 38.

40 Ibid., p. 112.

41 Regarding this key notion of colonization as "thingification," see Aimé Césaire, *Discourse on Colonialism* (New York: Monthly Review Press, 1972), p. 21; and Fanon, *The Wretched of the Earth*, pp. 36–7.

42 Ibid., p. 40.

43 This is the contradiction between the state as the embodiment of "ethical life" and the unresolvable contradictions of "civil society," the realm of socio-economic existence. On this point, see my already cited paper, "The Idea of Colonialism in Hegel's *Philosophy of Right*."

44 Fanon, *The Wretched of the Earth*, p. 36.

45 Ibid., p. 41.

46 Loren Eisely, *Darwin's Century* (New York: Anchor Books, 1961), chap. 10. See also Edward Said, *The Question of Palestine* (New York: Vintage Books, 1980), pp. 56–83.

47 Fanon, *The Wretched of the Earth*, p. 118.

48 Ibid., pp. 152–6.

49 Ibid., p. 51.

50 Ibid., p. 43.

51 Ibid., p. 51, emphasis added.

52 Jean-Jacques Rousseau, *On the Social Contract*, trans. Donald A. Cress and introduced by Peter Gay (Indianapolis: Hackett, 1983), p. 17. The relevant lines read as follows: "Were I to consider only force and the effect that flows from it, I would say that so long as a people is constrained to obey and does obey, it does well. As soon as it can shake off the yoke and

does shake it off, it does even better. For by recovering its liberty by means of the same right that stole it, either the populace is justified in getting it back or else those who took it away were not justified in their actions."

53 Fanon, *The Wretched of the Earth*, p. 69, emphasis added.

54 Memmi, *The Colonizer and the Colonized*, p. 92, emphasis added.

55 Oliva Blanchette, *For a Fundamental Social Ethic* (New York: Philosophical Library, 1973), p. 28.

56 Heidegger, *Being and Time* (New York: Harper & Row, 1962), p. 255. In this regard see also "Letter on Humanism," in *Basic Writings*, ed. David Farrell Krell (New York: Harper & Row, 1977), p. 209; and Heidegger's last statement of his views, "Modern Natural Science and Technology," in *Radical Phenomenology*, ed. J. Sallis (Atlantic Highlands, N.J.: Humanities Press, 1978), p. 4. For Heidegger's overall perspective on technology and the situation of the modern world, see *The Question concerning Technology and Other Essays*, trans. William Lovitt (New York: Harper & Row, 1977).

57 Fanon, *The Wretched of the Earth*, p. 51.

58 Albert Memmi, *Dominated Man* (Boston: Beacon Press, 1969), in section 4 "The Domestic Servant," p. 178. It is important to note that the condition of utter humiliation and sexual domination that Memmi highlights based on his reflections on the film *The Servant* (by Harold Pinter and Joseph Losey) is a rather accurate representation of the reality of life, especially for female servants, in most African countries. This is particularly true if the master or employer is himself a Westernized African and a member of the neocolonial ruling class, who culturally aspires and "sees" himself as incarnating European culture.

59 Ibid., p. 179.

60 Ibid.

61 Fanon, *The Wretched of the Earth*, pp. 36–7.

62 Hegel, *Phenomenology of Spirit*, p. 10, para. 18. As is well known, for Hegel *Wirklichkeit* (actuality) is grounded on the adequation of concept and object.

63 Frantz Fanon, *Les damnés de la terre* (Paris: François Maspero, 1974), p. 6.

64 Patrick Taylor, *The Narrative of Liberation*, p. 49. On this point it is necessary to emphasize that Taylor's position, if left unqualified, suffers from a naive essentialism which is grounded on reifying and elevating above the historicity of existence the pre-colonial humanity of the colonized.

65 On this point see the upcoming discussion later in this chapter. In *The Wretched of the Earth*, please see pp. 55–9.

66 For an interesting exposition of this point, please see Michael Ryan, *Marxism and Deconstruction* (Baltimore: Johns Hopkins University Press, 1984), p. 6.

67 Martin Heidegger, *An Introduction to Metaphysics*

(New Haven: Yale University Press, 1977), p. 62.

68 Ibid., p. 152.

69 Ibid., p. 155, and the additional exploration of this point on pp. 143–65.

70 Taylor, *The Narrative of Liberation*, p. 60.

71 Jean-Paul Sartre, in the preface to *The Wretched of the Earth*, p. 14.

72 Hannah Arendt, *On Violence* (New York: Harcourt Brace Jovanovich, 1970), p. 65.

73 Hannah Arendt, *Between Past and Future* (New York: Penguin Books, 1980), p. 4.

74 In this regard see Edward W. Said, "An Ideology of Difference," *Critical Inquiry*, vol. 12, no. 1 (Autumn 1985), p. 47. To my knowledge the one European philosopher that is not snared by this Eurocentric double standard is Jean-Paul Sartre. On the other hand, one of the most blatant offenders on this score is Albert Camus. On this last point, see Albert Camus, *Resistance, Rebellion and Death* (New York: Vintage Books, 1974), specifically contrast "Letters to a German Friend" and the section titled "Algeria."

75 As V. Y. Mudimbe points out: "Until the 1950s – and I am not certain at all that things have changed today for the general public in the West – Africa is widely perceived and presented as the continent without memory, without past, without history. More precisely, her history is supposed to commence with her contacts with Europe, specifically with the progressive European invasion of the continent that begins at the end of the fifteenth century." *The Surreptitious Speech* (Chicago: University of Chicago Press, 1992), p. xx.

76 It should be noted, as Fanon points out in his article, "Accra: Africa Affirms Its Unity and Defines Its Strategy" (first published in *El Moudjahid*, no. 34, Dec. 24, 1958; presently collected in *Towards the African Revolution*, section 16 [Grove Press, 1988]), that the counterclaim of the colonized has to do with the relation of forces within which the colonizer–colonized confrontation unfolds. It is only when this relation – globally or regionally – tilts against the colonizing power that we here talk of "non-violent decolonization" (p. 155).

77 Frantz Fanon, *A Dying Colonialism* (New York: Grove Press, 1965), p. 78. In her already cited work *On Violence*, Arendt writes that, "if only the practice of violence would make it possible to interrupt automatic processes in the realm of human affairs, the preachers of violence would have won an important point" (p. 30). In point of fact, as Fanon points out, in the quotation just cited, this is precisely the case in the colonial context. The inertness of submission to colonial tyranny is replaced by the vitality of anti-colonial resistance and revolution.

78 Ironically Albert Camus was one of the "prestigious French intellectuals" (V.Y. Mudimbe, *The Surreptitious Speech*, p. xvii) who in 1947 was sympathetic to and supportive of Alioune Diop's efforts to establish

Présence Africaine, a solitary African cultural institution in the heart of post-war France.

79 Memmi, *The Colonizer and the Colonized*, p. 3.

80 Amilcar Cabral, *Return to the Source: Selected Speeches* (New York: Monthly Review Press, 1973), p. 79. In *On Violence*, Arendt is of the opinion that the "civil-rights movement . . . was entirely nonviolent" (p. 76). For a detailed discussion which contradicts Arendt's unsubstantiated assertion, see William R. Jones, "Liberation Strategies in Black Theology: Mao, Martin or Malcolm?" *Philosophy Born of Struggle* (Kendal/Hunt Publishing Co., 1983).

81 Fanon, *The Wretched of the Earth*, p. 56.

82 On this point see, Paul Nizan's interesting short novel, *Aden Arabie* (Boston: Beacon Press, 1960).

83 Fanon, *The Wretched of the Earth*, p. 58.

84 Ibid.

85 Aimé Césaire, *The Tragedy of King Christophe* (New York: Grove Press, 1969), p. 13.

86 On this point see Michel Foucault, "The Ethic of Care for the Self as a Practice of Freedom," an interview translated by J. D. Gauthier, S.J., in *The Final Foucault*, ed. J. Bernauer and D. Rasmussen (Cambridge, Mass.: MIT Press, 1988), p. 3.

87 Césaire, *The Tragedy of King Christophe*, p. 19.

88 Fanon, *The Wretched of the Earth*, p. 47.

89 Memmi, *The Colonizer and the Colonized*, pp. 51–66.

90 On this point see Memmi, *The Colonizer and the Colonized*, pp. 58–62. See also in this chapter note 7 and the related discussion of fascism and colonialism.

91 Fanon, *The Wretched of the Earth*, p. 60.

92 Memmi, *The Colonizer and the Colonized*, part two, the sections titled, "Mythical Portrait of the Colonized," and "Situations of the Colonized," *passim*.

93 On this point see Fanon's pioneering discussion in *Black Skin, White Masks*, chapter 4, "The So-called Dependency Complex of Colonized Peoples." See also what Memmi calls *"The Usurper's Role* (or the Nero complex)," *The Colonizer and the Colonized*, pp. 52, 53.

94 The film, a 1968 production is based on Sembene's short novel, *The Money Order* (Portsmouth, N.H.: Heinemann Educational Books, 1988).

95 Fanon, *The Wretched of the Earth*, p. 150. On this point Sembene's novels and specifically *The Money Order and Xala* (Chicago: Lawrence Hill Books, 1976) are indispensable reading.

96 Taylor, *The Narrative of Liberation*, p. 10. As Taylor points out, for Fanon, neocolonialism and the domination of the liberation struggle, by the degenerate and counterfeit African "national bourgeoisie" – i.e., "Caliban become Prospero" – is the negative possibility that can develop (as indeed has happened in most of Africa) as a result of the failure of the African liberation struggle to concretely institutionalize its emancipatory possibilities. The obverse of this tragic situation is the as of yet unrealized possibility of concretely consolidating the gains of the African

liberation struggle. For Fanon's pioneering discussion of this crucial point, see the section of *The Wretched of the Earth* titled, "The Pitfalls of National Consciousness."

97 I borrow this notion from Hans-Georg Gadamer, *Truth and Method* (New York: Crossroad Publishing Co., 1982), pp. 273–4. By the qualification "sociological" I mean only to suggest that, for me, "the fusion of horizons" is a concrete historical and ontic process that occurs in engaging real life issues and problems within the context of a specific historicalness. On the fundamental importance of this moment in the African liberation struggle, see Cabral, *Return to the Source: Selected Speeches*, p. 63.

98 Fanon, *The Wretched of the Earth*, p. 41.

99 Ibid., p. 146.

100 Ibid., p. 150.

101 On this point, see Marx's third thesis in "Theses on Feuerbach," in Karl Marx and Frederick Engels, *The German Ideology* (New York: International Publishers, 1973), p. 121.

30

Cultural Nationalism in the Colonial Period

R. L. Okonkwo

With the advent of colonialism the traditional society was disrupted by Christianity, Western education, and other forces. European influences seemed to have swept away the African culture before it. Missionaries saw little of value in the African way of life and sought to re-make their wards into Europeans or black Englishmen. Whereas the Africans seemed willing pupils, ready to copy the European models at first, the cultural nationalists later rebelled against the denationalization of the African by the missionaries and the colonial authorities.

The cultural nationalist movement, which grew up at the end of the nineteenth century in West Africa, exhorted Africans to regain touch with their own culture. The cultural nationalists studied the institutions of the traditional society and sought, as much as possible, to cast off the European life style and to live according to African traditions.

The difficulties this first generation of African nationalists faced in restoring their African nationality was a sign of the everbearing influence European education had had. In their attempt to define the African personality and portray the true African culture, the nationalists could not divorce themselves completely from Western influences. They remained hybrids, a mixture of European and African influences. They could never identify completely with the uncontaminated African.[1]

From *Readings in African Humanities*, ed. Ogbu U. Kalu (1978); by kind permission of Fourth Dimension Co. Ltd.

The problem of the loss of African identity which the cultural nationalists first brought to light is as timely today as it was in the early part of the century. When Western education and religion first spread to the interior, pupils experienced conflicts of culture. Today, in reaction to Western-oriented university education, Africans are turning more and more to the study of themselves. They wish to study the traditions of their ancestors, to know the institutions and values which are peculiar to Africa and which should be retained in any more towards modernization.

It may be that the earlier generation of cultural nationalists were too intellectual in their attitudes to the traditional society. Their backgrounds were, in fact, unique in the degree to which they severed their ties to the village society. On the other hand, the Europeanization of the African life style has become more and more widespread with the urbanization of the interior. Otonti Nduka's book, *Western Education and the Nigerian Cultural Background*, highlights the fact that even after independence, Africa still needs emancipation from European culture. Nduka calls for the preservation of indigenous values and institutions and a blending of Western and African culture.[2]

Origins of Cultural Nationalism

Cultural nationalism was a movement of the Western-educated elite of West Africa. The type of education of the European missionaries gave their nineteenth-century pupils was at the root of the grievances of the cultural nationalists. The missionaries conceived that the teaching of Christianity and the skills of reading, writing, and arithmetic had to be accompanied by the adoption of Western dress names, food, and life style. They insisted that a good Christian must drink tea and take walks with his wife. They could see little but barbarism in the traditional African institutions and sought to destroy the vestiges of African culture.

Sierra Leone was the first centre of missionary activity in British West Africa. Fourah Bay College, established in 1827, was the only institution of higher learning of that time in West Africa. Thus, Nigerians, Ghanaians, Gambians, as well as Creoles, came to Freetown to study. Their common education and friendships created a class of West African intellectuals who had more in common with each other than with their brothers in the interior. Thus, cultural nationalism was not actually a movement within any one nation, but was a response of the West African educated elite who had shared similar experiences at the hands of the ethnocentric missionaries.

The first generation of educated Nigerians were known as the *Saros*. They were originally captured as slaves in the tribal wars of the early nineteenth century. The British Navy, which was patrolling the Atlantic in an effort to stop the iniquitous slave trade, recaptured the slaves and sent them to Sierra Leone. The liberated Africans were so grateful to their British mentors for saving them from slavery, that they willingly adopted European civilization along with the Christian religion.

In the 1840s the recaptives began returning to Nigeria to re-establish ties with their families. With the advantages of Western education and a knowledge of English, they became leaders in the society. They were valuable to the Europeans and traditional rulers as middlemen between the two groups. The Saros settled mainly in Lagos and Abeokuta, Calabar, Opobo and other coastal areas where, as doctors, lawyers, traders, and clergymen, they emerged as leaders.[3] The Saros came with the European names given to them by the missionaries. They included Thomas Babington Macaulay, father of Herbert Macaulay, Samuel Crowther, John Randall, and James Johnson. With such English-sounding names, they saw themselves more as Europeans than Africans.

Michael Echeruo's recent book, *Victorian Lagos*, described the extent to which the Saros imitated the European life style. Their entertainment included races, fancy dress balls, cricket, musical and dramatic concerts, levees, soirées, conversazione, and at-homes.[4] They held elaborate weddings, with dresses complete with plumes, stockings, gloves, fans, and parasols. The wedding gifts included Morocco visiting cards and gold cheese dishes.[5]

It was from this class of Saros that the cultural nationalists recruited their supporters. The impetus for a re-examination of their European life styles came from two quarters, from the attitudes of the Europeans and from the indigenes. The ridicule of the Europeans was a great blow to their erstwhile pupils; the Europeans found the Africans dressing up in Victorian top hats and spats a caricature and a mockery. Lord Lugard, for example, refused to recognize the African elite as spokesmen for the traditional rulers and considered them dangerous spoilers of the traditional society.[6]

The Saros, who craved acceptance in European society, were deeply hurt by the growing movement towards racial discrimination and segregation at the turn of the century. Whereas in the earlier period, the two groups had socialized freely, in the 1890s, the racial climate changed. The increasing racial prejudice was revealed in the attempt to make Christ Church a colonial church for whites only, and in the harsh treatment of Bishop Samuel Ajayi Crowther, a Saro who was the first black bishop in West Africa and a symbol of the potential of the black man to rise in the European church. The educated African also suffered discrimination in civil service promotions. Some, such as Herbert Macaulay, resigned from the government service during this due to unfair treatment. The scorn and humiliation they suffered caused the Saros to question their association with the European way of life. They began to see their destinies as allied to their brothers in the interior.

The second impetus to cultural nationalism came from the reaction of the indigenes to the Victorian Africans. At first the Saros were condescending to the natives, and the natives were hostile to them. After they became disillusioned with the whites, the Saros allied with the Africans. By 1910, the old Lagos society had changed into two groups, the whites and the blacks.[7]

Cultural Renaissance

Cultural nationalism thus grew up in the late nineteenth century in West African as a reaction to increasing discrimination against educated Africans in the church and colonial government. The movement embraced the elite in the major coastal cities, Freetown, Cape Coast, Accra, and Lagos. It was marked by a cultural renaissance, a re-awakening of interest in traditional African culture.

As an important symbol of their new sense of African identity, the elite abandoned their European names given them by the missionaries and took African names. In Nigeria, Rev. David B. Vincent became Majola Agbebi. Others retained their surnames, but adopted African first names. George William Johnson became Oshokale Tejumade Johnson and J. Augustus Payne became J. Otonba Payne, and in Freetown, William J. Davis took the name Orishatukeh Faduma.

Another important sign of the new African awareness was the wearing of African traditional dress instead of the Victorian heavy woolen suits. In Freetown, the Creoles organized a Dress Reform society in 1887 to encourage others to abandon European dress, which was not only unsuitable for the climate, but made the African an object of ridicule. Mrs Adelaide Casely Hayford, a Creole, was one of the few women who wore traditional dress, the buba and lappah, to all formal occasions.[8] Rev. Mojola Agbebi wore traditional dress in Europe and America, as well as at home in Nigeria, and became an international symbol of the African personality.[9]

The cultural nationalists took a renewed interest in the achievements of the traditional African society and wrote many learned books on African art, religion, and history. Mojola Agbebi, for example, published a collection of Yoruba riddles in Yoruba, and began a Yoruba dictionary. Some of the published histories are still important sources for the modern historian, such as Samuel Johnson's *History of the Yorubas*, J. O. George's *Historical Notes on the Yoruba Country and its Tribes*, and Otonba Payne's *Tables of Principal Events in Yoruba History*. In the Gold Coast, J. E. Casely Hayford wrote *Gold Coast Native Institutions*, a study of the political institutions of the traditional Fanti society, and J. Mensah Sarbah was the author of a book entitled *Fanti Customary Laws*.

Education was an area of crucial importance to the cultural nationalists. They sought to run their own schools, which would teach traditional culture, the native languages, and African history. African-run schools were the answer to the denationalizing effects of the missionary and colonial government education.

Adelaide Casely Hayford founded the Girls' Vocational School in Freetown, 1923–40, to give to the pupils a pride in their race and a love for their country. She introduced the teaching of traditional crafts such as spinning and weaving to foster and appreciate of African art, which she deemed one of Africa's original contributions to the world. Mrs Hayford lamented that the urban woman had lost the artistic skills of her grandmother as well as an appreciation of the beauty of African artwork. The Creole women preferred to import cloth to decorate their homes rather than use the fine native materials. Mrs Hayford encouraged her pupils to wear African dress and to learn the songs and dances. She sought to foster creativity as well as practical skills which were being lost in urban society.[10]

J. H. Casely Hayford, husband to Adelaide, stressed the need for an African university. He wanted to situate the university in the interior, closer to the true African culture. Hayford called for professorships of African history and African languages.[11] Edward Wilmot Blyden of Liberia stressed the importance of an indigenous university to counteract the harmful effects of Africans travelling abroad for higher studies, believing overseas travel to be harmful to health and the preservation of African identity. Education should take place in Africa, amid the scenes of future labours, with more access to the people of the interior.[12]

As many of the early cultural nationalists were clergymen, their reforms centred around the church. Edward Wilmot Blyden (1832–1912), often called the Father of Cultural Nationalism, spoke against the attempts of the European missionaries to destroy African culture. In his famous speech, "The Return of the Exiles and the West African Church," delivered during his visit to Lagos in early 1891, Blyden called for the Lagosians to organize an independent African Church, free from European control and missionaries. He spoke of the need for Africans to convert Africans with a truer understanding of the African's deep religious instincts which only needed to be shown the way to salvation. Blyden believed Christianity was universal and could be adapted to the African culture.[13]

As part of the cultural nationalist movement, the Lagosians organized the United Native African Church in August, 1891. There were four independent churches established in Nigeria before 1917. They accepted polygamy and other traditional institutions which was judged compatible with the universal tenets of Christianity. They held services in the vernacular and wrote African hymns and songs.[14]

In addition to the clergy, African newspapers were an important force in cultural nationalism. *The Sierra Leone Weekly News, The Gold Coast Leader*, and in Lagos, *The Lagos Weekly Record* and *The Lagos Standard* exhorted the educated elite to abandon their servile imitation of European culture and become Africans. John Payne Jackson, editor of the *Lagos Weekly Record* called the Europeanized African, "a non-descript, a libel on his country, and a blot on civilization."[15]

The cultural nationalists were forerunners of the poets of the Negritude movement in their attempt to define the "African personality." The cultural nationalists believed that the Africans were not backward or inferior to the whites. Each race was unique and had an independent destiny and contribution to make to world civilization. The greatest danger to the educated African was that he would lose his special African genius.

What was the "African personality"? Blyden stressed that the African was a spiritual being. The African's deeply religious nature and his humanitarianism would serve as an antidote to the materialism of the West. The African way of life was, in many ways, superior to that of the European. Blyden applauded the cooperative principles of African village life. "We, not I, is the law of African life."[16] In traditional African society, wrote Blyden, there were no hospitals as the family was responsible for its sick. There were not thieves and no papers as everyone had enough. Blyden's idyllic picture was an antidote to the European view of the primitive and barbaric practices of traditional society.

J. E. Casely Hayford echoed Blyden's emphasis on the peculiar spirituality of the African, seeing Africa as a moral force to bring peace to the world.[17] The cultural nationalists continually quoted the passage, "Ethiopia shall stretch forth her hands unto God" as proof of the religious destiny of the African race.

The concept of the "African personality," originated by the cultural nationalists, was later used by Kwame Nkrumah as a force in the struggle for freedom from colonialism. Nkrumah also stressed the humanistic principles of traditional African society, the communalism in which members cooperated for the well being of all.[18]

The Legacy of Cultural Nationalism

The cultural nationalists were never a large group among the educated classes. Yet, through the church and newspapers, they publicized their ideas and gradually molded a new national consciousness among the people. The first generation of nationalists were Saros. As education spread to the interior, other groups joined in the protest against the imposition of Western-oriented institutions. Dr Nnamdi Azikiwe and Mazi Mbonu Ojike were important cultural nationalists of a later period. Ojike's slogan, "Boycott the boycottables," sought to induce Africans to use African products rather than imported articles.[19]

Cultural nationalism has been viewed as the first step in the growth of the nationalist movements which eventually demanded independence from the colonial authorities.[20] Consciousness of belonging to a nationality preceded the political movements which came later in the twentieth century. While political nationalism took prominence from 1940 to 1960, cultural nationalism has again assumed importance following independence. Western incursions into Africa have continued to threaten the African heritage, and latterly cultural nationalists continue the fight to preserve the traditional institutions and the African identity.

Notes

1 E. A. Ayandele, *Holy Johnson Pioneer of African Nationalism* (London: Frank Cass, 1970), p. 287.

2 Otonti Nduka, *Western Education and the Nigerian Cultural Background* (London: Oxford University Press, 1975), p. vi.

3 For more about the Saros see Jean Herskovits Kopytoff, *A Preface to Modern Nigeria: The "Sierra Leoneans" in Yoruba, 1830–1890* (Madison: University of Wisconsin Press, 1965).

4 Michael Echeruo, *Victorian Lagos: Aspects of Nineteenth-Century Lagos Life* (London: Macmillan, 1977),
p. 30.

5 Ibid., p. 31

6 James Coleman, *Nigeria: Background to Nationalism* (Berkeley: University of California Press, 1958), p. 156.

7 Patrick Cole, *Modern and Traditional Elites in the Politics of Lagos* (Cambridge: Cambridge University Press, 1975), p. 75.

8 R. L. Okonkwo, "Adelaide Casely Hayford: Cultural Nationalist and Feminist," unpublished paper submitted to the 23rd Annual Congress of the Historical

Society of Nigeria, Zaria, April, 1978.

9 E. A. Ayandele, *A Visionary of the African Church: Mojola Agbebi* (Nairobi: East Africa Publishing House, 1971) p. 13.

10 R. L. Okonkwo.

11 J. E. Casely Hayford, *Ethiopia Unbound: Studies in Race Emancipation* (London: Frank Cass, 1969), p. 95.

12 E. W. Blyden, "Aims of Liberia College," quoted in M. Echeruo, p. 65.

13 E. W. Blyden, "The Return of the Exiles and the West African Church," in H. Lynch, ed., *Black Spokesman: Selected Published Writings of Edward Wilmot Blyden* (London: Frank Cass, 1971), pp. 191–4.

14 For more information about independent churches in Yorubaland, see J. B. Webster, *The African Churches Among the Yoruba 1888–1922* (Oxford: Clarendon

Press, 1964).

15 *Lagos Weekly Record* (March, 1896), quoted in M. Echeruo, p. 35.

16 E. W. Blyden, *African Life and Customs* (London: African Publication Society, 1969), p. 30.

17 J. E. Casely Hayford, p. 208.

18 Afari-Gyan, *Political Ideas of Kwame Nkrumah* (New York African Heritage Studies, 1970), p. 220.

19 P. M. Mbaeyi, "Culture in Nigerian Nationalism," unpublished paper delivered at the 22nd Annual Congress of the Historical Society of Nigeria, Benin, March 1977, pp. 15–16.

20 D. Kimble, *A Political History of Ghana: The Rise of Gold Coast Nationalism* (Oxford: Clarendon Press, 1963), p. 506.

31

National Liberation and Culture (Return to the Source)

Amilcar Cabral

When Goebbels, the brain behind Nazi propaganda, heard culture being discussed, he brought out his revolver. That shows that the Nazis – who were and are the most tragic expression of imperialism and of its thirst for domination – even if they were all degenerates like Hitler, had a clear idea of the value of culture as a factor of resistance to foreign domination.

History teaches us that, in certain circumstances, it is very easy for the foreigner to impose his domination on a people. But it also teaches us that, whatever may be the material aspects of this domination, it can be maintained only by the permanent, organized repression of the cultural life of the people concerned. Implantation of foreign domination can be assured definitively only by physical liquidation of a significant part of the dominated population.

In fact, to take up arms to dominate a people is, above all, to take up arms to destroy, or at least to neutralize, to paralyze, its cultural life. For, with a strong indigenous cultural life, foreign domination cannot be sure of its perpetuation. . . .

The ideal for foreign domination, whether imperialist or not, would be to choose:

- either to liquidate practically all the population of the dominated country, thereby eliminating the possibilities for cultural resistance;

From Amilcar Cabral, *Return to the Source: Selected Speeches* (1973), copyright © 1973 by PAIGC; by kind permission of Monthly Review Press.

- or to succeed in imposing itself without damage to the culture of the dominated people – that is, to harmonize economic and political domination of these people with their cultural personality.

The first hypothesis implies genocide of the indigenous population and creates a void which empties foreign domination of its content and its object: the dominated people. The second hypothesis has not, until now, been confirmed by history. The broad experience of mankind allows us to postulate that it has no practical viability: it is not possible to harmonize the economic and political domination of a people, whatever may be the degree of their social development, with the preservation of their cultural personality.

In order to escape this choice – which may be called the *dilemma of cultural resistance* – imperialist colonial domination has tried to create theories which, in fact, are only gross formulations of racism, and which, in practice, are translated into a permanent state of siege of the indigenous populations on the basis of racist dictatorship (or democracy).

This, for example, is the case with the so-called theory of progressive *assimilation* of native populations, which turns out to be only a more or less violent attempt to deny the culture of the people in question. The utter failure of this "theory," implemented in practice by several colonial powers, including Portugal, is the most obvious proof of its lack of viability, if not of its inhuman character. It attains the highest degree of absurdity in the Portuguese case, where Salazar affirmed that Africa does *not exist*.

This is also the case with the so-called theory of apartheid, created, applied and developed on the basis of the economic and political domination of the people of Southern Africa by a racist minority, with all the outrageous crimes against humanity which that involves. The practice of apartheid takes the form of unrestrained exploitation of the labor force of the African masses, incarcerated and repressed in the largest concentration camp mankind has ever known.

These practical examples give a measure of the drama of foreign imperialist domination as it confronts the cultural reality of the dominated people. They also suggest the strong, dependent and reciprocal relationships existing between the *cultural situation* and the *economic* (and political) *situation* in the behavior of human societies. In fact, culture is always in the life of a society (open or closed), the more or less conscious result of the economic and political activities of that society, the more or less dynamic expression of the kinds of relationships which prevail in that society, on the one hand between man (considered individually or collectively) and nature, and, on the other hand, among individuals, groups of individuals, social strata or classes.

The value of culture as an element of resistance to foreign domination lies in the fact that culture is the vigorous manifestation on the ideological or idealist plane of the physical and historical reality of the society that is dominated or to be dominated. Culture is simultaneously the fruit of a people's history and a determinant of history, by the positive or negative influence which it exerts on the evolution of relationships between man and his environment, among men or groups of men within a society, as well as among different societies. Ignorance of this fact may explain the failure of several attempts at foreign domination – as well as the failure of some international liberation movements.

Let us examine the nature of *national liberation*. We shall consider this historical phenomenon in its contemporary context, that is, national liberation in opposition to imperialist domination. The latter is, as we know, distinct both in form and in content from preceding types of foreign domination (tribal, military-aristocratic, feudal, and capitalist domination in the free competition era).

The principal characteristic, common to every kind of imperialist domination, is the negation of the *historical process* of the dominated people by

means of violently usurping the free operation of the process of development of the *productive forces*. Now, in any given society, the level of development of the productive forces and the system for social utilization of these forces (the ownership system) determine the *mode of production*. In our opinion, the mode of production whose contradictions are manifested with more or less intensity through the class struggle, is the principal factor in the history of any human group, the level of the productive forces being the true and permanent driving power of history.

For every society, for every group of people, considered as an evolving entity, the level of the productive forces indicates the stage of development of the society and of each of its components in relation to nature, its capacity to act or to react consciously in relation to nature. It indicates and conditions the type of material relationships (expressed objectively or subjectively) which exists among the various elements or groups constituting the society in question. Relationships and types of relationships between man and nature, between man and his environment. Relationships and type of relationships among the individual or collective components of a society. To speak of these is to speak of history, but it is also to speak of culture.

Whatever may be the ideological or idealistic characteristics of cultural expression, culture is an essential element of the history of a people. Culture is, perhaps, the product of this history just as the flower is the product of a plant. Like history, or because it is history, culture has as its material base the level of the productive forces and the mode of production. Culture plunges its roots into the physical reality of the environmental humus in which it develops, and it reflects the organic nature of the society, which may be more or less influenced by external factors. History allows us to know the nature and extent of the imbalances and conflicts (economic, political and social) which characterize the evolution of a society; culture allows us to know the dynamic syntheses which have been developed and established by social conscience to resolve these conflicts at each stage of its evolution, in the search for survival and progress.

Just as happens with the flower in a plant, in culture there lies the capacity (or the responsibility) for forming and fertilizing the seedling which will assure the continuity of history, at the same time assuring the prospects for evolution and progress of the society in question. Thus it is understood that imperialist domination, by denying the historical development of the dominated people, necessarily also denies their cultural development. It is also understood why imperialist domination, like all other foreign domination, for its own security, requires cultural oppression and the attempt at direct or indirect liquidation of the essential elements of the culture of the dominated people.

The study of the history of national liberation struggles shows that generally these struggles are preceded by an increase in expression of culture, consolidated progressively into a successful or unsuccessful attempt to affirm the cultural personality of the dominated people, as a means of negating the oppressor culture. Whatever may be the conditions of a people's political and social factors in practicing this domination, it is generally within the culture that we find the seed of opposition, which leads to the structuring and development of the liberation movement.

In our opinion, the foundation for national liberation rests in the inalienable right of every people to have their own history, whatever formulations may be adopted at the level of international law. The objective of national liberation is, therefore, to reclaim the right, usurped by imperialist domination, namely: the liberation of the process of development of national productive forces. Therefore, national liberation takes place when, and only when, national productive forces are completely free of all kinds of foreign domination. The liberation of productive forces and consequently the ability to determine the mode of production most appropriate to the evolution of the liberated people, necessarily opens up new prospects for the cultural development of the society in question, by returning to that society all its capacity to create progress.

A people who free themselves from foreign domination will be free culturally only if, without complexes and without under-estimating the importance of positive accretions from the oppressor and other cultures, they return to the upward paths of their own culture, which is nourished by the living reality of its environment, and which negates both harmful influences and any kind of subjection to foreign culture. Thus, it may be seen that if imperialist domination has the vital need to practice cultural oppression, national liberation is necessarily an act of *culture*. . . .

The experience of colonial domination shows that, in the effort to perpetuate exploitation, the colonizer not only creates a system to repress the cultural life of the colonized people; he also provokes and develops the cultural alienation of a part of the population, either by so-called assimilation of indigenous people, or by creating a social gap between the indigenous elites and the popular masses. As a result of this process of dividing or of deepening the divisions in the society, it happens that a considerable part of the population, notably the urban or peasant *petite bourgeoisie*, assimilates the colonizer's mentality, considers itself culturally superior to its own people and ignores or looks down upon their cultural values. This situation, characteristic of the majority of colonized intellectuals, is consolidated by increases in the social privileges of the assimilated or alienated group with direct implications for the behavior of individuals in this group in relation to the liberation movement. A reconversion of minds – of mental set – is thus indispensable to the true integration of people into the liberation movement. Such reconversion – re-Africanization, in our case – may take place before the struggle, but it is completed only during the course of the struggle, through daily contact with the popular masses in the communion of sacrifice required by the struggle. . . .

Recognizing this reality, the colonizer who represses or inhibits significant cultural activity on the part of the masses at the base of the social pyramid, strengthens and protects the prestige and the cultural influence of the ruling class at the summit. The colonizer installs chiefs who support him and who are to some degree accepted by the masses; he gives these chiefs material privileges such as education for their eldest children, creates chiefdoms where they did not exist before, develops cordial relations with religious leaders, builds mosques, organizes journeys to Mecca, etc. And above all, by means of the repressive organs of colonial administration, he guarantees economic and social privileges to the ruling class in their relations with the masses. All this does not make it impossible that, among these ruling classes, there may be individuals or groups of individuals who join the liberation movement, although less frequently than in the case of the assimilated "petite bourgeoisie." Several traditional and religious leaders join the struggle at the very beginning or during its development, making an enthusiastic contribution to the cause of liberation.

But here again vigilance is indispensable: preserving deep down the cultural prejudices of their class, individuals in this category generally see in the liberation movement the only valid means, using the sacrifices of the masses, to eliminate colonial oppression of their own class and to re-establish in this way their complete political and cultural domination of the people.

In the general framework of contesting colonial imperialist domination and in the actual situation to which we refer, among the oppressor's most loyal allies are found some high officials and intellectuals of the liberal professions, assimilated people, and also a significant number of representatives of the ruling class from rural areas. This fact gives some measure of the influence (positive or negative) of culture and cultural prejudices in the problem of political choice when one is confronted with the liberation movement. It also illustrates the limits of this influence and the supremacy of the class factor in the behavior of the different social groups. The high official or the assimilated intellectual, charac-terized by total cultural alienation, identifies him-self by political choice with the traditional or religious leader who has experienced no significant foreign cultural influences.

For these two categories of people place above all principles or demands of a cultural nature – and against the aspirations of the people – their own economic and social privileges, their own *class interests*. That is a truth which the liberation movement cannot afford to ignore without risking betrayal of the economic, political, social and cultural objectives of the struggle.

Without minimizing the positive contribution which privileged classes may bring to the struggle, the liberation movement must, on the cultural level just as on the political level, base its action in popular culture, whatever may be the diversity of levels of cultures in the country. The cultural combat against colonial domination – the first phase of the liberation movement – can be planned efficiently only on the basis of the culture of the rural and urban working masses, including the nationalist (revolutionary) "petite bourgeoisie" who have been re-Africanized or who are ready for cultural reconversion. . . .

The political and moral unity of the liberation movement and of the people it represents and directs implies achieving the cultural unity of the social groups which are of key importance for the liberation struggle. This unity is achieved on the one hand by total identification with the environ-mental reality and with the fundamental problems and aspirations of the people; and, on the other hand, by progressive cultural identification of the various social groups participating in the struggle. . . .

The time is past when it was necessary to seek arguments to prove the cultural maturity of African peoples. The irrationality of the racist "theories" of a Gobineau or a Lévy-Bruhl neither interests nor convinces anyone but racists. In spite of colonial domination (and perhaps even because of this domination), Africa was able to impose respect for her cultural values. She even showed herself to be one of the richest of continents in cultural values. From Carthage to Giza to Zimbabwe, from Meroe to Benin and Ife, from Sahara or Timbuktu to Kilwa, across the immensity and the diversity of the continent's natural conditions, the culture of Afri-can peoples is an undeniable reality: in works of art as well as in oral and written traditions, in cosmological conceptions as well as in music and dance, in religions and belief as well as in the dynamic balance of economic, political and social structures created by African man.

The universal value of African culture is now an incontestable fact; nevertheless, it should not be forgotten that African man, whose hands, as the poet said, "placed the stones of the foundations of the world," has developed his culture frequently, if not constantly, in adverse conditions: from deserts to equatorial forests, from coastal marshes to the banks of great rivers subject to frequent flooding, in spite of all sorts of difficulties, including plagues which have destroyed plants and animals and man alike. In agreement with Basil Davidson and other researchers in African history and culture, we can say that the accomplishments of the African genius in economic, political, social and cultural domains, despite the inhospitable character of the environ-ment, are epic – comparable to the major historical examples of the greatness of man.

Of course, this reality constitutes a reason for pride and a stimulus to those who fight for the liberation and the progress of African peoples. But it is important not to lose sight of the fact that no culture is a perfect, finished whole. Culture, like history, is an expanding and developing phenom-enon. Even more important, we must take account of the fact that the fundamental characteristic of a culture is the highly dependent and reciprocal nature of its linkages with the social and economic reality of the environment, with the level of productive forces and the mode of production of the society which created it.

Culture, the fruit of history, reflects at every moment the material and spiritual reality of society, of man-the-individual and of man-the-social-be-ing, faced with conflicts which set him against nature and the exigencies of common life. From this we see that all culture is composed of essential and secondary elements, of strengths and weaknesses, of virtues and failings, of positive and negative aspects, of factors of progress and factors of stagnation or regression. From this also we can see that culture – the creation of society and the synthesis of the balances and the solutions which society engenders to resolve the conflicts which characterize each phase of its history – is a social reality, independent of the will of men, the color of their skins or the shape of their eyes.

A thorough analysis of cultural reality does not permit the claim that there exist continental or racial cultures. This is because, as with history, the development of culture proceeds in uneven fashion, whether at the level of a continent, a "race," or even a society. The coordinates of culture, like those of any developing phenomenon, vary in space and time, whether they be material (physical) or human (biological and social). The fact of recognizing the existence of common and particular features in the cultures of African peoples, independent of the color of their skin, does not necessarily imply that one and only one culture exists on the continent. In the same way that from a economic and political viewpoint we can recognize the existence of several Africas, so also there are many African cultures.

Without any doubt, underestimation of the cultural values of African peoples, based upon racist feelings and upon the intention of perpetuating foreign exploitation of Africans, has done much harm to Africa. But in the face of the vital need for progress, the following attitudes or behaviors will be no less harmful to Africa: indiscriminate compliments; systematic exaltation of virtues without condemning faults; blind acceptance of the values of the culture, without considering what presently or potentially regressive elements it contains; confusion between what is the expression of an objective and material historical reality and what appears to be a creation of the mind or the product of a peculiar temperament; absurd linking of artistic creations, whether good or not, with supposed racial characteristics; and finally, the non-scientific or a scientific critical appreciation of the cultural phenomenon.

Thus, the important thing is not to lose time in more or less idle discussion of the specific or unspecific characteristics of African cultural values, but rather to look upon these values as a conquest of a small piece of humanity for the common heritage of humanity, achieved in one or several phases of its evolution. The important thing is to proceed to critical analysis of African cultures in relation to the liberation movement and to the exigencies of progress – confronting this new stage in African history. It is important to be conscious of the value of African cultures in the framework of universal civilization, but to compare this value with that of other cultures, not with a view of deciding its superiority or inferiority, but in order to determine, in the general framework of the struggle for progress, what contribution African culture has made and can make, and what are the contributions it can or must receive from elsewhere. . . .

The more one realizes that the chief goal of the liberation movement goes beyond the achievement of political independence to the superior level of complete liberation of the productive forces and the construction of economic, social and cultural progress of the people, the more evident is the necessity of undertaking a selective analysis of the values of the culture within the framework of the struggle for liberation. The need for such an analysis of cultural values becomes more acute when, in order to face colonial violence, the liberation movement must mobilize and organize the people, under the direction of a strong and disciplined political organization, in order to resort to violence in the cause of freedom – *the armed struggle for the national liberation*. . . .

The armed struggle for liberation, launched in response to the colonialist oppressor, turns out to be a painful but efficient instrument for developing the cultural level of both the leadership strata in the liberation movement and the various social groups who participate in the struggle.

The leaders of the liberation movement, drawn generally from the "petite bourgeoisie" (intellectuals, clerks) or the urban working class (workers, chauffeurs, salary-earners in general), having to live day by day with the various peasant groups in the heart of the rural populations, come to know the people better. They discover at the grass roots the richness of their cultural values (philosophic, political, artistic, social and moral), acquire a clearer understanding of the economic realities of the country, of the problems, sufferings and hopes of the popular masses. The leaders realize, not without a certain astonishment, the richness of spirit, the capacity for reasoned discussion and clear exposition of ideas, the facility for understanding and assimilating concepts on the part of population groups who yesterday were forgotten, if not despised, and who were considered incompetent by the colonizer and even by some nationals. The leaders thus enrich their cultures – develop personally their capacity to serve the movement in the service of the people.

On their side, the working masses and, in particular, the peasants who are usually illiterate and never have moved beyond the boundaries of their village or region, in contact with other groups lose the complexes which constrained them in their relationships with other ethnic and social groups. They realize their crucial role in the struggle; they break the bounds of the village universe to integrate progressively into the country and the world; they acquire an infinite amount of new knowledge, useful for their immediate and future activity within the framework of the struggle, and they strengthen their political awareness by assimilating the principles of national and social revolution postulated by the struggle. They thereby become more able to play the decisive role of providing the principal force behind the liberation movement.

As we know, the armed liberation struggle requires the mobilization and organization of a significant majority of the population, the political and moral unity of the various social classes, the efficient use of modern arms and of other means of war, the progressive liquidation of the remnants of tribal mentality, and the rejection of social and religious rules and taboos which inhibit development of the struggle (gerontocracies, nepotism, social inferiority of women, rites and practices which are incompatible with the rational and national character of the struggle, etc.). The struggle brings about other profound modifications in the life of populations. The armed liberation struggle implies, therefore, a veritable forced march along the road to cultural progress.

Consider these features inherent in an armed liberation struggle: the practice of democracy, of criticism and self-criticism, the increasing responsibility of populations for the direction of their lives, literacy work, creation of schools and health services, training of cadres from peasant and worker backgrounds – and many other achievements. When we consider these features, we see that the armed liberation struggle is not only a product of culture but also a *determinant of culture*. This is without doubt for the people the prime recompense for the efforts and sacrifices which war demands. In this perspective, it behooves the liberation movement to define clearly the objectives of cultural resistance as an integral and determining part of the struggle.

From all that has just been said, it can be concluded that in the framework of the conquest of national independence and in the perspective of developing the economic and social progress of the people, the objectives must be at least the following: *development of a popular culture* and of all positive indigenous cultural values; *development of a national culture* based upon the history and the achievements of the struggle itself; constant promotion of the *political and moral awareness* of the people (of all social groups) as well as *patriotism*, of the spirit of sacrifice and devotion to the cause of independence, of justice, and of progress; development of a technical, technological, and *scientific culture*, compatible with the requirements for progress; development, on the basis of a critical assimilation of man's achievements in the domains of art, science, literature, etc., of a *universal culture* for perfect integration into the contemporary world, in the perspectives of its evolution; constant and generalized promotion of feelings of humanism, of solidarity, of respect and disinterested devotion to human beings.

The achievement of these objectives is indeed possible, because the armed struggle for liberation, in the concrete conditions of life of African peoples, confronted with the imperialist challenge, is an act of insemination upon history – the major expression of our culture and of our African essence. In the moment of victory, it must be translated into a significant leap forward of the culture of the people who are liberating themselves.

If that does not happen, then the efforts and sacrifices accepted during the struggle will have been made in vain. The struggle will have failed to achieve its objectives, and the people will have missed an opportunity for progress in the general framework of history.

Notes

This text was originally delivered 20 Feb. 1970 as part of the Eduardo Mondlane Memorial Lecture Series at Syracuse University, Syracuse, New York, under the auspicies of The Program of Eastern African Studies. It was translated from the French by Maureen Webster. Eduardo Mondlane, was the first President of the Mozambique Liberation Front (FRELIMO). He was assassinated by Portuguese agents on 3 Feb. 1969.

Philosophy and Race

32

The Conservation of Races

W. E. B. Du Bois

The American Negro has always felt an intense personal interest in discussions as to the origins and destinies of races: primarily because back of most discussions of race with which he is familiar, have lurked certain assumptions as to his natural abilities, as to his political, intellectual and moral status, which he felt were wrong. He has, consequently, been led to deprecate and minimize race distinctions, to believe intensely that out of one blood God created all nations, and to speak of human brotherhood as though it were the possibility of an already dawning tomorrow.

Nevertheless, in our calmer moments we must acknowledge that human beings are divided into races; that in this country the two most extreme types of the world's races have met, and the resulting problem as to the future relations of these types is not only of intense and living interest to us, but forms an epoch in the history of mankind.

It is necessary, therefore, in planning our movements, in guiding our future development, that at times we rise above the pressing, but smaller questions of separate schools and cars, wage-discrimination and lynch law, to survey the whole question of race in human philosophy and to lay, on a basis of broad knowledge and careful insight, those large lines of policy and higher ideals which may form our guiding lines and boundaries in the practical difficulties of every day. For it is certain that all human striving must recognize the hard limits of natural law, and that any striving, no matter how intense and earnest, which is against the constitution of the world, is vain. The question, then, which we must seriously consider is this: What is the real meaning of Race; what has, in the past, been the law of race development, and what lessons has the past history of race development to teach the rising Negro people?

When we thus come to inquire into the essential difference of races we find it hard to come at once to any definite conclusion. Many criteria of race differences have in the past been proposed, as color, hair, cranial measurements and language. And manifestly, in each of these respects, human beings differ widely. They vary in color, for instance, from the marble-like pallor of the Scandinavian to the rich, dark brown of the Zulu, passing by the creamy Slav, the yellow Chinese, the light brown Sicilian and the brown Egyptian. Men vary, too, in the texture of hair from the obstinately straight hair of the Chinese to the obstinately tufted and frizzled hair of the Bushman. In measurement of heads, again, men vary; from the broad-headed Tartar to the medium-headed European and the narrow-headed Hottentot; or, again in language, from the highly-inflected Roman tongue to the monosyllabic Chinese. All these physical characteristics are patent enough, and if they agreed with each other it would be very easy to classify mankind. Unfortunately for scientists, however, these criteria of race are most exasperatingly intermingled. Color does not agree with texture of hair, for many of the dark races have straight hair; nor does color agree with the breadth of the head, for the yellow

Tartar has a broader head than the German; nor, again, has the science of language as yet succeeded in clearing up the relative authority of these various and contradictory criteria. The final word of science, so far, is that we have at least two, perhaps three, great families of human beings – the whites and Negroes, possibly the yellow race. That other races have arisen from the intermingling of the blood of these two. This broad division of the world's races which men like Huxley and Raetzel have introduced as more nearly true than the old five-race scheme of Blumenbach, is nothing more than an acknowledgment that, so far as purely physical characteristics are concerned, the differences between men do not explain all the differences of their history. It declares, as Darwin himself said, that great as is the physical unlikeness of the various races of men their likenesses are greater, and upon this rests the whole scientific doctrine of Human Brotherhood.

Although the wonderful developments of human history teach that the grosser physical differences of color, hair and bone go but a short way toward explaining the different roles which groups of men have played in Human Progress, yet there are differences – subtle, delicate and elusive, though they may be – which have silently but definitely separated men into groups. While these subtle forces have generally followed the natural cleavage of common blood, descent, and physical peculiarities, they have at other times swept across and ignored these. At all times, however, they have divided human beings into races, which, while they perhaps transcend scientific definition, nevertheless, are clearly defined to the eye of the Historian and Sociologist.

If this be true, then the history of the world is the history, not of individuals, but of groups, not of nations, but of races, and he who ignores or seeks to override the race idea in human history ignores and overrides the central thought of all history. What, then, is a race? It is a vast family of human beings, generally of common blood and language, always of common history, traditions and impulses, who are both voluntarily and involuntarily striving together for the accomplishment of certain more or less vividly conceived ideals of life.

Turning to real history, there can be no doubt, first, as to the widespread, nay, universal, prevalence of the race idea, the race spirit, the race ideal, and as to its efficiency as the vastest and most ingenious invention for human progress. We, who have been reared and trained under the individu-

alistic philosophy of the Declaration of Independence and the *laisser-faire* philosophy of Adam Smith, are loath to see and loath to acknowledge this patent fact of human history. We see the Pharaohs, Caesars, Toussaints and Napoleons of history and forget the vast races of which they were but epitomized expressions. We are apt to think in our American impatience, that while it may have been true in the past that closed race groups made history, that here in conglomerate America *nous avons changer tout cela* – we have changed all that, and have no need of this ancient instrument of progress. This assumption of which the Negro people are especially fond, can not be established by a careful consideration of history.

We find upon the world's stage today eight distinctly differentiated races, in the sense in which History tells us the word must be used. They are, the Slavs of eastern Europe, the Teutons of middle Europe, the English of Great Britain and America, the Romance nations of southern and western Europe, the Negroes of Africa and America, the Semitic people of western Asia and northern Africa, the Hindoos of central Asia and the Mongolians of eastern Asia. There are, of course, other minor race groups, as the American Indians, the Esquimaux and the South Sea Islanders; these larger races, too, are far from homogeneous; the Slav includes the Czech, the Magyar, the Pole and the Russian; the Teuton includes the German, the Scandinavian and the Dutch; the English include the Scotch, the Irish and the conglomerate American. Under Romance nations the widely-differing Frenchman, Italian, Sicilian and Spaniard are comprehended. The term Negro is, perhaps, the most indefinite of all, combining the Mulattoes and Zamboes of America and the Egyptians, Bantus and Bushmen of Africa. Among the Hindoos are traces of widely differing nations, while the great Chinese, Tartar, Corean and Japanese families fall under the one designation – Mongolian.

The question now is: What is the real distinction between these nations? Is it the physical differences of blood, color and cranial measurements? Certainly we must all acknowledge that physical differences play a great part, and that, with wide exceptions and qualifications, these eight great races of today follow the cleavage of physical race distinctions; the English and Teuton represent the white variety of mankind; the Mongolian, the yellow; the Negroes, the black. Between these are many crosses and mixtures, where Mongolian and Teuton have blended into the Slav, and other mixtures have produced the Romance nations and the Semites. But while race differences have followed mainly physical race lines, yet no mere physical distinctions would really define or explain the deeper differences – the cohesiveness and continuity of these groups. The deeper differences are spiritual, psychical, differences – undoubtedly based on the physical, but infinitely transcending them. The forces that bind together the Teuton nations are, then, first, their race identity and common blood; secondly, and more important, a common history, common laws and religion, similar habits of thought and a conscious striving together for certain ideals of life. The whole process which has brought about these race differentiations has been a growth, and the great characteristic of this growth has been the differentiation of spiritual and mental differences between great races of mankind and the integration of physical differences.

The age of nomadic tribes of closely related individuals represents the maximum of physical differences. They were practically vast families, and there were as many groups as families. As the families came together to form cities the physical differences lessened, purity of blood was replaced by the requirement of domicile, and all who lived within the city bounds became gradually to be regarded as members of the group; i.e., there was a slight and slow breaking down of physical barriers. This, however, was accompanied by an increase of the spiritual and social differences between cities. This city became husbandmen, this, merchants, another warriors, and so on. The *ideals of life* for which the different cities struggled were different. When at last cities began to coalesce into nations there was another breaking down of barriers which separated groups of men. The larger and broader differences of color, hair and physical proportions were not by any means ignored, but myriads of minor differences disappeared, and the sociological and historical races of men began to approximate the present division of races as indicated by physical researches. At the same time the spiritual and physical differences of race groups which constituted the nations became deep and decisive. The English nation stood for constitutional liberty and commercial freedom; the German nation for science and philosophy; the Romance nations stood for literature and art, and the other race groups are striving, each in its own way, to develop for civilization its particular message, its particular ideal, which shall help to guide the world

nearer and nearer that perfection of human life for which we all long, that "one far off Divine event."

This has been the function of race differences up to the present time. What shall be its function in the future? Manifestly some of the great races of today – particularly the Negro race – have not as yet given to civilization the full spiritual message which they are capable of giving. I will not say that the Negro race has as yet given no message to the world, for it is still a mooted question among scientists as to just how far Egyptian civilization was Negro in its origin; if it was not wholly Negro, it was certainly very closely allied. Be that as it may, however the fact still remains that the full, complete Negro message of the whole Negro race has not as yet been given to the world: that the messages and ideal of the yellow race have not been completed, and that the striving of the mighty Slavs has but begun. The question is, then: How shall this message be delivered; how shall these various ideals be realized? The answer is plain: By the development of these race groups, not as individuals, but as races. For the development of Japanese genius, Japanese literature and art, Japanese spirit, only Japanese, bound and welded together, Japanese inspired by one vast ideal, can work out in its fullness the wonderful message which Japan has for the nations of the earth. For the development of Negro genius, of Negro literature and art, of Negro spirit, only Negroes bound and welded together, Negroes inspired by one vast ideal, can work out in its fullness the great message we have for humanity. We cannot reverse history; we are subject to the same natural laws as other races, and if the Negro is ever to be a factor in the world's history – if among the gaily-colored banners that deck the broad ramparts of civilization is to hang one uncompromising black, then it must be placed there by black hands, fashioned by black heads and hallowed by the travail of 200,000,000 black hearts beating in one glad song of jubilee.

For this reason, the advance guard of the Negro people – the 8,000,000 people of Negro blood in the United States of America – must soon come to realize that if they are to take their just place in the van of Pan-Negroism, then their destiny is *not* absorption by the white Americans. That if in America it is to be proven for the first time in the modern world that not only Negroes are capable of evolving individual men like Toussaint, the Saviour, but are a nation stored with wonderful possibilities of culture, then their destiny is not a servile imitation of Anglo-Saxon culture, but a stalwart originality which shall unswervingly follow Negro ideals.

It may, however, be objected here that the situation of our race in America renders this attitude impossible; that our sole hope of salvation lies in our being able to lose our race identity in the commingled blood of the nation; and that any other course would merely increase the friction of races which we call race prejudice, and against which we have so long and so earnestly fought.

Here, then, is the dilemma, and it is a puzzling one, I admit. No Negro who has given earnest thought to the situation of his people in America has failed, at some time in life, to find himself at these cross-roads; has failed to ask himself at some time: What, after all, am I? Am I an American or am I a Negro? Can I be both? Or is it my duty to cease to be a Negro as soon as possible and be an American? If I strive as a Negro, am I not perpetuating the very cleft that threatens and separates Black and White America? Is not my only possible practical aim the subduction of all that is Negro in me to the American? Does my black blood place upon me any more obligation to assert my nationality than German, or Irish or Italian blood would?

It is such incessant self-questioning and the hesitation that arises from it, that is making the present period a time of vacillation and contradiction for the American Negro; combined race action is stifled, race responsibility is shirked, race enterprises languish, and the best blood, the best talent, the best energy of the Negro people cannot be marshalled to do the bidding of the race. They stand back to make room for every rascal and demagogue who chooses to cloak his selfish deviltry under the veil of race pride.

Is this right? Is it rational? Is it good policy? Have we in America a distinct mission as a race – a distinct sphere of action and an opportunity for race development, or is self-obliteration the highest end to which Negro blood dare aspire?

If we carefully consider what race prejudice really is, we find it, historically, to be nothing but the friction between different groups of people; it is the difference in aim, in feeling, in ideals of two different races; if, now, this difference exists touching territory, laws, language, or even religion, it is manifest that these people cannot live in the same territory without fatal collision; but if, on the other hand, there is substantial agreement in laws, language and religion; if there is a satisfactory adjustment of economic life, then there is no reason why, in the same country and on the same street, two or three great national ideals might not thrive and develop, that man of different races might not strive together for their race ideals as well, perhaps even better, than in isolation. Here, it seems to me, is the reading of the riddle that puzzles so many of us. We are Americans, not only by birth and by citizenship, but by our political ideals, our language, our religion. Farther than that, our Americanism does not go. At that point, we are Negroes, members of a vast historic race that from the very dawn of creation has slept, but half awakening in the dark forests of its African fatherland. We are the first fruits of this new nation, the harbinger of that black tomorrow which is yet destined to soften the whiteness of the Teutonic today. We are that people whose subtle sense of song has given America its only American music, its only American fairy tales, its only touch of pathos and humor amid its mad money-getting plutocracy. As such, it is our duty to conserve our physical powers, our intellectual endowments, our spiritual ideals; as a race we must strive by race organization, by race solidarity, by race unity to the realization of that broader humanity which freely recognizes differences in men, but sternly deprecates inequality in their opportunities of development.

For the accomplishment of these ends we need race organizations: Negro colleges, Negro newspapers, Negro business organizations, a Negro school of literature and art, and an intellectual clearing house, for all these products of the Negro mind, which we may call a Negro Academy. Not only is all this necessary for positive advance, it is absolutely imperative for negative defense. Let us not deceive ourselves at our situation in this country. Weighted with a heritage of moral iniquity from our past history, hard pressed in the economic world by foreign immigrants and native prejudice, hated here, despised there and pitied everywhere; our one haven of refuge is ourselves, and but one means of advance, our own belief in our great destiny, our own implicit trust in our ability and worth. There is no power under God's high heaven that can stop the advance of eight thousand thousand honest, earnest, inspired and united people. But – and here is the rub – they *must* be honest, fearlessly criticizing their own faults, zealously correcting them; they must be *earnest*. No people that laughs at itself, and ridicules itself, and wishes to God it was anything but itself ever wrote its name in history; it *must* be inspired with the Divine faith of our black mothers, that out of the blood and dust of battle will march a victorious host, a mighty nation, a peculiar people, to speak to the nations of earth a Divine truth that shall make them free. And such a people must be united; not merely united for the organized theft of political spoils, not united to disgrace religion with whoremongers and ward-heelers; not united merely to protest and pass resolutions, but united to stop the ravages of consumption among the Negro people, united to keep black boys from loafing, gambling and crime; united to guard the purity of black women and to reduce that vast army of black prostitutes that is today marching to hell; and united in serious organizations, to determine by careful conference and thoughtful interchange of opinion the broad lines of policy and action for the American Negro.

This is the reason for being which the American Negro Academy has. It aims at once to be the epitome and expression of the intellect of the black-blooded people of America, the exponent of the race ideals of one of the world's great races. As such, the Academy must, if successful, be

(*a*) Representative in character.
(*b*) Impartial in conduct.
(*c*) Firm in leadership.

It must be representative in character; not in that it represents all interests or all factions, but in that it seeks to comprise something of the *best* thought, the most unselfish striving and the highest ideals. There are scattered in forgotten nooks and corners throughout the land, Negroes of some considerable training, of high minds, and high motives, who are unknown to their fellows, who exert far too little influence. These the Negro Academy should strive to bring into touch with each other and to give them a common mouthpiece.

The Academy should be impartial in conduct; while it aims to exalt the people it should aim to do so by truth – not by lies, by honesty – not by flattery. It should continually impress the fact upon the Negro people that they must not expect to have things done for them – they MUST DO FOR THEM-SELVES; that they have on their hands a vast work of self-reformation to do, and that a little less complaint and whining, and a little more dogged work and manly striving would do us more credit and benefit than a thousand Force or Civil Rights bills.

Finally, the American Negro Academy must point out a practical path of advance to the Negro people; there lie before every Negro today hundreds of questions of policy and right which must be settled and which each one settles now, not in accordance with any rule, but by impulse or individual preference; for instance: What should be the attitude of Negroes toward the educational qualification for voters? What should be our attitude toward separate schools? How should we meet discriminations on railways and in hotels? Such questions need not so much specific answers for each part as a general expression of policy, and nobody should be better fitted to announce such a policy than a representative honest Negro Academy.

All this, however, must come in time after careful organization and long conference. The immediate work before us should be practical and have direct bearing upon the situation of the Negro. The historical work of collecting the laws of the United States and of the various States of the Union with regard to the Negro is a work of such magnitude and importance that no body but one like this could think of undertaking it. If we could accomplish that one task we would justify our existence.

In the field of Sociology an appalling work lies before us. First, we must unflinchingly and bravely face the truth, not with apologies, but with solemn earnestness. The Negro Academy ought to sound a note of warning that would echo in every black cabin in the land: *Unless we conquer our present vices they will conquer us*; we are diseased, we are developing criminal tendencies, and an alarmingly large percentage of our men and women are sexually impure. The Negro Academy should stand and proclaim this over the housetops, crying with Garrison: *I will not equivocate, I will not retreat a single inch, and I will be heard*. The Academy should seek to gather about it the talented, unselfish men, the pure and noble-minded women, to fight an army of devils that disgraces our manhood and our womanhood. There does not stand today upon God's earth a race more capable in muscle, in intellect, in morals, than the American Negro, if he will bend his energies in the right direction; if he will

> Burst his birth's invidious bar
> And grasp the skirts of happy chance,
> And breast the blows of circumstance,
>   And grapple with his evil star.

In science and morals, I have indicated two fields of work for the Academy. Finally, in practical policy, I wish to suggest the following *Academy Creed*:

1. We believe that the Negro people, as a race, have a contribution to make to civilization and humanity, which no other race can make.

2. We believe it the duty of the Americans of Negro descent, as a body, to maintain their race identity until this mission of the Negro people is accomplished, and the ideal of human brotherhood has become a practical possibility.

3. We believe that, unless modern civilization is a failure, it is entirely feasible and practicable for two races in such essential political, economic and religious harmony as the white and colored people of America, to develop side by side in peace and mutual happiness, the peculiar contribution which each has to make to the culture of their common country.

4. As a means to this end we advocate, not such social equality between these races as would disregard human likes and dislikes, but such a social equilibrium as would, throughout all the complicated relations of life, give due and just consideration to culture, ability, and moral worth, whether they be found under white or black skins.

5. We believe that the first and greatest step toward the settlement of the present friction between the races – commonly called the Negro Problem – lies in the correction of the immorality, crime and laziness among the Negroes themselves, which still remains as a heritage from slavery. We believe that only earnest and long continued efforts on our own part can cure these social ills.

6. We believe that the second great step toward a better adjustment of the relations between the races, should be a more impartial selection of ability in the economic and intellectual world, and a greater respect for personal liberty and worth, regardless of race. We believe that only earnest efforts on the part of the white people of this country will bring much needed reform in these matters.

7. On the basis of the foregoing declaration, and firmly believing in our high destiny, we, as American Negroes, are resolved to strive in every honorable way for the realization of the best and highest aims, for the development of strong manhood and pure womanhood, and for the rearing of a race ideal in America and Africa, to the glory of God and the uplifting of the Negro people.

33

The Illusions of Race

Kwame Anthony Appiah

If this be true, the history of the world is the history, not of individuals, but of groups, not of nations, but of races . . .[1]

W. E. B. Du Bois

Alexander Crummell and Edward Wilmot Blyden began the intellectual articulation of a Pan-Africanist ideology, but it was W. E. B. Du Bois who laid both the intellectual and the practical foundations of the Pan-African movement. Du Bois's life was a long one, and his intellectual career – which he called the "autobiography of a race concept"[2] – encompassed almost the whole period of European colonial control of Africa. It is hard to imagine a more substantial rupture in political ideas than that which separates the division of Africa at the Congress of Berlin from the independence of Ghana, yet Du Bois was a teenager when the former happened in 1884, and, in 1957, he witnessed – and rejoiced in – the latter. And, as we shall see, there is an astonishing consistency in his position throughout the years. Not only did Du Bois live long, he wrote much; if any single person can offer us an insight into the archaeology of Pan-Africanism's idea of race, it is he.

Du Bois's first extended discussion of the concept of race is in "The Conservation of Races," a paper he delivered to the American Negro Academy in the year it was founded by Alexander Crummell. The "American Negro," he declares, "has been led to . . . minimize race distinctions" because "back of most of the discussions of race with which he is familiar, have lurked certain assumptions as to his natural abilities, as to his political, intellectual and moral status, which he felt were wrong." And he goes on: "Nevertheless, in our calmer moments we must acknowledge that human beings are divided into races," even if "when we come to inquire into the essential differences of races, we find it hard to come at once to any definite conclusion."[3] For what it is worth, however, "the final word of science, so far, is that we have at least two, perhaps three, great families of human beings – the whites and Negroes, possibly the yellow race."[4]

Du Bois is not, however, satisfied with the "final word" of the late-nineteenth-century science. For, as he thinks, what matter are not the "grosser physical differences of color, hair and bone" but the "differences – subtle, delicate and elusive, though they may be – which have silently but definitely separated men into groups."

> While these subtle forces have generally followed the natural cleavage of common blood, descent and physical peculiarities, they have at other times swept across and ignored these. At all times, however, they have divided human beings into races, which, while they perhaps transcend scientific definition, nevertheless, are clearly defined to the eye of the historian and sociologist.
>
> If this be true, then the history of the world is the history, not of individuals, but

of groups, not of nations, but of races . . .
What then is a race? It is a vast family of
human beings, generally of common blood
and language, always of common history,
traditions and impulses, who are both voluntarily and involuntarily striving together for
the accomplishment of certain more or less
vividly conceived ideals of life.[5]

We have moved, then, away from the "scientific"
– that is, biological and anthropological – conception of race to a sociohistorical notion. And, by this
sociohistorical criterion – whose breadth of sweep
certainly encourages the thought that no biological
or anthropological definition is possible – Du Bois
considers that there are not three but eight "distinctly differentiated races, in the sense in which
history tells us the word must be used."[6] The list
is an odd one: Slavs, Teutons, English (in both
Great Britain and America), Negroes (of Africa
and, likewise, America), the Romance race, Semites,
Hindus, and Mongolians.

Du Bois continues:

> The question now is: What is the real
> distinction between these nations? Is it
> physical differences of blood, color and
> cranial measurements? Certainly we must all
> acknowledge that physical differences play a
> great part . . . But while race differences
> have followed along mainly physical lines,
> yet no mere physical distinction would really
> define or explain the deeper differences – the
> cohesiveness and continuity of these groups.
> The deeper differences are spiritual, psy-
> chical, differences – undoubtedly based on
> the physical, but infinitely transcending
> them.[7]

The various races are

> striving, each in its own way, to develop for
> civilization its particular message, its par-
> ticular ideal, which shall help guide the
> world nearer and nearer that perfection of
> human life for which we all long, that "one
> far off Divine event."[8]

For Du Bois, then, the problem for the Negro is
the discovery and expression of the message of his
or her race.

> The full, complete Negro message of the

whole Negro race has not as yet been given
to the world. . . .

> The question is, then: how shall this
> message be delivered; how shall these vari-
> ous ideals be realized? The answer is plain:
> by the development of these race groups, not
> as individuals, but as races. . . . For the
> development of Negro genius, of Negro
> literature and art, of Negro spirit, only
> Negroes bound and welded together, Ne-
> groes inspired by one vast ideal, can work out
> in its fullness the great message we have for
> humanity. . . .
> For this reason, the advance guard of the
> Negro people – the eight million people of
> Negro blood in the United States of America
> – must soon come to realize that if they are
> to take their place in the van of Pan-
> Negroism, then their destiny is *not* absorp-
> tion by the white Americans.[9]

And so Du Bois ends by proposing his *Academy
Creed*, which begins with words that echo down
almost a century of American race relations:

1 We believe that the Negro people, as a race,
  have a contribution to make to civilization and
  humanity, which no other race can make.
2 We believe it is the duty of the Americans of
  Negro descent, as a body, to maintain their race
  identity until this mission of the Negro people
  is accomplished, and the ideal of human brotherhood has become a practical possibility.[10]

What can we make of this analysis and prescription?
On the face of it, Du Bois's argument in "The
Conservation of Races" is that "race" is not a
"scientific" – that is, biological – but a sociohistorical
concept. Sociohistorical races each have a "message" for humanity, a message that derives, in some
way, from God's purpose in creating races. The
Negro race has still to deliver its full message, and
so it is the duty of Negroes to work together –
through race organizations – so that this message
can be delivered.

We do not need the theological underpinnings of
this argument. What is essential is the thought that
Negroes, by virtue of their sociohistorical community, can achieve, through common action, worthwhile ends that will not otherwise be achieved. On
the face of it, then, Du Bois's strategy here is the
antithesis of a classic dialectic in the reaction to
prejudice. The thesis in this dialectic – which Du
Bois reports as the American Negro's attempt to

"minimize race distinctions" – is the denial of difference. Du Bois's antithesis is the acceptance of difference along with a claim that each group has its part to play, that the white and the Negro races are related not as superior to inferior but as complementaries; the Negro message is, with the white one, part of the message of humankind. What he espouses is what Sartre once called – in negritude – an "antiracist racism."[11]

I call this pattern a classic dialectic, and, indeed, we find it in feminism also. On the one hand, a simple claim to equality, a denial of substantial difference; on the other, a claim to a special message, revaluing the feminine "Other" not as the "helpmeet" of sexism but as the New Woman.

Because this *is* a classic dialectic, my reading of Du Bois's argument is a natural one. To confirm this interpretation we must establish that what Du Bois attempts, despite his own claims to the contrary, is not the transcendence of the nineteenth-century scientific conception of race – as we shall see, he relies on it – but rather, as the dialectic requires, a revaluation of the Negro race in the face of the sciences of racial inferiority. We can begin by analyzing the sources of tension in Du Bois's allegedly sociohistorical conception of race, which he explicitly sets over against the "scientific" conception. The tension is plain enough in his references to "common blood"; for this, dressed up with fancy craniometry, a dose of melanin, and some measure for hair curl, is what the scientific notion amounts to. If he has fully transcended the scientific notion, what is the role of this talk of "blood"?

We may leave aside for the moment the common "impulses" and the voluntary and involuntary "strivings." For these must be due either to a shared biological inheritance, "based on the physical, but infinitely transcending" it; or to a shared history; or, of course, to some combination of these. If Du Bois's notion is purely sociohistorical, then the issue is common history and traditions; otherwise, the issue is, at least in part, a common biology. We shall only know which when we understand the core of Du Bois's conception of race.

The claim that a race generally shares a common language is also plainly inessential: the "Romance" race is not of common language, nor, more obviously, is the Negro. And "common blood" can mean little more than "of shared ancestry," which is already implied by Crummellian talk of a "vast *family*." At the center of Du Bois's conception, then, is the claim that a race is "a vast family of

human beings, always of a common history [and] traditions."[12] So, if we want to understand Du Bois, our question must be: What is a "family . . . of common history"?

We already see that the scientific notion, which presupposes common features in virtue of a common biology derived from a common descent, is not fully transcended. It is true that a family can have adopted children, kin by social rather than biological law. By analogy, therefore, a vast human family might contain people joined together not by biology but by an act of choice. But it is plain enough that Du Bois cannot have been contemplating this possibility: like all of his contemporaries, he would have taken it for granted that race is a matter of birth. Indeed, to understand the talk of "family," we must distance ourselves from *all* of its sociological meaning. A family is usually defined culturally through either patrilineal or matrilineal descent alone.[13] But if an individual drew a "conceptual" family tree back over five hundred years and assumed that he or she was descended from each ancestor in only one way, the tree would have more than a million branches at the top. Although, in fact, many individuals would be represented on more than one branch – that far back, we are all going to be descended from many people by more than one route – it is plain, as a result, that a matri- or patrilineal conception of our family histories drastically under-represents the biological range of our ancestry.

Biology and social convention go startlingly different ways. Let's pretend, secure in our republicanism, that the claim of the queen of England to the throne depends partly on a single line from one of her ancestors nine hundred years ago. If there were no overlaps in her family tree, there would be more than fifty thousand billion such lines, though, of course, there have never been anywhere near that many people on the planet; even with reasonable assumptions about overlaps, there are millions of such lines. We chose one line, even though most of the population of England is probably descended from William the Conqueror by *some* uncharted route. Biology is democratic: all parents are equal. Thus to speak of two people being of common ancestry is to require that somewhere in the past a large proportion of the branches leading back in their family trees coincided.[14]

Already, then, Du Bois requires, as the scientific conception does, a common ancestry (in the sense just defined) with whatever – if anything – this biologically entails. Yet apparently this does not commit him to the scientific conception, for there are many groups of common ancestry – ranging, at its widest, from humanity in general to the narrower group of Slavs, Teutons, and Romance people taken together – that do not, for Du Bois, constitute races. Thus, Du Bois's "common history," which must be what is supposed to distinguish Slav from Teuton, is an essential part of his conception. The issue now is whether a common history is something that could be a criterion that distinguishes one group of human beings – extended in time – from another. Does adding a notion of common history allow us to make the distinctions between Slav and Teuton, or between English and Negro? The answer is no.

Consider, for example, Du Bois himself. As the descendant of Dutch ancestors, why does not the history of Holland in the fourteenth century (which he shares with all people of Dutch descent) make him a member of the Teutonic race? The answer is straightforward: the Dutch were not Negroes, Du Bois is. But it follows from this that the history of Africa is part of the common history of African-Americans not simply because African-Americans are descended from various peoples who played a part in African history but because African history is the history of people of the same race.

My general point is this: just as to recognize two events at different times as part of the history of a single individual, we have to have a criterion of identity for the individual at each of those times, independent of his or her participation in the two events, so, when we recognize two events as belonging to the history of one race, we have to have a criterion of membership of the race at those two times, independently of the participation of the members in the two events. To put it more simply: sharing a common group history cannot be a *criterion* for being members of the same group, for we would have to be able to identify the group in order to identify *its* history. Someone in the fourteenth century could share a common history with me through our membership in a historically extended race only if something accounts for their membership in the race in the fourteenth century and mine in the twentieth. That something cannot, on pain of circularity, be the history of the race.[15]

There is a useful analogy here, which I relied on a moment ago, between the historical continuity of races and the temporal continuity of people. Du Bois's attempt to make sense of racial identity through time by way of a figurative "long memory" subserves the same function as John Locke's

attempt – in his *Essay Concerning Human Understanding* – to make literal memory the core of the soul's identity through time. For Locke needed to have an account of the nature of the soul that did not rely on the physical continuity of the body, just as Du Bois wanted to rely on something more uplifting than the brute continuity of the germ plasm. Locke's view was that two souls at different times were, in the philosopher's jargon, "time slices" of the same individual if the later one had memories of the earlier one. But, as philosophers since Locke have pointed out, we cannot tell whether a memory is evidence of the rememberer's identity, even if what is "remembered" really did happen to an earlier person, unless we know already that the rememberer and the earlier person are one. For it is quite conceivable that someone should think that they recall something that actually happened to somebody else. I have simply applied this same strategy of argument against Du Bois. History may have made us what we are, but the choice of a slice of the past in a period before your birth as your own history is always exactly that: a choice. The phrase the "invention of tradition" is a pleonasm.[16]

Whatever holds Du Bois's races conceptually together, then, it cannot be a common history. It is only because they are already bound together that members of a race at different times can share a history at all. If this is true, Du Bois's reference to a common history cannot be doing any work in his individuation of races. And once we have stripped away the sociohistorical elements from Du Bois's definition of race, we are left with his true criterion.

Consequently, not only the talk of language, which Du Bois admits is neither necessary (the Romance race speaks many languages) nor sufficient (African-Americans generally speak the same language as other Americans) for racial identity, must be expunged from the definition; now we have seen that talk of common history and traditions must go too. We are left with common descent and the common impulses and strivings, which I put aside earlier. Since common descent, and the characteristics that flow from it are part of the nineteenth-century scientific conception of race, these impulses are all that is left to do the job that Du Bois had claimed for a sociohistorical conception: namely, to distinguish his conception from the biological one. Du Bois claims that the existence of races is "clearly defined to the eye of the historian and sociologist."[17] Since common ancestry is acknowledged by biology as a criterion, whatever extra insight is provided by sociohistorical understanding can only be gained by observation of the common impulses and strivings. Reflection suggests, however, that this cannot be true. For what common impulses – whether voluntary or involuntary – do Romance people share that the Teutons and the English do not?

Du Bois had read the historiography of the Anglo-Saxon school, which accounted for the democratic impulse in America by tracing it to the racial tradition of the Anglo-Saxon moot. He had read American and British historians in earnest discussion of the "Latin" spirit of Romance peoples, and perhaps he had believed some of it. Here, then, might be the source of the notion that history and sociology can observe the differing impulses of races.

In all these writings, however, such impulses are allegedly discovered to be the *a posteriori* properties of racial and national groups, not to be criteria of membership of them. It is, indeed, because the claim is *a posteriori* that historical evidence is relevant to it. And if we ask which common impulses that history has detected allow us to recognize the Negro, we shall see that Du Bois's claim to have found in these impulses a criterion of identity is mere bravado. If, without evidence about his or her impulses, we can say who is a Negro, then it cannot be part of what it is to be a Negro that he or she has them; rather it must be an *a posteriori* claim that people of a common race, defined by descent and biology, have impulses, for whatever reason, in common. Of course, the common impulses of a biologically defined group may be historically caused by common experiences, common history. But Du Bois's claim can only be that biologically defined races happen to share, for whatever reason, common impulses. The common impulses cannot be a criterion of membership of the group. And if that is so, we are left with the scientific conception.

How, then, is it possible for Du Bois's criteria to issue in eight groups, while the scientific conception issues in three? The reason is clear from the list. Slavs, Teutons, English, Hindus, and Romance peoples each live in a characteristic geographical region. (American English – and, for that matter, American Teutons, American Slavs, and American Romance people – share recent ancestry with their European "cousins" and thus share a mildly more complex relation to a place and its languages and traditions.) Semites (*modulo* such details as the Jewish Diaspora and the westward expansion of the

Islamized Arabs) and Mongolians (this is the whole population of eastern Asia) share a (rather larger) geographical region also. Du Bois's talk of common history conceals his superaddition of a geographical criterion: your history is, in part, the history of people who lived in the same place.[18]

The criterion Du Bois is actually using amounts, then, to this: people are members of the same race if they share features in virtue of being descended largely from people of the same region. Those features may be physical (hence African-Americans are Negroes) or cultural (hence Anglo-Americans are English). Focusing on one sort of feature – "grosser differences of color, hair and bone" – you get "whites and Negroes, possibly the yellow race," the "final word of science, so far." Focusing on a different feature – language or shared customs – you get Teutons, Slavs, and Romance peoples. The tension in Du Bois's definition of race reflects the fact that for the purposes of European historiography (of which his Harvard and University of Berlin trainings had made him aware), it was the latter that mattered, but for purposes of American social and political life it was the former.

The real difference in Du Bois's conception, therefore, is not that his definition of race is at odds with the scientific one: it is rather, as the dialectic requires, that he assigns to race a different moral and metaphysical significance from the majority of his white contemporaries. The distinctive claim is that the Negro race has a positive message, a message that is not only different but valuable. And that, it seems to me, is the significance of the sociohistorical dimension; for the strivings of a race are, as Du Bois viewed the matter, the stuff of history: "The history of the world is the history, not of individuals, but of groups, not of nations, but of races, and he who ignores or seeks to override the race idea in human history ignores and overrides the central thought of all history."[19] By studying history, we can discern the outlines of the message of each race.

We have seen that, for the purpose that concerned him most – namely for understanding the status of the Negro – Du Bois was thrown back on the "scientific" definition of race, which he officially rejected. But the scientific definition (Du Bois's uneasiness with which is reflected in his remark that races "perhaps transcend scientific definition") was itself already threatened as he spoke at the first meeting of the Negro Academy. In the latter nineteenth century most thinking people (like many even today) believed that what Du Bois called the "grosser differences" were a sign of an inherited racial essence, which accounted for the intellectual and moral deficiency of the "lower" races. In "The Conservation of Races" Du Bois elected, in effect, to admit that color was a sign of a racial essence but to deny that the cultural capacities of the black-skinned, curly-haired members of humankind – the capacities determined by their essence – were inferior to those of the white-skinned, straighter-haired ones. But the collapse of the sciences of racial inferiority led Du Bois to repudiate the connection between cultural capacity and gross morphology, to deny the familiar "impulses and strivings" of his earlier definition. We can find evidence of this change of mind in an article in the August 1911 issue of *The Crisis*, the journal of the American National Association for the Advancement of Colored People, which he edited vigorously through most of the early years of the century.

> The leading scientists of the world have come forward . . . and laid down in categorical terms a series of propositions[20] which may be summarized as follows:
> 1. (a) It is not legitimate to argue from differences in physical characteristics to differences in mental characteristics. . . .
> 2. The civilization of a . . . race at any particular moment of time offers no index to its innate or inherited capacities.[21]

The results have been amply confirmed since then. And we do well, I think, to remind ourselves of the current picture.

The evidence in the contemporary biological literature is, at first glance, misleading. For despite a widespread scientific consensus on the underlying genetics, contemporary biologists are not agreed on the question whether there are any human races. Yet, for our purposes, we can reasonably regard this issue as terminological. What most people in most cultures ordinarily believe about the significance of "racial"; difference is quite remote from what the biologists *are* agreed on, and, in particular, it is not consistent with what I have called *racialism*. Every reputable biologist will agree that human genetic variability between the populations of Africa or Europe or Asia is not much greater than that within those populations, though how much greater depends, in part, on the measure of genetic variability the biologist chooses. If biologists want to make

interracial difference seem relatively large, they can say that "the proportion of genic variation attributable to racial difference is . . . 9–11%."[22] If they want to make it seem small, they can say that, for two people who are both "Caucasoid," the chances of differing in genetic constitution at one site on a given chromosome have recently been estimated at about 14.3 per cent, while for any two people taken at random from the human population the same calculations suggest a figure of about 14.8 per cent. The underlying statistical facts about the distribution of variant characteristics in human populations and subpopulations are the same, whichever way you express the matter. Apart from the visible morphological characteristics of skin, hair, and bone, by which we are inclined to assign people to the broadest racial categories – black, white, yellow – there are few genetic characteristics to be found in the population of England that are not found in similar proportions in Zaire or in China, and few too (though more) that are found in Zaire but not in similar proportions in China or in England. All this, I repeat, is part of the consensus.

A more familiar part of the consensus is that the differences between peoples in language, moral affections, aesthetic attitudes, or political ideology – those differences that most deeply affect us in our dealings with each other – are not to any significant degree biologically determined.

This claim will, no doubt, seem outrageous to those who confuse the question whether biological difference accounts for our differences with the question whether biological similarity accounts for our similarities. Some of our similarities as human beings in these broadly cultural respects – the capacity to acquire human languages, for example, or the ability to smile – *are* to a significant degree biologically determined. We can study the biological basis of these cultural capacities, and give biological explanations of features of our exercise of them. But if biological difference between human beings is unimportant in these explanations – and it is – then racial difference, as a species of biological difference, will not matter either. We can see why if we attend to the underlying genetics.

Human characteristics are genetically determined,[23] to the extent that they are determined, by sequences of DNA in the chromosome – in other words, by genes.[24] A region of a chromosome occupied by a gene is called a *locus*. Some loci are occupied in different members of a population by different genes, each of which is called an *allele*; and a locus is said to be *polymorphic* in a population if there is at least a pair of alleles for it. Perhaps as many as half the loci in the human population are polymorphic; the rest, naturally enough, are said to be *monomorphic*.

Many loci have not just two alleles but several, and each has a frequency in the population. Suppose a particular locus has n alleles, which we can just call 1, 2, and so on up to n; then we can call the frequencies of these alleles $x_1, x_2, \ldots, x_n$. If you consider two members of a population chosen at random and look at the same locus on one chromosome of each of them, the probability that they will have the same allele at the locus is just the probability that they will both have the first allele (x_1^2), plus the probability that they'll both have the second $(x_2^2) \ldots$ plus the probability that they will both have the nth (x_n^2). We can call this number the *expected homozygosity* at that locus, for it is just the proportion of people in the population who would be homozygous at that locus – having identical alleles at that locus on each of the relevant chromosomes – provided the population was mating at random.[25]

Now if we take the average value of the expected homozygosity for all loci, polymorphic and monomorphic (which geneticists tend to label J), we have a measure of the chance that two people, taken at random from the population, will share the same allele at a locus on a chromosome taken at random. This is a good measure of how similar a randomly chosen pair of individuals should be expected to be in their biology, *and* a good guide to how closely – on the average – the members of the population are genetically related.

I can now express simply one measure of the extent to which members of those human populations we call races differ more from each other than they do from members of the same race. For the value of J for "Caucasoids" – estimated, in fact, largely from samples of the English population[26] – is estimated to be about 0.857, while that for the whole human population is estimated at 0.852. The chances, in other words, that two people taken at random from the human population will have the same characteristic at a random locus are about 85.2 per cent, while the chances for two (white) people taken from the population of England are about 85.7 per cent. And since 85.2 is 100 minus 14.8, and 85.7 is 100 minus 14.3, this is equivalent to what I said previously: the chances of two people who are both "Caucasoid" differing in genetic constitution at one site on a given chromosome are about 14.3 per cent, while, for any two people taken at random

from the human population, they are about 14.8 per cent.

The conclusion is obvious: given only a person's race, it is hard to say what his or her biological characteristics (apart from those that human beings share) will be, except in respect of the "grosser" features of color, hair, and bone (the genetics of which is, in any case, rather poorly understood) – features of "morphological differentiation," as the evolutionary biologist would say. As Nei and Roychoudhury express themselves, somewhat coyly, "The extent of genic differentiation between human races is not always correlated with the degree of morphological differentiation."[27] This may seem relatively untroubling to committed racialists. Race, they might say, is at least important in predicting morphological difference. But that, though true, is not a biological fact but a logical one, for Nei and Roychoudhury's races are defined by their morphology in the first place. The criterion for excluding from an American "Caucasoid" sample people with black skins is just the "gross" morphological fact that their skins are black. But recent immigrants of eastern European ancestry would be included in the sample, while dark-skinned people whose ancestors for the last ten generations had largely lived in the New World would be excluded.

To establish that this notion of race is relatively unimportant in explaining biological differences between people, where biological difference is measured in the proportion of differences in loci on the chromosome, is not yet to show that race is unimportant in explaining cultural difference. It could be that large differences in intellectual or moral capacity are caused by differences at very few loci, and that at these loci, all (or most) black-skinned people differ from all (or most) white-skinned or yellow-skinned ones. As it happens, there is little evidence for any such proposition and much against it. But suppose we had reason to believe it. In the biological conception of the human organism, in which characteristics are determined by the pattern of genes in interaction with environments, it is the presence of the alleles (which give rise to these moral and intellectual capacities) that accounts for the observed differences in those capacities in people in similar environments. So the characteristic racial morphology – skin and hair and bone – could be a sign of those differences only if it were (highly) correlated with those alleles. Since there are no such strong correlations, even those who think that intellectual and moral character are strongly genetically determined must accept that *race* is at best a poor indicator of capacity.

When I define *racialism* I [would say] that it [is] committed not just to the view that there are heritable characteristics, which constitute "a sort of racial essence," but also to the claim that the essential heritable characteristics account for more than the visible morphology – skin color, hair type, facial features – on the basis of which we make our informal classifications. To say that biological races existed because it was possible to classify people into a small number of classes according to their gross morphology would be to save racialism in the letter but lose it in the substance. The notion of race that was recovered would be of no biological interest – the interesting biological generalizations are about genotypes, phenotypes, and their distribution in geographical populations. We could just as well classify people according to whether or not they were redheaded, or redheaded and freckled, or redheaded, freckled, and broad-nosed too, but nobody claims that this sort of classification is central to human biology.

There are relatively straightforward reasons for thinking that large parts of humanity will fit into no class of people who can be characterized as sharing not only a common superficial morphology but also significant other biological characteristics. The nineteenth-century dispute between monogenesis and polygenesis, between the view that we are descended from one original population and the view that we descend from several, is over. There is no doubt that all human beings descend from an original population (probably, as it happens, in Africa), and that from there people radiated out to cover the habitable globe. Conventional evolutionary theory would predict that as these populations moved into different environments and new characters were thrown up by mutation, some differences would emerge as different characteristics gave better chances of reproduction and survival. In a situation where a group of people was isolated genetically for many generations, significant differences between populations could build up, though it would take a very extended period before the differences led to reproductive isolation – the impossibility of fertile breeding – and thus to the origin of a new pair of distinct species. We know that there is no such reproductive isolation between human populations, as a walk down any street in New York or Paris or Rio will confirm, but we also know that none of the major human population groups have been reproductively isolated for very many generations. If I may be excused what will

sound like a euphemism, at the margins there is always the exchange of genes.

Not only has there always been some degree of genetic linkage of this marginal kind; human history contains continued large-scale movements of people – the "hordes" of Attila the Hun, the Mediterranean jihads of the newly Islamized Arabs, the Bantu migrations – that represent possibilities for genetic exchange. As a consequence, all human populations are linked to each other through neighboring populations, *their* neighbors, and so on. We might have ended up as a "ring species," like the gulls of the *Larus argentatus* and *Larus fuscus* groups that circumscribe the North Pole, where there is inbreeding between most neighboring populations but reproductive isolation of the varieties that form the beginning and end of the chain of variation, but we did not.[28]

The classification of people into "races" would be biologically interesting if both the margins and the migrations had not left behind a genetic trail. But they have, and along that trail are millions of us (the numbers obviously depending on the criteria of classification that are used) who can be fitted into no plausible scheme at all. In a sense, trying to classify people into a few races is like trying to classify books in a library: you may use a single property – size, say – but you will get a useless classification, or you may use a more complex system of interconnected criteria, and then you will get a good deal of arbitrariness. No one – not even the most compulsive librarian! – thinks that book classifications reflect deep facts about books. Each of them is more or less useless for various purposes; all of them, as we know, have the kind of rough edges that take a while to get around. And nobody thinks that a library classification can settle which books we should value; the numbers in the Dewey decimal system do not correspond with qualities of utility or interest or literary merit.

The appeal of race as a classificatory notion provides us with an instance of a familiar pattern in the history of science. In the early phases of theory, scientists begin, inevitably, with the categories of their folk theories of the world, and often the criteria of membership of these categories can be detected with the unaided senses. Thus, in early chemistry, color and taste played an important role in the classification of substances; in early natural history, plant and animal species were identified largely by their gross visible morphology. Gradually, as the science develops, however, concepts are developed whose application requires more than the unaided senses; instead of the phenomenal properties of things, we look for "deeper," more theoretical properties. The price we pay is that classification becomes a more specialized activity; the benefit we gain is that we are able to make generalizations of greater power and scope. Few candidates for laws of nature can be stated by reference to the colors, tastes, smells, or touches of objects. It is hard for us to accept that the colors of objects, which play so important a role in our visual experience and our recognition of everyday objects, turn out neither to play an important part in the behavior of matter nor to be correlated with properties that do. Brown, for example, a color whose absence would make a radical difference to the look of the natural world, is hard to correlate in any clear way with the physical properties of reflecting surfaces.[29]

This desire to save the phenomena of our experience by way of objects and properties that are hidden from our direct view is, of course, a crucial feature of the natural sciences. At the heart of this project, as Heisenberg – one of the greatest physicists of our and any time – once pointed out, is a principle that he ascribed to Democritus:

> Democritus' atomic theory . . . realizes that it is impossible to explain rationally the perceptible qualities of matter except by tracing these back to the behaviour of entities which themselves no longer possess these qualities. If atoms are really to explain the origin of colour and smell of visible material bodies, then they cannot possess properties like colour and smell.[30]

The explanation of the phenotypes of organisms in terms of their genotypes fits well into this Democritean pattern. In the same way, nineteenth-century race science sought in a heritable racial essence an explanation of what its proponents took to be the observed phenomena of the differential distribution in human populations both of morphological and of psychological and social traits. What modern genetics shows is that there is no such underlying racial essence. There was nothing wrong with the Democritean impulse, only with the particular form it took and the prejudices that informed – perhaps one should say "deformed" – the theorists' views of the phenomena.

The disappearance of a widespread belief in the biological category of the Negro would leave nothing for racists to have an attitude toward. But it would offer, by itself, no guarantee that Africans would escape from the stigma of centuries. Extrinsic racists could disappear and be replaced by people who believed that the population of Africa had in its gene pool fewer of the genes that account for those human capacities that generate what is valuable in human life; fewer, that is, than in European or Asian or other populations. Putting aside the extraordinary difficulty of defining which genes these are, there is, of course, no scientific basis for this claim. A confident expression of it would therefore be evidence only of the persistence of old prejudices in new forms. But even this view would be, in one respect, an advance on extrinsic racism. For it would mean that each African would need to be judged on his or her own merits. Without some cultural information, being told that someone is of African origin gives you little basis for supposing anything much about them. Let me put the claim at its weakest: in the absence of a racial essence, there could be no guarantee that some particular person was not more gifted – in some specific respect – than any or all others in the populations of other regions.[31]

It was earlier evidence, pointing similarly to the conclusion that "the genic variation within and between the three major races of man . . . is small compared with the intraracial variation"[32] and that differences in morphology were not correlated strongly with intellectual and moral capacity, that led Du Bois in *The Crisis* to an explicit rejection of the claim that biological race mattered for understanding the status of the Negro:

> So far at least as intellectual and moral aptitudes are concerned we ought to speak of civilizations where we now speak of races . . . Indeed, even the physical characteristics, excluding the skin color of a people, are to no small extent the direct result of the physical and social environment under which it is living. . . . These physical characteristics are furthermore too indefinite and elusive to serve as a basis for any rigid classification or division of human groups.[33]

This is straightforward enough. Yet it would be too swift a conclusion to suppose that Du Bois here expresses his deepest convictions. After 1911 he went on to advocate Pan-Africanism, as he had advocated Pan-Negroism in 1897, and whatever African-Americans and Africans, from Asante to

Zulu, share, it is not a single civilization.

Du Bois managed to maintain Pan-Africanism while officially rejecting talk of race as anything other than a synonym for color. We can see how he did this if we turn to his second autobiography, *Dusk of Dawn*, published in 1940.

In *Dusk of Dawn* – the "essay toward the autobiography of a race concept" – Du Bois explicitly allies himself with the claim that race is not a "scientific" concept.

> It is easy to see that scientific definition of race is impossible; it is easy to prove that physical characteristics are not so inherited as to make it possible to divide the world into races; that ability is the monopoly of no known aristocracy; that the possibilities of human development cannot be circumscribed by color, nationality or any conceivable definition of race.[34]

But we need no scientific definition, for

> All this has nothing to do with the plain fact that throughout the world today organized groups of men by monopoly of economic and physical power, legal enactment and intellectual training are limiting with determination and unflagging zeal the development of other groups; and that the concentration particularly of economic power today puts the majority of mankind into a slavery to the rest.[35]

Or, as he puts it pithily a little later, "the black man is a person who must ride 'Jim Crow' in Georgia."[36]

Yet, just a few pages earlier, he has explained why he remains a Pan-Africanist, committed to a political program that binds all this indefinable black race together. This passage is worth citing extensively.

Du Bois begins with Countee Cullen's question – What is Africa to me? – and replies:

> Once I should have answered the question simply: I should have said "fatherland" or perhaps better "motherland" because I was born in the century when the walls of race were clear and straight; when the world consisted of mut[u]ally exclusive races; and even though the edges might be blurred, there was no question of exact definition and

understanding of the meaning of the word. . . .

Since [the writing of "The Conservation of Races"] the concept of race has so changed and presented so much of contradiction that as I face Africa I ask myself: what is it between us that constitutes a tie which I can feel better than I can explain? Africa is of course my fatherland. Yet neither my father nor my father's father ever saw Africa or knew its meaning or cared overmuch for it. My mother's folk were closer and yet their direct connection, in culture and race, became tenuous; still my tie to Africa is strong. On this vast continent were born and lived a large portion of my direct ancestors going back a thousand years or more. The mark of their heritage is upon me in color and hair. These are obvious things, but of little meaning in themselves; only important as they stand for real and more subtle differences from other men. Whether they do or not, I do not know nor does science know today.

But one thing is sure and that is the fact that since the fifteenth century these ancestors of mine and their descendants have had a common history; have suffered a common disaster and have one long memory. The actual ties of heritage between the individuals of this group vary with the ancestors that they have in common with many others: Europeans and Semites, perhaps Mongolians, certainly American Indians. But the physical bond is least and the badge of color relatively unimportant save as a badge; the real essence of this kinship is its social heritage of slavery; the discrimination and insult; and this heritage binds together not simply the children of Africa, but extends through yellow Asia and into the South Seas. It is this unity that draws me to Africa.[37]

This passage is affecting, powerfully expressed. We should like to be able to follow it in its conclusions. But, since it seduces us into error, we should begin distancing ourselves from the appeal of its argument by noticing how it echoes our earlier text. Color and hair are unimportant save "as they stand for real and more subtle differences," Du Bois says here, and we recall the "subtle forces" that "have generally followed the natural cleavage of common blood, descent and physical peculiarities" of "The Conservation of Races." There it was an essential part of the argument that these subtle forces – impulses and strivings – were the common property of those who shared a "common blood"; here, Du Bois does "not know nor does science" whether this is so. But if it is not so, then, on Du Bois's own admission, these "obvious things" are "of little meaning." And if they are of little meaning, then his mention of them marks, on the surface of his argument, the extent to which he cannot quite escape the appeal of the earlier conception of race.

Du Bois's yearning for the earlier conception that he has now prohibited himself accounts for the pathos of the chasm between the unconfident certainty that Africa is "of course" his fatherland and the concession that it is not the land of his father or his father's father. What use is such a fatherland? What use is a motherland with which even your mother's connection is "tenuous"? What does it matter that a large portion of his ancestors have lived on that vast continent, if there is no subtler bond with them than brute – that is, culturally unmediated – biological descent and its entailed "badge" of hair and color?

Even in the passage that follows his explicit disavowal of the scientific conception of race, the references to "common history" – the "one long memory," the "social heritage of slavery" – only lead us back into the now-familiar move to substitute for the biological conception of race a sociohistorical one. And that, as we have seen, is simply to bury the biological conception below the surface, not to transcend it. Because he never truly "speaks of civilization," Du Bois cannot ask if there is not in American culture – which undoubtedly *is* his – an African residue to take hold of and rejoice in, a subtle connection mediated not by genetics but by intentions, by meaning. Du Bois has no more conceptual resources here for explicating the unity of the Negro race – the Pan-African identity – than he had in "The Conservation of Races" half a century earlier. A glorious non sequitur must be submerged in the depths of the argument. It is easily brought to the surface.

If what Du Bois has in common with Africa is a history of "discrimination and insult," then this binds him, on his own account, to "yellow Asia and . . . the South Seas" also. How can something he shares with the whole nonwhite world bind him to a part of it? Once we interrogate the argument here, a further suspicion arises that the claim to this bond is based on a hyperbolic reading of the facts. The "discrimination and insult" that we know Du Bois experienced in his American childhood and as an adult citizen of the industrialized world were different in character from that experienced by, say, Kwame Nkrumah in colonized West Africa, and were absent altogether in large parts of "yellow Asia." What Du Bois shares with the nonwhite world is not insult but the *badge* of insult, and the badge, without the insult, is just the very skin and hair and bone that it is impossible to connect with a scientific definition of race.

Du Bois's question deserves a more careful answer than he gives it. What *does* cement together people who share a characteristic – the "badge of insult" – on the basis of which some of them have suffered discrimination? We might answer: "Just that; so there is certainly something that the nonwhite people of the world share." But if we go on to ask what harm exactly a young woman in Mali suffers from antiblack race prejudice in Paris, this answer misses all the important details. She *does* suffer, of course, because, for example, political decisions about North–South relations are strongly affected by racism in the metropolitan cultures of the North. But this harm is more systemic, less personal, than the affront to individual dignity represented by racist insults in the postindustrial city. If she is an intellectual, reflecting on the cultures of the North, she may also feel the mediated sense of insult: she may know, after all, that if she were there, in Paris, she would risk being subjected to some of the same discriminations; she may recognize that racism is part of the reason why she could not get a visa to go there; why she would not have a good time if she did.

Such thoughts are certainly maddening, as African and African-American and black European intellectuals will avow, if you ask them how they feel about the racist immigration policies of Europe or the institutionalized racism of apartheid. And they are thoughts that can be had by any nonwhite person anywhere who knows – in a phrase of Chinua Achebe's – "how the world is moving." The thought that if *I* were there now, I would be a victim strikes at you differently, it seems to me, from the thought – which can enrage any decent white human being – that if I were there and *if I were not white*, I would be a victim.[38] Yet we should always remember that this thought, too, has led many to an identification with the struggle against racism.

The lesson, I think, of these reflections must be that there is no one answer to the question what identifications our antiracism may lead us into. Du Bois writes as if he has to choose between Africa, on the one hand, and "yellow Asia and . . . the

South Seas," on the other. But that, it seems to me, is just the choice that racism imposes on us – and just the choice we must reject.

I [have] made the claim that there are substantial affinities between the racial doctrines of Pan-Africanism and other forms of nationalism rooted in the nineteenth century, in particular, with Zionism. Since we cannot forget what has been done to Jews in the name of race in this century, this claim is bound to invite controversy. I make it only to insist on the ways in which the Pan-Africanism of the African-American creators of black nationalist rhetoric was not untypical of European and American thought of its day, even of the rhetoric of the victims of racism. With Du Bois's position laid out before us, the comparison can be more substantially articulated.

But, given the sensitivity of the issue, I am bound to begin with caveats. It is no part of my brief to argue that Zionism has to be racialist – not the least because, as I shall be arguing finally, the Pan-Africanist impetus can also be given a nonracialist foundation. Nor is it my intention to argue for the claim that the origins of modern Zionism are *essentially* racialist, or that racialism is central to the thought of all the founders of modern Zionism. It seems to me, as I have said, that Judaism – the religion – and the wider body of Jewish practice through which the various communities of the Diaspora have defined themselves allow for a cultural conception of Jewish identity that cannot be made plausible in the case of Pan-Africanism. As evidence of this fact, I would simply cite the way that the fifty or so rather disparate African nationalities in our present world seem to have met the nationalist impulses of many Africans, while Zionism has, of necessity, been satisfied by the creation of a single state.

But despite these differences, it is important to be clear that there were Jewish racialists in the early story of modern Zionism; that they were not marginal figures or fringe madmen; and that they, like Crummell and, later, Du Bois, developed a nationalism rooted in nineteenth-century theories of race. It is important in the practical world of politics because a racialized Zionism continues to be one of the threats to the moral stability of Israeli nationalism; as witness the politics of the late Rabbi Meir Kahane. But it is theoretically important to my argument, because, as I say, it is central to my view that Crummell's inchoate *theoria*, which Du Bois turned to organized theory, was thoroughly conventional.

Now, of course, to establish that Crummell's view was conventional, we should need no more than to cite the historical writings of the first academic historians in the United States, with their charming fantasies of Puritan democracy as part of a continuous tradition derived from the Anglo-Saxon moot, or the works of British Anglo-Saxon historiography, which traced the evolution of British institutions back to Tacitus's Teutonic hordes. But *that* comparison would leave out part of what is so fascinating about the thought of these early nationalists. For, however anachronistic our reaction, our surprise at Crummell and those of his Zionist contemporaries that shared his racialized vision is that they, as victims of racism, endorsed racialist theories.

So that when we read "The Ethics of Zionism" by Horace M. Kallen, published in the *Maccabaean* in New York in August 1906, we may feel the same no-doubt-anachronistic astonishment.[39] Kallen's essay was based on a lecture he had given to a gathering of an American Zionist organization (the *Maccabaean* was its official publication). He says: "It is the race and not the man who, in the greater account of human destiny, struggles, survives or dies, and types of civilization have always reflected the natural character of the dominant races."[40] And we remember Du Bois's "the history of the world is the history, not of individuals . . . but of races." He asks: "What then has the Jew done for civilization? What is his place in the evolution of the human race? What is his moral worth to humanity?"[41] And we are reminded of Du Bois's races each "struggling . . . to develop for civilization its particular message."

There are, of course, instructive differences between Kallen's "ethics" and Du Bois's. Part of the historical divergence between African-American and Jewish-American conceptions of identity is revealed when Kallen explicitly rejects a religious or cultural conception of Jewish identity:

Here is an intensely united people of relatively unmixed blood, and intense race consciousness, sojourning in all parts of the earth, in some manner successfully, and the natural object of hatred of those among whom it lives. To avoid the effect of this hatred many of the race have tried to eliminate all resemblances between themselves and it. Their languages are as various as the countries in which they live; they proclaim their nationalities as Russian, English, French, Austrian, or American and relegate their racial character to a sectarian label. "We", they say, "are not Jews but Judaists.["][42]

... our duty i[s] to Judaize the Jew.[43]

For this argument presupposes as its antagonist a purely cultural nationalism of a kind that was to develop fully among African-Americans only later. Kallen saw "Culture-Zionism" of this sort as not "much better than assimilation,"[44] which, of course, he actively opposed also. But his resistance to assimilation could not be part of Du Bois's position, either: assimilation, which some took to be a possibility for a brief moment after the American Civil War, did not become more than a theoretical possibility again – save for the few African-Americans who could "pass for white" – until after the civil rights movement, and then, of course, it was largely rejected in favor of a cultural national-ism of Roots.

Nevertheless, mutatis mutandis, the operative ideology here is recognizable Du Bois's; American Jewish nationalism – at least in this manifestation – and American black nationalism are (unsurprisingly) part of the same scheme of things.[45]

If Du Bois's race concept seems an all-too-Ameri-can creation, its traces in African rhetoric are legion. When Kwame Nkrumah addressed the Gold Coast Parliament in presenting the "motion of destiny" accepting the independence constitu-tion, he spoke these words:

> Honourable Members . . . The eyes and ears of the world are upon you; yea, our op-pressed brothers throughout this vast conti-nent of Africa and the New World are looking to you with desperate hope, as an inspiration to continue their grim fight against cruelties which we in this corner of Africa have never known – cruelties which are a disgrace to humanity, and to the civilization which the white man has set himself to teach us.[46]

To a person unencumbered with the baggage of the history of the idea of race, it would surely seem strange that the independence of one nation of black men and women should resonate more with black people than with other oppressed people; strange too that it should be the whiteness of the oppressors – "the white man" – as opposed, say, to their

imperialism, that should stand out. It should seem a strange idea, even to those of us who live in a world formed by racial ideology, that your freedom from cruelties I have never known should spur me on in my fight for freedom because we are of the same color. Yet Du Bois died in Nkrumah's Ghana, led there by the dream of Pan-Africanism and the reality of American racism. If he escaped that racism, he never completed the escape from race. The logic of his argument leads naturally to the final repudiation of race as a term of difference – to speaking "of civilizations where we now speak of races." The logic is the same logic that has led us to speak of gender – the social construction out of the biological facts – where we once spoke of sex, and a rational assessment of the evidence requires that we should endorse not only the logic but the premises of each argument. I have only sketched the evidence for these premises in the case of race, but it is all there in the journals. Discussing Du Bois has been largely a pretext for adumbrating the argu-ment he never quite managed to complete.

I distinguish two kinds of racism – intrinsic and extrinsic: Du Bois's theoretical racism [is] in my view, extrinsic. Yet, in his heart, it seems to me that Du Bois's feelings were those of an intrinsic racist. He wanted desperately to find in Africa and with Africans a home, a place where he could feel, as he never felt in America, that he belonged. His reason would not allow him to be an intrinsic racist, however; and so he reacted to the challenges to racialism by seeking in more and more exotic ways to defend his belief in the connection between race and morally relevant properties.

The truth is that there are no races: there is nothing in the world that can do all we ask race to do for us. As we have seen, even the biologist's notion has only limited uses, and the notion that Du Bois required, and that underlies the more hateful racisms of the modern era, refers to nothing in the world at all. The evil that is done is done by the concept, and by easy – yet impossible – assumptions as to its application.

Talk of "race" is particularly distressing for those of us who take culture seriously. For, where race works – in places where "gross differences" of morphology are correlated with "subtle differ-ences" of temperament, belief, and intention – it works as an attempt at metonym for culture, and it does so only at the price of biologizing what is culture, ideology.

To call it "biologizing" is not, however, to consign our concept of race to biology. For what is present there is not our concept but our word only. Even the biologists who believe in human races use the term *race*, as they say, "without any social implication."[47] What exists "out there" in the world – communities of meaning, shading variously into each other in the rich structure of the social world – is the province not of biology but of the human sciences.

I have examined these issues through the writings of Du Bois, with the burden of his scholarly inheritance, seeking to transcend the system of oppositions whose acceptance would have left him opposed to the (white) norm of form and value. In his early work, Du Bois takes race for granted and seeks to revalue one pole of the opposition of white to black. The received concept is a hierarchy, a vertical structure, and Du Bois wishes to rotate the axis, to give race a "horizontal" reading. Challenge the assumption that there can be an axis, however oriented in the space of values, and the project fails for loss of presuppositions. In his later writings, Du Bois – whose life's work was, in a sense, an attempt at just this impossible project – was unable to escape the notion of race he explicitly rejected. [This] curious conjunction of a reliance on and a repudiation of race recurs in recent African theorizing.

We may borrow Du Bois's own metaphor: though he saw the dawn coming, he never faced the sun. And it would be hard to deny that he is followed in this by many in Africa – as in Europe and America – today: we all live in the dusk of that dawn.

Notes

1 W. E. B. Du Bois, "The Conservation of Races," 76.
2 Du Bois, *Dusk of Dawn: An Essay Toward an Autobiography of a Race Concept*.
3 Du Bois, "The Conservation of Races," 73–4.
4 Ibid. 75.
5 Ibid. 75–6.
6 Ibid. 76.
7 Ibid. 77.
8 Ibid. 78.
9 Ibid. 78–9. This talk of racial absorption, and similar talk of racial extinction, reflects the idea that African-Americans might disappear because their genetic heritage would be diluted by the white one. This idea might be thought to be absurd on any view that believes in a racial essence: either a person has it or they don't. But to think this way is to conceive of racial essences as being like genes, and Mendelian genetics was not yet "rediscovered" when Du Bois wrote this piece. What Du Bois is probably thinking of is the fact "passing for white"; on views of inheritance as the blending of parental "blood," it might be thought that the more it is the case that black "blood" is diluted, the more likely that every person of African descent in America could pass for white. And that *would* be a kind of extinction of the socially recognized Negro. It is an interesting question why those who discussed this question assumed that it would not be the extinction of the white also, and the creation of a "hybridized" human race. But, as I say, such speculation is ruled out by the coming of Mendelian genetics.
10 Ibid. 85.
11 Jean-Paul Sartre, "Orphée Noir," in *Anthologie de la Nouvelle Poésie Nègre et Malagache de Langue Francaise*, ed. L. S. Senghor, xiv. Sartre in this passage explicitly argues that this antiracist racism is a path to the "final unity . . . the abolition of differences of race."
12 Shared traditions do not help: the traditions of African-Americans that are African-derived are derived from *specific* African cultures, and are thus not a common black possession; and the American-ness of African-Americans has to do with traditions developed in the New World in interaction with the cultures brought by other Americans from Europe and Asia.
13 Even dual-descent systems, in which ancestry can be traced through both sexes, tend to follow one branch backward in each generation.
14 This way of thinking about the distance between social and biological ancestry I owe to R. B. Le Page and A. Tabouret-Keller's *Acts of Identity*, ch. 6. I am very grateful to Professor Le Page for allowing me to see a typescript many years ago.
15 It might be suggested in Du Bois's defense that he meant by two people sharing a common history only that two people at the present who are of the same race have common ancestry – the historical relationship between them being that each of them can trace their ancestry back to members of the same past group of people. But then this would clearly not be a sociohistorical conception of race but, once more, the biological one.
16 There is a different sense in which the discipline of history is always a matter of making as well as finding: all telling of the past is controlled by narrative conventions. Neither this point nor the one I make in the text here entails either that there are no facts about the past or that historical narratives are fictions, in the sense that we cannot make valid judgments of their truth and falsity.
17 Du Bois, "The Conservation of Races," 75.
18 This seems to me the very notion that the biologists

have ended up with: that of a population, which is a group of people (or, more generally, organisms) occupying a common region (or, more generally, an environmental niche), along with people in other regions who are largely descended from people of the same region. See M. Nei and A. K. Roychoudhury, "Genetic Relationship and Evolution of Human Races"; for useful background see also M. Nei and A. K. Roychoudhury, "Gene Differences between Caucasian, Negro and Japanese Populations."

19 Du Bois, "The Conservation of Races," 75.

20 This claim was prompted by G. Spiller, ed., *Papers in Inter-Racial Problems Communicated to the First Universal Races Congress Held at the University of London, July 26–29, 1911.*

21 Du Bois, "Races," 13.

22 Nei and Roychoudhury, "Genetic Relationship and Evolution of Human Races," 4.

23 I call a characteristic of an organism genetically *determined* if, roughly, the organism has a certain genetic constitution whose possession entails, within the normal range of the environments it inhabits, and in the course of an uninterrupted normal development, the possession of that characteristic. "Normal" and "interrupted" are concepts that need detailed explication, of course, but the general idea is enough for our purposes here.

24 Strictly we should say that the character of an organism is fixed by genes, along with sequences of nucleic acid in the cytoplasm and some other features of the cytoplasm of the ovum. But the differential influences of these latter sources of human characteristics are largely swamped by the nucleic DNA; they are substantially similar in almost all people. It is these facts that account, I think, for their not being generally mentioned.

25 It follows, from these definitions, of course, that where a locus is monomorphic the expected homozygosity is going to be one.

26 These figures come from Nei and Roychoudhury, "Genetic Relationship and Evolution of Human Races." I have used the figures derived from looking at proteins, not blood groups, since they claim these are likely to be more reliable. I have chosen a measure of "racial" biological difference that makes it look spectacularly small, but I would not wish to imply that it is not the case, as these authors say, that "genetic differentiation is real and generally statistically highly significant" (41). I *would* dispute their claim that their work shows there is a biological basis for the classification of human races: what it shows is that human populations differ in their distributions of genes. That *is* a biological fact. The objection to using this fact as a basis of a system of classification is that far too many people don't fit into just one category that can be so defined.

I should add that these are only illustrative figures. One way, which I would recommend, to get a sense of the current total picture, if you aren't familiar with this literature, is to read the two articles by these authors in the bibliography, in the order of publication. For purposes of cross-reference I should point out that the "average heterozygosity" they refer to is just 1 minus the average homozygosity, which I explain above.

27 Nei and Roychoudhury, "Genetic Relationship and Evolution of Human Races," 44.

28 See John Maynard-Smith, *The Theory of Evolution*, 212–14. The European crow is a similar reminder of the relative arbitrariness of some species boundaries: there is interbreeding of neighboring populations but reproductive isolation of the birds of the eastern and western limits.

29 See Jonathan Westphall's *Colour: Some Philosophical Problems from Wittgenstein.*

30 Heisenberg's *Philosophic Problems of Nuclear Science* (1952), as cited in Robin Horton's paper "Paradox and Explanation: A Reply to Mr Skorupski," 243.

31 In particular sociocultural settings supposedly "racial" characteristics may be highly predictive, of course, of social or cultural traits. African-Americans are much more likely to be poor, for example, than Americans taken at random; they are thus more likely to be poorly educated. Even here, though, just a small piece of sociocultural information can change the picture. First-generation Afro-Caribbean immigrants, for example, look very different statistically from other African-Americans.

32 Nei and Roychoudhury, "Genetic Relationship and Evolution of Human Races," 40.

33 Du Bois, "Races," 14.

34 Du Bois, *Dusk of Dawn*, 137.

35 Ibid. 137–8.

36 Ibid. 153.

37 Ibid. 116–17.

38 For further thoughts along these lines see my "But Would That Still Be Me? Notes on Gender, 'Race,' Ethnicity as Sources of Identity."

39 Kallen no doubt acquired some of his ideas from the same Harvard courses as Du Bois, and he plainly identified with the struggles of blacks against racial intolerance, on one occasion refusing to attend a Rhodes scholars' dinner at Oxford from which Alain Locke, as a black man, was excluded.

40 Kallen, "The Ethics of Zionism," 62.

41 Ibid.

42 Ibid. 69. Kallen also endorses various more specific racialist doctrines – notably a view of intermarriage as leading to sterility – that Afro-Americans were less likely to endorse. "That the Jew merits and must have his self-hood, must retain his individuality, is beyond question. He has the fundamental biological endowment and the transcendent efficiency of moral function which are the ethical conditions of such self-maintenance. . . . It is the Jew that dominates in the child of a mixed marriage, and after a few

generations, if sterility does not supervene, as it usually does, what is not Jewish dies out or is transmuted" (70). But notice that this view, *mutatis mutandis*, would be consistent with the American practice, endorsed by Du Bois, of treating people with *any* identifiable African ancestry as "black."

43 Ibid. 71.
44 Ibid. 70.

45 I am very grateful to Jeff Vogel for drawing Kallen's article to my attention, and for what I have learned from discussions of this issue with him.
46 Nkrumah, *Autobiography of Kwame Nkrumah*, pp. 166–71; this is the July 1953 motion that Nkrumah called the "Motion of Destiny."
47 Nei and Roychoudhury, "Genetic Relationship and Evolution of Human Races," 4.

References

Du Bois, W. E. B. "The Conservation of Races." American Negro Academy Occasional Papers, no. 2, 1897. Repr. in *W. E. B. Du Bois Speaks: Speeches and Addresses 1890–1919*, ed. P. S. Foner, 73–85. New York: Pathfinders Press, 1970.

Du Bois, W. E. B. *Dusk of Dawn: An Essay Toward an Autobiography of a Race Concept*. New York: Harcourt, Brace and Co., 1940. Repr. with an introduction by Herbert Aptheker. Milwood, NY: Kraus-Thomson, 1975.

Heisenberg, W. *Philosophic Problems of Nuclear Science*. New York: Pantheon, 1952.

Horton, R. "Paradox and Explanation: A Reply to Mr Skorupski." *Philosophy of Social Sciences* 3 (1973): 231–56.

Kallen, H. M. "The Ethics of Zionism." In *The Maccabaean*, New York, Aug. 1906.

Le Page, R. B., and A. Tabouret-Keller. *Acts of Identity: Creole-Based Approaches to Language and Ethnicity*. Cambridge and New York: Cambridge University Press, 1985.

Maynard-Smith, John. *The Theory of Evolution*. 3rd edn. London: Penguin, 1975.

Nei, M., and A. K. Roychoudhury. "Gene Differences between Caucasian, Negro and Japanese Populations." *Science* 177 (Aug. 1972): 434–5.

Nei, M., and A. K. Roychoudhury. "Genetic Relationship and Evolution of Human Races." *Evolutionary Biology* 14 (1983): 1–59.

Nkrumah, K. *Autobiography of Kwame Nkrumah*. London: Panaf Books, 1973.

Sartre, Jean-Paul. "Orphée Noir." In *Anthologie de la nouvelle poésie Nègre et Malagache de langue Française*, ed. L. S. Senghor. Paris: Presses Universitaires de France, 1948.

Spiller, G., ed. *Paper in Inter-Racial Problems Communicated to the First Universal Races Congress Held at the University of London, July 26–29, 1911*. London: P. S. King & Son, 1911. Republished with an introduction by H. Aptheker. Secaucus, NJ: Citadel Press, 1970.

Westphall, Jonathan. *Colour: Some Philosophical Problems from Wittgenstein*. Oxford: Blackwell, 1987.

34

Du Bois on the Invention of Race

Tommy L. Lott

In his well-known address to the newly founded American Negro Academy, W. E. B. Du Bois entertained the question of the fate and destiny of African-Americans as a group, asking somewhat rhetorically, "Does my black blood place upon me any more obligation to assert my nationality than German, or Irish or Italian blood would?"[1] His answer was that it is "the duty of the Americans of Negro descent, as a body, to maintain their race identity."[2] The argument he advanced to support this claim has sometimes been understood to suggest that African-Americans as a group are obligated to maintain and perpetuate their culture in order to retain their authenticity.[3] We should resist, however, becoming overly focused on this aspect of Du Bois's view, for it is fairly clear, on even the most cursory reading of his essay, that he was not particularly concerned with the African past as a standard for measuring the authenticity of African-American culture. Indeed, he proposed to resolve the dilemma of African-American double consciousness by appealing to a revisionist analysis of the concept of race that eschews a biological essentialist account of race identity.

One very good reason, frequently cited by commentators, for supposing that Du Bois was primarily concerned with the question of authenticity is his repeated criticism of African-Americans striving for "self-obliteration," seeking "absorption by the white Americans," or pursuing "a servile

imitation of Anglo-Saxon culture."[4] Although there certainly was a concern with authenticity expressed in Du Bois's remarks, I believe that it is somewhat misleading to take this to have been his primary motivation for raising these issues, for there is a very important reason why such issues were not in the foreground of his discussion of race, and why they do not figure into his argument regarding the obligation of African-Americans to maintain their race identity. Hence, I shall present a reading of Du Bois's essay, that, with regard to the question of race identity, deviates from several recent interpretations.[5]

Du Bois's argument for the claim that African-Americans are obligated to retain their race identity is connected with his early view of the role of culture in the African-American quest for social equality.[6] In particular, he maintained that the cultural integrity of African-Americans is crucial for their gaining acceptance as social equals. The view Du Bois stated in 1897 displays the late nineteenth-century historical context of African-American social thought; consequently, many features of the argument he presented can be found in the writings of his contemporaries. By contextualizing his argument I aim to show that he presented a notion of race that was in keeping with his own version of a race uplift theory of social change. According to my interpretation, his revisionist account represents a view of race identity that accorded with the prevailing African-American social philosophy at the turn of the century. I will begin with a brief discussion of his definition of

Reproduced by kind permission of *Philosophical Forum*, Inc.

race, followed by a sketch of some of the historical sources from which he may have drawn certain ideas to develop his argument for the duty of African-Americans to retain their race identity. I want to defend the plausibility of Du Bois's sociohistorical view of race identity against several, quite damaging, criticisms and thereby salvage the major thrust of his argument.

A Revisionist Concept of Race

With the aim of presenting an account tailored to fit his theory of social change, Du Bois proposed the following definition of race,

> It is a vast family of human beings, generally of common blood and language, always of common history, traditions and impulses, who are both voluntarily and involuntarily striving together for the accomplishment of certain more or less vividly conceived ideals of life.[7]

Unless we bear in mind why Du Bois was motivated to write about African-American identity, his definition of race will seem quite implausible, especially his stipulation that a racial group must *always* share a common history, traditions, and impulses, but need not always share a common blood or language. The reason Du Bois's proposal seems implausible is because he meant to implicitly contest the way the received view, which places a greater emphasis on common blood, has been socially constructed. Unfortunately, the insight that underlies his definition is diminished by the twofold nature of his account, an account which involves both a deconstruction of the received view as well as a reconstruction of his alternative conception.

Du Bois opened his essay with the statement that African-Americans are always interested in discussions regarding the origins and destinies of races because such discussions usually presuppose assumptions about the natural abilities, and the social and political status of African-Americans, assumptions that impede African-American social progress. He noted that the undesirable implications of some of these assumptions have fostered a tendency for African-Americans "to deprecate and minimize race distinctions."[8] He took himself to be giving voice to their aspiration for social equality by advancing a conception of African-Americans that would allow a discussion of racial distinctions while accommodating the tendency of African-Americans, under the dominating influence of racism, to want to minimize references to physical differences in such discussions.

Du Bois was interested in formulating non-biological criteria for a definition of race mainly because he wanted to provide a more adequate ground for the group identity he considered a crucial component in the African-American's social agenda. He made this clear when, with the reference to the idea of race in general, he spoke of "its efficiency as the vastest and most ingenious invention for human progress."[9] He suggested that, following the success model of other groups, African-Americans must *invent* a conception of themselves that will contribute to their social elevation as a group. His revisionist notion of race was therefore proposed at the outset of something African-Americans must self-consciously adopt for political purposes. We can notice that he did not fail to acknowledge the social construction of the concept of race when, in his citation of the eight distinct racial groups, he qualified his reference to them with the phrase "in the sense in which history tells us the word must be used."[10] What shows us that he aimed to deconstruct the received view, however, is the way he juxtaposed his sociohistorical concept of race with what he referred to as "the present division of races," viz., the scientific conception of the three main biological groups; for he goes on to point out that biology cannot provide the criteria for race identity because, historically, there has been an "integration of physical differences."[11] This fact leads him to conclude that what really distinguishes groups of people into races are their "spiritual and mental differences."[12]

Some of Du Bois's readers have rejected his sociohistorical definition of race in favor of a definition based on physical differences.[13] What Du Bois's detractors tend to overlook, however, is the fact that his definition does not deny the obvious physical differences that constitute race, nor does his discussion of race display any special commitment to the sociohistorical view he sets forth. A close reading will reveal that he only meant to deny the *viability* of a strictly biological account of race, and, furthermore, to assert that an empirical study of history will show this to be the case. Based on his own survey of anthropological findings, he tells us that when different groups of people came together to form cities,

The larger and broader differences of color, hair and physical proportions were not by any means ignored, but myriads of minor differences disappeared, and the sociological and historical races of men began to approximate the present division of races as indicated by physical researches.[14]

The aim of Du Bois's deconstruction of the concept of race was to create a means of employing the prevailing definition of race based on genetics, i.e., to allow him to continue speaking of "the black-blooded people of America," or the "people of Negro blood in the United States," while at the same time leaving room for him to question any undesirable implications of such definitions, i.e., to override definitions that imply that the physical differences which typically characterize the various races somehow justify social inequality.

The African-American Cultural Imperative

But what bearing does Du Bois's revised notion of race have on his argument for the claim that African-Americans have a duty to retain their race identity? As Boxill has noted, one important reason Du Bois cites to support this imperative is that African-Americans have a distinct cultural mission as a racial group.[15] On behalf of the Negro Academy, Du Bois asserted that, "We believe that the Negro people, as a race, have a contribution to make to civilization and humanity, which no other race can make."[16] But what exactly is this unique contribution? I am not sure whether Du Bois had an answer to this question. He weakly stated that African-Americans are "a nation stored with wonderful possibilities of culture," which suggests that they do not yet have any such cultural contribution to make. He then goes on to speak of "a stalwart originality which shall unswervingly follow Negro ideals."[17] And, although he makes passing references to "Pan-Negroism" and the "African fatherland," at no point does he advocate reclaiming any African cultural retentions.[18] Instead, he prefers to tell us that "it is our duty to conserve our physical powers, our intellectual endowments, our spiritual ideals."[19]

What then did Du Bois mean when he spoke of the duty of African-Americans to conserve their race identity in order to make a cultural contribution? His view of what constitutes African-Ameri-

can culture seems especially problematic when we consider some of his remarks regarding African-American identity. He states that,

> We are Americans, not only by birth and by citizenship, but by our political ideals, our language, our religion. Farther than that, our Americanism does not go. At that point, we are Negroes, members of a vast historic race that from the very dawn of creation has slept, but half awakening in the dark forests of its African fatherland.[20]

If African-Americans share the same language, religion, and political ideals with other Americans there does not seem to be much left for them to uniquely contribute to American culture.[21] Although, in some places, Du Bois spoke of the African-American's special mission in terms of a distinct culture contribution he seems to have had more than simply culture in mind. I suspect that he really meant to speak of a *political* mission that culture in some way enables African-Americans to carry out. This is suggested, for instance, by his remarks regarding "that black to-morrow which is yet destined to soften the whiteness of the Teutonic to-day."[22] What Du Bois may have meant here is simply that, through the establishment of a culturally pluralistic society, white cultures will no longer dominate. Instead, social equality will be fostered through a cultural exchange between the various races.

If we consider Du Bois's sociohistorical definition of race, along with his belief that African-Americans have a special mission, his rejection of biological essentialism and his failure to make use of the idea of African cultural retentions, begin to appear quite troublesome.[23] For, as Appiah has keenly observed, his talk of Pan-Negroism requires that African-Americans and Africans share something in common other than oppression by whites.[24] This lacuna in Du Bois's argument can be explained to some extent by considering the *tentative* nature of the duty of African-Americans to conserve their race identity. According to Du Bois, this duty lasts only "until this mission of the Negro people is accomplished."[25] These remarks imply that the special mission of African-Americans has more to do with their struggle for social equality than with their making a cultural contribution; once social equality has been achieved, this duty no longer exists. We can see the explicitly *political* nature of this mission clearly expressed in the following remarks:

[African-Americans] must be inspired with the Divine faith of our black mothers, that out of the blood and dust of battle will march a victorious host, a mighty nation, a peculiar people, to speak to the nations of earth a Divine truth that shall make them free.[26]

Although the imperative to make a cultural contribution has more to do with politics than with culture, there is nonetheless a link between them, for African-Americans must be inspired "out of the blood and dust of battle" to produce a unique culture that will contribute to world civilization. What makes African-American culture unique is its hybrid genesis within the context of racial oppression in America. The need for African cultural retentions is diminished given that the culture forged out of this experience will enable African-Americans to assume a role of political leadership among other black people. Du Bois's argument for the claim that African-Americans have a duty to conserve their race identity is backward-looking in the sense that it makes reference to the historical oppression of African-Americans, as a diaspora group, as a ground for this duty. His argument is forward-looking in the sense that it foresees an end to this oppression and, hence, an eventual release from the imperative.

Nineteenth-century African-American Social Thought

Some commentators have invoked biographical facts about Du Bois's own racial background to explain why he wanted to advance a sociohistorical account of race.[27] While it is not unfair to see this as an important factor influencing his thinking about race, it is a plain misunderstanding to suppose that the reconstruction Du Bois proposed was wholly original. When we consider his argument within the context of African-American social thought at the turn of the century, certain quite noticeable details strongly indicate the influence of his contemporaries. He alludes to many concerns that had been expressed on both sides of the perennial separatist–integrationist debate by combining, under his own concept of cultural pluralism, certain tenets drawn from various doctrines of earlier emigrationist–assimilationist thinkers such as Blyden and Douglass. By far one of the most abiding and dominant influences on his thinking was clearly Booker T. Washington. We can notice

the traces of some of Du Bois's nineteenth-century influences by paying careful attention to certain ideas that crop up in his essay.

According to Wilson J. Moses, Du Bois's argument in "The Conservation of Races" was directly influenced by Alexander Crummell, whose inaugural address to the Negro Academy expressed a similar preoccupation with the idea of "civilization" as a means of social elevation.[28] Crummell, along with other nineteenth-century activists such as Henry Highland Garnet and Martin Delany, was prominent among the supporters of the African Civilization Society. The goals and values of nineteenth-century African-American nationalism were often situated in arguments regarding the development of "civilization" as a means of group elevation. With an eye to the place of African-Americans in a world civilization, Du Bois seems to reflect Blyden's earlier call of providence in his talk of an "advance guard" of African-Americans who must "take their just place in the van of Pan-Negroism."[29] Appiah has suggested this reading, perhaps inadvertently, in characterizing Du Bois's remarks regarding the African-American message for humanity as deriving from God's purpose in creating races.[30] The claim Du Bois makes here regarding the leadership role of African-Americans vis-à-vis other black people in Africa and the diaspora seems to capture the gist of Blyden's argument for emigration, although emigration was a proposal that Du Bois never embraced.

Despite the fact that his mention of "Pan-Negroism" presages the Pan-Africanism he would later adopt, Du Bois seems to have believed in 1897 that the uplift of Africa, and black people everywhere, could best be brought about by African-Americans pursuing cultural self-determination in America. Of course, the problem this poses for his sociohistorical account of race is that African-American and African cultures are significantly different. The idea of "Pan-Negroism" he derived from that account, i.e., "Negroes bound and welded together," failed to recognize the important cultural differences among the various groups of African and African diaspora people.[31]

By contrast with Blyden's African nationalism, Frederick Douglass saw ex-slaves as Americans. He believed that, once African-Americans were educated and allowed to demonstrate their equality with whites, assimilation into the American mainstream would someday be possible. In some of his remarks, Du Bois avers to Douglass's view that slavery had severely damaged the dignity and sense of self-worth of African-Americans. He maintained that the first step toward social equality will be "the correction of the immorality, crime and laziness among the Negroes themselves, which still remains as a heritage from slavery."[32]

Under the legal segregation that followed slavery Douglass's assimilationist view found a new expression in the philosophy of Booker T. Washington. Washington's strategy for changing the socioeconomic conditions of African-Americans was to appeal to the self-interest of whites. He gave priority to economic development as a key to the elevation of African-Americans as a group. Rather than demand social equality, Washington believed it would gradually come with the economic progress of the group. Notwithstanding their much-heralded disagreement over the role of political agitation, Du Bois seems to have accepted certain aspects of Washington's strategy. Along with Washington, for instance, Du Bois advocated social separation from whites "to avoid the friction of races."[33] And Du Bois's assertion that "No people that laughs at itself, and ridicules itself, and wishes to God it was anything but itself ever wrote its name in history" seems to be a rewording of Washington's famous statement at the Atlanta Exposition that "No race that has anything to contribute to the markets of the world is long, in any degree, ostracized."[34] Both claims are reminiscent of Douglass's earlier concern with the self-esteem of African-Americans as a group. Unlike Washington, however, Du Bois placed a greater emphasis on the cultural status of African-Americans. He argued against "a servile imitation of Anglo-Saxon culture" on the ground that African-Americans have a unique cultural contribution to make and that to accomplish this they must not assimilate.[35] For Du Bois, social equality would be attained through the distinctive cultural achievements of African-Americans, who must retain their race identity in order to accomplish this.

When we consider Du Bois's idea of African-Americans gaining social equality through their cultural achievements we must not overlook some of the earlier proponents of this suggestion, viz., members of the various literary societies in the early part of the nineteenth century and the New Negro literary movement at the beginning of the 1890s.[36] Maria W. Stewart followed David Walker in the tradition of advocating moral uprightness as the basis for elevating the race, a tradition which was perpetuated throughout the nineteenth century by various African-American voluntary associations.[37]

We can notice the sense of a mission, for instance, in Anna Julia Cooper's advocacy of an African-American literature "to give the character of beauty and power to the literary utterance of the race."[38] In this vein then we should understand Du Bois's statement that "it is our duty to conserve our physical powers, our intellectual endowments, our spiritual ideals." His somewhat vague proposition here emanated from a history of ideas that assigned a specific role to culture in the elevation of African-Americans as a group.

Indeed, as a cornerstone of many turn-of-the-century theories of social change, the African-American cultural imperative created a strong expectation that educated African-Americans would employ their intellectual resources in the service of race uplift. On the assumption that culture and politics must coincide, Frances E. W. Harper and Pauline E. Hopkins presented arguments in their novels for the obligation of the black elite, viz., mulattoes, to refrain from marrying whites, or passing, and instead devote themselves to the betterment of African-Americans as a group.[39] They aimed to influence some members of the group to remain loyal and to assume responsibility for elevating other members by arguing that there is a special duty requiring a sacrifice of social privilege. Du Bois seems to have heeded their teachings when he spoke against the loss of race identity in "the commingled blood of the nation," and when he raised the question "is self-obliteration the highest end to which Negro blood dare aspire?"[40]

The duty to conserve African-American race identity so as to develop a distinct culture derives from an historical context in which the oppression of African-Americans as a group obtains. Under such conditions the function of culture is to resist oppression. Even if we accept the idea that African-Americans are, in some sense, collectively obligated to resist oppression we might still wonder whether they are, for this reason, obligated to conserve their race identity so as to develop a distinctive culture. With regard to the oppression experienced by African-Americans it seems that, for Du Bois, the right of resistance is tantamount to the right of cultural self-determination. Although African-Americans are, perhaps collectively, obligated to resist oppression in the sense that every African-American has a *right* not to acculturate into the American mainstream, this does not establish that African-Americans have a *duty* to conserve a distinctive culture.[41]

Race, Ethnicity, and Biology

When Du Bois defines race in terms of sociohistorical, rather than biological, or physical, criteria he seems to have blurred an important distinction between race and ethnicity, where the former is understood to refer to biological characteristics and the latter refers chiefly to cultural characteristics.[42] Several commentators have taken him to task for lapsing into this confusion. Their criticisms, however, seem to presuppose that people can be divided into biologically distinct racial groups that develop in relative isolation. Du Bois's contention was that this ideal-type model of racial and ethnic groups lacks empirical validity, for socio-historical factors have a greater significance for understanding the essentially *political* genesis, structure, and function of such groups.

Appiah, for instance, objects to Du Bois's sociohistorical definition on the ground that a group's history or culture *presupposes* a group identity and, therefore, cannot be a criterion of that group's identity.[43] He attempts to refurbish Du Bois's talk of a common history by adding a geographical criterion such that a group's history is to be understood as (in part) the history of people from the same place. This move, however, seems needless on two counts. First, Du Bois makes clear that an important part of the history of African-Americans is their African past, and since he had little concern with cultural retentions, his point was largely a matter of geography. Secondly, as a criterion of group identity, geography does not add much, given that there are racially and culturally diverse people in various locations.

A similar objection has been raised by Boxill who points out that it is simply false to maintain that every black American shares a common culture. Instead, Boxill offers a physical definition of race that is reflected in the way the racist classifies people into races, whether they share a common culture or not:

> I propose that, insofar as black people are a race, they are people who either themselves look black – that is, have a certain kind of physical appearance – or are, at least in part, descended from such a group of people.[44]

Boxill, however, is a bit too hasty in his dismissal of the obvious fact that the American system of classification, constructed on the basis of a racist

ideology, breaks down when people of mixed blood do not neatly fit into the prescribed racial categories. He makes reference to the notion of "passing" to show that, with regard to people of mixed blood, a physical definition of race still offers the best account. But he overlooks the fact that this notion is fairly limited to the United States and perhaps to similar societies with a majority white population.[45] Moreover, as I shall indicate shortly, many times the practice of racism, which informs Boxill's definition, seems to conveniently disregard the biological criteria he takes to be essential.

The best way to meet the objection that a definition of race based primarily on sociohistorical criteria confuses race with ethnicity is to accept it. In the United States the alleged confusion seems to have become a matter of institutionalized practice. College application forms, for instance, frequently display some such confusion when under the ethnic identity category they list *racial* designations such as "black" and "white" along with *ethnic* designations such as "Japanese" and "Hispanic." It becomes clear that such a system of racial and ethnic classification is constructed for political purposes when we take note of certain combined categories such as "Hispanic, not black."[46] As primarily a linguistic designation, the term "Hispanic" can apply to groups of people who consider themselves white, black, or mixed-blood. Why then is there a need for a special category which designates a racial distinction that only singles out black people?

The idea that various notions of race have been constructed by racists for political purposes was well recognized in nineteenth-century African-American social thought. In his 1854 essay. "The Claims of the Negro Ethnologically Considered," Douglass accused the slaveholders of seeking a justification in science for the oppression of slaves. He pointed out that by engaging arguments that amount to "scientific moonshine that would connect men with monkeys," they wanted "to separate the Negro race from every intelligent nation and tribe in Africa." Douglass surmised that "they aimed to construct a theory in support of a foregone conclusion."[47]

A similar accusation was published anonymously in 1859 in an article in the *Anglo-African Magazine*. The author begins with the claim that there is no pure unmixed Anglo-Saxon race, arguing that all whites with ethnic backgrounds (even with Egyptian blood) still claim to be Anglo-Saxon. The author then refers to the construction of the Anglo-Saxon race as "a legendary theory."[48] The underlying racism of this theory, which relies on the Bible, is exposed by raising the question: if the curse of Canaan is used to prove that black blood is contaminated, what about the curse that marked out Anglo-Saxons for slavery? According to the author, Noah's curse did not point specifically to black people since Cush and Canaan were both sons of Ham. Ethnologists who use Biblical references to establish racial distinctions that imply black inferiority employ "a curious chain of evidence," for there is no African race, i.e., no group with pure African blood. The author reduces to absurdity the Biblical evidence for this belief, according to which:

> First, Abyssinians belong to a white race. Secondly, Ethiopians were the same as the Abyssinians. Lastly, the Negroes were Ethiopians.[49]

The conclusion drawn from this *reductio* argument was that Negroes (Ethiopians) belong to the white race. The author's purpose in presenting this argument seems to have been to urge that all racial terms be treated as misnomers.

These nineteenth-century discussions of race indicate two of the most important factors underlying Du Bois's deconstruction of the biological concept of race, viz., racism and intermingling. Although the identity of every racial or ethnic group will involve both (a) physical or biological criteria and (b) cultural or sociohistorical criteria, whether, in any given society, (a) gains precedence over (b) seems to be a matter of politics, i.e., racism. But even in societies such as the United States where biological criteria have gained precedence, the fact of intermingling has rendered any attempt to establish rigid biological racial classifications problematic. When we consider groups such as Chicanos, Amerasians, or Cape Verdians it becomes clear that ethnic designations are needed to accommodate interminglings that have resulted in the creation of group identities that are based almost entirely on sociohistorical criteria.[50]

The Dilemma of Biological Essentialism

One major shortcoming of Du Bois's sociohistorical concept of race is that it fails to make clear how, in the face of racism, African-Americans are supposed to invent, or reconstruct, a concept of black identity that will contribute to the progress of the group.

Racism is firmly grounded in scientific thinking regarding biologically determined racial types such that, for conceptual reasons, it seems undeniable that there are fundamentally yellow, black, and white people, despite any other ethnic, or cultural, designation that applies to them.[51] As Appiah has noted, Du Bois's proposal to replace the biological concept of race with a sociohistorical one "is simply to bury the biological conception below the surface, not to transcend it."[52] What is at issue, however, is whether the rigid dichotomy between race and ethnicity is tenable. Du Bois introduced sociohistorical criteria as a way to give an account of African-American group identity without presupposing this dichotomy. His insight was to draw from the history of racial intermingling in the United States both an objection to the biological essentialism of scientific classifications, as well as a ground on which to reconstruct African-American group identity in a social context dominated by a racist ideology.

With regard to the political aspect of Du Bois's reconstructionist project there is a dilemma posed by the ideological competition between Pan-African nationalists and Pan-Indian nationalists, both of whom have made appeals for unity to the same mixed-blood populations.[53] Each nationalist group wants to lay claim to much of the same constituency as rightfully belonging to it, and each would justify this claim by reference to the relevant biological ancestry. Their respective injunctions regarding group loyalty make use of this essentialized conception of group membership for political purposes. In keeping with the biology inherent in their respective appeals for group loyalty, persons mixed with both African and Indian ancestry are asked to identify with the group that best represents their physical appearance.[54]

It is worth noting that the nationalist's motivation for establishing such rigid biological criteria for group membership is strictly political. Since black people and Indians are oppressed on the basis of race, rather than culture, the nationalists are rightfully inclined to seek to reconstruct the group identity of black people, or Indians, on strictly racial grounds. Du Bois, of course, recognized this and sought to achieve the same political ends as the nationalists, but without invoking the biological categories handed down from scientific racism. He wanted to accommodate the fact that intermingling had become an important feature of the history of African-Americans as a group. For Du Bois, then, group loyalty need not rely on a biological essentialism, given that most African-Americans are of mixed blood. As a criterion of group identity, he proposed to give culture a greater weight than physical characteristics.

The way biology is used to rationalize the American system of racial classification gives rise to an interesting puzzle regarding the dichotomy between race and ethnicity. Consider, for instance, the case in which two siblings are racially distinct, in some genetic sense, but have the same physical characteristics, as when a white male has offspring by both a black and a white female.[55] We can speak of the offspring as being racially distinct on wholly genetic grounds, given that one child has two white parents and the other is of mixed parentage. The fact that this particular genetic difference should matter with regard to racial classification suggests a reason for the belief that race and ethnicity are not interchangeable concepts, viz., only the offspring of two white parents can be considered white.[56]

This particular application of biological criteria becomes much more problematic, however, when the practice of tracing genetic background fails to neatly correlate with the practice of using physical characteristics as a basis for racial classification. We can see this problem by considering an example that involves a multiracial ethnic group that overlaps both black and white racial categories. Suppose that the female offspring of black/white mixed-blood parents has the same physical characteristics as the male offspring of non-black Hispanic parents, and further that they marry and have two children (a boy and a girl) who both, in turn, marry whites. Both are genetically black due to their mother's mixed blood, but since the girl no longer has a Spanish surname her children will be classified as white, while her brother's children will be classified as Hispanic. What this shows, I think, is not only that concepts of race and ethnicity are sometimes interchangeable, but also that, for sociological reasons, at some point genetics frequently drops out of consideration as a basis for racial classification.[57]

We might wonder whether the emphasis Du Bois placed on sociohistorical criteria avoids the nationalist dilemma that arises on the biological essentialist account. Suppose that there are two persons with the same racial and cultural profile, i.e., each is of mixed heritage (with one black parent), each has the physical characteristics of a white person, and each has been acculturated into a white community. What if one decides to adopt a black identity despite her white cultural background? Can her newly acquired consciousness allow her to transcend her

cultural background? Given the American system of racial classification, based on genetics, she is entitled to claim a black identity, something which seems to be ruled out on strictly sociohistorical grounds.[58]

In many cases where members of multiracial ethnic groups seem to have pretty much adopted some version of Du Bois's sociohistorical criteria for their own group identity we can notice that the race–culture ambivalence engendered by the American system of racial classification is frequently resolved along cultural lines. For black Latinos, such as Puerto Ricans, Cubans, or Dominicans, language exerts an overriding influence on their group identity. Persons with black ancestry who have acculturated into these Latino groups would, in many instances, be more inclined to identify with people who share their cultural orientation than with people who share their physical characteristics, despite a great deal of pressure from the dominant society to abide by the prescribed racial classifications.[59]

Du Bois has been taken to task for giving insufficient attention to the cultural differences among different groups of black people in various parts of the world. Indeed, his sociohistorical notion seems to break down when applied to culturally distinct groups of black people. But if in many cases culture gains precedence over race as a basis for group identity, he must have thought that there is something universal, or essential, in the cultures of all the various black ethnic groups, viz., a common history of oppression. Appiah has objected to Du Bois's sociohistorical essentialism by pointing out that it fails to uniquely apply to black people, for African-Americans share a history of oppression with many groups other than Africans or diaspora black people. This objection must be questioned, for I do not think it does much damage to Du Bois's suggestion that a commonly shared history of oppression provides a basis for African-American identity and for Pan-African unity.

What Du Bois was after with his reconstructed notion of race is best exemplified by considering its application to Jews. Membership in this group is determined mainly, but not exclusively, by a blood relationship (i.e., matrilineal descent) with other members of the group.[60] Yet Jews are represented in all three of the biological races, most likely as a result of having intermingled.[61] Jewish identity does not seem to be strictly a matter of culture, i.e., religion, or language, for during the Inquisition many people who were Jewish "by birth" were forced to convert to Catholicism (hence the term "Jewish Catholic"), and, presently, there are many individuals who have chosen not to learn Hebrew, or to practice a religion, yet in both cases they would still be considered Jews, and by and large they would themselves accept this designation. What then is essential to having a Jewish identity?

One very important factor which plays a major role in the construction of Jewish identity is the history of oppression commonly shared by Jews of all races and cultures.[62] With regard to this oppression there is a sociohistorical continuity to the consciousness which unifies the group that is perpetuated by the persistence of antisemitism. Moreover, this consciousness seems to extend uniquely throughout the Jewish diaspora and, since the holocaust, has provided a rallying call for the maintenance of a homeland in Israel. What is important to notice in this regard is that contemporary Zionists in Israel have been accused of racism toward non-Jews, while antisemitism directed toward Jews seems to be virtually identical with other varieties of racism.[63] What this shows, I think, is that there seems to be some sense in which racist practices can be attributed to a multiracial ethnic group, and equally, a sense in which such groups can be considered the victims of racism.

In considering how Du Bois's reconstructed notion of race can be applied to multiracial ethnic groups we must not assume that this is always by virtue of intermingling in the sense of some form of racial amalgamation. In both the United States and in Latin American societies where so-called "miscegenation" has occurred, the mixed-blood populations are largely the result of involuntary sexual contact between white masters and their slaves.[64] In this historical context racism toward ex-slaves and their offspring has produced a value system such that "whitening" has become the racial ideal.[65] Although this is, understandably, a dominant tendency among oppressed Third World people generally, we must not allow the influence of racism to blind us to a quite different sense in which racial identities have been constructed.

Consider, for instance, the fact that British colonialists sometimes referred to the natives of India and Australia as "blacks" and "niggers." Pan-African nationalism may very well be viewed as a response to colonialism, but can it therefore be restricted to groups of people of black African origin? There seems to be a clear sense in which people who are not of black African descent share

a common oppression with black Africans and diaspora black people. In Australia there has developed a black consciousness movement among the aboriginals, who have appropriated a black identity heavily influenced by the sixties Civil Rights struggle in the United States.[66] In England the term "black" is often used politically to include people of both West Indian and Asian descent. The reason for this development is that the Asian immigrant populations from Pakistan and India are politically aligned (in a way that is temporary and strained at times) with the West Indian immigrant population. The basis for the formation of this multiracial coalition under the rubric "black people" is the common history of oppression they share as ex-colonial immigrant settlers in Britain.[67] The extension of the racial term "black" to non-African people in Australia, as well as to Asians in contemporary Britain, provides some indication that there is a sense in which a racial concept can be reconstructed to extend to a multiracial group that has not intermingled in the sense of having mixed blood.

Du Bois's proposal regarding group identity requires an adjustment in the biological essentialist criteria to account for intermingling in the sense of racial amalgamation, but what about multiracial group coalitions? By shifting the emphasis to sociohistorical consciousness he wanted to modify the biological requirement (influenced by scientific racism) to specify only a vague blood tie. Given the fact of racial amalgamation in the United States, he rightly maintained that African-American identity can only reside in sociohistorical consciousness. It is far from clear that he would have embraced all that this implies, viz., that sociohistorical consciousness figures into the social formation of racial and ethnic groups on the model of multiracial group coalitions as well.

Racism and Color Stratification

What if a peculiar sort of cultural exchange were to suddenly occur such that the sociohistorical consciousness that once resided in the biological group now known as "black people" also begins to manifest itself in the biological group now known as "white people"? Suppose further that, at some time in the future, the former group is exterminated (by genocide) or disappears (through amalgamation), and that the latter group inherits this consciousness. To what extent do we continue to apply the term "black people"? It seems that on Du Bois's account some such transference of consciousness would be allowed as long as there is, perhaps, a blood tie (say, "traceable") and the inheritors have a sociohistorical connection with their ancestors. If we treat Du Bois's stipulation regarding common blood as inessential it seems that his sociohistorical criteria provide a sufficient ground on which to establish the black identity of this biological white group.[68]

While it may appear odd to speak of "white African-Americans," such an expression could conceivably be applied in some sense that parallels the present usage of the expression "black Anglo-Saxons," which does not seem odd.[69] In each instance the respective expression would be applied by virtue of a transference of consciousness from one biological group to another, even when there is no blood tie between them. The reason that the expression "white African-American" may seem odd is because in the United States the concept of race applies strictly to blacks and whites in the sense that "traceable ancestry" really means that to be white is to have *no* non-white ancestry and to be black is to have *any* black ancestry. With few exceptions we can safely assume that there will be only a one-way transference of consciousness, i.e., black people will acculturate into the dominant white mainstream.[70]

It would be a mistake, however, to rule out entirely the possibility of a group of white people appropriating something very much akin to the racial consciousness of African-Americans. In 1880 Gustave de Molinari documented his observation that the English press "allow no occasion to escape them of treating the Irish as an inferior race – a kind of white negroes."[71] What is most interesting about this instance of bigotry by one white ethnic group directed toward another is that it was justified by appealing to the same scientific racism used to justify the oppression of black people, i.e., the idea that the Irish were a lower species closer to the apes. Moreover, presently in Northern Ireland, Irish Catholics are sometimes referred to by Protestants as "white niggers" – and, in turn, have appropriated and politically valorized this appellation. The link between African-Americans and, say, black South Africans is largely sociohistorical such that an important feature of African-American identity includes a commonly shared history of oppression, but only in this attenuated sense. Similarly, there is no reason to suppose that Irish Catholic identity could not conceivably include, as fellow colonial subjects, a commonly shared history of oppression, in this attenuated sense, with African-Americans and black South Africans.[72]

The oddness of the concept of "white Negroes" or "white African-Americans" is a result of a special norm that places black people into a rock bottom category to which others can be assimilated for political purposes.[73] The simianized portrayal of Irish Catholics figures into their oppression and degradation in a fashion similar to the function of such portrayals of African-Americans. What must be noted, however, is that black people are the paradigm for any such category.[74] This indicates that racism is an ideology regarding the superiority of white people and the inferiority of nonwhite people. Du Bois made reference to the fact that this color spectrum is defined mainly by the black and white extremes. Although certain white ethnic groups, such as the Irish and the Jews, have experienced their own peculiar brand of racial oppression by other whites, they are not above engaging in racial discrimination against blacks.

The most telling criticism of Du Bois's attempt to reconstruct an African-American identity in terms of culture, rather than biology or physical characteristics, is the fact that so much racism is based on color discrimination.[75] Unlike most racial and ethnic groups, for black people physical characteristics are more fundamental than cultural characteristics with regard to racism. It is for this reason that black Jews experience discrimination by other Jews, or that there is a need to distinguish black Hispanics from all others.[76] Racism based on color indicates that black people occupy an especially abhorrent category such that even hybrid groups that include mulattoes discriminate against them.[77]

Although certain considerations regarding the intermingling of different racial and ethnic groups motivated Du Bois's revision of the notion of race his main concern was with the impact of racism on African-American group identity. He aimed to address the problem of color discrimination within the group by providing a concept of race that would bring African-Americans of different colors together.[78] To the extent that color was an indication of class position among African-Americans he also dealt with the issue of group pride by rejecting the extremely divisive assimilationist racial ideal. He challenged the assimilationist doctrine of "whitening" by formulating the criteria of group identity in nonbiological terms, a strategy designed to include African-Americans on both ends of the color spectrum. Group elevation does not require amalgamation and self-obliteration. Instead, social progress for African-Americans requires a conservation of physical characteristics (already multiracial) in order to foster cultural development. The strength of a group lies in its cultural integrity, which has to be situated in a dynamic historical process, rather than in a biologically fixed category.

Notes

My research for this essay was partially supported by a Ford Postdoctoral Fellowship, 1989–90, and by a grant from Stanford University, 1991, hereby gratefully acknowledged.

1 W. E. B. Du Bois, "The Conservation of Races," in Howard Brotz (ed.), *Negro Social and Political Thought, 1850–1920* (New York: Basic Books, 1966), p. 491. All subsequent references to Du Bois will be to this work unless otherwise indicated.

2 Du Bois, p. 491.

3 Bernard R. Boxill, *Blacks and Social Justice* (Totowa, NJ: Rowman & Allanheld, 1984), p. 180.

4 Du Bois, p. 488.

5 Joseph P. DeMarco, *The Social Thought of W. E. B. Du Bois* (Lanham, Md.: University Press of America, 1983), pp. 31–62; Boxill, *Blacks and Social Justice*, pp. 173–85; Anthony Appiah, "The Uncompleted Argument: Du Bois and the Illusion of Race" in Henry L. Gates, Jr. (ed.), *"Race," Writing, and Difference* (Chicago: University of Chicago Press, 1985), pp. 21–37.

6 In this essay I do not take on the larger task of comparing Du Bois's claims in "The Conservation of Races" with modifications that appeared in his later writings. For useful analyses in this regard see the above cited works by DeMarco and Appiah.

7 Du Bois, p. 485.

8 Du Bois, p. 485.

9 Du Bois, p. 485.

10 Du Bois, p. 485.

11 Du Bois, pp. 486–7.

12 Du Bois, p. 486.

13 Boxill, *Blacks and Social Justice*, p. 178; Appiah, "The Uncompleted Argument," p. 28.

14 Du Bois, p. 487.

15 Boxill, *Blacks and Social Justice*, p. 183.

16 Du Bois, p. 491.

17 Du Bois, p. 488. Du Bois leaves open the question of whether Egyptian civilization was "Negro in its origin" and stresses that "the full, complete Negro message of the whole Negro race has not as yet been given to the world" (p. 487).

18 Du Bois, pp. 487 and 489.

19 Du Bois, p. 489.

20 Du Bois, p. 489. Du Bois's reference to Negroes in Africa as having "slept, but half awakening" reflects his lack of knowledge of African history at this early stage of his career. He later wrote the following about his reaction to Franz Boas's 1906 Atlanta University commencement address on the topic of black kingdoms south of the Sahara: "I was too astonished to speak. All of this I had never heard. . . ." *Black Folk: Then and Now* (New York: Henry Holt, 1939), p. vii.

21 Du Bois cites the fact that African Americans have given America "its only American music, its only American fairy tales, its only touch of pathos" (p. 489). Later Du Bois spoke of African-American music as "the greatest gift of the Negro people." *The Souls of Black Folk* (New York: Fawcett World Library. 1961), p. 181.

22 Du Bois, p. 489.

23 In a much later work Du Bois rejects what he calls "the physical bond" but goes on to assert that "the real essence of this kinship is its social heritage of slavery." *Dusk of Dawn: An Essay Toward an Autobiography of a Race Concept* (New York: Schocken, 1968), pp. 116–17, quoted in Appiah, "The Uncompleted Argument," p. 33.

24 Appiah, p. 32.

25 Du Bois, p. 491.

26 Du Bois, p. 489.

27 DeMarco, *Social Thought of W. E. B. Du Bois*, p. 33; Appiah, "The Uncompleted Argument," p. 27.

28 Wilson J. Moses, *Alexander Crummell: A Study of Civilization and Discontent* (Oxford: Oxford University Press, 1989), p. 262. With regard to the notion of "civilization" Du Bois's European influences must also be acknowledged. Bernard W. Bell maintains that although there is no documentary evidence of his having read Herder "it is unlikely that Du Bois remained untouched by the spirit and thought of Herder, Goethe, and Rousseau." *Folk Roots of Contemporary Afro-American Poetry* (Detroit: Broadside Press, 1974), p. 23. For a discussion of Du Bois's known academic influences see Francis L. Broderick, "German Influence on the Scholarship of W. E. B. Du Bois," *Phylon* 19 (Dec. 1958) and "The Academic Training of W. E. B. Du Bois," *Journal of Negro Education* 27 (Winter 1958).

29 Du Bois, p. 487.

30 Appiah, "The Uncompleted Argument," p. 25.

31 Du Bois did acknowledge that "The term Negro is, perhaps, the most indefinite of all" and applies to a wide variety of people, but he does not hesitate to override this consideration with remarks such as "200,000,000 black hearts beating in one glad song of jubilee" (pp. 486–7).

32 Du Bois, p. 491.

33 Du Bois, p. 488.

34 Du Bois, p. 489; Booker T. Washington, "Atlanta Exposition Address" in Brotz, *Negro Social and Political Thought*, p. 359. Du Bois seems even closer to Washington when he implores the Academy to "continually impress the fact upon the Negro people that . . . they MUST DO FOR THEMSELVES . . . that a little less complaint and whining, and a little more dogged work and manly striving would do us more credit and benefit than a thousand Force or Civil Rights bills" (p. 490).

35 Du Bois, p. 488.

36 See Dorothy Porter, "The Organized Educational Activities of Negro Literary Societies, 1828–1846," *Journal of Negro Education* 5 (Oct. 1936), pp. 556–66.

37 See C. M. Wiltse (ed.) *David Walker's Appeal* (New York: Hill and Wang, 1965); Maria W. Stewart, "An Address Delivered Before the Afric-American Female Intelligence Society of America" and "Mrs. Stewart's Farewell Address to Her Friends in the City of Boston" in Marilyn Richardson (ed.), *Maria W. Stewart, America's First Black Woman Political Writer* (Bloomington: Indiana University Press, 1987); Howard H. Bell, "National Negro Conventions of the Middle 1840s: Moral Suasion vs. Political Action," *Journal of Negro History* 42 (Oct. 1957), pp. 247–60; Howard H. Bell, *A Survey of the Negro Convention Movement 1830–1861* (New York: Arno Press, 1969).

38 W. H. A. Moore, "The New Negro Literary Movement," *AME Church Review* 21 (1904), p. 52.

39 Cf. Frances E. W. Harper, "Iola," and Pauline E. Hopkins, "Sappho," in Mary Helen Washington (ed.), *Invented Lives* (New York: Anchor, 1987), pp. 87–129. For a discussion of why some African-Americans choose to pass see James E. Conyers and T. H. Kennedy, "Negro Passing: To Pass or Not to Pass," *Phylon* 25, 3 (Fall 1963), pp. 215–23, and Virginia R. Dominguez, *White by Definition* (New Brunswick, NJ: Rutgers University Press, 1986), pp. 200–204.

40 Du Bois, p. 488.

41 Cf. Boxill, *Blacks and Social Justice*, p. 185.

42 For a discussion of the rather tenuous racial basis for ethnicity see R. B. LePage and Andree Tabouret-Keller, *Acts of Identity: Creole-Based Approaches to Language and Ethnicity* (Cambridge: Cambridge University Press, 1985), pp. 207–49. Lucius Outlaw has argued a similar line regarding the social construction of race and ethnicity. See his "Toward a Critical Theory of 'Race'" in David T. Goldberg (ed.), *Anatomy of Racism* (Minneapolis: University of Minnesota Press, 1990), pp. 58–82.

43 Appiah, "The Uncompleted Argument," p. 27. In this regard Du Bois may have followed the view of Herder. According to Herder, "[Races] belong not, therefore, so properly to systematic natural history, as to the physico-geographical history of man." F. McEachran,

The Life and Philosophy of Johann Gottfried Herder (Oxford: Clarendon Press, 1939), p. 298, cited in Cedric Dover, "The Racial Philosophy of Johann Herder," *British Journal of Sociology* 3 (1952) p. 125. See also Vernon J. Williams, Jr., *From A Caste to A Minority: Changing Attitudes of American Sociologists Toward Afro-Americans, 1896–1945* (New York: Greenwood Press, 1989), pp. 86–7.

44 Boxill, *Blacks and Social Justice*, p. 178.

45 For an historical account of racial classification see Michael Banton, "The Classification of Races in Europe and North America: 1700–1850," *International Social Science Journal* 111 (Feb. 1987), pp. 45–60. According to Robert E. Park, "In South America and particularly in Brazil, where Negroes and mixed bloods constitute more than 60 per cent of the population, there is, strictly speaking, no color line . . . [although] the white man is invariably at the top, and the black man and the native Indian are at the bottom." *Race and Culture* (Glencoe, Ill.: Free Press, 1950), p. 381. Similarly, Julian Pitt-Rivers reports that "A man who would be considered Negro in the United States might, by traveling to Mexico, become *moreno* or *prieto*, then *canela* or *trigueno* in Panama, and end up in Barranquilla white." "Race, Color, and Class in Central America and the Andes" in John Hope Franklin (ed.), *Color and Race* (Boston: Houghton Mifflin Co., 1968), p. 270. With reference to black people of lighter skin Philip Mason tells us that " 'The white man' in Jamaica sometimes means a well-to-do person who behaves as though he came from Europe and would often not be classed as 'white' in the United States." "The Revolt Against Western Values" in Franklin (ed.), *Color and Race*, p. 61.

46 See the California State University and University of Massachusetts Application Forms, 1991–92. For a discussion of the definitions of affirmative action categories see David H. Rosenbloom, "The Federal Affirmative Action Policy" in D. Nachimias (ed.), *The Practice of Policy Evaluation* (New York: Saint Martin's Press, 1980), pp. 169–86, cited in Dvora Yanow, "The Social Construction of Affirmative Action and Other Categories," a paper presented at the Fifth National Symposium on Public Administration Theory, Chicago, April 9–10, 1992. For a discussion of the political implications of treating the concepts of race and ethnicity as interchangeable see Michael Omi and Howard Winant, *Racial Formation in the United States: From the 1960s to the 1980s* (New York: Routledge & Kegan Paul, 1986), pp. 14–37.

47 Frederick Douglass, "The Claims of the Negro Ethnologically Considered" in Brotz. *Negro Social and Political Thought*. p. 250.

48 S. S. N., "Anglo Saxons and Anglo Africans." *The Anglo African Magazine*, vol. 1, 1859 (New York: Arno Press, 1968), p. 250.

49 "Anglo Saxons," p. 250.

50 According to Margot Pepper, "Although *Chicano* has

been misused to identify all Mexican Americans, it actually refers to a specific political and cultural attitude; it is not an ethnic category." "Resistance and Affirmation," *San Francisco Guardian* (June 26, 1991), p. 33. Velina Hasu Houston, president of the Amerasian League, informs us that "The term (*Amerasian*) referred to all multiracial Asians, whether their American half was Anglo, African American or Latino." "Broadening the Definition of Amerasians," *Los Angeles Times* (July 11, 1991). p. E5. Cape Verdians are a mixed Portuguese/African group who speak a creole language, but, in Massachusetts, are not classified as either black or Hispanic.

51 Cf. Ruth Benedict and Gene Weltfish, *The Races of Mankind*, Public Affairs Pamphlet no. 85 (Sept. 1980), p. 8.

52 Appiah, "The Uncompleted Argument," p. 34. DeMarco suggests that Du Bois may have believed that the original world population was divided into the three different races, since he "characterized the growth of racial units as one which proceeds from physical heterogeneity to an increasing physical homogeneity." DeMarco, *Social Thought*, p. 41. Arnold Rampersad, however, has pointed out that by 1915 Du Bois shifted more toward a common ancestry view. *The Art and Imagination of W. E. B. Du Bois* (Cambridge, Mass.: Harvard University Press, 1976), pp. 230–1.

53 Cf. Robert A. Hill and Barbara Bair (eds.), *Marcus Garvey Life and Lessons* (Berkeley: University of California Press, 1987), p. 206, and V. R. H. de la Torre, "Indo–America" and "Thirty years of Aprismo" in *The Ideologies of the Developing Nations* (New York: Simon and Schuster, 1972), pp. 790–800.

54 In 1885, Croatan Indians in Robeson County, North Carolina, sought to distinguish themselves from African-Americans, with whom they had mixed, by getting the legislature to pass laws that made them the final judges on questions of genealogy. They adopted the pragmatic definition, "an Indian is a person called an Indian by other Indians." Guy B. Johnson, "Personality in a White-Indian-Negro Community," in Alain Locke and Bernhard J. Stern (eds.), *When Peoples Meet* (New York: Progressive Education Association, 1942), p. 577.

55 See, for instance, Jean Fagan Yellin (ed.), Harriet Jacobs, *Incidents in the Life of a Slave Girl* (Cambridge, Mass.: Harvard University Press, 1987), p. 29.

56 In the mid-seventeenth century, Virginia enacted legislation that stipulated that children born of a black woman would inherit her status, even when the father was white. This measure allowed slaveholders to literally reproduce their own labor force. See Paula Giddings, *When and Where I Enter* (New York: Bantam, 1985), p. 37. Marvin Harris argues that the difference between the United States and Latin America in applying this rule of descent must be understood in terms of it being "materially advanta-

geous to one set of planters, while it was the opposite to another." *Patterns of Race in the Americas* (New York: W. W. Norton, 1964), p. 81.

57 Indeed, in many cases where phenotypical characteristics are ambiguous with regard to an individual's genotype, self-identification (i.e., cultural criteria) becomes more of a possibility. C. Eric Lincoln informs us that "Reliable estimates on the basis of three hundred and fifty years of miscegenation and passing suggest that there are several million 'Caucasians' in this country who are part Negro insofar as they have Negro blood or Negro ancestry." "Color and Group Identity in the United States," in Franklin (ed.), *Color and Race*, p. 250. To see that the issue of genetic heritage is mostly a matter of politics we need only consider the fact that the Louisiana state legislature recently repealed a 1970 statute that established a mathematical formula to determine if a person was black. The "one thirty-second rule" was changed to "traceable amount." Frances Frank Marcus, "Louisiana Repeals Black Blood Law," *New York Times* (July 6, 1983), p. A10. For a detailed historical account of the politics surrounding the Louisiana law see Dominguez, chs 2 & 3. When Hawaii became a United States Territory in 1990 the "one thirty-second rule" was lobbied against by five large landholding companies. For economic reasons they favored the present law which requires 50% native blood to be eligible for a land grant. See Timothy Egan, "Aboriginal Authenticity to Be Decided in a Vote," *New York Times* (Jan. 1, 1990), p. A12.

58 See the discussion of Hansen's Law by Werner Sollors in his *Beyond Ethnicity: Consent and Descent in American Culture* (New York: Oxford University Press, 1986), pp. 214–21. For a discussion of its application to Louisiana creoles see Dominguez, ch. 7.

59 Boxill's definition of black people cannot accommodate such cases for he would insist on phenotype and descent as overriding factors such that black Latinos who operate with a primarily *cultural* identity must be viewed as in some sense "passing."

60 According to Israel's Law of Return anyone born to a Jewish mother who has not taken formal steps to adopt a different religion has the right to become a citizen of Israel.

61 Cf. Benedict and Weltfish, *The Races of Mankind*, p. 10; Abram Leon Sachar, *A History of the Jews* (New York: Alfred A. Knopf, 1979), p. 250.

62 According to Louis Wirth, "What has held the Jewish community together in spite of all disintegrating forces is . . . the fact that the Jewish community is treated as a community by the world at large." "Why the Jewish Community Survives" in Locke and Stern (eds). *When Peoples Meet*, p. 493.

63 Cf. Peter Singer, "Is Racial Discrimination Arbitrary?," *Philosophia* 8, 2–3 (Nov. 1978), p. 185. See also Edward W. Said, "Zionism from the Standpoint

Tommy L. Lott

of Its Victims" in Goldberg *Anatomy of Racism*, pp. 210–46.

64 Webster's dictionary emphasizes the fact that this term applies primarily to marriage or inter-breeding between whites and blacks.

65 See Thomas E. Skidmore, "Racial Ideas and Social Policy in Brazil, 1870–1940," in Richard Graham (ed.), *The Idea of Race in Latin America, 1870–1940* (Austin: University of Texas Press, 1990), pp. 7–36; and Parks, *Race and Culture*, p. 385.

66 For an account of the aboriginal struggle for social equality in Australia, see Roberta B. Sykes, *Black Majority* (Victoria, Australia: Hudson Publishing, 1989).

67 Consider, for instance, the following quote: "Now, a comment about the title of the book and why we have chosen the term "black population." What the immigrants from New Commonwealth and Pakistan (NCWP) and their children born have in common is the material consequences and, in very many cases, the direct experience of discrimination. Discrimination, as the studies, by Political and Economic Planning (PEP) have demonstrated, is based upon colour. Hence, the reference to Britain's black population. It can, of course, be argued that some immigrants and their children do not and would not want to be labelled as *black*. That is not denied, but the defence of this terminology in this context lies with the fact that, irrespective of their own particular beliefs, experiences and the wide range of cultural variations, racism and racial discrimination is a crucial determinant of their economic and social situation." The Runnymede Trust and the Radical Statistics Race Group, *Britain's Black Population* (London: Heinemann Educational Books, 1980), p. xii. See also Kobena Mercer, "'1968': Periodizing Postmodern Politics and Identity," in Lawrence Grossberg, Cary Nelson, Paula Treichler (eds), *Cultural Studies* (New York: Routledge, 1992), pp. 424–38; Frank Reeves, *British Racial Discourse* (Cambridge: Cambridge University Press, 1983), p. 255; Lionel Morrison, *As They See It* (London: Community Relations Commission, 1976), pp. 35–49; Brian D. Jacobs, *Black Politics and Urban Crisis in Britain* (Cambridge: Cambridge University Press, 1986), pp. 41–62; Paul Gilroy, "*There Ain't No Black In The Union Jack*" (London: Hutchinson, 1987).

68 In *Worlds of Color*, written near his ninetieth birthday, Du Bois gave the following description of Jean Du Bignon: "a 'white Black Girl' from New Orleans; that is, a well educated young white woman who was classed as "Colored" because she had a Negro great-grandfather." *Worlds of Color* (Millwood. NY: Kraus-Thomson, 1976), p. 9. It should be noted here that Du Bois seems to have inconsistently treated his own blood tie with his Dutch ancestors as inessential. Most likely this was due to his *cultural* identification with black people, as well as with his tacit commitment to

the "census" definition of a black person – viz., that a black person is a person who "passes" for a black person in the community where he lives. See Parks, *Race and Culture*, p. 293.

69 In the nineteenth century black Americans sometimes referred to themselves nonpejoratively as "Anglo-Africans." With a similar reference to a white cultural influence Nathan Hare's book, *The Black Anglo Saxons* (New York: Collier Books, 1965), was offered as a criticism of the assimilationist mentality of certain segments of the black middle class.

70 One notable exception is the white rap group, *Young Black Teenagers*, who explain their appropriation of this title (along with tunes such as "Proud to Be Black" and "Daddy Kalled Me Niga Cause I Likeded To Rhyme") as an expression of their having grown up in a predominately black youth culture in New York City. See Joe Wood, "Cultural Consumption, From Elvis Presley to the Young Black Teenagers," *Village Voice Rock & Roll Quarterly*, pp. 10–11.

71 Quoted in L Perry Curtis, Jr., *Apes and Angels: The Irishman in Victorian Caricature* (Washington, DC: Smithsonian Institution Press, 1971), p. 1.

72 In his very interesting documentary film, *The Black and the Green*, Saint Claire Bourne explores the theme of black consciousness in the Irish Catholics' struggle for social equality.

73 See Norman Mailer's "The White Negro" in his *Advertisements for Myself* (New York: Andre Deutsch, 1964).

74 Kobena Mercer cites a passage from Arthur Rimbaud's "A Season in Hell" (1873) in which the claim is made: "I am a beast, a Negro." Mercer, "'1968,'" p. 432.

75 With regard to his discussion of Du Bois's concept of race, Anthony Appiah was sharply criticized by Houston Baker for downplaying the role of color discrimination in everyday affairs. See his "Caliban's Triple Play" in Gates (ed.), "*Race*," *Writing, and Difference*, pp. 384–5. and Appiah's reply "The Conservation of 'Race'," *Black American Literature Forum*, 23, 1 (Spring 1989), pp. 37–60.

76 Cf. Morris Lounds, Jr., *Israel's Black Hebrews: Black Americans in Search of Identity* (Washington, DC: University Press of America, 1981), pp. 209–13.

77 Cf. Ozzie L. Edwards, "Skin Color as a Variable in Racial Attitudes of Black Urbanites," *Journal of Black Studies*, 3, 4 (June, 1972), pp. 473–83; Robert E. Washington, "Brown Racism and the Formation of a World System of Racial Stratification," *International Journal of Politics, Culture, and Society*, 4, 2, 1990; Lincoln, "Color and Group Identity," pp. 249–63.

78 With regard to the "self-questioning," "hesitation," "vacillation," and "contradiction" faced by mulattoes Du Bois remarked that "combined race action is stifled, race responsibility is shirked, race enterprises languish, and the best blood, the best talent, the best energy of the Negro people cannot be marshalled to do the bidding of the race" (p. 488).

304

35

Racism and Culture

Frantz Fanon

The unilaterally decreed normative value of certain cultures deserves our careful attention. One of the paradoxes immediately encountered is the rebound of egocentric, sociocentric definitions.

There is first affirmed the existence of human groups having no culture; then of a hierarchy of cultures; and finally, the concept of cultural relativity.

We have here the whole range from overall negation to singular and specific recognition. It is precisely this fragmented and bloody history that we must sketch on the level of cultural anthropology.

There are, we may say, certain constellations of institutions, established by particular men, in the framework of precise geographical areas, which at a given moment have undergone a direct and sudden assault of different cultural patterns. The technical, generally advanced development of the social group that has thus appeared enables it to set up an organized domination. The enterprise of deculturation turns out to be the negative of a more gigantic work of economic, and even biological, enslavement.

The doctrine of cultural hierarchy is thus but one aspect of a systematized hierarchization implacably pursued.

The modern theory of the absence of cortical integration of colonial peoples is the anatomic-

From Frantz Fanon, *Toward the African Revolution* (1988), copyright © 1988 Monthly Review Press; reproduced by kind permission of Monthly Review Press.

physiological counterpart of this doctrine. The apparition of racism is not fundamentally determining. Racism is not the whole but the most visible, the most day-to-day and, not to mince matters, the crudest element of a given structure.

To study the relations of racism and culture is to raise the question of their reciprocal action. If culture is the combination of motor and mental behavior patterns arising from the encounter of man with nature and with his fellow-man, it can be said that racism is indeed a cultural element. There are thus cultures with racism and cultures without racism.

This precise cultural element, however, has not become encysted. Racism has not managed to harden. It has had to renew itself, to adapt itself, to change its appearance. It has had to undergo the fate of the cultural whole that informed it.

The vulgar, primitive, over-simple racism purported to find in biology – the Scriptures having proved insufficient – the material basis of the doctrine. It would be tedious to recall the efforts then undertaken: the comparative form of the skulls, the quantity and the configuration of the folds of the brain, the characteristics of the cell layers of the cortex, the dimensions of the vertebrae, the microscopic appearance of the epiderm, etc. . . .

Intellectual and emotional primitivism appeared as a banal consequence, a recognition of existence.

Such affirmations, crude and massive, give way to a more refined argument. Here and there, however, an occasional relapse is to be noted. Thus the "emotional instability of the Negro," the "subcritical integration of the Arab," "the quasi-generic culpability of the Jew" are data that one comes upon among a few contemporary writers. The monograph by J. Carothers, for example, sponsored by the World Health Organization, invokes "scientific arguments" in support of a physiological lobotomy of the African Negro.

These old-fashioned positions tend in any case to disappear. This racism that aspires to be rational, individual, genotypically and phenotypically determined, becomes transformed into cultural racism. The object of racism is no longer the individual man but a certain form of existing. At the extreme, such terms as "message" and "cultural style" are resorted to. "Occidental values" oddly blend with the already famous appeal to the fight of the "cross against the crescent."

The morphological equation, to be sure, has not totally disappeared, but events of the past thirty years have shaken the most solidly anchored convictions, upset the checkerboard, restructured a great number of relationships.

The memory of Nazism, the common wretchedness of different men, the common enslavement of extensive social groups, the apparition of "European colonies," in other words the institution of a colonial system in the very heart of Europe, the growing awareness of workers in the colonizing and racist countries, the evolution of techniques, all this has deeply modified the problem and the manner of approaching it.

We must look for the consequences of this racism on the cultural level.

Racism, as we have seen, is only one element of a vaster whole: that of the systematized oppression of a people. How does an oppressing people behave? Here we rediscover constants.

We witness the destruction of cultural values, of ways of life. Language, dress, techniques, are devalorized. How can one account for this constant? Psychologists, who tend to explain everything by movements of the psyche, claim to discover this behavior on the level of contacts between individuals: the criticism of an original hat, of a way of speaking, of walking . . .

Such attempts deliberately leave out of account the special character of the colonial situation. In reality the nations that undertake a colonial war have no concern for the confrontation of cultures. War is a gigantic business and every approach must be governed by this datum. The enslavement, in the strictest sense, of the native population is the prime necessity.

For this its systems of reference have to be broken. Expropriation, spoliation, raids, objective murder, are matched by the sacking of cultural patterns, or at least condition such sacking. The social panorama is destructured; values are flaunted, crushed, emptied.

The lines of force, having crumbled, no longer give direction. In their stead a new system of values is imposed, not proposed but affirmed, by the heavy weight of cannons and sabers.

The setting up of the colonial system does not of itself bring about the death of the native culture. Historic observation reveals, on the contrary, that the aim sought is rather a continued agony than a total disappearance of the pre-existing culture. This culture, once living and open to the future, becomes closed, fixed in the colonial status, caught in the yoke of oppression. Both present and mummified, it testifies against its members. It defines them in fact without appeal. The cultural mummification leads to a mummification of individual thinking. The apathy so universally noted among colonial peoples is but the logical consequence of this operation. The reproach of inertia constantly directed at "the native" is utterly dishonest. As though it were possible for a man to evolve otherwise than within the framework of a culture that recognizes him and that he decides to assume.

Thus we witness the setting up of archaic, inert institutions, functioning under the oppressor's supervision and patterned like a caricature of formerly fertile institutions . . .

These bodies appear to embody respect for the tradition, the cultural specificities, the personality of the subjugated people. This pseudo-respect in fact is tantamount to the most utter contempt, to the most elaborate sadism. The characteristic of a culture is to be open, permeated by spontaneous, generous, fertile lines of force. The appointment of "reliable men" to execute certain gestures is a deception that deceives no one. Thus the Kabyle *djemaas* named by the French authority are not recognized by the natives. They are matched by another *djemaa* democratically elected. And naturally the second as a rule dictates to the first what his conduct should be.

The constantly affirmed concern with "respecting the culture of the native populations" accordingly does not signify taking into consideration the values borne by the culture, incarnated by men. Rather, this behavior betrays a determination to objectify, to confine, to imprison, to harden. Phrases such as "I know them," "that's the way they are," show this maximum objectification success-fully achieved. I can think of gestures and thoughts that define these men.

Exoticism is one of the forms of this simplifica-tion. It allows no cultural confrontation. There is on the one hand a culture in which qualities of dynamism, of growth, of depth can be recognized. As against this, we find characteristics, curiosities, things, never a structure.

Thus in an initial phase the occupant establishes his domination, massively affirms his superiority. The social group, militarily and economically sub-jugated, is dehumanized in accordance with a polydimensional method.

Exploitation, tortures, raids, racism, collective liquidations, rational oppression take turns at dif-ferent levels in order literally to make of the native an object in the hands of the occupying nation.

This object man, without means of existing, without a *raison d'être*, is broken in the very depth of his substance. The desire to live, to continue, becomes more and more indecisive, more and more phantom-like. It is at this stage that the well-known guilt complex appears. In his first novels, Wright gives a very detailed description of it.

Progressively, however, the evolution of tech-niques of production, the industrialization, limited though it is, of the subjugated countries, the increasingly necessary existence of collaborators, impose a new attitude upon the occupant. The complexity of the means of production, the evolu-tion of economic relations inevitably involving the evolution of ideologies, unbalance the system. Vulgar racism in its biological form corresponds to the period of crude exploitation of man's arms and legs. The perfecting of the means of production inevitably brings about the camouflage of the techniques by which man is exploited, hence of the forms of racism.

It is therefore not as a result of the evolution of people's minds that racism loses its virulence. No inner revolution can explain this necessity for racism to seek more subtle forms, to evolve. On all sides men become free, putting an end to the lethargy to which oppression and racism had condemned them.

In the very heart of the "civilized nations" the workers finally discover that the exploitation of man, at the root of a system, assumes different faces. At this stage racism no longer dares appear without disguise. It is unsure of itself. In an ever greater number of circumstances the racist takes to cover. He who claimed to "sense," to "see through"

those others, finds himself to be a target, looked at, judged. The racist's purpose has become a purpose haunted by bad conscience. He can find salvation only in a passion-driven commitment such as is found in certain psychoses. And having defined the symptomatology of such passion-charged deliria is not the least of Professor Baruk's merits.

Racism is never a super-added element discov-ered by chance in the course of the investigation of the cultural data of a group. The social constella-tion, the cultural whole, are deeply modified by the existence of racism.

It is a common saying nowadays that racism is a plague of humanity. But we must not content ourselves with such a phrase. We must tirelessly look for the repercussions of racism at all levels of sociability. The importance of the racist problem in contemporary American literature is significant. The Negro in motion pictures, the Negro and folklore, the Jew and children's stories, the Jew in the café, are inexhaustible themes.

Racism, to come back to America, haunts and vitiates American culture. And this dialectical gangrene is exacerbated by the coming to awareness and the determination of millions of Negroes and Jews to fight this racism by which they are victimized.

This passion-charged, irrational, groundless phase, when one examines it, reveals a frightful visage. The movement of groups, the liberation, in certain parts of the world, of men previously kept down, make for a more and more precarious equilibrium. Rather unexpectedly, the racist group points accus-ingly to a manifestation of racism among the oppressed. The "intellectual primitivism" of the period of exploitation gives way to the "medieval, in fact prehistoric fanaticism" of the period of the liberation.

For a time it looked as though racism had disappeared. This soul-soothing, unreal impression was simply the consequence of the evolution of forms of exploitation. Psychologists spoke of a prejudice having become unconscious. The truth is that the rigor of the system made the daily affirmation of a superiority superfluous. The need to appeal to various degrees of approval and support, to the native's cooperation, modified relations in a less crude, more subtle, more "culti-vated" direction. It was not rare, in fact, to see a "democratic and humane" ideology at this stage. The commercial undertaking of enslavement, of cultural destruction, progressively gave way to a verbal mystification.

The interesting thing about this evolution is that racism was taken as a topic of meditation, sometimes even as a publicity technique.

Thus the blues – "the black slave lament" – was offered up for the admiration of the oppressors. This modicum of stylized oppression is the exploiter's and the racist's rightful due. Without oppression and without racism you have no blues. The end of racism would sound the knell of great Negro music . . .

As the all-too-famous Toynbee might say, the blues are the slave's response to the challenge of oppression.

Still today, for many men, even colored, Armstrong's music has a real meaning only in this perspective.

Racism bloats and disfigures the face of the culture that practices it. Literature, the plastic arts, songs for shopgirls, proverbs, habits, patterns, whether they set out to attack it or to vulgarize it, restore racism. This means that a social group, a country, a civilization, cannot be unconsciously racist.

We say once again that racism is not an accidental discovery. It is not a hidden, dissimulated element. No superhuman efforts are needed to bring it out.

Racism stares one in the face for it so happens that it belongs in a characteristic whole: that of the shameless exploitation of one group of men by another which has reached a higher stage of technical development. This is why military and economic oppression generally precedes, makes possible, and legitimizes racism.

The habit of considering racism as a mental quirk, as a psychological flaw, must be abandoned.

But the men who are a prey to racism, the enslaved, exploited, weakened social group – how do they behave? What are their defense mechanisms?

What attitudes do we discover here?

In an initial phase we have seen the occupying power legitimizing its domination by scientific arguments, the "inferior race" being denied on the basis of race. Because no other solution is left it, the racialized social group tries to imitate the oppressor and thereby to deracialize itself. The "inferior race" denies itself as a different race. It shares with the "superior race" the convictions, doctrines, and other attitudes concerning it.

Having witnessed the liquidation of its systems of reference, the collapse of its cultural patterns, the native can only recognize with the occupant that "God is not on his side." The oppressor, through the inclusive and frightening character of his authority, manages to impose on the native new ways of seeing, and in particular a pejorative judgement with respect to his original forms of existing.

This event, which is commonly designated as alienation, is naturally very important. It is found in the official texts under the name of assimilation.

Now this alienation is never wholly successful. Whether or not it is because the oppressor quantitatively and qualitatively limits the evolution, unforeseen, disparate phenomena manifest themselves.

The inferiorized group had admitted, since the force of reasoning was implacable, that its misfortunes resulted directly from its racial and cultural characteristics.

Guilt and inferiority are the usual consequences of this dialectic. The oppressed then tries to escape these, on the one hand by proclaiming his total and unconditional adoption of the new cultural models, and on the other, by pronouncing an irreversible condemnation of his own cultural style.[1]

Yet the necessity that the oppressor encounters at a given point to dissimulate the forms of exploitation does not lead to the disappearance of this exploitation. The more elaborate, less crude economic relations require a daily coating, but the alienation at this level remains frightful.

Having judged, condemned, abandoned his cultural forms, his language, his food habits, his sexual behavior, his way of sitting down, of resting, of laughing, of enjoying himself, the oppressed *flings himself* upon the imposed culture with the desperation of a drowning man.

Developing his technical knowledge in contact with more and more perfected machines, entering into the dynamic circuit of industrial production, meeting men from remote regions in the framework of the concentration of capital, that is to say, on the job, discovering the assembly line, the team, production "time," in other words yield per hour, the oppressed is shocked to find that he continues to be the object of racism and contempt.

It is at this level that racism is treated as a question of persons. "There are a few hopeless racists, but you must admit that on the whole the population likes . . ."

With time all this will disappear.

This is the country where there is the least amount of race prejudice . . .

At the United Nations there is a commission to fight race prejudice.

Films on race prejudice, poems on race prejudice, messages on race prejudice . . .

Spectacular and futile condemnations of race prejudice. In reality, a colonial country is a racist country. If in England, in Belgium, or in France, despite the democratic principles affirmed by these respective nations, there are still racists, it is these racists who, in their opposition to the country as a whole, are logically consistent.

It is not possible to enslave men without logically making them inferior through and through. And racism is only the emotional, affective, sometimes intellectual explanation of this inferiorization.

The racist in a culture with racism is therefore normal. He has achieved a perfect harmony of economic relations and ideology. The idea that one forms of man, to be sure, is never totally dependent on economic relations, in other words – and this must not be forgotten – on relations existing historically and geographically among men and groups. An ever greater number of members belonging to racist societies are taking a position. They are dedicating themselves to a world in which racism would be impossible. But everyone is not up to this kind of objectivity, this abstraction, this solemn commitment. One cannot with impunity require of a man that he be against "the prejudices of his group."

And, we repeat, every colonialist group is racist. "Acculturized" and deculturized at one and the same time, the oppressed continues to come up against racism. He finds this sequel illogical, what he has left behind him inexplicable, without motive, incorrect. His knowledge, the appropriation of precise and complicated techniques, sometimes his intellectual superiority as compared to a great number of racists, lead him to qualify the racist world as passion-charged. He perceives that the racist atmosphere impregnates all the elements of the social life. The sense of an overwhelming injustice is correspondingly very strong. Forgetting racism as a consequence, one concentrates on racism as cause. Campaigns of deintoxication are launched. Appeal is made to the sense of humanity, to love, to respect for the supreme values . . .

Race prejudice in fact obeys a flawless logic. A country that lives, draws its substance from the exploitation of other peoples, makes those peoples inferior. Race prejudice applied to those peoples is normal.

Racism is therefore not a constant of the human spirit.

It is, as we have seen, a disposition fitting into a well-defined system. And anti-Jewish prejudice is no different from anti-Negro prejudice. A society has race prejudice or it has not. There are no degrees of prejudice. One cannot say that a given country is racist but that lynchings or extermination camps are not to be found there. The truth is that all that and still other things exist on the horizon. These virtualities, these latencies circulate, carried by the life-stream of psycho-affective, economic relations . . .

Discovering the futility of his alienation, his progressive deprivation, the inferiorized individual, after this phase of deculturation, of extraneousness, comes back to his original positions.

This culture, abandoned, sloughed off, rejected, despised, becomes for the inferiorized an object of passionate attachment. There is a very marked kind of overvaluation that is psychologically closely linked to the craving for forgiveness.

But behind this simplifying analysis there is indeed the intuition experienced by the inferiorized of having discovered a spontaneous truth. This is a psychological datum that is part of the texture of History and of Truth.

Because the inferiorized rediscovers a style that had once been devalorized, what he does is in fact to cultivate culture. Such a caricature of cultural existence would indicate, if it were necessary, that culture must be lived, and cannot be fragmented. It cannot be had piecemeal.

Yet the oppressed goes into ecstasies over each rediscovery. The wonder is permanent. Having formerly emigrated from his culture, the native today explores it with ardor. It is a continual honeymoon. Formerly inferiorized, he is now in a state of grace.

Not with impunity, however, does one undergo domination. The culture of the enslaved people is sclerosed, dying. No life any longer circulates in it. Or more precisely, the only existing life is dissimulated. The population that normally assumes here and there a few fragments of life, which continues to attach dynamic meanings to institutions, is an anonymous population. In a colonial system these are the traditionalists.

The former emigré, by the sudden ambiguity of his behavior, causes consternation. To the anonymity of the traditionalist he opposes a vehement and aggressive exhibitionism.

The state of grace and aggressiveness are the two constants found at this stage. Aggressiveness being the passion-charged mechanism making it possible to escape the sting of paradox.

Because the former emigré is in possession of

precise techniques, because his level of action is in the framework of relations that are already complex, these rediscoveries assume an irrational aspect. There is an hiatus, a discrepancy between intellectual development, technical appropriation, highly differentiated modes of thinking and of logic, on the one hand, and a "simple, pure" emotional basis on the other . . .

Rediscovering tradition, living it as a defense mechanism, as a symbol of purity, of salvation, the decultured individual leaves the impression that the mediation takes vengeance by substantializing itself. This falling back on archaic positions having no relation to technical development is paradoxical. The institutions thus valorized no longer correspond to the elaborate methods of action already mastered.

The culture put into capsules, which has vegetated since the foreign domination, is revalorized. It is not reconceived, grasped anew, dynamized from within. It is shouted. And this headlong, unstructured, verbal revalorization conceals paradoxical attitudes.

It is at this point that the incorrigible character of the inferiorized is brought out for mention. Arab doctors sleep on the ground, spit all over the place, etc. . . .

Negro intellectuals consult a sorcerer before making a decision, etc. . . .

"Collaborating" intellectuals try to justify their new attitude. The customs, traditions, beliefs, formerly denied and passed over in silence are violently valorized and affirmed.

Tradition is no longer scoffed at by the group. The group no longer runs away from itself. The sense of the past is rediscovered, the worship of ancestors resumed . . .

The past, becoming henceforth a constellation of values, becomes identified with the Truth.

This rediscovery, this absolute valorization almost in defiance of reality, objectively indefensible, assumes an incomparable and subjective importance. On emerging from these passionate espousals, the native will have decided, "with full knowledge of what is involved," to fight all forms of exploitation and of alienation of man. At this same time, the occupant, on the other hand, multiplies appeals to assimilation, then to integration, to community.

The native's hand-to-hand struggle with his culture is too solemn, too abrupt an operation to tolerate the slightest slip-up. No neologism can mask the new certainty: the plunge into the chasm of the past is the condition and the source of freedom.

The logical end of this will to struggle is the total liberation of the national territory. In order to achieve this liberation, the inferiorized man brings all his resources into play, all his acquisitions, the old and the new, his own and those of the occupant.

The struggle is at once total, absolute. But then race prejudice is hardly found to appear.

At the time of imposing his domination, in order to justify slavery, the oppressor had invoked scientific argument. There is nothing of the kind here.

A people that undertakes a struggle for liberation rarely legitimizes race prejudice. Even in the course of acute periods of insurrectional armed struggle one never witnesses the recourse to biological justifications.

The struggle of the inferiorized is situated on a markedly more human level. The perspectives are radically new. The opposition is the henceforth classical one of the struggles of conquest and of liberation.

In the course of struggle the dominating nation tries to revive racist arguments but the elaboration of racism proves more and more ineffective. There is talk of fanaticism, of primitive attitudes in the face of death, but once again the now crumbling mechanism no longer responds. Those who were once unbudgeable, the constitutional cowards, the timid, the eternally inferiorized, stiffen and emerge bristling.

The occupant is bewildered.

The end of race prejudice begins with a sudden incomprehension.

The occupant's spasmed and rigid culture, now liberated, opens at last to the culture of people who have really become brothers. The two cultures can affront each other, enrich each other.

In conclusion, universality resides in this decision to recognize and accept the reciprocal relativism of different cultures, once the colonial status is irreversibly excluded.

Notes

Text of Frantz Fanon's speech before the First Congress of Negro Writers and Artists in Paris, Sept. 1956. Published in the Special Issue of *Présence Africaine*, June-Nov., 1956.

1 A little-studied phenomenon sometimes appears at this stage. Intellectuals, students, belonging to the dominant group, make "scientific" studies of the dominated society, its art, its ethical universe.

In the universities the rare colonized intellectuals find their own cultural system being revealed to them. It even happens that scholars of the colonizing countries grow enthusiastic over this or that specific feature. The concepts of purity, naïveté, innocence appear. The native intellectual's vigilance must here be doubly on the alert.

36

Racism and Feminism

bell hooks

American women of all races are socialized to think of racism solely in the context of race hatred. Specifically in the case of black and white people, the term racism is usually seen as synonymous with discrimination or prejudice against black people by white people. For most women, the first knowledge of racism as institutionalized oppression is engendered either by direct personal experience or through information gleaned from conversations, books, television, or movies. Consequently, the American woman's understanding of racism as a political tool of colonialism and imperialism is severely limited. To experience the pain of race hatred or to witness that pain is not to understand its origin, evolution, or impact on world history. The inability of American women to understand racism in the context of American politics is not due to any inherent deficiency in woman's psyche. It merely reflects the extent of our victimization.

No history books used in public schools informed us about racial imperialism. Instead we were given romantic notions of the "new world," the "American dream," America as the great melting pot where all races come together as one. We were taught that Columbus *discovered* America; that "Indians" were scalphunters, killers of innocent women and children; that black people were enslaved because of the biblical curse of Ham, that God "himself" had decreed they would be hewers of wood, tillers of the field, and bringers of water.

From bell hooks, *Ain't I a Woman?* (1988); by kind permission of South End Press.

No one talked of Africa as the cradle of civilization, of the African and Asian people who came to America before Columbus. No one mentioned mass murders of Native Americans as genocide, or the rape of Native American and African women as terrorism. No one discussed slavery as a foundation for the growth of capitalism. No one described the forced breeding of white wives to increase the white population as sexist oppression.

I am a black woman. I attended all-black public schools. I grew up in the south where all around me was the fact of racial discrimination, hatred, and forced segregation. Yet my education as to the politics of race in American society was not that different from that of white female students I met in integrated high schools, in college, or in various women's groups. The majority of us understood racism as a social evil perpetuated by prejudiced white people that could be overcome through bonding between blacks and liberal whites, through militant protest, changing of laws or racial integration. Higher educational institutions did nothing to increase our limited understanding of racism as a political ideology. Instead professors systematically denied us truth, teaching us to accept racial polarity in the form of white supremacy and sexual polarity in the form of male dominance.

American women have been socialized, even brainwashed, to accept a version of American history that was created to uphold and maintain racial imperialism in the form of white supremacy and sexual imperialism in the form of patriarchy. One measure of the success of such indoctrination is that we perpetuate both consciously and unconsciously the very evils that oppress us. I am certain that the black female sixth grade teacher who taught us history, who taught us to identify with the American government, who loved those students who could best recite the pledge of allegiance to the American flag was not aware of the contradiction; that we should love this government that segregated us, that failed to send schools with all black students supplies that went to schools with only white pupils. Unknowingly she implanted in our psyches a seed of the racial imperialism that would keep us forever in bondage. For how does one overthrow, change, or even challenge a system that you have been taught to admire, to love, to believe in? Her innocence does not change the reality that she was teaching black children to embrace the very system that oppressed us, that she encouraged us to support it, to stand in awe of it, to die for it.

That American women, irrespective of their education, economic status, or racial identification, have undergone years of sexist and racist socialization that has taught us to blindly trust our knowledge of history and its effect on present reality, even though that knowledge has been formed and shaped by an oppressive system, is nowhere more evident than in the recent feminist movement. The group of college-educated white middle and upper class women who came together to organize a women's movement brought a new energy to the concept of women's rights in America. They were not merely advocating social equality with men. They demanded a transformation of society, a revolution, a change in the American social structure. Yet as they attempted to take feminism beyond the realm of radical rhetoric and into the realm of American life, they revealed that they had not changed, had not undone the sexist and racist brainwashing that had taught them to regard women unlike themselves as Others. Consequently, the Sisterhood they talked about has not become a reality, and the women's movement they envisioned would have a transformative effect on American culture has not emerged. Instead, the hierarchical pattern of race and sex relationships already established in American society merely took a different form under "feminism": the form of women being classed as an oppressed group under affirmative action programs further perpetuating the myth that the social status of all women in America is the same; the form of women's studies programs being established with all-white faculty teaching literature almost exclusively by white women about white women and

frequently from racist perspectives; the form of white women writing books that purport to be about the experience of American women when in fact they concentrate solely on the experience of white women; and finally the form of endless argument and debate as to whether or not racism was a feminist issue.

If the white women who organized the contemporary movement toward feminism were at all remotely aware of racial politics in American history, they would have known that overcoming barriers that separate women from one another would entail confronting the reality of racism, and not just racism as a general evil in society but the race hatred they might harbor in their own psyches. Despite the predominance of patriarchal rule in American society, America was colonized on a racially imperialistic base and not on a sexually imperialistic base. No degree of patriarchal bonding between white male colonizers and Native American men overshadowed white racial imperialism. Racism took precedence over sexual alliances in both the white world's interaction with Native Americans and African Americans, just as racism overshadowed any bonding between black women and white women on the basis of sex. Tunisian writer Albert Memmi emphasizes in *The Colonizer and the Colonized* the impact of racism as a tool of imperialism:

> Racism appears ... not as an incidental detail, but as a consubstantial part of colonialism. It is the highest expression of the colonial system and one of the most significant features of the colonialist. Not only does it establish a fundamental discrimination between colonizer and colonized, a sine qua non of colonial life, but it also lays the foundation for the immutability of this life.

While those feminists who argue that sexual imperialism is more endemic to all societies than racial imperialism are probably correct, American society is one in which racial imperialism supersedes sexual imperialism.

In America, the social status of black and white women has never been the same. In nineteenth- and early twentieth-century America, few if any similarities could be found between the life experiences of the two female groups. Although they were both subject to sexist victimization, as victims of racism black women were subjected to oppressions no white woman was forced to endure. In fact, white

313

racial imperialism granted all white women, however victimized by sexist oppression they might be, the right to assume the role of oppressor in relationship to black women and black men. From the onset of the contemporary move toward feminist revolution, white female organizers attempted to minimize their position in the racial caste hierarchy of American society. In their efforts to disassociate themselves from white men (to deny connections based on shared racial caste), white women involved in the move toward feminism have charged that racism is endemic to white male patriarchy and have argued that they cannot be held responsible for racist oppression. Commenting on the issue of white female accountability in her essay "'Disloyal to Civilization': Feminism, Racism, and Gynephobia," radical feminist Adrienne Rich contends:

> If Black and White feminists are going to speak of female accountability, I believe the word racism must be seized, grasped in our bare hands, ripped out of the sterile or defensive consciousness in which it so often grows, and transplanted so that it can yield new insights for our lives and our movement. An analysis that places the guilt for active domination, physical and institutional violence, and the justifications embedded in myth and language, on white women not only compounds false consciousness; it allows us all to deny or neglect the charged connection among black and white women from the historical conditions of slavery on, and it impedes any real discussion of women's instrumentality in a system which oppresses all women and in which hatred of women is also embedded in myth, folklore, and language.

No reader of Rich's essay could doubt that she is concerned that women who are committed to feminism work to overcome barriers that separate black and white women. However, she fails to understand that from a black female perspective, if white women are denying the existence of black women, writing "feminist" scholarship as if black women are not a part of the collective group American women, or discriminating against black women, then it matters less that North America was colonized by white patriarchal *men* who institutionalized a racially imperialistic social order than that white women who purport to be feminists support

and actively perpetuate anti-black racism.

To black women the issue is not whether white women are more or less racist than white men, but that they are racist. If women committed to feminist revolution, be they black or white, are to achieve any understanding of the "charged connections" between white women and black women, we must first be willing to examine woman's relationship to society, to race, and to American culture as it is and not as we would ideally have it be. That means confronting the reality of white female racism. Sexist discrimination has prevented white women from assuming the dominant role in the perpetuation of white racial imperialism, but it has not prevented white women from absorbing, supporting, and advocating racist ideology or acting individually as racist oppressors in various spheres of American life.

Every women's movement in America from its earliest origin to the present day has been built on a racist foundation – a fact which in no way invalidates feminism as a political ideology. The racial apartheid social structure that characterized nineteenth- and early twentieth-century American life was mirrored in the women's rights movement. The first white women's rights advocates were never seeking social equality for all women; they were seeking social equality for white women. Because many nineteenth-century white women's rights advocates were also active in the abolitionist movement, it is often assumed they were anti-racist. Historiographers and especially recent feminist writing have created a version of American history in which white women's rights advocates are presented as champions of oppressed black people. This fierce romanticism has informed most studies of the abolitionist movement. In contemporary times there is a general tendency to equate abolitionism with a repudiation of racism. In actuality, most white abolitionists, male and female, though vehement in their anti-slavery protest, were totally opposed to granting social equality to black people. Joel Kovel, in his study *White Racism: A Psychohistory*, emphasizes that the "actual aim of the reform movement, so nobly and bravely begun, was not the liberation of the black, but the fortification of the white, conscience and all."

It is a commonly accepted belief that white female reformist empathy with the oppressed black slave, coupled with her recognition that she was powerless to end slavery, led to the development of a feminist consciousness and feminist revolt. Contemporary historiographers and in particular white female scholars accept the theory that the white women's rights advocates' feelings of solidarity with black slaves were an indication that they were anti-racist and were supportive of social equality of blacks. It is this glorification of the role white women played that leads Adrienne Rich to assert:

> It is important for white feminists to remember that – despite lack of constitutional citizenship, educational deprivation, economic bondage to men, laws and customs forbidding women to speak in public or to disobey fathers, husbands, and brothers – our white foresisters have, in Lillian Smith's words, repeatedly been "disloyal to civilization" and have "smelled death in the word 'segregation',", often defying patriarchy for the first time, not on their own behalf but for the sake of black men, women, and children. We have a strong anti-racist female tradition despite all efforts by the white patriarchy to polarize its creature-objects, creating dichotomies of privilege and caste, skin color, and age and condition of servitude.

There is little historical evidence to document Rich's assertion that white women as a collective group or white women's rights advocates are part of an anti-racist tradition. When white women reformers in the 1830s chose to work to free the slave, they were motivated by religious sentiment. They attacked slavery, not racism. The basis of their attack was moral reform. That they were not demanding social equality for black people is an indication that they remained committed to white racist supremacy despite their anti-slavery work. While they strongly advocated an end to slavery, they never advocated a change in the racial hierarchy that allowed their caste status to be higher than that of black women or men. In fact, they wanted that hierarchy to be maintained. Consequently, the white women's rights movement which had a lukewarm beginning in earlier reform activities emerged in full force in the wake of efforts to gain rights for black people precisely because white women wanted to see no change in the social status of blacks until they were assured that their demands for more rights were met.

White women's rights advocate and abolitionist Abby Kelly's comment, "We have good cause to be grateful to the slave for the benefit we have received to ourselves, in working for him. In striving to strike his irons off, we found most surely, that we were manacled ourselves," is often quoted by scholars as evidence that white women became conscious of their own limited rights as they worked to end slavery. Despite popular nineteenth-century rhetoric, the notion that white women had to learn from their efforts to free the slave of their own limited rights is simply erroneous. No nineteenth-century white woman could grow to maturity without an awareness of institutionalized sexism. White women did learn via their efforts to free the slave that white men were willing to advocate rights for blacks while denouncing rights for women. As a result of negative reaction to their reform activity and public effort to curtail and prevent their anti-slavery work, they were forced to acknowledge that without outspoken demands for equal rights with white men they might ultimately be lumped in the same social category with blacks – or even worse, black men might gain a higher social status than theirs.

It did not enhance the cause of oppressed black slaves for white women to make synonymous their plight and the plight of the slave. Despite Abby Kelly's dramatic statement, there was very little if any similarity between the day-to-day life experiences of white women and the day-to-day experiences of the black slave. Theoretically, the white woman's legal status under patriarchy may have been that of "property," but she was in no way subjected to the de-humanization and brutal oppression that was the lot of the slave. When white reformers made synonymous the impact of sexism on their lives, they were not revealing an awareness of or sensitivity to the slave's lot; they were simply appropriating the horror of the slave experience to enhance their own cause.

The fact that the majority of white women reformers did not feel political solidarity with black people was made evident in the conflict over the vote. When it appeared that white men might grant black men the right to vote while leaving white women disenfranchised, white suffragists did not respond as a group by demanding that all women and men deserved the right to vote. They simply expressed anger and outrage that white men were more committed to maintaining sexual hierarchies than racial hierarchies in the political arena. Ardent white women's rights advocates like Elizabeth Cady Stanton who had never before argued for women's rights on a racially imperialistic platform expressed outrage that inferior "niggers" should be granted the vote while "superior" white women remained disenfranchised. Stanton argued:

If Saxon men have legislated thus for their own mothers, wives and daughters, what can we hope for at the hands of Chinese, Indians, and Africans? ... I protest against the enfranchisement of another man of any race or clime until the daughters of Jefferson, Hancock, and Adams are crowned with their rights.

White suffragists felt that white men were insulting white womanhood by refusing to grant them privileges that were to be granted black men. They admonished white men not for their sexism but for their willingness to allow sexism to overshadow racial alliances. Stanton, along with other white women's rights supporters, did not want to see blacks enslaved, but neither did she wish to see the status of black people improved while the status of white women remained the same.

At the beginning of the twentieth-century, white women suffragists were eager to advance their own cause at the expense of black people. In 1903 at the National American Woman's Suffrage Convention held in New Orleans, a southern suffragist urged the enfranchisement of white women on the grounds that it "would insure immediate and durable white supremacy." Historian Rosalyn Terborg-Penn discusses white female support of white supremacy in her essay "Discrimination Against Afro-American Women in the Woman's Movement 1830–1920":

As early as the 1890s, Susan B. Anthony realized the potential to the woman suffrage cause in wooing southern white women. She chose expedience over loyalty and justice when she asked veteran feminist supporter Frederick Douglass not to attend the National American Woman Suffrage Association convention scheduled in Atlanta. ...

During the National American Woman Suffrage Association meeting of 1903 in New Orleans, the *Times Democrat* assailed the association because of its negative attitude on the question of black women and the suffrage for them. In a prepared statement signed by Susan B. Anthony, Carrie C. Catt, Anna Howard Shaw, Kate N. Gordon, Alice Stone Blackwell, Harriet Taylor Upton, Laura Clay, and Mary Coggeshall, the board of officers of the NAWSA endorsed the organization's states' rights position, which was tantamount to an endorsement of white supremacy in most states, particularly in the south.

Racism within the women's rights movement did not emerge simply as a response to the issue of suffrage; it was a dominant force in all reform groups with white female members. Terborg-Penn contends:

Discrimination against Afro-American women reformers was the rule rather than the exception within the woman's rights movement from the 1830s to 1920. Although white feminists Susan B. Anthony, Lucy Stone, and some others encouraged black women to join the struggle against sexism during the nineteenth century, antebellum reformers who were involved with women's abolitionist groups as well as women's rights organizations actively discriminated against black women.

In their efforts to prove that solidarity existed between nineteenth-century black and white female reformers, contemporary women activists often cite the presence of Sojourner Truth at Women's Rights conventions to support their argument that white female suffragists were anti-racist. But on every occasion Sojourner Truth spoke, groups of white women protested. In *The Betrayal of the Negro*, Rayford Logan writes:

When the General Federation of Women's Clubs was faced with the question of the color line at the turn of the century, Southern clubs threatened to secede. One of the first expressions of the adamant opposition to the admission of colored clubs was disclosed by the Chicago *Tribune* and the *Examiner* during the great festival of fraternization at the Atlanta Exposition, the Encampment of the GAR in Louisville, and the dedication of the Chickamauga battlefield. ... The Georgia Women's Press Club felt so strongly on the subject that members were in favor of withdrawing from the Federation if colored women were admitted there. Miss Corinne Stocker, a member of the Managing Board of the Georgia Women's Press Club and one of the editors of the *Atlanta Journal*, stated on September 19: "In this matter the Southern women are not narrow-minded or bigoted, but they simply cannot recognize the colored women socially. ... At the same time we feel that the South is the colored woman's best friend."

Southern white women's club members were most vehement in their opposition to black women joining their ranks, but northern white women also supported racial segregation. The issue of whether black women would be able to participate in the women's club movement on an equal footing with white women came to a head in Milwaukee at the General Federation of Women's Clubs conference when the question was raised as to whether black feminist Mary Church Terrell, then president of the National Association of Colored Women, would be allowed to offer greetings, and whether Josephine Ruffin, who represented the black organization the New Era Club, would be recognized. In both cases white women's racism carried the day. In an interview in the Chicago *Tribune*, the president of the federation, Mrs Lowe, was asked to comment on the refusal to acknowledge black female participants like Josephine Ruffin, and she responded: "Mrs Ruffin belongs among her own people. Among them she would be a leader and could do much good, but among us she can create nothing but trouble." Rayford Logan comments on the fact that white women like Mrs Lowe had no objection to black women trying to improve their lot; they simply felt that racial apartheid should be maintained. Writing of Mrs Lowe's attitude toward black women, Logan comments:

> Mrs Lowe had assisted in establishing kindergartens for colored children in the South, and the colored women in charge of them were all her good friends. She associated with them in a business way, but, of course they would not think of sitting beside her at a convention. Negroes were "a race by themselves, and among themselves they can accomplish much, assisted by us and by the federation, which is ever ready to do all in its power to help them." If Mrs Ruffin were the "cultured lady every one says she is, she should put her education and her talents to good uses as a colored woman among colored women."

Anti-black feelings among white female club members were much stronger than anti-black sentiment among white male club members. One white male wrote a letter to the Chicago *Tribune* in which he stated:

> Here we have the spectacle of educated, refined, and Christian women who have

been protesting and laboring for years against the unjust discrimination practiced against them by men, now getting together and the first shot out of their reticules is fired at one of their own because she is black, no other reason or pretence of reason.

Prejudices white women activists felt toward black women were far more intense than their prejudices toward black men. As Rosalyn Penn states in her essay, black men were more accepted in white reform circles than black women. Negative attitudes toward black women were the result of prevailing racist-sexist stereotypes that portrayed black women as morally impure. Many white women felt that their status as ladies would be undermined were they to associate with black women. No such moral stigma was attached to black men. Black male leaders like Frederick Douglass, James Forten, Henry Garnett and others were occasionally welcome in white social circles. White women activists who would not have considered dining in the company of black women welcomed individual black men to their family tables.

Given white fear of amalgamation between the races and the history of white male sexual lust for black females, we cannot rule out the possibility that white women were reluctant to acknowledge black women socially for fear of sexual competition. In general, white women did not wish to associate with black women because they did not want to be contaminated by morally impure creatures. White women saw black women as a direct threat to their social standing – for how could they be idealized as virtuous, goddess-like creatures if they associated with black women who were seen by the white public as licentious and immoral? In her speech to the 1895 delegates from black women's clubs, Josephine Ruffin told her audience that the reason white women club members did not want to join with black women was because of the supposed "black female immorality," and she urged them to protest the perpetuation of negative stereotypes about black womanhood:

> All over America there is to be found a large and growing class of earnest, intelligent, progressive colored women who, if not leading full, useful lives, are only waiting for the opportunity to do so, many of them still warped and cramped for lack of opportunity, not only to do more but to be more; and yet, if an estimate of the colored women of

America is called for, the inevitable reply, glibly given, is: "For the most part, ignorant and immoral, some exceptions of course, but these don't count."

... Too long have we been silent under unjust and unholy charges. ... Year after year southern women have protested against the admission of colored women into any national organization on the ground of the immorality of these women, and because all refutation has only been tried by individual work, the charge had never been crushed, as it could and should have been at first. ... It is to break this silence, not by noisy protestation of what we are not, but by a dignified showing of what we are and hope to become, that we are impelled to take this step, to make of this gathering an object lesson to the world.

The racism white females felt toward black women was as apparent in the work arena as it was in the women's rights movement and in the women's club movement. During the years between 1880 and World War I, white women's rights activists focused their attention on obtaining for women the right to work in various occupations. They saw work for pay as the way for women like themselves to escape economic dependence on white men. Robert Smut, author of *Women and Work in America* (a work that would be more accurtely titled *White Women and Work in America*), writes:

If a woman could support herself in honor, she could refuse to marry or stay married, except on her own terms. Thus, work was seen by many feminists as an actual or potential alternative to marriage, and consequently, as an instrument for reforming the marriage relationship.

The efforts of white women activists to expand employment opportunities for women were focused exclusively on improving the lot of white women workers, who did not identify with black women workers. In fact, the black woman worker was seen as a threat to white female security; she represented more competition. Relationships between white and black women workers were characterized by conflict. That conflict became more intense when black women tried to enter the industrial labor force and were forced to confront racism. In 1919, a study of black women in industry in New York City was published called *A New Day for the Colored Woman Worker*. The study began by stating:

For generations Colored women have been working in the fields of the south. They have been the domestic servants of both the south and the north, accepting the position of personal service open to them. Hard work and unpleasant work has been their lot, but they have been almost entirely excluded from our shops and factories. Tradition and race prejudice have played the largest part in their exclusion. The tardy development of the south, and the failure of the Colored women to demand industrial opportunities have added further barriers. ... For these reasons, the Colored women have not entered the ranks of the industrial army in the past.

That they are doing so today cannot be disputed. War expediency, for a time at least, partially opened the door of industry to them. Factories which had lost men to the war and White women to the war industries, took on Colored women in their places. The demand for more skilled, semi-skilled and unskilled labor had to be met. The existing immigrant labor supply had already been tapped and the flow of immigration stopped, and semi-skilled White workers were being forced up into the really skilled positions by the labor shortage. Cheap labor had to be recruited from somewhere. For the first time employment bureaus and advertisements inserted the word "Colored" before the word "wanted." Colored women, untried as yet, were available in large numbers.

Black female workers who entered the industrial labor force worked in commercial laundries, food industries, and the less skilled branches of the needle trades, like the lamp shade industry which depended heavily on the labor of black women. Hostility between black and white female workers was the norm. White women did not want to compete with black women for jobs nor did they want to work alongside black women. To prevent white employers from hiring black females, white female workers threatened to cease work. Often white women workers would use complaints about black women workers as a way of discouraging an employer from hiring them.

White women employed by the federal government insisted that they be segregated from black women. In many work situations separate work rooms, washrooms, and showers were installed so that white women would not have to work or wash alongside black women. The same argument white women club members used to explain their exclusion of black women was presented by white women workers, who claimed black women were immoral, licentious, and insolent. They further argued that they needed the protection of segregation so that they would not catch "Negro" diseases. Some white women claimed to have seen black women with vaginal diseases. In one instance a white woman working in the office of the Recorder of Deeds, Maud B. Woodward, swore out an affidavit asserting:

> That the same toilet is used by whites and blacks, and some of said blacks have been diseased evidence thereof being very apparent; that one negro woman Alexander has been for years afflicted with a private disease, and for dread of using the toilet after her some of the white girls are compelled to suffer mentally and physically.

Competition between black and white women workers for jobs was usually decided in favor of white women. Often black women were forced to accept jobs that were considered too arduous or taxing for white women. In candy factories black women not only wrapped and packed candy, they worked as bakers and in this capacity were constantly lifting heavy trays from table to machine and from machine to table. They were doing "loosening" in tobacco factories, a process formerly done solely by men. Investigators for the New York City Study reported:

> Colored women were found on processes that White women refuse to perform. They were replacing boys at cleaning window shades, work which necessitates constant standing and reaching. They were taking men's places in the dyeing of furs, highly objectionable and injurious work involving standing, reaching, the use of a weighted brush, and ill smelling dye. In a mattress factory they were found replacing men at "baling," working in pairs, wrapping five mattresses together and sewing them up ready for shipment. These women had to

bend constantly and lift clumsy 160 pound bales.

In racially segregated work situations black women workers were usually paid a lower wage than white women workers. As there was little if any association between the two groups, black women did not always know of the disparity between their salaries and those of white women. Workers for the New York City study found that most employers refused to pay black women workers as much as white women for doing the same job.

> Throughout the trades, differences in the wages of the Colored and White were unmistakable. While every other Colored woman was receiving less than $10.00 a week, of the White workers only one out of every six was so poorly paid. . . . A great many employers justified the payment of better wages to White women on the grounds of their greater speed. Foremen in the millinery factories, however, admitted that they paid the Colored workers less, even though they were more satisfactory than the White. . . .
>
> This wage discrimination seems to have taken three forms. Employers have sometimes segregated the Colored workers, keeping the wage scale of the Colored departments lower than that of similar departments made up of White workers. . . . A second method has been to deny the Colored the opportunity of competing in piece work, as in the case of the Colored pressers in the needle trades who were paid $10.00 a week on a time rate basis, while the White pressers averaged $12.00 a week at piece work. The third form of discrimination has been the frank refusal of employers to pay a Colored woman as much as a White woman for a week's work.

As a group, white women workers wanted to maintain the racial hierarchy that granted them higher status in the labor force than black women. Those white women who supported employment of black women in unskilled trades felt they should be denied access to skilled process. Their active support of institutionalized racism caused constant hostility between them and black women workers. To avoid uprisings, many plants chose to hire either one race or the other. In plants where both groups were present, the conditions under which black women worked were much worse than those of white female workers. The refusal of white women to share dressing rooms, bathrooms, or lounge areas with black women often meant that black women were denied access to these comforts. In general black women workers were continually abused because of the racist attitudes of white women workers, and of the white working public as a whole. Researchers for the New York City study summed up their findings by making a plea that more consideration be given the black woman worker in industry:

> It has been apparent throughout this discussion that the coming of the Colored woman into our industries is not without its problems. She is doing work which the White woman is refusing to do, and at a wage which the White woman is refusing the accept. She replaced White women and men and Colored men at a lower wage and is performing tasks which may easily prove to be detrimental to her health. She is making no more mistakes than are common to a new and inexperienced industrial worker, yet she has the greatest of all handicaps to overcome.
>
> What is the status of the Colored woman in industry with the coming of peace? At the time of greatest need for production and the greatest labor shortage in the history of this country Colored women were the last to be employed: they were not called into industry until there was no other available labor supply. They did the most uninteresting work, the most menial work and by far the most underpaid work. . . .
>
> The American people will have to go very far in its treatment of the Colored industrial woman to square itself with that democratic ideal of which it made so much during the war.

Relationships between white and black women were charged by tensions and conflicts in the early part of the twentieth century. The women's rights movement had not drawn black and white women close together. Instead, it exposed the fact that white women were not willing to relinquish their support of white supremacy to support the interests of all women. Racism in the women's rights movement and in the work arena was a constant reminder to black women of the distances that separated the two experiences, distances that white women did not want bridged. When the contempo-

rary movement toward feminism began, white women organizers did not address the issue of conflict between black and white women. Their rhetoric of sisterhood and solidarity suggested that women in America were able to bond across both class and race boundaries – but no such coming together had actually occurred. The structure of the contemporary women's movement was no different from that of the earlier women's rights movement. Like their predecessors, the white women who initiated the women's movement launched their efforts in the wake of the 1960s black liberation movement. As if history were repeating itself, they also began to make synonymous their social status and the social status of black people. And it was in the context of endless comparisons of the plight of "women" and "blacks" that they revealed their racism. In most cases, this racism was an unconscious, unacknowledged aspect of their thought, suppressed by their narcissism – a narcissism which so blinded them that they would not admit two obvious facts: one, that in a capitalist, racist, imperialist state there is no one social status women share as a collective group; and second, that the social status of white women in America has never been like that of black women or men.

When the women's movement began in the late 1960s, it was evident that the white women who dominated the movement felt it was "their" movement, that is the medium through which a white woman would voice her grievances to society. Not only did white women act as if feminist ideology existed solely to serve their own interests because they were able to draw public attention to feminist concerns. They were unwilling to acknowledge that non-white women were part of the collective group women in American society. They urged black women to join "their" movement or in some cases the women's movement, but in dialogues and writings, their attitudes toward black women were both racist and sexist. Their racism did not assume the form of overt expressions of hatred; it was far more subtle. It took the form of simply ignoring the existence of black women or writing about them using common sexist and racist stereotypes. From Betty Friedan's *The Feminine Mystique* to Barbara Berg's *The Remembered Gate* and on to more recent publications like *Capitalist Patriarchy and the Case for Socialist Feminism*, edited by Zillah Eisenstein, most white female writers who considered themselves feminist revealed in their writing that they had been socialized to accept and perpetuate racist ideology.

In most of their writing, the white American woman's experience is made synonymous with *the* American woman's experience. While it is in no way racist for any author to write a book exclusively about white women, it is fundamentally racist for books to be published that focus solely on the American white woman's experience in which that experience is assumed to be *the* American woman's experience. For example, in the course of research for this book, I sought to find information about the life of free and slave black women in colonial America. I saw listed in a bibliography Julia Cherry Spruill's work *Women's Life and Work in the Southern Colonies*, which was first published in 1938 and then again in 1972. At the Sisterhood bookstore in Los Angeles I found the book and read a blurb on the back which had been written especially for the new edition:

> One of the classic works in American social history, *Women's Life and Work in the Southern Colonies* is the first comprehensive study of the daily life and status of women in southern colonial America. Julia Cherry Spruill researched colonial newspapers, court records, and manuscript material of every kind, drawing on archives and libraries from Boston to Savannah. The resulting book was, in the words of Arthur Schlesinger, Sr., "a model of research and exposition, an important contribution to American social history to which students will constantly turn."
>
> The topics include women's function in the settlement of the colonies; their homes, domestic occupation, and social life; the aims and methods of their education; their role in government and business affairs outside the home; and the manner in which they were regarded by the law and by society in general. Out of a wealth of documentation, and often from the words of colonial people themselves, a vivid and surprising picture – one that had never been seen before – emerges of the many different aspects of these women's lives.

I expected to find in Spruill's work information about various groups of women in American society. I found instead that it was another work solely about white women and that both the title and blurb were misleading. A more accurate title would have been *White Women's Life and Work in*

the Southern Colonies. Certainly, if I or any author sent a manuscript to an American publisher that focused exclusively on the life and work of black women in the south, also called *Women's Life and Work in the Southern Colonies*, the title would be automatically deemed misleading and unacceptable. The force that allows white feminist authors to make no reference to racial identity in their books about "women" that are in actuality about white women is the same one that would compel any author writing exclusively on black women to refer explicitly to their racial identity. That force is racism. In a racially imperialist nation such as ours, it is the dominant race that reserves for itself the luxury of dismissing racial identity while the oppressed race is made daily aware of their racial identity. It is the dominant race that can make it seem that their experience is representative.

In America, white racist ideology has always allowed white women to assume that the word woman is synonymous with white woman, for women of other races are always perceived as Others, as de-humanized beings who do not fall under the heading woman. White feminists who claimed to be politically astute showed themselves to be unconscious of the way their use of language suggested they did not recognize the existence of black women. They impressed upon the American public their sense that the word "woman" meant white woman by drawing endless analogies between "women" and "blacks." Examples of such analogies abound in almost every feminist work. In a collection of essays published in 1975 titled *Women: A Feminist Perspective*, an essay by Helen Hacker is included called "Women as a Minority Group" which is a good example of the way white women have used comparisons between "women" and "blacks" to exclude black women and to deflect attention away from their own racial caste status. Hacker writes:

> The relation between women and Negroes is historical, as well as analogical. In the seventeenth century the legal status of Negro servants was borrowed from that of women and children, who were under the patria potestas, and until the Civil War there was considerable cooperation between the Abolitionists and woman suffrage movement.

Clearly Hacker is referring solely to white women. An even more glaring example of the white feminist comparison between "blacks" and "women" occurs in Catherine Stimpson's essay "'Thy Neighbor's Wife, Thy Neighbor's Servants': Women's Liberation and Black Civil Rights." She writes:

> The development of an industrial economy, as Myrdal points out, has not brought about the integration of women and blacks into the adult male culture. Women have not found a satisfactory way to bear children and to work. Blacks have not destroyed the hard doctrine of their unassimilability. What the economy gives both women and blacks are menial labor, low pay, and few promotions. White male workers hate both groups, for their competition threatens wages and their possible job equality, let alone superiority, threatens nothing less than the very nature of things. The tasks of women and blacks are usually grueling, repetitive, slogging, and dirty. . . .

Throughout Stimpson's essay she makes woman synonymous with white women and black synonymous with black men.

Historically, white patriarchs rarely referred to the racial identity of white women because they believed that the subject of race was political and therefore would contaminate the sanctified domain of "white" woman's reality. By verbally denying white women racial identity, that is by simply referring to them as women when what they really meant was white women, their status was further reduced to that of non-person. In much of the literature written by white women on the "woman question" from the nineteenth century to the present day, authors will refer to "white men" but use the word "woman" when they really mean "white woman." Concurrently, the term "blacks" is often made synonymous with black men. In Hacker's article she draws a chart comparing the "castelike status of Women and Negroes." Under the heading "Rationalization of Status" she writes for blacks "Thought all right in his place."(?) Hacker's and Stimpson's assumption that they can use the word "woman" to refer to white women and "black" to refer to black men is not unique; most white people and even some black people make the same assumption. Racist and sexist patterns in the language Americans use to describe reality support the exclusion of black women. During the recent political uprisings in Iran, newspapers throughout the US carried headlines that read "Khomeini Frees Women and Blacks." In fact, the American

hostages freed from the Iranian Embassy were white women and black men.

White feminists did not challenge the racist-sexist tendency to use the word "woman" to refer solely to white women; they supported it. For them it served two purposes. First, it allowed them to proclaim white men world oppressors while making it appear linguistically that no alliance existed between white women and white men based on shared racial imperialism. Second, it made it possible for white women to act as if alliances did exist between themselves and non-white women in our society, and by so doing they could deflect attention away from their classism and racism. Had feminists chosen to make explicit comparisons between the status of white women and that of black people, or more specifically the status of black women and white women, it would have been more than obvious that the two groups do not share an identical oppression. It would have been obvious that similarities between the status of women under patriarchy and that of any slave or colonized person do not necessarily exist in a society that is both racially and sexually imperialistic. In such a society, the woman who is seen as inferior because of her sex can also be seen as superior because of her race, even in relationship to men of another race. Because feminists tended to evoke an image of women as a collective group, their comparisons between "women" and "blacks" were accepted without question. This constant comparison of the plight of "women" and "blacks" deflected attention away from the fact that black women were extremely victimized by both racism and sexism – a fact which, had it been emphasized, might have diverted public attention away from the complaints of middle and upper class white feminists.

Just as nineteenth-century white woman's rights advocates attempted to make synonymous their lot with that of the black slave was aimed at drawing attention away from the slave toward themselves, contemporary white feminists have used the same metaphor to attract attention to their concerns. Given that America is a hierarchical society in which white men are at the top and white women are second, it was to be expected that should white women complain about not having rights in the wake of a movement by black people to gain rights, their interests would overshadow those of groups lower on the hierarchy, in this case the interests of black people. No other group in America has used black people as metaphors as extensively as white women involved in the women's movement. Speaking about the purpose of a metaphor, Ortega Y Gasset comments:

> A strange thing, indeed, the existence in many of this mental activity which substitutes one thing for another – from an urge not so much to get at the first as to get rid of the second. The metaphor disposes of an object by having it masquerade as something else. Such a procedure would make no sense if we did not discern beneath it an instinctive avoidance of certain realities.

When white women talked about "Women as Niggers," "The Third World of Women," "Woman as Slave," they evoked the sufferings and oppressions of non-white people to say "look at how bad our lot as white women is, why we are like niggers, like the Third World." Of course, if the situation of upper and middle class white women were in any way like that of the oppressed people in the world, such metaphors would not have been necessary. And if they had been poor and oppressed, or women concerned about the lot of oppressed women, they would not have been compelled to appropriate the black experience. It would have been sufficient to describe the oppression of woman's experience. A white woman who has suffered physical abuse and assault from a husband or lover, who also suffers poverty, need not compare her lot to that of a suffering black person to emphasize that she is in pain.

If white women in the women's movement needed to make use of a black experience to emphasize woman's oppression, it would seem only logical that they focus on the black female experience – but they did not. They chose to deny the existence of black women and to exclude them from the women's movement. When I use the word "exclude" I do not mean that they overtly discriminated against black women on the basis of race. There are other ways to exclude and alienate people. Many black women felt excluded from the movement whenever they heard white women draw analogies between "women" and "blacks." For by making such analogies white women were in effect saying to black women: "We don't acknowledge your presence as women in American society." Had white women desired to bond with black women on the basis of common oppression they could have done so by demonstrating any awareness or knowledge of the impact of sexism on the status of black women. Unfortunately, despite all the rhetoric about sisterhood and bonding, white women were not sincerely committed to bonding with black women and other groups of women to fight sexism. They were primarily interested in drawing attention to their lot as white upper and middle class women.

It was not in the opportunistic interests of white middle and upper class participants in the women's movement to draw attention to the plight of poor women, or the specific plight of black women. A white woman professor who wants the public to see her as victimized and oppressed because she is denied tenure is not about to evoke images of poor women working as domestics receiving less than the minimum wage struggling to raise a family single-handed. Instead it is far more likely she will receive attention and sympathy if she says, "I'm a nigger in the eyes of my white male colleagues." She evokes the image of innocent, virtuous white womanhood being placed on the same level as blacks and most importantly on the same level as black men. It is not simply a coincidental detail that white women in the women's movement chose to make their race-sex analogies by comparing their lot as white women to that of black men. In Catherine Stimpson's essay on women's liberation and black civil rights, in which she argues that "black liberation and women's liberation must go their separate ways," black civil rights is associated with black men and women's liberation with white women. When she writes of the nineteenth-century women's rights movement, she quotes from the work of black male leaders even though black women were far more active in that movement than any black male leader.

Given the psychohistory of American racism, for white women to demand more rights from white men and stress that without such rights they would be placed in a social position like that of black men, not like that of black people, was to evoke in the minds of racist white men an image of white womanhood being degraded. It was a subtle appeal to white men to protect the white female's position on the race/sex hierarchy. Stimpson writes:

> White men, convinced of the holy primacy of sperm, yet guilty about using it, angry at the loss of the cosy sanctuary of the womb and the privilege of childhood, have made their sex a claim to power and then used their power to claim control of sex. In fact and fantasy, they have violently segregated black men and white women. The most notorious fantasy claims that the black man is sexually

evil, low, subhuman; the white woman sexually pure elevated, superhuman. Together they dramatize the polarities of excrement and disembodied spirituality. Blacks and women have been sexual victims, often cruelly so: the black man castrated, the woman raped and often treated to a psychic clitoridectomy.

For Stimpson, black is black male and woman is white female, and though she is depicting the white male as racist, she conjures an image of white women and black men sharing oppression only to argue that they must go their separate ways, and in so doing she makes use of the sex/race analogy in such a way as to curry favor from racist white men. Ironically, she admonishes white women not to make analogies between blacks and themselves but she continues to do just that in her essay. By suggesting that without rights they are placed in the same category as black men, white women appeal to the anti-black-male racism of white patriarchal men. Their argument for "women's liberation" (which for them is synonymous with white women's liberation) thus becomes an appeal to white men to maintain the racial hierarchy that grants white women a higher social status than black men.

Whenever black women tried to express to white women their ideas about white female racism or their sense that the women who were at the forefront of the movement were not oppressed women they were told that "oppression cannot be measured." White female emphasis on "common oppression" in their appeals to black women to join the movement further alienated many black women. Because so many of the white women in the movement were employers of non-white and white domestics, their rhetoric of common oppression was experienced by black women as an assault, an expression of the bourgeois woman's insensitivity and lack of concern for the lower class woman's position in society.

Underlying the assertion of common oppression was a patronizing attitude toward black women. White women were assuming that all they had to do was express a desire for sisterhood, or a desire to have black women join their groups, and black women would be overjoyed. They saw themselves as acting in a generous, open, non-racist manner and were shocked that black women responded to their overtures with anger and outrage. They could not see that their generosity was directed at themselves, that it was self-centered and motivated by their own opportunistic desires.

Despite the reality that white upper and middle class women in America suffer from sexist discrimination and sexist abuse, they are not as a group as oppressed as *poor* white, or black, or yellow women. Their unwillingness to distinguish between various degrees of discrimination or oppression caused black women to see them as enemies. As many upper and middle class white feminists who suffer least from sexist oppression were attempting to focus all attention on themselves, it follows that they would not accept an analysis of woman's lot in America which argued that not all women are equally oppressed because some women are able to use their class, race, and educational privilege to effectively resist sexist oppression.

Initially, class privilege was not discussed by white women in the women's movement. They wanted to project an image of themselves as victims and that could not be done by drawing attention to their class. In fact, the contemporary women's movement was extremely class bound. As a group, white participants did not denounce capitalism. They chose to define liberation using the terms of white capitalist patriarchy, equating liberation with gaining economic status and money power. Like all good capitalists, they proclaimed work as the key to liberation. This emphasis on work was yet another indication of the extent to which the white female liberationists' perception of reality was totally narcissistic, classist, and racist. Implicit in the assertion that work was the key to women's liberation was a refusal to acknowledge the reality that, for masses of American working class women, working for pay neither liberated them from sexist oppression nor allowed them to gain any measure of economic independence. In *Liberating Feminism*, Benjamin Barber's critique of the women's movement, he comments on the white middle and upper class women's liberationist focus on work:

Work clearly means something very different to women in search of an escape from leisure than it has to most of the human race for most of history. For a few lucky men, for far fewer women, work has occasionally been a source of meaning and creativity. But for most of the rest it remains even now forced drudgery in front of the ploughs, machines, words or numbers – pushing products, pushing switches, pushing papers to eke out the wherewithal of material existence.
... To be able to work and to have work are

two different matters. I suspect, however, that few liberationist women are to be found working as menials and unskilled laborers simply in order to occupy their time and identify with the power structure. For status and power are not conferred by work per se, but by certain kinds of work generally reserved to the middle and upper classes. . . . As Studs Terkel shows in *Working*, most workers find jobs dull, oppressive, frustrating and alienating – very much what women find housewifery.

When white women's liberationists emphasized work as a path to liberation, they did not concentrate their attention on those women who are most exploited in the American labor force. Had they emphasized the plight of working class women, attention would have shifted away from the college-educated suburban housewife who wanted entrance into the middle and upper class work force. Had attention been focused on women who were already working and who were exploited as cheap surplus labor in American society, it would have de-romanticized the middle class white woman's quest for "meaningful" employment. While it does not in any way diminish the importance of women resisting sexist oppression by entering the labor force, work has not been a liberating force for masses of American women. And for some time now, sexism has not prevented them from being in the work force. White middle and upper class women like those described in Betty Friedan's *The Feminine Mystique* were housewives not because sexism would have prevented them from being in the paid labor force, but because they had willingly embraced the notion that it was better to be a housewife than to be a worker. The racism and classism of white women's liberationists was most apparent whenever they discussed work as the liberating force for women. In such discussions it was always the middle class "housewife" who was depicted as the victim of sexist oppression and not the poor black and non-black women who are most exploited by American economics.

Throughout woman's history as a paid laborer, white women workers have been able to enter the work force much later than black women yet advance at a much more rapid pace. Even though all women were denied access to many jobs because of sexist discrimination, racism ensured that the lot of the white women would always be better than that of the black female worker. Pauli Murray compared the status of the two groups in her essay "The Liberation of Black Women" and noted:

> When we compare the position of the black woman to that of the white woman, we find that she remains single more often, bears more children, is in the labor market longer and in greater proportion, has less education, earns less, is widowed earlier, and carries a relatively heavier economic responsibility as family head than her white counterpart.

Often in discussions of woman's status in the labor force, white women liberationists choose to ignore or minimize the disparity between the economic status of black women and that of white women. White activist Jo Freeman addresses the issue in *The Politics of Women's Liberation* when she comments that black women have the "highest unemployment rates and lowest median income of any race/sex group." But she then minimizes the impact of this assertion in a sentence that follows: "Of all race/sex groups of full-time workers, non-white women have had the greatest percentage increase in their median income since 1939, and white women have had the lowest." Freeman does not inform readers that the wages black women received were not a reflection of an advancing economic status so much as they were an indication that the wages paid them, for so long considerably lower than those paid white women, were approaching the set norm.

Few, if any, white women liberationists are willing to acknowledge that the women's movement was consciously and deliberately structured to exclude black and other non-white women and to serve primarily the interests of middle and upper class college-educated white women seeking social equality with middle and upper class white men. While they may agree that white women involved with women's liberationist groups are racist and classist they tend to feel that this in no way undermines the movement. But it is precisely the racism and classism of exponents of feminist ideology that has caused a large majority of black women to suspect their motives, and to reject active participation in any effort to organize a women's movement. Black woman activist Dorothy Bolden, who worked 42 years as a maid in Atlanta, one of the founders of the National Domestic Workers, Inc., voiced her opinions of the movement in *Nobody Speaks for Me! Self Portraits of Working Class Women*:

I was very proud to see them stand up and speak up when it started. I'm glad to see any group do that when they're righteous and I know they have been denied something. But they're not talking about the masses of people. You've got different classes of people in all phases of life and all races, and those people have to be spoken up for too.

... You can't talk about women's rights until we include all women. When you deny one woman of her rights, you deny all. I'm getting tired of going to those meetings, because there's none of us participating.

They're still trying to put their amendment to the constitution, but they're not going to be able to do it until they include us. Some of these states know this, that you don't have all women up front supporting that amendment. They are talking about women's rights but which women?

It is often assumed that all black women are simply not interested in women's liberation. White women's liberationists have helped to perpetuate the belief that black women would rather remain in stereotypically female roles than have social equality with men. Yet a Louis Harris Virginia Slims poll conducted in 1972 revealed that 62 percent of black women supported efforts to change woman's status in society as compared to 45 per cent of white women, and that 67 per cent of black women were sympathetic to women's liberation groups compared with only 35 per cent of white women. The findings of the Harris poll suggest it is not opposition to feminist ideology that has caused black women to reject involvement in the women's movement.

Feminism as a political ideology advocating social equality for all women was and is acceptable to many black women. They rejected the women's movement when it became apparent that middle and upper class college-educated white women who were its majority participants were determined to shape the movement so that it would serve their own opportunistic ends. While the established definition of feminism is the theory of the political, economic, and social equality of the sexes, white women liberationists used the power granted them by virtue of their being members of the dominant race in American society to interpret feminism in such a way that it was no longer relevant to all women. And it seemed incredible to black women that they were being asked to support a movement whose majority participants were eager to maintain race and class hierarchies between women.

Black women who participated in women's groups, lectures, and meetings initially trusted the sincerity of white female participants. Like nineteenth-century black women's rights advocates, they assumed that any women's movement would address issues relevant to all women and that racism would be automatically cited as a force that had divided women, that would have to be reckoned with for true Sisterhood to emerge, and also that no radical revolutionary women's movement could take place until women as a group were joined in political solidarity. Although contemporary black women were mindful of the prevalence of white female racism, they believed it could be confronted and changed.

As they participated in the women's movement they found, in their dialogues with white women in women's groups, in women's studies classes, at conferences, that their trust was betrayed. They found that white women had appropriated feminism to advance their own cause, i.e., their desire to enter the mainstream of American capitalism. They were told that white women were in the majority and that they had the power to decide which issues would be considered "feminist" issues. White women liberationists decided that the way to confront racism was to speak out in consciousness-raising groups about their racist upbringings, to encourage black women to join their cause, to make sure they hired one non-white woman in "their" women's studies program, or to invite one non-white woman to speak on a discussion panel at "their" conference.

When black women involved with women's liberation attempted to discuss racism, many white women responded by angrily stating: "We won't be guilt-tripped." For them the dialogue ceased. Others seemed to relish admitting that they were racist but felt that admitting verbally to being racist was tantamount to changing their racist values. For the most part, white women refused to listen when black women explained that what they expected was not verbal admissions of guilt but conscious gestures and acts that would show that white women liberationists were anti-racist and attempting to overcome their racism. The issue of racism within the women's movement would never have been raised had white women shown in their writings and speeches that they were in fact "liberated" from racism.

As concerned black and white individuals tried

to stress the importance to the women's movement of confronting and changing racist attitudes because such sentiments threatened to undermine the movement, they met with resistance from those white women who saw feminism solely as a vehicle to enhance their own individual, opportunistic ends. Conservative, reactionary white women, who increasingly represented a large majority of the participants, were outspoken in their pronouncements that the issue of racism should not be considered worthy of attention. They did not want the issue of racism raised because they did not want to deflect attention away from their projection of the white woman as "good," i.e., non-racist victim, and the white man as "bad," i.e., racist oppressor. For them to have acknowledged woman's active complicity in the perpetuation of imperialism, colonialism, racism, or sexism would have made the issue of women's liberation far more complex. To those who saw feminism solely as a way to demand entrance into the white male power structure, it simplified matters to make all men oppressors and all women victims.

Some black women who were interested in women's liberation responded to the racism of white female participants by forming separate "black feminist" groups. This response was reactionary. By creating segregated feminist groups, they both endorsed and perpetuated the very "racism" they were supposedly attacking. They did not provide a critical evaluation of the women's movement and offer to all women a feminist ideology uncorrupted by racism or the opportunistic desires of individual groups. Instead, as colonized people have done for centuries, they accepted the terms imposed upon them by the dominant groups (in this instance white women liberationists) and structured their groups on a racist platform identical to that of the white-dominated groups they were reacting against. White women were actively excluded from black groups. In fact, the distinguishing characteristic of the black "feminist" group was its focus on issues relating specifically to black women. The emphasis on black women was made public in the writings of black participants. The Combahee River Collective published "A Black Feminist Statement" to explain their group's focus. In their opening paragraph they declared:

We are a collective of black feminists who have been meeting together since 1974. During that time we have been involved in the process of defining and clarifying our politics, while at the same time doing political work within our own group and in coalition with other progressive organizations and movements. The most general statement of our politics at the present time would be that we are actively committed to struggling against racial, sexual, heterosexual, and class oppression and see as our particular task the development of integrated analysis and practice based upon the fact that the major systems of oppression are interlocking. The synthesis of these oppressions creates the conditions of our lives. As black women we see black feminism as the logical political movement to combat the manifold and simultaneous oppression that all women of color face.

The emergence of black feminist groups led to a greater polarization of black and white women's liberationists. Instead of bonding on the basis of shared understanding of woman's varied collective and individual plight in society, they acted as if the distance separating their experiences from one another could not be bridged by knowledge or understanding. Rather than black women attacking the white female attempt to present them as an Other, an unknown, unfathomable element, they acted as if they were an Other. Many black women found an affirmation and support of their concern with feminism in all-black groups that they had not experienced in women's groups dominated by white women; this has been one of the positive features of black women's groups. However, all women should experience in racially mixed groups affirmation and support. Racism is the barrier that prevents positive communication and it is not eliminated or challenged by separation. White women supported the formation of separate groups because it confirmed their preconceived racist-sexist notion that no connection existed between their experiences and those of black women. Separate groups meant they would not be asked to concern themselves with race or racism. While black women condemned the anti-black racism of white women, the mounting animosity between the two groups gave rise to overt expression of their anti-white racism. Many black women who had never participated in the women's movement saw the formation of separate black groups as confirmation of their belief that no alliance could ever take place between black and white women. To express their anger and rage at white women, they evoked the negative stereotypical image of the white woman as a passive, parasitic, privileged being living off the labor of others as a way to mock and ridicule the white women liberationists. Black woman Lorraine Bethel published a poem entitled "What Chou Mean We, White Girl? Or. The Cullud Lesbian Feminist Declaration of Independence" prefaced with the statement:

I bought a sweater at a yard sale from a white-skinned (as opposed to Anglo-Saxon) woman. When wearing it I am struck by the smell – it reeks of a soft, privileged life without stress, sweat, or struggle. When wearing it I often think to myself, this sweater smells of a comfort, a way of being in the world I have never known in my life, and never will. It's the same feeling I experience walking through Bonwit Teller's and seeing white-skinned women buying trinkets that cost enough to support the elderly Black Woman elevator operator, who stands on her feet all day taking them up and down, for the rest of her life. It is moments/infinities of conscious pain like these that make me want to cry/kill/roll my eyes suck my teeth hand on my hip scream at so-called radical white lesbians/feminist(s) "WHAT CHOU MEAN WE, WHITE GIRL?"

Animosity between black and white women's liberationists was not due solely to disagreement over racism within the women's movement; it was the end result of years of jealousy, envy, competition, and anger between the two groups. Conflict between black and white women did not begin with the twentieth-century women's movement. It began during slavery. The social status of white women in America has to a large extent been determined by white people's relationship to black people. It was the enslavement of African people in colonized America that marked the beginning of a change in the social status of white women. Prior to slavery, patriarchal law decreed white women were lowly inferior beings, the subordinate group in society. The subjugation of black people allowed them to vacate their despised position and assume the role of a superior.

Consequently, it can be easily argued that even though white men institutionalized slavery, white women were its most immediate beneficiaries. Slavery in no way altered the hierarchical social status of the white male but it created a new status

for the white female. The only way that her new status could be maintained was through the constant assertion of her superiority over the black woman and man. All too often colonial white women, particularly those who were slave mistresses, chose to differentiate their status from the slave's by treating the slave in a brutal and cruel manner. It was in her relationship to the black female slave that the white woman could best assert her power. Individual black slave women were quick to learn that sex-role differentiation did not mean that the white mistress was not to be regarded as an authority figure. Because they had been socialized via patriarchy to respect male authority and resent female authority, black women were reluctant to acknowledge the "power" of the white mistress. When the enslaved black woman expressed contempt and disregard for white female authority, the white mistress often resorted to brutal punishment to assert her authority. But even brutal punishment could not change the fact that black women were not inclined to regard the white female with the awe and respect they showed to the white male.

By flaunting their sexual lust for the bodies of black women and their preference for them as sexual partners, white men successfully pitted white women and enslaved black women against one another. In most instances, the white mistress did not envy the black female slave her role as sexual object; she feared only that her newly acquired social status might be threatened by white male sexual interaction with black women. His sexual involvement with black women (even if that involvement was rape) in effect reminded the white female of her subordinate position in relationship to him. For he could exercise his power as racial imperialist and sexual imperialist to rape or seduce black women, while white women were not free to rape or seduce black men without fear of punishment. Though the white female might condemn the actions of a white male who chose to interact sexually with black female slaves, she was unable to dictate to him proper behavior. Nor could she retaliate by engaging in sexual relationships with enslaved or free black men. Not surprisingly, she directed her anger and rage at the enslaved black women. In those cases where emotional ties developed between white men and black female slaves, white mistresses would go to great lengths to punish the female. Severe beatings were the method most white women used to punish black female slaves. Often in a jealous rage a mistress might use disfigurement to punish a lusted-after black female slave. The mistress might cut off her breast, blind an eye, or cut off another body part. Such treatment naturally caused hostility between white women and enslaved black women. To the enslaved black woman, the white mistress living in relative comfort was the representative symbol of white womanhood. She was both envied and despised – envied for her material comfort, despised because she felt little concern or compassion for the slave woman's lot. Since the white woman's privileged social status could only exist if a group of women were present to assume the lowly position she had abdicated, it follows that black and white women would be at odds with one another. If the white woman struggled to change the lot of the black slave woman, her own social position on the race-sex hierarchy would be altered.

Manumission did not bring an end to conflicts between black and white women; it heightened them. To maintain the apartheid structure slavery had institutionalized, white colonizers, male and female, created a variety of myths and stereotypes to differentiate the status of black women from that of white women. White racists and even some black people who had absorbed the colonizer's mentality depicted the white woman as a symbol of perfect womanhood and encouraged black women to strive to attain such perfection by using the white female as her model. The jealousy and envy of white women that had erupted in the black woman's consciousness during slavery was deliberately encouraged by the dominant white culture. Advertisements, newspaper articles, books, etc., were constant reminders to black women of the difference between their social status and that of white women, and they bitterly resented it. Nowhere was this dichotomy as clearly demonstrated as in the materially privileged white household where the black female domestic worked as an employee of the white family. In these relationships, black women workers were exploited to enhance the social standing of white families. In the white community, employing domestic help was a sign of material privilege and the person who directly benefited from a servant's work was the white woman, since without the servant she would have performed domestic chores. Not surprisingly, the black female domestic tended to see the white female as her "boss," her oppressor, not the white male whose earnings usually paid her wage.

Throughout American history white men have deliberately promoted hostility and divisiveness between white and black women. The white patriarchal power structure pits the two groups against each other, preventing the growth of solidarity between women and ensuring that woman's status as a subordinate group under patriarchy remains intact. To this end, white men have supported changes in the white woman's social standing only if there exists another female group to assume that role. Consequently, the white patriarch undergoes no radical change in his sexist assumption that woman is inherently inferior. He neither relinquishes his dominant position nor alters the patriarchal structure of society. He is, however, able to convince many white women that fundamental changes in "woman's status" have occurred because he has successfully socialized her, via racism, to assume that no connection exists between her and black women.

Because women's liberation has been equated with gaining privileges within the white male power structure, white men – and not women, either white or black – have dictated the terms by which women are allowed entrance into the system. One of the terms male patriarchs have set is that one group of women is granted privileges that they obtain by actively supporting the oppression and exploitation of other groups of women. White and black women have been socialized to accept and honor these terms, hence the fierce competition between the two groups; a competition that has always been centered in the arena of sexual politics, with white and black women competing against one another for male favor. This competition is part of an overall battle between various groups of women to be the chosen female group.

The contemporary move toward feminist revolution was continually undermined by competition between various factions. In regards to race, the women's movement has become simply another arena in which white and black women compete to be the chosen female group. This power struggle has not been resolved by the formation of opposing interest groups. Such groups are symptomatic of the problem and are no solution. Black and white women have for so long allowed their idea of liberation to be formed by the existing status quo that they have not yet devised a strategy by which we can come together. They have had only a slave's idea of freedom. And to the slave, the master's way of life represents the ideal free lifestyle.

Women's liberationists, white and black, will always be at odds with one another as long as our idea of liberation is based on having the power white men have. For that power denies unity, denies common connections, and is inherently divisive. It is woman's acceptance of divisiveness as a natural order that has caused black and white women to cling religiously to the belief that bonding across racial boundaries is impossible, to passively accept the notion that the distances that separate women are immutable. Even though the most uninformed and naive women's liberationist knows that Sisterhood as political bonding between women is necessary for feminist revolution, women have not struggled long or hard enough to overcome the societal brainwashing that has impressed on our psyches the belief that no union between black and white women can ever be forged. The methods women have employed to reach one another across racial boundaries have been shallow, superficial, and destined to fail.

Resolution of the conflict between black and white women cannot begin until all women acknowledge that a feminist movement which is both racist and classist is a mere sham, a cover-up for women's continued bondage to materialist patriarchal principles, and passive acceptance of the status quo. The sisterhood that is necessary for the making of feminist revolution can be achieved only when all women disengage themselves from the hostility, jealousy, and competition with one another that has kept us vulnerable, weak, and unable to envision new realities. That sisterhood cannot be forged by the mere saying of words. It is the outcome of continued growth and change. It is a goal to be reached, a process of becoming. The process begins with action, with the individual woman's refusal to accept any set of myths, stereotypes, and false assumptions that deny the shared commonness of her human experience; that deny her capacity to experience the Unity of all life; that deny her capacity to bridge gaps created by racism, sexism, or classism; that deny her ability to change. The process begins with the individual woman's acceptance that American women, without exception, are socialized to be racist, classist, and sexist, in varying degrees, and that labeling ourselves feminists does not change the fact that we must consciously work to rid ourselves of the legacy of negative socialization.

If women want a feminist revolution – ours is a world that is crying out for feminist revolution – then we must assume responsibility for drawing women together in political solidarity. That means we must assume responsibility for eliminating all the forces that divide women. Racism is one such force. Women, all women, are accountable for racism continuing to divide us. Our willingness to assume responsibility for the elimination of racism need not be engendered by feelings of guilt, moral responsibility, victimization, or rage. It can spring from a heartfelt desire for sisterhood and the personal, intellectual realization that racism among women undermines the potential radicalism of feminism. It can spring from our knowledge that racism is an obstacle in our path that must be removed. More obstacles are created if we simply engage in endless debate as to who put it there.

PART VIII

Philosophy and Gender

37

The Woman Question: African and Western Perspectives

Marie Pauline Eboh

Introduction

The problem with a comparative study of this
nature is that the modern African woman, who
should have been compared with her Western
counterpart, is not seen as an authentic African. She
is regarded as "a philistine woman" or as "a
Westernized woman tinctured with traditionalism." The inability to reach the real traditional
Western woman with whom to compare the traditional African woman makes this study end up
comparing the traditional African woman with the
modern Western woman. However, this is not
totally out of order given that the feminine problem
is the same in all cultures, the difference is a
question of degree or a matter of nuances. As
patriarchal structure did repress or still represses
female potential and wholeness in Europe and
America, so it does in Africa. Women in these
continents have sweated heavily under the woe-
begone patriarchal burden of male superiority and
dominance on the one hand, and female subjugation
(lack of voice and choice) on the other hand.

Whether in Africa or in the West,

> woman is fundamentally manacled by the
> legacy of cultural domination and thraldom.
> Viewed essentially as a mere object, woman
> is grossly marginalised by a patriarchal

culture which assigns her the "sacred and
vital" role of wife and mother in the domestic sphere. Practically relegated to the confines of the private domain, [she] undergoes
a socialisation process that celebrates the
self-fulfillment of the male while undermining the autonomy of the female. Women's
education while precluding female social and
political growth, is primarily directed towards the affirmation of "eternal female
virtues such as docility, self-abnegation and
chasity."[1]

I. The African Woman Bears a Double Yoke

Just as the Igboman segregated against women in
the formula: "Did you see any of your fellow
women here?" – a rhetorical question which told a
woman that she was unwanted in certain circles and
spheres, so were the German women confined to
their biological role in the slogan: "Kinder, Küche,
Kirche" (Children, Kitchen, Church); and Freud
did the same in the euphemism: "Anatomy is
destiny." In short: From primeval times, the female
cycle has defined and confined women's role. As the
African woman was made to believe that her sole
purpose in life was to marry and beget children, so
also were American women told that their role was
to seek fulfillment as wives and mothers. The voices
of tradition and of Freudian sophistication re-
echoed that they could desire no greater destiny
than to glory in their femininity. Experts taught

From *Postkoloniales Philosophieren: Afrika*, eds. Herta
Nagl-Docekal and Franz Martin Wimmer, R. Oldenbourg
Verlag (1992); by kind permission of the editors.

them how to catch a man and keep him, how to dress, look and act more feminine, how to breast-feed children, etc. Up to the middle of the twentieth century, they were still taught to devote their lives from earliest childhood to finding a husband and bearing children; and they were so indoctrinated that good feminine women do not need careers, high education or political rights – the independence and opportunities which feminists fought for – that by the mid fifties, 60 percent of the women attending college dropped out to marry, or for fear that education would be a marriage bar.[2] So serious was this culture of the subjection of women that the renowned feminist, Lucy Stone, had to practice public speaking secretly in the woods.

> Even at Oberlin, the girls were forbidden to speak in public. Washing the men's clothes, caring for their rooms, serving them at table, listening to their orations, but themselves remaining respectfully silent in public as-semblages, the Oberlin "Co-eds" were being prepared for intelligent motherhood and a properly subservient wifehood".[3]

Worse still, "to become a wife was to die as a person. The concept "femme couverte" (*covered woman*) written into the law, suspended the "very being or legal existence of a woman" upon mar-riage."[4] The same is no less true in Africa where

> The woman as daughter or sister has greater status and more rights in her lineage. Mar-ried, she becomes a possession, voiceless and often rightless in her husband's family, except for what accrues to her through her children."[5]

Wrong as this may be, the aetiology of it is that whatever is bought has a utilitarian value. It does not matter whether it is christened bride price, dowry or a token that marriage has been contracted. If a man acquires a wife, by the law of accretion, whatever she will acquire should accrue to him. Here lies the wisdom of the Igboman, who when their belongings were shared between him and his wife (at the request of the latter) to mark the demise of their marriage, chose only one thing. "I choose my wife," he said, "she can take the rest of the things." As far as he was concerned, his wife was part of the property to be shared and having chosen her, the rest of the things were his by implication.

Bride wealth has a depersonalizing effect on the married woman. It was only when dowry disap-peared from the American scene that women began to be wooed for themselves, and marriage of choice or marriage of love utterly replaced arranged marriages, and the valuation placed on female qualities: meekness, home-abidingness, timorous clinging to the saddle of a husband as he rode away for a two-mile journey (which were all very well in the Old World), gave way to the concept of the frontier woman. Strong women with character and determination, in fact, women with guts became more and more acceptable in America.[6]

Given that African and Western women have suffered and still suffer similar indignities, and Asian women are not spared the same, the feminine issue is, by its very nature, a global problem. The magnitude of the problem calls for international female bonding, the achievement of which would have been easy if all things were equal. African women recognize the need for international femi-nism, but they rejected the Western model. The question to be posited is, Is there anything that prevents Western feminists from accepting the African alternative? If the mountain does not go to Mohammed, Mohammed will go to the mountain. Besides, African women's reasons are cogent enough to merit due consideration. She who wears the shoe more, knows more where it pinches.

The African woman bears a double yoke.

> In the modern world, she is in a difficult position of fighting sexist institutions of her own culture, as well as those bequeathed from the West, in the educational, religious and occupational spheres. Therefore the demands of feminists in Western countries are equally relevant to the needs of African women.[7]

In fact, one would expect African women to be in the vanguard of international feminism because they bear international yokes. On the contrary, they hardly want to associate themselves with the term "feminists," they prefer to be known as "womanists."

II. African Womanism and Western Feminism

Is there anything in feminism which does not quite agree with the Black woman? The fact that black writers like Flora Nwapa, Chikwenye Ogunyemi, etc., prefer the term "womanist" to "feminist" logically raises the questions: What makes a piece of writing feminist? Who is a womanist? Why does the black woman who has earnestly pitched against the victimization, exploitation and the subjugation of women reluct to fully identify with her Western counterpart? What is the philosophy of womanism?

Feminist literary works make it their duty to flay the unjust marginalisation of women in patriarchal societies. In these works, women are portrayed as assertive beings seeking recognition and parity in a sexist society that relegates womanhood to the sex/gender roles. While for Virginia Woolf transcendence presupposes androgyny and for Simone de Beauvoir it is the negation of immanence, for the African feminist writer it is the extirpation of retrogressive cultural norms.[8]

A study of African feminism which includes "female autonomy and cooperation and emphasis on nature over culture, the centrality of children, multiple mothering and kinship, the use of ridicule in the African woman's worldview, a number of traditional rights and responsibilities of women," Filomena Steady concludes, makes the African woman, in practice, much more a feminist than her Western counterpart. According to her.

True feminism is an abnegation of male protection and a determination to be resourceful and reliant. The majority of the black women in Africa and the diaspora have developed these characteristics, though not always by choice.[9]

Among what makes African feminism different, Steady lists lack of choice in motherhood and marriage, oppression of barren women, genital mutilation, enforced silence, etc., and she suggests that these should be at the crux of the African feminist theory, but she is mistaken. These phenomena did not and do not exclusively plague African women. A quick glance over Margaret Mead's *Male and Female*, Betty Friedon's *The Feminine Mystique*, etc., reveals that lack of choice in motherhood and marriage, enforced silence and so on, were as Western as they were African. As for the new breed of African woman, she, like her Western counterpart, now has a voice and choice within and outside marriage. There is a greater female awakening and a better life. She has force-

fully made her point and she has been heard.[10] But this does not mean that African customs have changed any more than those of the West. It is almost impossible for women either in the West or in Africa to claim total liberation from men. The point is that we need to look elsewhere for clarification as to what makes African womanism different from Western feminism.

A womanist, Alice Walter would say, is in part a black feminist, a feminist of color committed to the survival and wholeness of an entire people, male and female, but who loves herself nonetheless. African womanism tends to marry African perturbation with the feminine problem. For the African womanist, the double allegiance to woman's emancipation and African liberation are inseparable. This is the philosophy of African womanism. For

although the African woman is repressed by the normative patterns of her male-dominated culture, she is well-informed of other social and political forces in the society which may take precedence over sexual politics. She would rather identify more with the African man in the struggle for social and political freedom than with the middle class white feminist who ignores the fact that racism and capitalism are concomitants of sexism. Given a society where sexual prejudice consists in the circumvention of female potentials, it is only logical that the African woman should rely on male support in her war against sexism, capitalism and neo-colonialism. She is alive to the fact that her individual freedom is, to an extent, interlocked with the freedom of her continent which is still under Western hegemony.[11]

The failure of Western feminists to deal with issues that directly affect Black women and their tendency to sensationalize others create antagonisms as does the fact that white women are often partners in the oppression of both African women and men as in South Africa, for instance.[12] If only Western feminists will make these points part of their agenda, international feminism will be greatly enhanced.

Apart from this core issue, other minor differences consist in the fact that (as Toni Morrison rightly points out) black womanists, unlike white feminists, eschew bitterness in their confrontation and relationship with men. They do not negate men, rather they accommodate them; men are central to their lives not merely as husbands but also as sons and brothers and their continuous presence is assured. This does not mean that they cannot do without men or stand on their own. The success of African womanism derives from the discovered awareness by women of their indispensability to the male. This is the bedrock of their actions, this gives the anchor, and the voice. Thus, the myth of male superiority disappears, for the woman looks inward for a fresh appreciation of self.[13]

African womanism is characterized by female bonding or solidarity and it surprisingly enlists male support. It is not apprehensive of wifehood and motherhood. Western feminism, on the other hand, is marked by man-hating even though Ernestine Rose always insisted, in the bitterest days of the fight for women's rights, that women's enemy was not man but bad principles. However, the excesses of Western feminists may have arisen from their helplessness in the face of so many odds. They had too many rights to fight: the right to equal education, the right to speak in public, the right to own property, the right to work at a job or profession and control their own earnings, etc., – some of which were either taken for granted in Africa or were handed over to the African woman on a platter of gold.

The African womanist lacks the radicalism of the Western feminists. In spite of that, she is gaining a lot of ground in the fight against sexist segregation. Just as it was not until the 1940s (and really only as a result of need during World War II) that single or married women were granted equal employment opportunities in the West, in the present-day Africa, the need to mobilize all available human resources for moral renaissance, national reconstruction and development has forced

African governments to take the lead in speeding up women's emancipation. It is interesting that the African woman is almost being begged to venture into spheres that were formally male preserves. She is even accused of lethargy and political apathy by those well aware that the average African woman relucts against politics simply because she was made to internalize that she is a *persona non grata* in such a sphere.

Apart from the differences enumerated above, a womanist, just like every other feminist, seeks to raise awareness as to the plight of women who, as it were, are struggling to co-exist in a man's world where they are regarded as appendages. As Anna Aidoo puts it,

> a womanist commits her energies, actively, to exposing the sexist tragedy of women's history; protesting the ongoing degradation of women; celebrating their physical and intellectual capabilities and above all, unfolding revolutionary vision of their role.[14]

This paper cannot be ended without mentioning that the woman question elicits more and more consciousness or female awakening daily, and that the higher status to which both Western and African women have arisen has made for greater autonomy in their relationship with men. Nonetheless, women should strive harder to enter in their thousands into politics, and into all decision-making bodies, not only to bring to bear on the system their resourcefulness and intuitive potentials but also because so long as the women "in these roles are few, so long will the values of society continue to be formulated to the disadvantage of women."[15]

Notes

1 Chioma Opara, "Hunters and Gatherers: Poetics as Gender Politics in Sam Ukala's 'The Slave Wife and the Log in Your Eye,'" *Review of English and Literary Studies*, vol. 7, no. 1.

2 Betty Friedan, *The Feminine Mystique* (New York: Penguin Books, 1983), pp. 13, 14.

3 Eleanor Flexner, *Century of Struggle: The Woman's Rights in the United States* (Cambridge, Mass., 1959); cf. Friedan, *Feminine Mystique*, p. 78.

4 Friedan, p. 80.

5 Omolara Ogundipe-Leslie, "Not Spinning on the Axis of Maleness," *Sisterhood is Global*, pp. 500–1, quoted in Ngambika, *Feminist Consciousness and Afri-*

can Literary Criticism (Trento: African World Press, 1986), p. 9.

6 Margaret Mead, *Male and Female* (Middlesex: Penguin Books, 1964), pp. 267–77.

7 M. N. Kisekka, "Polygyny and the Status of African Women," in Ogunsheye et al., eds, *Nigerian Women and Development* (Ibadan: Ibadan University Press, 1988).

8 C. Opara, "The Foot as Metaphor in Female Dreams: Analysis of Zaynab Alkali's Novels," *Literature and Black Aesthetics* (Calabar: Heinemann, 1990), pp. 158–66.

9 Filomena Steady, *The Black Woman Cross-Culturally*

(Cambridge, Mass: Schenkman Publishing Company, 1981), pp. 7–41.

10 Helen Chukwuma, "Voices and Choices: The Feminist Dilemma in Four African Novels," *Literature and Black Aesthetics* (Calabar: Heinemann, 1990), pp. 131–42.

11 Opara, pp. 158, 159.

12 Carole Boyce Davies, "Introduction: Feminist Consciousness and African Literary Criticism," in Ngambika, pp. 1–13.

13 Chukwuma, p. 140.

14 T. Ezeigbo, "Reflecting the Times; Radicalism in Recent Female-Oriented Fiction," *Literature and Black Aesthetics* (Calabar: Heinemann, 1990), pp. 143–57.

15 Grace Alele Williams, "Education and the Status of Nigerian Women," in Ogunsheye, pp. 170–9.

38

Black Women: Shaping Feminist Theory

bell hooks

Feminism in the United States has never emerged from the women who are most victimized by sexist oppression; women who are daily beaten down, mentally, physically, and spiritually – women who are powerless to change their condition in life. They are a silent majority. A mark of their victimization is that they accept their lot in life without visible question, without organized protest, without collective anger or rage. Betty Friedan's *The Feminine Mystique* is still heralded as having paved the way for the contemporary feminist movement – it was written as if these women did not exist. Friedan's famous phrase, "the problem that has no name," often quoted to describe the condition of women in this society, actually referred to the plight of a select group of college-educated, middle and upper class, married white women – housewives bored with leisure, with the home, with children, with buying products, who wanted more out of life. Friedan concludes her first chapter by stating: "We can no longer ignore that voice within women that says: 'I want something more than my husband and my children and my house.'" That "more" she defined as careers. She did not discuss who would be called in to take care of the children and maintain the home if more women like herself were freed from their house labor and given equal access with white men to the professions. She did not speak of the needs of women without men, without children, without homes. She ignored the existence of all non-white women and poor white women. She did not tell readers whether it was more fulfilling to be a maid, a babysitter, a factory worker, a clerk, or a prostitute, than to be a leisure class housewife.

She made her plight and the plight of white women like herself synonymous with a condition affecting all American women. In so doing, she deflected attention away from her classism, her racism, her sexist attitudes towards the masses of American women. In the context of her book, Friedan makes clear that the women she saw as victimized by sexism were college-educated, white women who were compelled by sexist conditioning to remain in the home. She contends:

> It is urgent to understand how the very condition of being a housewife can create a sense of emptiness, non-existence, nothingness in women. There are aspects of the housewife role that make it almost impossible for a woman of adult intelligence to retain a sense of human identity, the firm core of self or "I" without which a human being, man or woman, is not truly alive. For women of ability, in America today, I am convinced that there is something about the housewife state itself that is dangerous.

Specific problems and dilemmas of leisure class white housewives were real concerns that merited consideration and change but they were not the pressing political concerns of masses of women. Masses of women were concerned about economic

From bell hooks, *Black Women Shaping Feminist Theory*; by kind permission of South End Press.

survival, ethnic and racial discrimination, etc. When Friedan wrote *The Feminine Mystique*, more than one third of all women were in the work force. Although many women longed to be housewives, only women with leisure time and money could actually shape their identities on the model of the feminine mystique. They were women who, in Friedan's words, were "told by the most advanced thinkers of our time to go back and live their lives as if they were Noras, restricted to the doll's house by Victorian prejudices."

From her early writing, it appears that Friedan never wondered whether or not the plight of college-educated, white housewives was an adequate reference point by which to gauge the impact of sexism or sexist oppression on the lives of women in American society. Nor did she move beyond her own life experience to acquire an expanded perspective on the lives of women in the United States. I say this not to discredit her work. It remains a useful discussion of the impact of sexist discrimination on a select group of women. Examined from a different perspective, it can also be seen as a case study of narcissism, insensitivity, sentimentality, and self-indulgence which reaches its peak when Friedan, in a chapter titled "Progressive Dehumanization," makes a comparison between the psychological effects of isolation on white housewives and the impact of confinement on the self-concept of prisoners in Nazi concentration camps.

Friedan was a principal shaper of contemporary feminist thought. Significantly, the one-dimensional perspective on women's reality presented in her book became a marked feature of the contemporary feminist movement. Like Friedan before them, white women who dominate feminist discourse today rarely question whether or not their perspective on women's reality is true to the lived experiences of women as a collective group. Nor are they aware of the extent to which their perspectives reflect race and class biases, although there has been a greater awareness of biases in recent years. Racism abounds in the writings of white feminists, reinforcing white supremacy and negating the possibility that women will bond politically across ethnic and racial boundaries. Past feminist refusal to draw attention to and attack racial hierarchies suppressed the link between race and class. Yet class structure in American society has been shaped by the racial politic of white supremacy; it is only by analyzing racism and its function in capitalist society that a thorough understanding of class relationships can

emerge. Class struggle is inextricably bound to the struggle to end racism. Urging women to explore the full implication of class in an early essay, "The Last Straw," Rita Mae Brown explained:

> Class is much more than Marx's definition of relationship to the means of production. Class involves your behavior, your basic assumptions about life. Your experience (determined by your class) validates those assumptions, how you are taught to behave, what you expect from yourself and from others, your concept of a future, how you understand problems and solve them, how you think, feel, act. It is these behavioral patterns that middle class women resist recognizing although they may be perfectly willing to accept class in Marxist terms, a neat trick that helps them avoid really dealing with class behavior and changing that behavior in themselves. It is these behavioral patterns which must be recognized, understood, and changed.

White women who dominate feminist discourse, who for the most part make and articulate feminist theory, have little or no understanding of white supremacy as a racial politic, of the psychological impact of class, of their political status within a racist, sexist, capitalist state.

It is this lack of awareness that, for example, leads Leah Fritz to write in *Dreamers and Dealers*, a discussion of the current women's movement published in 1979:

> Women's suffering under sexist tyranny is a common bond among all women, transcending the particulars of the different forms that tyranny takes. *Suffering cannot be measured and compared quantitatively.* Is the enforced idleness and vacuity of a "rich" woman, which leads her to madness and/or suicide, greater or less than the suffering of a poor woman who barely survives on welfare but retains somehow her spirit? There is no way to measure such difference, but should these two women survey each other without the screen of patriarchal class, they may find a commonality in the fact that they are both oppressed, both miserable.

Fritz's statement is another example of wishful thinking, as well as the conscious mystification of social divisions between women, that has characterized much feminist expression. While it is evident that many women suffer from sexist tyranny, there is little indication that this forges "a common bond among all women." There is much evidence substantiating the reality that race and class identity creates differences in quality of life, social status, and lifestyle that take precedence over the common experience women share – differences which are rarely transcended. The motives of materially privileged, educated, white women with a variety of career and lifestyle options available to them must be questioned when they insist that "suffering cannot be measured." Fritz is by no means the first white feminist to make this statement. It is a statement that I have never heard a poor woman of any race make. Although there is much I would take issue with in Benjamin Barber's critique of the women's movement, *Liberating Feminism*, I agree with his assertion:

> Suffering is not necessarily a fixed and universal experience that can be measured by a single rod: it is related to situations, needs, and aspirations. But there must be some historical and political parameters for the use of the term so that political priorities can be established and different forms and degrees of suffering can be given the most attention.

A central tenet of modern feminist thought has been the assertion that "all women are oppressed." This assertion implies that women share a common lot, that factors like class, race, religion, sexual preference, etc. do not create a diversity of experience that determines the extent to which sexism will be an oppressive force in the lives of individual women. Sexism as a system of domination is institutionalized but it has never determined in an absolute way the fate of all women in this society. Being oppressed means the *absence of choices*. It is the primary point of contact between the oppressed and the oppressor. Many women in this society do have choices, (as inadequate as they are) therefore exploitation and discrimination are words that more accurately describe the lot of women collectively in the United States. Many women do not join organized resistance against sexism precisely because sexism has not meant an absolute lack of choices. They may know they are discriminated against on the basis of sex, but they do not equate this with oppression. Under capitalism, patriarchy is structured so that sexism restricts women's behavior in some realms even as freedom from limitations is allowed in other spheres. The absence of extreme restrictions leads many women to ignore the areas in which they are exploited or discriminated against; it may even lead them to imagine that no women are oppressed.

There are oppressed women in the United States, and it is both appropriate and necessary that we speak against such oppression. French feminist Christine Delphy makes the point in her essay, "For a Materialist Feminism," that the use of the term oppression is important because it places feminist struggle in a radical political framework:

> The rebirth of feminism coincided with the use of the term "oppression." The ruling ideology, i.e. common sense, daily speech, does not speak about oppression but about a "feminine condition." It refers back to a naturalist explanation: to a constraint of nature, exterior reality out of reach and not modifiable by human action. The term "oppression," on the contrary, refers back to a choice, an explanation, a situation that is political. "Oppression" and "social oppression" are therefore synonyms or rather social oppression is a redundance: the notion of a political origin, i.e. social, is an integral part of the concept of oppression.

However, feminist emphasis on "common oppression" in the United States was less a strategy for politicization than an appropriation by conservative and liberal women of a radical political vocabulary that masked the extent to which they shaped the movement so that it addressed and promoted their class interests.

Although the impulse towards unity and empathy that informed the notion of common oppression was directed at building solidarity, slogans like "organize around your own oppression" provided the excuse many privileged women needed to ignore the differences between their social status and the status of masses of women. It was a mark of race and class privilege, as well as the expression of freedom from the many constraints sexism places on working class women, that middle class white women were able to make their interests the primary focus of feminist movement and employ a rhetoric of commonality that made their condition synonymous with "oppression." Who was there to demand a change in vocabulary? What other group of women in the United States had the same access to universities, publishing houses, mass media, money? Had middle class black women begun a movement in which they had labeled themselves "oppressed," no one would have taken them seriously. Had they established public forums and given speeches about their "oppression," they would have been criticized and attacked from all sides. This was not the case with white bourgeois feminists for they could appeal to a large audience of women, like themselves, who were eager to change their lot in life. Their isolation from women of other class and race groups provided no immediate comparative base by which to test their assumptions of common oppression.

Initially, radical participants in women's movement demanded that women penetrate that isolation and create a space for contact. Anthologies like *Liberation Now, Women's Liberation: Blueprint for the Future, Class and Feminism, Radical Feminism,* and *Sisterhood Is Powerful,* all published in the early 1970s, contain articles that attempted to address a wide audience of women, an audience that was not exclusively white, middle class, college-educated, and adult (many have articles on teenagers). Sookie Stambler articulated this radical spirit in her introduction to *Women's Liberation: Blueprint for the Future*:

> Movement women have always been turned off by the media's necessity to create celebrities and superstars. This goes against our basic philosophy. We cannot relate to women in our ranks towering over us with prestige and fame. We are not struggling for the benefit of the one woman or for one group of women. We are dealing with issues that concern all women.

These sentiments, shared by many feminists early in the movement, were not sustained. As more and more women acquired prestige, fame, or money from feminist writings or from gains from feminist movement for equality in the workforce, individual opportunism undermined appeals for collective struggle. Women who were not opposed to patriarchy, capitalism, classism, or racism labeled themselves "feminist." Their expectations were varied. Privileged women wanted social equality with men of their class; some women wanted equal pay for equal work; others wanted an alternative lifestyle. Many of these legitimate concerns were easily co-

opted by the ruling capitalist patriarchy. French feminist Antoinette Fouque states:

> The actions proposed by the feminist groups are spectacular, provoking. But provocation only brings to light a certain number of social contradictions. It does not reveal radical contradictions within society. The feminists claim that they do not seek equality with men, but their practice proves the contrary to be true. Feminists are a bourgeois avant-garde that maintains, in an inverted form, the dominant values. Inversion does not facilitate the passage to another kind of structure. Reformism suits everyone! Bourgeois order, capitalism, phallocentrism are ready to integrate as many feminists as will be necessary. Since these women are becoming men, in the end it will only mean a few more men. The difference between the sexes is not whether one does or doesn't have a penis, it is whether or not one is an integral part of a phallic masculine economy.

Feminists in the United States are aware of the contradictions. Carol Ehrlich makes the point in her essay, "The Unhappy Marriage of Marxism and Feminism: Can It Be Saved?," that "feminism seems more and more to have taken on a blind, safe, nonrevolutionary outlook" as "feminist radicalism loses ground to bourgeois feminism," stressing that "we cannot let this continue":

> Women need to know (and are increasingly prevented from finding out) that feminism is *not* about dressing for success, or becoming a corporate executive, or gaining elective office; it is *not* being able to share a two career marriage and take skiing vacations and spend huge amounts of time with your husband and two lovely children because you have a domestic worker who makes all this possible for you, but who hasn't the time or money to do it for herself; it is *not* opening a Women's Bank, or spending a weekend in an expensive workshop that guarantees to teach you how to become assertive (but not aggressive); it is most emphatically *not* about becoming a police detective or CIA agent or marine corps general.

> But if these distorted images of feminism have more reality than ours do, it is partly our own fault. We have not worked as hard

as we should have at providing clear and meaningful alternative analyses which relate to people's lives, and at providing active, accessible groups in which to work.

It is no accident that feminist struggle has been so easily co-opted to serve the interests of conservative and liberal feminists since feminism in the United States has so far been a bourgeois ideology. Zillah Eisenstein discusses the liberal roots of North American feminism in *The Radical Future of Liberal Feminism*, explaining in the introduction:

> One of the major contributions to be found in this study is the role of the ideology of liberal individualism in the construction of feminist theory. Today's feminists either do not discuss a theory of individuality or they unself-consciously adopt the competitive, atomistic ideology of liberal individualism. There is much confusion on this issue in the feminist theory we discuss here. Until a conscious differentiation is made between a theory of individuality that recognizes the importance of the individual within the social collectivity and the ideology of individualism that assumes a competitive view of the individual, there will not be a full accounting of what a feminist theory of liberation must look like in our Western society.

The ideology of "competitive, atomistic liberal individualism" has permeated feminist thought to such an extent that it undermines the potential radicalism of feminist struggle. The usurpation of feminism by bourgeois women to support their class interests has been to a very grave extent justified by feminist theory as it has so far been conceived. (For example, the ideology of "common oppression.") Any movement to resist the co-optation of feminist struggle must begin by introducing a different feminist perspective – a new theory – one that is not informed by the ideology of liberal individualism.

The exclusionary practices of women who dominate feminist discourse have made it practically impossible for new and varied theories to emerge. Feminism has its party line and women who feel a need for a different strategy, a different foundation, often find themselves ostracized and silenced. Criticisms of or alternatives to established feminist ideas are not encouraged, e.g. recent controversies

about expanding feminist discussions of sexuality. Yet groups of women who feel excluded from feminist discourse and praxis can make a place for themselves only if they first create, via critiques, an awareness of the factors that alienate them. Many individual white women found in the women's movement a liberatory solution to personal dilemmas. Having directly benefited from the movement, they are less inclined to criticize it or to engage in rigorous examination of its structure than those who feel it has not had a revolutionary impact on their lives or the lives of masses of women in our society. Non-white women who feel affirmed within the current structure of feminist movement (even though they may form autonomous groups) seem to also feel that their definitions of the party line, whether on the issue of black feminism or on other issues, is the only legitimate discourse. Rather than encourage a diversity of voices, critical dialogue, and controversy, they, like some white women, seek to stifle dissent. As activists and writers whose work is widely known, they act as if they are best able to judge whether other women's voices should be heard. Susan Griffin warns against this overall tendency towards dogmatism in her essay, "The Way of All Ideology":

> ... when a theory is transformed into an ideology, it begins to destroy the self and self-knowledge. Originally born of feeling, it pretends to float above and around feeling. Above sensation. It organizes experience according to itself, without touching experience. By virtue of being itself, it is supposed to know. To invoke the name of this ideology is to confer truthfulness. No one can tell it anything new. Experience ceases to surprise it, inform it, transform it. It is annoyed by any detail which does not fit into its world view. Begun as a cry against the denial of truth, now it denies any truth which does not fit into its scheme. Begun as a way to restore one's sense of reality, now it attempts to discipline real people, to remake natural beings after its own image. All that it fails to explain it records as its enemy. Begun as a theory of liberation, it is threatened by new theories of liberation; it builds a prison for the mind.

We resist hegemonic dominance of feminist thought by insisting that it is a theory in the making, that we must necessarily criticize, question, re-examine, and explore new possibilities. My persistent critique has been informed by my status as a member of an oppressed group, experience of sexist exploitation and discrimination, and the sense that prevailing feminist analysis has not been the force shaping my feminist consciousness. This is true for many women. There are white women who had never considered resisting male dominance until the feminist movement created an awareness that they could and should. My awareness of feminist struggle was stimulated by social circumstance. Growing up in a Southern, black, father-dominated, working class household, I experienced (as did my mother, my sisters, and my brother) varying degrees of patriarchal tyranny and it made me angry – it made us all angry. Anger led me to question the politics of male dominance and enabled me to resist sexist socialization. Frequently, white feminists act as if black women did not know sexist oppression existed until they voiced feminist sentiment. They believe they are providing black women with "the" analysis and "the" program for liberation. They do not understand, cannot even imagine, that black women, as well as other groups of women who live daily in oppressive situations, often acquire an awareness of patriarchal politics from their lived experience, just as they develop strategies of resistance (even though they may not resist on a sustained or organized basis).

These black women observed white feminist focus on male tyranny and women's oppression as if it were a "new" revelation and felt such a focus had little impact on their lives. To them it was just another indication of the privileged living conditions of middle and upper class white women that they would need a theory to inform them that they were "oppressed." The implication being that people who are truly oppressed know it even though they may not be engaged in organized resistance or are unable to articulate in written form the nature of their oppression. These black women saw nothing liberatory in party line analyses of women's oppression. Neither the fact that black women have not organized collectively in huge numbers around the issues of "feminism" (many of us do not know or use the term) nor the fact that we have not had access to the machinery of power that would allow us to share our analyses or theories about gender with the American public negate its presence in our lives or place us in a position of dependency in relationship to those white and non-white feminists who address a larger audience.

The understanding I had by age thirteen of patriarchal politics created in me expectations of the feminist movement that were quite different from those of young, middle class, white women. When I entered my first women's studies class at Stanford University in the early 1970s, white women were revelling in the joy of being together – to them it was an important, momentous occasion. I had not known a life where women had not been together, where women had not helped, protected, and loved one another deeply. I had not known white women who were ignorant of the impact of race and class on their social status and consciousness (Southern white women often have a more realistic perspective on racism and classism than white women in other areas of the United States). I did not feel sympathetic to white peers who maintained that I could not expect them to have knowledge of or understand the life experiences of black women. Despite my background (living in racially segregated communities) I knew about the lives of white women, and certainly no white women lived in our neighborhood, attended our schools, or worked in our homes.

When I participated in feminist groups, I found that white women adopted a condescending attitude towards me and other non-white participants. The condescension they directed at black women was one of the means they employed to remind us that the women's movement was "theirs" – that we were able to participate because they allowed it, even encouraged it; after all, we were needed to legitimate the process. They did not see us as equals. They did not treat us as equals. And though they expected us to provide first hand accounts of black experience, they felt it was their role to decide if these experiences were authentic. Frequently, college-educated black women (even those from poor and working class backgrounds) were dismissed as mere imitators. Our presence in movement activities did not count, as white women were convinced that "real" blackness meant speaking the patois of poor black people, being uneducated, streetwise, and a variety of other stereotypes. If we dared to criticize the movement or to assume responsibility for reshaping feminist ideas and introducing new ideas, our voices were tuned out, dismissed, silenced. We could be heard only if our statements echoed the sentiments of the dominant discourse.

Attempts by white feminists to silence black women are rarely written about. All too often they have taken place in conference rooms, classrooms, or the privacy of cozy living room settings, where one lone black woman faces the racist hostility of a group of white women. From the time the women's liberation movement began, individual black women went to groups. Many never returned after a first meeting. Anita Cornwall is correct in "Three for the Price of One: Notes from a Gay Black Feminist," when she states, "sadly enough, fear of encountering racism seems to be one of the main reasons that so many black womyn refuse to join the women's movement." Recent focus on the issue of racism has generated discourse but has had little impact on the behavior of white feminists towards black women. Often the white women who are busy publishing papers and books on "unlearning racism" remain patronizing and condescending when they relate to black women. This is not surprising given that frequently their discourse is aimed solely in the direction of a white audience and the focus solely on changing attitudes rather than addressing racism in a historical and political context. They make us the "objects" of their privileged discourse on race. As "objects," we remain unequals, inferiors. Even though they may be sincerely concerned about racism, their methodology suggests they are not yet free of the type of paternalism endemic to white supremacist ideology. Some of these women place themselves in the position of "authorities" who must mediate communication between racist white women (naturally they see themselves as having come to terms with their racism) and angry black women whom they believe are incapable of rational discourse. Of course, the system of racism, classism, and educational elitism remain intact if they are to maintain their authoritative positions.

In 1981, I enrolled in a graduate class on feminist theory where we were given a course reading list that had writings by white women and men, one black man, but no material by or about black, Native American Indian, Hispanic, or Asian women. When I criticized this oversight, white women directed an anger and hostility at me that was so intense I found it difficult to attend the class. When I suggested that the purpose of this collective anger was to create an atmosphere in which it would be psychologically unbearable for me to speak in class discussions or even attend class, I was told that they were not angry. *I* was the one who was angry. Weeks after class ended, I received an open letter from one white female student acknowledging her anger and expressing regret for her attacks. She wrote:

> I didn't know you. You were black. In class after a while I noticed myself, that I would always be the one to respond to whatever you said. And usually it was to contradict. Not that the argument was always about racism by any means. But I think the hidden logic was that if I could prove you wrong about one thing, then you might not be right about anything at all.

And in another paragraph:

> I said in class one day that there were some people less entrapped than others by Plato's picture of the world. I said I thought we, after fifteen years of education, courtesy of the ruling class, might be more entrapped than others who had not received a start in life so close to the heart of the monster. My classmate, once a close friend, sister, colleague, has not spoken to me since then. I think the possibility that we were not the best spokespeople for all women made her fear for her self-worth and for her Ph.D.

Often in situations where white feminists aggressively attacked individual black women, they saw themselves as the ones who were under attack, who were the victims. During a heated discussion with another white female student in a racially mixed women's group I had organized, I was told that she had heard how I had "wiped out" people in the feminist theory class, that she was afraid of being "wiped out" too. I reminded her that I was one person speaking to a large group of angry, aggressive people; I was hardly dominating the situation. It was I who left the class in tears, not any of the people I had supposedly "wiped out."

Racist stereotypes of the strong, superhuman black woman are operative myths in the minds of many white women, allowing them to ignore the extent to which black women are likely to be victimized in this society and the role white women may play in the maintenance and perpetuation of that victimization. In Lillian Hellman's autobiographical work *Pentimento*, she writes, "All my life, beginning at birth, I have taken orders from black women, wanting them and resenting them, being superstitious the few times I disobeyed." The black women Hellman describes worked in her household as family servants and their status was never that of an equal. Even as a child, she was always in the dominant position as they questioned, advised, or guided her: they were free to exercise these rights because she or another white authority figure allowed it. Hellman places power in the hands of these black women rather than acknowledge her own power over them; hence she mystifies the true nature of their relationship. By projecting onto black women a mythical power and strength, white women both promote a false image of themselves as powerless, passive victims and deflect attention away from their aggressiveness, their power (however limited in a white supremacist, male-dominated state), their willingness to dominate and control others. These unacknowledged aspects of the social status of many white women prevent them from transcending racism and limit the scope of their understanding of women's overall social status in the United States.

Privileged feminists have largely been unable to speak to, with, and for diverse groups of women because they either do not understand fully the inter-relatedness of sex, race, and class oppression or refuse to take this inter-relatedness seriously. Feminist analyses of woman's lot tend to focus exclusively on gender and do not provide a solid foundation on which to construct feminist theory. They reflect the dominant tendency in Western patriarchal minds to mystify woman's reality by insisting that gender is the sole determinant of woman's fate. Certainly it has been easier for women who do not experience race or class oppression to focus exclusively on gender. Although socialist feminists focus on class and gender, they tend to dismiss race or they make a point of acknowledging that race is important and then proceed to offer an analysis in which race is not considered.

As a group, black women are in an unusual position in this society, for not only are we collectively at the bottom of the occupational ladder, but our overall social status is lower than that of any other group. Occupying such a position, we bear the brunt of sexist, racist, and classist oppression. At the same time, we are the group that has not been socialized to assume the role of exploiter/oppressor in that we are allowed no institutionalized "other" that we can exploit or oppress. (Children do not represent an institutionalized other even though they may be oppressed by parents.) White women and black men have it both ways. They can act as oppressor or be oppressed. Black men may be victimized by racism, but sexism allows them to act as exploiters and oppressors of women. White women may be victimized by sexism, but racism enables them to act as exploiters and oppressors of black people. Both groups have led liberation movements that favor their interests and support the continued oppression of other groups. Black male sexism has undermined struggles to eradicate racism just as white female racism undermines feminist struggle. As long as these two groups or any group defines liberation as gaining social equality with ruling class white men, they have a vested interest in the continued exploitation and oppression of others.

Black women with no institutionalized "other" that we may discriminate against, exploit, or oppress often have a lived experience that directly challenges the prevailing classist, sexist, racist social structure and its concomitant ideology. This lived experience may shape our consciousness in such a way that our world view differs from those who have a degree of privilege (however relative within the existing system). It is essential for continued feminist struggle that black women recognize the special vantage point our marginality gives us and make use of this perspective to criticize the dominant racist, classist, sexist hegemony as well as to envision and create a counter-hegemony. I am suggesting that we have a central role to play in the making of feminist theory and a contribution to offer that is unique and valuable. The formation of a liberatory feminist theory and praxis is a collective responsibility, one that must be shared. Though I criticize aspects of feminist movement as we have known it so far, a critique which is sometimes harsh and unrelenting, I do so not in an attempt to diminish feminist struggle but to enrich, to share in the work of making a liberatory ideology and a liberatory movement.

39

Mammies, Matriarchs, and Other Controlling Images

Patricia Hill Collins

Called Matriarch, Emasculator and Hot Momma. Sometimes Sister, Pretty Baby, Auntie, Mammy and Girl. Called Unwed Mother, Welfare Recipient and Inner City Consumer. The Black American Woman has had to admit that while nobody knew the troubles she saw, everybody, his brother and his dog, felt qualified to explain her, even to herself.

Harris 1982, 4

Race, class, and gender oppression could not continue without powerful ideological justifications for their existence. As Cheryl Gilkes contends, "Black women's assertiveness and their use of every expression of racism to launch multiple assaults against the entire fabric of inequality have been a consistent, multifaceted threat to the status quo. As punishment, Black women have been assaulted with a variety of negative images" (1983a, 294). Portraying African-American women as stereotypical mammies, matriarchs, welfare recipients, and hot mommas has been essential to the political economy of domination fostering Black women's oppression. Challenging these controlling images has long been a core theme in Black feminist thought.

As part of a generalized ideology of domination, these controlling images of Black womanhood take on special meaning because the authority to define these symbols is a major instrument of power. In order to exercise power, elite white men and their representatives must be in a position to manipulate appropriate symbols concerning Black women.

They may do so by exploiting already existing symbols, or they may create new ones relevant to their needs (Patterson 1982). Hazel Carby suggests that the objective of stereotypes is "not to reflect or represent a reality but to function as a disguise, or mystification, of objective social relations" (1987, 22). These controlling images are designed to make racism, sexism, and poverty appear to be natural, normal, and an inevitable part of everyday life.

Even when the political and economic conditions that originally generated controlling images disappear, such images prove remarkably tenacious because they not only keep Black women oppressed but are key in maintaining interlocking systems of race, class, and gender oppression. The status of African-American women as outsiders or strangers becomes the point from which other groups define their normality. Ruth Shays, a Black inner-city resident, describes how the standpoint of a subordinate group is discredited: "It will not kill people to hear the truth, but they don't like it and they would much rather hear it from one of their own than from a stranger. Now, to white people your colored person is always a stranger. Not only that, we are supposed to be dumb strangers, so we can't tell them anything!" (Gwaltney 1980, 29). As the "Others" of society who can never really belong, strangers threaten the moral and social order. But they are simultaneously essential for its survival because those individuals who stand at the margins of society clarify its boundaries. African-American women, by not belonging, emphasize the significance of belonging.

The Objectification of Black Women as the Other

Black feminist critic Barbara Christian asserts that in America, "the enslaved African woman became the basis for the definition of our society's *Other*" (1985, 160). Maintaining images of Black women as the Other provides ideological justification for race, gender, and class oppression.

Certain basic ideas crosscut all three systems. Claimed by Black feminist theorist bell hooks to be "the central ideological component of all systems of domination in Western society," one such idea is either/or dichotomous thinking (1984, 29). Either/or dichotomous thinking categorizes people, things, and ideas in terms of their difference from one another (Keller 1985, 8). For example, the terms in the dichotomies black/white (Richards 1980; Irele 1983), male/female (Eisenstein 1983), reason/emotion (Hochschild 1975; Halpin 1989), culture/nature (Asante 1987), fact/opinion (Westkott 1979; Bellah 1983), mind/body (Spelman 1982), and subject/object (Halpin 1989) gain meaning only in *relation* to their counterparts.

Another basic idea concerns the relationship between notions of differences in either/or dichotomous thinking and objectification. In either/or dichotomous thinking, difference is defined in oppositional terms. One part is not simply different from its counterpart; it is inherently opposed to its "other." Whites and Blacks, males and females, thought and feeling are not complementary counterparts – they are fundamentally different entities related only through their definition as opposites. Feeling cannot be incorporated into thought or even function in conjunction with it because in either/or dichotomous thinking, feeling retards thought, values obscure facts, and judgment clouds knowledge.

Objectification is central to this process of oppositional difference. In either/or dichotomous thinking, one element is objectified as the Other, and is viewed as an object to be manipulated and controlled. Social theorist Dona Richards (1980) suggests that Western thought requires objectification, a process she describes as the "separation of the 'knowing self' from the 'known object'" (p. 72). Intense objectification is a "prerequisite for the despiritualization of the universe,"

notes Richards, "and through it the Western cosmos was made ready for ever increasing materialization" (p. 72). A Marxist assessment of the culture/nature dichotomy argues that history can be seen as one in which human beings constantly objectify the natural world in order to control and exploit it (Brittan and Maynard 1984, 198). Culture is defined as the opposite of an objectified nature that, if left alone, would destroy culture.[1] Feminist scholars point to the identification of women with nature as being central to women's subsequent objectification by men as sex objects (Eisenstein 1983). Black scholars contend that defining people of color as less human, animalistic, or more "natural" denies African and Asian people's subjectivity and supports a political economy of domination (Asante 1987).

Domination always involves attempts to objectify the subordinate group. "As subjects, people have the right to define their own reality, establish their own identities, name their history," asserts bell hooks (1989, 42). "As objects, one's reality is defined by others, one's identity created by others, one's history named only in ways that define one's relationship to those who are subject" (p. 42). The treatment afforded Black women domestic workers exemplifies the many forms that objectification can take. Making Black women work as if they were animals or "mules uh de world" represents one form of objectification. Deference rituals such as calling Black domestic workers "girls" and by their first names enable employers to treat their employees like children, as less capable human beings. Objectification can be so severe that the Other simply disappears, as was the case when Judith Rollins's employer treated her as if she were invisible by conducting a conversation while ignoring Rollins's presence in the room. But in spite of these pressures, Black women have insisted on our right to define our own reality, establish our own identities, and name our history. One significant contribution of work by Judith Rollins (1985), Bonnie Thornton Dill (1980, 1988a), Elizabeth Clark-Lewis (1985), and others is that they document Black women's everyday resistance to this attempted objectification.

Finally, because oppositional dichotomies rarely represent different but equal relationships, they are inherently unstable. Tension is resolved by subordinating one half of the dichotomy to the other. Thus whites rule Blacks, men dominate women, reason is thought superior to emotion in ascertaining truth, facts supersede opinion in evaluating knowledge, and subjects rule objects. The foundations of a complex social hierarchy become grounded in the interwoven concepts of either/or dichotomous thinking, oppositional difference, and objectification. With domination based on difference forming an essential underpinning for this entire system of thought, these concepts invariably imply relationships of superiority and inferiority, hierarchical bonds that mesh with political economies of race, gender, and class oppression.

African-American women occupy a position whereby the inferior half of a series of these dichotomies converge, and this placement has been central to our subordination. The allegedly emotional, passionate nature of Black women has long been used to justify Black women's sexual exploitation. Similarly, restricting Black women's literacy, then claiming that we lack the facts for sound judgment, relegates African-American women to the inferior side of the fact/opinion dichotomy. Denying Black women status as fully human subjects by treating us as the objectified Other in a range of such dichotomies demonstrates the power that dichotomous either/or thinking, oppositional difference, and objectification wield in maintaining interlocking systems of oppression. Analyzing the specific, externally defined, controlling images applied to African-American women both reveals the specific contours of Black women's objectification and offers a clearer view of how systems of race, gender, and class oppression actually interlock.

Controlling Images and Black Women's Oppression

"Black women emerged from slavery firmly enshrined in the consciousness of white America as 'Mammy' and the 'bad black woman,'" contends Cheryl Gilkes (1983a, 294). The dominant ideology of the slave era fostered the creation of four interrelated, socially constructed controlling images of Black womanhood, each reflecting the dominant group's interest in maintaining Black women's subordination. Given that both Black and white women were important to slavery's continuation, the prevailing ideology functioned to mask contradictions in social relations affecting all women. According to the cult of true womanhood, "true" women possessed four cardinal virtues: piety, purity, submissiveness, and domesticity. Elite white women and those of the emerging middle class were encouraged to aspire to these virtues. African-American women encountered a different set of controlling images. The sexual ideology of the period as is the case today "confirmed the differing material circumstances of these two groups of women ... by balancing opposing definitions of womanhood and motherhood, each dependent on the other for its existence" (Carby 1987, 25).

The first controlling image applied to African-American women is that of the mammy – the faithful, obedient domestic servant. Created to justify the economic exploitation of house slaves and sustained to explain Black women's long-standing restriction to domestic service, the mammy image represents the normative yardstick used to evaluate all Black women's behavior. By loving, nurturing, and caring for her white children and "family" better than her own, the mammy symbolizes the dominant group's perceptions of the ideal Black female relationship to elite white male power. Even though she may be well loved and may wield considerable authority in her white "family," the mammy still knows her "place" as obedient servant. She has accepted her subordination.

Black women intellectuals have aggressively deconstructed the image of African-American women as contented mammies by challenging traditional views of Black women domestics (Dill 1980, 1988a; Clark-Lewis 1985; Rollins 1985). Literary critic Trudier Harris's (1982) volume *From Mammies to Militants: Domestics in Black American Literature* investigates prominent differences in how Black women have been portrayed by others in literature and how they portray themselves. In her work on the difficulties faced by Black women leaders, Rhetaugh Dumas (1980) describes how Black women executives are hampered by being treated as mammies and penalized if they do not appear warm and nurturing. But despite these works, the mammy image lives on in scholarly and popular culture. Audre Lorde's account of a shopping trip offers a powerful example of its tenacity: "I wheel my two-year-old daughter in a shopping cart through a supermarket in ... 1967, and a little white girl riding past in her mother's cart calls out excitedly, 'Oh look, Mommy, a baby maid!'" (1984, 126).[2]

The mammy image is central to interlocking systems of race, gender, and class oppression. Since efforts to control African-American family life require perpetuating the symbolic structures of racial oppression, the mammy image is important because it aims to shape Black women's behavior as mothers. As the members of African-American families who are most familiar with the skills needed for Black accommodation, Black women are encouraged to transmit to their own children the deference behavior many are forced to exhibit in mammy roles. By teaching Black children their assigned place in white power structures, Black women who internalize the mammy image potentially become effective conduits for perpetuating racial oppression. In addition, employing mammies buttresses the racial superiority of white women employers and weds them more closely to their fathers, husbands, and sons as sources of elite white male power (Rollins 1985).

The mammy image also serves a symbolic function in maintaining gender oppression. Black feminist critic Barbara Christian argues that images of Black womanhood serve as a reservoir for the fears of Western culture, "a dumping ground for those female functions a basically Puritan society could not confront" (1985, 2). Juxtaposed against the image of white women promulgated through the cult of true womanhood, the mammy image as the Other symbolizes the oppositional difference of mind/body and culture/nature thought to distinguish Black women from everyone else. Christian comments on the mammy's gender significance: "All the functions of mammy are magnificently physical. They involve the body as sensuous, as funky, the part of woman that white southern America was profoundly afraid of. Mammy, then, harmless in her position of slave, unable because of her all-giving nature to do harm, is needed as an image, a surrogate to contain all those fears of the physical female" (1985, 2). The mammy image buttresses the ideology of the cult of true womanhood, one in which sexuality and fertility are severed. "Good" white mothers are expected to deny their female sexuality and devote their attention to the moral development of their offspring. In contrast, the mammy image is one of an asexual woman, a surrogate mother in blackface devoted to the development of a white family.

No matter how loved they were by their white "families," Black women domestic workers remained poor because they were economically exploited. The restructured post – World War II economy in which African-American women moved from service in private homes to jobs in the low-paid service sector has produced comparable economic exploitation. Removing Black women's labor from African-American families and exploiting it denies Black extended family units the benefits of either decent wages or Black women's unpaid labor

in their homes. Moreover, many white families in both the middle class and working class are able to maintain their class position because they have long used Black women as a source of cheap labor (Rollins 1985; Byerly 1986). The mammy image is designed to mask this economic exploitation of social class (King 1973).

For reasons of economic survival, African-American women may play the mammy role in paid work settings. But within African-American communities these same women often teach their own children something quite different. Bonnie Thornton Dill's (1980) work on child-rearing patterns among Black domestics shows that while the participants in her study showed deference behavior at work, they discouraged their children from believing that they should be deferent to whites and encouraged their children to avoid domestic work. Barbara Christian's analysis of the mammy in Black slave narratives reveals that, "unlike the white southern image of mammy, she is cunning, prone to poisoning her master, and not at all content with her lot" (1985, 5).

The fact that the mammy image cannot control Black women's behavior as mothers is tied to the creation of the second controlling image of Black womanhood. Though a more recent phenomenon, the image of the Black matriarch fulfills similar functions in explaining Black women's placement in interlocking systems of race, gender and class oppression. Ironically, Black scholars such as William E. B. Du Bois (1969) and E. Franklin Frazier (1948) described the connections among higher rates of female-headed households in African-American communities, the importance that women assume in Black family networks, and the persistence of Black poverty. However, neither scholar interpreted Black women's centrality in Black families as a *cause* of African-American social class status. Both saw so-called matriarchal families as an *outcome* of racial oppression and poverty. During the eras when Du Bois and Frazier wrote, the oppression of African-Americans was so total that control was maintained without the controlling image of matriarch. But what began as a muted theme in the works of these earlier Black scholars grew into a full-blown racialized image in the 1960s, a time of significant political and economic mobility for African-Americans. Racialization involves attaching racial meaning to a previously racially unclassified relationship, social practice, or group (Omi and Winant 1986). Prior to the 1960s, female-headed households were certainly higher in African-American communities, but an ideology racializing female-headedness as a causal feature of Black poverty had not emerged. Moreover, "the public depiction of Black women as unfeminine, castrating matriarchs came at precisely the same moment that the feminist movement was advancing its public critique of American patriarchy" (Gilkes 1983a, 296).

While the mammy typifies the Black mother figure in white homes, the matriarch symbolizes the mother figure in Black homes. Just as the mammy represents the "good" Black mother, the matriarch symbolizes the "bad" Black mother. The modern Black matriarchy thesis contends that African-American women fail to fulfill their traditional "womanly" duties (Moynihan 1965). Spending too much time away from home, these working mothers ostensibly cannot properly supervise their children and are a major contributing factor to their children's school failure. As overly aggressive, unfeminine women, Black matriarchs allegedly emasculate their lovers and husbands. These men, understandably, either desert their partners or refuse to marry the mothers of their children. From an elite white male standpoint, the matriarch is essentially a failed mammy, a negative stigma applied to those African-American women who dared to violate the image of the submissive, hard-working servant.

Black women intellectuals examining the role of women in African-American families discover few matriarchs and even fewer mammies (Hale 1980; Myers 1980; Sudarkasa 1981b; Dill 1988b). Instead they portray African-American mothers as complex individuals who often show tremendous strength under adverse conditions. In *A Raisin in the Sun*, the first play presented on Broadway written by a Black woman, Lorraine Hansberry (1959) examines the struggles of widow Lena Younger to actualize her dream of purchasing a home for her family. In *Brown Girl, Brownstones*, novelist Paule Marshall (1959) presents Mrs Boyce, a Black mother negotiating a series of relationships with her husband, her daughters, the women in her community, and the work she must perform outside her home. Ann Allen Shockley's *Loving Her* (1974) depicts the struggle of a lesbian mother trying to balance her needs for self-actualization with the pressures of child-rearing in a homophobic community. Like these fictional analyses, Black women's scholarship on Black single mothers also challenges the matriarchy thesis (Ladner 1972; McCray 1980; Lorde 1984; McAdoo 1985; Brewer 1988).

Like the mammy, the image of the matriarch is central to interlocking systems of race, gender, and class oppression. Portraying African-American women as matriarchs allows the dominant group to blame Black women for the success or failure of Black children. Assuming that Black poverty is passed on intergenerationally via value transmission in families, an elite white male standpoint suggests that Black children lack the attention and care allegedly lavished on white, middle-class children and that this deficiency seriously retards Black children's achievement. Such a view diverts attention from the political and economic inequality affecting Black mothers and children and suggests that anyone can rise from poverty if he or she only received good values at home. Those African-Americans who remain poor are blamed for their own victimization. Using Black women's performance as mothers to explain Black economic subordination links gender ideology to explanations of class subordination.

The source of the matriarch's failure is her inability to model appropriate gender behavior. In the post-World War II era, increasing numbers of white women entered the labor market, limited their fertility, and generally challenged their proscribed roles in white patriarchal institutions. The image of the Black matriarch emerged at that time as a powerful symbol for both Black and white women of what can go wrong if white patriarchal power is challenged. Aggressive, assertive women are penalized – they are abandoned by their men, end up impoverished, and are stigmatized as being unfeminine.

The image of the matriarch also supports racial oppression. Much social science research implicitly uses gender relations in African-American communities as one putative measure of Black cultural disadvantage. For example, the Moynihan Report (1965) contends that slavery destroyed Black families by creating reversed roles for men and women. Black family structures are seen as being deviant because they challenge the patriarchal assumptions underpinning the construct of the ideal "family." Moreover, the absence of Black patriarchy is used as evidence for Black cultural inferiority (Collins 1989). Black women's failure to conform to the cult of true womanhood can then be identified as one fundamental source of Black cultural deficiency. Cheryl Gilkes posits that the emergence of the matriarchal image occurred as a counterideology to efforts by African-Americans and women who were confronting interlocking systems of race, gender, and class oppression: "The image of dangerous

Black women who were also deviant castrating mothers divided the Black community at a critical period in the Black liberation struggle and created a wider gap between the worlds of Black and white women at a critical period in women's history" (1983a, 297).

Taken together, images of the mammy and the matriarch place African-American women in an untenable position. For Black women workers in domestic work and other occupations requiring long hours and/or substantial emotional labor, becoming the ideal mammy means precious time and energy spent away from husbands and children. But being employed when Black men have difficulty finding steady work exposes African-American women to the charge that Black women emasculate Black men by failing to be submissive, dependent, "feminine" women. Moreover, Black women's financial contributions to Black family well-being have also been cited as evidence supporting the matriarchy thesis (Moynihan 1965). Many Black women are the sole support of their families, and labeling these women "matriarchs" erodes their self-confidence and ability to confront oppression. In essence, African-American women who must work are labeled mammies, then are stigmatized again as matriarchs for being strong figures in their own homes.

A third, externally defined, controlling image of Black womanhood – that of the welfare mother – appears tied to Black women's increasing dependence on the post-World War II welfare state. Essentially an updated version of the breeder woman image created during slavery, this image provides an ideological justification for efforts to harness Black women's fertility to the needs of a changing political economy.

During slavery the breeder woman image portrayed Black women as more suitable for having children than white women. By claiming that Black women were able to produce children as easily as animals, this objectification of Black women as the Other provided justification for interference in the reproductive rights of enslaved Africans. Slaveowners wanted enslaved Africans to "breed" because every slave child born represented a valuable unit of property, another unit of labor, and, if female, the prospects for more slaves. The externally defined, controlling image of the breeder woman served to justify slaveowner intrusion into Black women's decisions about fertility (King 1973; Davis 1981).

The post-World War II political economy has offered African-Americans rights not available in former historical periods (Fusfeld and Bates 1984; Wilson 1987). African-Americans have successfully acquired basic political and economic protections from a greatly expanded welfare state, particularly Social Security, Aid to Families with Dependent Children, unemployment compensation, affirmative action, voting rights, antidiscrimination legislation, and the minimum wage. In spite of sustained opposition by Republican administrations in the 1980s, these programs allow many African-Americans to reject the subsistence-level, exploitative jobs held by their parents and grandparents. Job export, deskilling, and increased use of illegal immigrants have all been used to replace the loss of cheap, docile Black labor (Braverman 1974; Gordon et al. 1982; Nash and Fernandez-Kelly 1983). The large numbers of undereducated, unemployed African-Americans, most of whom are women and children, who inhabit inner cities cannot be forced to work. From the standpoint of the dominant group, they no longer represent cheap labor but instead signify a costly threat to political and economic stability.

Controlling Black women's fertility in such a political economy becomes important. The image of the welfare mother fulfills this function by labeling as unnecessary and even dangerous to the values of the country the fertility of women who are not white and middle class. A closer look at this controlling image reveals that it shares some important features with its mammy and matriarch counterparts. Like the matriarch, the welfare mother is labeled a bad mother. But unlike the matriarch, she is not too aggressive – on the contrary, she is not aggressive enough. While the matriarch's unavailability contributed to her children's poor socialization, the welfare mother's accessibility is deemed the problem. She is portrayed as being content to sit around and collect welfare, shunning work and passing on her bad values to her offspring. The image of the welfare mother represents another failed mammy, one who is unwilling to become "de mule uh de world."

The image of the welfare mother provides ideological justifications for interlocking systems of race, gender, and class oppression. African-Americans can be racially stereotyped as being lazy by blaming Black welfare mothers for failing to pass on the work ethic. Moreover, the welfare mother has no male authority figure to assist her. Typically portrayed as an unwed mother, she violates one cardinal tenet of Eurocentric masculinist thought: she is a woman alone. As a result, her treatment reinforces the dominant gender ideology positing that a woman's true worth and financial security should occur through heterosexual marriage. Finally, in the post-World War II political economy, one of every three African-American families is officially classified as poor. With such high levels of Black poverty, welfare state policies supporting poor Black mothers and their children have become increasingly expensive. Creating the controlling image of the welfare mother and stigmatizing her as the cause of her own poverty and that of African-American communities shifts the angle of vision away from structural sources of poverty and blames the victims themselves. The image of the welfare mother thus provides ideological justification for the dominant group's interest in limiting the fertility of Black mothers who are seen as producing too many economically unproductive children (Davis 1981).

The fourth controlling image – the Jezebel, whore, or sexually aggressive woman – is central in this nexus of elite white male images of Black womanhood because efforts to control Black women's sexuality lie at the heart of Black women's oppression. The image of Jezebel originated under slavery when Black women were portrayed as being, to use Jewelle Gomez's words, "sexually aggressive wet nurses" (Clarke et al. 1983, 99). Jezebel's function was to relegate all Black women to the category of sexually aggressive women, thus providing a powerful rationale for the widespread sexual assaults by white men typically reported by Black slave women (Davis 1981; Hooks 1981; D. White 1985). Yet Jezebel served another function. If Black slave women could be portrayed as having excessive sexual appetites, then increased fertility should be the expected outcome. By suppressing the nurturing that African-American women might give their own children which would strengthen Black family networks, and by forcing Black women to work in the field or "wet nurse" white children, slaveowners effectively tied the controlling images of Jezebel and Mammy to the economic exploita-

tion inherent in the institution of slavery.

The fourth image of the sexually denigrated Black woman is the foundation underlying elite white male conceptualizations of the mammy, matriarch, and welfare mother. Connecting all three is the common theme of Black women's sexuality. Each image transmits clear messages about the proper links among female sexuality, fertility, and Black women's roles in the political economy. For example, the mammy, the only somewhat positive figure, is a desexed individual. The mammy is typically portrayed as overweight, dark, and with characteristically African features – in brief, as an unsuitable sexual partner for white men. She is asexual and therefore is free to become a surrogate mother to the children she acquired not through her own sexuality. The mammy represents the clearest example of the split between sexuality and motherhood present in Eurocentric masculinist thought. In contrast, both the matriarch and the welfare mother are sexual beings. But their sexuality is linked to their fertility, and this link forms one fundamental reason they are negative images. The matriarch represents the sexually aggressive woman, one who emasculates Black men because she will not permit them to assume roles as Black patriarchs. She refuses to be passive and thus is stigmatized. Similarly, the welfare mother represents a woman of low morals and uncontrolled sexuality, factors identified as the cause of her impoverished state. In both cases Black female control over sexuality and fertility is conceptualized as antithetical to elite white male interests.

Taken together, these four prevailing interpretations of Black womanhood form a nexus of elite white male interpretations of Black female sexuality and fertility. Moreover, by meshing smoothly with systems of race, class, and gender oppression, they provide effective ideological justifications for racial oppression, the politics of gender subordination, and the economic exploitation inherent in capitalist economies.

Notes

1 Dona Richards (1980) offers an insightful analysis of the relationship between Christianity's contributions to an ideology of domination and the culture/nature dichotomy. She notes that European Christianity is predicated on a worldview that sustains the exploitation of nature: "Christian thought provides a view of man, nature, and the universe which supports not only the ascendancy of science, but of the technical order, individualism, and relentless progress. Emphasis within this world view is placed on humanity's dominance over *all* other beings, which become 'objects' in an 'objectified' universe. There is no emphasis on an awe-inspiring God or cosmos. Being 'made in God's image,' given the European ethos, translates into

'acting *as* God,' recreating the universe. Humanity is separated from nature" (p. 69).

2 Brittan and Maynard (1984) note that ideology (1) is common sense and obvious; (2) appears natural, inevitable, and universal; (3) shapes lived experience and behavior; (4) is sedimented in people's consciousness; and (5) consists of a system of ideas embedded in the social system as a whole. This example captures all dimensions of how racism and sexism function ideologically. The status of Black woman as servant is so "common sense" that even a child knows it. That the child saw a Black female child as a baby maid speaks to the naturalization dimension and to the persistence of controlling images in individual consciousness and the social system overall.

References

Asante, Molefi Kete. 1987. *The Afrocentric Idea.* Philadelphia: Temple University Press.

Bellah, Robert N. 1983. "The Ethical Aims of Social Inquiry." In *Social Science as Moral Inquiry*, edited by Norma Haan, Robert Bellah, Paul Rabinow, and William Sullivan, 360–81. New York: Columbia University Press.

Braverman, Harry. 1974. *Labor and Monopoly Capital.* New York: Monthly Review Press.

Brewer, Rose. 1988. "Black Women in Poverty: Some Comments on Female-Headed Families." *Signs* 13(2): 331–39.

Brittan, Arthur, and Mary Maynard. 1984. *Sexism, Racism and Oppression.* New York: Basil Blackwell.

Byerly, Victoria. 1986. *Hard Times Cotton Mills Girls.* Ithaca, NY: Cornell University Press.

Carby, Hazel. 1987. *Reconstructing Womanhood: The Emergence of the Afro-American Woman Novelist.* New York: Oxford.

Christian, Barbara. 1985. *Black Feminist Criticism, Perspectives on Black Women Writers.* New York: Pergamon.

Clarke, Cheryl, Jewell L. Gomez, Evelyn Hammonds, Bonnie Johnson, and Linda Powell. 1983. "Conversations and Questions: Black Women on Black Women Writers." *Conditions: Nine* 3(3): 88–137.

Clark-Lewis, Elizabeth. 1985. *"This Work Had a' End":* *The Transition from Live-In to Day Work.* Southern Women: The Intersection of Race, Class and Gender. Working Paper no 2. Memphis, TN: Center for Research on Women, Memphis State University.

Collins, Patricia Hill. 1989. "A Comparison of Two Works on Black Family Life." *Signs* 14(4): 875–84.

Davis, Angela Y. 1981. *Women, Race and Class.* New York: Random House.

Dill, Bonnie Thornton. 1980. "'The Means to Put My Children Through': Child-Rearing Goals and Strategies among Black Female Domestic Servants." In *The Black Woman*, edited by La Frances Rodgers-Rose, 107–23. Beverly Hills, CA: Sage.

—— 1988a. "'Making Your Job Good Yourself': Domestic Service and the Construction of Personal Dignity." In *Women and the Politics of Empowerment*, edited by Ann Bookman and Sandra Morgen, 33–52. Philadelphia: Temple University Press.

—— 1988b. "Our Mothers' Grief: Racial Ethnic Women and the Maintenance of Families." *Journal of Family History* 13(4): 415–31.

Du Bois, William E. B. 1969. *The Negro American Family.* New York: Negro Universities Press.

Eisenstein, Hester. 1983. *Contemporary Feminist Thought.* Boston: G. K. Hall.

Frazier, E. Franklin. 1948. *The Negro Family in the United States.* New York: Dryden Press.

Fusfield, Daniel R., and Timothy Bates. 1984. *The Political Economy of the Urban Ghetto.* Carbondale: Southern Illinois University Press.

Gilkes, Cheryl Townsend. 1983a. "From Slavery to Social Welfare: Racism and the Control of Black Women." In *Class, Race, and Sex: The Dynamics of Control*, edited by Amy Swerdlow and Hanna Lessinger, 288–300. Boston: G. K. Hall.

Gordon, David M., Richard Edwards, and Michael Reich. 1982. *Segmented Work, Divided Workers.* New York: Cambridge University Press.

Gwaltney, John Langston. 1980. *Drylongso, A Self-Portrait of Black America.* New York: Vintage.

Hale, Janice. 1980. "The Black Woman and Child Rearing." In *The Black Woman*, edited by La Frances Rodgers-Rose, 79–88. Beverly Hills, CA: Sage.

Halpin, Zuleyma Tang. 1989. "Scientific Objectivity and the Concept of "The Other." *Women's Studies International Forum* 12(3): 285–94.

Hansberry, Lorraine. 1959. *A Raisin in the Sun.* New York: Signet.

Harris, Trudier. 1982. *From Mammies to Militants: Domestics in Black American Literature.* Philadelphia: Temple University Press.

Hochschild, Arlie Russell. 1975. "The Sociology of Feeling and Emotion: Selected Possibilities." In *Another Voice: Feminist Perspectives on Social Life and Social Science*, edited by Marcia Millman and Rosabeth Kanter, 280–307. Garden City, NY: Anchor.

hooks, bell. 1981. *Ain't I a Woman: Black Women and Feminism.* Boston: South End Press.

—— 1984. *From Margin to Center.* Boston: South End Press.

—— 1989. *Talking Back: Thinking Feminist, Thinking Black.* Boston: South End Press.

Irele, Abiola. 1983. "Introduction." In *African Philosophy, Myth and Reality*, by Paulin J. Houtondji, 7–32. Bloomington: Indiana University Press.

Keller, Evelyn Fox. 1985. *Reflections on Gender and Science*. New Haven, CT: Yale University Press.

King, Mae. 1973. "The Politics of Sexual Stereotypes." *Black Scholar* 4 (6–7): 12–23.

Ladner, Joyce. 1972. *Tomorrow's Tomorrow*. Garden City, NY: Doubleday.

Lorde, Audre. 1984. *Sister Outsider*. Trumansberg, NY: The Crossing Press.

Marshall, Paule. 1959. *Brown Girl, Brownstones*. New York: Avon.

McAdoo, Harriette Pipes. 1985. "Strategies Used by Black Single Mothers against Stress." *Review of Black Political Economy* 14(2–3): 153–66.

McCray, Carrie Allen. 1980. "The Black Woman and Family Roles." In *The Black Woman*, edited by La Frances Rodgers-Rose, 67–78. Beverly Hills, CA: Sage.

Moynihan, Daniel Patrick. 1965. *The Negro Family: The Case for National Action*. Washington, DC: GPO.

Myers, Lena Wright. 1980. *Black Women: Do They Cope Better?* Englewood Cliffs, NJ: Prentice-Hall.

Nash, June, and Maria Patricia Fernandez-Kelly, eds. 1983. *Women, Men and the International Division of Labor*. Albany: State University of New York.

Omi, Michael, and Howard Winant. 1986. *Racial Formation in the United States: From the 1960s to the 1980s.* New York: Routledge & Kegan Paul.

Patterson, Orlando. 1982. *Slavery and Social Death*. Cambridge, MA: Harvard University Press.

Richards, Dona. 1980. "European Mythology: The Ideology of 'Progress.'" In *Contemporary Black Thought*, edited by Molefi Kete Asante and Abdulai Sa. Vandi, 59–79. Beverly Hills, CA: Sage.

Rollins, Judith. 1985. *Between Women, Domestics and Their Employers*. Philadelphia: Temple University Press.

Shockley, Ann Allen. 1974. *Loving Her*. Tallahassee, FL: Naiad Press.

Spelman, Elizabeth V. 1982. "Theories of Race and Gender: The Erasure of Black Women." *Quest* 5(4): 36–62.

Sudarkasa, Niara. 1981b. "Interpreting the African Heritage in Afro-American Family Organization." In *Black Families*, edited by Harriette Pipes McAdoo, 37–53. Beverly Hills, CA: Sage.

Westkott, Marcia. 1979. "Feminist Criticism of the Social Sciences." *Harvard Educational Review* 49(4): 422–30.

White, Evelyn. 1985. *Chain Chain Change. For Black Women Dealing with Physical and Emotional Abuse*. Seattle: The Seal Press.

Wilson, William Julius. 1987. *The Truly Disadvantaged: The Inner City, the Underclass, and Public Policy*. Chicago: University of Chicago Press.

40

The Erasure of Black Women

Elizabeth V. Spelman

Recent feminist theory has not totally ignored white racism, though white feminists have paid much less attention to it than have black feminists. Nor have white feminists explicitly enunciated and espoused positions of white superiority. Yet much of feminist theory has reflected and contributed to what Adrienne Rich has called "white solipsism": to think, imagine, and speak as if whiteness described the world.

> not the consciously held *belief* that one race is inherently superior to all others, but a tunnel-vision which simply does not see nonwhite experience or existence as precious or significant, unless in spasmodic, impotent guilt-reflexes, which have little or no long-term, continuing momentum or political usefulness.

In this essay, I shall focus on what I take to be instances and sustaining sources of such solipsism in recent theoretical works by, or of interest to, feminists – in particular, certain ways of comparing sexism and racism, and some well-ingrained habits of thought about the source of women's oppression and the possibility of our liberation. . . . To begin, I will examine some recent prominent claims to the effect that sexism is more fundamental than racism. . . . Before turning to the evidence that has been

From *Twenty Questions: An Introduction to Philosophy*, eds B. Lee Bowie, M. W. Michaels and R. Solomin, Harcourt Brace (1995), copyright © Elizabeth Spelman; reproduced by kind permission of Elizabeth Spelman.

given in behalf of that claim, we need to ask what it means to say that sexism is more fundamental than racism. It has meant or might mean several different though related things.

- It is harder to eradicate sexism than it is to eradicate racism.
- There might be sexism without racism but not racism without sexism: any social and political changes which eradicate sexism will have eradicated racism, but social and political changes which eradicate racism will not have eradicated sexism.
- Sexism is the first form of oppression learned by children.
- Sexism is historically prior to racism.
- Sexism is the cause of racism.
- Sexism is used to justify racism.

In the process of comparing racism and sexism, Richard Wasserstrom describes ways in which women and blacks have been stereotypically conceived of as less fully developed than white men. "Men and women are taught to see men as independent, capable, and powerful; men and women are taught to see women as dependent, limited in abilities, and passive." But who is taught to see black men as "independent, capable, and powerful," and by whom are they taught? Are black men taught that? Black women? White men? White women? Similarly, who is taught to see black women as "dependent, limited in abilities, and passive"? If this stereotype is so prevalent, why then have black women had to defend themselves against the images of matriarch and whore?

Wasserstrom continues:

> As is true for race, it is also a significant social fact that to be a female is to be an entity or creature viewed as different from the standard, fully developed person who is male as well as white. *But to be female, as opposed to being black*, is not to be conceived of as simply a creature of less worth. That is one important thing that differentiates sexism from racism: the ideology of sex, as opposed to the ideology of race, is a good deal more complex and confusing. *Women are both put on a pedestal* and deemed not fully developed persons. [emphasis mine]

In this brief for the view that sexism is a "deeper phenomenon" than racism, Wasserstrom leaves no room for the black woman. For a black woman cannot be "female, as opposed to being black"; she is female *and* black. Since Wasserstrom's argument proceeds from the assumption that one is either female or black, it cannot be an argument that applies to black women. Moreover, we cannot generate a composite image of the black woman from the above, since the description of women as being put on a pedestal, or being dependent, never generally applied to black women in the United States and was never meant to apply to them.

Wasserstrom's argument about the priority of sexism over racism has an odd result, which stems from the erasure of black women in his analysis. He wishes to claim that in this society sex is a more fundamental fact about people than race. Yet his description of woman does not apply to the black woman, which implies that being black is a more fundamental fact about her than being a woman. I am not saying that Wasserstrom actually believes this is true, but that paradoxically the terms of his theory force him into that position. . . .

Additive Analyses

. . . [S]exism and racism do not have different "objects" in the case of black women. Moreover, it is highly misleading to say, without further explanation, that black women experience sexism and racism. For to say *merely* that suggests that black women experience one form of oppression, as *blacks* – the same thing black men experience – and that they experience another form of oppression, as *women* – the same thing white women experience.

But this way of describing and analyzing black women's experience seems to me to be inadequate. For while it is true that images and institutions that are described as sexist affect both black and white women, they are affected in different ways, depending upon the extent to which they are affected by other forms of oppression.

For example, . . . it will not do to say that women are oppressed by the image of the "feminine" woman as fair, delicate, and in need of support and protection by men. While all women are oppressed by the use of that image, we are not oppressed in the same ways. As Linda Brent puts it so succinctly, "That which commands admiration in the white woman only hastens the degradation of the female slave." More specifically, as Angela Davis reminds us, "the alleged benefits of the ideology of femininity did not accrue" to the black female slave – she was expected to toil in the fields for just as long and hard as the black male was.

Reflection on the experience of black women also shows that it is not as if one form of oppression is merely piled upon another. As Barbara Smith has remarked, the effect of multiple oppression "is not merely arithmetic." Such an "additive" analysis informs, for example, Gerda Lerner's remark about the nature of the oppression of black women under slavery: "Their work and duties were the same as that of the men, while childbearing and rearing fell upon them as an added burden." But, as Angela Davis has pointed out, the mother-housewife role (even the words seem inappropriate) doesn't have the same *meaning* for women who experience racism as it does for those who are not so oppressed:

> In the infinite anguish of ministering to the needs of the men and children around her (who were not necessarily members of her immediate family), she was performing the *only* labor of the slave community which could not be directly and immediately claimed by the oppressor. . . . Even as she was suffering from her unique oppression as female, she was thrust by the force of circumstances into the center of the slave community.

The meaning and the oppressive nature of the "housewife" role has to be understood in relation to the roles against which it is contrasted. The work of mate/mother/nurturer has a different meaning depending on whether it is contrasted to work which has high social value and ensures economic independence, or to labor which is forced, degrading, and unpaid. All of these factors are left out in a simple additive analysis. How one form of oppression (e.g., sexism) is experienced, is influenced by and influences how another form (i.e., racism) is experienced. So it would be quite misleading to say simply that black women and white women both are oppressed as *women*, and that a black woman's oppression as a black is thus separable from her oppression as a woman because she shares the latter but not the former with the white woman. An additive analysis treats the oppression of a black woman in a sexist and racist society as if it were a *further* burden than her oppression in a sexist but non-racist society, when, in fact, it is a *different* burden. As the article by Davis, among others, shows, to ignore the difference is to deny or obscure the particular reality of the black woman's experience.

If sexism and racism must be seen as interlocking, and not as piled upon each other, serious problems arise for the claim that one of them is more fundamental than the other. As we saw, one meaning of the claim that sexism is more fundamental than racism is that sexism causes racism: racism would not exist if sexism did not, while sexism could and would continue to exist even in the absence of racism. In this connection, racism is sometimes seen as something which is both derivative from sexism and in the service of it: racism keeps women from uniting in alliance against sexism. This view has been articulated by Mary Daly in *Beyond God the Father*. According to Daly, sexism is "root and paradigm" of other forms of oppression such as racism. Racism is a "deformity *within* patriarchy . . . it is most unlikely that racism will be eradicated as long as sexism prevails."

Daly's theory relies on an additive analysis, and we can see again why such an analysis fails to describe adequately black women's experience. Daly's analysis makes it look simply as if both black and white women experience sexism, while black women also experience racism. Black women should realize, Daly says, that they must see what they have in common with white women – shared sexist oppression – and see that black and white women are "pawns in the racial struggle, which is basically not the struggle that will set them free as *women*." The additive analysis obscures the differences between black and white women's struggles. Insofar as she is oppressed by racism in a sexist context and sexism in a racist context, the black woman's struggle cannot be compartmentalized into two struggles – one as a black and one as a woman. But that way of speaking about her struggle is required by a theory which insists not only that sexism and racism are distinct but that one might be eradicated before the other. Daly rightly points out that the black woman's struggle can easily be, and has usually been, subordinated to the black man's struggle in anti-racist organizations. But she does not point out that the black woman's struggle can easily be, and usually has been, subordinated to the white woman's struggle in anti-sexist organizations.

Daly's line of thought also promotes the idea that, were it not for racism, there would be no important differences between black and white women. Since sexism is the fundamental form of oppression, and racism works in its service, the only significant differences between black and white women are differences which men have created and which are the source of antagonism between women. What is really crucial about us is our sex; racial distinctions are one of the many products of sexism, of patriarchy's attempt to keep women from uniting. It is through our shared sexual identity that we are oppressed together; it is through our shared sexual identity that we shall be liberated together.

A serious problem in thinking or speaking this way, however, is that it seems to deny or ignore the positive aspects of "racial" identities. It ignores the fact that being black is a source of pride, as well as an occasion for being oppressed. It suggests that once racism is eliminated (!), black women no longer need be concerned about or interested in their blackness – as if the only reason for paying attention to one's blackness is that it is the source of pain and sorrow and agony. But that is racism pure and simple, if it assumes that there is nothing positive about having a black history and identity. . . .

Racism and Somatophobia

. . . [F]eminist theorists as politically diverse as Simone de Beauvoir, Betty Friedan, and Shulamith Firestone have described the conditions of women's liberation in terms which suggest that the identification of woman with her body has been the source of our oppression, and that, hence, the source of our liberation lies in sundering that connection. For example, de Beauvoir introduces *The Second Sex* with the comment that woman has been regarded as "womb"; woman is thought of as planted firmly

Elizabeth Spelman

in the world of "immanence," that is, the physical world of nature, her life defined by the dictates of their "biologic fate." In contrast, men live in the world of "transcendence," actively using their minds to create "values, mores, religions," the world of culture as opposed to the world of nature. Among Friedan's central messages is that women should be allowed and encouraged to be "culturally" as well as "biologically" creative, because the former activities, which are "mental," are of "highest value to society" in comparison to childbearing and rearing – "mastering the secrets of atoms, or the stars, composing symphonies, pioneering a new concept in government or society." . . .

I bring up the presence of somatophobia in the work of Firestone and others because I think it is a force that contributes to white solipsism in feminist thought, in at least three related ways.

First, insofar as feminists do not examine somatophobia, but actually accept it and embrace it in prescriptions for women's liberation, we will not be examining what often has been an important element in racist thinking. For the superiority of men to women is not the only hierarchical relationship that has been linked to the superiority of the mind to the body. Certain kinds, or "races," of people have been held to be more body-like than others, and this has been meant as more animal-like and less god-like.

For example, in *The White Man's Burden*, Winthrop Jordan describes ways in which white Englishmen portrayed black Africans as beastly, dirty, highly sexed beings. Lillian Smith tells us in *Killers of the Dream* how closely run together were her lessons about the evil of the body and the evil of blacks.

Derogatory stereotypes of blacks versus whites (as well as of manual workers versus intellectuals) have been very similar to the derogatory stereotypes of women versus men. Indeed, the grounds on which Plato ridiculed women were so similar to those on which he ridiculed slaves, beasts, and children that he typically ridiculed them in one breath. He also thought it sufficient ridicule of one such group to accuse it of being like another (women are like slaves, slaves are like children, etc.). Aristotle's defense of his claim about the inferiority of women to men in the *Politics* is almost the same as his defense of the view that some people are meant to be slaves. (Aristotle did not identify what he called the natural class of slaves by skin color, but he says that identifying that class would be much easier if there were readily available physical characteristics by which one could do that.) Neither in women nor in slaves does the rational element work the way it ought to. Hence women and slaves are, though in different ways, to attend to the physical needs of the men/masters/intellectuals. . . .

So we need to examine and understand somatophobia and look for it in our own thinking, for the idea that the work of the body and for the body has no part in real human dignity has been part of racist as well as sexist ideology. That is, oppressive stereotypes of "inferior races" and of women have typically involved images of their lives as determined by basic bodily functions (sex, reproduction, appetite, secretions and excretions) and as given over to attending to the bodily functions of others (feeding, washing, cleaning, doing the "dirty work"). Superior groups, we have been told from Plato on down, have better things to do with their lives. As Hannah Arendt has pointed out, the position of women and slaves has been directly tied to the notion that their lives are to be devoted to taking care of bodily functions. It certainly does not follow from the presence of somatophobia in a person's writings that she or he is a racist or a sexist. But somatophobia historically has been symptomatic of sexist and racist (as well as classist) attitudes.

Human groups know that the work of the body and for the body is necessary for human existence, and they make provisions for that fact. And so even when a group views its liberation in terms of being free of association with, or responsibility for, bodily tasks, explicitly or implicitly, its own liberation may be predicated on the oppression of other groups – those assigned to do the body work. For example, if feminists decide that women are not going to be relegated to doing such work, who do we think is going to do it? Have we attended to the role that racism (and classism) historically has played in settling that question?

Finally, if one thinks – as de Beauvoir, Friedan, and Firestone do – that the liberation of women requires abstracting the notion of woman from the notion of woman's body, then one perhaps also will think that the liberation of blacks requires abstracting the notion of a black person from the notion of a black body. Since the body is thought to be the culprit (or anyway certain aspects of the body are thought to be the culprits), the solution may seem to be: keep the person and leave the occasion for oppression behind. Keep the woman, somehow, but leave behind her woman's body; keep the black person but leave the blackness behind. . . .

Once the concept of woman is divorced from the concept of woman's body, conceptual room is made for the idea of a woman who is no particular historical woman – she has no color, no accent, no particular characteristics that require having a body. She is somehow all and only woman; that is her only identifying feature. And so it will seem inappropriate or beside the point to think of women in terms of any physical characteristics, especially if it has been in the name of such characteristics that oppression has been rationalized. . . .

Rich on Embodiment

. . . Adrienne Rich is perhaps the only well-known white feminist to have noted "white solipsism" in feminist theorizing and activity. I think it is no coincidence that she also noticed and attended to the strong strain of somatophobia in feminist theory. . . .

. . . Both de Beauvoir and Firestone wanted to break it by insisting that women need be no more connected – in thought or deed – with the body than men have been. De Beauvoir and Firestone more or less are in agreement, with the patriarchal cultural history they otherwise question, that embodiment is a drag. Rich, however, insists that the negative connection between woman and body be broken along other lines. She asks us to think about whether what she calls "flesh-loathing" is the only attitude it is possible to have toward our bodies. Just as she explicitly distinguishes between motherhood as experience and motherhood as institution, so she implicitly asks us to distinguish between embodiment as experience and embodiment as institution. Flesh-loathing is part of the well-entrenched beliefs, habits, and practices epitomized in the treatment of pregnancy as a disease. But we need not experience our flesh, our body, as loathsome. . . . I think it is not a psychological or historical accident

that having reflected so thoroughly on flesh-loathing, Rich focused on the failure of white women to see black women's experience as different from their own. For looking at embodiment is one way (though not the only one) of coming to note and understand the *particularity* of experience. Without bodies we could not have personal histories, for without them we would not live at a particular time nor in a particular place. Moreover, without them we could not be identified as woman or man, black or white. This is not to say that reference to publicly observable bodily characteristics settles the question of whether someone is woman or man, black or white; nor is it to say that being woman or man, black or white, just means having certain bodily characteristics. But different meanings are attached to having those characteristics, in different places and at different times and by different people, and those differences make a huge difference in the kinds of lives we lead or experiences we have. Women's oppression has been linked to the meanings assigned to having a woman's body by male oppressors. Blacks' oppression has been linked to the meanings assigned to having a black body by white oppressors. We cannot hope to understand the meaning of a person's experiences, including her experiences of oppression, without first thinking of her as embodied, and second thinking about the particular meanings assigned to that embodiment. If, because of somatophobia, we think and write as if we are not embodied, or as if we would be better off if we were not embodied, we are likely to ignore the ways in which different forms of embodiment are correlated with different kinds of experience. . . . Rich does not run away from the fact that women have bodies, nor does she wish that women's bodies were not so different from men's. That healthy regard for the ground of our differences from men is logically connected to – though of course does not ensure – a healthy regard for the ground of the differences between black women and white women. . . .

41

The Curious Coincidence of Feminine and African Moralities

Sandra Harding

Carol Gilligan has persuasively argued that women and men have distinctive moralities. Men tend to believe that moral problems arise only from competing rights; that moral development requires the increased capacity for fairness; that the resolution of moral problems requires absolute judgments; and that such judgments should be arrived at through the formal, abstract thinking necessary for taking the role of the generalized other. Men worry about people interfering with one another's rights, and they tend to evaluate as immoral only objective unfairness – regardless of whether an act creates subjective hurt. While many women use this rights orientation, women also are concerned with a second set of moral issues that only rarely appear in men's thinking. In this second set, the care orientation, moral problems arise from conflicting responsibilities to particular, dependent others; moral development requires the increased capacity for understanding and care; the resolution of moral problems requires awareness of the possible limitations on any particular problem resolution; and such resolutions should be arrived at through the contextual and inductive thinking characteristic of taking the role of the particular other. Women worry about not helping others when they could, and within this care orientation, subjectively felt hurt appears immoral whether or not it can be justified as fair. Thus, in contrast to standard masculine views of women's morality, expressed through psychological and developmental theories throughout the history of modern Western ethical theory, Gilligan argues that women's morality is not deviant or immature relative to "human morality," but simply different from men's morality. She points out that both sets of concerns are necessary for the moral conduct of human social life.[1]

It should be noted at the start that, as Gilligan argues, these two orientations are not opposites. Justice, the goal of the rights orientation, need not be uncaring; and caring need not be unfair. Rather, they are complementary. However, Gilligan points out that the possibility of violence – or at least of force – stands behind only the rights mode of moral reasoning. Rights are violated at the risk of violence from both individuals and from the state or other authorities. The need for caring is ignored at no such direct risk of violence or force.

Ethical views are not isolated from an individual's total cultural beliefs. Thus, it is not surprising to see reflections of the gendered moralities Gilligan identifies also appearing in forms and processes of knowing. Hilary Rose, Jane Flax, Nancy Hartsock, and Dorothy Smith have all identified the distinctive masculine patterns in Western science, epistemology, and metaphysics.[2] Relatively rigid separations between mind and body, reason and the emotions, the public and the private, self and other, the abstract and the concrete, culture and nature, appear characteristic of (Western) masculine thinking. In each of these dichotomies, men fear that the feminine aspect will dominate and destroy the masculine, so therefore the masculine must domi-

From *Women and Moral Theory*, eds. Eva Kittay and Diana T. Myeres (1987); by kind permission of Rowman & Littlefield Publishers Inc.

nate. Many of the feminist critics of biology point to this androcentric perspective in the theories and concepts they criticize. Philosopher Sara Ruddick looks at the practices of mothering for a maternal thinking different from the paternal thinking that constitutes what is thought of as Western rationality.[3]

In the course of providing a casual account of gender differences, the feminist, psychoanalytic, object relations theorists perhaps provide the clearest picture of gender-differing ontologies.[4] Gender differences originate, they argue, in infantile developmental processes. As a result of male and female infants' different struggles to separate from their first caretaker, and to establish autonomous, individual identities as social persons, men tend toward an "objectifying" personality and women toward a "relational" one. Conceptions of self, of other people, of nature, and of the appropriate relationship of the self to community and nature are consequently different for men and women. Men tend toward abstract conceptions of their own self. This self is individualistic, separated from others and nature, and threatened by close relationships with others and nature. For men, other people are conceptualized as similarly autonomous individuals, isolated from each other, and threatening to infringe on each other's and the self's projects. Nature, too, is autonomous and separate from humans. It threatens to overwhelm human projects if not carefully controlled. Women tend toward concrete conceptions of the self and others. Their self is experienced as more continuous with women's bodies, with other selfs, and with nature, and threatened by too great separations between the self and these others. For women, other people and nature tend to be conceptualized as dependent parts of relational networks. Humans and nature are continuous with each other. Both Gilligan and many of the epistemologists have pointed to this developmental theory as one possible explanation of the origins of the androcentrism of Western philosophy, ethics, and social thought.

However, whether or not one accepts this psychoanalytic account of the origins of gendered ontologies, ethics, and modes of knowledge-seeking, the characteristic division of labor by sex/gender for adults appears to be sufficient to tend to cause gender-differentiated concepts of self, others, and the natural world, and the appropriate relationships between these three. Assigning domestic labor, and especially emotional labor, exclusively to women – in both the household and the workplace – divides human social experience and activity by sex/gender in such a way as to make it likely that women and men will think differently about themselves and their relationships to the world around them.[5] Whatever the origins of gendered concepts, it is clear that we are looking at dichotomized world views. A single set of gendered ontologies emerges within both moral views and cognitive styles.

I do not question that these differences exist between feminine and masculine moralities and between the world views these moralities are part of. Furthermore, far too much of adult social life is spent defensively working out unresolved infantile dilemmas. Different child rearing arrangements that would defuse or even eliminate gendering could help us to develop truly reciprocal selves. We could become persons who could acknowledge and incorporate difference instead of defensively needing to dominate whatever is defined as "other." There is something fundamentally right about the ontological, moral, and cognitive dichotomies and the psychoanalytic theories to which they appeal. Nevertheless, I think that there is also something wrong about these accounts. I am going to question the way we have conceptualized these differences. The problem is that the gender dichotomies appear to be embedded in a larger pattern of difference, one that separates ruling-class men in the West from the rest of us – not just, or perhaps, even, men from women in the West. If this is true, then the casual accounts that appeal to gendering processes are also thrown into doubt. Thus, the focus of my concern here is not Gilligan's work, but the more general characteristics of social relations that tend to produce the contrasting human problematics Gilligan locates in the moral preoccupations of the women and men she studied.

I want to explore some of the implications of the curious coincidence of the gender dichotomies with dichotomies claimed responsible for other forms of domination. It is in terms of similar dichotomies that Russell Means contrasts Native American and Eurocentric attitudes toward nature, and Joseph Needham contrasts Chinese and Western concepts of nature.[6] In particular, one stream of observers of both African and Afro-American social life focuses on the centrality of these kinds of dichotomies to racism, and on an "African World View" that represents the origins of an emancipatory politics, ethics, and epistemology. What these observers call the "African World View" is suspiciously similar to what the feminist literature has identified as a distinctively feminine world view. What they label

European or Euro-centric shares significant similarities with what we have been identifying as masculine or androcentric. Thus, on these separate accounts, people (men?) of African descent and (Western?) women appear to have similar ontologies, epistemologies, and ethics, and the world views of their respective rulers also appear to be similar.

It is no surprise to be able to infer that Western men hold a distinctively European world view, though Gilligan and other feminist theorists argue that not all people of European descent hold a masculine world view. And, the Africanist argument, like the European world view it rejects, apparently assumes that the human is identical to the masculine. However, it is startling to be led to the inference that Africans hold what in the West is characterized as a feminine world view, and that, correlatively, women in the West hold what Africans characterize as an African world view. Furthermore, how are we supposed to think of the world view of women of African descent? As doubly feminine? This particular reasonable inference from the correlation flies in the face of repeated observations that Black women, like women in other subjugated racial, class, and cultural groups, have been denied just the degree of "femininity" insisted upon for women in the dominant races, classes, and cultures.[7] And men in racially dominated groups are consistently denied just the degree of masculinity insisted upon for men in the dominant racial group. In racist societies, womanliness and manliness, femininity and masculinity, are always racial as well as gender categories. Of course, women of African descent, no less than white women, have presumably gone through distinctively feminine processes of development that bear at least some resemblance to the analogous Western processes. (For example, their first caretakers are primarily women; to become a woman is, at least in part, to become a potential mother, to become a potential wife, to become a person devalued relative to men.) The reader can already begin to see the array of conceptual problems generated by looking back and forth between these two literatures.

I must note here at the outset that this overgeneralizing tendency in both the Africanist and feminist literatures, which makes women of African descent disappear from both accounts and their world views incomprehensible when examined from the perspective of the two literatures together, has other unfortunate consequences. White feminists frequently balk at the very idea of an African world view shared by peoples of African descent in the many, very different cultures in which they live. Certainly this literature, produced primarily by Africans and Afro-Americans, draws our attention away from important cultural differences and may create fictitious commonalities. But certainly no more so than feminist accounts that attribute unitary world views to women and men respectively, ignoring differences created by the social contexts of being black or white, rural or industrialized, Western or non-Western, past or present. And there may well be very general commonalities in each case that can be found across all these cultural differences. After all, we are not uncomfortable speaking of a medieval world view or a modern world view, despite the cultural differences in the peoples to whom we attribute these very general conceptual schemes. I shall discuss these issues in somewhat greater detail later.[8]

Here, I will present the African world view and then draw attention to some problematic consequences of its correlation for feminist theorizing. Finally I will suggest some alternative ways in which we might conceptualize the nature and causes of these overlapping world views.

The African World View

A paradigm of the African vs. European dichotomy can be found in a paper entitled "World Views and Research Methodology," by the Black American economist, Vernon Dixon.[9] (I will quote extensively from Dixon's writings lest the reader think either Dixon or I use sexual metaphors to describe the phenomenon he examines.) Dixon outlines these world views in order to explain why it is that the economic behavior of Afro-Americans is persistently perceived as deviant when viewed in the context of neoclassical economic theory. Thus, his argument is that the "rational economic man" of this European theory is, in fact, only European. Aspects of Afro-American economic behavior that appear irrational from the perspective of neoclassical economic theory appear perfectly rational when understood from the perspective of an African world view.

Dixon locates the major difference between the two world views in the European "Man-to-Object" vs. the African "Man-to-Person" relationship, where this relationship is "between the 'I' or self (man) and everything that differs from that 'I' or self. This latter term means other men, things, nature, invisible beings, gods, wills, powers, etc., i.e., the phenomenal world."[10]

> In the Euro-American world view, there is a separation between the self and the nonself (phenomenal world). Through this process of separation, the phenomenal world becomes an Object, an "it." By Object, I mean the totality of phenomena conceived as constituting the nonself, that is, all the phenomena that are the antithesis of subject, ego, or self-consciousness. The phenomenal world becomes an entity considered as totally independent of the self. Events or phenomena are treated as external to the self rather than as affected by one's feelings or reflections. Reality becomes that which is set before the mind to be apprehended, whether it be things external in space or conceptions formed by the mind itself.[11]

Dixon cites empirical studies such as one that found in Euro-American students "a systematic . . . perception of conceptual distance between the observer and the observed; an objective attitude, a belief that everything takes place out there in the stimulus. This distance is sufficiently great so that the observer can study and manipulate the observed without being affected by it."[12]

This fundamental Euro-American separation of the self from nature and other people results in a characteristic "objectifying" of both. The presence of "empty perceptual space"[13] surrounding the self and separating it from everything else extracts the self from its natural and social surroundings and locates all the forces in the universe concerned with furthering the self's interests inside the circle of empty perceptual space – that is, in the self itself. Outside the self are only objects that can be acted upon or measured – i.e., known. Nature is an "external, impersonal system" which, since it "does not have his interest at heart, man should and can subordinate . . . to his own goals."[14] "The individual becomes the center of social space," and so "there is no conception of the group as a whole except as a collection of individuals."[15] Thus, "the responsibility of the individual to the total society and his place in it are defined in terms of goals and roles which are structured as autonomous."[16] "One's rise up the ladder of success is limited only by one's individual talents. Individual effort determines one's position."[17] This conception of the self, as

fundamentally an individual, also limits ones obligations and responsibilities.

> One retains the right to refuse to act in any capacity. It is not expected that a man, in pursuing his own goals of money-making and prestige, will remain dedicated to the goals of a given firm, college, or government agency if he receives an offer from another institution which will increase his salary or status. The individual only participates *in* a group; he does not feel *of* the group. In decision making, therefore, voting rather than unanimous consensus prevails.[18]

In the African world view, there is no gap between the self and the phenomenal world. "One is simply an extension of the other."[19] For people with this kind of ontology, there is

> a narrowing of perceived conceptual distance between the observer and the observed. The observed is perceived to be placed so close to the individual that it obscures what lies beyond it, and so that the observer cannot escape responding to it. The individual also appears to view the "field" as itself responding to him; i.e., although it may be completely objective and inanimate to others, because it demands response it is accorded a kind of life of its own.[20]

Given this conception of the self and its relationship to the phenomenal world, Africans

> experience man in harmony with nature. Their aim is to maintain balance or harmony among the various aspects of the universe. Disequilibrium may result in troubles such as human illness, drought, or social disruption. . . . According to this orientation, magic, voodoo, mysticism are not efforts to overcome a separation of man and nature, but rather the use of forces in nature to restore a more harmonious relationship between man and the universe. The universe is not static, inanimate or "dead"; it is a dynamic, animate, living and powerful universe.[21]

Furthermore, "the individual's position in social space is relative to others. . . . The individual is not a human being except as he is part of a social order."[22] "Whatever happens to the individual happens to the whole group, and whatever happens to the whole group happens to the individual."[23] In this communal rather than individualistic orientation, "an individual cannot refuse to act in any critical capacity when called upon to do so."[24] Thus Afro-Americans will often "unquestioningly go against their own personal welfare for other Blacks . . . even though the former know that the latter are wrong. They will co-sign loans for friends while aware that their friends will default and that their own finances will suffer."[25] An orientation toward interpersonal relationships has predominance over an orientation to the welfare of the self.

For Europeans, knowledge-seeking is a process of first separating the observer (the self) from what is to be known, and then categorizing and measuring it in an impartial, disinterested, dispassionate manner. In contrast, Africans "know reality predominantly through the interaction of affect and symbolic imagery."[26] The interaction of affect and symbolic imagery, in contrast to intuition, requires "inference from or reasoning about evidence."[27] But in contrast to European modes of gaining knowledge, it refuses to regard as value-free what is known, or as impartial, disinterested, and dispassionate either the knower or the process of coming to know. The self's feelings, emotions, and values are a necessary and positive part of his coming to know.

In summary, Dixon argues that the African world view is grounded in a conception of the self as intrinsically connected with, a part of, both the community and nature. The community is not a collection of fundamentally isolated individuals, but is ontologically primary. The individual develops his sense of self through his relationships within his community. His personal welfare depends fundamentally upon the welfare of the community, rather than the community's welfare depending upon the welfare of the individuals who constitute it. Because the self is continuous with nature rather than apart from and against it, the need to dominate nature as an impersonal object is replaced by the need to cooperate in nature's own projects. Coming to know is a process that involves concrete interactions that acknowledge the role that emotions, feelings, and values play in gaining knowledge, and that recognizes the world-to-be-known as having its own values and projects.

There are differences between the two dichotomies – not so much in what is attributed to Europeans and men as in the world views attributed to Africans and women. The feminist and Africanist accounts of our own realities are simply different. This should not be surprising since there are important differences between the life worlds of Africans and Afro-Americans on the one hand, and women of European descent on the other. I return to this point later. But the similarities are nevertheless striking. Europeans and men are thought to conceptualize the self as autonomous, individualistic, self-interested, fundamentally isolated from other people and from nature, and threatened by these "others" unless the "others" are dominated by the self. For both groups, the community is perceived as being merely a collection of similarly autonomous, isolated, self-interested individuals, with which one has no intrinsic relations. For both groups, nature replicates the image of the community. Nature too, is an autonomous system from which the self is fundamentally separated and that must be dominated to alleviate the threat of the self's being controlled by it. To Africans and women are attributed a concept of the self as dependent on others, as defined through relationships to others, as perceiving self-interest to lie in the welfare of the relational complex. Communities are relational complexes that are ontologically and morally more fundamental than the individuals defined through the relations to each other that constitute the community. Nature and culture are inseparable, continuous with each other.

From these contrasting ontologies "follow" contrasting ethics and epistemologies. To Europeans and men are attributed ethics that emphasize rule-governed adjudication of competing rights between self-interested, autonomous others, and epistemologies that conceptualize the knower as fundamentally separated from the known, and the known as an autonomous "object" that can be controlled through dispassionate, impersonal, "hand and brain" manipulations and measures. To Africans and women are attributed ethics that emphasize responsibilities to increasing the welfare of social complexes through contextual, inductive, and tentative decision processes, and epistemologies that conceptualize the knower as a part of the known, the known as affected by the process of coming to know, and that process as one that unites manual, mental, and emotional activity.

Obviously, there are many problems with taking the claims in these literatures at face value and in the form in which they have been presented. But I think these claims can be reconstructed to reveal some important theoretical and political truths.

Problems

Feminists and Africanists clearly have located differences in what we respectively call feminine vs. masculine, and African vs. European world views. However, before we noticed the correlation between the two dichotomies, there were already severe conceptual problems within each literature. Recognition of the correlation intensifies these problems.

As feminists, we need to apply the kind of criticism to our own theories that we have so effectively aimed at androcentric thinking. There, we have argued that what men define as a problem in need of explanation, and how that problem is conceptualized, are the major sources of the inadequate explanations of nature and social life that constitute what is counted as knowledge. For instance, as Gilligan has argued, it is not women's "deviant" morality that uniquely stands in need of explanation, but, more importantly, men's preoccupation with such limited moral focuses. How should the conceptual framework within which we feminists define our own problematics shift when we try to take account of this curious coincidence between African and feminine world views? Might we be led toward different kinds of casual explanations than those we have often favored?

In the interests of brevity, I shall simply identify three of these problems for the gender dichotomy that are exacerbated by recognition of the curious coincidence of this dichotomy with the racial one. The first is the ahistoricity of all such dichotomies. The second is a problem inherent to contrast schemas. The third is the problem of metaphoric explanation – what the anthropologist Judith Shapiro has happily called gender totemism.[28] These three problems all appear in similar form in the African/European dichotomy, and I leave it to the reader to identify those analogous problems.[29] Significantly, all the problems with these dichotomies originate, not in the emancipatory discourses of feminism and African liberation, but in the sexist and racist discourses that precede and accompany them. However, I suggest that rethinking these criticisms in this particular context – that of trying to account for the correlation between the dichotomized sets of world views – provides us with a constructive focus for our theorizing that has been missing from many earlier formulations of these criticisms.

Ahistoricity

A number of feminist critics have pointed out that generalizing from the gender-differing traits or behaviors observed in any particular culture or subculture to what is universally masculine and feminine ignores the effects of history and culture on human belief and behavior. Should we expect to find the ontological, epistemological, and moral configurations we can observe in women more or less like ourselves also in female gatherers, peasants, slaves, nineteenth-century industrial workers, heads of state, or members of aristocracies? Are the presumed commonalities of women's social experiences as female, and as daughters, wives, and mothers, strong enough to create shared world views in spite of the differences in the character and meanings of these experiences created by race, class, and culture? (I cannot remind the reader often enough that a similar problem appears in the Africanist literature.)

The apparent similarities between the world views of women and people of African descent escalate the force of this criticism. Given the usual androcentrism of both the Western anthropologists and the "native informants" who are reporting the Afro-American and African world view, we can be fairly confident that what we are hearing about in this literature is primarily African men's world view. (However, it is also possible that differences between the genders are not quite so marked in peoples who have been subjected to domestic and international imperialism. After all, as noted earlier, the dominant racial group tries to decrease the self-esteem of the dominated group by forbidding to it the forms of masculinity and femininity extolled for the dominant group. As Angela Davis has remarked about Black men and women subjected to the American slave experience, racism enforced a certain miserable form of gender equality.) At any rate, since the masculine and Euro-centric world views are not so surprisingly a relatively clear reflection of the assumptions underlying Western political, psychological, and philosophic thought, and especially since the Enlightenment, should we not seek their origins in historically narrower, more specific, social experiences than those common across gender difference or across racial difference? Perhaps the dichotomy we need is one between modern, Western men, and the rest of us.

Problems with Contrast Schemas

Feminine vs. masculine and African vs. European are contrast schemas.[30] These particular ones originated primarily in men's and Europeans' attempts to define as "other" and subhuman, groups they intended to and did subjugate. (It is an interesting and important question to what extent Africans and women, respectively, also participated as acts of rebellion in the conscious or unconscious construction of these contrast schemas.) While the original social process of creating the genders is lost to our view in the distant mists of human history,[31] the social process of creating races is entirely visible in relatively recent history. The concept of Europe and the distinctiveness of its peoples only began to appear during Charlemagne's unification of the Holy Roman Empire. The concept of Africa first appeared in European writings during the advent of Imperialism.[32] Plato and Aristotle did not think of themselves as Europeans, nor did they think of the "wooly headed Nubians" living on the southern shores of the Mediterranean as African. We can see differences between the races in the United States created and legitimated by slavery, the genocide of Native Americans, nineteenth- and early twentieth-century immigration, labor, and reproductive policies, institutionalized anti-Semitism, and other forms of racism. Historians describe similar political processes that have simultaneously legitimated and created modern forms of observable gender differences.

There are several points to be made here. Racial and gender contrast schemas originate within projects of social domination. Therefore, we should look to the history of those projects to locate the primary causes of subsequent differences between the races and genders. I suggest that when we look at these racial and gender domination projects together, we will notice that it is the same group of white, European, bourgeois men who have legitimated and brought into being for the rest of us life worlds different from theirs. In this sense, it is one contrast schema we have before us, not two. And it is not one primarily of our making, either ideologically or in actual experience. Moreover, any contrast schema distorts particular differences at the expense of other commonalities. Is it observable differences between men and women we want to emphasize in feminist theory, or differences between the social projects and fantasy lands of white, bourgeois males and the projects and hopes of the rest of us? Furthermore, such schemas also exalt commonalities

at the expense of differences. The masculine and Euro-centric world view(s) appears more coherent than do the collective world views of those it defines as "other." It is different subjugations to which we are assigned by our single set of rulers, and these differences occur within women's history and African history as well as between the two histories. Finally, while there is no denying that men and women in our culture live in different experiential worlds, there is something at least faintly anachronistic about our emphasis on these differences during a period when they are presumably disappearing for many of us. Imagine how much greater these differences were for the sex-segregated lives of the nineteenth-century bourgeoisie. As the divisions of human activity and social experience that created the "men" and "women" in the bourgeois nineteenth-century sense disappear, should we not expect feminine and masculine world views in these groups to begin to merge? As a woman doing "men's work" as well as traditional "women's work," I notice that my ethical concerns are more often rights oriented than are those of women who are still immersed full time in family and childrearing. Furthermore, was not the Counterculture of the 1960s objecting, much as do Gilligan's women, to the limited moral and political choices offered them? Does anyone really want to say that the 1960s expressed a feminine revolution?[33] Could anyone do so without falling into the problem of gender totemism I take up next?

The contrast schema is valuable for identifying the far less than human aspects of the Western world view within which we are all supposed to want to live out our lives. Focusing on women's and Africans' different realities clarifies how much less than human that world view is. My cautions here are about tendencies to exalt women's different reality when it is less than fully human, not the only alternative reality, and is disappearing.

The Problem of Metaphoric Explanation

Race and gender metaphors have often been used to explain other phenomena. The behavior of Africans, Afro-Americans, native Americans, and other racially dominated groups; male homosexual behavior; and the reproductive behavior of females (and sometimes even of males) among apes, sheep, bees, and other non-humans have all been characterized as "feminized" (and by scientists!). Women's subjugation or the condition of the proletariat is described as slavery where the rhetorical appeal is to the image of African slavery.

That is not happening in either of the literatures we are considering. But a more subtle kind of metaphoric explanation may be occurring. Namely, differences that correlate with sex difference are conceptualized as gender differences; those that correlate with race difference are conceptualized as racial differences. As we all know, correlation is not the most reliable form of explanation. For instance, because women in our culture tend to have an ethic of caring rather than of rights, this is conceptualized as feminine. If men of African descent also tend toward an ethic of caring rather than rights, we need to look beyond Western women's distinctive social experiences to identify the social conditions tending to produce this kind of ethics. Our gender totemism obscures for us the origins of the gender dichotomies we observe. What is interesting about the totemism anthropologists describe is not the relationship between the signifier and the thing signified, but between the signifiers. It is not the relationship between one tribe and wolves, and another tribe and snakes that anthropologists have found revealing, but between the meanings of wolves vs. snakes for both tribes.[34] Similarly, attention to gender totemism in our characterization of world views leads us to examine the meanings of masculinity and femininity for both men and women rather than the fit between these meanings and observable beliefs and behaviors. Why is it important for women and men to be culturally assigned different moralities? What social arrangements do such designations legitimate?

Towards a "Unified Field Theory"

Thinking about this curious coincidence directs us to seek different kinds of explanations of observable gender differences than those we have favored. What we need is something akin to a "unified field theory"; that is, one that can account for the gender differences, but also for the dichotomized Africanist/Euro-centric world views. If we had such a theory we would certainly have an intellectual structure quite as impressive as that provided by Newton's laws of mechanics, for it would be able to chart the "laws of tendency of patriarchy" and also the "laws of tendency of racism," their independent and conjoined consequences for social life and social

thought. I make no pretenses to be able to formulate such a useful conceptual apparatus. However, I can point to three analytical notions that illuminate different casual aspects of the correlated dichotomies, and out of which might be constructed the framework for such a powerful social theory.

However, before I turn to these three notions, I want to eliminate one popular idea from this collection of fruitful analytical instruments. The biological explanations that some feminists and Africanists (not to mention, of course, sexists and racists) have favored lose their last vestiges of plausibility once we acknowledge the coincidence.[35] Now, it cannot be denied that our sex-differing embodiments do and should tend to give us different kinds of life experiences. Feminism should not want to replicate Cartesian denial of the importance of our sexed embodiment. Menstruation, female orgasm, pregnancy, birthing, lactation, and menopause are distinctive to females, and it would be odd if these distinctive life experiences had no effect at all on our beliefs and behaviors.[36] But African men do not have these life experiences, and yet their world view apparently resembles European women's more than it does European men's. In the creation of world views, the effects of biologically differing experiences evidently are outweighed by other differences in life experiences. Perhaps these considerations will not convince those feminist and African emancipationists interested in exploring further possible casual relations between biological difference and mental life, but it should at least alert them to the need for more complex and empirically reliable explanatory accounts than any produced so far.

"The Feminine" and "The African" As Categories of Challenge

Historians have suggested that "the feminine" functioned as a "category of challenge" in eighteenth-century French thought.[37] Perhaps this notion can be used more generally to conceptualize the similarities in the world views of women and peoples of African descent. We can think of both "the feminine" and "the African" as having important functions as categories of challenge. The categories were, in the first place, but mirror images of the culturally created categories, "men" and "European." They had no substantive referents independent of the social relations created by, and self-images of, men and Europeans. Women were "not men" – they were what men reject in themselves. Africans were "not European" – they were what Europeans rejected in their own lives. (And, perhaps, these categories also express what women and Africans, respectively, claimed for themselves as unappropriatable by the increasing hegemony of a masculinized and Euro-centric world view.) As categories of challenge, the feminine and African world views name what is absent in the thinking and social activities of men and Europeans, what is relegated to "others" to think, feel, and do. In their calls for science and epistemologies, ethics and politics that are not loyal to gender or race dominance projects, we can see in Africanism and feminism "the return of the repressed."[38]

While this notion illuminates ideological aspects of the world views characteristic of Western men and the various groups making up "the rest," it needs to be supplemented by more concrete accounts of the differences in social activity and experience that make the dichotomized views appropriate for different peoples. The next two notions are useful for this task.

Conceptualizers vs. Executors

Marxists point out that it is the separation of the conception and execution of labor within capitalist economic production that permits the bourgeoisie to gain control of workers' labor.[39] Where craft laborers are the ones who know how to make a pair of shoes or a loaf of bread, in industrialized economies, this knowledge of the labor process is transferred to bosses and machines. Capitalist industrialization has increasingly infused all human labor processes. Now, industrial processes are responsible not only for the things made in factories, but also for such products of human labor as the results of scientific inquiry, social services, and encultured children.

This analysis of the increasing division of labor between conceptualizers and executors illuminates additional aspects of the shared relationship between European and African labor, on the one hand, and men's and women's labor, on the other. Imperialism can be understood as enforcing the transfer to Europeans and Americans of the conceptualization and control of the daily labor of Africans. The construction of an ideology that attributed different natures and world views to Europeans and Africans occurred as an attempt by Europeans and Americans to justify this imperial-

ism. This ideology justified the exploitation underway. With the coming of imperialism to Africa, Americans and Europeans seized the power to decide what labor Africans would perform and who would benefit from this labor. Henceforth, Africans would labor to benefit Euro-American societies, whether as diamond miners, as domestic servants, as the most menial of industrial wage laborers, or as wage or salve labor on plantations in Africa or America. But the practices of imperialism made the ideological distinctions between Europeans and Africans come true to some extent. Only Europeans were permitted to perform the conceptualizing, administrative labor that requires the kind of world view attributed to Europeans. Prior to the arrival of Europeans in Africa, vast trade networks had been organized by Africans; influential centers of African Islamic scholarship existed – Africans had conceptualized and administered a variety of pan-African activities. The conceptualization and administration of complex human activities by peoples of African descent was appropriated by imperialistic nations.[40] Thus, the African vs. the European world views are simultaneously ideological constructs of the imperialists, and also true reflections of the dichotomized social experience imperialism went on to create. (We have here, incidentally, a richer understanding of the nature of ideologies than various popular uses of the term suggest.)

Similarly, the emergence of male domination among our distant ancestors can be understood as the transfer of the conceptualization and control of women's sexuality, reproduction, and production labor to men – a process intensified and systematized in new ways during the last three centuries in the West. Engels referred to this original moment as "the world historic defeat of the female sex."[41] Here, too, the attribution of different natures and world views to women and men originally occurs, presumably, as an ideological construct by the dominators (we can certainly see this process in the last three centuries even if its origins in human history are only dimly graspable), but subsequently becomes true as the control of women's labor is shifted from women to men.

But now, peoples engaged in struggles against imperialism and male dominance are conceptualizing their own labor and experience counter to their rulers' conceptions. It is precisely the fact that Blacks and women increasingly conceptualize their own activities that permits the emergence of Africanism and feminism. Furthermore, this charge has economic, political, and social origins that lie outside Africanism and feminism. For women, the revolution in birth control, the increased need for women in public employment and the consequent double-day of work are key conditions that permit women to conceptualize their own labor and experience in new ways. For Africans, the "internal logic" of capitalism, which requires more consumers, higher-skilled labor, and legitimations of both by local, state, and international economic, political, and educational policies, is among the conditions that permit Africans to conceptualize their own labor and experience in new ways. The political dynamics that created "Africans" and "women" in the first place are disappearing, as are the Africans and women defined originally by the appropriation of the conceptualization of their activity and experience. (I am not arguing that racism and sexism are disappearing, but that they are taking new forms.) Those still caught in the economic, political, and intellectual confines of the "feminine" and the "African" are precisely not the movers and shakers of these movements for emancipation. Those who participate in Africanist and feminist political struggles have far more ambiguous race and gender options, respectively, than the Africans and women whose emancipation they would advance. At least among women, it is precisely those whose economic and political options remain only sex specific, only traditional, who are most resistant – and for good concrete reasons – to the feminist political agenda.[42]

Thus, we should expect differences in cognitive styles and world views from peoples engaged in different kinds of social activities. And we should expect similarities from peoples engaged in similar kinds of social activities. The kind of account I am suggesting here finds precedents in tendencies within the sociology of knowledge. Examinations of social structure reveal why adversarial modes of reasoning are prevalent in one culture and not in another; why instrumental calculation infuses one culture's content and style of thought but not another's. Why is it that the free will vs. determinism dispute does not surface in ancient Greek philosophy, but is so central in European thought from the seventeenth century on? Why is it that we hear nothing about individual rights in ancient Greek thought – a model of misogyny and appeals to the naturalness of many kinds of domination. Something happened to European, bourgeois men's life expectations during the fifteenth to seventeenth centuries to ensure that a focus on individuals, their

rights, the effect of the "value-neutral," impersonal "laws" to which men discovered their bodies were subject, and the power of men's wills would have to become crucial problematics if these men were to understand themselves and the new world they found themselves in. Was there anything in European women's social experience during this period (fifteenth to seventeenth century) to lead them to focus on such issues? Probably yes and no, if one freely reads the disputes in history. What about women in the purportedly traditional nuclear families in the West today? Why should they be expected to hold a world view organized around distinctions among forces within and outside their control, or on problems of adjudicating between the conflicting rights of autonomous individuals? What about the social experience of the peoples in the cultures Europe has colonized? We should not expect there to be much reason for slaves to find interest in the free will vs. determinism dispute, or issues of individual rights. For reasons originating in an analysis of social relations, we should expect white, bourgeois. European men to have cognitive styles and a world view that is different from the cognitive styles and world views of those whose daily activities permit the direction of social life by those men.

Developmental Processes

In the form in which they have been presented, the developmental explanations for the gender-differing world views cited as possible support for Gilligan's discoveries, and elaborated by the feminist object relations theorists, are thrown into doubt by this correlation. No doubt there are similar processes of producing gender in individuals cross-culturally. Gender- differing patterns of separation from the first caretaker, of being inserted in one's gender-proper place in the world of the father, and of gaining an individual and gendered identity are presumably common to all young humans in cultures structured by male-dominance. But these commonalities do not appear powerful enough to produce distinctively cross-cultural masculine and feminine world views – at least not the world views generalized from modern, Western gender differences.

Nevertheless, it is possible that object relations theory can be historicized in illuminating ways. One hint about how to do so is provided by Isaac Balbus.[43] He argues that if we take the intensity of the infant's initial identity with its caretaker (mother) as one cultural variable, and the severity of the infant's separation from that caretaker as another cultural variable, object relations theory can account for the growth of different forms of the state, and for different cultural attitudes toward nature. He points out that there are thoroughly misogynous cultures that are loath to dominate other cultural groups and/or nature, and less misogynous cultures that regularly engage in the domination of other groups and of nature. Balbus is not concerned with issues of racism, and he only begins to explore the anthropological and historical evidence that reveals cultural variations in the intensity of infant identity with the caretaker and the subsequent severity of separation that occurs.

Obviously, a great deal of theoretical and empirical work must be done for this intriguing theory to explain how Western men's infantile experience leads to one set of ontologies, ethics, and modes of knowledge-seeking, while the infantile experience of the rest of us tends to produce a different set. The core of the self we keep for life appears to be highly influenced by our prerational experiences as infants – by the opportunities child-rearing patterns offer us to identify with paternal authority, both as a reaction to and a refuge from initial maternal authority. Thus, it would be foolish to overlook the contributions a theory of infantile enculturation could make to the unified field theory that we need.

Conclusion

This essay appears to have traveled far afield of considerations of women's morality. However, I think such a trip is necessary in order to bring to this topic an enlarged vision of the social constraints within which moral concerns are formulated by women and men in different cultures. I am affirming the tendency in the most radical feminist and Africanist thought to identify and legitimate the distinctive cognitive styles and ethical concerns of women and people of African descent. Though the emancipation efforts of our foremothers and forefathers were brave and well-designed attacks on the biological determinist thinking and politics of the male-domination and racism that respectively they faced, we can see the problems with asserting that women's emancipation lies in wanting to be just like men, or that Black emancipation will occur when people of African descent become just like their oppressors. We are different, not primarily by nature's design, but as a result of the social subjugations we have lived through and continue to experience. And yet, those histories of social subjugation offer a hope for the future. From those small differences that we can now observe between the genders and among the races in different cultures can emerge a vast difference between the defensively gendered and raced cultures we are, and the reciprocity-seeking, difference-appreciating, raceless and genderless cultures we could become. We could have cultural difference without the cultural domination endemic to so much of the history of gender and race. (I take race, like gender, to be a social construct and, thus, to have a history.) But to move in that direction, we need a more adequate definition of the forces investing in sexism and racism.

The "women's morality" Gilligan has so astutely drawn to our attention is, most likely, the kind of morality appropriate for everyone in the daily interactions with those dependent upon us, and upon whom we depend, where we should be unwilling to use "rights" and force to obtain our moral goals. The pity is that Western men are not produced in such a way that they can recognize the inappropriateness of a rights orientation in many aspects of social life, and that Western women and non-Western peoples have such limited access to the rights available to Western men.[44]

Notes

1 Carol Gilligan, "Women's Place in Man's Life Cycle," *Harvard Educational Review* 49:4 (1979); *In a Different Voice: Psychological Theory and Women's Development* (Cambridge: Harvard University Press, 1982). Gilligan is careful to point out that girls and women appeal equally to the "rights orientation" and the "care orientation" in justifying their moral decisions. However, boys and men far less often reason through the "care orientation," and the incidence of their appeal to these concerns decreases as they age. In the talk she gave at the Stony Brook conference, she suggested that there is something about achieving adult masculine identity in our culture that appears to require the suppression of that concern for caring that is more evident in boys' youthful reasoning. Thus, in referring to these contrasting moral orientations as "femi-

nine" and "masculine," I am not implying that they are "natural" or even universally correlated with the actual moral reasoning exhibited by women and men, but only that the "care orientation" is less often and the "rights orientation" more often to be found in men's moral thinking. These two moral orientations appear to be associated with femininity and masculinity.

2 Hilary Rose, "Hand, Brain and Heart: A Feminist Epistemology for the Natural Sciences," *Signs* 9:1 (1983); Jane Flax, "Political Philosophy and the Patriarchal Unconscious: A Psychoanalytic Perspective on Epistemology and Metaphysics," in S. Harding and M. Hintikka, *Discovering Reality: Feminist Perspectives on Epistemology, Metaphysics, Methodology and Philosophy of Science*, (Dordrecht: D. Reidel, 1983); Nancy Hartsock, "The Feminist Standpoint: Developing the Ground for a Specifically Feminist Historical Materialism," in Harding and Hintikka; Dorothy Smith, "Women's Perspective as a Radical Critique of Sociology," *Sociological Inquiry* 44 (1974); "Some Implications of a Sociology for Women," in N. Glazer and H. Waehrer, eds., *Woman in a Man-Made World* (Chicago: Rand-McNally, 1977); "A Sociology for Women," in J. Sherman and E. Beck, eds., *The Prism of Sex: Essays in the Sociology of Knowledge* (Madison: University of Wisconsin Press, 1979). See also, Sandra Harding, "Is Gender a Variable in Conceptions of Rationality? A Survey of Issues," *Dialectica* 36: 2–3 (1982); reprinted in Carol Gould, ed., *Beyond Domination: New Perspectives on Women and Philosophy* (Totowa, N.J.: Rowman and Allenheld, 1983); and *The Science Question in Feminism* (Ithaca: Cornell University Press, 1986).

3 Sara Ruddick, "Maternal Thinking," *Feminist Studies* 6:2 (1980).

4 See Flax (cited above); Nancy Chodorow, *The Reproduction of Mothering* (Berkeley: University of California Press, 1978); Dorothy Dinnerstein, *The Mermaid and the Minotaur: Sexual Arrangements and Human Malaise* (New York: Harper and Row, 1976). See also the uses to which Dinnerstein's version of this theory is put in the last two chapters of Isaac Balbus, *Marxism and Domination* (Princeton: University Press, 1982). We shall raise questions about the ability of this account to provide a causal explanation of such general characteristics of human thought as these ontologies.

5 See the Hartsock and Smith papers cited above.

6 Russell Means, "The Future of the Earth," *Mother Jones*; Joseph Needham, "History and Human Values: A Chinese Perspective for World Science and Technology," in Hilary Rose and Steven Rose, eds., *Ideology of/in the Natural Sciences*: (Cambridge: Schenkman, 1979).

7 See Bettina Aptheker, *Woman's Legacy* (Amherst: University of Massachusetts Press, 1982); Angela Davis, "The Black Woman's Role in the Community of Slaves," *The Black Scholar*, Dec. 1971; Gisela Bock,

"Racism and Sexism in Nazi Germany: Motherhood, Compulsory Sterilization, and the State," *Signs* 8:3 (1983), bell hooks, *Ain't I a Woman* (Boston: South End Press, 1981), and *Feminist Theory From Margin to Center* (Boston: South End Press, 1984). In racially stratified cultures, androcentrism and sexism always prescribe different restrictions for women in the subjugated and dominant races; in gender stratified societies, racism takes different forms for men and women. In the Stony Brook lecture, Gilligan reported that the only group of women she had studied in which the "care orientation" did not figure in their moral reasoning was a (small) group of Black women medical students. See the novels of Buchi Emecheta, especially *The Slave Girl* (New York: George Braziller, 1977), and *The Joys of Motherhood* (London: Heinemann, 1980) for one vision of growing up female in Nigeria. The novels and poetry of Alice Walker, Tony Morrison, Audre Lorde, Paule Marshall, Ntozake Shange, and many other Black American writers present this experience on this side of the Atlantic.

8 The issues of this paper are developed from a much longer argument that appears as chapter 7 in *The Science Question in Feminism*. A number of the conceptual problems I can only point to here are explored more fully in this longer essay.

9 Vernon Dixon, "World Views and Research Methodology," in L. M. King, V. J. Dixon, W. W. Nobles, eds., *African Philosophy: Assumptions and Paradigms for Research on Black Persons* (Los Angeles: Fanon Center Publication, Charles R. Drew Postgraduate Medical School, 1976). See also the sources Dixon cites, and Gerald G. Jackson. "The African Genesis of the Black Perspective in Helping," in R. L. Jones, ed., *Black Psychology* (2nd edn) (New York: Harper & Row, 1980), 314–31.

10 Dixon, 54–5.

11 Dixon, 55.

12 Ibid., quoting Rosalie Cohen, "The Influence of Conceptual Rule-sets on Measures of Learning Ability," George Gamble and James Bond, *Race and Intelligence*, American Anthropologist (1971), 47.

13 Dixon, 58.

14 Ibid.

15 Ibid.

16 Ibid.

17 Ibid.

18 Dixon, 58–9.

19 Dixon, 61.

20 Ibid., quoting Rosalie Cohen (see note 12).

21 Dixon, 62–3.

22 Dixon, 63.

23 Ibid., quoting John S. Mbiti, *African Religions and Philosophy* (London: Heinemann, 1969), 108.

24 Dixon, 64.

25 Ibid.

26 Dixon, 69–70.

27 Dixon, 70.

28 Judith Sharpiro, "Gender Totemism and Feminist Thought," paper presented to the University of Pennsylvania Mid-Atlantic Seminar for the Study of Women and Society, Oct. 17, 1984.

29 As indicated earlier, I can only briefly point to these problems here. See chapter 7 of *The Science Question in Feminism* for a more comprehensive discussion.

30 For a discussion by an anthropologist of the problems with contrast schemas, see Robert Horton, "Lévy-Bruhl, Durkheim and the Scientific Revolution," in R. Horton and R. Finnegan, eds., *Modes of Thought: Essays on Thinking in Western and Non-Western Societies* (London: Faber and Faber, 1973). See also Paulin Hountondji, *African Philosophy: Myth and Reality* (Bloomington; University of Indiana Press, 1983), and Lanciany Keita, "African Philosophical Systems: A Rational Reconstruction," *The Philosophical Forum*, 9:2–3 (1977–8) for (African) philosophers' criticism of the African vs. European schema.

31 For an attempt to peer through those distant mists, see Salvatore Cucchiari. "The Gender Revolution and the Transition from Bisexual Horde to Patrilocal Band: The Origins of Gender Hierarchy," in Sherry B. Ortner and Harriet Whitehead, eds., *Sexual Meanings: The Cultural Construction of Gender and Sexuality* (New York: Cambridge University Press, 1981).

32 See Keita (cited above).

33 Some observers come pretty close to such a claim. See, e.g., David Riesman's characterization of the "other directed" young emerging in urban centers in the 1950s, in chapter 1 of *The Lonely Crowd* (New Haven: Yale University Press, 1973); Christopher Lasch's bewailing of *The Culture of Narcissism* (New York: Warner Books, 1979). See Balbus's discussion of the 1960s for a more sensitive analysis of the emergence of a cultural mentality that was in different respects both less masculinist and more intensely misogynous (cited above). See, also, Dennis Altman, *The Homosexualization of America* (Boston: Beacon Press, 1983) for clues to the continuation of these tendencies into the 1970s and 1980s.

34 See Shapiro (cited above).

35 Examples of biological determinist accounts by African emancipationists can be found in Dubois Phillip McGee, "Psychology: Melanin, the Physiological Basis for Psychological Oneness," in L. M. King, V. J. Dixon, W. W. Nobles, eds., *African Philosophy*. With respect to gender differences, the Lacanian followers of Freud appear to be arguing against their object relations colleagues that no variety of "alternative parenting" – by fathers, homosexual co-parents, etc. – can overcome the effects of the mother–child bond or the father's phallic presence. However, even the object relations theorists sometimes intimate that biology is to blame for "sexual arrangements and human malaise." Dinnerstein (cited above) discusses the legacy the "obstetrical dilemma" at the dawn of human history left for human gender relations. Again, while Mary O'Brien insists that biology is not destiny, her account of differences in the consciousnesses we have of our reproductive systems suggests a biological basis for gender ideology in *The Politics of Reproduction* (New York: Routledge and Kegan Paul, 1981). Whether or not they are in fact writing within the assumptions of feminist theory as they assume, Jean Elshtain and Carol MacMillan think feminism would be advanced by a better understanding of the significances of biological difference; see Jean Elshtain, "Feminists Against the Family," *The Nation*, Nov. 17, 1979; *Public Man, Private Woman: Women in Social and Political Thought* (Princeton: University Press, 1981); "Antigone's Daughters," *Democracy* 2:2 (1982); Carol MacMillan, *Woman, Reason and Nature* (Princeton: University Press, 1982).

36 And, at any rate, public policy needs to recognize these biological differences: pregnancy does not "contingently" happen to occur in female bodies, as the US Supreme Court has recently held; occupational hazards have different effects on male and female reproductive systems.

37 See Maurice Bloch and Jean Bloch, "Women and the Dialectics of Nature in Eighteenth Century French Thought," in Carol MacCormack and Marilyn Strathern, eds., *Nature, Culture and Gender* (Cambridge: University Press, 1980).

38 The phrase is Jane Flax's (cited above).

39 See Harry Braverman, *Labor and Monopoly Capital* (New York: Monthly Review Press, 1974.)

40 See Keita (cited above).

41 Friedrich Engels, *The Origin of the Family, Private Property and the State* (New York: International Publishers, 1942).

42 See e.g., Kristin Luker, *Abortion and the Politics of Motherhood* (Berkeley: University of California Press, 1984).

43 See chapter 9 in Balbus, *Marxism and Domination*.

44 I thank Eva Kittay and Diana Meyers for their helpful questions that enabled me to strengthen this paper.

PART IX

Philosophy and Transatlantic African Slavery

The Nature of Slavery

Frederick Douglass

More than twenty years of my life were consumed in a state of slavery. My childhood was environed by the baneful peculiarities of the slave system. I grew up to manhood in the presence of this hydra-headed monster – not as a master – not as an idle spectator – not as the guest of the slaveholder – but as A SLAVE, eating the bread and drinking the cup of slavery with the most degraded of my brother-bondmen, and sharing with them all the painful conditions of their wretched lot. In consideration of these facts, I feel that I have a right to speak, and to speak *strongly*. Yet, my friends, I feel bound to speak truly.

Goading as have been the cruelties to which I have been subjected – bitter as have been the trials through which I have passed – exasperating as have been, and still are, the indignities offered to my manhood – I find in them no excuse for the slightest departure from truth in dealing with any branch of this subject.

First of all, I will state, as well as I can, the legal and social relation of master and slave. A master is one – to speak in the vocabulary of the southern states – who claims and exercises a right of property in the person of a fellow-man. This he does with the force of the law and the sanction of southern religion. The law gives the master absolute power over the slave. He may work him, flog him, hire him out, sell him, and, in certain contingencies, *kill* him, with perfect impunity. The slave is a human being, divested of all rights – reduced to the level of a brute – a mere "chattel" in the eye of the law – placed beyond the circle of human brotherhood – cut off from his kind – his name, which the "recording angel" may have enrolled in heaven, among the blest is impiously inserted in a *master's ledger*, with horses, sheep, and swine. In law, the slave has no wife, no children, no country, and no home. He can own nothing, possess nothing, acquire nothing, but what must belong to another. To eat the fruit of his own toil, to clothe his person with the work of his own hands, is considered stealing. He toils that another may reap the fruit; he is industrious that another may live in idleness; he eats unbolted meal that another may eat the bread of fine flour; he labors in chains at home, under a burning sun and biting lash, that another may ride in ease and splendor abroad; he lives in ignorance that another may be educated; he is abused that another may be exalted; he rests his toil-worn limbs on the cold, damp ground that another may repose on the softest pillow; he is clad in coarse and tattered raiment that another may be arrayed in purple and fine linen; he is sheltered only by the wretched hovel that a master may dwell in a magnificent mansion; and to this condition he is bound down as by an arm of iron.

From this monstrous relation there springs an unceasing stream of most revolting cruelties. The very accompaniments of the slave system stamp it as the offspring of hell itself. To ensure good behavior, the slaveholder relies on the whip; to induce proper humility, he relies on the whip; to rebuke what he is pleased to term insolence, he relies on the whip; to supply the place of wages as an incentive to toil, he relies on the whip; to bind down the spirit of the slave, to imbrute and destroy his manhood, he relies on the whip, the chain, the gag, the thumb-screw, the pillory, the bowie-knife, the pistol, and the blood-hound. These are the necessary and unvarying accompaniments of the system. Whenever slavery is found, these horrid instruments are also found. Whether on the coast of Africa, among the savage tribes, or in South Carolina, among the refined and civilized, slavery is the same, and its accompaniments one and the same. It makes no difference whether the slaveholder worships the God of the Christians, or is a follower of Mahomet, he is the minister of the same cruelty, and the author of the same misery. *Slavery* is always *slavery*; always the same foul, haggard, and damning scourge, whether found in the eastern or in the western hemisphere.

There is a still deeper shade to be given to this picture. The physical cruelties are indeed sufficiently harassing and revolting; but they are as a few grains of sand on the sea shore, or a few drops of water in the great ocean, compared with the stupendous wrongs which it inflicts upon the mental, moral, and religious nature of its hapless victims. It is only when we contemplate the slave as a moral and intellectual being, that we can adequately comprehend the unparalleled enormity of slavery, and the intense criminality of the slaveholder. I have said that the slave was a man. "What a piece of work is man! How noble in reason! How infinite in faculties! In form and moving how express and admirable! In action how like an angel! In apprehension how like a God! the beauty of the world! the paragon of animals!"

The slave is a man, "the image of God," but "a little lower than the angels"; possessing a soul, eternal and indestructible; capable of endless happiness, or immeasurable woe; a creature of hopes and fears, of affections and passions, of joys and sorrows, and he is endowed with those mysterious powers by which man soars above the things of time and sense, and grasps, with undying tenacity, the elevating and sublimely glorious idea of a God. It is *such* a being that is smitten and blasted. The first work of slavery is to mar and deface those characteristics of its victims which distinguish *men* from *things*, and *persons* from *property*. Its first aim is to destroy all sense of high moral and religious responsibility. It reduces man to a mere machine. It cuts him off from his Maker, it hides from him the laws of God, and leaves him to grope his way

from time to eternity in the dark, under the arbitrary and despotic control of a frail, depraved, and sinful fellow-man. As the serpent-charmer of India is compelled to extract the deadly teeth of his venomous prey before he is able to handle him with impunity, so the slaveholder must strike down the conscience of the slave before he can obtain the entire mastery over his victim.

It is, then, the first business of the enslaver of men to blunt, deaden, and destroy the central principle of human responsibility. Conscience is, to the individual soul, and to society, what the law of gravitation is to the universe. It holds society together; it is the basis of all trust and confidence; it is the pillar of all moral rectitude. Without it, suspicion would take the place of trust; vice would be more than a match for virtue; men would prey upon each other, like the wild beasts of the desert; and earth would become a *hell*.

Nor is slavery more adverse to the conscience than it is to the mind. This is shown by the fact, that in every state of the American Union, where slavery exists, except the state of Kentucky, there are laws absolutely prohibitory of education among the slaves. The crime of teaching a slave to read is punishable with severe fines and imprisonment, and, in some instances, with *death itself*.

Nor are the laws respecting this matter a dead letter. Cases may occur in which they are disregarded, and a few instances may be found where slaves may have learned to read; but such are isolated cases, and only prove the rule. The great mass of slaveholders look upon education among the slaves as utterly subversive of the slave system. I well remember when my mistress first announced to my master that she had discovered that I could read. His face colored at once with surprise and chagrin. He said that "I was ruined, and my value as a slave destroyed; that a slave should know nothing but to obey his master; that to give a Negro an inch would lead him to take an ell; that having learned how to read, I would soon want to know how to write; and that by-and-by I would be running away." I think my audience will bear witness to the correctness of this philosophy, and to the literal fulfillment of this prophecy.

It is perfectly well understood at the south, that to educate a slave is to make him discontented with slavery, and to invest him with a power which shall open to him the treasures of freedom; and since the object of the slaveholder is to maintain complete authority over his slave, his constant vigilance is exercised to prevent everything which militates against, or endangers, the stability of his authority. Education being among the menacing influences, and, perhaps, the most dangerous, is, therefore, the most cautiously guarded against.

It is true that we do not often hear of the enforcement of the law, punishing as a crime the teaching of slaves to read, but this is not because of a want of disposition to enforce it. The true reason or explanation of the matter is this: there is the greatest unanimity of opinion among the white population in the south in favor of the policy of keeping the slave in ignorance. There is, perhaps, another reason why the law against education is so seldom violated. The slave is too poor to be able to offer a temptation sufficiently strong to induce a white man to violate it; and it is not to be supposed that in a community where the moral and religious sentiment is in favor of slavery, many martyrs will be found sacrificing their liberty and lives by violating those prohibitory enactments.

As a general rule, then, darkness reigns over the abodes of the enslaved, and "how great is that darkness!"

We are sometimes told of the contentment of the slaves, and are entertained with vivid pictures of their happiness. We are told that they often dance and sing; that their masters frequently give them wherewith to make merry; in fine, that they have little of which to complain. I admit that the slave does sometimes sing, dance, and appear to be merry. But what does this prove? It only proves to my mind, that though slavery is armed with a thousand stings, it is not able entirely to kill the elastic spirit of the bondman. That spirit will rise and walk abroad, despite of whips and chains, and extract from the cup of nature occasional drops of joy and gladness. No thanks to the slaveholder, nor to slavery, that the vivacious captive may sometimes dance in his chains; his very mirth in such circumstances stands before God as an accusing angel against his enslaver.

It is often said, by the opponents of the anti-slavery cause, that the condition of the people of Ireland is more deplorable than that of the American slaves. Far be it from me to underrate the sufferings of the Irish people. They have been long oppressed; and the same heart that prompts me to plead the cause of the American bondman, makes it impossible for me not to sympathize with the oppressed of all lands. Yet I must say that there is no analogy between the two cases. The Irishman is poor, but he is not a slave. He may be in rags, but he is not a slave. He is still the master of his own body, and can say with the poet, "The hand of Douglass is his own." "The world is all before him, where to choose"; and poor as may be my opinion of the British parliament, I cannot believe that it will ever sink to such a depth of infamy as to pass a law for the recapture of fugitive Irishmen! The shame and scandal of kidnapping will long remain wholly monopolized by the American congress. The Irishman has not only the liberty to emigrate from his country, but he has liberty at home. He can write, and speak, and cooperate for the attainment of his rights and the redress of his wrongs.

The multitude can assemble upon all the green hills and fertile plains of the Emerald Isle; they can pour out their grievances, and proclaim their wants without molestation; and the press, that "swift-winged messenger," can bear the tidings of their doings to the extreme bounds of the civilized world. They have their "Conciliation Hall," on the banks of the Liffey, their reform clubs, and their newspapers; they pass resolutions, send forth addresses, and enjoy the right of petition. But how is it with the American slave? Where may he assemble? Where is his Conciliation Hall? Where are his newspapers? Where is his right of petition? Where is his freedom of speech? his liberty of the press? and his right of locomotion? He is said to be happy; happy men can speak. But ask the slave what is his condition – what his state of mind – what he thinks of enslavement? and you had as well address your inquiries to the *silent dead*. There comes no *voice* from the enslaved. We are left to gather his feelings by imagining what ours would be, were our souls in his soul's stead.

If there were no other fact descriptive of slavery, than that the slave is dumb, this alone would be sufficient to mark the slave system as a grand aggregation of human horrors.

Most who are present, will have observed that leading men in this country have been putting forth their skill to secure quiet to the nation. A system of measures to promote this object was adopted a few months ago in congress. The result of those measures is known. Instead of quiet, they have produced alarm; instead of peace, they have brought us war; and so it must ever be.

While this nation is guilty of the enslavement of three millions of innocent men and women, it is as idle to think of having a sound and lasting peace, as it is to think there is no God to take cognizance of the affairs of men. There can be no peace to the wicked while slavery continues in the land. It will be condemned; and while it is condemned there will be agitation. Nature must cease to be nature; men must become monsters; humanity must be transformed; christianity must be exterminated; all ideas of justice and the laws of eternal goodness must be utterly blotted out from the human soul, – ere a system so foul and infernal can escape condemnation, or this guilty republic can have a sound, enduring peace – **December 1, 1850**.

43

The Concept of Slavery

Winthrop D. Jordan

At first glance, one is likely to see merely a fog of inconsistency and vagueness enveloping the terms *servant* and *slave* as they were used both in England and in seventeenth-century America. When Hamlet declaims "O what a rogue and peasant slave am I," the term seems to have a certain elasticity. When Peter Heylyn defines it in 1627 as "that ignominious word, *Slave*; whereby we use to call ignoble fellows, and the more base sort of people,"[1] the term seems useless as a key to a specific social status. And when we find in the American colonies a reference in 1665 to "Jacob a negro slave and servant to Nathaniel Utye,"[2] it is tempting to regard slavery as having been in the first half of the seventeenth century merely a not very elevated sort of servitude.

In one sense, it was, since the concept embodied in the terms *servitude*, *service*, and *servant* was widely embracive. *Servant* was more a generic term than *slave*. Slaves could be "servants" – as they were eventually and ironically to become in the antebellum South – but servants *should not* be "slaves." This injunction, which was common in England, suggests a measure of precision in the concept of slavery. In fact there was a large measure which merits closer inspection.

First of all, the "slave's" loss of freedom was complete. "Of all men which be destitute of libertie

From Winthrop D. Jordan, *White Over Black: American Attitudes Toward the Negro*, 1550–1812 (1968), published for the Institute of Early American History and Culture, copyright © 1968 by the University of North Carolina Press; by kind permission of the University of North Carolina Press.

or freedome," explained Henry Swinburne in his *Briefe Treatise of Testaments and Last Willes* (1590), "the slave is in greatest subjection, for a slave is that person which is in servitude or bondage to an other, even against nature." "Even his children," moreover, "are infected with the Leproise of his father's bondage." Swinburne was at pains to distinguish this condition from that of the villein, whom he likened to the *Ascriptitius Glebæ* of the civil law, "one that is ascrited or assigned to a ground or farme, for the perpetuall tilling or manuring thereof." "A villeine," he insisted, "howsoever he may seeme like unto a slave, yet his bondage is not so great."[3] Swinburne's was the prevailing view of bond slavery; only the preciseness of emphasis was unusual. At law, much more clearly than in literary usage, "bond slavery" implied utter deprivation of liberty.

Slavery was also thought of as a perpetual condition. While it had not yet come invariably to mean lifetime labor, it was frequently thought of in those terms. Except sometimes in instances of punishment for crime, slavery was open ended; in contrast to servitude, it did not involve a definite term of years. Slavery was perpetual also in the sense that it was often thought of as hereditary. It was these dual aspects of perpetuity which were to assume such importance in America.

So much was slavery a complete loss of liberty that it seemed to Englishmen somehow akin to loss of humanity. No theme was more persistent than the claim that to treat a man as a slave was to treat him as a beast. Almost half a century after Sir Thomas Smith had made this connection a Puritan divine was condemning masters who used "their servants as slaves, or rather as beasts" while Captain

John Smith was moaning about being captured by the Turks and "all sold for slaves, like beasts in a market-place."[4] No analogy could have better demonstrated how strongly Englishmen felt about total loss of personal freedom.

Certain prevalent assumptions about the origins of slavery paralleled this analogy at a different level of intellectual construction. Lawyers and divines alike assumed that slavery was impossible before the Fall, that it violated natural law, that it was instituted by positive human laws, and, more generally, that in various ways it was connected with sin. These ideas were as old as the church fathers and the Roman writers on natural law. In the social atmosphere of pre-Restoration England it was virtually inevitable that they should have been capsulated in the story of Ham. The Reverend Jeremy Taylor (an opponent of the Puritans) explained what it was "that brought servitude or slavery into the world": God had "consigned a sad example that for ever children should be afraid to dishonour their parents, and discover their nakedness, or reveal their turpitude, their follies and dishonours." Sir Edward Coke (himself scarcely a Puritan) declared, "This is assured, That Bondage or Servitude was first inflicted for dishonouring of Parents: For Cham the Father of Canaan . . . seeing the Nakedness of his Father Noah, and shewing it in Derision to his Brethren, was therefore punished in his Son Canaan with Bondage."[5]

The great jurist wrote this in earnest, but at least he did offer another description of slavery's genesis. In it he established what was perhaps the most important and widely acknowledged attribute of slavery: at the time of the Flood "all Things were common to all," but afterward, with the emergence of private property, there "arose battles"; "then it was ordained by Constitution of Nations . . . that he that was taken in Battle should remain Bond to his taker for ever, and he to do with him, all that should come of him, his Will and Pleasure, as with his Beast, or any other Cattle, to give, or to sell, or to kill." This final power, Coke noted, had since been taken away (owing to "the Cruelty of some Lords") and placed in the hands only of kings.[6] The animating rationale here was that captivity in war meant an end to a person's claim to life as a human being; by sparing the captive's life, the captor acquired virtually absolute power over the life of the man who had lost the power to control his own.

More than any other single quality, *captivity* differentiated slavery from servitude. Although there were other, subsidiary ways of becoming a slave, such as being born of slave parents, selling oneself into slavery, or being adjudged to slavery for crime, none of these were considered to explain the way slavery had originated. Slavery was a power relationship; servitude was a relationship of service. Men were "slaves" to the devil but "servants" of God. Men were "galley-slaves," not galley servants. Bondage had never existed in the county of Kent because Kent was "never vanquished by [William] the Conquerour, but yeelded it selfe by composition."[7]

This tendency to equate slavery with captivity had important ramifications. Warfare was usually waged against another people; captives were usually foreigners – "strangers" as they were termed. Until the emergence of nation-states in Europe, by far the most important category of strangers was the non-Christian. International warfare seemed above all a ceaseless struggle between Christians and Turks. Slavery, therefore, frequently appeared to rest upon the "perpetual enmity" which existed between Christians on the one hand and "infidels" and "pagans" on the other.[8] In the sixteenth and seventeenth centuries Englishmen at home could read scores of accounts concerning the miserable fate of Englishmen and other Christians taken into "captivity" by Turks and Moors and oppressed by the "verie worst manner of bondmanship and slaverie."[9] Clearly slavery was tinged by the religious disjunction.

Just as many commentators thought that the spirit of Christianity was responsible for the demise of bondage in England, many divines distinguished between ownership of Christian and of non-Christian servants. The Reverend William Gouge referred to "such servants as being strangers were bond-slaves, over whom masters had a more absolute power than others." The Reverend Henry Smith declared, "He which counteth his servant a slave, is in error: for there is difference betweene beleeving servants and infidell servants."[10] Implicit in every clerical discourse was the assumption that common brotherhood in Christ imparted a special quality to the master–servant relationship.

Slavery did not possess that quality, which made it fortunate that Englishmen did not enslave one another. As we have seen, however, Englishmen did possess a *concept* of slavery, formed by the clustering of several rough but not illogical equations. The slave was treated like a beast. Slavery was inseparable from the evil in men; it was God's punishment upon Ham's prurient disobedience. Enslavement was captivity, the loser's lot in a contest of power. Slaves were infidels or heathens.

On every count, Negroes qualified.

Notes

1 *Hamlet*, II, ii; Heylyn, ΜΙΚΡΌΚΟΣΜΟΣ, 175.

2 *Archives of Maryland*, XLIX, 489.

3 Henry Swinburne, *A Briefe Treatise of Testaments and Last Willes* . . . (London, 1590), 43.

4 William Gouge, *Of Domesticall Duties Eight Treatises* (London, 1622), 690; Edward Arber, ed., *Travels and Works of Captain John Smith* . . . , 2 vols. (Edinburgh, 1910), II, 853.

5 *The Whole Works of the Right Rev. Jeremy Taylor* . . . , 10 vols. (London, 1850–4), X, 453; Sir Edward Coke, *The First Part of the Institutes of the Laws of England: or, a Commentary upon Littleton* . . . , 12th edn (London, 1738), Lib. II, Cap. XI. For the long-standing assumption that slavery was brought about by man's sinfulness see R. W. and A. J. Carlyle, *A History of Medieval Political Theory in the West*, 6 vols. (Edinburgh and London, 1903–36), I, 116–24, II, 119–20.

6 Coke, *Institutes*, Lib. II, Cap. XI.

7 William Lambard[e], *A Perambulation of Kent* . . . (London, 1576), 11. The notion of selling oneself into slavery was very much subsidiary and probably derived from the Old Testament. Isaac Mendelsohn, *Slavery in the Ancient Near East* . . . (New York, 1949), 18, points out that the Old Testament was the only ancient law code to mention voluntary slavery and self-sale.

8 The phrases are from Michael Dalton, *The Countrey Justice* . . . (London, 1655), 191.

9 *The Estate of Christians, Living under the Subjection of the Turke* . . . (London, 1595), 5.

10 Gouge, *Domestical Duties*, 663; *The Sermons of Master Henry Smith* . . . (London, 1607), 40.

44

The Origin of Negro Slavery

Eric Williams

When in 1492 Columbus, representing the Spanish monarchy, discovered the New World, he set in train the long and bitter international rivalry over colonial possessions for which, after four and a half centuries, no solution has yet been found. Portugal, which had initiated the movement of international expansion, claimed the new territories on the ground that they fell within the scope of a papal bull of 1455 authorizing her to reduce to servitude all infidel peoples. The two powers, to avoid controversy, sought arbitration and, as Catholics, turned to the Pope – a natural and logical step in an age when the universal claims of the Papacy were still unchallenged by individuals and governments. After carefully sifting the rival claims, the Pope issued in 1493 a series of papal bulls which established a line of demarcation between the colonial possessions of the two states: the East went to Portugal and the West to Spain. The partition, however, failed to satisfy Portuguese aspirations and in the subsequent year the contending parties reached a more satisfactory compromise in the Treaty of Tordesillas, which rectified the papal judgment to permit Portuguese ownership of Brazil.

Neither the papal arbitration nor the formal treaty was intended to be binding on other powers, and both were in fact repudiated. Cabot's voyage to North America in 1497 was England's immediate reply to the partition. Francis I of France voiced his celebrated protest: "The sun shines for me as for others. I should very much like to see the clause in Adam's will that excludes me from a share of the world." The king of Denmark refused to accept the Pope's ruling as far as the East Indies were concerned. Sir William Cecil, the famous Elizabethan statesman, denied the Pope's right "to give and take kingdoms to whomsoever he pleased." In 1580 the English government countered with the principle of effective occupation as the determinant of sovereignty.[1] Thereafter, in the parlance of the day, there was "no peace below the line." It was a dispute, in the words of a later governor of Barbados, as to "whether the King of England or of France shall be monarch of the West Indies, for the King of Spain cannot hold it long. ..."[2] England, France, and even Holland, began to challenge the Iberian Axis and claim their place in the sun. The Negro, too, was to have his place, though he did not ask for it: it was the broiling sun of the sugar, tobacco and cotton plantations of the New World.

According to Adam Smith, the prosperity of a new colony depends upon one simple economic factor – "plenty of good land."[3] The British colonial possessions up to 1776, however, can broadly be divided into two types. The first is the self-sufficient and diversified economy of small farmers, "mere earth-scratchers" as Gibbon Wakefield derisively called them,[4] living on a soil which, as Canada was described in 1840, was "no lottery, with a few exorbitant prizes and a large number of

From Eric Williams, *Capitalism and Slavery* (1944); reproduced by kind permission of André Deutsch Ltd and Erica Williams.

blanks, but a secure and certain investment."[5] The second type is the colony which has facilities for the production of staple articles on a large scale for an export market. In the first category fell the Northern colonies of the American mainland; in the second, the mainland tobacco colonies and the sugar islands of the Caribbean. In colonies of the latter type, as Merivale pointed out, land and capital were both useless unless labor could be commanded.[6] Labor, that is, must be constant and must work, or be made to work, in co-operation. In such colonies the rugged individualism of the Massachusetts farmer, practising his intensive agriculture and wringing by the sweat of his brow niggardly returns from a grudging soil, must yield to the disciplined gang of the big capitalist practising extensive agriculture and producing on a large scale. Without this compulsion, the laborer would otherwise exercise his natural inclination to work his own land and toil on his own account. The story is frequently told of the great English capitalist, Mr Peel, who took £50,000 and three hundred laborers with him to the Swan River colony in Australia. His plan was that his laborers would work for him, as in the old country. Arrived in Australia, however, where land was plentiful – too plentiful – the laborers preferred to work for themselves as small proprietors, rather than under the capitalist for wages. Australia was not England, and the capitalist was left without a servant to make his bed or fetch him water.[7]

For the Caribbean colonies the solution for this dispersion and "earth-scratching" was slavery. The lesson of the early history of Georgia is instructive. Prohibited from employing slave labor by trustees who, in some instances, themselves owned slaves in other colonies, the Georgian planters found themselves in the position, as Whitefield phrased it, of people whose legs were tied and were told to walk. So the Georgia magistrates drank toasts "to the one thing needful" – slavery – until the ban was lifted.[8] "Odious resource" though it might be, as Merivale called it,[9] slavery was an economic institution of the first importance. It had been the basis of Greek economy and had built up the Roman Empire. In modern times it provided the sugar for the tea and the coffee cups of the Western world. It produced the cotton to serve as a base for modern capitalism. It made the American South and the Caribbean islands. Seen in historical perspective, it forms a part of that general picture of the harsh treatment of the underprivileged classes, the unsympathetic poor laws and severe feudal laws, and the indiffer-

ence with which the rising capitalist class was "beginning to reckon prosperity in terms of pounds sterling, and ... becoming used to the idea of sacrificing human life to the deity of increased production."[10]

Adam Smith, the intellectual champion of the industrial middle class with its new-found doctrine of freedom, later propagated the argument that it was, in general, pride and love of power in the master that led to slavery and that, in those countries where slaves were employed, free labor would be more profitable. Universal experience demonstrated conclusively that "the work done by slaves, though it appears to cost only their maintenance, is in the end the dearest of any. A person who can acquire no property can have no other interest than to eat as much as possible, and to labour as little as possible."[11]

Adam Smith thereby treated as an abstract proposition what is a specific question of time, place, labor, and soil. The economic superiority of free hired labor over slave is obvious even to the slave owner. Slave labor is given reluctantly, it is unskillful, it lacks versatility.[12] Other things being equal, free men would be preferred. But in the early stages of colonial development, other things are not equal. When slavery is adopted, it is not adopted as the choice over free labor; there is no choice at all. The reasons for slavery, wrote Gibbon Wakefield, "are not moral, but economical circumstances; they relate not to vice and virtue, but to production."[13] With the limited population of Europe in the sixteenth century, the free laborers necessary to cultivate the staple crops of sugar, tobacco, and cotton in the New World could not have been supplied in quantities adequate to permit large-scale production. Slavery was necessary for this, and to get slaves the Europeans turned first to the aborigines and then to Africa.

Under certain circumstances slavery has some obvious advantages. In the cultivation of crops like sugar, cotton, and tobacco, where the cost of production is appreciably reduced on larger units, the slaveowner, with his large-scale production and his organized slave gang, can make more profitable use of the land than the small farmer or peasant proprietor. For such staple crops, the vast profits can well stand the greater expense of inefficient slave labor.[14] Where all the knowledge required is simple and a matter of routine, constancy and cooperation in labor – slavery – is essential, until, by importation of new recruits and breeding, the population has reached the point of density and the land available for appropriation has been already apportioned. When that stage is reached, and only then, the expenses of slavery, in the form of the cost and maintenance of slaves, productive and unproductive, exceed the cost of hired laborers. As Merivale wrote: "Slave labour is dearer than free *wherever abundance of free labour can be procured.*"[15]

From the standpoint of the grower, the greatest defect of slavery lies in the fact that it quickly exhausts the soil. The labor supply of low social status, docile and cheap, can be maintained in subjection only by systematic degradation and by deliberate efforts to suppress its intelligence. Rotation of crops and scientific farming are therefore alien to slave societies. As Jefferson wrote of Virginia, "we can buy an acre of new land cheaper than we can manure an old one."[16] The slave planter, in the picturesque nomenclature of the South, is a "land-killer." This serious defect of slavery can be counter-balanced and postponed for a time if fertile soil is practically unlimited. Expansion is a necessity of slave societies; the slave power requires ever fresh conquests.[17] "It is more profitable," wrote Merivale, "to cultivate a fresh soil by the dear labour of slaves, than an exhausted one by the cheap labour of freemen."[18] From Virginia and Maryland to Carolina, Georgia, Texas, and the Middle West; from Barbados to Jamaica to Saint Domingue and then to Cuba; the logic was inexorable and the same. It was a relay race; the first to start passed the baton, unwillingly we may be sure, to another and then limped sadly behind.

Slavery in the Caribbean has been too narrowly identified with the Negro. A racial twist has thereby been given to what is basically an economic phenomenon. Slavery was not born of racism: rather, racism was the consequence of slavery. Unfree labor in the New World was brown, white, black, and yellow; Catholic, Protestant, and pagan.

The first instance of slave trading and slave labor developed in the New World involved, racially, not the Negro but the Indian. The Indians rapidly succumbed to the excessive labor demanded of them, the insufficient diet, the white man's diseases, and their inability to adjust themselves to the new way of life. Accustomed to a life of liberty, their constitution and temperament were ill-adapted to the rigors of plantation slavery. As Fernando Ortíz writes: "To subject the Indian to the mines, to their monotonous, insane and severe labor, without tribal sense, without religious ritual, . . . was like taking away from him the meaning of his life. . . . It was to enslave not only his

muscles but also his collective spirit."[19]

The visitor to Ciudad Trujillo, capital of the Dominican Republic (the present-day name of half of the island formerly called Hispaniola), will see a statue of Columbus, with the figure of an Indian woman gratefully writing (so reads the caption) the name of the Discoverer. The story is told, on the other hand, of the Indian chieftain, Hatuey, who, doomed to die for resisting the invaders, staunchly refused to accept the Christian faith as the gateway to salvation when he learned that his executioners, too, hoped to get to Heaven. It is far more probable that Hatuey, rather than the anonymous woman, represented contemporary Indian opinion of their new overlords.

England and France, in their colonies, followed the Spanish practice of enslavement of the Indians. There was one conspicuous difference – the attempts of the Spanish Crown, however ineffective, to restrict Indian slavery to those who refused to accept Christianity and to the warlike Caribs on the specious plea that they were cannibals. From the standpoint of the British government Indian slavery, unlike later Negro slavery which involved vital imperial interests, was a purely colonial matter. As Lauber writes: "The home government was interested in colonial slave conditions and legislation only when the African slave trade was involved. . . . Since it (Indian slavery) was never sufficiently extensive to interfere with Negro slavery and the slave trade, it never received any attention from the home government, and so existed as legal because never declared illegal."[20]

But Indian slavery never was extensive in the British dominions. Ballagh, writing of Virginia, says that popular sentiment had never "demanded the subjection of the Indian race *per se*, as was practically the case with the Negro in the first slave act of 1661, but only of a portion of it, and that admittedly a very small portion. . . . In the case of the Indian . . . slavery was viewed as of an occasional nature, a preventive penalty and not as a normal and permanent condition."[21] In the New England colonies Indian slavery was unprofitable, for slavery of any kind was unprofitable because it was unsuited to the diversified agriculture of these colonies. In addition the Indian slave was inefficient. The Spaniards discovered that one Negro was worth four Indians.[22] A prominent official in Hispaniola insisted in 1518 that "permission be given to bring Negroes, a race robust for labor, instead of natives, so weak that they can only be employed in tasks requiring little endurance, such as taking care of maize fields or farms."[23] The future staples of the New World, sugar and cotton, required strength which the Indian lacked, and demanded the robust "cotton nigger" as sugar's need of strong mules produced in Louisiana the epithet "sugar mules." According to Lauber, "When compared with sums paid for Negroes at the same time and place the prices of Indian slaves are found to have been considerably lower."[24]

The Indian reservoir, too, was limited, the African inexhaustible. Negroes therefore were stolen in Africa to work the lands stolen from the Indians in America. The voyages of Prince Henry the Navigator complemented those of Columbus, West African history became the complement of West Indian.

The immediate successor of the Indian, however, was not the Negro but the poor white. These white servants included a variety of types. Some were indentured servants, so called because, before departure from the homeland, they had signed a contract, indented by law, binding them to service for a stipulated time in return for their passage. Still others, known as "redemptioners," arranged with the captain of the ship to pay for their passage on arrival or within a specified time thereafter; if they did not, they were sold by the captain to the highest bidder. Others were convicts, sent out by the deliberate policy of the home government, to serve for a specified period.

This emigration was in tune with mercantilist theories of the day which strongly advocated putting the poor to industrious and useful labor and favored emigration, voluntary or involuntary, as relieving the poor rates and finding more profitable occupations abroad for idlers and vagrants at home. "Indentured servitude," writes C. M. Haar, "was called into existence by two different though complementary forces: there was both a positive attraction from the New World and a negative repulsion from the Old."[25] In a state paper delivered to James I in 1606 Bacon emphasized that by emigration England would gain "a double commodity, in the avoidance of people here, and in making use of them there."[26]

This temporary service at the outset denoted no inferiority or degradation. Many of the servants were manorial tenants fleeing from the irksome restrictions of feudalism, Irishmen seeking freedom from the oppression of landlords and bishops, Germans running away from the devastation of the Thirty Years War. They transplanted in their hearts a burning desire for land, an ardent passion for independence. They came to the land of opportunity to be free men, their imaginations powerfully wrought upon by glowing and extravagant descriptions in the home country.[27] It was only later when, in the words of Dr Williamson, "all ideals of a decent colonial society, of a better and greater England overseas, were swamped in the pursuit of an immediate gain,"[28] that the introduction of disreputable elements became a general feature of indentured service.

A regular traffic developed in these indentured servants. Between 1654 and 1685 10,000 sailed from Bristol alone, chiefly for the West Indies and Virginia.[29] In 1683 white servants represented one-sixth of Virginia's population. Two-thirds of the immigrants to Pennsylvania during the eighteenth century were white servants; in four years 25,000 came to Philadelphia alone. It has been estimated that more than a quarter of a million persons were of this class during the colonial period,[30] and that they probably constituted one-half of all English immigrants, the majority going to the middle colonies.[31]

As commercial speculation entered the picture, abuses crept in. Kidnapping was encouraged to a great degree and became a regular business in such towns as London and Bristol. Adults would be plied with liquor, children enticed with sweetmeats. The kidnappers were called "spirits," defined as "one that taketh upp men and women and children and sells them on a shipp to be conveyed beyond the sea." The captain of a ship trading to Jamaica would visit the Clerkenwell House of Correction, ply with drink the girls who had been imprisoned there as disorderly, and "invite" them to go to the West Indies.[32] The temptations held out to the unwary and the credulous were so attractive that, as the mayor of Bristol complained, husbands were induced to forsake their wives, wives their husbands, and apprentices their masters, while wanted criminals found on the transport ships a refuge from the arms of the law.[33] The wave of German immigration developed the "newlander," the labor agent of those days, who traveled up and down the Rhine Valley persuading the feudal peasants to sell their belongings and emigrate to America, receiving a commission for each emigrant."[34]

Much has been written about the trickery these "newlanders" were not averse to employing.[35] But whatever the deceptions practiced, it remains true, as Friedrich Kapp has written, that "the real ground for the emigration fever lay in the unhealthy political and economic conditions. . . . The misery and oppression of the conditions of the little (German) states promoted emigration much more dangerously and continuously than the worst 'newlander.' "[36]

Convicts provided another steady source of white labor. The harsh feudal laws of England recognized 300 capital crimes. Typical hanging offences included: picking a pocket for more than a shilling; shoplifting to the value of five shillings; stealing a horse or a sheep; poaching rabbits on a gentleman's estate.[37] Offenses for which the punishment prescribed by law was transportation comprised the stealing of cloth, burning stacks of corn, the maiming and killing of cattle, hindering customs officers in the execution of their duty, and corrupt legal practices.[38] Proposals made in 1664 would have banished to the colonies all vagrants, rogues and idlers, petty thieves, gipsies, and loose persons frequenting unlicensed brothels.[39] A piteous petition in 1667 prayed for transportation instead of the death sentence for a wife convicted of stealing goods valued at three shillings and four pence.[40] In 1745 transportation was the penalty for the theft of a silver spoon and a gold watch.[41] One year after the emancipation of the Negro slaves, transportation was the penalty for trade union activity. It is difficult to resist the conclusion that there was some connection between the law and the labor needs of the plantations, and the marvel is that so few people ended up in the colonies overseas.

Benjamin Franklin opposed this "dumping upon the New World of the outcasts of the Old" as the most cruel insult ever offered by one nation to another, and asked, if England was justified in sending her convicts to the colonies, whether the latter were justified in sending to England their rattlesnakes in exchange?[42] It is not clear why Franklin should have been so sensitive. Even if the convicts were hardened criminals, the great increase of indentured servants and free emigrants would have tended to render the convict influence innocuous, as increasing quantities of water poured in a glass containing poison. Without convicts the early development of the Australian colonies in the nineteenth century would have been impossible. Only a few of the colonists, however, were so particular. The general attitude was summed up by a contemporary: "Their labor would be more beneficial in an infant settlement, than their vices could be pernicious."[43] There was nothing strange about this attitude. The great problem in a new country is the problem of labor, and convict labor, as Merivale has pointed out, was equivalent to a free

present by the government to the settlers without burdening the latter with the expense of importation.[44] The governor of Virginia in 1611 was willing to welcome convicts reprieved from death as "a readie way to furnish us with men and not always with the worst kind of men."[45] The West Indies were prepared to accept all and sundry, even the spawn of Newgate and Bridewell, for "no goalebird [sic] can be so incorrigible, but there is hope of his conformity here, as well as of his preferment, which some have happily experimented."[46]

The political and civil disturbances in England between 1640 and 1740 augmented the supply of white servants. Political and religious nonconformists paid for their unorthodoxy by transportation, mostly to the sugar islands. Such was the fate of many of Cromwell's Irish prisoners, who were sent to the West Indies.[47] So thoroughly was this policy pursued that an active verb was added to the English language – to "barbadoes" a person.[48] Montserrat became largely an Irish colony,[49] and the Irish brogue is still frequently heard today in many parts of the British West Indies. The Irish, however, were poor servants. They hated the English, were always ready to aid England's enemies, and in a revolt in the Leeward Islands in 1689[50] we can already see signs of that burning indignation which, according to Lecky, gave Washington some of his best soldiers.[51] The vanquished in Cromwell's Scottish campaigns were treated like the Irish before them, and Scotsmen came to be regarded as "the general travaillers and soldiers in most foreign parts."[52] Religious intolerance sent more workers to the plantations. In 1661 Quakers refusing to take the oath for the third time were to be transported; in 1664 transportation, to any plantation except Virginia or New England, or a fine of one hundred pounds was decreed for the third offence for persons over sixteen assembling in groups of five or more under pretense of religion.[53] Many of Monmouth's adherents were sent to Barbados, with orders to be detained as servants for 10 years. The prisoners were granted in batches to favorite courtiers, who made handsome profits from the traffic in which, it is alleged, even the Queen shared.[54] A similar policy was resorted to after the Jacobite risings of the eighteenth century.

The transportation of these white servants shows in its true light the horrors of the Middle Passage – not as something unusual or inhuman but as a part of the age. The emigrants were packed like herrings. According to Mittelberger, each servant was allowed about two feet in width and six feet in length in bed.[55] The boats were small, the voyage long, the food, in the absence of refrigeration, bad, disease inevitable. A petition to Parliament in 1659 describes how 72 servants had been locked up below deck during the whole voyage of five and a half weeks, "amongst horses, that their souls, through heat and steam under the tropic, fainted in them."[56] Inevitably abuses crept into the system and Fearon was shocked by "the horrible picture of human suffering which this living sepulchre" of an emigrant vessel in Philadelphia afforded.[57] But conditions even for the free passengers were not much better in those days, and the comment of a Lady of Quality describing a voyage from Scotland to the West Indies on a ship full of indentured servants should banish any ideas that the horrors of the slave ship are to be accounted for by the fact that the victims were Negroes. "It is hardly possible," she writes, "to believe that human nature could be so depraved, as to treat fellow creatures in such a manner for so little gain."[58]

The transportation of servants and convicts produced a powerful vested interest in England. When the Colonial Board was created in 1661, not the least important of its duties was the control of the trade in indentured servants. In 1664 a commission was appointed, headed by the King's brother, to examine and report upon the exportation of servants. In 1670 an act prohibiting the transportation of English prisoners overseas was rejected; another bill against the stealing of children came to nothing. In the transportation of felons, a whole hierarchy, from courtly secretaries and grave judges down to the jailors and turnkeys, insisted on having a share in the spoils.[59] It has been suggested that it was humanity for his fellow countrymen and men of his own color which dictated the planter's preference for the Negro slave.[60] Of this humanity there is not a trace in the records of the time, at least as far as the plantation colonies and commercial production were concerned. Attempts to register emigrant servants and regularize the procedure of transportation – thereby giving full legal recognition to the system – were evaded. The leading merchants and public officials were all involved in the practice. The penalty for mansteeling was exposure in the pillory, but no missiles from the spectators were tolerated. Such opposition as there was came from the masses. It was enough to point a finger at a woman in the streets of London and call her a "spirit" to start a riot.

This was the situation in England when Jeffreys came to Bristol on his tour of the West to clean up the remnants of Monmouth's rebellion. Jeffreys has been handed down to posterity as a "butcher," the tyrannical deputy of an arbitrary king, and his legal visitation is recorded in the textbooks as the "Bloody Assizes." They had one redeeming feature. Jeffreys vowed that he had come to Bristol with a broom to sweep the city clean, and his wrath fell on the kidnapers who infested the highest municipal offices. The merchants and justices were in the habit of straining the law to increase the number of felons who could be transported to the sugar plantations they owned in the West Indies. They would terrify petty offenders with the prospect of hanging and then induce them to plead for transportation. Jeffreys turned upon the mayor, complete in scarlet and furs, who was about to sentence a pickpocket to transportation to Jamaica, forced him, to the great astonishment of Bristol's worthy citizens, to enter the prisoners' dock, like a common felon, to plead guilty or not guilty, and hectored him in characteristic language: "Sir, Mr Mayor, you I meane, Kidnapper, and an old Justice of the Peace on the bench. . . . I doe not knowe him, an old knave: he goes to the taverne, and for a pint of sack he will bind people servants to the Indies at the taverne. A kidnapping knave! I will have his ears off, before I goe forth of towne. . . . Kidnapper, you, I mean, Sir. . . . If it were not in respect of the sword, which is over your head, I would send you to Newgate, you kidnapping knave. You are worse than the pick-pockett who stands there. . . . I hear the trade of kidnapping is of great request. They can discharge a felon or a traitor, provided they will go to Mr Alderman's plantation at the West Indies." The mayor was fined one thousand pounds, but apart from the loss of dignity and the fear aroused in their hearts, the merchants lost nothing – their gains were left inviolate.[61]

According to one explanation, Jeffrey's insults were the result of intoxication or insanity.[62] It is not improbable that they were connected with a complete reversal of mercantilist thought on the question of emigration, as a result of the internal development of Britain herself. By the end of the seventeenth century the stress had shifted from the accumulation of the precious metals as the aim of national economic policy to the development of industry within the country, the promotion of employment, and the encouragement of exports. The mercantilists argued that the best way to reduce costs, and thereby compete with other countries, was to pay low wages, which a large population tended to ensure. The fear of overpopulation at the beginning of the seventeenth century gave way to a fear of underpopulation in the middle of the same century. The essential condition of colonization – emigration from the home country – now ran counter to the principle that national interest demanded a large population at home. Sir Josiah Child denied that emigration to America had weakened England, but he was forced to admit that in this view he was in a minority of possibly one in a thousand, while he endorsed the general opinion that "whatever tends to the depopulating of a kingdom tends to the impoverishment of it."[63] Jeffreys' unusual humanitarianism appears less strange and may be attributed rather to economic than to spirituous considerations. His patrons, the Royal Family, had already given their patronage to the Royal African Company and the Negro slave trade. For the surplus population needed to people the colonies in the New World the British had turned to Africa, and by 1680 they already had positive evidence, in Barbados, that the African was satisfying the necessities of production better than the European.

The status of these servants became progressively worse in the plantation colonies. Servitude, originally a free personal relation based on voluntary contract for a definite period of service, in lieu of transportation and maintenance, tended to pass into a property relation which asserted a control of varying extent over the bodies and liberties of the person during service as if he were a thing.[64] Eddis, writing on the eve of the Revolution, found the servants groaning "beneath a worse than Egyptian bondage."[65] In Maryland servitude developed into an institution approaching in some respects chattel slavery.[66] Of Pennsylvania it has been said that "no matter how kindly they may have been treated in particular cases, or how voluntarily they may have entered into the relation, as a class and when once bound, indentured servants were temporarily chattels."[67] On the sugar plantations of Barbados the servants spent their time "grinding at the mills and attending the furnaces, or digging in this scorching island; having nothing to feed on (notwithstanding their hard labour) but potatoe roots, nor to drink, but water with such roots washed in it, besides the bread and tears of their own afflictions; being bought and sold still from one planter to another, or attached as horses and beasts for the debts of their masters, being whipt at the whipping posts (as rogues,) for their masters' pleasure, and sleeping in sties worse than hogs in England."[68] As Professor Harlow concludes, the weight of evidence proves

incontestably that the conditions under which white labor was procured and utilized in Barbados were "persistently severe, occasionally dishonourable, and generally a disgrace to the English name."[69]

English officialdom, however, took the view that servitude was not too bad, and the servant in Jamaica was better off than the husbandman in England. "It is a place as grateful to you for trade as any part of the world. It is not so odious as it is represented."[70] But there was some sensitiveness on the question. The Lords of Trade and Plantations, in 1676, opposed the use of the word "servitude" as a mark of bondage and slavery, and suggested "service" instead.[71] The institution was not affected by the change. The hope has been expressed that the white servants were spared the lash so liberally bestowed upon their Negro comrades.[72] They had no such good fortune. Since they were bound for a limited period, the planter had less interest in their welfare than in that of the Negroes who were perpetual servants and therefore "the most useful appurtenances" of a plantation.[73] Eddis found the Negroes "almost in every instance, under more comfortable circumstances than the miserable European, over whom the rigid planter exercises an inflexible severity."[74] The servants were regarded by the planters as "white trash," and were bracketed with the Negroes as laborers. "Not one of these colonies ever was or ever can be brought to any considerable improvement without a supply of white servants and Negroes," declared the Council of Montserrat in 1680.[75] In a European society in which subordination was considered essential, in which Burke could speak of the working classes as "miserable sheep" and Voltaire as "canaille," and Linguet condemn the worker to the use of his physical strength alone, for "everything would be lost once he knew that he had a mind"[76] – in such a society it is unnecessary to seek for apologies for the condition of the white servant in the colonies.

Defoe bluntly stated that the white servant was a slave.[77] He was not. The servant's loss of liberty was of limited duration, the Negro was slave for life. The servant's status could not descend to his offspring, Negro children took the status of the mother. The master at no time had absolute control over the person and liberty of his servant as he had over his slave. The servant had rights, limited but recognized by law and inserted in a contract. He enjoyed, for instance, a limited right to property. In actual law the conception of the servant as a piece of property never went beyond that of personal estate and never reached the stage of a chattel or real estate. The laws in the colonies maintained this rigid distinction and visited cohabitation between the races with severe penalties. The servant could aspire, at the end of his term, to a plot of land, though, as Wertenbaker points out for Virginia, it was not a legal right,[78] and conditions varied from colony to colony. The serf in Europe could therefore hope for an early freedom in America which villeinage could not afford. The freed servants became small yeomen farmers, settled in the back country, a democratic force in a society of large aristocratic plantation owners, and were the pioneers in westward expansion. That was why Jefferson in America, as Saco in Cuba, favored the introduction of European servants instead of African slaves – as tending to democracy rather than aristocracy.[79]

The institution of white servitude, however, had grave disadvantages. Postlethwayt, a rigid mercantilist, argued that white laborers in the colonies would tend to create rivalry with the mother country in manufacturing. Better black slaves on plantations than white servants in industry, which would encourage aspirations to independence.[80] The supply moreover was becoming increasingly difficult, and the need of the plantations outstripped the English convictions. In addition, merchants were involved in many vexatious and costly proceedings arising from people signifying their willingness to emigrate, accepting food and clothes in advance, and then suing for unlawful detention.[81] Indentured servants were not forthcoming in sufficient quantities to replace those who had served their term. On the plantations, escape was easy for the white servant; less easy for the Negro who, if freed, tended, in self-defense, to stay in his locality where he was well known and less likely to be apprehended as a vagrant or runaway slave. The servant expected land at the end of his contract; the Negro, in a strange environment, conspicuous by his color and features, and ignorant of the white man's language and ways, could be kept permanently divorced from the land. Racial differences made it easier to justify and rationalize Negro slavery, to exact the mechanical obedience of a plough-ox or a cart-horse, to demand that resignation and that complete moral and intellectual subjection which alone make slave labor possible. Finally, and this was the decisive factor, the Negro slave was cheaper. The money which procured a white man's services for 10 years could buy a Negro for life.[82] As the governor of Barbados stated, the Barbadian planters found by experience that "three blacks work better and cheaper than one white man."[83]

But the experience with white servitude had been invaluable. Kidnaping in Africa encountered no such difficulties as were encountered in England. Captains and ships had the experience of the one trade to guide them in the other. Bristol, the center of the servant trade, became one of the centers of the slave trade. Capital accumulated from the one financed the other. White servitude was the historic base upon which Negro slavery was constructed. The felon-drivers in the plantations became without effort slave-drivers. "In significant numbers," writes Professor Phillips, "the Africans were latecomers fitted into a system already developed."[84]

Here, then, is the origin of Negro slavery. The reason was economic, not racial; it had to do not with the color of the laborer, but the cheapness of the labor. As compared with Indian and white labor, Negro slavery was eminently superior. "In each case," writes Bassett, discussing North Carolina, "it was a survival of the fittest. Both Indian slavery and white servitude were to go down before the black man's superior endurance, docility, and labor capacity."[85] The features of the man, his hair, color, and dentifrice, his "subhuman" characteristics so widely pleaded, were only the later rationalizations to justify a simple economic fact: that the colonies needed labor and resorted to Negro labor because it was cheapest and best. This was not a theory, it was a practical conclusion deduced from the personal experience of the planter. He would have gone to the moon, if necessary, for labor. Africa was nearer than the moon, nearer too than the more populous countries of India and China. But their turn was to come.

This white servitude is of cardinal importance for an understanding of the development of the New World and the Negro's place in that development. It completely explodes the old myth that the whites could not stand the strain of manual labor in the climate of the New World and that, for this reason and this reason alone, the European powers had recourse to Africans. The argument is quite untenable. A Mississippi dictum will have it that "only black men and mules can face the sun in July." But the whites faced the sun for well over a hundred years in Barbados, and the Salzburgers of Georgia indignantly denied that rice cultivation was harmful to them.[86] The Caribbean islands are well within the tropical zone, but their climate is more equable than tropical, the temperature rarely exceeds 80 degrees though it remains uniform the whole year round, and they are exposed to the gentle winds from the sea. The unbearable humidity of an August day in some parts of the United States has no equal in the islands. Moreover only the southern tip of Florida in the United States is actually tropical, yet Negro labor flourished in Virginia and Carolina. The southern parts of the United States are not hotter than South Italy or Spain, and de Tocqueville asked why the European could not work there as well as in those two countries?[87] When Whitney invented his cotton gin, it was confidently expected that cotton would be produced by free labor on small farms, and it was, in fact, so produced.[88] Where the white farmer was ousted, the enemy was not the climate but the slave plantation, and the white farmer moved westward, until the expanding plantation sent him on his wanderings again. Writing in 1857, Weston pointed out that labor in the fields of the extreme South and all the heavy outdoor work in New Orleans were performed by whites, without any ill consequences. "No part of the continental borders of the Gulf of Mexico," he wrote, "and none of the islands which separate it from the ocean, need be abandoned to the barbarism of negro slavery."[89] In our own time we who have witnessed the dispossession of Negroes by white sharecroppers in the South and the mass migration of Negroes from the South to the colder climates of Detroit, New York, Pittsburgh, and other industrial centers of the North, can no longer accept the convenient rationalization that Negro labor was employed on the slave plantations because the climate was too rigorous for the constitution of the white man.

A constant and steady emigration of poor whites from Spain to Cuba, to the very end of Spanish dominion, characterized Spanish colonial policy. Fernando Ortíz has drawn a striking contrast between the role of tobacco and sugar in Cuban history. Tobacco was a free white industry intensively cultivated on small farms; sugar was a black slave industry extensively cultivated on large plantations. He further compared the free Cuban tobacco industry with its slave Virginian counterpart.[90] What determined the difference was not climate but the economic structure of the two areas. The whites could hardly have endured the tropical heat of Cuba and succumbed to the tropical heat of Barbados. In Puerto Rico, the jíbaro, the poor white peasant, is still the basic type, demonstrating, in the words of Grenfell Price, how erroneous is the belief that after three generations the white man cannot

breed in the tropics.[91] Similar white communities have survived in the Caribbean, from the earliest settlements right down to our own times, in the Dutch West Indian islands of Saba and St Martin. For some 60 years French settlers have lived in St Thomas not only as fishermen but as agriculturalists, forming today the "largest single farming class" in the island.[92] As Dr Price concludes: "It appears that northern whites can retain a fair standard for generations in the trade-wind tropics if the location is free from the worst forms of tropical disease, if the economic return is adequate, and if the community is prepared to undertake hard, physical work."[93] Over 100 years ago a number of German emigrants settled in Seaford, Jamaica. They survive today, with no visible signs of deterioration, flatly contradicting the popular belief as to the possibility of survival of the northern white in the tropics.[94] Wherever, in short, tropical agriculture remained on a small farming basis, whites not only survived but prospered. Where the whites disappeared, the cause was not the climate but the supersession of the small farm by the large plantation, with its consequent demand for a large and steady supply of labor.

The climatic theory of the plantation is thus nothing but a rationalization. In an excellent essay on the subject Professor Edgar Thompson writes: "The plantation is not to be accounted for by climate. It is a political institution." It is, we might add, more: it is an economic institution. The climatic theory "is part of an ideology which rationalizes and naturalizes an existing social and economic order, and this everywhere seems to be an order in which there is a race problem."[95]

The history of Australia clinches the argument. Nearly half of this island continent lies within the tropical zone. In part of this tropical area, the state of Queensland, the chief crop is sugar. When the industry began to develop, Australia had a choice of two alternatives: black labor or white labor. The commonwealth began its sugar cultivation in the usual way – with imported black labor from the Pacific islands. Increasing demands, however, were made for a white Australia policy, and in the twentieth century non-white immigration was prohibited. It is irrelevant to consider here that as a result the cost of production of Australian sugar is prohibitive, that the industry is artificial and survives only behind the Chinese wall of Australian autarchy [The author writes in the 1940s – ed.] Australia was willing to pay a high price in order to remain a white man's country. Our sole concern here with the question is that this price was paid from the pockets of the Australian consumer and not in the physical degeneration of the Australian worker.

Labor in the Queensland sugar industry today is wholly white. "Queensland," writes H. L. Wilkinson, "affords the only example in the world of European colonization in the tropics on an extensive scale. It does more; it shows a large European population doing the whole of the work of its civilization from the meanest service, and most exacting manual labor, to the highest form of intellectualism."[96] To such an extent has science exploded superstition that Australian scientists today argue that the only condition on which white men and women can remain healthy in the tropics is that they must engage in hard manual work. Where they have done so, as in Queensland, "the most rigorous scientific examination," according to the Australian Medical Congress in 1920, "failed to show any organic changes in white residents which enabled them to be distinguished from residents of temperate climates."[97]

Negro slavery, thus, had nothing to do with climate. Its origin can be expressed in three words: in the Caribbean, Sugar; on the mainland, Tobacco and Cotton. A change in the economic structure produced a corresponding change in the labor supply. The fundamental fact was "the creation of an inferior social and economic organization of exploiters and exploited."[98] Sugar, tobacco, and cotton required the large plantation and hordes of cheap labor, and the small farm of the ex-indentured white servant could not possibly survive. The tobacco of the small farm in Barbados was displaced by the sugar of the large plantation. The rise of the sugar industry in the Caribbean was the signal for a gigantic dispossession of the small farmer. Barbados in 1645 had 11,200 small white farmers and 5,680 Negro slaves; in 1667 there were 745 large plantation owners and 82,023 slaves. In 1645 the island had 18,300 whites fit to bear arms, in 1667 only 8,300.[99] The white farmers were squeezed out. The planters continued to offer inducements to newcomers, but they could no longer offer the main inducement, land. White servants preferred the other islands where they could hope for land, to Barbados, where they were sure there was none.[100] In desperation the planters proposed legislation which would prevent a landowner from purchasing more land, compel Negroes and servants to wear dimity manufactured in Barbados (what would

English mercantilists have said?) to provide employment for the poor whites, and prevent Negroes from being taught to trade.[101] The governor of Barbados in 1695 drew a pitiful picture of these ex-servants. Without fresh meat or rum, "they are domineered over and used like dogs, and this in time will undoubtedly drive away all the commonalty of the white people." His only suggestion was to give the right to elect members of the Assembly to every white man owning two acres of land. Candidates for election would "sometimes give the poor miserable creatures a little rum and fresh provisions and such things as would be of nourishment to them," in order to get their votes – and elections were held every year.[102] It is not surprising that the exodus continued.

The poor whites began their travels, disputing their way all over the Caribbean, from Barbados to Nevis, to Antigua, and thence to Guiana and Trinidad, and ultimately Carolina. Everywhere they were pursued and dispossessed by the same inexorable economic force, sugar; and in Carolina they were safe from cotton only for a hundred years. Between 1672 and 1708 the white men in Nevis decreased by more than three-fifths, the black population more than doubled. Between 1672 and 1727 the white males of Montserrat declined by more than two-thirds, in the same period the black population increased more than eleven times.[103] "The more they buie," said the Barbadians, referring to their slaves, "the more they are able to buye, for in a yeare and a halfe they will earne with God's blessing as much as they cost."[104] King Sugar had begun his depredations, changing flourishing commonwealths of small farmers into vast sugar factories owned by a camarilla of absentee capitalist magnates and worked by a mass of alien proletarians. The plantation economy had no room for poor whites; the proprietor or overseer, a physician on the more prosperous plantations, possibly their families, these were sufficient. "If a state," wrote Weston, "could be supposed to be made up of continuous plantations, the white race would be not merely starved out, but literally squeezed out."[105] The resident planters, apprehensive of the growing disproportion between whites and blacks, passed Deficiency Laws to compel absentees, under penalty of fines, to keep white servants. The absentees preferred to pay the fines. In the West Indies today the poor whites survive in the "Redlegs" of Barbados, pallid, weak and depraved from inbreeding, strong rum, insufficient food and abstinence from manual labor. For, as Merivale wrote, "in a country where Negro slavery prevails extensively, no white is industrious."[106]

It was the triumph, not of geographical conditions, as Harlow contends,[107] but of economic. The victims were the Negroes in Africa and the small white farmers. The increase of wealth for the few whites was as phenomenal as the increase of misery for the many blacks. The Barbados crops in 1650, over a 20-month period, were worth over 3 million pounds,[108] about 15 millions in modern money. In 1666 Barbados was computed to be 17 times as rich as it had been before the planting of sugar. "The buildings in 1643 were mean, with things only for necessity, but in 1666, plate, jewels, and household stuff were estimated at £500,000, their buildings very fair and beautiful, and their houses like castles, their sugar houses and negroes huts show themselves from the sea like so many small towns, each defended by its castle."[109] The price of land skyrocketed. A plantation of 500 acres which sold for £400 in 1640 fetched £7,000 for a half-share in 1648.[110] The estate of one Captain Waterman, comprising 800 acres, had at one time been split up among no less than 40 proprietors.[111] For sugar was and is essentially a capitalist undertaking, involving not only agricultural operations but the crude stages of refining as well. A report on the French sugar islands stated that to make 10 hogsheads of sugar required as great an expenditure in beasts of burden, mills, and utensils as to make 100.[112] James Knight of Jamaica estimated that it required 400 acres to start a sugar plantation.[113] According to Edward Long, another planter and the historian of the island, it needed £5,000 to start a small plantation of 300 acres, producing from 30 to 50 hogsheads of sugar a year, £14,000 for a plantation of the same size producing 100 hogsheads.[114] There could be only two classes in such a society, wealthy planters and oppressed slaves.

The moral is reinforced by a consideration of the history of Virginia, where the plantation economy was based not on sugar but on tobacco. The researches of Professor Wertenbaker have exploded the legend that Virginia from the outset was an aristocratic dominion. In the early seventeenth century about two-thirds of the landholders had neither slaves nor indentured servants. The strength of the colony lay in its numerous white yeomanry. Conditions became worse as the market for tobacco was glutted by Spanish competition and the Virginians demanded in wrath that something be done about "those petty English plantations in the savage islands in the West Indies" through which quantities of Spanish tobacco reached England.[115] Nonetheless, though prices continued to fall, the exports of Virginia and Maryland increased more than six times between 1663 and 1699. The explanation lay in two words – Negro slavery, which cheapened the cost of production. Negro slaves, one-twentieth of the population in 1670, were one-fourth in 1730. "Slavery, from being an insignificant factor in the economic life of the colony, had become the very foundation upon which it was established." There was still room in Virginia, as there was not in Barbados, for the small farmer, but land was useless to him if he could not compete with slave labor. So the Virginian peasant, like the Barbadian, was squeezed out. "The Virginia which had formerly been so largely the land of the little farmer, had become the land of Masters and Slaves. For aught else there was no room."[116]

The whole future history of the Caribbean is nothing more than a dotting of the i's and a crossing of the t's. It happened earlier in the British and French than in the Spanish islands, where the process was delayed until the advent of the dollar diplomacy of our own time. Under American capital we have witnessed the transformation of Cuba, Puerto Rico, and the Dominican Republic into huge sugar factories (though the large plantation, especially in Cuba, was not unknown under the Spanish regime), owned abroad and operated by alien labor, on the British West Indian pattern. That this process is taking place with free labor and in nominally independent areas (Puerto Rico excepted) helps us to see in its true light the first importation of Negro slave labor in the British Caribbean – a phase in the history of the plantation. In the words of Professor Phillips, the plantation system was "less dependent upon slavery than slavery was upon it. . . . The plantation system formed, so to speak, the industrial and social frame of government . . . , while slavery was a code of written laws enacted for that purpose."[117]

Where the plantation did not develop, as in the Cuban tobacco industry, Negro labor was rare and white labor predominated. The liberal section of the Cuban population consistently advocated the cessation of the Negro slave trade and the introduction of white immigrants. Saco, mouthpiece of the liberals, called for the immigration of workers "white and free, from all parts of the world, of all races, provided they have a white face and can do honest labor."[118] Sugar defeated Saco. It was the sugar plantation, with its servile base, which retarded white immigration in nineteenth-century Cuba as it had banned it in seventeenth-century Barbados and eighteenth-century Saint Domingue. No sugar, no Negroes. In Puerto Rieo, which developed relatively late as a genuine plantation, and where, before the American regime, sugar never dominated the lives and thoughts of the population as it did elsewhere, the poor white peasants survived and the Negro slaves never exceeded 14 per cent of the population.[119] Saco wanted to "whiten" the Cuban social structure.[120] Negro slavery blackened that structure all over the Caribbean while the blood of the Negro slaves reddened the Atlantic and both its shores. Strange that an article like sugar, so sweet and necessary to human existence, should have occasioned such crimes and bloodshed!

After emancipation the British planters thought of white immigration, even convicts. The governor of British Guiana wrote in glowing terms in 1845 about Portuguese immigrants from Madeira.[121] But though the Portuguese came in large numbers, as is attested by their strength even today in Trinidad and British Guiana, they preferred retail trade to plantation labor. The governor of Jamaica was somewhat more cautious in his opinion of British and Irish immigrants. Sickness had broken out, wages were too low, the experiment could only be partially useful in making an immediate addition to the laboring population, and therefore indiscriminate importation was inadvisable.[122] The European immigrants in St Christopher bewailed their fate piteously, and begged to be permitted to return home. "There is not the slightest reluctance on our part to continue in the island for an honest livelihood by pleasing our employers by our industrious labour if the climate agreed with us, but unfortunately it do not; and we are much afraid if we continue longer in this injurious hot climate [the West Indies] death will be the consequence to the principal part of us. . . ."[123]

It was not the climate which was against the experiment. Slavery had created the pernicious tradition that manual labor was the badge of the slave and the sphere of influence of the Negro. The first thought of the Negro slave after emancipation was to desert the plantation, where he could, and set up for himself where land was available. White plantation workers could hardly have existed in a society side by side with Negro peasants. The whites would have prospered if small farms had been encouraged. But the abolition of slavery did not mean the destruction of the sugar plantation. The emancipation of the Negro and the inadequacy of the white worker put the sugar planter back to where he had been in the seventeenth century. He still needed labor. Then he had moved from Indian to white to Negro. Now, deprived of his Negro, he turned back to white and then to Indian, this time the Indian from the East. India replaced Africa; between 1833 and 1917, Trinidad imported 145,000 East Indians and British Guiana 238,000. The pattern was the same for the other Caribbean colonies. Between 1854 and 1883 39,000 Indians were introduced into Guadeloupe; between 1853 and 1924, over 22,000 laborers from the Dutch East Indies and 34,000 from British India were carried to Dutch Guiana.[124] Cuba, faced with a shortage of Negro slaves, adopted the interesting experiment of using Negro slaves side by side with indentured Chinese coolies,[125] and after emancipation turned to the teeming thousands of Haiti and the British West Indies. Between 1913 and 1924 Cuba imported 217,000 laborers from Haiti, Jamaica, and Puerto Rico.[126] What Saco wrote 100 years ago was still true, 60 years after Cuba's abolition of slavery.

Negro slavery therefore was only a solution, in certain historical circumstances, of the Caribbean labor problem. Sugar meant labor – at times that labor has been slave, at other times nominally free; at times black, at other times white or brown or yellow. Slavery in no way implied, in any scientific sense, the inferiority of the Negro. Without it the great development of the Caribbean sugar plantations, between 1650 and 1850, would have been impossible.

Notes

1 C. M. Andrews, *The Colonial Period of American History* (New Haven, 1934–8), I, 12–14, 19–20.

2 N. M. Crouse, *The French Struggle for the West Indies, 1665–1713* (New York, 1943), 7.

3 Adam Smith, *The Wealth of Nations* (Cannan edn, New York, 1937), 538. To this Smith added a political factor, "liberty to manage their own affairs in their own way."

4 H. Merivale, *Lectures on Colonization and Colonies* (Oxford, 1928 edn), 262.

5 Ibid, 385. The description is Lord Sydenham's, Governor-General of Canada.

6 Merivale, 256.

7 Ibid.

8 R. B. Flanders, *Plantation Slavery in Georgia* (Chapel Hill, 1933), 15–16, 20.

9 Merivale, 269.

10 M. James, *Social Problems and Policy during the Puritan Revolution, 1640–1660* (London, 1930), 111.

11 Adam Smith, 365.

12 J. Cairnes, *The Slave Power* (New York, 1862), 39.

13 G. Wakefield, *A View of the Art of Colonization* (London, 1849), 323.

14 Adam Smith, 365–6.

15 Merivale, 303. Italics Merivale's.

16 M. B. Hammond, *The Cotton Industry: An Essay in American Economic History* (New York, 1897), 39.

17 Cairnes, 44; Merivale, 305–6. On soil exhaustion and the expansion of slavery in the United States see W. C. Bagley, *Soil Exhaustion and the Civil War* (Washington, DC, 1942).

18 Merivale, 307–8.

19 J. A. Saco, *Historia de la Esclavitud de los Indios en el Nuevo Mundo* (La Habana, 1932 edn), I, Introduction, p. xxxviii. The Introduction is written by Fernando Ortiz.

20 A. W. Lauber, *Indian Slavery in Colonial Times within the Present Limits of the United States* (New York, 1913), 214–15.

21 J. C. Ballagh, *A History of Slavery in Virginia* (Baltimore, 1902), 51.

22 F. Ortiz, *Contrapunteo Cubano del Tabaco y el Azúcar* (La Habana, 1940), 353.

23 Ibid., 359.

24 Lauber, 302.

25 C. M. Haar, "White Indentured Servants in Colonial New York," *Americana* (July 1940), 371.

26 *Cambridge History of the British Empire* (Cambridge, 1929), I, 69.

27 See Andrews, I, 59; K. F. Geiser, *Redemptioners and Indentured Servants in the Colony and Commonwealth of Pennsylvania* (New Haven, 1901), 18.

28 *Cambridge History of the British Empire*, I, 236.

29 C. M. MacInnes, *Bristol, a Gateway of Empire* (Bristol, 1939), 158–9.

30 M. W. Jernegan, *Laboring and Dependent Classes in Colonial America, 1607–1783* (Chicago, 1931), 45.

31 H. E. Bolton and T. M. Marshall, *The Colonization of North America, 1492–1783* (New York, 1936), 336.

32 J. W. Bready, *England Before and After Wesley – The Evangelical Revival and Social Reform* (London, 1938), 106.

33 *Calendar of State Papers, Colonial Series*, V, 98. July 16, 1662.

34 Geiser, 18.

35 See G. Mittelberger, *Journey to Pennsylvania in the year 1750* (Philadelphia, 1898), 16; E. I. McCormac, *White Servitude in Maryland* (Baltimore, 1904), 44, 49; "Diary of John Harrower, 1773–1776," *American Historical Review* (Oct., 1900), 77.

36 E. Abbott, *Historical Aspects of the Immigration Problem, Select Documents* (Chicago, 1926), 12n.

37 Bready, 127.

38 L. F. Stock (ed.), *Proceedings and Debates in the British Parliament respecting North America* (Washington, DC, 1924–1941), I, 353n, 355; III, 437n, 494.

39 *Calendar of State Papers, Colonial Series*, V, 221.

40 Ibid., V, 463. April 1667 (?)

41 Stock, V, 229n.

42 Jernegan, 49.

43 J. D. Lang, *Transportation and Colonization* (London, 1837), 10.

44 Merivale, 125.

45 J. D. Butler, "British Convicts Shipped to American Colonies," *American Historical Review* (Oct., 1896), 25.

46 J. C. Jeaffreson (ed.), *A Young Squire of the Seventeenth Century. From the Papers (A.D. 1676–1686) of Christopher Jeaffreson* (London, 1878), I, 258. Jeaffreson to Poyntz, 6 May 1681.

47 For Cromwell's own assurance for this, see Stock, I, 211. Cromwell to Speaker Lenthall, 17 Sept. 1649.

48 V. T. Harlow, *A History of Barbados, 1625–1685* (Oxford, 1926), 295.

49 J. A. Williamson, *The Caribbee Islands Under the Proprietary Patents* (Oxford, 1926), 95.

50 *Calendar of State Papers, Colonial Series*, XIII, 65. Joseph Crispe to Col. Bayer, 10 June 1689 from St Christopher: "Besides the French we have a still worse enemy in the Irish Catholics." In Montserrat the Irish, three to every one of the English, threatened to turn over the island to the French (ibid., 73. 27 June 1689). Governor Codrington from Antigua preferred to trust the defence of Montserrat to the few English and their slaves rather than rely on the "doubtful fidelity" of the Irish (ibid., 112–13. 31 July 1689). He disarmed the Irish in Nevis and sent them to Jamaica (ibid., 123. 15 Aug. 1689).

51 H. J. Ford, *The Scotch-Irish in America* (New York, 1941), 208.

52 *Calendar of State Papers, Colonial Series*, V, 495. Petition of Barbados, 5 Sept. 1667.

53 Stock, I, 288n, 321n, 327.

54 Harlow, 297–8.

55 Mittelberger, 19.

56 Stock, I, 249. 25 March 1659.

57 Geiser, 57.

58 E. W. Andrews (ed.), *Journal of a Lady of Quality; Being the Narrative of a Journey from Scotland to the West Indies, North Carolina and Portugal, in the years 1774–1776* (New Haven, 1923), 33.

59 Jeaffreson, II, 4.

60 J. A. Doyle, *English Colonies in America – Virginia, Maryland, and the Carolinas* (New York, 1889), 387.

61 MacInnes, 164–5; S. Sever, *Memoirs Historical and Topographical of Bristol and its Neighbourhood* (Bristol, 1821–1823), II, 531; R. North, *The Life of the Rt. Hon. Francis North, Baron Guildford* (London, 1826), II, 24–7.

62 Seyer, II, 532.

63 *Cambridge History of the British Empire*, I, 563–5.

64 Ballagh, 42.

65 McCormac, 75.

66 Ibid., 111.

67 C. A. Herrick, *White Servitude in Pennsylvania* (Philadelphia, 1926), 3.

68 Stock, I, 249.

69 Harlow, 306.

70 Stock, I, 250. 25 March 1659.

71 *Calendar of State Papers, Colonial Series,* IX, 394. 30 May 1676.

72 Sir W. Besant, *London in the Eighteenth Century* (London, 1902), 557.

73 *Calendar of State Papers, Colonial Series,* V, 229. Report of Committee of Council for Foreign Plantations, Aug., 1664 (?).

74 G. S. Callender, *Selections from the Economic History of the United States, 1765–1860* (New York, 1909), 48.

75 *Calendar of State Papers, Colonial Series,* X, 574. 13 July 1680.

76 H. J. Laski, *The Rise of European Liberalism* (London, 1936), 199, 215, 221.

77 Daniel Defoe, *Moll Flanders* (Abbey Classics edition, London, n.d.), 71.

78 T. J. Wertenbaker, *The Planters of Colonial Virginia* (Princeton, 1922), 61.

79 Herrick, 278.

80 Ibid., 12.

81 *Calendar of State Papers, Colonial Series,* V, 220. Petition of Merchants, Planters, and Masters of Ships trading to the Plantations, 12 July 1664.

82 Harlow, 307.

83 *Calendar of State Papers, Colonial Series,* IX 445. 15 Aug. 1676.

84 U. B. Phillips, *Life and Labor in the Old South* (Boston, 1929), 25.

85 J. S. Bassett, *Slavery and Servitude in the Colony of North Carolina* (Baltimore, 1896), 77. On the docility of the Negro slave, see *infra*, pp. 201–8.

86 Flanders, 14.

87 Cairnes, 35n.

88 Callender, 764n.

89 Cairnes, 36.

90 Ortiz, 6, 84.

91 A. G. Price, *White Settlers in the Tropics* (New York, 1939), 83.

92 Ibid., 83, 95.

93 Ibid., 92.

94 Ibid., 94.

95 E. T. Thompson, "The Climatic Theory of the Plantation," *Agricultural History* (Jan., 1941), 60.

96 H. L. Wilkinson, *The World's Population Problems and a White Australia* (London, 1930), 250.

97 Ibid., 251.

98 R. Guerra, *Azúcar y Población en Las Antillas* (La Habana, 1935), 20.

99 Williamson, 157–8.

100 *Calendar of State Papers, Colonial Series,* X, 503.

Governor Atkins, 26 March 1680.

101 Ibid., VII, 141. Sir Peter Colleton to Governor Codrington, 14 Dec. 1670. A similar suggestion came from Jamaica in 1686. Permission was requested for the introduction of cotton manufacture, to provide employment for the poor whites. The reply of the British Customs authorities was that "the more such manufactures are encouraged in the Colonies the less they will be dependent on England." F. Cundall, *The Governors of Jamaica in the Seventeenth Century* (London, 1936), 102–3.

102 *Calendar of State Papers, Colonial Series,* XIV, 446–7. Governor Russell, 23 March 1695.

103 C. S. S. Higham, *The Development of the Leeward Islands under the Restoration, 1660–1688* (Cambridge, 1921), 145.

104 Harlow, 44.

105 Callender, 762.

106 Merivale, 62.

107 Harlow, 293.

108 Ibid., 41.

109 *Calendar of State Papers, Colonial Series,* V, 529. "Some Observations on the Island of Barbadoes," 1667.

110 Harlow, 41.

111 Ibid., 43.

112 Merivale, 81.

113 F. W. Pitman, *The Settlement and Financing of British West India Plantations in the Eighteenth Century,* in *Essays in Colonial History by Students of C. M. Andrews* (New Haven, 1931), 267.

114 Ibid., 267–9.

115 *Calendar of State Papers, Colonial Series,* I, 79. Governor Sir Francis Wyatt and Council of Virginia, 6 April 1626.

116 Wertenbaker, 59, 115, 122–3, 131, 151.

117 R. B. Vance, *Human Factors in Cotton Culture: A Study in the Social Geography of the American South* (Chapel Hill, 1929), 36.

118 J. A. Saco, *Historia de la Esclavitud de la Raza Africana en el Nuevo Mundo y en especial en los Países America-Hispanos* (La Habana, 1938), I, Introduction, p. xxviii. The Introduction is by Fernando Ortiz.

119 T. Blanco, "El Prejuicio Racial en Puerto Rico," *Estudios Afrocubanos,* II (1938), 26.

120 Saco, *Historia de la Esclavitud de la Raza Africana . . .* Introduction, p. xxx.

121 *Immigration of Labourers into the West Indian Colonies and the Mauritius,* Part II, *Parliamentary Papers,* 26 Aug. 1846, 60. Henry Light to Lord Stanley, 17 Sept. 1845: "As labourers they are invaluable, as citizens they are amongst the best, and rarely are brought before the courts of justice or the police."

122 *Papers Relative to the West Indies, 1841–1842, Jamaica-Barbados,* 18. C. T. Metcalfe to Lord John Russell, 27 Oct. 1841.

123 *Immigration of Labourers into the West Indian Colonies*

..., 111. William Reynolds to C. A. Fitzroy, 20 Aug. 1845.

124 These figures are taken from tables in I. Ferenczi, *International Migrations* (New York, 1929), I, 506–9, 516–18, 520, 534, 537.

125 The following table illustrates the use of Chinese labor on Cuban sugar plantations in 1857:

Plantation	Negroes	Chinese
Flor de Cuba	409	170
San Martín	452	125
El Progreso	550	40
Armonía	330	20
Santa Rosa	300	30
San Rafael	260	20
Santa Susana	632	200

The last plantation was truly cosmopolitan; the slave gang included 34 natives of Yucatan. These figures are taken from J. G. Cantero, *Los Ingenios de la Isla de Cuba* (La Habana, 1857). The book is not paged. There was some opposition to this Chinese labor, on the ground that it increased the heterogeneity of the population. "And what shall we lose thereby?" was the retort. *Anales de la Real Junta de Fomento y Sociedad Económica de La Habana* (La Habana, 1851), 187.

126 Ferenczi, I, 527.

45

The Interesting Narrative . . .

Olaudah Equiano

I hope the reader will not think I have trespassed on his patience in introducing myself to him with some account of the manners and customs of my country. They had been implanted in me with great care, and made an impression on my mind, which time could not erase, and which all the adversity and variety of fortune I have since experienced, served only to rivet and record: for, whether the love of one's country be real or imaginary, or a lesson of reason, or an instinct of nature, I still look back with pleasure on the first scenes of my life, though that pleasure has been for the most part mingled with sorrow.

I have already acquainted the reader with the time and place of my birth. My father, besides many slaves, had a numerous family, of which seven lived to grow up, including myself and sister, who was the only daughter. As I was the youngest of the sons, I became, of course, the greatest favorite with my mother, and was always with her; and she used to take particular pains to form my mind.[1] I was trained up from my earliest years in the art of war: my daily exercise was shooting and throwing javelins, and my mother adorned me with emblems, after the manner of our greatest warriors. In this way I grew up till I had turned the age of eleven, when an end was put to my happiness in the following manner: Generally, when the grown people in the neighborhood were gone far in the fields to labor, the children assembled together in some of the neighboring premises to play; and commonly some of us used to get up a tree to look

out for any assailant, or kidnapper, that might come upon us – for they sometimes took those opportunities of our parents' absence, to attack and carry off as many as they could seize. One day as I was watching at the top of a tree in our yard, I saw one of those people come into the yard of our next neighbor but one, to kidnap, there being many stout young people in it. Immediately on this I gave the alarm of the rogue, and he was surrounded by the stoutest of them, who entangled him with cords, so that he could not escape, till some of the grown people came and secured him. But, alas! ere long it was my fate to be thus attacked, and to be carried off, when none of the grown people were nigh.

One day, when all our people were gone out to their works as usual, and only I and my dear sister were left to mind the house, two men and a woman got over our walls, and in a moment seized us both, and, without giving us time to cry out, or make resistance, they stopped our mouths, and ran off with us into the nearest wood. Here they tied our hands, and continued to carry us as far as they could, till night came on, when we reached a small house, where the robbers halted for refreshment, and spent the night. We were then unbound, but were unable to take any food; and, being quite overpowered by fatigue and grief, our only relief was some sleep, which allayed our misfortune for a short time. The next morning we left the house, and continued travelling all the day. For a long time we had kept the woods, but at last we came into a road which I believed I knew. I had now some hopes of being delivered; for we had advanced but a little way before I discovered some people at a distance, on which I began to cry out for their assistance; but my cries had no other effect than to make them tie me faster and stop my mouth, and then they put me into a large sack. They also stopped my sister's mouth, and tied her hands; and in this manner we proceeded till we were out of sight of these people. When we went to rest the following night, they offered us some victuals, but we refused it; and the only comfort we had was in being in one another's arms all that night, and bathing each other with our tears. But alas! we were soon deprived of even the small comfort of weeping together.

The next day proved a day of greater sorrow than I had yet experienced; for my sister and I were then separated, while we lay clasped in each other's arms. It was in vain that we besought them not to part us; she was torn from me, and immediately carried away, while I was left in a state of distraction not to be described. I cried and grieved continually; and for several days did not eat anything but what they forced into my mouth. At length, after many days' travelling, during which I had often changed masters, I got into the hands of a chieftain, in a very pleasant country. This man had two wives and some children, and they all used me extremely well, and did all they could do to comfort me; particularly the first wife, who was something like my mother. Although I was a great many days' journey from my father's house, yet these people spoke exactly the same language with us. This first master of mine, as I may call him, was a smith, and my principal employment was working his bellows, which were the same kind as I had seen in my vicinity. They were in some respects not unlike the stoves here in gentlemen's kitchens, and were covered over with leather; and in the middle of that leather a stick was fixed, and a person stood up, and worked it in the same manner as is done to pump water out of a cask with a hand pump. I believe it was gold he worked, for it was a lovely bright yellow color, and was worn by the women on their wrists and ankles.

I was there I suppose about a month, and they at last used to trust me some little distance from the house. This liberty I used in embracing every opportunity to inquire the way to my own home; and I also sometimes, for the same purpose, went with the maidens, in the cool of the evenings, to bring pitchers of water from the springs for the use of the house. I had also remarked where the sun rose

in the morning, and set in the evening, as I had travelled along; and I had observed that my father's house was towards the rising of the sun. I therefore determined to seize the first opportunity of making my escape, and to shape my course for that quarter; for I was quite oppressed and weighed down by grief after my mother and friends; and my love of liberty, ever great, was strengthened by the mortifying circumstance of not daring to eat with the free-born children, although I was mostly their companion.

While I was projecting my escape, one day an unlucky event happened, which quite disconcerted my plan, and put an end to my hopes. I used to be sometimes employed in assisting an elderly slave to cook and take care of the poultry; and one morning, while I was feeding some chickens, I happened to toss a small pebble at one of them, which hit it on the middle, and directly killed it. The old slave, having soon after missed the chicken, inquired after it; and on my relating the accident (for I told her the truth, for my mother would never suffer me to tell a lie), she flew into a violent passion, and threatened that I should suffer for it; and, my master being out, she immediately went and told her mistress what I had done. This alarmed me very much, and I expected an instant flogging, which to me was uncommonly dreadful, for I had seldom been beaten at home. I therefore resolved to fly; and accordingly I ran into a thicket that was hard by, and hid myself in the bushes. Soon afterwards my mistress and the slave returned, and, not seeing me, they searched all the house, but not finding me, and I not making answer when they called to me, they thought I had run away, and the whole neighborhood was raised in the pursuit of me.

In that part of the country, as in ours, the houses and villages were skirted with woods, or shrubberies, and the bushes were so thick that a man could readily conceal himself in them, so as to elude the strictest search. The neighbors continued the whole day looking for me, and several times many of them came within a few yards of the place where I lay hid. I expected every moment, when I heard a rustling among the trees, to be found out, and punished by my master; but they never discovered me, though they were often so near that I even heard their conjectures as they were looking about for me; and I now learned from them that any attempts to return home would be hopeless. Most of them supposed I had fled towards home; but the distance was so great, and the way so intricate, that they thought I could never reach it, and that I should be lost in the woods. When I heard this I was seized with a violent panic, and abandoned myself to despair. Night, too, began to approach, and aggravated all my fears. I had before entertained hopes of getting home, and had determined when it should be dark to make the attempt; but I was now convinced it was fruitless, and began to consider that, if possibly I could escape all other animals, I could not those of the human kind; and that, not knowing the way, I must perish in the woods. Thus was I like the hunted deer –

– Every leaf and every whisp'ring breath,
Convey'd a foe, and every foe a death.

I heard frequent rustlings among the leaves, and being pretty sure they were snakes, I expected every instant to be stung by them. This increased my anguish, and the horror of my situation became now quite insupportable. I at length quitted the thicket, very faint and hungry, for I had not eaten or drank anything all the day, and crept to my master's kitchen, from whence I set out at first, which was an open shed, and laid myself down in the ashes with an anxious wish for death, to relieve me from all my pains. I was scarcely awake in the morning, when the old woman slave, who was the first up, came to light the fire, and saw me in the fireplace. She was very much surprised to see me, and could scarcely believe her own eyes. She now promised to intercede for me, and went for her master, who soon after came, and, having slightly reprimanded me, ordered me to be taken care of, and not ill treated.

Soon after this, my master's only daughter, and child by his first wife, sickened and died, which affected him so much that for sometime he was almost frantic, and really would have killed himself, had he not been watched and prevented. However, in a short time afterwards he recovered, and I was again sold. I was now carried to the left of the sun's rising, through many dreary wastes and dismal woods, amidst the hideous roarings of wild beasts. The people I was sold to used to carry me very often, when I was tired, either on their shoulders or on their backs. I saw many convenient well-built sheds along the road, at proper distances, to accommodate the merchants and travellers, who lay in those buildings along with their wives, who often accompany them; and they always go well armed.

From the time I left my own nation, I always found somebody that understood me till I came to the sea coast. The languages of different nations did not totally differ, nor were they so copious as those of the Europeans, particularly the English. They were therefore easily learned; and, while I was journeying thus through Africa, I acquired two or three different tongues. In this manner I had been travelling for a considerable time, when, one evening, to my great surprise, whom should I see brought to the house where I was but my dear sister! As soon as she saw me, she gave a loud shriek, and ran into my arms – I was quite overpowered; neither of us could speak, but, for a considerable time, clung to each other in mutual embraces, unable to do anything but weep. Our meeting affected all who saw us; and, indeed, I must acknowledge, in honor of those sable destroyers of human rights, that I never met with any ill treatment, or saw any offered to their slaves, except tying them, when necessary, to keep them from running away.

When these people knew we were brother and sister, they indulged us to be together; and the man, to whom I supposed we belonged, lay with us, he in the middle, while she and I held one another by the hands across his breast all night; and thus for a while we forgot our misfortunes, in the joy of being together; but even this small comfort was soon to have an end; for scarcely had the fatal morning appeared when she was again torn from me forever! I was now more miserable, if possible, than before. The small relief which her presence gave me from pain, was gone, and the wretchedness of my situation was redoubled by my anxiety after her fate, and my apprehensions lest her sufferings should be greater than mine, when I could not be with her to alleviate them. Yes, thou dear partner of all my childish sports! thou sharer of my joys and sorrows! happy should I have ever esteemed myself to encounter every misery for you and to procure your freedom by the sacrifice of my own. Though you were early forced from my arms, your image has been always riveted in my heart, from which neither time nor fortune have been able to remove it; so that, while the thoughts of your sufferings have damped my prosperity, they have mingled with adversity and increased its bitterness. To that Heaven which protects the weak from the strong, I commit the care of your innocence and virtues, if they have not already received their full reward, and if your youth and delicacy have not long since fallen victims to the violence of the African trader, the pestilential stench of a Guinea ship, the seasoning in the European colonies, or the lash and lust of a brutal and unrelenting overseer.

I did not long remain after my sister. I was again

sold, and carried through a number of places, till after travelling a considerable time, I came to a town called Tinmah, in the most beautiful country I had yet seen in Africa.[2] It was extremely rich, and there were many rivulets which flowed through it, and supplied a large pond in the centre of the town, where the people washed. Here I saw for the first time cocoanuts, which I thought superior to any nuts I had ever tasted before; and the trees, which were loaded, were also interspersed among the houses, which had commodious shades adjoining, and were in the same manner as ours, the insides being neatly plastered and whitewashed. Here I also saw and tasted for the first time, sugar-cane. Their money consisted of little white shells, the size of the finger nail. I was sold here for one hundred and seventy-two of them, by a merchant who lived and brought me there.

I had been about two or three days at his house, when a wealthy widow, a neighbor of his, came there one evening, and brought with her an only son, a young gentleman about my own age and size. Here they saw me; and, having taken a fancy to me, I was bought of the merchant, and went home with them. Her house and premises were situated close to one of those rivulets I have mentioned, and were the finest I ever saw in Africa: they were very extensive, and she had a number of slaves to attend her.

The next day I was washed and perfumed, and when meal time came, I was led into the presence of my mistress, and ate and drank before her with her son. This filled me with astonishment; and I could scarce help expressing my surprise that the young gentleman should suffer me, who was bound, to eat with him who was free; and not only so, but that he would not at any time either eat or drink till I had taken first, because I was the eldest, which was agreeable to our custom. Indeed, every thing here, and all their treatment of me, made me forget that I was a slave. The language of these people resembled ours so nearly, that we understood each other perfectly. They had also the very same customs as we. There were likewise slaves daily to attend us, while my young master and I, with other boys, sported with our darts and bows and arrows, as I had been used to do at home. In this resemblance to my former happy state, I passed about two months; and I now began to think I was to be adopted into the family, and was beginning to be reconciled to my situation, and to forget by degrees my misfortunes, when all at once the delusion vanished; for, without the least previous

knowledge, one morning early, while my dear master and companion was still asleep, I was awakened out of my reverie to fresh sorrow, and hurried away even amongst the uncircumcised.

Thus, at the very moment I dreamed of the greatest happiness, I found myself most miserable; and it seemed as if fortune wished to give me this taste of joy only to render the reverse more poignant. The change I now experienced was as painful as it was sudden and unexpected. It was a change indeed, from a state of bliss to a scene which is inexpressible by me, as it discovered to me an element I had never before beheld, and till then had no idea of, and wherein such instances of hardship and cruelty continually occurred, as I can never reflect on but with horror.

All the nations and people I had hitherto passed through, resembled our own in their manners, customs, and language; but I came at length to a country, the inhabitants of which differed from us in all those particulars. I was very much struck with this difference, especially when I came among a people who did not circumcise, and ate without washing their hands. They cooked also in iron pots, and had European cutlasses and cross bows, which were unknown to us, and fought with their fists among themselves. Their women were not so modest as ours, for they ate, and drank, and slept with their men. But above all, I was amazed to see no sacrifices or offerings among them. In some of those places the people ornamented themselves with scars, and likewise filed their teeth very sharp. They wanted sometimes to ornament me in the same manner, but I would not suffer them; hoping that I might some time be among a people who did not thus disfigure themselves, as I thought they did. At last I came to the banks of a large river which was covered with canoes, in which the people appeared to live with their household utensils, and provisions of all kinds. I was beyond measure astonished at this, as I had never before seen any water larger than a pond or a rivulet; and my surprise was mingled with no small fear when I was put into one of these canoes, and we began to paddle and move along the river. We continued going on thus till night, and when we came to land, and made fires on the banks, each family by themselves; some dragged their canoes on shore, others stayed and cooked in theirs, and laid in them all night. Those on the land had mats, of which they made tents, some in the shape of little houses; in these we slept; and after the morning meal, we embarked again and proceeded as before. I was often very much astonished to see some of the women, as well as the men, jump into the water, dive to the bottom, come up again, and swim about.

Thus I continued to travel, sometimes by land, sometimes by water, through different countries and various nations, till, at the end of six or seven months after I had been kidnapped, I arrived at the sea coast. It would be tedious and uninteresting to relate all the incidents which befell me during this journey, and which I have not yet forgotten; of the various hands I passed through, and the manners and customs of all the different people among whom I lived – I shall therefore only observe, that in all the places where I was, the soil was exceedingly rich; the pumpkins, eadas, plantains, yams, &c. &c., were in great abundance, and of incredible size. There were also vast quantities of different gums, though not used for any purpose, and everywhere a great deal of tobacco. The cotton even grew quite wild, and there was plenty of red-wood. I saw no mechanics whatever in all the way, except such as I have mentioned. The chief employment in all these countries was agriculture, and both the males and females, as with us, were brought up to it, and trained in the arts of war.

The first object which saluted my eyes when I arrived on the coast, was the sea, and a slave ship, which was then riding at anchor, and waiting for its cargo. These filled me with astonishment, which was soon converted into terror, when I was carried on board. I was immediately handled, and tossed up to see if I were sound, by some of the crew; and I was now persuaded that I had gotten into a world of bad spirits, and that they were going to kill me. Their complexions, too, differing so much from ours, their long hair, and the language they spoke (which was very different from any I had ever heard), united to confirm me in this belief. Indeed, such were the horrors of my views and fears at the moment, that, if ten thousand worlds had been my own, I would have freely parted with them all to have exchanged my condition with that of the meanest slave in my own country. When I looked round the ship too, and saw a large furnace of copper boiling, and a multitude of black people of every description chained together, every one of their countenances expressing dejection and sorrow, I no longer doubted of my fate; and, quite overpowered with horror and anguish, I fell motionless on the deck and fainted. When I recovered a little, I found some black people about me, who I believed were some of those who had brought me on board, and had been receiving their pay; they talked to me in order to cheer me, but all in vain. I asked them if we were not to be eaten by those white men with horrible looks, red faces, and long hair. They told me I was not, and one of the crew brought me a small portion of spirituous liquor in a wine glass; but being afraid of him, I would not take it out of his hand. One of the blacks therefore took it from him and gave it to me, and I took a little down my palate, which, instead of reviving me, as they thought it would, threw me into the greatest consternation at the strange feeling it produced, having never tasted any such liquor before. Soon after this, the blacks who brought me on board went off, and left me abandoned to despair.

I now saw myself deprived of all chance of returning to my native country, or even the least glimpse of hope of gaining the shore, which I now considered as friendly; and I even wished for my former slavery in preference to my present situation, which was filled with horrors of every kind, still heightened by my ignorance of what I was to undergo. I was not long suffered to indulge my grief; I was soon put down under the decks, and there I received such a salutation in my nostrils as I had never experienced in my life: so that, with the loathsomeness of the stench, and crying together, I became so sick and low that I was not able to eat, nor had I the least desire to taste anything. I now wished for the last friend, death, to relieve me; but soon, to my grief, two of the white men offered me eatables; and, on my refusing to eat, one of them held me fast by the hands, and laid me across, I think, the windlass, and tied my feet, while the other flogged me severely. I had never experienced anything of this kind before, and, although not being used to the water, I naturally feared that element the first time I saw it, yet, nevertheless, could I have got over the nettings, I would have jumped over the side, but I could not; and besides, the crew used to watch us very closely who were not chained down to the decks, lest we should leap into the water; and I have seen some of these poor African prisoners most severely cut, for attempting to do so, and hourly whipped for not eating. This indeed was often the case with myself.

In a little time after, amongst the poor chained men, I found some of my own nation, which in a small degree gave ease to my mind. I inquired of these what was to be done with us? They gave me to understand, we were to be carried to these white people's country to work for them. I then was a little revived, and thought, if it were no worse than working, my situation was not so desperate; but still

I feared I should be put to death, the white people looked and acted, as I thought, in so savage a manner; for I had never seen among any people such instances of brutal cruelty; and this not only shown towards us blacks, but also to some of the whites themselves. One white man in particular I saw, when we were permitted to be on deck, flogged so unmercifully with a large rope near the foremast, that he died in consequence of it; and they tossed him over the side as they would have done a brute. This made me fear these people the more; and I expected nothing less than to be treated in the same manner. I could not help expressing my fears and apprehensions to some of my countrymen; I asked them if these people had no country, but lived in this hollow place (the ship)? They told me they did not, but came from a distant one. "Then," said I, "how comes it in all our country we never heard of them?" They told me because they lived so very far off. I then asked where were their women? had they any like themselves? I was told they had. "And why," said I, "do we not see them?" They answered, because they were left behind. I asked how the vessel could go? They told me they could not tell; but that there was cloth put upon the masts by the help of the ropes I saw, and then the vessel went on; and the white men had some spell or magic they put in the water when they liked, in order to stop the vessel. I was exceedingly amazed at this account, and really thought they were spirits. I therefore wished much to be from amongst them, for I expected they would sacrifice me; but my wishes were vain – for we were so quartered that it was impossible for any of us to make our escape.

While we stayed on the coast I was mostly on deck; and one day, to my great astonishment, I saw one of these vessels coming in with the sails up. As soon as the whites saw it, they gave a great shout, at which we were amazed; and the more so, as the vessel appeared larger by approaching nearer. At last, she came to an anchor in my sight, and when the anchor was let go, I and my countrymen who saw it, were lost in astonishment to observe the vessel stop – and were now convinced it was done by magic. Soon after this the other ship got her boats out, and they came on board of us, and the people of both ships seemed very glad to see each other. Several of the strangers also shook hands with us black people, and made motions with their hands, signifying I suppose, we were to go to their country, but we did not understand them.

At last, when the ship we were in, had got in all her cargo, they made ready with many fearful noises, and we were all put under deck, so that we could not see how they managed the vessel. But this disappointment was the least of my sorrow. The stench of the hold while we were on the coast was so intolerably loathsome, that it was dangerous to remain there for any time, and some of us had been permitted to stay on the deck for the fresh air; but now that the whole ship's cargo were confined together, it became absolutely pestilential. The closeness of the place, and the heat of the climate, added to the number in the ship, which was so crowded that each had scarcely room to turn himself, almost suffocated us. This produced copious perspirations, so that the air soon became unfit for respiration, from a variety of loathsome smells, and brought on a sickness among the slaves, of which many died – thus falling victims to the improvident avarice, as I may call it, of their purchasers. This wretched situation was again aggravated by the galling of the chains, now became insupportable, and the filth of the necessary tubs,[3] into which the children often fell, and were almost suffocated. The shrieks of the women, and the groans of the dying, rendered the whole a scene of horror almost inconceivable. Happily perhaps, for myself, I was soon reduced so low here that it was thought necessary to keep me almost always on deck; and from my extreme youth I was not put in fetters. In this situation I expected every hour to share the fate of my companions, some of whom were almost daily brought upon deck at the point of death, which I began to hope would soon put an end to my miseries. Often did I think many of the inhabitants of the deep much more happy than myself. I envied them the freedom they enjoyed, and as often wished I could change my condition for theirs. Every circumstance I met with, served only to render my state more painful, and heightened my apprehensions, and my opinion of the cruelty of the whites.

One day they had taken a number of fishes; and when they had killed and satisfied themselves with as many as they thought fit, to our astonishment who were on deck, rather than give any of them to us to eat, as we expected, they tossed the remaining fish into the sea again, although we begged and prayed for some as well as we could, but in vain; and some of my countrymen, being pressed by hunger, took an opportunity, when they thought no one saw them, of trying to get a little privately; but they were discovered, and the attempt procured them some very severe floggings.

One day, when we had a smooth sea and

moderate wind, two of my wearied countrymen who were chained together (I was near them at the time), preferring death to such a life of misery, somehow made through the nettings and jumped into the sea; immediately, another quite dejected fellow, who, on account of his illness, was suffered to be out of irons, also followed their example; and I believe many more would very soon have done the same, if they had not been prevented by the ship's crew, who were instantly alarmed. Those of us that were the most active, were in a moment put down under the deck; and there was such a noise and confusion amongst the people of the ship as I never heard before, to stop her, and get the boat out to go after the slaves. However, two of the wretches were drowned, but they got the other, and afterwards flogged him unmercifully, for thus attempting to prefer death to slavery. In this manner we continued to undergo more hardships than I can now relate, hardships which are inseparable from this accursed trade. Many a time we were near suffocation from the want of fresh air, which we were often without for whole days together. This, and the stench of the necessary tubs, carried off many.

During our passage, I first saw flying fishes, which surprised me very much; they used frequently to fly across the ship, and many of them fell on the deck. I also now first saw the use of the quadrant; I had often with astonishment seen the mariners make observations with it, and I could not think what it meant. They at last took notice of my surprise; and one of them, willing to increase it, as well as to gratify my curiosity, made me one day look through it. The clouds appeared to me to be land, which disappeared as they passed along. This heightened my wonder; and I was now more persuaded than ever, that I was in another world, and that every thing about me was magic.

At last we came in sight of the island of Barbadoes, at which the whites on board gave a great shout, and made many signs of joy to us. We did not know what to think of this; but as the vessel drew nearer, we plainly saw the harbor, and other ships of different kinds and sizes, and we soon anchored amongst them, off Bridgetown. Many merchants and planters now came on board, though it was in the evening. They put us in separate parcels, and examined us attentively. They also made us jump, and pointed to the land, signifying we were to go there. We thought by this, we should be eaten by these ugly men, as they appeared to us; and, when soon after we were all put down under the deck again, there was much dread and trembling among us, and nothing but bitter cries to be heard all the night from these apprehensions, insomuch, that at last the white people got some old slaves from the land to pacify us. They told us we were not to be eaten, but to work, and were soon to go on land, where we should see many of our country people. This report eased us much. And sure enough, soon after we were landed, there came to us Africans of all languages.

We were conducted immediately to the merchant's yard, where we were all pent up together, like so many sheep in a fold, without regard to sex or age. As every object was new to me, everything I saw filled me with surprise. What struck me first, was, that the houses were built with bricks and stories, and in every other respect different from those I had seen in Africa; but I was still more astonished on seeing people on horseback. I did not know what this could mean; and, indeed, I thought these people were full of nothing but magical arts. While I was in this astonishment, one of my fellow prisoners spoke to a countryman of his, about the horses, who said they were the same kind they had in their country. I understood them, though they were from a distant part of Africa; and I thought it odd I had not seen any horses there; but afterwards, when I came to converse with different Africans, I found they had many horses amongst them, and much larger than those I then saw.

We were not many days in the merchant's custody, before we were sold after their usual manner, which is this: On a signal given (as the beat of a drum), the buyers rush at once into the yard where the slaves are confined, and make choice of that parcel they like best. The noise and clamor with which this is attended, and the eagerness visible in the countenances of the buyers, serve not a little to increase the apprehension of terrified Africans, who may well be supposed to consider them as the ministers of that destruction to which they think themselves devoted. In this manner, without scruple, are relations and friends separated, most of them never to see each other again.

I remember, in the vessel in which I was brought over, in the men's apartment, there were several brothers, who, in the sale, were sold in different lots; and it was very moving on this occasion, to see and hear their cries at parting. O, ye nominal Christians! might not an African ask you – Learned you this from your God, who says unto you, Do unto all men as you would men should do unto you? Is it not enough that we are torn from our country and friends, to toil for your luxury and lust of gain?

Must every tender feeling be likewise sacrificed to your avarice? Are the dearest friends and relations, now rendered more dear by their separation from their kindred, still to be parted from each other, and thus prevented from cheering the gloom of slavery, with the small comfort of being together, and mingling their sufferings and sorrows? Why are parents to lose their children, brothers their sisters, or husbands their wives? Surely, this is a new refinement in cruelty, which, while it has no advantage to atone for it, thus aggravates distress, and adds fresh horrors even to the wretchedness of slavery.

Notes

1 Acholonu identifies Equiano's father as Ichie Ekwealuo, born about 1700, and his mother as Nwansoro, from the village of Uli. (See Catherine O. Acholonu, *The Igbo Roots of Olaudah Equiano*. Owerri, Nigeria: AFA, 1989, 42–3.)

2 Possibly Utuma, Utu Etim, or Tinan, villages on the border between Ibo and Ibibio. (Acholonu, *Igbo Roots*, 7–9.)

3 Latrines.

46

Thoughts and Sentiments on the Evil of Slavery

Ottobah Cugoano, a Native of Africa

One law, and one manner shall be for you, and for the stranger that sojourneth with you; and therefore, all things whatsoever ye would that men should do to you, do ye even so to them.

Numb. xv.16. – Math. vii.12.

As several learned gentlemen of distinguished abilities, as well as eminent for their great humanity, liberality and candour, have written various essays against that infamous traffic of the African Slave Trade, carried on with the West-India planters and merchants, to the great shame and disgrace of all Christian nations wherever it is admitted in any of their territories, or in any place or situation amongst them; it cannot be amiss that I should thankfully acknowledge these truly worthy and humane gentlemen with the warmest sense of gratitude, for their beneficent and laudable endeavours towards a total suppression of that infamous and iniquitous traffic of stealing, kid-napping, buying, selling, and cruelly enslaving men!

Those who have endeavoured to restore to their fellow-creatures the common rights of nature, of which especially the poor unfortunate Black People have been so unjustly deprived, cannot fail in meeting with the applause of all good men, and the approbation of that which will for ever redound to their honor; they have the warrant of that which is divine: *Open thy mouth, judge righteously, plead the*

From *Black Atlantic Writers of the 18th Century*, by Adam Potkay and Sandra Burr (1996), copyright © Adam Potkay and Sandra Burr; by kind permission of Macmillan Press Ltd and St Martin's Press.

cause of the poor and needy; for the liberal deviseth liberal things, and by liberal things shall stand.[1] And they can say with the pious Job, *Did not I weep for him that was in trouble; was not my soul grieved for the poor?*[2]

The kind exertions of many benevolent and humane gentlemen, against the iniquitous traffic of slavery and oppression, has been attended with much good to many, and must redound with great honor to themselves, to humanity and their country; their laudable endeavours have been productive of the most beneficent effects in preventing that savage barbarity from taking place in free countries at home. In this, as well as in many other respects, there is one class of people (whose virtues of probity and humanity are well known) who are worthy of universal approbation and imitation, because, like men of honor and humanity, they have jointly agreed to carry on no slavery and savage barbarity among them; and, since the last war,[3] some mitigation of slavery has been obtained in some respective districts of America, though not in proportion to their own vaunted claims of freedom; but it is to be hoped, that they will yet go on to make a further and greater reformation. However, notwithstanding all that has been done and written against it, that brutish barbarity, and unparalleled injustice, is still carried on to a very great extent in the colonies, and with an avidity as insidious, cruel and oppressive as ever. The longer that men continue in the practice of evil and wickedness, they grow the more abandoned; for nothing in history can equal the barbarity and cruelty of the tortures and murders committed under various pretences in modern slavery, except the annals of the Inquisition and the bloody edicts of Popish massacres.

It is therefore manifest, that something else ought yet to be done; and what is required, is evidently the incumbent duty of all men of enlightened understanding, and of every man that has any claim or affinity to the name of Christian, that the base treatment which the African Slaves undergo, ought to be abolished; and it is moreover evident, that the whole, or any part of that iniquitous traffic of slavery, can no where, or in any degree, be admitted, but among those who must eventually resign their own claim to any degree of sensibility and humanity, for that of barbarians and ruffians.

But it would be needless to arrange an history of all the base treatment which the African Slaves are subjected to, in order to shew the exceeding wickedness and evil of that insidious traffic, as the whole may easily appear in every part, and at every view, to be wholly and totally inimical to every idea of justice, equity, reason and humanity. What I intend to advance against that evil, criminal and wicked traffic of enslaving men, are only some Thoughts and Sentiments which occur to me, as being obvious from the Scriptures of Divine Truth, or such arguments as are chiefly deduced from thence, with other such observations as I have been able to collect. Some of these observations may lead into a larger field of consideration, than that of the African Slave Trade alone; but those causes from wherever they originate, and become the production of slavery, the evil effects produced by it, must shew that its origin and source is of a wicked and criminal nature.

No necessity, or any situation of men, however poor, pitiful and wretched they may be, can warrant them to rob others, or oblige them to become thieves, because they are poor, miserable and wretched: But the robbers of men, the kid-nappers, ensnarers and slave-holders, who take away the common rights and privileges of others to support and enrich themselves, are universally those pitiful and detestable wretches; for the ensnaring of others, and taking away their liberty by slavery and oppression, is the worst kind of robbery, as most opposite to every precept and injunction of the Divine Law, and contrary to that command which enjoins that *all men should love their neighbours as themselves*,[4] and *that they should do unto others, as they would that men should do to them.* As to any other laws that slave-holders may make among themselves, as respecting slaves, they can be of no better kind, nor give them any better character, than what

is implied in the common report – that there may be some honesty among thieves. This may seem a harsh comparison, but the parallel is so coincident that, I must say, I can find no other way of expressing my Thoughts and Sentiments, without making use of some harsh words and comparisons against the carriers on of such abandoned wickedness. But, in this little undertaking, I must humbly hope the impartial reader will excuse such defects as may arise from want of better education; and as to the resentment of those who can lay their cruel lash upon the backs of thousands, for a thousand times less crimes than writing against their enormous wickedness and brutal avarice, is what I may be sure to meet with.

However, it cannot but be very discouraging to a man of my complexion in such an attempt as this, to meet with the evil aspersions of some men, who say, "That an African is not entitled to any competent degree of knowledge, or capable of imbibing any sentiments of probity; and that nature designed him for some inferior link in the chain, fitted only to be a slave."[5] But when I meet with those who make no scruple to deal with the human species, as with the beasts of the earth, I must think them not only brutish, but wicked and base; and that their aspersions are insidious and false: And if such men can boast of greater degrees of knowledge, than any African is entitled to, I shall let them enjoy all the advantages of it unenvied, as I fear it consists only in a greater share of infidelity, and that of a blacker kind than only skin deep. And if their complexion be not what I may suppose, it is at least the nearest in resemblance to an infernal hue. A good man will neither speak nor do as a bad man will; but if a man is bad, it makes no difference whether he be a black or a white devil.

By some of such complexion, as whether black or white it matters not, I was early snatched away from my native country, with about eighteen or twenty more boys and girls, as we were playing in a field. We lived but a few days journey from the coast where we were kid-napped, and as we were decoyed and drove along, we were soon conducted to a factory,[6] and from thence, in the fashionable way of traffic, consigned to Grenada. Perhaps it may not be amiss to give a few remarks, as some account of myself, in this transposition of captivity.

I was born in the city of Agimaque, on the coast of Fantyn; my father was a companion to the chief in that part of the country of Fantee,[7] and when the old king died I was left in his house with his family; soon after I was sent for by his nephew, Ambro

Accasa, who succeeded the old king in the chiefdom of that part of Fantee known by the name of Agimaque and Assinee.[8] I lived with his children, enjoying peace and tranquillity, about twenty moons, which, according to their way of reckoning time, is two years. I was sent for to visit an uncle, who lived at a considerable distance from Agimaque. The first day after we set out we arrived at Assinee, and the third day at my uncle's habitation, where I lived about three months, and was then thinking of returning to my father and young companion at Agimaque; but by this time I had got well acquainted with some of the children of my uncle's hundreds of relations, and we were some days too ventursome in going into the woods to gather fruit and catch birds, and such amusements as pleased us. One day I refused to go with the rest, being rather apprehensive that something might happen to us; till one of my play-fellows said to me, because you belong to the great men, you are afraid to venture your carcase, or else of the *bounsam*, which is the devil.[9] This enraged me so much, that I set a resolution to join the rest, and we went into the woods as usual; but we had not been above two hours before our troubles began, when several great ruffians came upon us suddenly, and said we had committed a fault against their lord, and we must go and answer for it ourselves before him.

Some of us attempted in vain to run away, but pistols and cutlasses were soon introduced, threatening, that if we offered to stir we should all lie dead on the spot. One of them pretended to be more friendly than the rest, and said, that he would speak to their lord to get us clear, and desired that we should follow him; we were then immediately divided into different parties, and drove after him. We were soon led out of the way which we knew, and towards the evening, as we came in sight of a town, they told us that this great man of theirs lived there, but pretended it was too late to go and see him that night. Next morning there came three other men, whose language differed from ours, and spoke to some of those who watched us all the night, but he that pretended to be our friend with the great man, and some others, were gone away. We asked our keepers what these men had been saying to them, and they answered, that they had been asking them, and us together, to go and feast with them that day, and that we must put off seeing the great man till after; little thinking that our doom was so nigh, or that these villains meant to feast on us as their prey. We went with them again about half a day's journey, and came to a great multitude of people, having different music playing; and all the day after we got there, we were very merry with the music, dancing and singing. Towards the evening, we were again persuaded that we could not get back to where the great man lived till next day; and when bed-time came, we were separated into different houses with different people. When the next morning came, I asked for the men that brought me there, and for the rest of my companions; and I was told that they were gone to the sea side to bring home some rum, guns and powder, and that some of my companions were gone with them, and that some were gone to the fields to do something or other. This gave me strong suspicion that there was some treachery in the case, and I began to think that my hopes of returning home again were all over. I soon became very uneasy, not knowing what to do, and refused to eat or drink for whole days together, till the man of the house told me that he would do all in his power to get me back to my uncle; then I eat a little fruit with him, and had some thoughts that I should be sought after, as I would be then missing at home about five or six days. I enquired every day if the men had come back, and for the rest of my companions, but could get no answer of any satisfaction. I was kept about six days at this man's house, and in the evening there was another man came and talked with him a good while, and I heard the one say to the other he must go, and the other said the sooner the better; that man came out and told me that he knew my relations at Agimaque, and that we must set out to-morrow morning, and he would convey me there. Accordingly we set out next day, and travelled till dark, when we came to a place where we had some supper and slept. He carried a large bag with some gold dust, which he said he had to buy some goods at the sea side to take with him to Agimaque. Next day we travelled on, and in the evening came to a town, where I saw several white people, which made me afraid that they would eat me, according to our notion as children in the inland parts of the country.[10] This made me rest very uneasy all the night, and next morning I had some victuals brought, desiring me to eat and make haste, as my guide and kid-napper told me that he had to go to the castle with some company that were going there, as he had told me before, to get some goods. After I was ordered out, the horrors I soon saw and felt, cannot be well described; I saw many of my miserable countrymen chained two and two, some hand-cuffed, and some with their hands tied behind. We were conducted along by a guard, and when we arrived at the castle,

I asked my guide what I was brought there for, he told me to learn the ways of the *browfow*, that is the white faced people.[11] I saw him take a gun, a piece of cloth, and some lead for me, and then he told me that he must now leave me there, and went off. This made me cry bitterly, but I was soon conducted to a prison, for three days, where I heard the groans and cries of many, and saw some of my fellow-captives. But when a vessel arrived to conduct us away to the ship, it was a most horrible scene; there was nothing to be heard but rattling of chains, smacking of whips, and the groans and cries of our fellow-men. Some would not stir from the ground, when they were lashed and beat in the most horrible manner. I have forgot the name of this infernal fort; but we were taken in the ship that came for us, to another that was ready to sail from Cape Coast.[12] When we were put into the ship, we saw several black merchants coming on board, but we were all drove into our holes, and not suffered to speak to any of them. In this situation we continued several days in sight of our native land; but I could find no good person to give any information of my situation to Accasa at Agimaque. And when we found ourselves at last taken away, death was more preferable than life, and a plan was concerted amongst us, that we might burn and blow up the ship, and to perish all together in the flames;[13] but we were betrayed by one of our own countrywomen, who slept with some of the head men of the ship, for it was common for the dirty filthy sailors to take the African women and lie upon their bodies; but the men were chained and pent up in holes. It was the women and boys which were to burn the ship, with the approbation and groans of the rest; though that was prevented, the discovery was likewise a cruel bloody scene.

But it would be needless to give a description of all the horrible scenes which we saw, and the base treatment which we met with in this dreadful captive situation, as the similar cases of thousands, which suffer by this infernal traffic, are well known. Let it suffice to say, that I was thus lost to my dear indulgent parents and relations, and they to me. All my help was cries and tears, and these could not avail; nor suffered long, till one succeeding woe, and dread, swelled up another. Brought from a state of innocence and freedom, and, in a barbarous and cruel manner, conveyed to a state of horror and slavery: This abandoned situation may be easier conceived than described. From the time that I was kid-napped and conducted to a factory, and from thence in the brutish, base, but fashionable way of

traffic, consigned to Grenada, the grievous thoughts which I then felt, still pant in my heart; though my fears and tears have long since subsided. And yet it is still grievous to think that thousands more have suffered in similar and greater distress, under the hands of barbarous robbers, and merciless task-masters; and that many even now are suffering in all the extreme bitterness of grief and woe, that no language can describe[.] The cries of some, and the sight of their misery, may be seen and heard afar; but the deep sounding groans of thousands, and the great sadness of their misery and woe, under the heavy load of oppressions and calamities inflicted upon them, are such as can only be distinctly known to the ears of Jehovah Sabaoth.[14]

This Lord of Hosts, in his great Providence, and in great mercy to me, made a way for my deliverance from Grenada. – Being in this dreadful captivity and horrible slavery, without any hope of deliverance, for about eight or nine months, beholding the most dreadful scenes of misery and cruelty, and seeing my miserable companions often cruelly lashed, and as it were cut to pieces, for the most trifling faults; this made me often tremble and weep, but I escaped better than many of them. For eating a piece of sugar-cane, some were cruelly lashed, or struck over the face to knock their teeth out. Some of the stouter ones, I suppose often reproved, and grown hardened and stupid with many cruel beatings and lashings, or perhaps faint and pressed with hunger and hard labour, were often committing trespasses of this kind, and when detected, they met with exemplary punishment. Some told me they had their teeth pulled out to deter others, and to prevent them from eating any cane in future. Thus seeing my miserable companions and countrymen in this pitiful, distressed and horrible situation, with all the brutish baseness and barbarity attending it, could not but fill my little mind with horror and indignation. But I must own, to the shame of my own countrymen, that I was first kid-napped and betrayed by some of my own complexion, who were the first cause of my exile and slavery; but if there were no buyers there would be no sellers. So far as I can remember, some of the Africans in my country keep slaves, which they take in war, or for debt; but those which they keep are well fed, and good care taken of them, and treated well; and, as to their cloathing, they differ according to the custom of the country. But I may safely say, that all the poverty and misery that any of the inhabitants of Africa meet with among themselves, is far inferior to those inhospitable regions of misery which they meet with in the West-Indies, where their hard-hearted overseers have neither regard to the laws of God, nor the life of their fellow-men.

Thanks be to God, I was delivered from Grenada, and that horrid brutal slavery. – A gentleman coming to England, took me for his servant, and brought me away, where I soon found my situation more agreeable.[15] After coming to England, and seeing others write and read, I had a strong desire to learn, and getting what assistance I could, I applied myself to learn reading and writing, which soon became my recreation, pleasure, and delight; and when my master perceived that I could write some, he sent me to a proper school for that purpose to learn. Since, I have endeavoured to improve my mind in reading, and have sought to get all the intelligence I could, in my situation of life, towards the state of my brethren and countrymen in complexion, and of the miserable situation of those who are barbarously sold into captivity, and unlawfully held in slavery.

But, among other observations, one great duty I owe to Almighty God, (the thankful acknowledgement I would not omit for any consideration) that, although I have been brought away from my native country, in that torrent of robbery and wickedness, thanks be to God fo[r] his good providence towards me; I have both obtained liberty, and acquired the great advantages of some little learning, in being able to read and write, and, what is still infinitely of greater advantage, I trust, to know something of HIM *who is that God whose providence rules over all, and who is the only Potent One that rules in the nations over the children of men. It is unto Him, who is the Prince of the Kings of the earth, that I would give all thanks.*[16] And, in some manner, I may say with Joseph, as he did with respect to the evil intention of his brethren, when they sold him into Egypt, that whatever evil intentions and bad motives those insidious robbers had in carrying me away from my native country and friends, I trust, was what the Lord intended for my good.[17] In this respect, I am highly indebted to many of the good people of England for learning and principles unknown to the people of my native country. But, above all, what have I obtained from the Lord God of Hosts, the God of the Christians! in that divine revelation of the only true God, and the Saviour of men, what a treasure of wisdom and blessings are involved? How wonderful is the divine goodness displayed in those invaluable books the Old and New Testaments, that inestimable compilation of books, the Bible? And, O what a treasure to have, and one of the greatest advantages to be able to read therein, and a divine blessing to understand! . . .

"Some pretend that the Africans, in general, are a set of poor, ignorant, dispersed, unsociable people; and that they think it no crime to sell one another, and even their own wives and children; therefore they bring them away to a situation where many of them may arrive to a better state than ever they could obtain in their own native country." This specious pretence is without any shadow of justice and truth, and, if the argument was even true, it could afford no just and warrantable matter for any society of men to hold slaves. But the argument is false; there can be no ignorance, dispersion, or unsociableness so found among them, which can be made better by bringing them away to a state of a degree equal to that of a cow or a horse.

But let their ignorance in some things (in which the Europeans have greatly the advantage of them) be what it will, it is not the intention of those who bring them away to make them better by it; nor is the design of slave-holders of any other intention, but that they may serve them as a kind of engines and beasts of burden; that their own ease and profit may be advanced, by a set of poor helpless men and women, whom they despise and rank with brutes, and keep them in perpetual slavery, both themselves and children, and merciful death is the only release from their toil. By the benevolence of some, a few may get their liberty, and by their own industry and ingenuity, may acquire some learning, mechanical trades, or useful business; and some may be brought away by different gentlemen to free countries, where they get their liberty but no thanks to slave-holders for it. But amongst those who get their liberty, like all other ignorant men, are generally more corrupt in their morals, than they possibly could have been amongst their own people in Africa; for, being mostly amongst the wicked and apostate Christians,[18] they sooner learn their oaths and blasphemies, and their evil ways, than any thing else. Some few, indeed, may eventually arrive at some knowledge of the Christian religion, and the great advantages of it. Such was the case of Ukawsaw Groniosaw, an African prince, who lived in England. He was a long time in a state of great poverty and distress, and must have died at one time for want, if a good and charitable Attorney had not supported him. He was long after in a very poor state, but he would not have given his faith in the Christian religion, in exchange for all the kingdoms of Africa, if they could have been given to him, in place of his poverty, for it. And such was A. Morrant in America.[19] When a boy, he could stroll away into a desart, and prefer the society of wild beasts to the absurd Christianity of his mother's house. He was conducted to the king of the Cherokees, who, in a miraculous manner, was induced by him to embrace the Christian faith. This Morrant was in the British service last war, and his royal convert, the king of the Cherokee Indians, accompanied General Clinton at the siege of Charles-Town.[20]

But the supporters and favourers of slavery make other things a pretence and an excuse in their own defence; such as, that they find that it was admitted under the Divine institution by Moses,[21] as well as the long continued practice of different nations for ages; and that the Africans are peculiarly marked out by some signal prediction in nature and complexion for that purpose.

This seems to be the greatest bulwark of defence which the advocates and favourers of slavery can advance, and what is generally talked of in their favour by those who do not understand it. I shall consider it in that view, whereby it will appear, that they deceive themselves and mislead others. Men are never more liable to be drawn into error, than when truth is made use of in a guileful manner to seduce them. Those who do not believe the scriptures to be a Divine revelation, cannot, consistently with themselves, make the law of Moses, or any mark or prediction they can find respecting any particular set of men, as found in the sacred writings, any reason that one class of men should enslave another. In that respect, all that they have to enquire into should be, whether it be right, or wrong, that any part of the human species should enslave another; and when that is the case, the Africans, though not so learned, are just as wise as the Europeans; and when the matter is left to human wisdom, they are both liable to err. But what the light of nature, and the dictates of reason, when rightly considered, teach, is, that no man ought to

enslave another; and some, who have been rightly guided thereby, have made noble defences for the universal natural rights and privileges of all men. But in this case, when the learned take neither revelation nor reason for their guide, they fall into as great, and worse errors, than the unlearned; for they only make use of that system of Divine wisdom, which should guide them into truth, when they can find or pick out any thing that will suit their purpose, or that they can pervert to such – the very means of leading themselves and others into error. And, in consequence thereof, the pretences that some men make use of for holding of slaves, must be evidently the grossest perversion of reason, as well as an inconsistent and diabolical use of the sacred writings. For it must be a strange perversion of reason, and a wrong use or disbelief of the sacred writings, when any thing found there is so perverted by them, and set up as a precedent and rule for men to commit wickedness. They had better have no reason, and no belief in the scriptures, and make no use of them at all, than only to believe, and make use of that which leads them into the most abominable evil and wickedness of dealing unjustly with their fellow men.

But this will appear evident to all men that believe the scriptures, that every reason necessary is given that they should be believed; and, in this case, that they afford us this information: "That all mankind did spring from one original, and that there are no different species among men. For God who made the world, hath made of one blood all the nations of men that dwell on all the face of the earth."[22] Wherefore we may justly infer, as there are no inferior species, but all of one blood and of one nature, that there does not an inferiority subsist, or depend, on their colour, features or form, whereby some men make a pretence to enslave others; and consequently, as they have all one creator, one original, made of one blood, and all brethren descended from one father, it never could be lawful and just for any nation, or people, to oppress and enslave another.

Notes

1 Isaiah 32:8.
2 Job 30:25. These joined quotations from Isaiah and Job are also found in Olaudah Equiano's letter to the Senate of Great Britain in the *Public Advertiser* of 13 Feb. 1788 and his letter to the "Humanity" poet Samuel Jackson Pratt in the 27 June 1788 edition of

the *Morning Chronicle and London Advertiser*. Furthermore, these quotations appear together again in Equiano's *Narrative*.
3 The American Revolution, 1775–83.
4 The New Testament is filled with exhortations to love one's neighbor. See Matthew 19:19 and 22:39, Mark

12:31, 33, Romans 13:9, Galatians 5:14, and James 2:8.

5 The "chain" referred to here is the Great Chain of Being, the widespread Western notion that all of God's creatures had been assigned hierarchical ranks in the cosmos. Between God and man there intervened a hierarchy of angels and other "spiritous beings"; of all creatures on the earth, man occupied the highest link. See Milton, *Paradise Lost*, Bk. V, II. 470–505; Alexander Pope, *An Essay on Man*, Epistle I, II. 233–46. Beginning in the eighteenth century, certain thinkers sought to establish a graduated scale of perfection within the category of "Man." The concept of racial hierarchy may be found in the classification work of Carl Linné (Linnaeus), who regarded white skin as characteristic of preeminent members of the human species. In a similar manner, in their respective studies of human skulls, Johann Friedrich Blumenbach, Pieter Camper, John Hunter, and Samuel Thomas von Soemmerring gave the cranial characteristics of Caucasian skulls a preferential ranking over those from Ethiopia. Blumenbach, in fact, coined the now-familiar term *Caucasian*, after the Caucasus Mountains in southern Russia, the provenance of those skulls in his collection that he inferred to be European. For more information, see William Stanton, *The Leopard's Spots: Scientific Attitudes toward Race in America 1815–59* (Chicago: University of Chicago Press, 1965); and Winthrop D Jordan's "Introduction" to his critical edition of Samuel Stanhope Smith's *An Essay on the Causes of the Variety of Complexion and Figure in the Human Species* (Cambridge, MA: Harvard University Press, 1965), pp. vii–liii.

6 The word *factory* derives from the Portuguese *feitorias*, land-based European trade depots, which were thickly clustered along the West African coast by the eighteenth century. In his second edition of *An Essay on the Slavery and Commerce of the Human Species, Particularly the African* (enlarged and revised, London, 1788; rpt. New York: AMS Press, 1972), Thomas Clarkson notes the addition of "a new kind of factory established by the British merchants" in African waters: "It consists of a large ship, stationed along the coast, and is called a factory ship. Slaves are brought down and put on board, where they remain as in the factories upon land, till the ships from Europe come along-side, receive them, and carry them off" (p. 26n). He appends this statement to his discussion of the usual methods through which Europeans procured slaves, to wit, "by sending their boats to the villages situated up the creeks and rivers, or upon the sea shore; by dispatching tenders to different parts: or by an application to the factories, either publickly or privately, established there" (pp. 25–6).

7 Cugoano hails from the Fanti (Fante) tribal region of West Africa, located in modern Ghana. His birthplace, "the city of Agimaque," is the town or district of Ajumako. Fantyn may be a reference to Infantin,

which according to Albert van Dantzig and Adam Jones, was "the nucleus of what later became the 'Fantin' or 'Fante' confederacy." The present-day port of Biriwa (earlier known as Anishan) covers an area believed to correspond with the former Infantin, where the Fante chiefs would often meet. See Van Dantzig's and Jones's reprint of Pieter de Marees, *Description and Historical Account of the Gold Kingdom of Guinea (1602)* (rpt. Oxford: Oxford University Press, 1987), pp. 94 n. 1, 84 n. 22.

8 "Agimaque and Assinee," where Cugoano lived with Ambro Accasa, are the districts or towns of Ajumako and Assin. In 1853 Brodie Cruickshank noted that the people from Fanti and Assin, as well as those from Wassaw, Tufel, Denkera, Akim, Aquapim, and Ashantee – areas immediately surrounding or relatively close to Fanti – "all speak dialects of the same language." See *Eighteen Years on the Gold Coast of Africa including an account of the native tribes, and their intercourse with the Europeans*, 2nd ed., 2 vols. (1853; rpt. New York: Barnes & Noble, 1966), vol. 1, p. 46.

9 Paul Edwards notes that *bounsam* in modern Fanti is *abunsam* "a devil or any other evil or dangerous creature." See his introduction to the reprint of Cugoano's *Thoughts and Sentiments on the Evil of Slavery* (London: Dawsons of Pall Mall, 1969), p. xiv.

10 John Matthews reveals in *A Voyage to the River Sierra-Leone* (London, 1788; rpt. London: Frank Cass, 1966) that Europeans were quite familiar with the Africans' fears about the white man's plans for them: once enslaved, an African "imagines the white man buys him either to offer him as a sacrifice to his God, or to devour him as food." Matthews adds that the natives tended to respond to these fears either by falling into a catatonic state, refusing all nourishment, or by laughing – presumably at the white man's foreign, and therefore strange and absurd, appearance (p. 152). Both Cugoano and Olaudah Equiano refused to eat when they were captured.

11 According to Paul Edwards ("introduction," 1969), *browfow* corresponds with the plural modern Fanti word *abrofo*, which means "white men" (p. xiv).

12 The words *castle* and *fort* appear to be relatively synonymous in Cugoano's text, and not without reason. Cape Coast Castle, for example, was both a major European town and fort in which the slave trade was vigorously practiced, so much so that the town and the fort became virtually indistinguishable from each other in ordinary speech. Cugoano tells us that he sailed to Grenada from Cape Coast Castle, but it is virtually impossible to determine which castle or fort the slavers took him to first; approximately forty European forts dotted the Gold Coast landscape in the latter half of the eighteenth century.

13 Slave revolts aboard ship were not uncommon. In *Sketches Taken during Ten Voyages to Africa, Between the Years 1786 and 1800* (n.d.; rpt. New York: Johnson Reprint, 1970) English captain John Adams states,

"Whenever insurrections have occurred on board of slave ships on the Gold Coast, as the Fantees and Ashantees were invariably the promoters of them, the Chambas [a people who lived north of the Ashante], as if to be revenged on them, always assisted the crews in suppressing these mutinies, and keeping them in subjection" (p. 9).

14 Sabaoth is the Greek form of the Hebrew *tsebâóth*, "armies"; to the ancient Hebrews, Yahweh-*tsebâóth* was God as the leader of the Israelite armies, who "went forth with them" (Psalms 44:9). In the KJV New Testament, the phrase "Lord of Sabaoth" appears in Romans 9:29 and James 5:4.

15 Cugoano's account of his rescue from the island of Grenada differs from that of Henri Grégoire in *An Enquiry concerning the Intellectual and Moral Faculties, and Literature of Negroes; Followed with an Account of the Life and Works of Fifteen Negroes & Mulattoes, Distinguished in Science, Literature and the Arts* (Paris, 1808; Eng. trans. D. B. Warden [Brooklyn, New York: Printed by Thomas Kirk, 1810]), pp. 188–96. In a brief biographical passage gummed into the front matter of *Thoughts and Sentiments*, Cugoano writes that Alexander Campbell brought him to England; Grégoire avers that one "Lord Hoth" had done so. These conflicting reports may have arisen (at least in part) because Cugoano's short biography was not inserted in all copies of his work; therefore, distribution of his biography would not have been widespread. Apparently Grégoire was not aware of it. Where or how he discovered his own version of events remains unknown to us; compounding the problem is Grégoire's noted proclivity for error. Lord Hoth could possibly be a title belonging to Alexander Campbell.

16 See I Timothy 6:15 and Revelation 1:5.

17 See Genesis 45:5–7.

18 An apostate is a person who has abandoned his or her religious faith, political beliefs, or ethical principles.

19 Cugoano means John Marrant.

20 For General Clinton and the siege of Charleston, South Carolina, see Marrant's *Narrative*, note 60.

21 Exodus 21:2–6.

22 Acts 17:24, 26. Equiano favored this verse.

47

Autobiographical Acts and the Voice of the Southern Slave

Houston A. Baker, Jr.

The southern slave's struggle for terms for order is recorded by the single, existential voice engaged in what Elizabeth Bruss calls "autobiographical acts."[1] How reliable are such acts? Benedetto Croce called autobiography "a by-product of an egotism and a self-consciousness which achieve nothing but to render obvious their own futility and should be left to die of it." And a recent scholar of black autobiography expresses essentially the same reservations: "Admittedly, the autobiography has limitations as a vehicle of truth. Although so long an accepted technique toward understanding, the self-portrait often tends to be formal and posed, idealized or purposely exaggerated. The author is bound by his organized self. Even if he wishes, he is unable to remember the whole story or to interpret the complete experience."[2] A number of eighteenth- and nineteenth-century American thinkers would have taken issue with these observations. Egotism, self-consciousness, and a deep and abiding concern with the individual are at the forefront of American intellectual traditions, and the formal limitations of autobiography were not of great concern to those white authors who felt all existent literary forms were inadequate for representing their unique experiences. The question of the autobiography's adequacy, therefore, entails questions directed not only toward the black voice in the South, but also toward the larger context of the American experiment as a whole.

Envisioning themselves as God's elect and imbued with a sense of purpose, the Puritans braved the Atlantic on a mission into the wilderness. The emptiness of the New World, the absence of established institutions and traditions, reinforced their inclination to follow the example of their European forebears and brothers in God. They turned inward for reassurance and guidance. Self-examination became the *sine qua non* in a world where some were predestined for temporal leadership and eventual heavenly reward and others for a wretched earthly existence followed by the fires of hell. The diary, the journal, the meditation, the book of evidences drawn from personal experiences were the literary results of this preoccupation with self, and even documents motivated by religious controversy often took the form of apology or self-justification. A statement from Jonathan Edwards's *Personal Narrative* offers a view of this tradition: "I spent most of my time in thinking of divine things, year after year: often walking alone in the woods, and solitary places, for meditation, soliloquy, and prayer, and converse with God; and it was always my manner at such time, to sing forth my contemplations."[3]

The man alone, seeking self-definition and salvation, certain that he has a God-given duty to perform, is one image of the white American writer. Commenting on Edwards and the inevitable growth of autobiography in a land without a fully articulated social framework, Robert Sayre writes: "Edwards could and had to seek self-discovery within himself because there were so few avenues to it outside himself. The loneliness and the need for new forms really go together. They are consequences of one another and serve jointly as inducements and as difficulties to autobiography."[4] This judgment must be qualified, since Edwards's form does not differ substantially from John Bunyan's, and his isolated meditations fit neatly into a Calvinistic spectrum, but Sayre is fundamentally correct when he specifies a concern with solitude and a desire for unique literary expression as key facets of the larger American experience.

Despite the impression of loneliness left by Edwards and the sense of a barren and unpromising land for literature left by comments like those of Hawthorne in his preface to *The Marble Faun* or James in *Hawthorne*, there were a number of *a priori* assumptions available to the white American thinker. They developed over a wide chronological span (the original religious ideals becoming, like those treated in the discussion of black writers above, increasingly secular) and provided a background ready to hand. There was the white writer's sense that he was part of a new cultural experience, that he had gotten away from what D. H. Lawrence calls his old masters and could establish a new and fruitful way of life in America. There was the whole panoply of spiritual sanctions; as one of the chosen people, he was responsible for the construction of a new earthly paradise, one that would serve as a holy paradigm for the rest of the world. There was the white writer's belief, growing out of the liberal, secular thought of Descartes, Locke, and Newton, that the individual was unequivocally responsible for his own actions; a man was endowed with inalienable rights, and one of these was the right to educate himself and strive for commercial success. There was also the feeling that America offered boundless opportunities for creative originality: a unique culture with peculiar sanctions should produce a *sui generis* art.

Thus, while James's "extraordinary blankness – a curious paleness of colour and paucity of detail" was characteristic for some early white Americans, there were also more substantial aspects or qualities of the American experience that stood in contrast to this "blankness." The writer could look to a Puritan ontology and sense of mission, to conceptions of the self-made man, or to a prevailing American concern for unique aesthetic texts as preshaping influences for his work. The objective world provided both philosophical and ideological justifications for his task. When Emerson wrote, "Dante's praise is that he dared to write his autobiography in colossal cipher, or into universality," he optimistically stated the possibilities immanent in the white author's situation. The writer of comprehensive soul who dared to project his experiences on a broad plane would stand at the head of a great tradition. According to Emerson, the world surrounding such a person – that supposedly void externality – offered all the necessary supports. The permanence and importance of works such as Edward's *Personal Narrative*, Whitman's *Leaves of Grass*, and Adam's *The Education of Henry Adams* in American literature confirm his insight. As the American autobiographer turned inward to seek "the deepest *whole* self of man" (Lawrence's phrase), he carried with him the preexistent codes of his culture. They aided his definition of self and are fully reflected in the resultant texts – self-conscious literary autobiographies.

This perspective on white American autobiography highlights the distinctions between two cultures. Moved to introspection by the apparent "blankness" that surrounded him, the black, southern field slave had scarcely any *a priori* assumptions to act as stays in his quest for self-definition. He was a man of the diaspora, a displaced person imprisoned by an inhumane system. He was among alien gods in a strange land. Vassa describes his initial placement in the New World:

> We were landed up a river a good way from the sea, *about Virginia country*, where we saw few or none of our native Africans, and not one soul who could talk to me. I was a few weeks weeding grass and gathering stones in a plantation; and at last all my companions were distributed different ways, and only myself was left. I was now exceedingly miserable, and thought myself worse off than any of the rest of my companions, for they could talk to each other, but I had no person to speak to that I could understand. In this state, I was constantly grieving and pining, and wishing for death rather than anything else. [*Life*, p. 34]

For the black slave, the white externality provided no ontological or ideological certainties; in fact, it explicitly denied slaves the grounds of being. The seventeenth- and eighteenth-century black codes defined blacks as slaves in perpetuity, removing their chance to become free, participating citizens in the American City of God. The Constitution reaffirmed the slave's bondage, and the repressive legislation of the nineteenth century categorized him as "chattel personal." Instead of the ebullient sense of a new land offering limitless opportunities, the slave, staring into the heart of whiteness around him, must have felt as though he had been flung into existence without a human purpose. The white externality must have loomed like the Heideggerian "nothingness," the negative foundation of being. Jean Wahl's characterization of Heidegger's theory of existence captures the point of view a black American slave might justifiably have held: "Man is in this world, a world limited by death and experienced in anguish; is aware of himself as essentially anxious; is burdened by his solitude within the horizon of his temporality."[5]

There were at least two alternatives to this vision. There was the recourse of gazing idealistically back to "Guinea." Sterling Stuckey has shown that a small, but vocal, minority of blacks have always employed this strategy.[6] There was also the possibility of adopting the God of the enslaver as solace. A larger number of blacks chose this option and looked to the apocalyptic day that would bring their release from captivity and vengeance on the oppressors. (Tony McNeill's words, "between Africa and heaven," come to mind.) Finally, though, the picture that emerges from the innumerable accounts of slaves is charged with anguish – an anguish that reveals the black bondsman to himself as cast into the world, forlorn and without refuge.

And unlike white Americans who could assume literacy and familiarity with existing literary models as norms, the slave found himself without a system of written language – "uneducated," in the denotative sense of the word. His task was not simply one of moving toward the requisite largeness of soul and faith in the value of his experience. He first had to seize the word. His being had to erupt from nothingness. Only by grasping the word could he engage in the speech acts that would ultimately define his selfhood. Further, the slave's task was primarily one of creating a human and liberated self rather than of projecting one that reflected a peculiar landscape and tradition. His problem was not to answer Crèvecoeur's question: "What then is the American, this new man?" It was, rather, the problem of being itself.

The *Narrative of the Life of Frederick Douglass*, one of the finest black American slave narratives, serves to illustrate the black autobiographer's quest for being.[7] The recovered past, the journey back,

represented in the work is a sparse existence characterized by brutality and uncertainty:

I have no accurate knowledge of my age. The opinion was . . . whispered about that my master was my father; but of the correctness of this opinion, I know nothing. [pp. 21–2]

My mother and I were separated when I was but an infant. [p. 22]

I was seldom whipped by my old master, and suffered little from anything else than hunger and cold. [p. 43]

Our food was coarse corn meal boiled. This was called *mush*. It was put into a large wooden trough, and set down upon the ground. The children were then called, like so many pigs, and like so many pigs they would come out and devour the mush. [p. 44]

Unlike David Walker who, in his *Appeal*, attempts to explain why blacks are violently held in bondage, the young Douglass finds no explanation for his condition. And though he does describe the treatment of fellow slaves (including members of his own family), the impression left by the first half of the *Narrative* is one of a lone existence plagued by anxiety. The white world rigorously suppresses all knowledge and action that might lead the narrator to a sense of his humanity.

The total process through which this subjugation is achieved can be seen as an instance of the imposed silence suggested by Forten's address. Mr Hugh Auld, whom Douglass is sent to serve in Baltimore, finding that his wife – out of an impulse to kindness rare among whites in the *Narrative* – has begun to instruct the slave in the fundamentals of language, vociferously objects that "learning would *spoil* the best nigger in the world." Not only is it illegal to teach slaves, but it is also folly. It makes them aspire to exalted positions. The narrator's reaction to this injunction might be equated with the "dizziness" that, according to Heidegger, accompanies a sudden awareness of possibilities that lie beyond anguish:

These words sank into my heart, stirred up sentiments within that lay slumbering, and called into existence an entirely new train of thought. It was a new and special revelation, explaining dark and mysterious things, with which my youthful understanding had struggled, but struggled in vain. I now understood what had been to me a most perplexing difficulty – to wit, the white man's power to enslave the black man. [*Narrative*, p. 49]

Douglass had come to understand, by the "merest accident," the power of the word. His future is determined by this moment of revelation: he resolves, "at whatever cost of trouble, to learn how to read." He begins to detach himself from the white externality around him, declaring:

What he [Mr Auld] most dreaded, that I most desired. What he most loved, that I most hated. That which to him was a great evil, to be carefully shunned, was to me a great good to be diligently sought; and the argument which he so warmly urged, against my learning to read, only served to inspire me with a desire and determination to learn. [*Narrative*, p. 50]

The balanced antithesis of the passage is but another example – an explicit and forceful one – of the semantic competition involved in culture contact. Mr Auld is a representation of those whites who felt that by superimposing the cultural sign *nigger* on vibrant human beings like Douglass, they would be able to control the meanings and possibilities of life in America. One marker for the term *nigger* in Auld's semantic field is «subhuman agency of labor». What terrifies and angers the master, however, is that Douglass's capacities – as revealed by his response to Mrs Auld's kindness and instructions – are not accurately defined by this marker. For Douglass and others of his group are capable of learning. Hence, the markers in Auld's mapping of *nigger* must also include «agent capable of education». The semantic complexity, indeed the wrenching irony, of Auld's "nigger" is forcefully illustrated by the fact that the representation of Auld and *his* point of view enters the world of the learned by way of a narrative written by a "nigger." Douglass, that is to say, ultimately controls the competition among the various markers of *nigger* because he has employed meanings (e.g., agent having the power of literacy) drawn from his own field of experience to represent the competition in a way that invalidates «subhuman agency of labor». The nature of the autobiographical act, in this instance, is one of self-enfolding ironies. Douglass, the literate narrator, represents a Douglass who is

perceived by Auld as a "nigger." Certainly the narrator himself, who is a learned writer, can see this "nigger" only through Auld, who is the "other." And it is the "otherness" of Auld that is both repudiated and controlled by the narrator's balanced antithesis. By converting the otherness of Auld (and, consequently, his "nigger") into discourse, Douglass becomes the master of his own situation. And the white man, who wants a silently laboring brute, is finally (and ironically) visible to himself and a learned reading public only through the discourse of the articulate black spokesman.

Much of the remainder of the *Narrative* counterpoints the assumption of the white world that the slave is a brute[8] against the slave's expanding awareness of language and its capacity to carry him toward new dimensions of experience. Chapter 7 (the one following the Auld encounter), for example, is devoted to Douglass's increasing command of the word. He discovers *The Columbian Orator*, with its striking messages of human dignity and freedom and its practical examples of the results of fine speaking. He also learns the significance of that all-important word *abolition*. Against these new perceptions, he juxtaposes the unthinking condition of slaves who have not yet acquired language skills equal to his own. At times he envies them, since they (like the "meanest reptile") are not fully and self-consciously aware of their situation. For the narrator, language brings the possibility of freedom but renders slavery intolerable. It gives rise to his decision to escape as soon as his age and the opportunity are appropriate. Meanwhile, he bides his time and perfects his writing, since (as he says in a telling act of autobiographical conflation) "I might have occasion to write my own pass" (*Narrative*, p. 57).

Douglass's description of his reaction to ships on the Chesapeake illustrates that he did, effectively, write his own pass: "Those beautiful vessels, robed in purest white, so delightful to the eye of freemen, were to me so many shrouded ghosts to terrify and torment me with thoughts of my wretched condition" (*Narrative*, p. 76). He continues with a passionate apostrophe that shows how dichotomous are his own condition and that of these white, "swift-winged angels."

You are loosed from your moorings, and are free: I am fast in my chains, and am a slave! You move merrily before the gentle gale, and I sadly before the bloody whip! You are freedom's swift-winged angels, that fly around

the world; I am confined in bands of iron! O
that I were free! O, that I were on one of your
gallant decks, and under your protecting
wing! Alas! betwixt me and you, the turbid
waters roll. Go on, go on. O that I could also
go! Could I but swim! If I could fly! O, why
was I born a man, of whom to make a brute!
The glad ship is gone; she hides in the dim
distance. I am left in the hottest hell of
unending slavery. O God, save me! God,
deliver me! Let me be free! Is there any God?
Why am I a slave? I will run away. I will not
stand it. Get caught, or get clear, I'll try it.
[*Narrative*, p. 76]

When clarified and understood through language, the deathly, terrifying nothingness around
him reveals the grounds of being. Freedom, the
ability to chose one's own direction, makes life
beautiful and pure. Only the man free from
bondage has a chance to obtain the farthest reaches
of humanity. From what appears a blank and
awesome backdrop, Douglass wrests significance.
His subsequent progression through the roles of
educated leader, freeman, abolitionist, and autobiographer marks his firm sense of being.

But while it is the fact that the ships are loosed
from their moorings that intrigues the narrator, he
also drives home their whiteness and places them
in a Christian context. Here certain added difficulties for the black autobiographer reveal themselves.
The acquisition of language, which leads to being,
has ramifications that have been best stated by the
West Indian novelist George Lamming, drawing on
the relationship between Prospero and Caliban in
The Tempest:

Prospero has given Caliban Language; and
with it an unstated history of consequences,
an unknown history of future intentions.
This gift of language meant not English, in
particular, but speech and concept as a way,
a method, a necessary avenue towards areas
of the self which could not be reached in any
other way. It is in this way, entirely Prospero's
enterprise, which makes Caliban aware of
possibilities. Therefore, all of Caliban's
future – for future is the very name for
possibilities – must derive from Prospero's
experiment, which is also his risk.[9]

Mr Auld had seen that "learning" could lead to the
restiveness of his slave. Neither he nor his

represerter, however, seem to understand that it
might be possible to imprison the slave even more
thoroughly in the way described by Lamming. The
angelic Mrs Auld, however, in accord with the
evangelical codes of her era, has given Douglass the
rudiments of a system that leads to intriguing
restrictions. True, the slave can arrive at a sense of
being only through language. But it is also true that,
in Douglass's case, a conception of the preeminent
form of being is conditioned by white, Christian
standards.

To say this is not to charge him with treachery.
Africa was for the black southern slave an idealized
backdrop, which failed to offer the immediate
tangible means of his liberation. Moreover, whites
continually sought to strip Africans of their distinctive cultural modes. Vassa's isolation and perplexity
upon his arrival in the New World, which are
recorded in a passage previously cited, give some
notion of the results of this white offensive. Unable
to transplant the institutions of his homeland in the
soil of America – as the Puritans had done – the
black slave had to seek means of survival and
fulfillment on that middle ground where the
European slave trade had deposited him. He had to
seize whatever weapons came to hand in his
struggle for self-definition. The range of instruments was limited. Evangelical Christians and
committed abolitionists were the only discernible
groups standing in the path of America's hypocrisy
and inhumanity. The dictates of these groups,
therefore, suggested a way beyond servitude. And
these were the only signs and wonders in an
environment where blacks were deemed animals, or
"things." Determined to move beyond a subservient status, cut off from the alternatives held out to
whites, endowed with the "feeling" that freedom is
the natural condition of life, Douglass adopted a
system of symbols that seemed to promise him an
unbounded freedom. Having acquired language
and a set of dictates that specified freedom and
equality as norms, Douglass becomes more assured.
His certainty is reflected by the roles he projects for
himself in the latter part of his *Narrative*. They are
all in harmony with a white, Christian, abolitionist
framework.

During his year at Mr Freeland's farm, for
example, he spends much of his time "doing something that looked like bettering the condition of my
race" (*Narrative*, p. 90). His enterprise is a Sabbath
school devoted to teaching his "loved fellow-slaves"
so they will be able "to read the will of God"
(*Narrative*, p. 89). His efforts combine the philan-

thropic impulse of the eighteenth-century man of sympathy with a zeal akin to Jupiter Hammon's.

Having returned to Mr Auld's house after an absence of three years, he undertakes a useful trade and earns the right to hire out his own time. All goes well until he attends a religious camp meeting one Saturday night and fails to pay the allotted weekly portion of his wages to his master. When Auld rebukes him, the demands of the "robber" are set against the natural right of a man to worship God freely. Once again, freedom is placed in a Christian context. Infuriated, Douglass decides that the time and circumstances are now right for his escape. When he arrives in New York, he feels like a man who has "escaped a den of hungry lions" (a kind of New World Daniel), and one of his first acts is to marry Anna Murray in a Christian ceremony presided over by the Reverend James W. C. Pennington. It would not be an overstatement to say that the liberated self portrayed by Douglass is firmly Christian, having adopted cherished values from the white world that held him in bondage. It is not surprising, therefore, to see the narrator moving rapidly into the ranks of the abolitionists – that body of men and women bent on putting America in harmony with its professed ideals. Nor is it striking that the *Narrative* concludes with an appendix in which the narrator justifies himself as a true Christian.

In recovering the details of his past, then, the autobiographer shows a progression from baffled and isolated existent to Christian abolitionist lecturer and writer. The self in the autobiographical moment (the present, the time in which the work is composed), however, seems unaware of the limitations that have accompanied this progress. Even though the writer seems to have been certain (given the cohesiveness of the *Narrative*) how he was going to picture his development and how the emergent self should appear to the reader, he seems to have suppressed the fact that one cannot transcend existence in a universe where there is *only* existence. One can realize one's humanity through "speech and concept," but one cannot distinguish the uniqueness of the self if the "avenue towards areas of the self" excludes rigorously individualizing definitions of a human, black identity.

Douglass grasps language in a Promethean act of will, but he leaves unexamined its potentially devastating effects. One reflection of his uncritical acceptance of the perspective made available by

literacy is the *Narrative* itself, which was written at the urging of white abolitionists who had become the fugitive slave's employers. The work was written to prove that the narrator had indeed been a slave. And while autobiographical conventions forced him to portray as accurately as possible the existentiality of his original condition, the light of abolitionism is always implicitly present, guiding the narrator into calm, Christian, and publicly accessible harbors. The issue here is not simply one of intentionality (how the author wished his utterances to be taken). It is, rather, one that combines Douglass's understandable desire to keep his job with more complex considerations governing "privacy" as a philosophical concept.

Language, like other social institutions, is public; it is one of the surest means we have of communicating with the "other," the world outside ourselves. Moreover, since language seems to provide the principal way in which we conceptualize and convey anything (thoughts, feelings, sensations, and so forth), it is possible that no easily describable "private" domain exists. By adopting language as his instrument for extracting meaning from nothingness, being from existence, Douglass becomes a public figure.

He is comforted, but also restricted, by the system he adopts. The results are shown in the hierarchy of preferences that, finally, constitute value in the *Narrative*. The results are additionally demonstrated by those instances in the *Narrative* where the work's style is indistinguishable from that of the sentimental-romantic oratory and creative writing that marked the American nineteenth century. Had there been a separate, written black language available, Douglass might have fared better. What is seminal to this discussion, however, is that the nature of the autobiographer's situation seemed to force him to move to a public version of the self – one molded by the values of white America. Thus Mr Auld can be contained and controlled within the slave narrator's abolitionist discourse because Auld is a stock figure of such discourse. He is the penurious master corrupted by the soul-killing effects of slavery who appears in poetry, fiction, and polemics devoted to the abolitionist cause.

But the slave narrator must also accomplish the almost unthinkable (since thought and language are inseparable) task of transmuting an authentic, unwritten self – a self that exists outside the conventional literary discourse structures of a white reading public – into a literary representation. The simplest, and perhaps the most effective, way of proceeding is for the narrator to represent his "authentic" self as a figure embodying the public virtues and values esteemed by his intended audience. Once he has seized the public medium, the slave narrator can construct a public message, or massage, calculated to win approval for himself and (provided he has one) his cause. In the white abolitionist William Lloyd Garrison's preface to Douglass's *Narrative*, for example, the slave narrator is elaborately praised for his seemingly godlike movement "into the field of public usefulness" (*Narrative*, pp. v–vi). Garrison writes of his own reaction to Douglass's first abolitionist lecture to a white audience:

I shall never forget his first speech at the convention – the extraordinary emotion it excited in my own mind – the powerful impression it created upon a crowded auditory, completely taken by surprise – the applause which followed from the beginning to the end of his felicitous remarks. I think I never hated slavery so intensely as at that moment; certainly, my perception of the enormous outrage which is inflicted by it, on the godlike nature of its victims, was rendered far more clear than ever. There stood one, in physical proportion and stature commanding and exact – in intellect richly endowed – in natural eloquence a prodigy – in soul manifestly "created but a little lower than the angels" – trembling for his safety, hardly daring to believe that on the American soil, a single white person could be found who would befriend him at all hazards, for the love of God and humanity. Capable of high attainments as an intellectual and moral being – needing nothing but a comparatively small amount of cultivation to make him an ornament to society and a blessing to his race – by the law of the land, by the voice of the people, by the terms of the slave code, he was only a piece of property, a beast of burden, a chattel personal, nevertheless! [*Narrative*, p. vi]

Obviously, a talented, heroic, and richly endowed figure such as Garrison describes here was of inestimable "public usefulness" to the abolitionist crusade. And the Nantucket Convention of 1841 where Garrison first heard Douglass speak may be compared to a communicative context in which the sender and receiver employ a common channel (i.e., the English language) to arrive at, or to reinforce for each other, an agreed-upon message. Douglass transmits the "heroic fugitive" message to an abolitionist audience that has made such a figure part of its conceptual, linguistic, and rhetorical repertoire.

The issue that such an "autobiographical" act raises for the literary analyst is that of authenticity. Where, for example, in Douglass's *Narrative* does a prototypical black American self reside? What are the distinctive narrative elements that combine to form a representation of this self? In light of the foregoing discussion, it seems that such elements would be located in those episodes and passages of the *Narrative* that chronicle the struggle for literacy. For once literacy has been achieved, the black self, even as represented in the *Narrative*, begins to distance itself from the domain of experience constituted by the oral-aural community of the slave quarters (e.g., the remarks comparing fellow slaves to the meanest reptiles). The voice of the unwritten self, once it is subjected to the linguistic codes, literary conventions, and audience expectations of a literate population, is perhaps never again the authentic voice of black American slavery. It is, rather, the voice of a self transformed by an autobiographical act into a sharer in the general public discourse about slavery.

How much of the lived (as opposed to the represented) slave experience is lost in this transformation depends upon the keenness of the narrator's skill in confronting both the freedom and the limitations resulting from his literacy in Prospero's tongue. By the conclusion of Douglass's *Narrative*, the represented self seems to have left the quarters almost entirely behind. The self that appears in the work's closing moments is that of a public spokesman, talking about slavery to a Nantucket convention of whites:

while attending an anti-slavery convention at Nantucket, on the 11th of August 1841, I felt strongly moved to speak, and was at the same time much urged to do so by Mr William C. Coffin, a gentleman who had heard me speak in the colored people's meeting at New Bedford. It was a severe cross, and I took it up reluctantly. The truth was, I felt myself a slave, and the idea of speaking to white people weighed me down. I spoke but a few moments, when I felt a degree of freedom, and said what I desired with considerable ease. From that time until now, I have been engaged in pleading the cause of my brethren – with what success, and with what devotion, I leave to those acquainted with my labors to decide. [*Narrative*, pp. 118–19]

The Christian imagery ("a severe cross"), strained reluctance to speak before whites, discovered ease of eloquence, and public-spirited devotion to the cause of his brethren that appear in this passage are all in keeping with the image of the publicly useful and ideal fugitive captured in Garrison's preface. Immediately before telling the reader of his address to the Nantucket convention, Douglass notes that "he had not long been a reader of the 'Liberator' [Garrison's abolitionist newspaper]" before he got "a pretty correct idea of the principles, measures and spirit of the anti-slavery reform"; he adds that he "took right hold of the cause . . . and never felt happier than when in an anti-slavery meeting" (*Narrative*, p. 118). This suggests to me that the communication between Douglass and Garrison begins long before their face-to-face encounter at Nantucket, with the fugitive slave's culling from the white publisher's newspaper those virtues and values esteemed by abolitionist readers. The fugitive's voice is further refined by his attendance and speeches at the "colored people's meeting at New Bedford," and it finally achieves its emotionally stirring participation in the white world of public discourse at the 1841 Nantucket convention.

Of course, there are tangible reasons within the historical (as opposed to the autobiographical) domain for the image that Douglass projects. The feeling of larger goals shared with a white majority culture has always been present among blacks. We need only turn to the writings of Hammon, Wheatley, and Vassa to see this. From at least the third decade of the nineteenth century this feeling of a common pursuit was reinforced by men like Garrison and Wendell Phillips, by constitutional amendments, civil rights legislation, and perennial assurances that the white man's dream is the black man's as well. Furthermore, what better support for this assumption of commonality could Douglass find than in his own palpable achievements in American society?

When he revised his original *Narrative* for the third time, therefore, in 1893, the work that resulted represented the conclusion of a process that began for Douglass at the home of Hugh Auld. *The Life and Times of Frederick Douglass Written by*

Himself is public, rooted in the language of its time, and considerably less existential in tone than the 1845 *Narrative*. What we have is a verbose and somewhat hackneyed story of a life, written by a man of achievement. The white externality has been transformed into a world where sterling deeds by blacks are possible. Douglass describes his visit to the home of his former master who, forty years after the slave's escape, now rests on his deathbed:

> On reaching the house I was met by Mr Wm. H. Buff, a son-in-law of Capt. Auld, and Mrs Louisa Buff, his daughter, and was conducted to the bedroom of Capt. Auld. We addressed each other simultaneously, he called me "Marshal Douglass," and I, as I had always called him, "Captain Auld." Hearing myself called by him "Marshal Douglass," I instantly broke up the formal nature of the meeting by saying, "not *Marshal*, but Frederick to you as formerly." We shook hands cordially and in the act of doing so, he, having been long stricken with palsy, shed tears as men thus afflicted will do when excited by any deep emotion. The sight of him, the changes which time had wrought in him, his tremulous hands constantly in motion, and all the circumstances of his condition affected me deeply, and for a time choked my voice and made me speechless.[10]

A nearly tearful silence by the black "Marshal" (a term repeated three times in very brief space) of the District of Columbia as he gazes with sympathy on the body of his former master – this is a great distance, to be sure, from the aggressive young slave who appropriated language in order to do battle with the masters.

A further instance of Douglass's revised perspective is provided by his return to the home plantation of Colonel Lloyd on the Wye River in Talbot County, Maryland:

> Speaking of this desire of mine [to revisit the Lloyd Plantation] last winter, to Hon. John L. Thomas, the efficient collector at the Port of Baltimore, and a leading Republican of the State of Maryland, he urged me very much to go, and added that he often took a trip to the Eastern Shore in his revenue cutter *Guthrie* (otherwise known in time of war as the *Ewing*), and would be much pleased to have me accompany him on one of these

trips. . . . In four hours after leaving Baltimore we were anchored in the river off the Lloyd estate, and from the deck of our vessel I saw once more the stately chimneys of the grand old mansion which I had last seen from the deck of the *Sally Lloyd* when a boy. I left there as a slave, and returned as a freeman; I left there unknown to the outside world, and returned well known; I left there on a freight boat and returned on a revenue cutter; I left on a vessel belonging to Col. Edward Lloyd, and returned on one belonging to the United States. [*Life and Times*, pp. 445–6]

The "stately chimneys of the grand old mansion" sounds very much like the Plantation Tradition, and how different the purpose of the balanced antithesis is in this passage from that noted in the delineation of the slave's realization of language as a key to freedom ("What he most dreaded, that I most desired . . ."). This passage also stands in marked contrast to the description of ships on the Chesapeake cited earlier ("those beautiful vessels . . . so many shrouded ghosts"). The venerable status of the *Guthrie* is now matched by the eminence of the marshal of the District of Columbia.

Douglass, in his public role, often resembles the courteous and gentlemanly narrator of Vassa's work – a man determined to put readers at ease by assuring them of his accomplishments (and the sterling company he keeps) in language that is careful not to offend readers' various sensibilities. It is strikingly coincidental that *The Life and Times of Frederick Douglass* was reprinted in 1895, the year in which its author died and Booker T. Washington emerged as one of the most influential black public spokesmen America had ever known.

In 1901, Washington's *Up from Slavery* appeared, and it offers a perfect illustration of the black autobiographer's assumption of the public mantle. Unlike Douglass's 1845 *Narrative* (but like the 1893 version), Washington's work is primarily a life-and-times account that views the self within the larger American social current. Instead of apology, or the justification of rebellion, one finds in *Up from Slavery* gratitude – even joy – that the self has been swept along by the current and acknowledged for aiding its progressive flow. Moral uplift and financial success quickly run together as Washington accepts Economic Man as the norm in his own ascent from ignorance, poverty, and vice to property ownership and a sound bank account. Of course, the first president of Tuskegee Institute cannot be immediately denounced for portraying himself in this manner, since such a condemnation would require censuring the entire age in which he lived. Situated in the Gilded Age and surrounded by a set of conditions that the historian Rayford Logan has called the "nadir" in American race relations, Washington adopted a public mask that displayed a black self in harmony with its era. The problem with this strategy was that it forced the narrator to violate the governing conventions of autobiography at the very outset. He set truth aside from the beginning and simply ignored facts that did not agree with his mask.

Washington, therefore, is no bold historian who has surveyed chaos and given us the verifiable details of his journey. We cannot grasp the uniqueness of a black self because a self distinguishable from those of Huntington, Carnegie, Vanderbilt, and other white capitalists never emerges. Further, the sense that black being can emerge only by erupting through a white nothingness is contradicted by the countless white friends who aid Washington on his way to language, education, and financial stability. Rebecca Chalmers Barton has defined Washington and all black autobiographers who followed his lead as "accommodators," i.e., pseudoidealists who concealed their ambitiousness and feelings of inferiority in religious rhetoric and oratory dedicated to a cause.[11] Given the nature of *Up from Slavery*, this assessment seems just. It is difficult to understand how a more recent writer[12] has set such store by those turn-of-the-century black autobiographies which, time and again, reveal their narrators drawn into the linguistic prisons – the confining public discourse – of the white world.

Difficult, but not impossible. For if one takes language in a broad social sense and treats *Up from Slavery* as a social document, then Washington was simply an imitator of the commercial, industrial utterances that guided his age. His narrative is filled with the kind of observation one would expect to find in a primer devoted to principles of success in business and the conduct of the moral life in an industrialist society:

> One thing I was determined to do from the first, and that was to keep the credit of the school high, and this, I think I can say without boasting, we have done all through these years. I shall always remember a bit of advice given me by Mr George W. Campbell,

the white man to whom I have referred as the one who induced General Armstrong to send me to Tuskegee. Soon after I entered upon the work Mr Campbell said to me, in his fatherly way: "Washington, always remember that credit is capital."[13]

On the subject of soliciting contributions for Tuskegee:

Such work gives one a rare opportunity to study human nature. It also has its compensation in giving one an opportunity to meet some of the best people in the world – to be more correct, I think I should say *the best* people in the world. When one takes a broad survey of the country, he will find that the most useful and influential people in it are those who take the deepest interest in institutions that exist for the purpose of making the world better. [p. 127]

On interaction with the wealthy:

I have found that strict business methods go a long way in securing the interest of rich people. It has been my constant aim at Tuskegee to carry out, in our financial and other operations, such business methods as would be approved of by any New York banking house. [p. 132]

Two of his improving maxims read:

In meeting men, in many places, I have found that the happiest people are those who do the most for others; the most miserable are those who do the least. I have also found that few things, if any, are capable of making one so blind and narrow as race prejudice. [p. 152]

I have a strong feeling that every individual owes it to himself, and to the cause which he is serving, to keep a vigorous, healthy body, with the nerves steady and strong, prepared for great efforts and prepared for disappointments and trying positions. [p. 171]

Finally, one of the most infamous examples of Washington's employment of the language and concepts of the commercial industrial estate of his era appears in his speech to the Atlanta Cotton

States and International Exposition, which was delivered in 1895, and which is set down in full in *Up from Slavery*. He advises his recently emancipated fellow blacks:

when it comes to business, pure and simple, it is in the South that the Negro is given a man's chance in the commercial world, and in nothing is this Exposition more eloquent than in emphasizing this chance. Our greatest danger is that in the great leap from slavery to freedom we may overlook the fact that the masses of us are to live by the productions of our hands, and fail to keep in mind that we shall prosper in proportion as we learn to dignify and glorify common labour and put brains and skill into the common occupations of life. . . . It is at the bottom of life we must begin, and not at the top. [*Up from Slavery*, p. 147]

Founded on the assumption that only through hard work and abundant evidence that one has something to contribute to the white community can the black American rise, Washington's statement implicitly sanctioned the violently racist practices of his day. When Governor Bullock of Georgia introduced him at the Exposition as "a representative of Negro enterprise and Negro civilization," he surely had a clear idea of the type of representation of black life and culture Washington would present. The occasion, as it appears in *Up from Slavery*, is yet another instance of the coming together of a white audience and a black speaker who has molded a publicly useful "autobiographical" self. In Washington's case, unfortunately, Governor Bullock (and not William Lloyd Garrison) was the exemplary member of the white audience. Thus Washington, as a black public spokesman, became the compromiser of his own people's rights, and the Barton view of the author of *Up from Slavery* is reinforced by an analysis of the work as a social document.

But if language is considered not in the broad social sense but in the more restricted context of fictive discourse, then Washington's narrative, as a fictive account, presents a coherent structure signaling a particular domain of meaning. Rather than the "pseudoidealism" deplored by Barton, it implies propositions of the form "If X then Y."[14] For example, the world of the slave is one of unlimited opportunity; the black man can, if only he will. This amounts to a tacit agreement between the propositions governing *Up from Slavery* and the professed ideals of the larger white American culture. The work is designed as a validation of what the psychologists Hans Vaihinger and Alfred Adler called "fictional ideas" or "fictional finalism."[15] The notion captured by these phrases is that human beings are motivated in their present actions by their expectations of the future, by their orientation toward a goal which has no counterpart in reality. "This final goal may be a fiction, that is, an ideal that is impossible to realize but which is nonetheless a very real spur to human striving and the ultimate explanation of conduct."[16] Statements such as "all men are created equal," that is to say, or "honesty is the best policy," govern conduct. Washington's work, under the aspect of fictive discourse, can be interpreted as saying: "The propositions are analytic (basic, beyond question). Here is a story to prove it." In this light, *Up from Slavery* offers a stirring account. The differences between black and white fade; the disruptions of the triangular trade and chattel slavery are excusable failings of a past that is best forgotten. The motivation is directed entirely toward the future.

The problem with this interpretive strategy, however, is that while it provides one means of apprehending and valuing the text, it also ignores the significant conventions surrounding the genre that Washingtion and his cohorts chose to employ. Autobiography – the recounting of the self's or the selves' history – does not presuppose analytic propositions. It is, rather, a gathering together of synthetic propositions – factual statements whose truth-value is assumed to be historically determinate. Its statements are taken to accord with an actual past that is amenable to investigation. The difference between the fictive and the autobiographical can be suggested by the responses each entails to a statement like the following:

> The "Ku Klux" period was, I think, the darkest part of the Reconstruction days. I have referred to this unpleasant part of the history of the South simply for the purpose of calling attention to the great change that has taken place since the days of the "Ku Klux." To-day there are no such organizations in the South, and the fact that such ever existed is almost forgotten by both races. There are few places in the South now where public sentiment would permit such organizations to exist. [*Up from Slavery*, p. 71]

The truth-value of this assertion if it appeared in a novel would not be a very fruitful analytical issue to pursue. In an autobiography, however, the statement must be set against historical evidence as we know it. Only then can a reader judge the author's relationship to fundamental conventions, or rules, of the autobiographical genre.[17] And in the example cited, the narrator's assertion is a patent falsification.

One cannot dismiss Washington's work, however, as simply the effort of a writer confused about two realms of discourse, the fictive and the autobiographical. There is no more justification for such a course than there is for ignoring Wheatley because she used heroic couplets. What is demanded from the literary investigator is an analysis that will reveal the intersections between the two worlds of discourse. This discovery might lead, in turn, to a wider inquiry into the nature of black narrative. The school of "accommodators" can serve as a starting point, that is to say, in the search for higher-order rules that condition the fictionalizing of the self in autobiography and the construction of an autobiographical self in fiction that mark such narratives as Richard Wright's *Black Boy* and James Weldon Johnson's *The Autobiography of an Ex-Colored Man*. The question is how such works achieve their effects and eventually come to hold valued positions in Black intellectual and literary history.

Though Washington's voice is surely not the one Forten had in mind when he spoke of the slaves who might trouble their masters' quiet, it is nonetheless a distinctive voice and raises its own set of problems about Caliban's presence in the New World. *Up from Slavery*, like Wheatley's poetry and Vassa's narrative, stands as a verbal structure that compels our attention. If it falsifies details of the journey, it promises much for our understanding of the voyage into language. The wholeness of the self, the self as public man, the autobiographical self engaged in fictive discourse – these, too, represent attempts to find terms for order in a complex world.

The culturally unique aspects of *Up from Slavery* reside, like those in the works of the authors already discussed, at a level of functional oppositions. In this case, the disparity is between a graphically depicted hell of rural, impoverished, illiterate black southern life and an intriguingly displayed heaven of black southern urbanity, thrift, and education. Two distinct modes of discourse sustain this opposition – the autobiographical self exists in the former, while the fictive self lives in (and testifies to the possibility of) the latter.

Notes

1 *Autobiographical Acts* (Baltimore: Johns Hopkins University Press, 1976). "All reading (or writing) involves us in choice: we choose to pursue a style or subject matter, to struggle with or against a design. We also choose, as passive as it may seem, to take part in an interaction, and it is here that generic labels have their use. The genre does not tell us the style or construction of a text as much as how we should expect to 'take' that style or mode of construction – what force it should have for us" (p. 4). Professor Bruss is drawing on a speech-act theory as delineated by J. L. Austin, Paul Strawson, and John Searle. The nature, or force, of the speech act combines context, conditions, and intentions; it is called by the philosophers of language mentioned above the *illocutionary force* of an utterance. If the illocutionary force of a speech act is one involving certain rules, contexts, and intentions of self-revelation, the act can be called autobiographical. What I shall be investigating in the next few pages is the peculiar illocutionary force of certain black autobiographies produced during the nineteenth century. For an account of black autobiography, see Stephen Butterfield, *Black Autobiography in America* (Amherst: University of Massachusetts Press, 1974).

2 Rebecca Chalmers Barton, *Witnesses for Freedom* (New York: Harper, 1948), p. xii.

3 George McMichael, ed., *Anthology of American Literature* (New York: Macmillan, 1974), 1:228.

4 *The Examined Self* (Princeton: Princeton University Press, 1964), p. 39.

5 *A Short History of Existentialism* (New York: Philosophical Library, 1949), p. 31. See also Jean Wahl, *Philosophies of Existence: An Introduction to the Basic Thought of Kierkegaard, Heidegger, Jaspers, Marcel, Sartre* (New York: Schocken, 1959).

6 *The Ideological Origins of Black Nationalism* (Boston: Beacon, 1972).

7 *Narrative of the Life of Frederick Douglass, an American Slave. Written by Himself* (New York: Signet, 1968), p. 21.

8 In a fine analysis of the *Narrative* ("Animal Farm Unbound," *New Letters* 43 (1977): 25–48), H. Bruce Franklin explores the significance for American literature of white assumptions that blacks are outside the human family. But cf. my own treatment of animal imagery in Douglass, which appeared in my collection of essays *Long Black Song* (Charlottesville: University Press of Virginia, 1972); and Albert Stone, "Identity and Art in Frederick Douglass' Narrative," *CLA Journal* 17 (1973): 192–213.

9 Quoted from Janheinz Jahn, *Neo-African Literature* (New York: Grove, 1969), p. 240.

10 *The Life and Times of Frederick Douglass Written by Himself* (New York: Collier, 1973), p. 442.

11 *Witnesses for Freedom*, pp. 3–40.

12 John Blassingame, "Black Autobiographies as History and Literature," *Black Scholar* 5 (1973–4): 2–9.

13 *Up from Slavery*, in Franklin, ed., *Three Negro Classics*, p. 107. Unless otherwise specified, all citations refer to this edition.

14 The concept of "fictive discourse" is drawn from the work of Barbara Herrnstein Smith. Professor Smith makes a distinction between "natural discourse" and fictive discourse. While "a natural utterance is an historical *event* [and] like any other event, it occupies a specific and unique point in time and space," a fictive utterance is historically indeterminate. It is possible, therefore, for it to postulate and explore propositions that are considered "timeless." Works of imaginative literature, that is to say, may be thought of as discourse structures that imply analytical propositions. An analytical proposition, according to philosophy, is one of the conditions of possibility of reason. All men of reason understand that "If X then Y." The truth-value of such propositions is not contingent upon empirical reference, but upon reason, operating in a timeless dimension. See "Poetry as Fiction," in Cohen, ed., *New Directions in Literary History*, pp. 165–87. See also her book *On the Margins of Discourse* (Chicago: University of Chicago Press, 1978). For a discussion of analytic propositions in relation to speech acts, see Searle, *Speech Acts*.

15 The discussion here is based on C. S. Hall and Gardner Lindzey, *Theories of Personality* (New York: Wiley, 1978), pp. 160–1.

16 Ibid., p. 161.

17 Bruss, in stating her rules, or appropriateness conditions, for autobiographical acts of discourse says: "(a) under existing conventions, a claim is made for the truth-value of what the autobiography reports – no matter how difficult that truth-value might be to ascertain, whether the report treats of private experiences or publicly observable occasions. (b) The audience is expected to accept these reports as true, and is free to 'check up' on them or attempt to discredit them" (*Autobiographical Acts*, p. 11).

PART X

Ontology and the Nature of Art

48

Breath

Birago Diop

Listen more to things
Than to words that are said.
The water's voice sings
And the flame cries
And the wind that brings
The woods to sighs
Is the breathing of the dead.

Those who are dead have never gone away.
They are in the shadows darkening around,
They are in the shadows fading into day,
The dead are not under the ground.
They are in the trees that quiver,
They are in the woods that weep,
They are in the waters of the rivers,
They are in the waters that sleep.
They are in the crowds, they are in the
    homestead.
The dead are never dead.

Listen more to things
Than to words that are said.
The water's voice sings
And the flame cries
And the wind that brings
The woods to sighs
Is the breathing of the dead.
Who have not gone away
Who are not under the ground
Who are never dead.

From Birago Diop, *Leurres et Lueurs* (1961), by kind
permission of Présence Africaine.

Those who are dead have never gone away.
They are at the breast of the wife.
They are in the child's cry of dismay
And the firebrand bursting into life.
The dead are not under the ground.
They are in the fire that burns low
They are in the grass with tears to shed,
In the rock where whining winds blow
They are in the forest, they are in the
    homestead.
The dead are never dead.

Listen more to things
Than to words that are said.
The water's voice sings
And the flame cries
And the wind that brings
The woods to sighs
Is the breathing of the dead.

And repeats each day
The Covenant where it is said
That our fate is bound to the law,
And the fate of the dead who are not dead
To the spirits of breath who are stronger than
    they.
We are bound to Life by this harsh law
And by this Covenant we are bound
To the deeds of the breathings that die
Along the bed and the banks of the river,
To the deeds of the breaths that quiver
In the rock that whines and the grasses that cry
To the deeds of the breathings that lie
In the shadow that lightens and grows deep

Birago Diop

In the tree that shudders, in the woods that
  weep,
In the waters that flow and the waters that sleep,
To the spirits of breath which are stronger than
  they
That have taken the breath of the deathless dead
Of the dead who have never gone away
Of the dead who are not now under the ground.

Listen more to things
Than to words that are said.
The water's voice sings
And the flame cries
And the wind that brings
The woods to sighs
Is the breathing of the dead.

49

Bantu Ontology

Placide Tempels

Certain words are constantly being used by Africans. They are those which express their supreme values; and they recur like variations upon a leitmotiv present in their language, their thought, and in all their acts and deeds.

This supreme value is life, force, to live strongly, or vital force.

The Bantu say, in respect of a number of strange practices in which we see neither rime nor reason, that their purpose is to acquire life, strength or vital force, to live strongly, that they are to make life stronger, or to assure that force shall remain perpetually in one's posterity.

Used negatively, the same idea is expressed when the Bantu say: we act thus to be protected from misfortune, or from a diminution of life or of being, or in order to protect ourselves from those influences which annihilate or diminish us.

Force, the potent life, vital energy are the object of prayers and invocations to God, to the spirits and to the dead, as well as of all that is usually called magic, sorcery or magical remedies. The Bantu will tell you that they go to a diviner to learn the words of life, so that he can teach them the way of making life stronger. In every Bantu language it is easy to recognize the words or phrases denoting a force, which is not used in an exclusively bodily sense, but in the sense of the integrity of our whole being.

The bwanga (which has been translated "magical remedy") ought not, they say, to be applied to the wound or sick limb. It does not necessarily possess local therapeutic effects, but it strengthens, it increases the vital force.

In calling upon God, the spirits, or the ancestral spirits, the heathen ask above all, "give me force". If one urges them to abandon magical practices, as being contrary to the will of God and therefore evil, one will get the reply, "wherein are they wicked?" What we brand as magic is, in their eyes, nothing but setting to work natural forces placed at the disposal of man by God to strengthen man's vital energy.

When they try to get away from metaphors and periphrases, the Bantu speak of God himself as "the Strong One," he who possesses Force in himself. He is also the source of the Force of every creature. God is the "Dijina dikatampe": the great name, because he is the great Force, the "mukomo," as our Baluba have it, the one who is stronger than all other.

The spirits of the first ancestors, highly exalted in the super-human world, possess extraordinary force inasmuch as they are the founders of the human race and propagators of the divine inheritance of vital human strength. The other dead are esteemed only to the extent to which they increase and perpetuate their vital force in their progeny.

In the minds of the Bantu, all beings in the universe possess vital force of their own . . . Each being has been endowed by God with a certain force, capable of strengthening the vital energy of the strongest being of all creation: man.

Supreme happiness, the only kind of blessing, is,

From Placide Tempels, *Bantu Philosophy* (1959), by kind permission of Présence Africaine.

to the Bantu, to possess the greatest vital force: the worst misfortune and, in very truth, the only misfortune, is, he thinks, the diminution of this power.

Every illness, wound or disappointment, all suffering, depression, or fatigue, every injustice and every failure: all these are held to be, and are spoken of by the Bantu as, a diminution of vital force.

Illness and death do not have their source in our own vital power, but result from some external agent who weakens us through his greater force. It is only by fortifying our vital energy through the use of magical recipes, that we acquire resistance to malevolent external forces.

We need not be surprised that the Bantu allude to this vital force in their greetings one to another, using such forms of address as: "You are strong," or "you have life in you," "you have life strongly in you"; and that they express sympathy in such phrases as "your vital force is lowered," "your vital energy has been sapped." A similar idea is found in the form of sympathy, "wafwa ko!" which we translate "you are dying"; and by reason of our mistranslation, we are quite unable to understand the Bantu and find them given to ridiculous exaggeration when they continually say that they are "dead" of hunger or of fatigue, or that the least obstacle or illness is "killing" them. In their own minds they are simply indicating a diminution of vital force, in which sense their expression is reasonable and sensible enough. In their languages, too, are words like "kufwa" and "fukwididila," indicating the progressing stages of loss of force, of vitality, and the superlative of which signifies total paralysis of the power to live. It is quite erroneous for us to translate these words by "to die" and "to die entirely."

This explains what has, indeed, been true, that the thing which most inhibits pagans from conversion to Christianity and from giving up magical rites is the fear of attenuating this vital energy through ceasing to have recourse to the natural powers which sustain it.

In 1936 I gave my Normal Class students at Lukonzolwa (Lake Moëro) as an essay subject, "Obstacles to conversion among pagan peoples." To my astonishment, so far from setting out a list of practices, all of them declared that the great obstacle could be summed up in a conviction that to abandon the customs appointed by their ancestors would lead to death. The objection, therefore, was rather a matter of principle than of practice, their fear being grounded in the "truths" of Bantu ontology.

These various aspects of Bantu behaviour already enable us to see that the key to Bantu thought is the idea of vital force, of which the source is God.[1] Vital force is the reality which, though invisible, is supreme in man. Man can renew his vital force by tapping the strength of other creatures.

a) The general notion of being

We have seen that the Bantu soul hankers after life and force. The fundamental notion under which being is conceived lies within the category of forces.

Metaphysics studies this reality, existing in everything and in every being in the universe. It is in virtue of this reality that all beings have something in common, so that the definition of this reality may be applied to all existent forms of being.

To arrive at this reality common to all beings, or rather, which is identical in all beings, it is necessary to eliminate all forms of reality which belong to one category only among beings.

We pay attention to the elements only, but to all the elements, which are common to all beings. Such elements are, e.g., the origin, the growth, the changes, the destruction, or the achievement of the beings, passive and active causality, and particularly the nature of the being as such supporting those universal phenomena. These elements constitute the object of metaphysical knowledge, that is to say, of knowledge embracing all the physical or the real.

Metaphysics does not treat of the abstract or the unreal: these are but its notions, its definitions, its laws, which are abstract and general, as the notions, definitions and laws of every science always are.

Christian thought in the West, having adopted the terminology of Greek philosophy and perhaps under its influence, has defined this reality common to all beings, or, as one should perhaps say, being as such: "the reality that is," "anything that exists," "what is." Its metaphysics has most generally been based upon a fundamentally static conception of being.

Herein is to be seen the fundamental difference between Western thought and that of the Bantu and other primitive people. (I compare only systems which have inspired widespread "civilizations.")

We can conceive the transcendental notion of "being" by separating it from its attribute, "Force," but the Bantu cannot. "Force" in his thought is a necessary element in "being," and the concept "force" is inseparable from the definition of "being." There is no idea among Bantu of "being" divorced from the idea of "force." Without the element "force," "being" cannot be conceived.

We hold a static conception of "being," they a dynamic.

What has been said above should be accepted as the basis of Bantu ontology: in particular. The concept "force" is bound to the concept "being" even in the most abstract thinking upon the notion of being.

At least it must be said that the Bantu have a double concept concerning being, a concept which can be expressed: "being is that which has force."

But I think we must go further. Our statement of Bantu philosophy should press as closely as possible its distinctive characteristics. It seems to me that we shall not attain this precision by formulating the notion of being in Bantu thought as "being is that which possesses force."

I believe that we should most faithfully render the Bantu thought in European language by saying that Bantu speak, act, live as if, for them, beings were forces. Force is not for them an adventitious, accidental reality. Force is even more than a necessary attribute of beings: Force is the nature of being, force is being, being is force.

When we think in terms of the concept "being," they use the concept "force." Where we see concrete beings, they see concrete forces. When we say that "beings" are differentiated by their essence or nature, Bantu say that "forces" differ in their essence or nature. They hold that there is the divine force, celestial or terrestrial forces, human forces, animal forces, vegetable and even material or mineral forces.

The reader will be able to form his own opinion at the end of this study as to the validity, the exact worth of this hypothesis: in contradistinction to our definition of being as "that which is," or "the thing insofar as it is," the Bantu definition reads, "that which is force," or "the thing insofar as it is force," or "an existent force." We must insist once again that "force" is not for Bantu a necessary, irreducible attribute of being: no, the notion "force" takes for them the place of the notion "being" in our philosophy. Just as we have, so have they a transcendental, elemental, simple concept: with them "force," with us "being."

It is because all being is force and exists only in that it is force, that the category "force" includes of necessity all "beings": God, men living and departed, animals, plants, minerals. Since being is force, all these beings appear to the Bantu as forces. This universal concept is hardly used by the Bantu, but they are susceptible to philosophical abstractions though they express them in concrete terms only. They give a name to each thing, but the inner life of these things presents itself to their minds as such specific forces and not at all as static reality.

It would be a misuse of words to call the Bantu "dynamists" or "energists," as if the universe were animated by some universal force, a sort of unique magical power encompassing all existence, as certain authors seem to believe, judging from their treatment of "mana," "bwanga," or "kanga." Such is an European presentation of a primitive philosophy that is but imperfectly understood. The Bantu make a clear distinction and understand an essential difference between different beings, that is to say, different forces. Among the different kinds of forces they have come to recognize, just as we do, unity, individuality but individuality clearly understood as meaning individuality of forces.

That is why it seems to me necessary to reject as foreign to Bantu philosophy the dualism of good and evil as two forces; and also what has been called "common being" or "community of nature," when these terms are so used as to eliminate the individuality of forces.

In the category of visible beings the Bantu distinguish that which is perceived by the senses and the "thing in itself." By the "thing in itself" they indicate its individual inner nature, or, more precisely, the force of the thing. They are expressing themselves in figurative language when they say "in every thing there is another thing; in every man a little man." But one would grossly deceive oneself in wishing to attribute to this piece of imagery any exact verbal expression of the Bantu notion of being. Their allegory merely brings into relief the distinction they make between the contingent, the visible phenomenon of being or of force, and the intrinsic visible nature of that force.

When "we" differentiate in man the soul and the body, as is done in certain Western writings, we are at a loss to explain where "the man" has gone after these two components have been separated out. If, from our European outlook, we wish to seek Bantu terms adequate to express this manner of speaking, we are up against very great difficulties, especially if we are proposing to speak about the soul of man. Unless under European influence, the Bantu do not thus express themselves. They distinguish in man body, shadow and breath. This breath is the assumed manifestation, the evident sign, of life, though it is mortal and in no way corresponds with what we understand by the soul, especially the soul as subsisting after death, when the body with its shadow and its breath will have disappeared. What lives on after death is not called by the Bantu by a term indicating part of a man. I have always heard their elders speak of "the man himself," "himself," "aye mwine"; or it is "the little man" who was formerly hidden behind the perceptible manifestation of the man; or the "muntu," which, at death, has left the living.

It seems to me incorrect to translate this word "muntu" by "the man." The "muntu" certainly possesses a visible body, but this body is not the "muntu." A Bantu one day explained to one of my colleagues that the "muntu" is rather what you call in English the "person" and not what you connote by "the man." "Muntu" signifies, then, vital force, endowed with intelligence and will. This interpretation gives a logical meaning to the statement which I one day received from a Bantu: "God is a great muntu" ("Vidye i muntu mukatampe"). This meant "God is the great Person"; that is to say, The great, powerful and reasonable living force.

The "bintu" are rather what we call things; but according to Bantu philosophy they are beings, that is to say forces not endowed with reason, not living.

b) All force can be strengthened or enfeebled. That is to say, all being can become stronger or weaker

We say of a man that he grows, develops, acquires knowledge, exercises his intelligence and his will; and that in so doing he increases them. We do not hold that by these acquisitions and by this development he has become more a man; at least, not in the sense that his human nature no longer remains what it was. One either has human nature or one hasn't. It is not a thing that is increased or diminished. Development operates in a man's qualities or in his faculties.

Bantu ontology – or, to be more exact, the Bantu theory of forces – is radically opposed to any such conception. When a Bantu says "I am becoming stronger," he is thinking of something quite different from what we mean when we say that our powers are increasing. Remember that, for the Bantu, being is force and force being. When he says that a force is increasing, or that a being is reinforced, his thought must be expressed in our language and according to our mental outlook as "this being has grown as such," his nature has been made stronger, increased, made greater. What Catholic theology teaches concerning, in particular, the supernatural realities of grace, that it is a

supernal reinforcement of our being, that it is able to grow and to be strengthened in itself, is an idea similar to what the Bantu accept in the natural order as true of all being, of all force.

This is the sense in which it seems that we should understand the expressions which have been quoted to show that the behaviour of the Bantu is centred on the idea of vital energy: "to be strong," "to reinforce your life," "you are powerful," "be strong"; or again, "your vital force is declining, has been affected."

It is in this sense also that we must understand Fraser, when he writes in *The Golden Bough*, "The soul like the body can be fat or thin, great or small"; or again, "the diminution of the shadow is considered to be the index of a parallel enfeeblement in the vital energy of its owner."

The same idea again is envisaged by M. E. Possoz when he writes in his *Elements of Negro Customary Law*: "For the African, existence is a thing of variable intensity"; and further on when he mentions "the diminution or the reinforcement of being."

We must speak next of the existence of things or of forces. The origin, the subsistence or annihilation of beings or of forces, is expressly and exclusively attributed to God. The term "to create" in its proper connotation of "to evoke from not being" is found in its full signification in Bantu terminology (kupanga in Kiluba). It is in this sense that the Bantu see, in the phenomenon of conception, a direct intervention of God in creating life.

Those who think that, according to the Bantu, one being can entirely annihilate another, to the point that he ceases to exist, conceive a false idea. Doubtless one force that is greater than another can paralyse it, diminish it, or even cause its operation totally to cease, but for all that the force does not cease to exist. Existence which comes from God cannot be taken from a creature by any created force.

c) The interaction of forces: One being influencing another

We speak of the mechanical, chemical and psychical interactions between beings. Realists and idealists meet in recognizing yet another causality conditioning being itself, the cause of the existence of being as such. It is a metaphysical causality which binds the creature to the Creator. The relationship of the creature to the Creator is a constant. I mean to say that the creature is by his nature permanently dependent upon his Creator for existence and means of survival. We do not conceive of any equivalent relationship between creatures. Created beings are denoted in scholastic philosophy as substances, that is to say, beings who exist, if not by themselves, at any rate in themselves, *in se, non in alio*. The child is, from birth, a new being, a complete human being. It has the fullness of human nature and its human existence as such is independent of that of its progenitors. The human nature of a child does not remain in permanent causal relationship with that of its parents.

This concept of separate beings, of substance (to use the Scholastic term again) which find themselves side by side, entirely independent one of another, is foreign to Bantu thought. Bantu hold that created beings preserve a bond one with another, an intimate ontological relationship, comparable with the causal tie which binds creature and Creator. For the Bantu there is interaction of being with being, that is to say, of force with force. Transcending the mechanical, chemical and psychological interactions, they see a relationship of forces which we should call ontological. In the created force (a contingent being) the Bantu sees a causal action emanating from the very nature of that created force and influencing other forces. One force will reinforce or weaken another. This causality is in no way supernatural in the sense of going beyond the proper attributes of created nature. It is, on the contrary, a metaphysical causal action which flows out of the very nature of a created being. General knowledge of these activities belongs to the realm of natural knowledge and constitutes philosophy properly so called. The observation of the action of these forces in their specific and concrete applications would constitute Bantu natural science.

This interaction of beings has been denoted by the word "magic." If it is desired to keep the term, it must be modified so that it is understood in conformity with the content of Bantu thought. In what Europeans call "primitive magic" there is, to primitive eyes, no operation of supernatural, indeterminate forces, but simply the interaction between natural forces, as they were created by God and as they were put by him at the disposal of men.

In their studies of magic, authors distinguish "imitative magic," "sympathetic magic," "contagious magic," "magic of expressed desire," etc. Whatever the resemblance, contact, or the expression of desire, does not arise out of the essence of what is indicated by magic, that is to say, the

interaction of creatures. The very fact that there should have been recourse to different terms to distinguish the "kinds" of magic, proves that any attempt to penetrate to the real nature of magic has been given up in favour of a classification in terms of secondary characters only.

The child, even the adult, remains always for the Bantu a man, a force, in causal dependence and ontological subordination to the forces which are his father and mother. The older force ever dominates the younger. It continues to exercise its living influence over it. This is said to give a first example of the Bantu conception in accordance with which the "beings-forces" of the universe are not a multitude of independent forces placed in juxtaposition from being to being. All creatures are found in relationship according to the laws of a hierarchy. Nothing moves in this universe of forces without influencing other forces by its movement. The world of forces is held like a spider's web of which no single thread can be caused to vibrate without shaking the whole network.

It has been maintained that "beings" only acquire "power" to act upon other beings or forces through the intervention of spirits and manes. This contention emanates from European observers, it does not exist in the minds of Africans. The dead intervene on occasion to make known to the living the nature and quality of certain forces, but they do not thereby change that nature or those qualities which are preordained as belonging to that force. Africans expressly say that creatures are forces, created by God as such; and that the intervention of spirits or manes changes nothing: such changes are a White man's idea.

d) The hierarchy of forces: Primogeniture

As with Indian castes and as the Israelites distinguished the "pure" from the "impure," so beings are differentiated in Bantu ontology into species according to their vital power ("levenskracht") or their inherent vital rank ("levensrang"). Above all force is God, Spirit and Creator, the mwine bukomo bwandi. It is he who has force, power, in himself. He gives existence, power of survival and of increase, to other forces. In relation to other forces, he is "He who increases force." After him come the first fathers of men, founders of the different clans. These archi-patriarchs were the first to whom God communicated his vital force, with the power of exercising their influences on all posterity. They constitute the most important chain binding men to God. They occupy so exalted a rank in Bantu thought that they are not regarded merely as ordinary dead. They are no longer named among the manes; and by the Baluba they are called bavidye, spiritualized beings, beings belonging to a higher hierarchy, participating to a certain degree in the divine Force.

After these first parents come the dead of the tribe, following their order of primogeniture. They form a chain, through the links of which the forces of the elders exercise their vitalizing influence on the living generation. Those living on earth rank, in fact, after the dead. The living belong in turn to a hierarchy, not simply following legal status, but as ordered by their own being in accordance with primogeniture and their vital rank: that is to say, according to their vital power.

But man is not suspended in thin air. He lives on his land, where he finds himself to be the sovereign vital force, ruling the land and all that lives on it: man, animal, or plant. The eldest of a group or of a clan is, for Bantu, by Divine law the sustaining link of life, binding ancestors and their descendants. It is he who "reinforces" the life of his people and of all inferior forces, animal, vegetable and inorganic, that exist, grow, or live on the foundation which he provides for the welfare of his people. The true chief, then, following the original conception and political set up of clan peoples, is the father, the master, the king; he is the source of all zestful living; he is as God himself. This explains what the Bantu mean when they protest against the nomination of a chief, by government intervention, who is not able, by reason of his vital rank or vital force, to be the link binding dead and living. "Such an one cannot be chief. It is impossible. Nothing would grow in our soil, our women would bear no children and everything would be struck sterile." Such considerations and such despair are entirely mysterious and incomprehensible so long as we have not grasped the Bantu conception of existence and their interpretation of the universe. Judged, however, according to the theory of forces, their point of view becomes logical and clear.

After the category of human forces come the other forces, animal, vegetable and mineral. But within each of these categories is found a hierarchy based on vital power, rank and primogeniture.

From that it follows that an analogy can be found between a human and a lower group (e.g. in the animal class), an analogy based on the relative place of these groups in relation to its own class. Such would be an analogy founded on primogeniture or upon a pre-determined order of subordination. A human group and an animal species can occupy in their respective classes a rank relatively equal or relatively different. Their vital rank can be parallel or different. A Chief in the class of humans shows his royal rank by wearing the skin of a royal animal. The respect for this ranking in life, the care not to place oneself higher than one's legitimate place, the necessity not to approach the higher forces as if they were our equals, all that can supply the key to the so much disputed problem of "tabu" and "totem."

50

The Igbo World and Its Art

Chinua Achebe

The Igbo world is an arena for the interplay of forces. It is a dynamic world of movement and of flux. Igbo art, reflecting this world-view, is never tranquil but mobile and active, even aggressive.

Ike, energy, is the essence of all things human, spiritual, animate and inanimate. Everything has its own unique energy which must be acknowledged and given its due. *Ike di na awaja na awaja* is a common formulation of this idea: "Power runs in many channels." Sometimes the saying is extended by an exemplifying coda about a mild and gentle bird, *obu*, which nonetheless possesses the power to destroy a snake. *Onye na nkie, onye na nkie* – literally, "everyone and his own" – is a social expression of the same notion often employed as a convenient formula for saluting *en masse* an assembly too large for individual greetings.

In some cultures a person may worship one of the gods or goddesses in the pantheon and pay scant attention to the rest. In Igbo religion such selectiveness is unthinkable. All the people must placate all the gods all the time! For there is a cautionary proverb which states that even when a person has satisfied the deity Udo completely he may yet be killed by Ogwugwu. The degree of peril propounded by this proverb is only dimly apprehended until one realizes that Ogwugwu is not a stranger to Udo but his very consort!

It is the striving to come to terms with a multitude of forces and demands which gives Igbo life its tense and restless dynamism and its art an outward, social and kinetic quality. But it would be a mistake to take the extreme view that Igbo art has no room for contemplative privacy. In the first place, all extremism is abhorrent to the Igbo sensibility; but specifically, the Igbo word which is closest to the English word "art" is *nka*, and Igbo people do say: *Onye nakwa nka na-eme ka ona-adu iru*, which means that an artist at work is apt to wear an unfriendly face. In other words, he is excused from the normal demands of sociability! If further proof is required of this need for privacy in the creative process, it is provided clearly and definitively in the ritual seclusion of the makers of *mbari*, to which we shall return shortly.

But once made, art emerges from privacy into the public domain. There are no private collections among the Igbo beyond personal ritual objects like the *ikenga*. Indeed, the very concept of collections would be antithetical to the Igbo artistic intention. Collections by their very nature will impose rigid, artistic attitudes and conventions on creativity which the Igbo sensibility goes out of its way to avoid. The purposeful neglect of the painstakingly and devoutly accomplished *mbari* houses with all the art objects in them, as soon as the primary mandate of their creation has been served, provides a significant insight into the Igbo aesthetic value as process rather than product. Process is motion while product is rest. When the product is preserved or venerated, the impulse to repeat the process is compromised. Therefore the Igbo choose to eliminate the product and retain the process so that every occasion and every generation will receive its own impulse and kinesis of creation. Interestingly, this aesthetic disposition receives powerful endorsement from the tropical climate which provides an abundance of materials for making art, such as wood, as well as formidable enemies of stasis, such as humidity and the termite. Visitors to Igboland are often shocked to see that artefacts are rarely accorded any particular value on account of age alone.

In popular contemporary usage the Igbo formulate their view of the world as: "No condition is permanent." In Igbo cosmology even gods could fall out of use; and new forces are liable to appear without warning in the temporal and metaphysical firmament. The practical purpose of art is to channel a spiritual force into an aesthetically satisfying physical form that captures the presumed attributes of that force. It stands to reason, therefore, that new forms must stand ready to be called into being as often as new (threatening) forces appear on the scene. It is like "earthing" an electrical charge to ensure communal safety.

The frequent representation of the alien district officer among traditional *mbari* figures is an excellent example of the mediating role of art between old and new, between accepted norms and extravagant aberrations. Art must interpret all human experience, for anything against which the door is barred can cause trouble. Even if harmony is not achievable in the heterogeneity of human experience, the dangers of an open rupture are greatly lessened by giving to everyone his due in the same forum of social and cultural surveillance. The alien district officer may not, after all, be a greater oddity than a local woman depicted in the act of copulating with a dog, and such powerful aberrations must be accorded tactful artistic welcome-cum-invigilation.

Of all the art forms, the dance and the masquerade would appear to have satisfied the Igbo artistic appetite most completely. If the masquerade were not limited to the male sex alone, one might indeed call it the art form *par excellence* for it subsumes not only the dance but all other forms – sculpture, music, painting, drama, costumery, even architecture, for the Ijele masquerade is indeed a most fabulously extravagant construction.

What makes the dance and the masquerade so satisfying to the Igbo disposition is, I think, their artistic deployment of motion, of agility, which informs the Igbo concept of existence. The masquerade (which is really an elaborated dance) not only moves spectacularly but those who want to enjoy its motion fully must follow its progress up and down the arena. This seemingly minor observation was nonetheless esteemed important enough by the Igbo to be elevated into a proverb of general application: *Ada-akwu ofu ebe enene mmuo*, "You do not stand in one place to watch a masquerade." You must imitate its motion. The kinetic energy of the masquerade's art is thus instantly transmitted to a whole arena of spectators.

So potent is motion stylized into dance that the Igbo have sought to defeat with its power even the final immobility of death by contriving a funeral rite in which the bearers of the corpse perform the *abia* dance with their burden, transforming by their motion the body's imminent commitment to earth into an active rite of passage.

This body, appropriately transfigured, will return on festival or ritual occasions or during serious social crises, as a masquerade to participate with an enhanced presence and authority in the affairs of the community, speaking an esoteric dialect in which people are referred to as bodies: "The body of so-and-so, I salute you!"

Masquerades are of many kinds representing the range of human experience – from youth to age; from playfulness to terror; from the delicate beauty of the maiden spirit, *agbogho mmuo*, to the candid ugliness of *njo ka-oya*, "ugliness greater than disease"; from the athleticism of *ogolo* to the legless and armless inertia of *ebu-ebu*, a loquacious masquerade that has to be carried from place to place on the head of its attendant from which position it is wont to shout: Off we go! *(Ije abulu ufia!)*; from masquerades that appear at every festival to the awesome ancestors that are enticed to the world by rare crises such as the desecration of a masked spirit; from the vast majority that appear in daytime to the dreaded invisible chorus, *ayaka*, and the night-runner, *ogbazulobodo*.

I hasten to add that the examples given above are merely localized impressionistic illustrations taken from my own experience of growing up in Ogidi in the 1930s and 1940s. There are variations from one village community to the next and certainly from one region of Igboland to another. Nothing here can do justice, for instance, to the extraordinary twin traditions of Odo and Omabe of the Nsukka region. To encounter an Omabe masquerade just descended from the hills for a brief sojourn in the world after an absence of three years, its body of tiny metal discs throwing back the dying lights of dusk, can be a truly breathtaking experience!

The awesomeness of masquerades has suffered in modern times. This is not due, as some imagine, to the explosion of the secret concerning what lies behind the mask. Even in the past the women merely pretended not to know! I remember as a child a masquerade whose name was *Omanu kwue* – meaning, "If you know, speak." This was a dare, of course, and nobody was about to take up the challenge. But this masquerade was of such towering height that there was only one man in the whole of Ogidi, perhaps even in the whole world, who could carry it; the same man, incidentally, whose brief career as a policeman at the beginning of the century had left a powerful enough legend for him to be represented in his uniform in an *mbari* house in faraway Owerri and simply called Ogidi.

In the past, knowing who walked within the mask did not detract from the numinous, dramatic presence of a representative of the ancestors on a brief mission to the living. Disbelief was easily suspended! The decline today is merely a symptom of the collapse of a whole eschatology. But at least in my dreams masquerades have not ceased to bring forth the panic terror of childhood.

Originally published as Foreword to *Igbo Arts: Community and Cosmos*, by Herbert M. Cole and Chike C. Aniakor, Museum of Cultural History, University of California at Los Angeles, 1984.

51

The Fourth Stage: Through the Mysteries of Ogun[1] to the Origin of Yoruba Tragedy

Wole Soyinka

The persistent search for the meaning of tragedy, for a re-definition in terms of cultural or private experience is, at the least, man's recognition of certain areas of depth-experience which are not satisfactorily explained by general aesthetic theories; and, of all the subjective unease that is aroused by man's creative insights, that wrench within the human psyche which we vaguely define as 'tragedy' is the most insistent voice that bids us return to our own sources. There, illusively, hovers the key to the human paradox, to man's experience of being and non-being, his dubiousness as essence and matter, intimations of transience and eternity, and the harrowing drives between uniqueness and Oneness.

Our course to the heart of the Yoruba Mysteries leads by its own ironic truths through the light of Nietzsche[2] and the Phrygian deity; but there are the inevitable, key departures. 'Blessed Greeks!' sings our mad votary in his recessional rapture, 'how great must be your Dionysos, if the Delic god thinks such enchantments necessary to cure you of your Dithyrambic madness'. Such is Apollo's resemblance to the serene art of Obatala[3] the pure unsullied one, to the 'essence' idiom of his rituals, that it is tempting to place him at the end of a creative axis with Ogun, in a parallel evolutionary

relationship to Nietzsche's Dionysos – Apollo brotherhood. But Obatala the sculptural god is not the artist of Apollonian illusion but of inner essence. The idealist bronze and terra-cotta of Ife which may tempt the comparison implicit in 'Apollonian' died at some now forgotten period, evidence only of the universal surface culture of courts, never again resurrected. It is alien to the Obatala spirit of Yoruba 'essential' art. Obatala finds expression, not in Nietzsche's Apollonian 'mirror of enchantment' but as a statement of world resolution. The mutual tempering of illusion and will, necessary to an understanding of the Hellenic spirit, may mislead us, when we are faced with Yoruba art, for much of it has a similarity in its aesthetic serenity to the plastic arts of the Hellenic. Yoruba traditional art is not ideational however, but 'essential'. It is not the idea (in religious arts) that is transmitted into wood or interpreted in music or movement, but a quintessence of inner being, a symbolic interaction of the many aspects of revelations (within a universal context) with their moral apprehension.

Ogun, for his part, is best understood in Hellenic values as a totality of the Dionysian, Apollonian and Promethean virtues. Nor is that all. Transcending even today, the distorted myths of his terrorist reputation, traditional poetry records him as 'protector of orphans', 'roof over the homeless', 'terrible guardian of the sacred oath'; Ogun stands for a transcendental, humane but rigidly restorative jus-

From Wole Soyinka, *Myth, Literature and the African World* (1976); reproduced by kind permission of Cambridge University Press.

tice. (Unlike Sango, who is primarily retributive.) The first artist and technician of the forge, he evokes like Nietzsche's Apollonian spirit, a 'massive impact of image, concept, ethical doctrine and sympathy'. Obatala is the placid essence of creation; Ogun the creative urge and instinct, the essence of creativity.

> Rich-laden is his home, yet decked in palm
> fronds
> He ventures forth, refuge of the down-
> trodden,
> To rescue slaves he unleashed the judgment
> of war
> Because of the blind, plunged into forests
> Of curative herbs, Bountiful One
> Who stands bulwark to offsprings of the dead
> of heaven
> Salutations, O lone being, who swims in
> rivers of blood.

Such virtues place Ogun apart from the distorted dances to which Nietzsche's Dionysiac frenzy led him in his search for a selective 'Aryan' soul, yet do not detract from Ogun's revolutionary grandeur. Ironically, it is the depth-illumination of Nietzsche's intuition into basic universal impulses which negates his race exclusivist conclusions on the nature of art and tragedy. In our journey to the heart of Yoruba tragic art which indeed belongs in the Mysteries of Ogun and the choric ecstasy of revellers, we do not find that the Yoruba, as the Greek did, 'built for his chorus the scaffolding of a fictive chthonic realm and placed thereon fictive nature spirits . . .' on which foundation, claims Nietzsche, Greek tragedy developed: in short, the principle of illusion.

Yoruba tragedy plunges straight into the 'chthonic realm', the seething cauldron of the dark world will and psyche, the transitional yet inchoate matrix of death and becoming. Into this universal womb once plunged and emerged Ogun, the first actor, disintegrating within the abyss. His spiritual re-assemblage does not require a 'copying of actuality' in the ritual re-enactment of his devotees, any more than Obatala does in plastic representation, in the art of Obatala. The actors in Ogun Mysteries are the communicant chorus, containing within their collective being the essence of that transitional abyss. But only as essence, held, contained and mystically expressed. Within the mystic summons of the chasm the protagonist actor (and every god-suffused choric individual) resists, like Ogun before him, the final step toward complete annihilation. From this alone steps forward the eternal actor of the tragic rites, first as the unresisting mouthpiece of the god, uttering visions symbolic of the transitional gulf, interpreting the dread power within whose essence he is immersed as agent of the choric will. Only later, in the evenness of release from the tragic climax, does the serene self-awareness of Obatala reassert its creative control. He, the actor, emerges still as the mediant voice of the god, but stands now as it were beside himself, observant, understanding, creating. At this stage is known to him the sublime *aesthetic* joy, not within Nietzsche's heart of original oneness but in the distanced celebration of the cosmic struggle. This resolved aesthetic serenity is the link between Ogun's tragic art and Obatala's plastic beauty. The unblemished god, Obatala, is the serene womb of chthonic reflections (or memory), a passive strength awaiting and celebrating each act of vicarious restoration of his primordial being. (We shall come later to the story of that first severance.) His beauty is enigmatic, expressive only of the resolution of plastic healing through the wisdom of acceptance. Obatala's patient suffering is the well-known aesthetics of the saint.

For the Yoruba, the gods are the final measure of eternity, as humans are of earthly transience. To think, because of this, that the Yoruba mind reaches intuitively toward absorption in godlike essence is to misunderstand the principle of religious rites, and to misread, as many have done, the significance of religious possession. Past, present and future being so pertinently conceived and woven into the Yoruba world view, the element of eternity which is the god's prerogative does not have the same quality of remoteness or exclusiveness which it has in Christian or Buddhist culture. The belief of the Yoruba in the contemporaneous existence within his daily experience of these aspects of time has long been recognized but again misinterpreted. It is no abstraction. The Yoruba is not, like European man, concerned with the purely conceptual aspects of time; they are too concretely realized in his own life, religion, sensitivity, to be mere tags for explaining the metaphysical order of his world. If we may put the same thing in fleshed-out cognitions, life, present life, contains within it manifestations of the ancestral, the living and the unborn. All are vitally within the intimations and affectiveness of life, beyond mere abstract conceptualization.

And yet the Yoruba does not for that reason fail to distinguish between himself and the deities, between himself and the ancestors, between the unborn and his reality, or discard his awareness of the essential gulf that lies between one area of existence and another. This gulf is what must be constantly diminished by the sacrifices, the rituals, the ceremonies of appeasement to those cosmic powers which lie guardian to the gulf. Spiritually, the primordial disquiet of the Yoruba psyche may be expressed as the existence in collective memory of a primal severance in transitional ether,[4] whose first effective defiance is symbolized in the myth of the gods' descent to earth and the battle with immense chaotic growth which had sealed off reunion with man. For they were coming down, not simply to be acknowledged but to be re-united with human essence, to reassume that portion of re-creative transient awareness which the first deity Orisanla possessed and expressed through his continuous activation of man images – brief reflections of divine facets – just as man is grieved by a consciousness of the loss of the eternal essence of his being and must indulge in symbolic transactions to recover his totality of being.

Tragedy, in Yoruba traditional drama, is the anguish of this severance, the fragmentation of essence from self. Its music is the stricken cry of man's blind soul as he flounders in the void and crashes through a deep abyss of aspirituality and cosmic rejection. Tragic music is an echo from that void; the celebrant speaks, sings and dances in authentic archetypal images from within the abyss. All understand and respond, for it is the language of the world.

It is necessary to emphasize that the gods were coming down to be reunited with man, for this tragedy could not be, the anguish of severance would not attain such tragic proportions, if the gods' position on earth (i.e. in man's conception) was to be one of divine remoteness. This is again testified to by the form of worship, which is marked by camaraderie and irreverence just as departure to ancestorhood is marked by bawdiness in the midst of grief. The anthropomorphic origin of uncountable deities is one more leveller of divine class-consciousness but, finally, it is the innate humanity of the gods themselves, their bond with man through a common animist relation with nature and phenomena. Continuity for the Yoruba operates both through the cyclic concept of time and the animist interfusion of all matter and consciousness.

The first actor – for he led the others – was Ogun, first suffering deity, first creative energy, the first challenger, and conqueror of transition. And his,

the first art, was tragic art, for the complementary drama of the syncretic successor to Orisa-nla, Obatala's 'Passion' play, is only the plastic resolution of Ogun's tragic engagement. The Yoruba metaphysics of accommodation and resolution could only come *after* the passage of the gods through the transitional gulf, after the demonic test of the self-will of Ogun the explorer-god in the creative cauldron of cosmic powers. Only after such testing could the harmonious Yoruba world be born, a harmonious will which accommodates every alien material or abstract phenomenon within its infinitely stressed spirituality. The artefact of Ogun's conquest of separation, the 'fetish', was iron ore, symbol of earth's womb-energies, cleaver and welder of life. Ogun, through his redemptive action became the first symbol of the alliance of disparities when, from earth itself, he extracted elements for the subjugation of chthonic chaos. In tragic consciousness the votary's psyche reaches out beyond the realm of nothingness (or spiritual chaos) which is potentially destructive of human awareness, through areas of terror and blind energies, into a ritual empathy with the gods, the eternal presence, who once preceded him in parallel awareness of their own incompletion. Ritual anguish is therefore experienced as that primal transmission of the god's despair – vast, numinous, always incomprehensible. In vain we seek to capture it in words; there is only for the protagonist the certainty of the experience of this abyss – the tragic victim plunges into it in spite of ritualistic earthing and is redeemed only by action. Without acting and yet in spite of it, he is forever lost in the maul of tragic tyranny.

Acting is therefore a contradiction of the tragic spirit, yet it is also its natural complement. To act, the Promethean instinct of rebellion, channels anguish into a creative purpose which releases man from a totally destructive despair, releasing from within him the most energetic, deeply combative inventions which, without usurping the territory of the infernal gulf, bridges it with visionary hopes. Only the battle of the will is thus primally creative; from its spiritual stress springs the soul's despairing cry which proves its own solace, which alone reverberating within the cosmic vaults, usurps (at least, and however briefly) the power of the abyss. At the charged climatic moments of the tragic rites we understand how music came to be the sole art from which can contain tragic reality. The votary is led by no other guide into the pristine heart of tragedy. Music as the embodiment of the tragic spirit has been more than perceptively exhausted in the philosophy of Europe; there is little to add, much to qualify. And the function and nature of music in Yoruba tragedy is peculiarly revealing of the shortcomings of long accepted conclusions of European intuition.

The European concept of music does not fully illuminate the relationship of music to ritual and drama among the Yoruba. We are inhibited even by recognition of a universality of concepts in the European intuitive grasp of the emotions of the will. First, it is 'unmusical' to separate Yoruba musical form from myth and poetry. The nature of Yoruba music is intensively the nature of its language and poetry, highly charged, symbolic, myth-embryonic. We acknowledge quite readily the technical lip-service paid to the correspondence of African music to the tonal patterns (meaning and allusion) of the language, but the aesthetic and emotional significance of this relationship has not been truly absorbed, one which springs from the primal simultaneity of art forms in a culture of total awareness and phenomenal involvement. Language therefore is not a barrier to the profound universality of music but a cohesive dimension and clarification of that wilfully independent art-form which we label music. Language reverts in religious rites to its pristine existence, eschewing the sterile limits of particularization. In cult funerals, the circle of initiate mourners, an ageless swaying grove of dark pines, raises a chant around a mortar of fire, and words are taken back to their roots, to their original poetic sources when fusion was total and the movement of words was the very passage of music and the dance of images. Language is still the embryo of thought and music where myth is daily companion, for there language is constantly mythopoeic.

Language in Yoruba tragic music therefore undergoes transformation through myth into a secret (masonic) correspondence with the symbolism of tragedy, a symbolic medium of spiritual emotions within the heart of the choric union. It transcends particularization (of meaning) to tap the tragic source whence spring the familiar weird disruptive melodies. This masonic union of sign and melody, the true tragic music, unearths cosmic uncertainties which pervade human existence, reveals the magnitude and power of creation, but above all creates a harrowing sense of omnidirectional vastness where the creative Intelligence resides and prompts the soul to futile exploration. The senses do not at such moments interpret myth in their particular concretions; we are left only with the emotional and spiritual values, the essential experience of cosmic reality. The forms of music are not correspondences at such moments to the physical world, not at this nor at any other moment. The singer is a mouthpiece of the chthonic forces of the matrix and his somnambulist 'improvisations' – a simultaneity of musical and poetic forms – are not representations of the ancestor, recognitions of the living or unborn, but of the no man's land of transition between and around these temporal definitions of experience. The past is the ancestors', the present belongs to the living, and the future to the unborn. The deities stand in the same situation to the living as do the ancestors and the unborn, obeying the same laws, suffering the same agonies and uncertainties, employing the same masonic intelligence of rituals for the perilous plunge into the fourth area of experience, the immeasurable gulf of transition. Its dialogue is liturgy, its music takes form from man's uncomprehending immersion in this area of existence, buried wholly from rational recognition. The source of the possessed lyricist, chanting hitherto unknown mythopoeic strains whose antiphonal refrain is, however, instantly caught and thrust with all its terror and awesomeness into the night by swaying votaries, this source is residual in the numinous area of transition.

This is the fourth stage, the vortex of archetypes and home of the tragic spirit.

It is necessary to recall again that the past is not a mystery and that although the future (the unborn) is yet unknown, it is not a mystery to the Yoruba but co-existent in present consciousness. Tragic terror exists therefore neither in the evocation of the past nor of the future. The stage of transition is, however, the metaphysical abyss both of god and man, and if we agree that, in the European sense, music is the 'direct copy or the direct expression of the will', it is only because nothing rescues man (ancestral, living or unborn) from loss of self within this abyss but a titanic resolution of the will whose ritual summons, response, and expression is the strange alien sound to which we give the name of music. On the arena of the living, when man is stripped of excrescences, when disasters and conflicts (the material of drama) have crushed and robbed him of self-consciousness and pretensions, he stands in present reality at the spiritual edge of this gulf, he has nothing left in physical existence which successfully impresses upon his spiritual or psychic perception. It is at such moments that transitional memory takes over and intimations rack him of that intense parallel of his progress through the gulf of transition, of the dissolution of his self and his struggle and triumph over subsumation through the agency of will. It is this experience that the modern tragic dramatist recreates through the medium of physical contemporary action, reflecting emotions of the first active battle of the will through the abyss of dissolution.[5] Ogun is the first actor in that battle, and Yoruba tragic drama is the re-enactment of the cosmic conflict.

To recognize why Ogun was elected for his role (and the penalty of horror which he had to pay for his challenge) is to penetrate the symbolism of Ogun both as essence of anguish and as combative will within the cosmic embrace of the transitional gulf. We have said that nothing but the will (for that alone is left untouched) rescues being from annihilation within the abyss. Ogun is embodiment of Will, and the Will is the paradoxical truth of destructiveness and creativeness in acting man. Only one who has himself undergone the experience of disintegration, whose spirit has been tested and whose psychic resources laid under stress by the forces most inimical to individual assertion, only he can understand and be the force of fusion between the two contradictions. The resulting sensibility is also the sensibility of the artist, and he is a profound artist only to the degree to which he comprehends and expresses this principle of destruction and re-creation.

We must not lose sight of the fact that Ogun is the artistic spirit, and not in the sentimental sense in which rhapsodists of négritude would have us conceive the negro as pure artistic intuition. The significant creative truth of Ogun is affirmation of the recreative intelligence; this is irreconcilable with naive intuition. The symbolic artefact of his victory is metallic ore, at once a technical medium as it is symbolic of deep earth energies, a fusion of elemental energies, a binding force between disparate bodies and properties. Thus Ogan, tragic actor, primordial voice of creative man is also, without a contradiction of essences, the forerunner and ancestor of palaeotechnic man. The principle of creativity when limited to pastoral idyllism, as negritude has attempted to limit it, shuts us off from the deeper, fundamental resolutions of experience and cognition. The tragic actor for the future age (already the present for Europe) is that neotechnic ancestor Sango,[6] god of electricity, whose tragedy stems similarly from the principle of a preliminary self-destruction, represented (as in a later penalty of Ogun) in the blind ignorant destruction of his own flesh and blood. What, for Ogun, was a destructive penalty leading to a secondary drama of 'Passion' was in Sango the very core of his tragedy. The historic process of dilution in tragic challenge is manifested in the relationship of these two myths. Sango is an anthropomorphic deity; his history revolved around petty tyranny; his self-destruction was the violent, central explosion from ego-inflation. Where Ogun's human alienation was the postscript error, an exaction for his basic victory over the transitional guardians of the gulf, Sango's was 'in character', a wild vengeful slaughter upon menials who had dared to defy his authority. But the 'terror and pity' of Sango is undeniable, only it is the 'terror and pity' of human disavowal for that new disciple standing on the edge of the sublimating abyss already subdued by Ogun. We will not find the roots of tragedy in the Mysteries of Sango.

Yoruba myth is a recurrent exercise in the experience of disintegration, and this is significant for the seeming distancing of will among a people whose mores, culture and metaphysics are based on apparent resignation and acceptance but which are, experienced in depth, a statement of man's penetrating insight into the final resolution of things and the constant evidence of harmony. What moral values do we encounter in the drama of Obatala, representative though it also is of the first disintegration experienced by godhead? We are further back in Origin, not now engaged in the transitional battle of Ogun, but in the fragmentation of Orisa-nla, the primal deity, from whom the entire Yoruba pantheon was born. Myth informs us that a jealous slave rolled a stone down the back of the first and only deity and shattered him in a thousand and one fragments. From this first act of revolution was born the Yoruba pantheon.

The drama which stems from this is not the drama of acting man but that of suffering spirit, the drama of Obatala. Yoruba myth syncretizes Obatala, god of purity, god also of creation (but not of creativity!), with the first deity Orisa-nla. And the ritual of Obatala is a play of form, a moving celebration whose nearest equivalent in the European idioms is the Passion play. The drama is all essence: captivity, suffering and redemption. Obatala is symbolically captured, confined and ransomed. At every stage he is the embodiment of the suffering spirit of man, uncomplaining, agonized, full of the redemptive qualities of endurance and martyrdom. The music that accompanies the rites of Obatala is all clear tone and winnowed lyric, of order and harmony, stately and saintly. Significantly, the motif is white for transparency of heart and mind; there is a rejection of mystery; tones of vesture and music combine to banish mystery and terror; the poetry of the song is litanic, the dramatic idiom is the processional or ceremonial. It is a drama in which the values of conflict or the revolutionary spirit are excluded, attesting in their place the adequacy and certainty of a harmomious resolution which belongs in time and human faith. It is antithetical to the tragic challenge of Ogun in man.

Proportion in tragedy is governed by an element of the unknown in the forces of opposition or by a miscalculation by the tragic victim of such powers. The drama of Obatala dispenses with the effect of the unknown, and his agony is an evocation of the loneliness of the first deity, for this drama is, as we have stated, all pathos. And the essence is the emotional prelude to the creation of man, the limited, serene aesthetics of moulding man, not to be compared to the cosmic eruption within consciousness brought about by the re-creation of the self. The sympathetic need to be redeemed by evidence of love and human contact, by extension of the self into recognizable entities and other units of potential consciousness – this is the province of Obatala, the delicate shell of the original fullness. The profounder aspect of self-re-creation, the anguish of the Will, is the portion of original restoration which has been left to the peculiar talents of Ogun, and the statement of Yoruba tragic rites is the complement of his Will to the essence of anguish. The latter by itself is crystallized in the Passion play. The drama of Obatala is prelude, suffering and aftermath. It symbolizes firstly the god's unbearable loneliness and next, the memory of his incompleteness, the missing essence. And so it is also with the other gods who did not avail themselves, as did Ogun, of the chance for a redemptive combat where each might re-create each by submission to a disintegrating process within the matrix of cosmic creativity, whence the Will performs the final reassemblage. The weightiest burden of severance is that of each from self, not of godhead from mankind, and the most perilous aspect of the god's journey is that in which the deity must truly undergo the experience of transition. It is look into the very heart of phenomena. To fashion a bridge across it was not only Ogun's task but his very nature, and he had first to experience it, to surrender his individuation once again (the first time, as a part of the original Orisa-nla

Oneness) to the fragmenting process; to be reabsorbed within universal Oneness, the Unconscious, the deep black whirlpool of mythopoeic forces, to immerse himself thoroughly within it, understand its nature and yet by the combative value of the will to rescue and re-assemble himself and emerge wiser, powerful from the draught of cosmic secrets, organizing the mystic and the technical forces of earth and cosmos to forge a bridge for his companions to follow.

It is true that to understand, to understand profoundly, is to be unnerved, deprived of the will to act. For is not human reality dwarfed by the awe and wonder, the inevitability of this cosmic gulf? It must be remembered that within this abyss are the activities of birth, death and resorption in phenomena (for the abyss is the transition between the various stages of existence). Life, the paltry reflection of the forces of the matrix, becomes suddenly inadequate, patronizing and undignified when the source of creative and destructive energies is glimpsed. Suffering cancels the opaque pleasure of human existence; suffering, the truly overwhelming suffering of Sango, of Lear, of Oedipus, this suffering hones the psyche to a finely self-annihilating perceptiveness and renders further action futile and, above all, lacking in dignity. And what has the struggle of the tragic hero been, after all, but an effort to maintain that innate concept of dignity which impels to action only to that degree in which the hero possesses a true nobility of spirit? At such moments he is close to the acceptance and wisdom of Obatala in which faith is rested, not on the self, but on a universal selfhood to which individual contributions are fundamentally meaningless. It is the faith of 'knowing', the enigmatic wisdom of spiritual serenity. It is this which is often narrowly interpreted as the philosophy of the African. But philosophies are the result of primal growth and formative experience; the oracular wisdom of a race based on and continually acted upon by the collective experience of the past, present and unborn (prognostic) realities, complements the intuitive glimpse and memory of the heart of transitional being.

Yoruba 'classical' art is mostly an expression of the Obatala resolution and human beneficence, utterly devoid, on the surface, of conflict and irruption. The masks alone occasionally suggest a correspondence to the chthonic realm and hint at the archetypes of transition, yet even the majority of them flee the full power of cosmic vision, take refuge in deliberately grotesque and comic attitudes. Such distortions are easily recognized as the technique of evasion from the fullness of numinous powers. Terror is both contained by art in tragic form and released by art through comic presentation and sexual ambience. The tragic mask, however, also functions from the same source as its music – from the archetypal essences whose language derives not from the plane of physical reality or ancestral memory (the ancestor is no more than agent or medium), but from the numinous territory of transition into which the artist obtains fleeting glimpses by ritual, sacrifice and a patient submission of rational awareness to the moment when fingers and voice relate the symbolic language of the cosmos. The deft, luminous peace of Yoruba religious art blinds us therefore to the darker powers of the tragic art into which only the participant can truly enter. The grotesquerie of the terror cults misleads the unwary into equating fabricated fears with the exploration of the Yoruba mind into the mystery of his individual will and the intimations of divine suffering to which artistic man is prone. Ifa's cycle of masonic poetry – curative, prognostic, aesthetic and omniscient – expresses a philosophy of optimism in its oracular adaptiveness and unassailable resolution of all phenomena; the gods are accommodating and embrace within their eternal presence manifestations which are seemingly foreign or contradictory. It is no wonder therefore that the overt optimistic nature of the total culture is the quality attributed to the Yoruba himself, one which has begun to affect his accommodation toward the modern world, a spiritual complacency with which he encounters threats to his human and unique validation. Alas, in spite of himself, from time to time, the raw urgent question beats in the blood of his temples demanding, what is the will of Ogun? For the hammering of the Yoruba will was done at Ogun's forge, and any threat of disjunction is, as with the gods, a memory code for the resurrection of the tragic myth.

Yoruba morality has also contributed to the mistaken exclusion of tragic myth from present consciousness; for, as always, the placid surface of the process of healing for spiritual or social rupture is mistaken for the absence of the principles of psychic experience that went into the restoration. Morality for the Yoruba is that which creates harmony in the cosmos, and reparation for disjunction within the individual psyche cannot be seen as compensation for the individual accident to that personality. Thus good and evil are not measured in terms of offences against the individual or even

the physical community, for there is knowledge from within the corpus of Ifa oracular wisdoms that a rupture is often simply one aspect of the destructive-creative unity, that offences even against nature may be part of the exaction by deeper nature from humanity of acts which alone can open up the deeper springs of man and bring about a constant rejuvenation of the human spirit. Nature in turn benefits by such broken taboos, just as the cosmos does by demands made upon its will by man's cosmic affronts. Such acts of hubris compel the cosmos to delve deeper into its essence to meet the human challenge. Penance and retribution are not therefore aspects of punishment for crime but the first acts of a resumed awareness, an invocation of the principle of cosmic adjustment. Tragic fate is the repetitive cycle of the taboo in nature, the karmic act of hubris witting or unwitting, into which the demonic will within man constantly compels him. Powerful tragic drama follows upon the act of hubris, and myth exacts this attendant penalty from the hero where he has actually emerged victor of a conflict. Sango's taboo is based on an elementary form of hubris. Over-reaching even beyond the generous toleration due to a monarch, he fell victim to a compulsion for petty intriguing which finally led to his downfall. A final, desperate invocation of unnatural strength gave him temporary ascendancy and he routed his disloyal men. Then came the desecration of nature in which he spilt the blood of his kin. Ogun not only dared to look into transitional essence but triumphantly bridged it with knowledge, with art, with vision and the mystic creativity of science – a total and profound hubristic assertiveness that is beyond any parallel in Yoruba experience. The penalty came later when, as a reward and acknowledgement of his leadership of the divinities, gods and humans joined to offer him a crown. At first he declined but later he consented to the throne of Ire. At the first battle the same demonic energies were aroused but this was no world womb, no chthonic lair, no playground of cosmic monsters, nor could the divisions between man and man, between I and you, friend and foe, be perceived by the erstwhile hero of the transitional abyss. Enemy and subjects fell alike until Ogun alone was left, sole survivor of the narrowness of human separation. The battle is symbolic of tragic hindsight common alike to god and man. In the Ogun Mysteries this drama is a 'Passion' of a different kind, released into quietist wisdom, a ritual exorcism of demonic energies. There is no elation, not even at the end of purgation, nothing like the beatified elation of Obatala after his redemption, only a world-weariness on the rock-shelf of Promethean shoulders, a profound sorrow in the chanting of the god's recessional.[7]

Once we recognize, to revert to his Hellenic equation, the Dionysian-Apollonian-Promethean essence of Ogun, the element of hubris is seen as innate to his tragic being, requiring definition in Yoruba terms, taking it to its cyclic resolution of man's metaphysical situation. Of the profound anguish of Dionysos, the mythic disintegration of his origin is the now familiar cause, and the process of the will, no less, is what rescues the ecstatic god from being, literally, scattered to the cosmic winds. The will of Zeus is as conceptually identifiable with that of Dionysos as the elemental fragmentation of Orisa-nla can be recognized as the recurrent consciousness within Ogun (and other gods) of this kernel of terror of a previous rendering. Ripped in pieces at the hands of the titans for the (by him) unwilled acts of hubris, a divine birth, Dionysos-Zagreus commences divine existence by this experience of the destruction of the self, the transitional horror. For it is an act of hubris not only to dare the gulf of transition but to mingle essences for extra measure. We approach, it seems, the ultimate pessimism of existence as pronounced by Nietzche's sage Silenus: it is an act of hubris to be born. It is a challenge to the jealous chthonic powers, to *be*. The answer of the Yoruba to this is just as clear: it is no less an act of hubris to *die*. And the whirlpool of transition requires both hubristic complements as catalyst to its continuous regeneration. This is the serene wisdom and essential art of Obatala. All acts are subordinate to these ultimates of the human condition and recreative will. To dare transition is the ultimate test of the human spirit, and Ogun is the first protagonist of the abyss.

The Phrygian god and his twin Ogun exercise irresistible fascination. Dionysos' thyrsus is physically and functionally paralleled by the *opa Ogun* borne by the male devotees of Ogun. But the thyrsus of Dionysos is brighter; it is all light and running wine, Ogun's stave is more symbolic of his labour through the night of transition. A long willowy pole, it is topped by a frond-bound lump of ore which strains the pole in wilful curves and keeps it vibrant. The bearers, who can only be men, are compelled to move about among the revellers as the effort to keep the ore-head from toppling over keeps them perpetually on the move. Through town and village, up the mountain to the grove of Ogun this dance of the straining phallus-heads pocks the air above men and women revellers who are decked in palm fronds and bear palm branches in their hands. A dog is slaughtered in sacrifice, and the mock-struggle of the head priest and his acolytes for the carcass, during which it is literally torn limb from limb, inevitably brings to mind the dismemberment of Zagreus, son of Zeus. Most significant of all is the brotherhood of the palm and the ivy. The mystery of the wine of palm, bled straight from the tree and potent without further ministration, is a miracle of nature acquiring symbolic significance in the Mysteries of Ogun. For it was instrumental in the tragic error of the god and his sequent Passion. Like Obatala also, the gods commit their error after an excess of the potent draught. Ogun was full of wine before his battle at the head of the Ire army. After his dark deed, the wine fog slowly lifted and he was left with nothing but dread truth. Obatala, moulder of men, fell also to the fumes of wine; his craftsman's fingers lost their control and he moulded cripples, albinos, the blind and other deformed. Obatala the eternal penitent therefore forbids wine to his worshippers in or out of his seasonal rites while Ogun, in proud acceptance of the need to create a challenge for the constant exercise of will and control, enjoins the liberal joy of wine. The palm fronds are a symbol of his wilful, ecstatic being.

And how else may the inhibiting bonds of man be dissolved when he goes to meet his god, how else may be quickly enter into the god's creative being, or his inner ear and eye respond to the fleeting presences which guard the abode of gods, how else partake in the psychic revelry of the world when it celebrates a crossing of the abyss of non-being? The sculpted rites of the worship of Obatala are rapturous also, but lacking in ecstasy. His is a dance of amelioration to tyrannic powers, not a celebration of the infinite will of the Promethean spirit. The one is withdrawal, the other an explosion of the forces of darkness and joy, explosion of the sun's kernel, an eruption of fire which is the wombfruit of pristine mountains, for no less, no different were the energies within Ogun whose ordering and control through the will brought him safely through the tragic gulf. Even through the medium of this ecstasy, a glimpse is obtained of the vastness of the abyss; the true devotee knows, understands and penetrates the god's anguish. In the centre of the swaying, milling, ecstatic horde where his individuation is routed and he submits to a union of joy, the inner being encounters the precipice.

Poised on the heights of the physical mountain-home of Ogun he experiences a yawning gulf within him, a menacing maul of chthonic strength yawning ever wider to annihilate his being; he is saved only by channelling the dark torrent into the plastic light of poetry and dance; not, however, as a reflection or illusion of reality, but as the celebrative aspects of the resolved crisis of his god.

Notes

1 Ogun: God of creativity, guardian of the road, god of metallic lore and artistry, Explorer, hunter, god of war, Custodian of the sacred oath.

2 Nietzsche, *The Birth of Tragedy*.

3 Obatala: God of creation (by syncretist tradition with Orisa-nla), essence of the serene arts. Obatala moulds the forms but the breath of life is administered by Edumare the Supreme deity. The art of Obatala is thus essentially plastic and formal.

4 I would render this more cogently today in terms of race origination, uprooting, wandering and settling. This group experience is less remote, and parallels the mythology of primordial chaos, as well as the rites of transition (birth, death etc.).

5 Or again the collective memory of dispersion and re-assemblage in racial coming-in-being. All these, and of course the recurring experience of birth and death, are psycho-historic motifs for the tragic experience: the essence of transition.

6 Sango: God of lightning and electricity. A tyrant of Oyo, he was forced to commit suicide by factions, through his own over-reaching. His followers there-upon deified him and he assumed the agency of lightning.

7 In contemporary (public) festivals of Ogun the usual intermingling of idioms has occurred – the ritual dismembering of a surrogate dog, enactment of the massacre at Ire, the dispute between Sango and Ogun, Ogun's battle triumphs, etc. The note is summatively festive.

52

The Duke's Blues

Stanley Crouch

You wouldn't think he had the time to do all that he did. He was so busy being gracious. So many autographs to sign. The women, they were lining up to lie down. Hmm. His musicians were such a bunch of royal-blue pains, weren't they? Didn't ruffle him. He was smiling wide and big. He was having himself a very good time. Had to fly first class. Said his musicians wouldn't work for a man who didn't. Ate steak every day. Look at that wardrobe. Definitely spent a lot of time with his tailor. That processed hair stayed in place. Must have had his own barber. Now, you got the unmitigated audacity to say he was an artist, too? A great, great artist, you say? Duke Ellington? Sell that ice to some Eskimos.

Duke Ellington considered himself "the world's greatest listener." In music, hearing is all. Given the two or three thousand pieces of music Ellington wrote, he could probably hear a flea scratching itself and put that rhythm into one of his compositions. For him the sounds of the world were the ingredients he mixed into appetizers, main courses, and desserts for the appetite of his worldwide audience. He wasn't averse to going out in a boat to catch the fish himself. He would raise the fowl and the livestock and slaughter them all himself if there was no one else to do it. But when that musical meal appeared before you none of the drudgery showed. It seemed perfectly natural, as if it had all appeared from behind an invisible door in the air.

In fact, Ellington maintained such a commanding touch with his art and the world that his fifty years of development constitute what just might be the most impressive evolution in the American arts. The blues was the key, and Ellington was surely the greatest manipulator of blues form and blues feeling that jazz has ever known. He understood the blues as both music and mood. He knew that those who thought of the blues as merely a vehicle for primitive complaint had their drawers or their brassieres on backward. The blues knows its way around. It can stretch from the backwoods to the space shuttle, from the bloody floor of a dive to the neurotic confusion of a beautifully clothed woman in a Manhattan penthouse. The blues – happy, sad, or neither – plays no favorites.

The hundreds of compositions and arrangements that Ellington wrote and recorded between 1924 and 1973 make the case for their creator as the most protean of American geniuses. In his music he assayed a multitude of forms and voices as successfully as Herman Melville, satirized the skin off pomposity as gleefully as Mark Twain, matched Buster Keaton for surreal slapstick, equalled the declarative lyricism Ernest Hemingway brought to lonely moments of tragic resolution, rivalled William Faulkner in the dense intricacy of his tonal colors, conjured up a combination of Bill (Bojangles) Robinson and Fred Astaire in the way his percussive accents danced through suave billows of harmony, was a twin to John Ford in the deployment of his phenomenal repertory team of players,

From *The New Yorker*, April 29 and May 6, 1996; reproduced by kind permission of Stanley Crouch.

mixed satire and gloom with as much innovation as his good friend Orson Welles. And, as the master bluesologist Albert Murray has observed, he had much in common with Frank Lloyd Wright in that he was the inventor of a musical architecture that blended perfectly with the shifting inner and outer landscapes of American life.

Just as Faulkner had his Yoknapatawpha County, Duke Ellington had his Harlem: that Harlem was not the piss-stained slum of those suicidal or smothered jungle bunnies you find in the protest writing of James Baldwin. The Ellingtonian Harlem is what Ralph Ellison recalled as "an outpost of American optimism, a gathering place for the avant-garde in music, dance, and democratic inter-racial relationships; and, as the site and symbol of America's free-wheeling sense of possibility, it was our homegrown version of Paris." In "Harlem," his own long paean to the place, written in 1950, Ellington signalled the mythic dimensions of the neighborhood in the opening two notes – the trumpet's plunger-muted statement of the title.

It's easy to understand why there is so much rich stuff in his canon dedicated to women, for no one's appreciation and experience of the opposite sex inspired more legendary tales than his. Tall, handsome, a former athlete, gifted with a grasp of gab that could mutate into honey, Ellington drew women of all races, places, and classes to him. Those intimate experiences are evoked in "A Drum Is a Woman," his 1956 fairy-tale history of jazz, narrated by Ellington himself. There, Madam Zajj – the dark enchantress, muse, and bitch goddess of his art – says to Ellington, "Come with me to my emerald rock garden, just off the moon, where darkness is only a translucency, and the cellophane trees grow a mile high. Come climb with me to the top of my tree, where the fruit is ripe and the taste is like the sky. Star rubies are budding in my diamond-encrusted hothouse." In "Sophisticated Lady," "The Gal from Joe's," "Lady of the Lavender Mist,' "The Tattooed Bride," and "Princess Blue," the sensuality of his women takes on greater emotional and psychological complexity. Ellington's musical women are combinations of grief and vivacity, insecurity and confidence, the childlike and the worldly, the down-home and the regal.

Because Ellington was such a man of the world, his bandstand encompassed every sort of human experience: it all ended up in his music. As a fledgling bandleader in the 1920s, he had worked for gangsters at the old Cotton Club, a segregated Harlem room that was off limits to all but the most celebrated Negroes. Often, after hours, he'd be summoned down to the city morgue to identify the corpse of someone who had been partying in the club the night before. In his memoir, "Music Is My Mistress" (1973), Ellington wrote that whether or not he recognized the murdered man on the slab, he always answered, "No," on being asked if he knew him. It was impossible for him to be a naïf. In his long career, he performed in Harlem benefits for the Scottsboro Boys Defense Fund, observed the racial double standard of show-business success, saw one of his musicians playing the tuba with the bones in his face periodically slipping out of place because he'd been roughed up by gangsters, watched colleagues slowly dissolve themselves in the acids of drink and drugs, and recognized the yearning for a fair shot that lay behind the eyes of so many. His was an art distilled from glamour, racism, murder, and good, good times, and Ellington became a show-business hero because he never stooped to the conventions of Uncle Tomming. Some of the startling dissonances in his music had to be acknowledgments of just how hard and cold the blues could get.

In order to tell us his epic tale, in which everything and everyone ends up in the arms of the blues, Ellington had to stay out there for more than five decades, writing for everyone from the clarinet-tist to the baritone saxophonist, the trumpet player to the trombonist, the string-bass player to the trap drummer. He wrote show tunes for singers, composed musicals, did scores for movies and television, and always kept himself well afloat. Beneath those blue suede gloves were homemade brass knuckles. Duke Ellington learned early that his was a world both sweet and rough and that he had to be ready for anything.

Born on 29 April 1899, in Washington, DC, to middle-class parents, Edward Kennedy Ellington was – like many Negro jazz innovators – a favored child. Like Coleman Hawkins, Charlie Parker, Thelonious Monk, and Miles Davis, he was pampered, tucked in, read to, and reared to believe in himself without reservation. The usual discriminations had little to do with how such artists viewed themselves as they struggled to give voice to their imaginations. Ellington got the nickname Duke because he liked fancy pants and was a charmer, ever quick with the kind of aristocratic lines that pulled in women and later made it easy for him to fire musicians so gracefully that some of them took the firing as a compliment. He was no snob. Long after he became a big success, he would leave his Harlem apartment in silk robe, pajamas, and slippers to sit up all night in a greasy spoon listening to the stories of other night owls and telling his own.

Like many Negro musicians of the time, Ellington was bitten by the new night creature of jazz. He was thrilled first by the Harlem "stride" piano style he heard on James P. Johnson's 1917 recording of "Carolina Shout." He picked it up by ear and quickly got a reputation among Washington musicians. Since there were no formal ways to study this new music, he learned his art in jam sessions, during which the discussions of craft and technique were often as fierce as the music. He had taken piano lessons as a child, but his most important education came from the exchanges between trained musicians and untrained players, each group drawing something from the other. From these exchanges, Ellington sensed that music from both the "serious" and "casual" worlds could be fused – a goal he worked at all his life. During those formative years, Ellington would sit with his drummer, Sonny Greer, way, way up in the balconies of concert halls and think about how to achieve European orchestral effects in the language of jazz. Alone in his Harlem apartment, he studied the harmony books he would later pretend to have ignored because he was too busy bandleading.

Before long, Ellington had figured out what would become the four most enduring elements of his art: the basic rhythmic structure of 4/4 swing, whether fast, medium, or slow; the blues; the romantic ballad; and Afro-Hispanic rhythms. That quartet of fundamentals has been reinterpreted over and over throughout the history of jazz innovation, from the playing of Louis Armstrong to the most fruitful work of Ornette Coleman and John Coltrane. It was Ellington's profound grasp of these essences of jazz that allowed him to maintain such superb aesthetic focus throughout his life, regardless of the shifting trends around him.

In his 1943 "Black, Brown, and Beige," an over-forty-minute work in which all his innovations up to that time reached a culmination, Ellington built what was then the most adventurous long composition in jazz. What began as a simple motif, like the opening of Beethoven's Fifth Symphony, was developed into many different kinds of themes, some lyric, some propulsive. He used or bypassed conventional phrasing lengths, twisted the blues

into and out of shape, wrote smooth or dissonant harmonies, and called upon a host of rhythmic modulations that moved from march beats to swing to jaunty Afro-Hispanic syncopations. This constantly mutating musical adventure shows why Ellington was the truest sort of innovator: he remade the earthy fundamentals of jazz so thoroughly that they blossomed into a whole new life.

He was a man who wanted his own language, and, because he knew that the foundation for that language – for any expressive language – was the human voice, he made his orchestrations extensions and refinements of the vocal styles of various blues and jazz singers. He liked to refer to himself as "no more than a primitive minstrel" – one of the many masks he wore when throwing historical daggers around obliquely. In the sixties, he rejected Charles Mingus's tongue-in-cheek suggestion that the two of them make an "avant-grade" recording together by imitating the chaotic squeaking and honking of the day. Ellington said there was no point in taking music back *that* far. In other words, he remembered exactly how it had been before jazz became a music of casual virtuosity, how it had been when so many musicians truly *couldn't* play, when they hadn't been able to control their instruments well enough to perform the simplest passages.

It was in 1921, when he was still an easygoing bandleader in Washington, especially popular among the black professional class, that he experienced the epiphany of hearing the cantankerous, pistol-packing New Orleans genius Sidney Bechet play "I'm Coming, Virginia." Ellington always referred to Bechet as "one of the truly great originals," and a few years later he employed him for a brief period in New York. On Ellington's bandstand at the Kentucky Club, on 49th Street and Broadway, Bechet's soprano saxophone did nightly battle with the growling plunger trumpet of Bubber Miley, whose sound had finally persuaded Ellington never to play "sweet music" again. Bechet was a grand master of both the improvised blues line and a bag of trick vocal effects that made it possible, he said, to call his dog with his horn. Miley had absorbed the growl techniques from listening to King Oliver, mentor to Louis Armstrong. The elements Bechet and Miley brought into Ellington's world never left it. His star alto saxophonist, Johnny Hodges, had been taught his way around the soprano sax by Bechet and was to retain ever after the older man's melodic ideas and inflections in almost every phrase of his own style, albeit in a tone so original that the Hodges sound became one of the century's great instrumental colors. Miley's plunger-muted influence – surely the most fascinating extension of the African talking drum in American music – was just as enduring. It spread through the entire Ellington brass section, establishing growl imitations of the Negro American voice's timbres, inflections, and speech patterns as an indelible aspect of the Ellington palette.

The results were frequently operatic. The Ellington brass and reed players delivered arias, duets, and choruses – laced, often, with a mockery of the sentimental. A head-snapping example is "The Mystery Song," of 1931, which contrasts frivolity with a fear of the grotesque. (It was perhaps no coincidence that 1931 was the year of James Whale's classic movie "Frankenstein.") The superb sensuality of Ellington's many romantic ballads made them the perfect catalysts for real-life courtships played out within hearing distance of the radio or record-player. The "plot" of these Ellington mini-operas was always the blues, with its complex mingling of sorrow and celebration, erotic ambition and romantic defeat. Ellington's deep blues sensibility was anything but restricted. It could find expression at any tempo. Its timbres could color any mood, from the swagger of the street to the heat of the boudoir, from violent rage to the pomp and pride of the dance floor. Always there was that plaintive lyricism, made spiritual by its unspecified object of desire.

One of the things Ellington perfected was something I call "timbral harmony." He once said that when he composed a particular note, he always had to decide *whose* note it would be. That jazz's very best brass or reed players have distinctly individual tones, even when they are playing perfectly in tune, was especially true of Ellington's musicians. (He called them a gathering of "tonal personalities.") This meant that a given note in his three-trombone section could have at least as many different colors as players. Moreover, Ellington liked to alter the effect of a harmonic voicing by moving the players around to different *positions* in the chord – top, middle, bottom.

Ellington was a master at exploiting the emotional riddles inherent in the blues to enrich the contrast between the mood of the melody line and the surrounding context of orchestration and rhythm. Fundamental to the blues is its double consciousness, allowing unhappy revelations to be stated over a jaunty rhythm. (A classic example is Ellington's surging 1940 arrangement of "St Louis Blues," recorded at a dance in Fargo North Dakota.)

Ellington also understood that the quixotic emotional turns of the blues could add zest to non-blues numbers, and he discouraged any type-casting among his star players. For example, the tenor saxophonist Ben Webster could step forward as a Kansas City Siegfried – innocent, romantic, erotic, and combatively heroic in the course of a single, multi-tempo arrangement of "How High the Moon." The lyric voice of Johnny Hodges could encompass the spiritual raptness of "Come Sunday," the glowing sensuality of "Warm Valley," and the adolescent yearning of "The Star-Crossed Lovers." Ray Nance's trumpet and cornet, abetted by mutes, plungers, and his refined control of open tone, could juggle the puckish, the plaintive, the buffoonish, the high-minded, and the translucently erotic.

In effect, Ellington made chameleons of his players. The Ellington Orchestra could *become* all sorts of weather, impersonate all sorts of technology, assume endless tonal disguises. In the opening measures of "Rude Interlude" (1934), Ellington has the trombone quite confidently create the effect of a French horn! A year earlier, he had produced the startling virtuoso display of "Daybreak Express," one of the best musical imitations of a roaring train ever written. Ellington would have Harry Carney blow his baritone sax so strongly that the overtones added "imaginary" notes; or he'd demand that two tenor saxophones play the same note in unison to create a timbre that seemed to come from an instrument never heard before.

Ellington often mentioned that he had thought in his early years of being a painter. Then, as he told the story, he commented on how he had replaced the brush and the palette with brass, reeds, string bass, and percussion. Certainly he avoided unvarnished abstraction at every opportunity. Just about every Ellington sound is connected to something particular in his experience or mind. Although it often suggests a dream, a fantasy, a myth, there is always the pressure of real life in his music – a real life that inevitably includes mystery and ambivalence. The sense of heartache you hear in Ellington is invariably countered by the transcendent moxie of swing.

Great innovators are great absorbers, and Ellington learned from everyone. The unmistakable Ellington colors were grounded in the New Orleans sound he had heard when he was starting out, with its use of the cornet to carry the melody, while the clarinet and trombone played obbligati above and below. Works such as the 1926 "Black Bottom Stomp," by

Jelly Roll Morton, taught him crucial lessons about tension and release, even though Ellington despised Morton for his braggadocio and was never mum about it.

From the Manhattan stride piano of James P. Johnson, Willie (The Lion) Smith, and Fats Waller to the Broadway songs of Tin Pan Alley and the work of such orchestrally innovative peers as Don Redman, Horace Henderson, and Benny Carter, Ellington was alive to everything around him. What he made of it perpetually revealed how broad and rich were the possibilities of jazz. Virtually alone among the musicians of his generation, he was perfectly comfortable performing not only with the giants who created the fundamental vocabulary for their instruments during the twenties and thirties – Armstrong, Bechet, Hawkins – but also with such later pathbreakers as Charlie Parker, Dizzy Gillespie, Charles Mingus, Max Roach, and Coltrane. With just two exceptions – Bechet and Parker – he made classic recordings with all of them.

Ellington maintained an orchestra longer than any other composer ever has – almost 50 years. Its only rival for longevity in Western music may be the orchestra Prince Esterházy provided in the eighteenth century for Haydn, which had a life of 29 years. Unlike Haydn, however, Ellington was artist *and* sponsor, using the royalties from his many hit recordings to meet his payroll, which made it possible for his latest music to be heard as soon as he wrote it. The Ellington Orchestra was jazz's answer to the John Ford Stock Company, which employed the faces, voices, bodies, and personalities of performers such as John Wayne, Donald Crisp, John Carradine, Ben Johnson, and a host of other lesser-known actors as often as possible. As those actors turned in their best work for Ford, so Johnny Hodges, Lawrence Brown, Ray Nance, Jimmy Hamilton, Paul Gonsalves, and others did for Ellington, because the contexts he created for them were so much more challenging than those which anyone else could provide. In addition to being composer, arranger, coach, and rhythm-section accompanist, Ellington was screenwriter, director, lighting technician, dialect coach, costume designer, set designer, special-effects and even makeup man. While his legendary patience was such that he once ignored a fistfight in a Japanese hotel lobby between his son, Mercer, and a veteran band member, asking only if his suite was ready, Ellington could also explode. He once knocked an inebriated musician to the floor because the man had been drunk onstage one time too many.

Yes, Ellington and John Ford had more than a bit in common.

One of the deepest accomplishments of the music of Duke Ellington is its epic expression of American feeling. In evocation after evocation, Ellington proves that he knew in his cells what William Carlos Williams meant when he observed in his classic "In the American Grain" that by truly exploring the specific an artist will achieve the universal. Ellington's music contains so many characteristics of the nation: the intricate dialogues between individuals and communities, the awesome and heartbreaking difficulties to "make it" or just plain survive, the urban skylines and rural landscapes. We hear the stone, glass, and steel of industrial achievement summoned up by brass, reeds, and percussion. No other music has so piercingly captured the bitter-sweet energy of modern life, the throbbing vitality that found its way onto the dance floor of the old Savoy Ballroom and made Easter uptown on Seventh Avenue such a voluminous display of elegance. All this fuelled the incredible momentum in Ellington's big city of music.

If the context was rural or Southern – as in various three-minute works and the longer "Deep South Suite" (1946) and "New Orleans Suite" (1971) – Ellington's music became pictorial, festive, epic. One could taste the home brew drunk from jars, hear the railroad rhythms that so influenced the inflections of the blues, groan at the hard labor done in the fields, see the old folks sitting and rocking on front porches, witness the visceral dignity of church services. With every new Ellington piece, one met the black, brown, beige, and bone people whose sufferings and celebrations have been beacons for our culture. Underneath was the hard blues, mutated into a love song or swung until the cows came home.

Over a forty-year stretch, the Ellington Orchestra made tours of Europe, the Middle East, Africa, Japan, Australia, and South America. These experiences proved the universality of Ellington's jazz, and also added generously to his canvas. He was always ready to wrestle or coax the spirit of a foreign place into melody, harmony, tonal colors, and rhythm – into the brew of the blues.

Ellington once told his nephew Michael James, "It's not about this or that generation. The issue in art is *regeneration*." That he sustained this credo is often lost on critics who have written that the last 30 years of his work saw a falling off from his "greatest period" of 1940–2. Their charges are mainly two: first, that in his later, more extended compositions he overreached the limits of his talent; second, that the quality of his ensemble wasn't up to what it had been.

Behind the criticism is a misunderstanding that bedevilled Ellington to the end of his life, and it demands serious rebuttal. It is true that the early forties were a kind of golden period for the Ellington Orchestra. In 1939, Ellington had brought the marvellous composing talent of Billy Strayhorn into the organization and was soon rewarded with Strayhorn's "Take the A Train." Strayhorn went on to write such standards as "Midriff," "Passion Flower," "Rain-check," "Johnny Come Lately," and "Chelsea Bridge." His arrival virtually coincided with that of two of the most thrilling players ever to join the Ellington organization, the bassist Jimmy Blanton and the tenor saxophonist Ben Webster – and they were prominently featured in such classics as "Jack the Bear," "Sepia Panorama," "Cotton Tail," and "What Am I Here For?" There is no doubt that in the Blanton–Webster years the Ellington Orchestra achieved an ideal balance of composition, personnel, and musicianship.

But what the critics fail to recognize is that Ellingtonia is a mountain range – not a series of hills leading to one great peak, followed by a descending line of more hills. It was a constantly *evolving* landscape. Ellington worked collectively – so much so that his musicians could laugh at the poorly written parts and throw them back at him. He usually left holes open for improvisation, and encouraged players to devise counterlines to the written parts. In this way, he was much like the makers of early Hollywood comedies, who would arrive on the set with no more than a plot outline or a few situations and would see such rudimentary beginnings improvised into form. Yet the determining sensibility was always Ellington's, which is why the music maintained its identity through so many changes in the players, no matter how strong their individual personalities.

Although Ellington's creative output after 1940–2 was characterized by longer pieces, he was capable to the end of writing the immaculate miniatures demanded by the 78-r.p.m. era, when disks held no more than three minutes on a side. (A wonderful example is "Feetbone," released in 1958.) Like his ancestors Bach and Handel, he was an inveterate recycler. Classic Ellington melodies inspired by women were extended by the late forties into 15-minute masterpieces, such as the 1948 "Tattooed

Bride," which advances upon such earlier concerti as "Clarinet Lament."

"Tonal portraits" of uptown New York – "Echoes of Harlem," "Harmony in Harlem," "Harlem Speaks," and so on – evolved into Ellington's favorite longer work, the 14-minute "Harlem," of 1950. It is one of Ellington's most thorough and masterly explorations of blues harmony. (A wonderful example of Ellingtonian counterpoint can be heard in the depiction of a funeral, near the end.) The Afro-Hispanic and exotic rhythms from all over the world which he explored in such Blanton–Webster classics as "Conga Brava" and "The Flaming Sword" formed the basis for such greater works in the sixties and seventies as "Afro-Bossa," "The Far East Suite," "The Latin American Suite," "Afro-Eurasian Eclipse," and "The Togo Brava Suite."

In his later years, Ellington brought new authority and depth to his arrangements of popular songs. His re-inventions of American show tunes on his album "At the Bal Masqué" and of French popular songs on the album "Midnight in Paris" are astonishing. His joyously sardonic 1934 arrangement of the "Ebony Rhapsody," based on a "Hungarian Rhapsody" by Liszt, is exceeded by the exhilarating complexity of the "Nut-cracker Suite" and "Peer Gynt Suite," of 1960. The same is true when one compares his beautiful 1934 score for the film "Symphony in Black" with the 1959 "Anatomy of a Murder" score and with the 1961 "Paris Blues" score, featuring Louis Armstrong. He had employed the jazz female voice as far back as the 1927 "Creole Love Call" to imitate musical instruments. By the 1946 "Transblucency," he was using a concert soprano, Kay Davis, to add classical tone color to the Ellington mix. He raised that innovation to new heights in such later "diva" pieces as the 1956 "A Drum Is a Woman" (for Margaret Tynes) and the writing done for Alice Babs in the second Sacred Concert that occupied much of his time near the end of his life.

One reason Ellington has been so misunderstood is that we don't always know how to assess ongoing musical creativity outside the tradition of European concert music. We expect the finest concert musicians to ripen and deepen with middle age but assume that jazz musicians will deteriorate once they leave the heady province of youth. In fact, Ellington's greatest band existed not in the forties but between 1956 and 1968, and he was still able to inspire strong performances from his musicians after that, too. Beginning in the middle fifties, what he got from Johnny Hodges, Paul Gonsalves, Harry Carney, Lawrence Brown, Ray Nance, Cootie Williams, Russell Procope, Jimmy Hamilton, and the others could only have been achieved by men who had lived beyond forty or fifty. By then, having played every note and register in every key on their instruments for so long, they had developed an intimacy with their horns that no younger players could match. What's more, they had seen their children become adults, friends die, and wars come and go. It's all in their playing.

After the deaths of such "irreplaceable" collaborators as Strayhorn (1967) and Hodges (1970), Ellington continued to feed his voracious muse.

Right up until his death, in 1974, the great listener lived and worked according to the terms he had declared in 1959: "I don't want to be modern . . . futuristic . . . and neither do I want to be hung by the plaintiveness of something we might have done years ago, even with success. I don't want to feel obliged to play something with the same styling that we became identified with at some specific period. I have no ambition to reach some intellectual plateau and look down on people. And, by the same token, I don't want anyone to challenge my right to sound completely mad, to screech like a wild man, to create the mauve melody of a simpering idiot, or to write a song that praises God."

PART XI

Philosophy of Religion

53

God, Faith, and the Nature of Knowledge

Zera Yacob

Later on I thought, saying to myself: "Is everything that is written in the Holy Scriptures true?" Although I thought much about these things I understood nothing, so I said to myself: "I shall go and consult scholars and thinkers; they will tell me the truth." But afterwards I thought, saying to myself: "What will men tell me other than what is in their heart?" Indeed each one says: "My faith is right, and those who believe in another faith believe in falsehood, and are the enemies of God." These days the *Frang* [Europeans, Catholics] tell us: "Our faith is right, yours is false." We on the other hand tell them: "It is not so; your faith is wrong, ours is right." If we also ask the Mohammedans and the Jews, they will claim the same thing, and who would be the judge for such a kind of argument? No single human being can judge: for all men are plaintiffs and defendants between themselves. Once I asked a *Frang* scholar many things concerning our faith; he interpreted them all according to his own faith. Afterwards I asked a well-known Ethiopian scholar and he also interpreted all things according to his own faith. If I had asked the Mohammedans and the Jews, they also would have interpreted according to their own faith; then, where could I obtain a judge that tells the truth? As my faith appears true to me, so does another one find his own faith true; but truth is one. While thinking over this matter, I said: "O my creator, wise among the wise and just among

From *The Source of African Philosophy* by Claude Sumner (1986); by kind permission of Franz Steiner Verlag Wiesbaden GmbH.

the just, who created me with an intelligence, help me to understand, for men lack wisdom and truthfulness; as David said: 'No man can be relied upon.'"

I thought further and said: "Why do men lie over problems of such great importance, even to the point of destroying themselves?" and they seemed to do so because although they pretend to know all, they know nothing. Convinced they know all, they do not attempt to investigate the truth. As David said: "Their hearts are curdled like milk." Their heart is curdled because they assume what they have heard from their predecessors and they do not inquire whether it is true or false. But I said: "O Lord! who strike me down with such torment, it is fitting that I know your judgement. You chastise me with truth and admonish me with mercy. But never let my head be anointed with the oil of sinners and of masters in lying: make me understand, for you created me with intelligence." I asked myself: "If I am intelligent, what is it I understand?" And I said: "I understand there is a creator, greater than all creatures; since from his overabundant greatness, he created things that are so great. He is intelligent who understands all, for he created us as intelligent from the abundance of his intelligence; and we ought to worship him, for he is the master of all things. If we pray to him, he will listen to us; for he is almighty." I went on saying in my thought: "God did not create me intelligent without a purpose, that is to look for him and to grasp him and his wisdom in the path he has opened for me and to worship him as long as I live." And still thinking on the same subject, I said to myself:

"Why is it that all men do not adhere to truth, instead of believing falsehood?" The cause seemed to be the nature of man which is weak and sluggish. Man aspires to know truth and the hidden things of nature, but his endeavour is difficult and can only be attained with great labour and patience, as Solomon said: "With the help of wisdom I have been at pains to study all that is done under heaven; oh, what a weary task God has given mankind to labour at!" Hence people hastily accept what they have heard from their fathers and shy from any critical examination. But God created man to be the master of his own actions, so that he will be what he wills to be, good or bad. If a man chooses to be wicked he can continue in this way until he receives the punishment he deserves for his wickedness. But being carnal, man likes what is of the flesh; whether they are good or bad, he finds ways and means through which he can satisfy his carnal desire. God did not create man to be evil, but to choose what he would like to be, so that he may receive his reward if he is good or his condemnation if he is bad. If a liar, who desires to achieve wealth or honours among men, needs to use foul means to obtain them, he will say he is convinced this falsehood was for him a just thing. To those people who do not want to search, this action seems to be true, and they believe in the liar's strong faith. I ask you in how many falsehoods do our people believe in? They believe wholeheartedly in astrology and other calculations, in the mumbling of secret words, in omens, in the conjuration of devils and in all kinds of magical art and in the utterances of soothsayers. They believe in all these because they did not investigate the truth but listened to their predecessors. Why did these predecessors lie unless it was for obtaining wealth and honours? Similarly those who wanted to rule the people said: "We were sent by God to proclaim the truth to you"; and the people believed them. Those who came after them accepted their fathers' faith without question: rather, as a proof of their faith, they added to it by including stories of signs and omens. Indeed they said: "God did these things"; and so they made God a witness of falsehood and a party to liars.

The Law of Moses and the Meditation of Mohammed

To the person who seeks it, truth is immediately revealed. Indeed he who investigates with the pure intelligence set by the creator in the heart of each man and scrutinizes the order and laws of creation, will discover the truth. Moses said: "I have been sent by God to proclaim to you his will and his law"; but those who came after him added stories of miracles that they claimed had been wrought in Egypt and on Mount Sinai and attributed them to Moses. But to an inquisitive mind they do not seem to be true. For in the Books of Moses, one can find a wisdom that is shameful and that fails to agree with the wisdom of the creator or with the order and the laws of creation. Indeed by the will of the creator, and the law of nature, it has been ordained that man and woman would unite in a carnal embrace to generate children, so that human beings will not disappear from the earth. Now this mating, which is willed by God in his law of creation, cannot be impure since God does not stain the work of his own hands. But Moses considered that act as evil; but our intelligence teaches us that he who says such a thing is wrong and makes his creator a liar. Again they said that the law of Christianity is from God, and miracles are brought forth to prove it. But our intelligence tells and confirms to us with proofs that marriage springs from the law of the creator; and yet monastic law renders this wisdom of the creator ineffectual, since it prevents the generation of children and extinguishes mankind. The law of Christians which propounds the superiority of monastic life over marriage is false and cannot come from God. How can the violation of the law of the creator stand superior to his wisdom, or can man's deliberation correct the word of God? Similarly Mohammed said: "The orders I pass to you are given to me by God"; and there was no lack of writers to record miracles proving Mohammed's mission, and people believed in him. But we know that the teaching of Mohammed could not have come from God; those who will be born both male and female are equal in number; if we count men and women living in an area, we find as many women as men; we do not find eight or ten women for every man; for the law of creation orders one man to marry one woman. If one man marries ten women, then nine men will be without wives. This violates the order of creation and the laws of nature and it ruins the usefulness of marriage; Mohammed, who taught in the name of God, that one man could marry many wives, is not sent from God. These few things I examined about marriage.

Similarly when I examine the remaining laws, such as the Pentateuch, the law of the Christians and the law of Islam, I find many things which disagree with the truth and the justice of our creator that our intelligence reveals to us. God indeed has illuminated the heart of man with understanding by which he can see the good and evil, recognize the licit and the illicit, distinguish truth from error, "and by your light we see the light, oh Lord"! If we use this light of our heart properly, it cannot deceive us; the purpose of this light which our creator gave us is to be saved by it, and not to be ruined by it. Everything that the light of our intelligence shows us comes from the source of truth, but what men say comes from the source of lies and our intelligence teaches us that all that the creator established is right. The creator in his kind wisdom has made blood to flow monthly from the womb of women. And the life of a woman requires this flow of blood in order to generate children; a woman who has no menstruation is barren and cannot have children, because she is impotent by nature. But Moses and Christians have defiled the wisdom of the creator; Moses even considers impure all the things that such a woman touches; this law of Moses impedes marriage and the entire life of a woman and it spoils the law of mutual help, prevents the bringing up of children and destroys love. Therefore this law of Moses cannot spring from him who created woman. Moreover, our intelligence tells us that we should bury our dead brothers. Their corpses are impure only if we follow the wisdom of Moses; they are not, however, if we follow the wisdom of our creator who made us out of dust that we may return to dust. God does not change into impurity the order he imposes on all creatures with great wisdom, but man attempts to render it impure that he may glorify the voice of falsehood.

The Gospel also declares: "He who does not leave behind father, mother, wife and children is not worthy of God." This forsaking corrupts the nature of man. God does not accept that his creature destroy itself, and our intelligence tells us that abandoning our father and our mother helpless in their old age is a great sin; the Lord is not a god that loves malice; those who desert their children are worse than the wild animals, that never forsake their offspring. He who abandons his wife abandons her to adultery and thus violates the order of creation and the laws of nature. Hence what the Gospel says on this subject cannot come from God. Likewise the Mohammedans said that it is right to go and buy a man as if he were an animal. But with our intelligence we understand that this Mohammedan law cannot come from the creator of man who made us equal, like brothers, so that we call our

creator our father. But Mohammed made the weaker man the possession of the stronger and equated a rational creature with irrational animals; can this depravity be attributed to God?

God does not order absurdities, nor does he say: "Eat this, do not eat that; today eat, tomorrow do not eat; do not eat meat today, eat it tomorrow," unlike the Christians who follow the laws of fasting. Neither did God say to the Mohammedans: "Eat during the night, but do not eat during the day," nor similar and like things. Our reason teaches us that we should eat of all things which do no harm to our health and our nature, and that we should eat each day as much as is required for our sustenance. Eating one day, fasting the next endangers health; the law of fasting reaches beyond the order of the creator who created food for the life of man and wills that we eat it and be grateful for it; it is not fitting that we abstain from his gifts to us. If there are people who argue that fasting kills the desire of the flesh, I shall answer them: "The concupiscence of the flesh by which a man is attracted to a woman and a woman to a man springs from the wisdom of the creator; it is improper to do away with it; but we should act according to the well-known law that God established concerning legitimate intercourse." God did not put a purposeless concupiscence into the flesh of men and of all animals; rather he planted it in the flesh of man as a root of life in this world and a stabilizing power for each creature in the way destined for it. In order that this concupiscence lead us not to excess, we should eat according to our needs, because overeating and drunkenness result in ill health and shoddiness in work. A man who eats according to his needs on Sunday and during the fifty days does not sin, similarly he who eats on Friday and on the days before Easter does not sin. For God created man with the same necessity for food on each day and during each month. The Jews, the Christians and the Mohammedans did not understand the work of God when they instituted the law of fasting; they lie when they say that God imposed fasting upon us and forbade us to eat; for God our creator gave us food that we support ourselves by it, not that we abstain from it.

The Law of God and the Law of Man

I said to myself: "Why does God permit liars to mislead his people?" God has indeed given reason to all and everyone so that they may know truth and falsehood, and the power to choose between the two as they will. Hence if it is truth we want, let us seek it with our reason which God has given us so that with it we may see that which is needed for us from among all the necessities of nature. We cannot, however, reach truth through the doctrine of man, for all men are liars. If on the contrary we prefer falsehood, the order of the creator and the natural law imposed on the whole of nature do not perish thereby, but we ourselves perish by our own error. God sustains the world by his order which he himself has established and which man cannot destroy, because the order of God is stronger than the order of men. Therefore those who believe that monastic life is superior to marriage are they themselves drawn to marriage because of the might of the order of the creator; those who believe that fasting brings righteousness to their soul eat when they feel hungry; and those who believe that he who has given up his goods is perfect are drawn to seek them again on account of their usefulness, as many of our monks have done. Likewise all liars would like to break the order of nature: but it is not possible that they do not see their lie broken down. But the creator laughs at them, the Lord of creation derides them. God knows the right way to act, but the sinner is caught in the snare set by himself. Hence a monk who holds the order of marriage as impure will be caught in the snare of fornication and of other carnal sins against nature and of grave sickness. Those who despise riches will show their hypocrisy in the presence of kings and of wealthy persons in order to acquire these goods. Those who desert their relatives for the sake of God lack temporal assistance in times of difficulty and in their old age, they begin to blame God and men and to blaspheme. Likewise all those who violate the law of the creator fall into the trap made by their own hands. God permits error and evil among men because our souls in this world live in a land of temptation, in which the chosen ones of God are put to the test, as the wise Solomon said: "God has put the virtuous to the test and proved them worthy to be with him; he has tested them like gold in a furnace, and accepted them as a holocaust." After our death, when we go back to our creator, we shall see how God made all things in justice and great wisdom and that all his ways are truthful and upright. It is clear that our soul lives after the death of our flesh; for in this world our desire for happiness is not fulfilled; those in need desire to possess, those who possess desire more, and though man owned the whole world, he is not satisfied and craves for

more. This inclination of our nature shows us that we are created not only for this life, but also for the coming world; there the souls which have fulfilled the will of the creator will be perpetually satisfied and will not look for other things. Without this inclination the nature of man would be deficient and would not obtain that of which it has the greatest need. Our soul has the power of having the concept of God and of seeing him mentally; likewise it can conceive of immortality. God did not give this power purposelessly; as he gave the power, so did he give the reality. In this world complete justice is not achieved: wicked people are in possession of the goods of this world in a satisfying degree, the humble starve; some wicked men are happy, some good men are sad, some evil men exult with joy; some righteous men weep. Therefore, after our death there must needs be another life and another justice, a perfect one, in which retribution will be made to all according to their deeds, and those who have fulfilled the will of the creator revealed through the light of reason and have observed the law of their nature will be rewarded. The law of nature is obvious, because our reason clearly propounds it, if we examine it. But men do not like such inquiries; they choose to believe in the words of men rather than to investigate the will of their creator.

The Nature of Knowledge

The will of God is known by this short statement from our reason that tells us: "Worship God your creator and love all man as yourself." Moreover our reason says: "Do not do unto others that which you do not like done to you, but do unto others as you would like others to do unto you." The decalogue of the Pentateuch expresses the will of the creator excepting the precept about the observance of the Sabbath, for our reason says nothing of the observance of the Sabbath. But the prohibitions of killing, stealing, lying, adultery: our reason teaches us these and similar ones. Likewise the six precepts of the Gospel are the will of the creator. For indeed we desire that men show mercy to us; it therefore is fitting that we ourselves show the same mercy to the others, as much as it is within our power. It is the will of God that we keep our life and existence in this world. It is the will of the creator that we come into and remain in this life, and it is not right for us to leave it against his holy will. The creator himself wills that we adorn our life with science and work; for such an end did he give us reason and power. Manual labour comes from the will of God, because without it the necessities of our life cannot be fulfilled. Likewise marriage of one man with one woman and education of children. Moreover there are many other things which agree with our reason and are necessary for our life or for the existence of mankind. We ought to observe them, because such is the will of our creator, and we ought to know that God does not create us perfect but creates us with such a reason as to know that we are to strive for perfection as long as we live in this world, and to be worthy for the reward that our creator has prepared for us in his wisdom. It was possible for God to have created us perfect and to make us enjoy beatitude on earth; but he did not will to create us in this way; instead he created us with the capacity of striving for perfection, and placed us in the midst of the trials of the world so that we may become perfect and deserve the reward that our creator will give us after our death; as long as we live in this world we ought to praise our creator and fulfill his will and be patient until he draws us unto him, and beg from his mercy that he will lessen our period of hardship and forgive our sins and faults which we committed through ignorance, and enable us to know the laws of our creator and to keep them.

Now as to prayer, we always stand in need of it because our rational nature requires it. The soul endowed with intelligence that is aware that there is a God who knows all, conserves all, rules all, is drawn to him so that it prays to him and asks him to grant things good and to be freed from evil and sheltered under the hand of him who is almighty and for whom nothing is impossible, God great and sublime who sees all that is above and beneath him, holds all, teaches all, guides all, our Father, our creator, our Protector, the reward for our souls, merciful, kind, who knows each of our misfortunes, takes pleasure in our patience, creates us for life and not for destruction, as the wise Solomon said: "You, Lord, teach all things, because you can do all things and overlook men's sins so that they can repent. You love all that exists, you hold nothing of what you have made in abhorrence, you are indulgent and merciful to all." God created us intelligent so that we may meditate on his greatness, praise him and pray to him in order to obtain the needs of our body and soul. Our reason which our creator has put in the heart of man teaches all these things to us. How can they be useless and false?

54

Must God Remain Greek?

Robert E. Hood

Why is God so Greek to most Christians? This may sound like an odd question when many of us hardly consciously associate a nationality with God. And the term *Greek* is certainly not one most of us would connect with God – rather it conjures up a small, picturesque Mediterranean country in southern Europe, an exotic kind of cuisine, the setting for a delightfully sensuous and earthy film called *Never on Sunday*, or possibly, in some circles, it may evoke images of the Greek Orthodox Church. However, *Greek* is also descriptive of the way Christians think about God intellectually and talk about God theologically, for that thought and discourse have been shaped and defined by ancient Greek philosophical thought. To this extent, we can say that Christian theology has given God an "ethnic" or "ethnocentric" character that is Greek. Depending on how much they feel "at home" with this legacy, Christians can be divided into three groups: the "homies," the "adopted homies," and the "homeless."

Home, a word and concept with all sorts of associations, can be a place of nurture and formation, a source of good and bad experiences, and a metaphor for familiar surroundings, as in the expression "I feel at home." Home can also be a space for refuge and rest, a place to relax after the weariness of the heat of the day, or a shelter where we can complain, shout, laugh, and cry. It can be a place of protestation and a focus of conversation,

a lodge of jubilation and self-affirmation.

Homey, a less familiar word to many, is a street expression in black culture. A "homey" is a person with whom you are at home and can relax, laugh, and cry because that person has been through the same stages of formation and rites of passage as you. You do not feel threatened by a "homey" even when disagreements arise. Doctrines about God in the Christian tradition have reflected what scholars call a "Eurocentric" character. This means that in terms of theological concepts and doctrines, God has been transformed into a "homey" for large numbers of Christians in European cultures. The dominant intellectual concepts and thought patterns in these cultures reflect assumptions of what some conservative scholars call "Western civilization," which in turn is a descendant of ancient Graeco-Roman culture and of a Christendom that dominated Europe, North Africa, and Egypt until the Islamic invasion in the eighth century. Thus the term *homies* refers to those European Christians who are at home with concepts of God that have their roots in Graeco-Roman culture.

The second group, the "adopted homies," are New World offspring of the "homies." They should more appropriately be described as Euro-Americans because of their cultural and intellectual roots in Europe. "Adopted homies" are members of either the dominant white North American culture or the European-rooted South American cultures. Indeed the caste systems operating in much of Latin America are anchored historically and racially in European assumptions about indigenous cultures, traditional religion, and color. The assumptions were derived from European ideas about ancient Greek culture and its superiority, particularly in lands where aboriginal peoples and African descendants predominated. The religious worldview of those at the top of these American caste systems has been heavily influenced by the religion of their former European colonial rulers, hence the expression *adopted homies.*

But there is a third group, the "homeless": those whose cultures have not been shaped or greatly influenced by Graeco-Roman concepts and culture as found in European or Euro-American cultures and their attendant religion. They have their own ancient heritages and cultures, yet viewed from within the hegemony of Western culture and its domination of the Christian theological tradition, these cultures are homeless. This is especially the case for the cultures of the Caribbean and of Africa south of the Sahara, where the Christian church is currently mushrooming. The fundamental worldview in these cultures – a worldview rooted in African antiquity, in African survivals from slavery and the plantation era, and in the indigenous Indian cultures that European Christians tried to supplant – has not been primarily shaped by the Graeco-Roman legacy as it passed through European and American cultures. Thus the latter's hegemony in preserving and shaping Christian theology and doctrine has in effect rendered these African and African-based cultures intellectually homeless, even though they are well represented demographically in the church.

The European hegemony is furthered by classifying aboriginal, indigenous cultures and their traditions as "primitive." This allows the West (1) to internalize its own definition of what constitutes "advanced" thinking and civilization; (2) to construct an intellectual and historical hierarchy of thought and traditions with Graeco-Roman culture and its descendants at the top; (3) to distance itself from what it perceives as underdeveloped thought; and (4) to justify a morality of paternalism toward "primitive" cultures and worldviews. Less subtly, it provides cultures descended from the Graeco-Roman worldview with a foundation for claiming authority to determine what is worthy to preserve in the Christian tradition and who is worthy to interpret that tradition.

Some are prone to dismiss African traditionalist culture as limited in influence because many Africans have been educated in Europe and the United States and because former African and Caribbean colonies now have Western-style educa-

tional systems. The continued influence of these traditional cultures and customs, however, was attested to even as recently as 1987. The Kenyan Court of Appeal was called upon to rule in a dispute about whether a deceased husband, who was a member of the Luo tribe, should be buried according to the wishes of his wife, who was of a different tribe, or according to the traditions of the Luo. The wife claimed that her husband, a prominent lawyer, was Westernized and while living, paid little heed to tribal or ethnic traditions. Therefore, she contended, he ought not be bound to such traditions in death. Members of his tribe, however, contended that were he not given a proper tribal burial in the soil of his ancestors, his spirit would be restless and continue to torment the tribe and his survivors.

The court, consisting solely of Western-educated judges, decided *unanimously* against the wife and in favor of the husband's tribe. The court ruled that it is not possible for an African to dispossess himself or herself of the tribe and its culture and that this is particularly true of tribes, such as the Luo, that trace kinship patrilineally. Thus the tribe had prior claim on the husband's corpse and could bury him according to tradition.[1]

Such a judgment will seem alien to those who simply and spontaneously take for granted the Greek claims that have shaped Western civilization and Christian doctrine. These persons are Christians and others who no doubt laud as "civilized" (meaning sufficient and superior) the abiding ideas of such pre-Christian Greek classics as the writings of Aeschylus, Sophocles, Euripides, Plato, and Aristotle, works formerly read at university under the admonition that a well-educated, civilized person is expected to be conversant with these classical foundations of Western civilization. Implicitly, such a claim reinforces the idea of Greek civilization and literature as organizing tools for defining our own identity culturally and even our understanding of God and Jesus Christ theologically. When made explicit, it may strike some as too abstract, and others as foreign. But we all are products of a historical legacy and of educational systems whose cultural and intellectual values, ideals, and methods of thinking have been hugely influenced and shaped by ancient Greek intellectual thought. We take it for granted, like breathing, until challenged.

But in addition to the Greek influence, much of Western thought and values has been shaped by Roman patterns of thought. These have been handed down to us through the Latin writings of such people as Cicero, Julius Caesar, Lucretius, and Virgil, through the works of Seneca, Juvenal, and Pliny, through medieval Scholasticism and the Renaissance, and through the Protestant Reformation. Indeed the aim of the Renaissance was to revive classical antiquity and recapture the thought patterns and literature of the ancient Greeks and Romans as progenitors of European culture. Much of ancient Rome's influence lay with its being the capital of a Greek-speaking empire, even though it was a latinized city. The key bodies and officials dealing with law were located there: the senate, the ordinary magistrates, the consuls (chief judges who controlled the treasury), the praetors (urban magistrates who decided legal disputes between citizens), and the quaestors (judges with criminal and treasury jurisdiction). Its free citizens had a special status as a nationality unto themselves in the empire. Furthermore, when Emperor Constantine endowed the church in Rome with vast lands mainly in the West – for example in Gaul and Greece – he ensured the Latin church's influence in the culture. Indeed when he became emperor, Rome was already a Latin city with a latinized populace, while the dominant Greek culture was dwindling. With the decline of the empire's central government in the third century AD, the power of the provinces and of Rome began to wane.

Examples of the Graeco-Roman legacy that we in the West take for granted abound. We assume uncritically that there are fundamental, unchanging "principles" that anchor humanity and cultures. We speak of "truth" as a natural given in human affairs and discourse. It is customary to think of "action based on one's principles" and to speak of the "spiritual" being dissimilar to the "material," of "essences" in contrast to "becoming." Theologians and other intellectuals like to talk about "being" and "God as the ground or source of being," about "Jesus Christ as the Logos," about "God as the alpha and the omega," about "essences and accidents," and about "form and matter." All of these demonstrate the conquest of Greek metaphysics and philosophical patterns of thought in our ordinary and conceptual lives. They are commonplace and "natural," so much so that we have determined that such is the most appropriate way to preach and interpret God and Jesus Christ to other cultures.

Such a determination is characteristic not only of mainstream Christian denominations and churches. It also has shaped the character, message, and mission of pietists, fundamentalists, televangelists, Christian Scientists, and Mormons, among others.

Adolf von Harnack noted that the person who played a major role as a conduit for funneling the church's hitherto variform Greek theology into the uniformed tidiness of Roman culture was the latinized African lawyer Tertullian (c. 160–225):

> He not only transferred the technical terms of the jurists into the ecclesiastical language of the West, but he also contemplated, from a legal standpoint, all relations of the individual and the Church to the Deity, and *vice versa*, all duties and rights, the moral imperative as well as the actions of God and Christ, nay, their mutual relationship. ... God appears as the mighty partner who watches jealously over his rights.[2]

In three centuries the small primitive Christian church emerged in the vortex of the Graeco-Roman culture of the Roman Empire and established itself as an imperial, inclusive institution by appealing to the intellectual and educated classes of the empire. The overarching environment of the empire in turn exercised a permanent influence on the Christian church's interpretation of the oriental Semitic God revealed in the Old Testament and the Aramaic-speaking Semitic figure of Jesus Christ in the New Testament. That this environment encouraged coherence, explanation, clarification, and inclusion as well as exclusion within the Christian church for these many centuries is to be applauded and commended.

The bequest of Graeco-Roman antiquity and of the Christian Latin Fathers, generously preserved and handed down by the Catholic Church in the West, particularly came into its own during the Reformation and Counter Reformation. The legacy of Greek antiquity and the Christian Greek Fathers and the Orthodox tradition was championed and handed down mainly in Byzantium, where it still governs thinking and spirituality in Eastern Orthodoxy today. So one may generalize and speak of Western culture and indeed mainstream Christian faith as descendants of Graeco-Roman thought, which also greatly shaped early and later Christian doctrines about God. At the same time, as we know from church history and the history of Christian doctrine, this also applies to theology about Jesus Christ, for only in Christ and through Christ do Christians know the true revelation of God.

This does not mean that there were not other competing cultural claims in the shaping of the Christian cultures of Western Europe, the New

World, and the East. They are evidenced by the number of synods and councils convoked in the East to deal with other claims often cataloged by the Church Catholic as "heresy." Nor is it the case, as some claim, that Africa south of the Sahara was uncivilized in antiquity. Not only did some Greeks of antiquity, such as Herodotus (fifth century BC), who visited Egypt and Ilé-Ifè (in modern Nigeria), acknowledge the antiquity of African worldviews and traditions, but also, as I shall show later, the idea of Africa had some meaning even in the New Testament community, although biblical scholars gloss over it. What all of this means is simply that the power of the emperors, and later of the conquerors, "discoverers," colonizers, victors, and other ruling powers made them players in the history of Christian thought. They also helped to effect the claims of cultures shaped by Graeco-Roman and subsequent Renaissance and Enlightenment values. Their power stood behind declarations of the West's cultural supremacy to other cultures, including those of Africa south of the Sahara and the indigenous or aboriginal cultures already in place when Westerners descended upon their lands.

So Graeco-Roman and Renaissance/Enlightenment cultural dominance in Christian thought is also implicitly linked with conquest and power rather than just with natural selection and emergence of the fittest . . . even the university contributed toward sanctioning this Graeco-Roman cultural and intellectual hegemony. Its disciplines of social anthropology and Egyptology were founded on eighteenth- and nineteenth-century European claims about the natural superiority of classical antiquity and the inferiority of most non-European cultures and ethnic groups, certainly those south of Egypt.

The Graeco-Roman packaging of Christian theology, dogmatics, languages, and traditions particularly raises acute issues of cultural and religious hegemony, called by less charitable people "cultural imperialism." Western Christians continue to exercise exclusive guardianship over the shape of Christian theology and over the debate about the meaning of Jesus Christ for a multicultural church and world; this is an especially crucial matter in Afro cultures, such as Africa and the Caribbean, where the church is growing rapidly. According to *The World Christian Encyclopedia*, as the Christian church began to institutionalize itself after AD 100 through its bishops, theologians, and, soon thereafter, its synods and councils, some 400,000

Christians lived in Africa, and many others were "evangelized": the "evangelized" being those who were aware of the gospel and the Christian faith but who did not yet confess to be members of the Christian faith. At the turn of this century, with missionary Christianity in full bloom in Africa, there were 10 million Christians and some 25 million evangelized people on that continent. It is projected that by AD 2000 there will be some 393.3 million Christians and some 695 million evangelized people in Africa.[3]

In 1900 there were only 369,430 Africans identified as Anglicans. By 1970 there were 7.8 million, and by the end of 1985 there were roughly 12.2 million – a growth rate of over 3000 percent since 1900. According to the most recent statistics, in 1988 there were over 14.9 million Anglicans in Africa, most of whom lived south of the Sahara.[4] By contrast, in England, where the Anglican Church was founded and is still the official established church of the realm, in 1900 25 million were registered Anglicans; by 1970 that number had expanded, but only to 29.3 million. By the end of 1985 that number was expected to have shrunk to 28 million. However, according to the 1985 electoral rolls, out of some 25 million baptized Anglicans, only some 1.6 million are active. In North America, a similar story can be told in comparison to Africa, even though statistically a majority of Americans claim belief in God and occasional visits to church. Not only has the Episcopal Church shriveled to 2.5 million members, but mainstream Protestant denominations in general are declining.[5]

The spread of the Christian faith in Africa is even more impressive when the rapidly growing African independent churches are considered; these are estimated to number 5000–6000 different bodies. These churches have radically changed a Christianity received from the European colonizers, and their membership is said to be in the millions. The independent churches are concentrated south of the Sahara, instead of being in North Africa, Egypt, and Ethiopia, where the faith was planted a long time ago.

And what about the Caribbean with its blend of the original Indian cultures, the European cultures, and the African cultures, all of which have formed and informed its religious traditions? The membership of churches affiliated with the Caribbean Council of Churches (CCC), which includes Roman Catholics, Anglicans, and Protestants, in 1985 numbered more than 2 million or 38 per cent of the population. When other churches not affiliated with the CCC – such as the various Evangelical, Seventh-Day Adventist, and indigenous churches – are added to this total, Christians make up at least 55 per cent of the population in the English-speaking Caribbean. And this figure does not include many of the Pentecostalists, whose numbers are growing swiftly in the Caribbean.

Hence, the critical issue is whether Christianity within the traditions of these Third World cultures, where the Christian faith is going from strength to strength in contrast to the West and the East where it is in a state of "suspended animation," must be filtered through Graeco-Roman religious thought and patterns in order to be considered legitimate and authentically Christian. In other words: Do Christians from Third World cultures have to become imitation Europeans or imitation North Americans before they can be considered fitting contributors to the formation and shaping of Christian thought? Must they steadily continue to contribute to their own *invisibility* within Christian thought by surrendering traditions and cultures long dismissed as "pagan," "animistic," "heathen," and "polytheistic"? We cannot neglect, overlook, or replace the major contributions of Graeco-Roman thought in formulating theologically the witness to and experience of the Christian God in the world, be those contributions from the apologetic, patristic, medieval, Scholastic, Reformation, Enlightenment, or colonial era. Still we also must remind ourselves that these contributions have in effect been universalized and sanctified by the church primarily based on the triumph of certain power factions that subsequently legitimized that victory and its accompanying ethnocentric claims by insisting that the Holy Spirit had led the assault. As Walter Bauer points out in his study of how orthodox doctrines came to be universalized, much had to do with the powerful position of Rome and of the church in Rome:

> At the beginning of the second century, Christianity as a whole is still called the "catholic church" by Ignatius, but by the end of that century it has become divided, as far as the Roman or Roman influenced outlook is concerned, into two distinct parts, the catholic or "great" church on the one hand and the *massa perditionis* ("condemned masses") of the heretics on the other. . . . This extremely powerful organism, although under great stress, knew how to rid itself

even of the highly dangerous poison of Marcionism in the middle of the second century.[6]

Hence, a crucial question for the worldwide Christian church as it tries to take seriously Third World cultures, particularly those in Africa and in the African diaspora (e.g., in the Caribbean), is whether Greek metaphysics will continue to be used as a filter to authenticate its claims and understanding of God in Jesus Christ. For the Third World cultures in Africa and the Caribbean, must God remain Greek?

Or can there be a diversity of theological concepts about God's revelation that allows for alternatives to the Greek model, certainly for Afro cultures? Can the the theological treasure house of Christianity open up yet another account with African and Afro Caribbean cultures, an account in which those cultures are contributors rather than merely being recipients of the inheritances of Europe and North America? An answer to these questions may be provided by examining concepts in the cultural and religious milieu and in some of the indigenous churches in Africa and the Caribbean. These concepts in turn can be deployed in constructing theological alternatives and in thereby expanding the wealth of Christian doctrine. Such alternatives are intended to be a critical aid to Euro-Americans and Afro Americans and an assistance to African and Caribbean Christians. The issue is whether the thought patterns and worldviews of Afro cultures can be molds for reconfigurating the Christian vision of God, Jesus Christ, and the Spirit/spirits. Can these reconfigurations be as exportable as the Graeco-Roman models? Or must God remain in the Greek mode doctrinally for all of Christianity?

Consequently, Tertullian's question about what Athens had to do with Jerusalem is no longer the key question before us. Or at best his question may still be raised by Europeans and North Americans for their own doctrines. Rather, in light of the critical issue about inherited ethnocentric Christian doctrines, perhaps a more appropriate question is: What do Athens and Rome have to do with Egypt, Ethiopia, West Africa, East Africa, and South Africa? Likewise, what do Wittenberg, Geneva, Zürich, Canterbury, Edinburgh, Richmond (Virginia), and New York have to do with sub-Saharan Africa and the Afro Caribbean come of age?

Notes

1 *New York Times*, May 16, 1987.
2 Adolf von Harnack, *History of Dogma*, trans. Neil Buchanan, 7 vols. (New York: Dover Publications, 1961), 5:16–17.
3 David B. Barrett, ed., *The World Christian Encyclopedia* (Oxford: Oxford University Press, 1982), 778, 798.
4 *Who Are the Anglicans? Profiles and Maps of the Anglican Communion* (Cincinnati: Forward Movement Publications, 1988), 12–31.
5 See "Mainline Churches," in *Emerging Trends* (Princeton, NJ: Gallup Organization, May 1989), 1.
6 Walter Bauer, *Orthodoxy and Heresy in Earliest Christianity*, trans. and ed. Robert A. Kraft *et al.* (Philadelphia: Fortress Press, 1971), 229–30.

55

The Problem of Evil: An Akan Perspective

Kwame Gyekye

Because Akan thinkers hold that moral evil stems from the exercise of man's free will, it is appropriately treated here. The problem of evil appears to be more complex in Akan thought than Western thought. The reason is that whereas in Western thought the problem centers round God, in Akan thought the problem centers round both the Supreme Being (God: Onyame) and the deities (that is, lesser spirits). In Western thought the problem arises out of seeming conflicts between the attributes of God and the existence of evil. In Akan thought the problem is conceived in terms not only of the attributes of God but also of those of the deities. When the problem of evil in Akan thought is pushed to its logical limits, however, its philosophical nature is quite similar to that in Western philosophy and theology.

The problem of evil in Western philosophy arises out of the contradiction between God's attributes of omnipotence and goodness (benevolence) on the one hand and the existence of evil on the other hand. Thus, given the three propositions:

A   God is omnipotent,
B   God is wholly good,
C   evil exists,

C is considered to be incompatible with *A* and *B*, individually or jointly. If God is omnipotent, then He can completely eliminate evil, since there are no

limits to what an omnipotent being can do, and if God is wholly good or benevolent then He would be willing to eliminate evil. Yet evil exists. The existence of evil, it is argued in Western philosophy, implies that either God does not exist or if He does exist He is not omnipotent or not wholly good or both. Of course various attempts have been made by philosophers and theologians to explain the sources of evil in this world.

In Akan philosophy and theology God is conceived as omnipotent and wholly good. Yet the Akan thinkers do not appear to find these attributes of God incompatible with the fact of the existence of moral evil. One might suppose that the Akan thinkers are dodging the philosophical issue here, but this is not so. Rather, they locate the source of the problem of evil elsewhere than in the logic of the relationships between the attributes of God and the fact of existence of evil.

For the Akan, evil is not a creation of God; that would be inconsistent with the goodness of God. Akan thinkers generally believe that it was not God who created evil (*Nyame ambō bōne*). Then how is the existence of evil explained? According to them, there are two main sources of evil: the deities (*abosom*, including all supernatural forces such as magical forces, witches, etc.) and mankind's own will. About half a dozen assembled discussants were unanimous in asserting that "evil derives from evil spirits" (*bōne firi obonsam*).[1] The deities are held either to be good and evil or to have powers of good and evil. Thus, unlike Onyame (God), they are not wholly good, and hence they are the authors of evil things. Although the deities were created by God,

---

From Kwame Gyekye, *An Essay on African Philosophical Thought*, Cambridge University Press (1987); by kind permission of Kwame Gyekye.

they are considered in Akan theology and cosmology to have independent existence of some sort; they operate independently of God and in accordance with their own desires and intentions.

Since the deities that constitute one source of evil in this world are held not to be wholly good, one might suppose that the problem of evil is thereby solved. Busia, for instance, thought that

> the problem of evil so often discussed in Western philosophy and Christian theology does *not* arise in the African concept of deity. It is when a God who is not only all powerful and omniscient but also perfect and loving is postulated that the problem of the existence of evil becomes an intellectual and philosophical hurdle. The Supreme Being of the African is the Creator, the source of life, *but between Him and man lie many powers and principalities good and bad, gods, spirits, magical forces, witches to account for the strange happenings in the world.*[2]

It is not clear what Busia means by "deity" here; perhaps he means the Supreme Being, God. If so, his view of the attributes of the Supreme Being – a view that implies some limitation on the Supreme Being as conceived in African thought – is disputable. Be that as it may, the view that the African concept of the Supreme. Being does not give rise to the problem of evil is of course predicated on the assumption that the lesser spirits created by Him are conceived of as good *and* bad, so that the quandaries arising out of the conflict of omnipotence and perfect goodness on the one hand and evil on the other hand cease to exist. But this conclusion is premature and unsatisfactory philosophically.

The immediate question that arises is this: Why should a wholly good God create a being that embodies in itself both good *and* evil powers or dispositions? One possible answer may be that it was not God who created the evil powers or actions of a lesser spirit, but that these result from the operations of the independent will of the spirit itself. But this answer is not wholly satisfactory either. First, God, being a higher entity, can destroy the lesser spirits as well as the other powers and forces. Consequently, God has the power to eliminate or control the evil wills and actions of the lower beings such as the lesser spirits and so to eliminate evil from the world. Second, since God is wholly good and eschews evil (*Nyame mpē bōne*), as an Akan proverb has it, he would not refrain from eliminating evil or controlling evil wills. Even if it were granted that God endowed the lesser spirits with independent wills, it might be expected that the wholly good God would be willing to intervene when he sees them using their wills to choose to act wrongly and so to cause evil. Would it have been wrong for God to intervene in the evil operations of the independent free wills of the lesser spirits in order to eliminate evil? But if he had done so, would he not have disrupted the free wills with which he endowed them? (These questions come up again in discussing mankind as a source of evil.) Thus, contrary to Busia's assertion, it is clear that the Akan concept of deity does generate the philosophical problem of evil. Busia's assertion would be true only if a lesser spirit, held to be both good *and* bad, were considered as the supreme or ultimate spiritual being. But this is not the case. It is Onyame who is the Supreme and Absolute Being.

The other source of evil, according to Akan thought, is human will. On this some of my discussants advanced the following views:

> Evil comes from man's character.
> (*bōne fi onipa suban*)[3]

In the view of this discussant, character determines the nature of our actions; bad character gives rise to evil actions, and good character gives rise to good actions. The person with bad character, he asserted, thinks evil, and it is such evil thoughts that translate or issue in morally evil actions. According to him, it is impossible for evil to come from Onyame (God) because (1) Onyame is good (*Onyame ye*), and (2) our character, from which evil proceeds, is of our own making; what our character is, or will be, is the person's responsibility, not God's. In a discussion with a different group of three elders,[4] two of them also blamed evil on human character, but the third one, criticizing the other two, asked: "Is it not *Onyame* who created the world and us and all that we are?" He answered his own question by saying: "If Onyame made us what we are, then he created, along with everything else, evil too." To this one of the others retorted: "It is surely *not* Onyame who tells or forces a person to go and rape, steal, and kill. It is the person's own desires and mind" (*n'apēde ne n'adwen*). But the conception of the human source of moral evil was shared by two other discussants, both from different communities. One of them maintained that "Onyame did not create evil; evil comes from man's own actions" (*Onyame ambō bōne; bōne firi onipa nneyēe*),[5] and the other that

"Onyame is not the cause of evil, but our own thinking and deliberation" (*bōne mfi Onyame; efi yēn ankasa adwendwen mu*).[6]

Arguing that God is not the author of evil, another discussant maintained that "evil comes from man's conscience" (*tiboa*).[7] His position is that a human being has what is called *tiboa*, conscience (moral sense, that is, a sense of right and wrong), which enables one to see the difference (*nsoe*) between good and evil. Putting it bluntly, he said, "Man is not a beast (*aboa*) to fail to distinguish between the good and evil." The comparison between man and beast is intended as a distinction between moral sense and amoral sense on the one hand, and between rationality (intelligence) and irrationality (non-intelligence) on the other hand. The implication is that it is only conscienceless, irrational beasts that cannot distinguish between good and evil. Since, according to this traditional thinker, our possession of *tiboa* enables (or, should enable) us to do correct moral thinking, evil stems from our inability to exercise the moral sense. But this argument is not persuasive. Having the ability to do correct moral thinking, or to distinguish between good and evil, does not necessarily imply possession of the moral will to carry out the implications of the distinction. This traditional wise man assumes that it does, but this assumption, I think, is mistaken. So that the statement "Evil comes from man's conscience" must perhaps be taken to mean that evil stems from the inability to exercise either our moral sense or our moral will.

In sum, the basic premise of the arguments of the Akan thinkers on the problem of evil is generally that God does not like evil (*Nyame mpē bōne*) and hence did not create it (*Nyame ambō bōne*). Evil, according to most of them, proceeds from man's character, conscience, desires, and thoughts – all of which suggest, within the Akan conceptual system, that evil stems from the exercise by the person of his or her own free will (*onipa ne pē*), as was in fact explicitly stated by a discussant.[8]

... The general nature of destiny (*nkrabea*) allows for the concept of human freedom, and therefore of choice, and within the context of human actions – which are *not* to be considered as events – the concept of determinism is inapplicable. Thus, the view of the human source of moral evil appears to stem from a set of related concepts in the Akan metaphysical system.

This argument seems to me a potent one. Nevertheless, some difficult questions might be raised against it. For instance: Why did not God, if he is omnipotent and wholly good, make human beings such that they always choose the good and avoid the evil? Or, having endowed them with freedom of the will, why does God not intervene when he sees them using this freedom to choose the wrong thing and so to cause evil? Is God unable to control human will? Is he unable to control what he has created? And if he is able, why does he not do so? Can the argument that evil results from the exercise of human free will really be sustained?

If God is omnipotent, then he certainly could have made human beings such that they always choose the good and avoid the evil, that he could also intervene in the event of human freedom of the will leading to evil, and that he could thus control human will. But if God had done all this, humans would act in a wholly determined way, without any choice whatever – a situation that would run counter to the *general* nature of the concept of destiny and the notion of human action as held by Akan thinkers. That would also have led to the subversion of rationality, which not only distinguishes human beings from beasts, but also enables human beings generally to judge before acting. The argument that God should have made humans such that they always choose the good implies that God should have made them nonrational and thus less human, wholly without the ability to choose. Thus, the subversion of rationality together with its concomitants of choice, deliberation, judgment, etc. constitutes a *reductio ad absurdum* of the view that the wholly good God should have created humans such that they always choose the good. The Akan thinkers, like thinkers in most other cultures, would rather have humankind endowed with rationality and conscience than to have them fashioned to behave like a beast. Hence. God's provision of rationality and freedom of the will and of choice is justified. If humans debase this provision, knowing that this would bring evil in its wake, then they, not their Creator, should be held responsible.

What if God made humans such that they use their rationality always to choose the good? Would they have been free under such circumstances? The answer must be no, inasmuch as the choice of the good would have been predetermined, which means that no choice ever existed.

This discussion shows that the problem of evil does indeed arise in Akan philosophy and theology. The Akan thinkers, although recognizing the existence of moral evil in the world, generally do not believe that this fact is inconsistent with the assertion that God is omnipotent and wholly good. Evil, according to them, is ultimately the result of the exercise by humans of their freedom of the will with which they were endowed by the Creator, *Obōadeē*.

Notes

1 Interview with some elders in Pano, near Kibi, 12 Aug. 1974.
2 K. A. Busia, "The African World-View," in *African Heritage*, ed. J. Drachler (New York: Crowell Collier & Macmillan, 1963), p. 148; my italics.
3 Interview with the Ankobeahene of Kibi, 15 Aug. 1974.
4 Interview in Apapam, near Kibi, 16 Aug. 1974.
5 Interview with Nana Dawson of Cape Coast, 4 Sept. 1976.
6 Interview with Opanin Kofi Adu of Asikam, near Kibi, 13 Aug. 1974.
7 Interview with Oheneba Kwabena Bekoe of Akropong-Akuapem, 6 Aug. 1976.
8 Interview with J. A. Annobil, 3 Sept. 1976: "Evil comes from man's will" (*bōne fi onipa ne pē*).

56

Black Women and Men: Partnership in the 1990s

bell hooks and Cornel West

b. h. I requested that Charles sing "Precious Lord" because the conditions that led Thomas Dorsey to write this song always make me think about gender issues, issues of black masculinity. Mr Dorsey wrote this song after his wife died in childbirth. That experience caused him to have a crisis of faith. He did not think he would be able to go on living without her. That sense of unbearable crisis truly expresses the contemporary dilemma of faith. Mr Dorsey talked about the way he tried to cope with this "crisis of faith." He prayed and prayed for a healing and received the words to this song. This song has helped so many folk when they are feeling low, feeling as if they can't go on. It was my grandmother's favorite song. I remembered how we sang it at her funeral. She died when she was almost ninety. And I am moved now as I was then by the knowledge that we can take our pain, work with it, recycle it, and transform it so that it becomes a source of power.

Let me introduce to you my "brother," my comrade Cornel West.

C. W. First I need to just acknowledge the fact that we as black people have come together to reflect on our past, present, and objective future. That, in and of itself, is a sign of hope. I'd like to thank the Yale African-American Cultural Center for bringing us together. bell and I thought it would be best to present in dialogical form a series of reflections on

the crisis of black males and females. There is a state of siege raging now in black communities across this nation linked not only to drug addiction but also consolidation of corporate power as we know it, and redistribution of wealth from the bottom to the top, coupled with the ways with which a culture and society centered on the market, preoccupied with consumption, erode structures of feeling, community, tradition. Reclaiming our heritage and sense of history are prerequisities to any serious talk about black freedom and black liberation in the twenty-first century. We want to try to create that kind of community here today, a community that we hope will be a place to promote understanding. Critical understanding is a prerequisite for any serious talk about coming together, sharing, participating, creating bonds of solidarity so that black people and other progressive people can continue to hold up the blood-stained banners that were raised when that song was sung in the civil rights movement. It was one of Dr Martin Luther King's favorite songs, reaffirming his own struggle and that of many others who have tried to link some sense of faith, religious faith, political faith, to the struggle for freedom. We thought it would be best to have a dialogue to put forth analysis and provide a sense of what form a praxis would take. That praxis will be necessary for us to talk seriously about black power, black liberation in the twenty-first century.

b. h. Let us say a little bit about ourselves. Both Cornel and I come to you as individuals who believe in God. That belief informs our message.

Reproduced by kind permission of South End Press.

C. W. One of the reasons we believe in God is due to the long tradition of religious faith in the black community. I think that, as a people who have had to deal with the absurdity of being black in America, for many of us it is a question of God and sanity, or God and suicide. And if you are serious about black struggle you know that in many instances you will be stepping out on nothing, hoping to land on something. That is the history of black folks in the past and present, and it continually concerns those of us who are willing to speak out with boldness and a sense of the importance of history and struggle. You speak knowing that you won't be able to do that for too long because America is such a violent culture. Given those conditions you have to ask yourself what links to a tradition will sustain you given the absurdity and insanity we are bombarded with daily. And so the belief in God itself is not to be understood in a noncontextual manner. It is understood in relation to a particular context, to specific circumstances.

b. h. We also come to you as two progressive black people on the left.

C. W. Very much so.

b. h. I will read a few paragraphs to provide a critical framework for our discussion of black power, just in case some of you may not know what black power means. We are gathered to speak with one another about black power in the twenty-first century. In James Boggs's essay, "Black Power: A Scientific Concept Whose Time Has Come," first published in 1968, he called attention to the radical political significance of the black power movement, asserting: "Today the concept of black power expresses the revolutionary social force which must not only struggle against the capitalist but against the workers and all who benefit by and support the system which has oppressed us." We speak of black power in this very different context to remember, reclaim, revision, and renew. We remember first that the historical struggle for black liberation was forged by black women and men who were concerned about the collective welfare of black people. Renewing our commitment to this collective struggle should provide a grounding for new direction in contemporary political practice. We speak today of political partnership between black men and women. The late James Baldwin wrote in his autobiographical preface to *Notes of a Native Son*: "I think that the past is all that makes the present coherent and further that the past will remain horrible for as long

as we refuse to accept it honestly." Accepting the challenge for this prophetic statement as we look at our contemporary past as black people, the space between the sixties and the nineties, we see a weakening of political solidarity between black men and women. It is crucial for the future black liberation struggle that we remain ever mindful that ours is a shared struggle, that we are each other's faith.

C. W. I think we can even begin by talking about the kind of existentialist chaos that exists in our own lives and our inability to overcome the sense of alienation and frustration we experience when we try to create bonds of intimacy and solidarity with one another. Now part of this frustration is to be understood again in relation to structures and institutions. In the way in which our culture of consumption has promoted an addiction to stimulation – one that puts a premium on bottled commodified stimulation. The market does this in order to convince us that our consumption keeps oiling the economy in order for it to reproduce itself. But the effect of this addiction to stimulation is an undermining, a waning of our ability for qualitatively rich relationships. It's no accident that crack is the postmodern drug, that it is the highest form of addiction known to humankind, that it provides a feeling ten times more pleasurable than orgasm.

b. h. Addiction is not about relatedness, about relationships. So it comes as no surprise that as addiction becomes more pervasive in black life it undermines our capacity to experience community. Just recently, I was telling someone that I would like to buy a little house next door to my parents' house. This house used to be Mr Johnson's house but he recently passed away. And they could not understand why I would want to live near my parents. My explanation that my parents were aging did not satisfy. Their inability to understand or appreciate the value of sharing family life intergenerationally was a sign to me of the crisis facing our communities. It's as though as black people we have lost our understanding of the importance of mutual interdependency, of communal living. That we no longer recognize as valuable the notion that we collectively shape the terms of our survival is a sign of crisis.

C. W. And when there is crisis in those communities and institutions that have played a fundamental role in transmitting to younger generations our values and sensibility, our ways of life and our ways of struggle, we find ourselves distanced, not simply from our predecessors but from the critical project of black liberation. And so more and more we seem to have young black people who are very difficult to understand, because it seems as though they live in two very different worlds. We don't really understand their music. Black adults may not be listening to NWA (Niggers With Attitude) straight out of Compton, California. They may not understand why they are doing what Stetsasonic is doing, what Public Enemy is all about, because young people have been fundamentally shaped by the brutal side of American society. Their sense of reality is shaped on the one hand by a sense of coldness and callousness, and on the other hand by a sense of passion for justice, contradictory impulses which surface simultaneously. Mothers may find it difficult to understand their children. Grandparents may find it difficult to understand us – and it's this slow breakage that has to be restored.

b. h.   That sense of breakage, or rupture, is often tragically expressed in gender relations. When I told folks that Cornel West and I were talking about partnership between black women and men, they thought I meant romantic relationships. I replied that it was important for us to examine the multi-relationships between black women and men, how we deal with fathers, with brothers, with sons. We are talking about all our relationships across gender because it is not just the heterosexual love relationships between black women and men that are in trouble. Many of us can't communicate with parents, siblings, etc. I've talked with many of you and asked, "What is it you feel should be addressed?" And many of you responded that you wanted to talk about black men and how they need to "get it together."

Let's talk about why we see the struggle to assert agency – that is, the ability to act in one's best interest – as a male thing. I mean, black men are not the only ones among us who need to "get it together." And if black men collectively refuse to educate themselves for critical consciousness, to acquire the means to be self-determined, should our communities suffer, or should we not recognize that both black women and men must struggle for self-actualization, must learn to "get it together"? Since the culture we live in continues to equate blackness with maleness, black awareness of the extent to which our survival depends on mutual partnership between women and men is under-

mined. In renewed black liberation struggle, we recognize the position of black men and women, the tremendous role black women played in every freedom struggle.

Certainly Septima Clark's book *Ready from Within* is necessary reading for those of us who want to understand the historical development of sexual politics in black liberation struggle. Clark describes her father's insistence that she not fully engage herself in civil rights struggle because of her gender. Later, she found the source of her defiance in religion. It was the belief in spiritual community, that no difference must be made between the role of women and that of men, that enabled her to be "ready within." To Septima Clark, the call to participate in black liberation struggle was a call from God. Remembering and recovering the stories of how black women learned to assert historical agency in the struggle for self-determination in the context of community and collectivity is important for those of us who struggle to promote black liberation, a movement that has at its core a commitment to free our communities of sexist domination, exploitation, and oppression. We need to develop a political terminology that will enable black folks to talk deeply about what we mean when we urge black women and men to "get it together."

C. W.   I think again that we have to keep in mind the larger context of American society, which has historically expressed contempt for black men and black women. The very notion that black people are human beings is a new notion in western civilization and is still not widely accepted in practice. And one of the consequences of this pernicious idea is that it is very difficult for black men and women to remain attuned to each other's humanity, so when bell talks about black women's agency and some of the problems black men have when asked to acknowledge black women's humanity, it must be remembered that this refusal to acknowledge one another's humanity is a reflection of the way we are seen and treated in the larger society. And it's certainly not true that white folks have a monopoly on human relationships. When we talk about a crisis in western civilization, black people are a part of that civilization even though we have been beneath it, our backs serving as a foundation for the building of that civilization, and we have to understand how it affects us so that the partnership that bell talks about can take on real substance and content. I think partnerships between black men and black women can be made when we learn how to be supportive and think in terms of critical affirmation.

b. h. Certainly black people have not talked enough about the importance of constructing patterns of interaction that strengthen our capacity to be affirming.

C. W. We need to affirm one another, support one another, help, enable, equip, and empower as one another to deal with the present crisis, but it can't be uncritical, because if it's uncritical then we are again refusing to acknowledge other people's humanity. If we are serious about acknowledging and affirming other people's humanity then we are committed to trusting and believing that they are forever in process. Growth, development, maturation happens in stages. People grow, develop, and mature along the lines in which they are taught. Disenabling critique and contemptuous feedback hinders.

b. h. We need to examine the function of critique in traditional black communities. Often it does not serve as a constructive force. Like we have that popular slang word "dissin" and we know that "dissin" refers to a kind of disenabling contempt – when we "read" each other in ways that are so painful, so cruel, that the person can't get up from where you have knocked them down. Other destructive forces in our lives are envy and jealousy. These undermine our efforts to work for a collective good. Let me give a minor example. When I came in this morning I saw Cornel's latest book on the table. I immediately wondered why my book was not there and caught myself worrying about whether he was receiving some gesture of respect or recognition denied me. When he heard me say, "Where's my book?" he pointed to another table. Often when people are suffering a legacy of deprivation, there is a sense that there are never any goodies to go around, so that we must viciously compete with one another. Again this spirit of competition creates conflict and divisiveness. In a larger social context, competition between black women and men has surfaced around the issue of whether black female writers are receiving more attention than black male writers. Rarely does anyone point to the reality that only a small minority of black women writers are receiving public accolades. Yet the myth that black women who succeed are taking something away from black men continues to permeate black psyches and inform how we as black women and men respond to one another. Since capitalism is rooted in unequal distribution of resources, it is not surprising that we as black women and men find ourselves in situations of competition and conflict.

C. W. I think part of the problem is deep down in our psyche we recognize that we live in such a conservative society, a society of business elites, a society in which corporate power influences are assuring that a certain group of people do get up higher.

b. h. Right, including some of you in this room.

C. W. And this is true not only between male and female relations but also black and brown relations and black and Korean, and black and Asian relations. We are struggling over crumbs because we know that the bigger part of lower corporate America is already received. One half of one percent of America owns 22 percent of the wealth, one percent owns 32 percent and the bottom 45 percent of the population has 20 percent of the wealth. So, you end up with this kind of crabs-in-the-barrel mentality. When you see someone moving up you immediately think they'll get a bigger cut in big-loaf corporate America and you think that's something real because we're still shaped by the corporate ideology of the larger context.

b. h. Here at Yale many of us are getting a slice of that mini-loaf and yet are despairing. It was discouraging when I came here to teach and found in many black people a quality of despair which is not unlike that we know is felt in "crack neighbourhoods." I wanted to understand the connection between underclass black despair and that of black people here who have immediate and/or potential access to so much material privilege. This despair mirrors the spiritual crisis that is happening in our culture as a whole. Nihilism is everywhere. Some of this despair is rooted in a deep sense of loss. Many black folks who have made it or are making it undergo an identity crisis. This is especially true for individual black people working to assimilate into the "mainstream." Suddenly, they may feel panicked, alarmed by the knowledge that they do not understand their history, that life is without purpose and meaning. These feelings of alienation and estrangement create suffering. The suffering many black people experience today is linked to the suffering of the past, to "historical memory." Attempts by black people to understand that suffering, to come to terms with it, are the conditions which enable a work like Toni Morrison's *Beloved* to receive so much attention. To look back, not just to describe slavery but to try and reconstruct a psycho-social history of its impact has only recently been fully understood as a necessary stage in the process of collective black self-recovery.

C. W. The spiritual crisis that has happened, especially among the well-to-do blacks, has taken the form of the quest for therapeutic release. So that you can get very thin, flat, and unidimensional forms of spirituality that are simply an attempt to sustain the well-to-do black folks as they engage in their consumerism and privatism. The kind of spirituality we're talking about is not the kind that remains superficial just physically but serves as an opium to help you justify and rationalize your own cynicism vis-à-vis the disadvantaged folk in our community. We could talk about churches and their present role in the crisis of America, religious faith as the American way of life, the gospel of health and wealth, helping the bruised psyches of the black middle class make it through America. That's not the form of spirituality that we're talking about. We're talking about something deeper – you used to call it conversion – so that notions of service and risk and sacrifice once again become fundamental. It's very important, for example, that those of you who remember the days in which black colleges were hegemonic among the black elite remember them critically but also acknowledge that there was something positive going on there. What was going on was that you were told every Sunday, with the important business of chapel, that you had to give service to the race. Now it may have been a bourgeois form, but it created a moment of accountability, and with the erosion of the service ethic the very possibility of putting the needs of others alongside of one's own diminishes. In this syndrome, me-ness, selfishness, and egocentricity become more and more prominent, creating a spiritual crisis where you need more psychic opium to get you over.

b. h. We have experienced such a change in that communal ethic of service that was so necessary for survival in traditional black communities. That ethic of service has been altered by shifting class relations. And even those black folks who have little or no class mobility may buy into a bourgeois class sensibility; TV shows like *Dallas* and *Dynasty* teach ruling class ways of thinking and being to underclass poor people. A certain kind of bourgeois individualism of the mind prevails. It does not correspond to actual class reality or circumstances of deprivation. We need to remember the many economic structures and class politics that have led to a shift of priorities for "privileged" blacks. Many privileged black folks obsessed with living out a bourgeois dream of liberal individualistic success no longer feel as though they have any accountability in relation to the black poor and underclass.

C. W. We're not talking about the narrow sense of guilt privileged black people can feel, because guilt usually paralyzes action. What we're talking about is how one uses one's time and energy. We're talking about the ways in which the black middle class, which is relatively privileged vis-à-vis the black working class, working poor, and underclass, needs to acknowledge that along with that privilege goes responsibility. Somewhere I read that for those to whom much is given, much is required. And the question becomes, "How do we exercise that responsibility given our privilege?" I don't think it's a credible notion to believe the black middle class will give up on its material toys. No, the black middle class will act like any other middle class in the human condition; it will attempt to maintain its privilege. There is something seductive about comfort and convenience. The black middle class will not return to the ghetto, especially given the territorial struggles going on with gangs and so forth. Yet, how can we use what power we do have to be sure more resources are available to those who are disadvantaged? So the question becomes, "How do we use our responsibility and privilege?" Because, after all, black privilege is a result of black struggle.

I think the point to make here is that there is a new day in black America. It is the best of times and the worst of times in black America. Political consciousness is escalating in black America, among black students, among black workers, organized black workers and trade unions, increasingly we are seeing black leaders with vision. The black church is on the move, black popular music, political themes and motifs are on the move. So don't think in our critique we somehow ask you to succumb to a paralyzing pessimism. There are grounds for hope and when that corner is turned, and we don't know what particular catalytic event will serve as the take-off for it (just like we didn't know December 1955 would be the take-off), but when it occurs we have got to be ready. The privileged black folks can play a rather crucial role if we have a service ethic, if we want to get on board, if we want to be part of the progressive, prophetic bandwagon. And that is the question we will have to ask ourselves and each other.

b. h. We also need to remember that there is a joy in struggle. Recently, I was speaking on a panel at a conference with another black woman from a privileged background. She mocked the notion of struggle. When she expressed. "I'm just tired of hearing about the importance of struggle; it doesn't interest me," the audience clapped. She saw struggle solely in negative terms, a perspective which led me to question whether she had ever taken part in any organized resistance movement. For if you have, you know that there is joy in struggle. Those of us who are old enough to remember segregated schools, the kind of political effort and sacrifice folks were making to ensure we would have full access to educational opportunities, surely remember the sense of fulfillment when goals that we struggled for were achieved. When we sang together "We shall overcome" there was a sense of victory, a sense of power that comes when we strive to be self-determining. When Malcolm X spoke about his journey to Mecca, the awareness he achieved, he gives expression to that joy that comes from struggling to grow. When Martin Luther King talked about having been to the mountaintop, he was sharing with us that he arrived at a peak of critical awareness, and it gave him great joy. In our liberatory pedagogy we must teach young black folks to understand that struggle is process, that one moves from circumstances of difficulty and pain to awareness, joy, fulfillment. That the struggle to be critically conscious can be that movement which takes you to another level, that lifts you up, that makes you feel better. You feel good, you feel your life has meaning and purpose.

C. W. A rich life is fundamentally a life of serving others, a life of trying to leave the world a little better than you found it. That rich life comes into being in human relationships. This is true at the personal level. Those of you who have been in love know what I am talking about. It is also true at the organizational and communal level. It's difficult to find joy by yourself even if you have all the right toys. It's difficult. Just ask somebody who has got a lot of material possessions but doesn't have anybody to share them with. Now that's at the personal level. There is a political version of this. It has to do with what you see when you get up in the morning and look in the mirror and ask yourself whether you are simply wasting time on the planet

or spending time in an enriching manner. We are talking fundamentally about the meaning of life and the place of struggle. bell talks about the significance of struggle and service. For those of us who are Christians there are certain theological foundations on which our commitment to serve is based. Christian life is understood to be a life of service. Even so, Christians have no monopoly on the joys that come from service and those of you who are part of secular culture can also enjoy this sense of enrichment. Islamic brothers and sisters share in a religious practice which also places emphasis on the importance of service. When we speak of commitment to a life of service we must also talk about the fact that such a commitment goes against the grain, especially the foundations of our society. To talk this way about service and struggle we must also talk about strategies that will enable us to sustain this sensibility, this commitment.

b. h. When we talk about that which will sustain and nurture our spiritual growth as a people, we must once again talk about the importance of community. For one of the most vital ways we sustain ourselves is by building communities of resistance, places where we know we are not alone. In *Prophetic Fragments*, Cornel began his essay on Martin Luther King by quoting the lines of the spiritual, "He promised never to leave me, never to leave me alone." In black spiritual tradition the promise that we will not be alone cannot be heard as an affirmation of passivity. It does not mean we can sit around and wait for God to take care of business. We are not alone when we build community together. Certainly there is a great feeling of community in this room today. And yet when I was here at Yale I felt that my labor was not appreciated. It was not clear that my work was having meaningful impact. Yet I feel that impact today. When I walked into the room a black woman sister let me know how much my teaching and writing had helped her. There's more of the critical affirmation Cornel spoke of. That critical affirmation says, "Sister, what you're doing is uplifting me in some way." Often folk think that those folks who are spreading the message are so "together" that we do not need affirmation, critical dialogue about the impact of all that we teach and write about and how we live in the world.

C. W. It is important to note the degree to which black people in particular, and progressive people in general, are alienated and estranged from communities that would sustain and support us.

We are often homeless. Our struggles against a sense of nothingness and attempts to reduce us to nothing are ongoing. We confront regularly the question, "Where can I find a sense of home?" That sense of home can only be found in our construction of those communities of resistance bell talks about and the solidarity we can experience within them. Renewal comes through participating in community. That is the reason so many folks continue to go to church. In religious experience they find a sense of renewal, a sense of home. In community one can feel that we are moving forward, that struggle can be sustained. As we go forward as black progressives, we must remember that community is not about homogeneity. Homogeneity is dogmatic imposition, pushing your way of life, your way of doing things onto somebody else. That is not what we mean by community. Dogmatic insistence that everybody think and act alike causes rifts among us, destroying the possibility of community. That sense of home that we are talking about and searching for is a place where we can find compassion, recognition of difference, of the importance of diversity, of our individual uniqueness.

b. h. When we evoke a sense of home as a place where we can renew ourselves, where we can know love and the sweet communication of shared spirit, I think it's important for us to remember that this location of well-being cannot exist in a context of sexist domination, in a setting where children are the objects of parental domination and abuse. On a fundamental level, when we talk about home, we must speak about the need to transform the African-American home, so that there, in that domestic space we can experience the renewal of political commitment to the black liberation struggle. So that there in that domestic space we learn to serve and honor one another. If we look again at the civil rights, at the black power movement, folks organized so much in homes. They were the places where folks got together to educate themselves for critical consciousness. That sense of community, cultivated and developed in the home, extended outward into a larger, more public context. As we talk about black power in the twenty-first century, about political partnership between black women and men, we must talk about transforming our notions of how and why we bond. In *Beloved*, Toni Morrison offers a paradigm for relationships between black men and women. Sixo describes his love for Thirty-Mile Woman, declaring, "She is a friend of mind. She gather me, man. The pieces I am, she gather them and give them back to me in all the right order. It's good, you know, when you got a woman who is a friend of your mind." In this passage Morrison evokes a notion of bonding that may be rooted in passion, desire, even romantic love, but the point of connection between black women and men is that space of recognition and understanding, where we know one another so well, our histories, that we can take bits and pieces, the fragments of who we are, and put them back together, remember them. It is this joy of intellectual bonding, or working together to create liberatory theory and analysis that black women and men can give one another, that Cornel and I give to each other. We are friends of one another's mind. We find a home with one another. It is that joy in community we celebrate and share with you this morning.

Index

479

Index